Salvator Rosa in French Literature

Studies in Romance Languages
John E. Keller, Editor

Salvator Rosa in French Literature

From the Bizarre to the Sublime

James S. Patty

THE UNIVERSITY PRESS OF KENTUCKY

Publication of this volume was made possible in part
by a grant from the National Endowment for the Humanities.

Editorial and Sales Offices: The University Press of Kentucky
663 South Limestone Street, Lexington, Kentucky 40508-4008
www.kentuckypress.com

09 08 07 06 05   5 4 3 2 1

Library of Congress Cataloging-in-Publication Data
Patty, James S.
Salvator Rosa in French literature : from the bizarre
to the sublime / James S. Patty.
          p.   cm.
Includes bibliographical references and index.
ISBN 0-8131-2330-5 (hardcover : alk. paper)
1. French literature—19th century—History and criticism.
2. Rosa, Salvator, 1615–1673—In literature.
3. Rosa, Salvator, 1615–1673—Influence. I. Title.
PQ283.P29   2004
840.9'351—dc22
2004024344

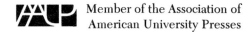

Contents

Preface

For about two centuries, the paintings of Salvator Rosa (1615–1673) enjoyed great popularity in Europe, and his works were on view in many major museums and private collections. His name was often mentioned with those of Poussin and Claude Lorrain as a master of landscape. He was especially popular in England; English travelers on the Grand Tour bought many Rosas—not all of them authentic—and took them back to their home country. In France the situation was a little different: while there had been a fairly brisk trade in Rosa's paintings in the second half of the eighteenth century, what mattered most was that several major works could be seen at the Louvre from the revolutionary period on. Because of the "pre-romantic qualities" of his landscapes, Rosa came to be regarded as a kindred spirit by the romantics. Once described as "bizarre," his pictures, especially his landscapes, were seen as "savage" and even "sublime." Rosa's colorful personality, that of a stormy, passionate, and proudly independent artist, suited the romantic mood. The legend, then accepted as historical fact, that he had participated in a popular revolt against the Spanish in Naples in 1647 reinforced the image. This image received a powerful boost from the vivid biography published in both English and French in 1824, which came from the pen of the Anglo-Irish writer known as Lady Morgan (ca. 1776–1859). The two volumes of her biography provided information and critical viewpoints, not only to art historians and art critics, but to poets, fiction writers, and dramatists as well. Rosa was the hero of a full-fledged romantic drama by Ferdinand Dugué; the play received an elaborate production at the Théâtre de la Porte-Saint-Martin in 1851 and was revived several times.

Rosa was born near Naples and spent most of his early life in that city.

But it was in Rome and Tuscany, especially the former, that he had his artistic career. He began to enjoy significant patronage by the age of twenty and was patronized by several Medici princes in the early 1640s. In 1649 he settled for good in Rome, where by the force of his personality he established himself as a successful, independent artist. His work attracted attention abroad and led to invitations and commissions from several foreign rulers.

Rosa practiced a number of genres: history painting, marines, battle scenes, portraits, and landscapes. His productions in this last-named genre were primarily responsible for his growing popularity, both in Italy and abroad. His pictures may be found in many major museums in Europe and the United States; the largest number are to be seen in Italy, Great Britain, and France. Rosa was a controversial but rather popular poet because of his seven satires. And several hundred of his letters have survived.

It was the availability of several of his works in the Louvre from the nineteenth century on that accounts for many of the most interesting references to Rosa by French writers. Among those who discuss Rosa are Staël, Stendhal, Balzac, Sand, Hugo, Dumas, Michelet, Gautier, and Baudelaire. References to Rosa are particularly numerous in the work of Gautier, one of the most prolific French art critics in the nineteenth century.

Rosa's popularity is linked to the rise of romanticism. Early art critics and art historians in French often judged him by classical criteria and found his work "bizarre." But in the decades leading to the triumph of romanticism, his landscapes came to match the dominant mood, with their somber and "wild" scenes of rugged scenery. Joined to several myths circulated by writers like Lady Morgan, his work was regarded as romantic before romanticism.

The fading of the more histrionic strains in romanticism and the coming, after midcentury, of such movements as realism and impressionism, led to some decline in Rosa's vogue in France. But he was not forgotten; art critics and art historians continued to write about him, and several of his major works remained and still remain on view in the Louvre. And, during some recent remodeling of that museum, a large room was rechristened the Salle Salvator Rosa. Thus Rosa now has a permanent place in the cultural life of France. A study of the documents that substantiate the process by which this phenomenon came about would seem to be in order.

Acknowledgments

In putting this study together, I have received help from a number of colleagues, most of whom are also good friends: Professors Lois Cassandra Hamrick, John E. Keller, Luigi Monga, Claude Pichois, Helen and Raymond Poggenburg, Laurence M. Porter, Claude Schopp, Albert B. Smith, James K. Wallace, and Dr. Graham Robb. Special thanks are owed to Mrs. Mary Monga for turning a rather messy manuscript into an expertly typed text and for providing, in the process, numerous important improvements through her suggestions and questions. I am also greatly indebted to the readers who evaluated my text for their valuable criticisms and suggestions. May all these persons find here a heartfelt expression of my gratitude for their contributions.

Introduction

In late 1831, Samuel F. B. Morse, the American painter—and future inventor of the telegraph—began work on a huge picture, *Gallery of the Louvre*, showing the Salon carré as a sort of *musée imaginaire*, a crowded collection of the paintings that Morse evidently considered outstanding and representative.[1] On display are copies of thirty-eight paintings by twenty-three artists, mostly Italian, French, and Flemish. In the place of honor, near the center of the bottom row, is, not surprisingly, the *Mona Lisa*. On the top row, well right of center and well above the imaginary viewer's eye level, in shadow, is a representation of Salvator Rosa's *Landscape with Soldiers and Hunters*. The inclusion of Rosa's picture, its place in Morse's imaginary exposition, and his choice of the recently acquired *Landscape* rather than any of the several other Rosas in the Louvre are revealing: In the early nineteenth century Salvator Rosa was a name to be reckoned with, an artist whose work had won its way into public and critical favor and who was known primarily as a landscapist. But, clearly, his place was not as prominent as those of Titian and Van Dyck or Rubens and Murillo (with three pictures each) or Guido Reni, Veronese, Rembrandt, and Poussin, all of whom had two pictures in Morse's ideal Louvre. One must not make too much out of these numbers—one *Mona Lisa* or one Raphael *Madonna* easily outshone the Rosa *Landscape*, high on the wall and dimly lit. But Rosa has at least made it into Morse's picture and, quite significantly, is represented by a landscape. All in all, Rosa's appearance in *Gallery of the Louvre* may be seen as depicting, quite literally, the high point of his reputation.

Another point deserves to be made: Rosa's picture has been given a place in a real museum, one of the world's greatest, certainly the greatest in France.

The vogue for Rosa's work may have been greater in England in the eighteenth and early nineteenth centuries, but, obviously, it was not negligible in France. This present study of Rosa's reception in France seems justified by that fact alone, especially since the English vogue for Rosa has been rather well studied by such authorities as Elizabeth W. Manwaring[2] and William Gaunt.[3] But it will not simply seek to do for France what Manwaring and Gaunt have done for England. Though it necessarily strives for some of the same ends and uses many of the same methods, it has been conceived in a somewhat different spirit. First of all, this study focuses exclusively on Rosa. Then it has cast its net wider and has sought to achieve something closer to a complete examination of French texts containing references to Rosa, regardless of genre. Thus it deals with a great variety of texts, ranging from the belletristic to the expository, from the intensely personal to the journalistic; it draws on encyclopedias, biographical dictionaries, art criticism, art history, literary history, travel books, biography, correspondence, works left unpublished by their authors, as well as poetry, fiction, and theater.

The main purposes of this study are (1) to follow the general outlines of Rosa's reputation and to document this narrative with quotations from as many authors as possible, sometime quoting *in extenso,* sometimes more briefly or in summary; (2) to identify the literary documents that account for Rosa's reputation and, where possible, to show the relationship between them: "literary" has been loosely defined so that prose in reference works will be treated as well as poetry, fiction, and drama; and (3) to identify the works by Rosa that inspired these materials and determine whether the writers actually saw the works in question or drew on texts by other writers.

The documents uncovered in this search vary greatly in quality and length. Many are by little-known, sometimes completely forgotten authors. But even if these texts are of extremely varied quality, they have been given their say. This material, conceivably, could have been presented more economically in the form of an annotated bibliography; indeed, all annotation might have been omitted. But it has seemed to me that a sort of narrative would prove to be a more readable presentation; for one thing, it would make possible the creation of contexts for the documents consulted, by surrounding them with historical facts and relating them to each other. Like any work essentially historical and chronological in character, it must be subdivided into chapters representing stages or periods in the development of Rosa's reception. I hope to have marked out without obvious arbitrariness the dividing lines between these stages or periods in the form of the chapters of this study. At the same time, I hope to be forgiven if these chronological divisions have, from time to time, been violated in order to link topics together logically or thematically rather than strictly chronologically. This has occasionally seemed desirable in the period—roughly 1830–1860—when the abundance of materials has called for treating them by genre.

Other decisions may be considered more controversial. First, and most important, I have annexed Lady Morgan's biography to French literature by using the French translation of her book as a major source, perhaps, in fact, *the* major source. This is defensible on several grounds: First, this was, with a possible exception, the version in which French readers knew her work in book-length form and where French authors found the makings of the poems, plays, fictions, biographical sketches, and critical studies they wrote about Rosa. Of course, after a certain amount of time, her information might be discovered indirectly in other texts as well as directly in hers (in reference works, for example, that drew on her book). Lady Morgan had many ties to France; she traveled there, frequented liberal circles in Paris, and wrote a book about France that aspired to be the counterpart of Madame de Staël's *De l'Allemagne*. Her book was published in Paris, in the original English, and in French, at almost the same moment as the original British edition appeared in London. Somewhat less relevant, but still of some importance, is the strong possibility that the German and other translators of her book worked from the French version rather than the English original.[4]

Some may question my decision to seek the presence of Rosa in what might be called subterranean regions, that is, in works where Rosa's influence is not offered directly or with specific reference to Rosa. This is true especially in my discussion of Diderot, whose descriptions of several contemporary painters, in his *Salons,* deal vividly with pictures close to Rosa in spirit, subject, and style, by artists who can be called his descendents. Similarly, apropos of Lamartine, I have found Rosaesque landscapes in his poetry and quoted extensively from relevant passages. The case of Vigny is a little different: I have treated his relationship to Rosa by pointing to affinities between the two artists that did not eventuate in actual texts by the French writer. Both Lamartine and Vigny did, however, reveal knowledge of and interest in Rosa's work in a few salient quotations.

Finally, a discussion of certain shortcomings of which I am aware is in order. First of all, a study of this type, at least as I conceive it, aims to be complete; theoretically, it would track down and deal with every reference to Rosa ever written down in French. I have pursued this goal, but done so in full awareness of the impossibility of attaining it. The sheer quantity of French texts where one might find references to Rosa, discussions of his life and work, or other evidence of his presence is, I think, an obstacle that any student of similar subjects will understand. The rise of the periodical press, especially after the fall of Napoleon, led to a production of documents on a staggering scale when compared to earlier centuries. Thus there are certainly texts involving Rosa that have eluded me, possibly even major ones. Perhaps, at least, the rather large quantity of texts that I have found and treated will have cleared the ground somewhat for other searchers in this field. Logistical problems have produced other inadequacies of which I am aware. I have sometimes had to quote from the English translation of certain documents, and, especially for recent French writings on Rosa, I have had to content myself with referring to them without quoting from them in cases where I was unable to consult them.

I have tried to limit the number of footnotes in several ways. First of all, references subsequent to the initial one are indicated simply by page number when the context makes it clear—and volume number if necessary—what work is being referred to. Later references, to the extent possible, are indicated by citing short titles. References to Lady Morgan's biography, in its French translation, are indicated parenthetically by volume number and page number (e.g., I, 179). References to standard reference works important in this study are, unless otherwise indicated, to the most recent edition; these include Michaud's *Biographie universelle,* Pierre Larousse's *Grand Dictionnaire universel du XIXe siècle, La Grande Encyclopédie*, E. Bénézit's *Dictionnaire,* Thieme and Becker's *Allgemeines Lexikon der bildender Künstler.* The fundamental early Italian sources of our knowledge of Rosa and his work—Baldinucci, Passeri, Pascoli, and De Dominici—have been handled in the same way. In general, full references, complete with the standard publication facts, to all works that have furnished substantive material to this study are listed in more complete form in the bibliography. In quotations from earlier periods, spellings now considered obsolete in French have been left as in the original, and marked [*sic*] sparingly. Little-known or forgotten writers are identified where I have been able to provide their dates of birth and death and, where possible, a few relevant biographical facts, occasionally bibliographical references (it has not seemed necessary to do the same for, say, Balzac or George Sand).

There are many references to the important modern works by the eminent Rosa specialist Luigi Salerno, i.e., *Salvator Rosa* (Milan: Edizioni per il Club del libro, 1963) and *L'opera completa di Salvator Rosa* (Milan: Rizzoli, 1975); normally, I have referred to these fundamental works simply as Salerno (1963) and Salerno (1975). Works by Rosa appearing in the catalogue provided in the latter publication are identified by Salerno's numbers preceded by an S.

Abbreviations

BM	*Burlington Magazine*
GBA	*Gazette des Beaux-Arts*
OC	*Œuvres complètes*
RDM	*Revue des deux mondes*
RHLF	*Revue d'histoire littéraire de la France*
RLC	*Revue de littérature comparée*

CHAPTER ONE

Crossing the Alps

Near the midpoint of his century and of his career, Salvator Rosa's reputation began to take on an international dimension. While still in Florence, Rosa had earned a brief but flattering entry in the third volume of Pierre Guillebaud's *Trésor chronologique et historique* (1647), in a list of more or less contemporary painters: "En Italie, particulièrement à Florence, le sieur Salvator Rose Napolitain, la fleur des Peintres de cette ville, et mesme des Poëtes, car il fait fort bien une Comedie."[1] Guillebaud's book is largely forgotten, and his survey of painting in his time is, in Jacques Thuillier's view, "assez déconcertant" (p. 130), that is, eccentric. But, as the earliest published reference to Rosa in French that I have located, this passage is precious evidence that Rosa's fame had transcended the Italian cities—Naples, Rome, and Florence—in which he had worked by the time Guillebaud was writing and had crossed the Alps. Alongside those of several lesser, even obscure artists, appear the names of Rubens, Pietro da Cortona, Poussin, La Hyre, and Vouet. More evidence of Rosa's growing reputation can be found a few years later in the efforts made by European rulers outside Italy to attach him to their courts. In 1650 he declined an invitation to go to the court of the Austrian emperor (Salerno 1963, p. 94) and in 1652 treated an invitation from Queen Christina of Sweden similarly (p. 95). In the latter year, Neri Corsini, newly appointed papal nuncio to France, commissioned Rosa to do a battle picture intended as a gift to the young Louis XIV. It seems unlikely the fourteen-year-old monarch had personally expressed an interest in Rosa's work or knew anything about it—it is much more likely that Corsini's choice of Rosa was his own and reflected the artist's growing fame in his native country and, specifically, his reputation as a painter of battle pictures;

Rosa's letters for 1652 (August 27 and October 19) show no evidence of contacts with France. By the mid-1660s the situation is quite different. In 1664 the battle picture commissioned by Corsini reached Versailles with Cardinal Flavio Chigi as donor. At the same time, the Cardinal bestowed on the French king Rosa's *Democritus and Protagoras* (S 184), also known as *The Call of Protagoras to Philosophy,* now in the Hermitage in St. Petersburg. Nothing more is heard of this picture until its appearance in the Walpole collection in the mid-eighteenth century; how it came to leave the French royal collection is unclear.[2] The following year, in 1665, presumably impressed by Rosa's work, Louis XIV invited Rosa to his court; this royal summons was declined like its predecessors. But the *Bataille* had entered the royal collection and eventually worked its way to the Louvre.

Meanwhile, stealing a march on Rosa's battle scene, Rosa's *Apollo and the Sibyl of Cumae* (S 128) had arrived in France, the first of his works to appear there. Its owner was, however, not the king but his chief minister Mazarin. This event must have occurred between 1653 and 1661: the inventory of Mazarin's collections made in the former year lists no such picture, or any other by Rosa, while the inventory made shortly after his death in early 1661 contains the following entry:

> 1240—Un autre faict par Salvator Rosa sur toile, représentant un Grand Paysage où est Apollon assis et appuyé sur la lyre avecq une femme près de luy et deux aultres plus loing, hault de cinq pieds quatre pouces et large de huict piedz, garny de sa bordure de bois couleur gris clair avecq un fillet d'or, prisé, la somme de sept cent cinquante livres, cy.[3]

Presumably Mazarin's Italian origins and ecclesiastical position put him in touch with the Roman art world and account for his interest in Rosa. Or it may be that the picture was an unsolicited gift from somebody in Rome seeking to please the all-powerful cardinal, an avid collector.[4] Despite the glittering context provided by Mazarin and his heirs, this picture does not seem to have won a place in the French wing of the *musée imaginaire* devoted to Rosa's work, probably because it left France before the peak of the pre-romantic vogue for Rosa and before it could attract critical attention.

A fourth picture by Rosa, one that ultimately attracted much attention and indeed admiration, is listed in the 1683 Le Brun inventory of Louis XIV's paintings: *Saül et la Pythonisse.* Since the circumstances in which this picture entered the royal collection are not known, it is difficult to say why the king acquired it. Did the subject interest him? Was the picture a purchase or a gift? When did it arrive in Versailles? The present state of our knowledge does not permit us to answer such questions.[5] At least one rather large collection of Rosa's etchings arrived in France sometime before 1666. In the catalogue he compiled of the huge collection of prints, which were eventually bought by Colbert for the royal cabinet and which came to rest in what is now called the Cabinet des estampes of the Bibliothèque Nationale, the abbé Michel de Marolles writes: "J'ai recueilli les œuvres de plusieurs maîtres, dans un grand volume couvert en veau lépreux desquels est ce Salvator Rosa peintre romain qui a lui-même gravé en eau forte de son dessein 74 pièces lesquelles il a dédiées à son ami Charles de Rubens."[6] As a collector, Marolles had done his work well—though today the total number of Rosa etchings totals over 120. He knew that Rosa—still alive, of course, in 1666—worked in Rome. It would be quibbling to criticize him for claiming that all 74 prints in his collection were dedicated to "Charles de Rubens," i.e., Carlo de' Rossi— there are 85 prints in the *Figurine* series as catalogued by Wallace. I have found no other references to Rosa etchings by seventeenth-century French writers or any other evidence that French print collectors were interested in Rosa. But the Marolles reference, though skimpy and a bit misleading, is suggestive of the future, and the Rosa prints he gathered up laid the foundation for Rosa's "fortune" as etcher.

Thus, by the end of the seventeenth century four major paintings by Rosa and a large body of his prints were housed in prestigious French collections, the most prestigious in fact. But, curiously, we find that Rosa enjoyed little reflected glory in the world of art writing in the age of Louis XIV. The first critical evaluation of him in print that I have located is a rather dry and unenthusiastic paragraph in André Félibien's *Noms des peintres les plus célèbres et les plus connus anciens et modernes*, of 1679:[7] "SALVATOR Rose dit SALVATORIEL, estoit Napolitain. Son principal talent estoit de peindre des batailles, n'estant pas agreable dans les autres grands sujets. Il faisait assez bien les ports de mer & les païsages, neanmoins toûjours d'une maniere bizarre & extraordinaire. Il estoit d'une conversation agreable, imaginatif, & faisoit des Vers. Il mourut vers 1673" (p. 55). In Félibien's ninth *Entretien* (1688), we find a slightly revised version of this text: The last sentence just quoted becomes: "Il mourut en 1673," and Félibien, who, as *Surintendant des bâtiments du Roi*, was in a good position to know, states: "Il y a de ses ouvrages dans le cabinet du Roi & au Palais Mazarin."[8] To put things into perspective, in his treatment of this period of Italian painting, Félibien devotes eight pages to Pietro da Cortona. Still, in these two passages, he has given Rosa a tiny place in French art historical writing. He obviously knows the king's huge *Battle* scene; one suspects that it was the *Saül et la Pythonisse d'Endor* that brought forth the epithet "bizarre et extraordinaire." And he was aware that the Mazarin collection contained at least one Rosa. How he came by his other information about Rosa is not clear, e.g., the fact that Rosa painted "les ports de mer," that his conversation was "agreable" (1679) or "aisée" (1688), that he wrote poetry, and that he died in 1673, though, given the fame Rosa enjoyed in the last decades of his career, it would not be difficult to learn such fundamental facts as the date of Rosa's death. Artistic contacts between Rome and Paris were close, numerous, and varied, thanks to the large French art colony in Rome, the establishment there of the Académie de France, and the long tradition of French royal patronage of Italian artists. Félibien had himself spent some time in Rome in France's diplomatic service—he arrived there (according to the *Dictionnaire de biographie française*) in 1647—but Rosa was in Florence in those years. Still, he may have heard of Rosa in the Roman art world, since Rosa had spent some years there earlier and, by 1647, had become, or was about to become, a major figure in Italian painting.

Printed references to Rosa are rare in France before the publication of the first volume of Dezallier d'Argenville's *Abrégé de la vie des plus fameux peintres* (1745), which offers the first substantial account in French of Rosa's life and work. Thus Félibien's thumbnail sketches were virtually the only ones available to most French readers for over half a century and so assumed great importance. They probably helped to shape the French view of Rosa for some time. The phrase "bizarre et extraordinaire" stands out in bold relief against the rest of Félibien's rather dim image of Rosa's work, and this assessment of Rosa's landscapes must have condemned him in the minds of those who read it. French taste would have to evolve a great deal before Félibien's "bizarre" could become Victor Hugo's "grotesque" or his "extraordinaire" could be replaced by "sublime." Writing at the very turn of the century, Florent Le Comte, in his *Cabinet de singularitez* (1699–1700), only reworked Félibien's text, varying slightly the latter's wording—as if he suffered from "anxiety of influence" or, more likely, feared the accusation of plagiarism. Only one sentence seems to add a new element: where Félibien, in 1679, had written "il faisoit assez bien les ports de mer & les païsages," Le Comte offers this variation: "il excelloit dans les Ports de mer; les Tempêtes & les païsages " (III, 190). Had he, perhaps, actually seen some Rosas and their supposedly stormy skies? Or had he heard Rosa's pictures described in these terms by some artist or collector who knew them directly? In any case, Le Comte, perhaps unwittingly, put into circulation one of the most popular images of Rose's landscapes but added nothing else substantive to Félibien's founding text.

French taste was not monolithic in the neoclassical era and its eighteenth-century prolongation; so it is not impossible that, despite Félibien and those for whom he spoke, Rosa found viewers and even admirers. The evidence from the turn of the century is mixed. Le Comte, as noted, merely echoed Félibien. Roger de Piles, probably the most important French art critic in the generation after Félibien, does not even mention Rosa in his *Abrégé de la vie des peintres* (1699), the counterpart of Félibien's *Noms des peintres* and *Entretiens,* nor is there any reference to Rosa in the early editions of Moréri or in Pierre Bayle's enormously influential *Dictionnaire historique et critique* (1697). On the other hand, the learned abbé Claude Nicaise (1623–1701), reminiscing near the very opening of the new century about the Roman art scene as he had known it on his trips to Rome in the late 1650s and in the 1660s, gave Salvator Rosa a prominent place:

> Parlons maintenant des beaux Arts qui regnent dans Rome, et de ceux qui en faisoient profession de mon temps, et que j'ai vû et pratiqué. Je devrois mettre d'abord à la tête, pour ce qui regarde la peinture, l'illustre et célèbre Mr. Poussin, si je n'avois déjà parlé de lui dans l'Ouvrage qui paraîtra bien tôt et que vous verrez. J'y parle aussi de l'excellent Pietro de Cortone, de Mr.Bellori, de Salvator Rosa, mon voisin, et du seigneur Carlo Maratti, qui l'était aussi.[9]

Nicaise's testimony as to Rosa's standing arrives several decades after the event, and we cannot tell whether it reflects the situation of the 1660s or that of the time of his writing, i.e., September 22, 1700. But it is interesting that he calls Rosa "mon voisin," and that he speaks of having "vû" and "pratiqué" the artists in his list. Thus he almost certainly knew Rosa in person. Even if Nicaise, as one would expect, places Poussin in a category by himself, it is no small tribute to Rosa that Nicaise includes him.

By the opening of the eighteenth century, then, a very small part of Salvator Rosa's work was known in France, several outstanding examples of his painted work were to be seen in important French collections, his prints were being collected, and he enjoyed a certain fame in a limited circle. On the other hand, little information about him was in circulation. Félibien's brief accounts of his life and work, each just a paragraph long, seem to be the only published texts dealing with Rosa before 1700.

Meanwhile, a body of art historical and biographical information about Rosa was building up in Italy. The eighteenth century saw the publication of four fundamental documents by writers who sought to update Vasari. Two of these were contemporaries of Rosa and, perhaps more important, knew him in person: Giovanni Battista Passeri (1610?–1679) and Filippo Baldinucci (1624?–1696). Lione Pascoli (1674–1744) and Bernardo De Dominici (1683–ca. 1750) were born too late to have known the artist. Baldinucci began to bring out his *Notizie dei professori del disegno da Cimabue in qua* in 1681, but publication was not completed until 1728; the article on Rosa was apparently written no earlier than 1693. Pascoli was the next to youngest of the four biographers; the two volumes of his *Vite de' pittori, scultori ed architetti moderni* appeared in 1730 and 1736. De Dominici's *Vite de' pittori, scultori ed architetti napoletani* came out in 1742–1744[10]. Passeri's presentation of Rosa was apparently the first written of the four, but his *Vite de' pittori, scultori ed architetti che hanno lavarato in Roma, morti dal 1641 fino al 1673* did not see publication until 1772, nearly a century after Rosa's death. Thus, in the second and third quarters of the eighteenth century, the four cornerstones of Rosa criticism and biography were put in place.

None of these texts was translated into French, either in the eighteenth century or thereafter. But the information—and misinformation—that they provided about Rosa and his work can be shown to have seeped into French art writing rather soon. In the "avertissement" of his *Abrégé de la vie des plus fameux peintres* (1745), which, especially in the enlarged edition of 1762, contains the fullest French account of Rosa's life and work in the eighteenth century and served as a standard reference for some decades, Antoine-Joseph Dezallier d'Argenville (1680–1765) refers to Baldinucci, but he seems to have consulted Pascoli as well. Dezallier's cousin, the great print collector Pierre-Jean Mariette (1694–1774), must have consulted De Dominici, since, in his entry on Aniello Falcone in his *Abecedario*,[11] he mentions the *Compagnia della morte* and its part in the 1647 revolt in Naples. In their *Dictionnaire des arts de peinture, sculpture et gravure* (1788–1791),[12] Claude-Henri Watelet and Pierre-Charles Lévesque refer to Passari (sic) in their article on Rosa (IV, 439–41), even though this text is largely a digest of Dezallier d'Argenville's fundamental document.

In this early French writing on Rosa, there are references to his literary efforts. In fact, Dezallier d'Argenville's sketch begins: "Il est assez rare qu'un peintre se soit autant distingué dans les lettres que dans son art, on trouve l'un & l'autre dans *Salvator Rosa* ou *Salvatoriel* fils d'un arpenteur" (p. 350). Later, he adds: "Il partageait son temps [à Florence] entre la peinture & la poësie; car *Salvator Rosa* était poëte satyrique, & ses satyres ont été imprimées plusieurs fois; il était encore musicien" (p. 351). But there was little direct knowledge of Rosa's satires on the part of French writers, at least those who wrote about Rosa.[13] All of the more or less complete editions of the *Satire* which were published from the beginning (1695) appeared in Italy.[14]

As has been suggested, published accounts in French of Rosa's life and work entered a new phase with the appearance in 1745–1752 of the first edition of Dezallier d'Argenville's *Abrégé de la vie des plus fameux peintres*. Dezallier, who was an important naturalist as well as an engraver and art writer, traveled in Italy in the years 1714–1716 and began to build up an important collection of his own as well as to acquire expertise in the fields that interested him the most: art and natural history. At the time of Dezallier's Italian trips, none of the major Italian biographies of Rosa had yet been published, so we cannot account for his knowledge of Baldinucci, De Dominici, and Pascoli on that basis. He must have bought his copies of these books after his return to Paris, unless he consulted copies belonging to his cousin Mariette.

In June 1727, Dezallier published in the *Mercure de France* (pp. 1295–1330) a *Lettre sur le choix et l'arrangement d'un cabinet curieux,* addressed to a certain M. de Fougeroux, and mostly devoted to the visual arts. Rosa's name occurs three times in this text, which largely consists of long lists of names of artists, unaccompanied by any details or any comments. Perhaps the best idea of Dezallier's estimate of Rosa is the presence of the latter's name (p. 1297) in a list of twenty-five Italian painters of the sixteenth and seventeenth centuries whose pictures deserve inclusion in a collector's *cabinet,* following up on similar lists of Flemish and French painters. (He rules out all living painters and, more revealingly, Leonardo, Michelangelo, Raphael, Giorgione, Titian, Parmigianino, Veronese, Tintoretto, Correggio, the Carracci, Guido Reni, Domenichino, Lanfranco, and Albani "comme hors de la portée d'un Particulier, s'ils sont originaux," i.e., too expensive for the average collector.) Later (p. 1309) Rosa's name appears in a long list of painters, engravings of whose works should be included in the collector's "six portes feuilles de sujets concernant l'Histoire Sacrée, mêlez des meilleurs Maîtres qui ont suivi les Anciens." Finally (p. 1313), "Salvatore-Roza" is one of dozens of landscapists who should be included in the "Six volumes de Paysages." Curiously, in the section "Des volumes de Grotesques, Bacchanales, Bambochades, Carmesses, Pastorales," Rosa's name does not appear, which suggests that Dezallier is unacquainted with Rosa's *Figurine,* though it may be that he simply does not believe that these armor-clad figures fit into these genres. (Callot is not mentioned either, incidentally, appearing only in the recommended "Quatre Portes feuilles remplis de petits morceaux sur toutes sortes de matieres" [p. 1312].) All in all, for Dezallier, writing in 1727, Rosa is just one name among many, a great many.

A little over a dozen years later, Mariette, in his catalogue of the fine collection of drawings that had belonged to Pierre Crozat (1665–1740), a rich financier and avid collector, produced the first discussion in French of Rosa's drawings and, all in all, the most favorable assessment to date of his work or any part of it:

L'on estime fort parmi les curieux, les Desseins de Salvator Rosa, une fougue de génie, souvent peu mesurée, a fait produire à ce Peintre des idées neuves & singulieres, qui piquent infiniment le goût; mais ce qu'il a fait de plus admirable, sont ses Païsages. Il les dessinoit avec tout l'esprit possible. Ceux qui recherchent les Desseins de ce Maître, trouveront ici de quoi se satisfaire.[15]

When he came to the compilation of the first edition (1745–1752) of his best-known work, the *Abrégé,* Dezallier felt obliged to devote a respectable entry to Salvator Rosa. By then, he had gained access to Baldinucci and to Pascoli, whose biographies of Rosa had appeared in the 1720s and 1730s. Dezallier digests the sixty-odd pages of Baldinucci and the twenty-odd pages of Pascoli into about six pages. Thus, for example, the dates of Rosa's birth and death are given simply as 1615 and 1673. More importantly, Baldinucci's approximately seventy references to specific Rosa paintings are reduced to about two dozen in Dezallier (Pascoli had listed only slightly over twenty). Still, French readers without access to the Italian sources found in Dezallier a great deal more on Rosa than had been available to them before: the essential biographical facts, a number of colorful anecdotes that the Italian writers had put into circulation, a list—admittedly too brief—of Rosa's paintings, an assessment of his personality, cursory discussion of his etchings and drawings, passing references to his literary works, and, as one might expect, a critical evaluation of Rosa's manner and achievement. In this latter domain, Dezallier, for the most part, elaborates on the judgment handed down by Félibien:

> *Salvator Rosa* est plus grand païsagiste qu'historien; ses tableaux sont ornés de belles figures de soldats, il a bien peint les animaux, les batailles, les marines et des caprices pictoresques [*sic*]. Mais il a excellé à faire du païsage, son feüiller est extrêmement léger et spirituel. On ne peut graver avec plus d'esprit et d'une plus belle touche, que ce que nous avons de sa main. (p. 352)

Despite the painter's great gifts ("gout . . . très-bon," "touche admirable," a totally individual style), "son génie était des plus bizarres." Failing or disdaining to consult nature, "il faisoit tout de pratique." His figures are "gigantesques et quelquefois peu correctes." Dezallier may be drawing on some earlier writer, but he gives the impression of having actually seen some Rosa landscapes in his notation of the painter's delicate foliage ("extrêmement léger et spirituel"), and after recording Rosa's ambition to be considered a history painter rather than a landscapist, Dezallier concedes that, in view of the many religious pictures he painted, Rosa gave proof of talent in this genre. Dezallier points, also, to the satirical and the philosophical or didactic sides of the artist's work, thus drawing suggestive links between his painting, his poetry, and literature in general. Indeed, echoing Pascoli's opening sentence, Dezallier begins, as we have seen, by stating: "Il est assez rare qu'un peintre se soit autant distingué dans les lettres que dans son art, on trouve l'un et l'autre dans *Salvatore Rosa* ou *Salvatoriel* fils d'un arpenteur" (p. 350).

Museologically, as already noted, Dezallier has less to offer than his Italian sources; in particular, his list of paintings is much briefer than Baldinucci's and only slightly longer than Pascoli's. On the other hand, he mentions a few pictures seemingly unknown to his predecessors: a *St. Nicolas of Bari* in Naples, and "un païsage avec beaucoup de figures" in Düsseldorf (no painting by Rosa on St. Nicolas is now listed among his works, and there is no Rosa now in Düsseldorf), and, as might be expected, the two Rosas in the French royal collection, that is, the huge *Battle* of 1652 and *Saül et la Pythonisse*. Dezallier is rather helpful in his discussion of Rosa's etchings, citing a number of titles and providing a total figure of eighty-four (Bartsch, in the early nineteenth century, lists eighty-six items). He also mentions some reproductive engravings of those paintings done by various modern engravers (Goupy, A. Pond, A. J. Prenner). He is particularly good on Rosa's drawings—thanks, perhaps, to his cousin Mariette, the cataloguer of Pierre Crozat's superb collection of drawings. While he mentions no specific drawings, one certainly has the impression that he—or Mariette?—has looked carefully at a number of them. His discussion of this part of Rosa's work deserves to be cited in full, as being the first serious criticism of Rosa in French:

> Les desseins de *Salvator Rosa* sont aussi estimés que ses tableaux, ils sont presque tous arrêtés d'un trait de plume lavés [*sic*] au bistre ou à l'encre de la Chine; d'autres ont quelques hachures de plume dans les ombres. On ne peut rien voir de plus léger ni de plus spirituel que la touche de ce maître, elle seule peut le distinguer des autres peintres, joint à sa manière de feüiller des arbres, qui souvent n'est qu'un trait de plume allongé sans être fermé et arrondi, comme sont ordinairement les feuilles des autres païsagistes, ses troncs d'arbres, ses rochers, ses terrasses sont admirables; on le reconnoît encore à ses figures gigantesques, à leurs extrémités qui ne sont pas proportionnées, à ses caractères de têtes et à son goût de draper. On peut dire que ses desseins sont très-chauds et ont beaucoup de couleur: comme ils sont griffonnés on les a souvent copiés, ainsi il faut examiner si la touche franche d'un maître s'y rencontre partout. (p. 354)

If Dezallier is uneven, incomplete, and—like his sources—ill-organized in his presentation of Rosa's life and work, his 1745 sketch inaugurated a new era in French writing about Rosa. The amount of biographical, art historical, and museological information he provided is a vast improvement over the scattered references from 1679 (Félibien) to 1745 and served as the principal source of French art writers for several generations. His view of Rosa reflects, to some extent, the neoclassical prejudices of the seventeenth century in favor of regularity and "correctness." When he writes, "son génie était des plus bizarres" (p. 352), he is echoing Félibien and not yet looking forward to Lady Morgan and Victor Hugo. But, like Félibien, he grants many virtues to Rosa's works, especially his landscapes, etchings, and drawings. After the brief and scattered references to Rosa from Félibien until the publication of Dezallier's *Abrégé,* and after the failure of Roger de Piles to say anything at all about Rosa in his *Abrégé* of 1699, Dezallier fills a serious gap and provides the principal fund of information on which French writers can draw for three quarters of a century.

Dezallier's 1762 revision of his book opens still other horizons. If one compares the 1745 text with the later one, a very important and interesting fact emerges: Dezallier has gained access to Bernardo De Dominici's *Vite de' pittori, scultori, ed architetti napoletani* (published in Naples in 1742–1744) but never mentions the author or his work. As we have seen, Mariette also consulted De Dominici—perhaps the cousins shared a copy of the book. In any case, Dezallier's 1762 text, as far as his chapter on Rosa is concerned, fully deserves to be called a new edition, "revue, corrigée et augmentée de la vie de plusieurs peintres," especially "augmentée." While the general structure of the new sketch remains the same as in 1745, and many passages are untouched except for occasional slight changes in wording, there are significant additions. Most of these are in Dezallier's early pages, on Rosa's origins, schooling, family situation, and—most interestingly—training as a painter. He maintains his statement—based on a misconstruction of his earlier Italian sources—that Ribera took Rosa to Rome on the occasion of the latter's first trip to the papal capital (1639?). Dezallier adds many details about Rosa's relations with Lanfranco, Fracanzano, Ribera, and Aniello Falcone. He refers to an early painting by Rosa that only De Dominici had mentioned: "une Agar avec l'ange qui lui apparoît" (De Dominici had described it more lengthily: "la storia di Agar schiava di Abramo, che languente in un bosco a cagion d'Ismaelle moribondo per la sete, vede apparir l'Angelo" [p. 217]).

The most interesting addition is so brief that it might pass unnoticed: relating the painter's sojourn at Viterbo, in the household of Cardinal Brancaccio, an episode that can be dated to 1639, Dezallier produces this surprising statement: "il y [at Viterbo] fit connoissance avec le poète *Abati,* et se trouva dans la fameuse revolte d'*Aniello;*[16] mais craignant le châtiment du Viceroi, il se retira à Rome, dont le séjour lui convenoit mieux" (p. 275). This nugget of misinformation seems to have lain unnoticed for decades. Art historians failed to notice the impossible chronology—not that Dezallier had given them many reliable *points de repère.* And nobody challenged the fundamental point: that Rosa participated in Masaniello's uprising in Naples in 1647. Thus the legend for which De Dominici is responsible appeared badly mangled, in French, over six decades before Lady Morgan gave it currency. The brevity and *sécheresse* of Dezallier's account, however, prevented the topic from being taken up by writers for political ends or becoming the stuff of fiction. In 1762 French readers and those who wrote for them were much less interested in a Neapolitan mutiny a century earlier than they would be later. Then, too, the figure of the artist as cultural hero and *artiste engagé* was not nearly as fully developed as it would be after the watershed of the French Revolution.

That Dezallier d'Argenville's sketch of Rosa contributed appreciably to the artist's reputation and, more demonstrably, added to the sum of knowledge about him, is indicated in the fact that, after mid-century, compilers of biographical dictionaries—unlike Pierre Bayle and Moréri—regularly saw fit to include entries on Rosa, all derived and digested from Dezallier. (François-Marie de Marsy had omitted Rosa from his *Dictionnaire abrégé de peinture et d'architecture* [1742]). Jacques Lacombe included a substantial article on Rosa in his *Dictionnaire portatif des beaux-arts* (1752), as did Louis-Mayeul Chaudon in his *Nouveau Dictionnaire historique-portatif* (Amsterdam [i.e., Avignon], 1769; 1771 edition, IV, p. 116–17) and the abbé de Fontenay in his *Dictionnaire des artistes* (1776, II, p. 502–04). The famous *Encyclopédie* of Diderot and D'Alembert contained a short passage on Rosa in the article on Naples (XI [1765], 18), but it barely enlarged on Félibien; an even briefer entry figured in the article "Peintre" (XII [1765], p. 266). Almost contemporary with the early phases of the Revolution, the *Dictionnaire des beaux-arts* of Claude-Henri Watelet and Pierre-Charles Lévesque—Volume 1 appeared in 1788, Volume 2 in 1791—contained an article on Rosa a little over two pages long, which may be considered the summing up of the tradition inaugurated by Dezallier d'Argenville.[17] The factual information, the anecdotes, and the critical assessment are essentially but an abridgment of the latter's founding text. Still, a new note is struck in two passages; after speaking of the genres practiced by Rosa, Lévesque's article continues: "il excelloit surtout à peindre des solitudes sauvages, le silence des eaux stagnantes, l'horreur des roches escarpées" (1792 edition, IV, 440).[18] A little later, apropos of Rosa's "tableaux historiques," Lévesque at first seems merely to echo Félibien, but quickly goes on to something new in the French writing on Rosa:

> Ses ouvrages en ce genre ont un merite [*sic*] qui lui est propre et qu'ils doivent à la force de ses conceptions bizarres et capricieuses. C'est un barbare, mais

qui étonne, qui effraye par sa fierté sublime. Quelque chose d'agreste domine dans toutes les parties de ses ouvrages: ses rochers, ses arbres, ses ciels, ses figures et même son exécution, ont quelque chose de rude et de sauvage. (Ibid.)

Within just a few lines, "bizarres" and "capricieuses" give way to "barbare," "étonne," "effraye," "fierté sublime," "rude," and "sauvage." It is as if Lévesque were consciously taking up the challenge posed several decades earlier by Diderot in *De la poésie dramatique* (1758): "La poésie veut quelque chose d'énorme, de barbare et de sauvage."[19] The storms of the Revolution raged at the time of publication of Watelet and Lévesque's *Dictionnaire*; perhaps they raged around Lévesque as he composed the article on Rosa. But he gives no hint of being aware of the legend of Rosa the revolutionary, the follower of Masaniello.

Nearly a century and a half had passed since Rosa's name first appeared in a French book (Guillebaud, 1647). In the second half of the seventeenth century four major paintings by Rosa had entered great French collections—Mazarin's and Louis XIV's.[20] Thumbnail sketches of Rosa and his work by Félibien (1679) remained for decades the principal source of information about the artist. Marolles collected Rosa etchings. For the seventeenth century, then, the Rosa harvest is sparse in most respects.

Still, the seeds had been planted. Rosa's drawings were collected by eminent *curieux* like Crozat and Mariette. And the body of information about Rosa built up in Italy by Passeri, Baldinucci, Pascoli, and, to a very slight degree, De Dominici began to filter into French writing. Most crucial is the article on Rosa in Dezallier d'Argenville's *Abrégé de la vie des plus fameux peintres* (1745, 1762), a text that furnished matter to reference works for at least the next half century.

These developments, however, seen in isolation, would suggest that the image of Rosa lived in somewhat uneasy harmony with the neoclassical aesthetic. His work aroused a certain admiration, but the enthusiasm for it was rather restrained; his reputation was cast in the shade by the glory of great Italian masters of the sixteenth and seventeenth centuries and several great French painters, especially Poussin and Claude Lorrain. We know that, occasionally, another Rosa had been glimpsed, a pre-romantic Rosa leading on to the one who loomed so large in the romantic era.

In the second half of the eighteenth century, before the Revolution and its upheavals, there is evidence of a sharpened taste for Rosa among French collectors—evidence to be examined later in this chapter—but, more important, evidence of a deep and widespread change in sensibility, a new aesthetic climate, which was beneficial to Rosa's reputation. While awaiting the events that would bring about the poetic revolution called for by Diderot ("La poésie veut quelque chose d'énorme, de barbare et de sauvage") a preromantic Zeitgeist was gathering. While the term *pre-romantic* is anachronistic, signs of a momentous shift in cultural reality were abundant. One of the most striking was the widening currency of the word *romantic*, a lexical breakthrough that has been studied in depth in the survey edited by Hans Eichner, *"Romantic" and its Cognates: The European History of a Word*.[21] As it happens, Rosa has a place in a text from the middle of the period under study that encapsulates much of the new Zeitgeist. In 1776, in the introduction to his ground-breaking translation of Shakespeare, Pierre Le Tourneur, discussing the words "romanesque," "pittoresque," and "romantique," produced a sentence fraught with great importance for our subject: "Les tableaux de Salvator Rosa, quelques sites des Alpes, plusieurs Jardins et Campagnes de l'Angleterre ne sont point *Romanesques; mais on peut dire qu'ils sont plus que pittoresques*, c'est-à-dire touchans et *Romantiques*."[22] The implicit link made here between Shakespeare and Rosa represents a new sort of *ut pictura, poesis rapprochement*, one that goes beyond a common thematics or shared formal qualities to posit an emotional affinity, a channel between the core of the great dramatist's plays and the painter's canvases. A half century later, Lady Morgan will offer a number of such *rapprochements* between Rosa and certain great writers, but in 1776 Le Tourneur was a pioneer. While Salvator Rosa's work is not described, the context of Le Tourneur's observation tells us that Rosa's painting is seen as parallel to some of the most salient aspects of the emerging pre-romanticism: the cult of Shakespeare, the vogue of the English-style garden, and the new appreciation for "sublime" mountainous scenery.

Unfortunately, Le Tourneur's pregnant words stand virtually alone in their time, and one might conclude that Rosa played but a modest role in ushering in the pre-romantic era. Direct evidence of his participation in the change is not abundant. But there is a good case to be made that, indirectly and clandestinely, he did indeed help to prepare the ground for what came to be called pre-romanticism. An examination of Diderot's writing on art will be crucial here. The striking sentence already quoted from his *Essai de la poésie dramatique* (1758) appears at the center of a passage that, if one did not know otherwise, might seem to be inspired by looking at Rosa's landscapes:

Qu'est-ce qu'il faut au poète? Est-ce une nature brute ou cultivée, paisible ou troublée? Préférera-t-il la beauté d'un jour pur et serein à l'horreur d'une nuit obscure, où le sifflement interrompu des vents se mêle par intervalles au murmure sourd et continu d'un tonnerre éloigné, et où il voit l'éclair allumer le ciel sur sa tête? Préférera-t-il le spectacle d'une mer tranquille à celui des flots agités? Le muet et froid aspect d'un palais, à la promenade parmi des ruines? Un édifice construit, un espace planté de la main des hommes, au touffu d'une antique forêt, au creux ignoré d'une roche déserte? Des nappes d'eau, des bassins, des cascades, à la vue d'une cataracte qui se brise en tombant à travers des rochers, et dont le bruit se fait entendre au loin du berger qui a conduit son troupeau dans la montagne, et qui l'écoute avec effroi? La poésie veut quelque chose d'énorme, de barbare et de sauvage.[23]

The sentence in which the critic answers his own question is followed by lines that could equally have been inspired by Rosa and, specifically, by the *Battle* in the royal collections, a picture Diderot certainly saw: "C'est lorsque la fureur de la guerre civile ou du fanatisme arme les hommes de poignards, et que le sang coule à grands flots sur la terre, que le laurier d'Apollon s'agite et verdit."

But Diderot's direct references to Rosa and his work are disappointingly rare, even when he is writing about the visual arts. In the *Salon de 1761,* in discussing one of Francesco Casanova's battle scenes, Diderot turns to the artist's "petits tableaux de paysages"[24]: "On dit que Salvator Rosa n'est pas plus beau que cela quand il est beau" (Œ, p. 588). Some years later, in the *Pensées détachées sur la peinture,* appear two observations that seem to be linked: "Quel que soit le coin de la nature que vous regardiez, sauvage ou cultivé, pauvre ou riche, désert ou peuplé, vous y trouverez toujours des qualités enchanteresses, la vérité et l'harmonie. Transportez Salvator Rosa dans les régions glacées voisines du pôle; et son génie les embellira" (Œ, p. 765). Moreover, the critic seems not to have seen much of Rosa's work or to have looked at it closely. And at least one of the two comments on Rosa lacks enthusiasm: "On dit que Salvator Rosa n'est pas plus beau que cela quand il est beau"—Diderot puts the now largely forgotten Casanova on a par with Rosa and, besides, concedes that the earlier Italian landscapist is uneven. Still, in the second passage, the critic speaks without qualification of Rosa's genius.

If Rosa is, so to speak, only a subtext in Diderot's art criticism, it needs to be said, first of all, that Diderot was primarily a critic of the work of his contemporaries as exhibited in the Paris salons. Then, the number of Rosa paintings to be seen in Paris, even by a diligent and enthusiastic *curieux* and *amateur,* was not very large. There were only two Rosas in the royal collections: the huge *Battle,* which seems to have spent the second half of the eighteenth century at the Luxembourg, the *Saül et la Pythonisse,* still presumably at Versailles, and perhaps *Tobie et l'ange.* There were, as we have seen, a fair number of Rosas in private collections, especially in the second half of the century, but it is difficult to say how many collectors made their *cabinets* and *galeries* accessible to the public or even to a famous writer like Diderot. Finally, one must admit that Rosa's reputation was not as towering as those of Leonardo, Michelangelo, Raphael, Correggio, Titian, and—closer to Rosa in time—the Carracci, Guido Reni, Rubens, and even Rembrandt, not to mention French masters like Poussin, Lorrain, and Le Brun.[25]

The case for seeing Diderot as, unwittingly, a follower of Rosa must be made on the grounds that, among the contemporary painters he most admired and about whom he wrote at greatest length, several were, in significant ways, heirs of Rosa, indirect pupils, so to speak: Joseph Vernet, Jacques-Philippe Loutherbourg, Francesco Casanova, and, to some extent, Hubert Robert. In his earliest *Salon* (1759), Diderot provides a capsule description of "une foule de Marines" by Vernet that might be seen as a glimpse into Rosa's world, only a little distorted: "Il est tout entier dans quatorze ou quinze tableaux. Les mers se soulèvent et se tranquillisent à son gré; le ciel s'obscurcit, l'éclair s'allume, le tonnerre gronde, la tempête s'élève; les vaisseaux s'embrasent; on entend le bruit des flots, les cris de ceux qui périssent; on voit . . . , on voit tout ce qui lui plaît" (*Œ*, p. 561). Rosa specialists have observed that none of his works literally depicts a storm, but the murky skies and wind-blown trees convince the viewer otherwise. (As for the human drama Diderot briefly evokes—"les cris de ceux qui périssent"— this is decidedly un-Rosa-like.) Even more elaborate descriptions of Vernet's storms can be found in the *Salons* of 1763 (*Œ*, pp. 562–63) and 1765 (pp. 568–69). In the *Salon de 1767*, Vernet's *Port de mer au clair de lune* provokes in Diderot a dithyramb reminiscent of his "Éloge de Richardson." The rather objective descriptive passage leading up to the lyrical outburst is not without suggesting Rosa, if one highlights certain details (and neglects certain others): "une fabrique . . . les débris d'un pilotis . . . des rochers escarpés . . . un massif de pierre . . . deux matelots, l'un assis par devant, l'autre accoudé par derrière . . . ces nuées sombres et chargées de leur mouvement" (*Œ*, pp. 575–76). The tribute to Vernet climaxes in a passage which exalts the painter's universality and also reminds us of Rosa at many points:

Que ne fait-il pas avec excellence! Figures humaines de tous les âges, de tous les états, de toutes les nations; arbres, animaux, marines, perspectives; toute sorte de poésie, rochers imposants, montagnes éternelles, eaux dormantes, agitées, précipitées; torrents, mers tranquilles, mers en fureur; sites variés à l'infini, fabriques grecques, romaines, gothiques; architecture civile, militaire, ancienne, moderne; ruines, palais, chaumières; constructions, gréements, manœuvres, vaisseaux, cieux, lointains, calme, temps orageux, temps serein; ciel de diverses saisons, lumières de diverses heures du jour; tempêtes, situations déplorables, victimes et scènes pathétiques de toute espèce; jour, nuit, lumières naturelles, artificielles, effets séparés ou confondus de ces lumières. (*Œ*, p. 577)

Granting that certain features of Vernet's universe, as defined by Diderot, are absent or unimportant in Rosa, it is still possible to point here, and here, and here to many that could be said to be derived, in one way or another, from Rosa.

Diderot so admired Vernet that he became—or imagined that he had become—the owner of a *Tempête* by this artist. In the *Salon de 1769* he speaks of the picture "que je tiens de son amitié" (*Salons,* IV, 88) and goes on to praise it ("le ciel, les eaux, l'arbre déchiré, les vues sont de la plus grande beauté" [IV, 89]), but not without giving vent to some reservations: "[J]e ne suis pas aussi content des roches, de la terrasse et des figures" (IV, 89). In the famous *Regrets sur ma vieille robe de chambre,* written a little later, his enthusiasm for this picture knows no bounds:

> Vois ce phare; vois cette tour adjacente qui s'élève à droite; vois ce viel [*sic*] arbre que les vents ont déchiré. Que cette masse est belle! Au dessous de cette masse obscure, vois ces rochers couverts de verdure. . . . Vois cette terrasse inégale qui s'étend du pré de ces rochers vers la mer. . . . O Dieu, reconnois les eaux que tu as créés [*sic*]. Reconnois les et lorsque ton souffle les agite, et lorsque ta main les appaise. Reconnois les sombres nuages que tu avois rassemblés et qu'il t'a plu de dissiper. . . . O mon ami, le beau Vernet que je possède! Le sujet est la fin d'une tempête sans catastrophe fâcheuse. Les flots sont encore agités; le ciel couvert de nuages; les matelots s'occupent sur leur navire échoué; les habitants accourent des montagnes voisines. . . . [C]omme ces montagnes de la droite sont vaporeuses; comme ces rochers et les édifices surimposés sont beaux; comme cet arbre est pittoresque; comme cette terrasse est éclairée; comme la lumière s'y dégrade.[26] (IV, 388–89)

Taking the passage as a whole, one notes that Diderot is at least as much absorbed in the melodramatic rescue of the human beings in Vernet's painting as in the stormy sea and rugged coast. Rosa's approach would have been more "philosophical," no doubt. Still, even if Vernet's landscapes have taken an approach that differs from Rosa's, they owe something, directly or indirectly, to the Italian artist. Vernet, like virtually all the more successful French painters in the seventeenth and eighteenth centuries, had spent considerable time (1734–1753) in Italy, mostly in Rome, and had opportunities to admire Rosa's work.[27] Clearly Rosa's works were not the only possible models for Vernet's mountainous scenes and storms at sea; but they are a major source—the current of such painting arose with Rosa or at least flowed through him. Whether Diderot actually owned Vernet's *Tempête* or merely wished that he did, he was looking at a picture that, while it contained elements that might not have appealed to Rosa, revealed the presence of Rosa even if the *philosophe* and art critic failed to acknowledge it.

Diderot's confrontation with the work of Francesco Casanova (1727–1802) follows much the same pattern. Here, however, it is mostly Rosa's battle pictures that are in the background. (Casanova had studied the work of Courtois in Italy and received advice from Charles Parrocel during a stay in Paris toward the end of the latter's life.)[28] As we have seen, one of the critic's few direct references to Rosa appears in the section on Casanova in the *Salon de 1761;* a look at the context of the reference to Rosa is in order:

> En vérité cet homme a bien du feu, bien de la hardiesse, une belle et vigoureuse couleur. Ce sont des rochers, des eaux, et pour figures des soldats qui sont en embuscade ou qui se reposent. On croirait que chaque objet est le produit d'un seul coup de pinceau; cependant on y remarque des nuances sans fin. On dit que Salvator Rosa n'est pas plus beau que cela quand il est beau.
>
> Ce Casanove est dès à présent un homme à imagination, un grand coloriste, une tête chaude et hardie, un bon poète, un grand peintre. (Œ, p. 588)

As noted earlier, these observations were inspired by some of Casanova's "petits tableaux de paysages," but it was usually his battle pictures that aroused Diderot's enthusiasm: "Le feu, la poussière et la fumée, éclairent d'un côté et couvrent de l'autre une multitude infinie d'acteurs qui remplissent un vaste champ de bataille. Quelle couleur! quelle lumière! quelle étendue de scène! Les cuirasses rouges, vertes ou bleues, selon les objets qui s'y peignent sont toujours d'acier" (Œ, p. 587). Of one of Casanova's battle pictures at the Salon of 1765, he writes: "C'est l'image que j'ai des horreurs d'une mêlée" (Œ, p. 594). Another picture in the same salon, *Une marche d'armée,* inspired one of Diderot's longest descriptions. Though his praise is seriously undercut by fault-finding, e.g., "Toute la toile ne vous offre que les divers accidents d'une grande croûte de pain brûlé" (Œ, p. 592), he obviously admires "l'effet de ces grandes roches, de cette grande masse de pierre élevée au centre de la toile, de ce merveilleux pont de bois, et de cette précieuse voûte de pierre, détruit et perdu" (Ibid.) and pronounces the picture to be "une des plus belles machines et des plus pittoresques que je connaisse"(Œ, p. 590) and "la plus belle production de Casanove" (Œ, p. 593). Twice (Œ, pp. 590, 593) he uses the word "poésie" to capture the essence of the picture's effect, and he pronounces it "un beau poème, bien conçu, bien conduit, et"—warning of negative criticism to come—"mal écrit" (Œ, p. 592). Whatever Diderot's reservations, it is obvious from his long description that the

subject is Rosaesque; indeed, one might say doubly Rosaesque, since it com-
bines a "sublime" landscape with a military theme. The former includes such
familiar motifs as "ce vieux château, des antiques tours dégradées," "cet autre pont en voûte" (cf. Rosa's *Il Ponte, S* 39, in the Pitti), "le torrent des
montagnes," "masse de pierre," "une masse de grandes roches de hauteurs
inégales," "cette tremblante fabrique de bois," "précipices obscurs et
profonds," "un vaste étang," "un arbre au pied du monticule," "pierres
dégradées," "des arbrisseaux et des plantes parasites," "ruines lointaines" (*Œ*,
pp. 590–91). As for the army, it is perhaps not so much Rosa's big battle
scenes like the one in the Louvre, then in the Luxembourg, that are evoked
as the landscapes in which small knots of soldiers and banditti appear:

> [L]es uns baignant leurs chevaux, les autres se désaltérant, ceux-ci étendus
> nonchalamment sur les bords de cet étang vaste et tranquille: ceux-là, sous
> une tente qu'ils ont formée d'un grand voile qui tient ici au tronc d'un arbre, là
> à un bout de roche, buvant, causant, riant, mangeant, dormant, assis, debout,
> couchés sur le dos, couchés sur le ventre. . . . On voit au sommet des roches
> quelques soldats en entier; à mesure qu'ils s'engagent dans le sentier escarpé,
> ils disparaissent; on les retrouve lorsqu'ils débouchent sur le pont de bois. (*Œ*,
> pp. 590–92)

Many of these figures could be Rosa *figurine* recruited into a large armed
force; those who appear, toward the end of this passage, remind us of those
Rosa landscapes in which soldiers and banditti appear in rocky settings, scenes
that were to inspire so much of the painting in the Rosa manner and so much
of the writing about him. In succeeding *Salons*—those of 1767 and 1769—
Diderot continues to focus on various military pictures by Casanova, often
high-lighting qualities or details which remind us of Rosa. His words often
might be just as well applied to Rosa's *Battaglia eroica* in Paris: "[Il] y a du
feu, du mouvement, de l'action dans toutes deux. On y frappe bien; on s'y
défend bien; on y attaque; on y tue bien" (*Œ*, p. 594). "Sur les ailes, mêlées
particulières dérobées par le feu, la poussière et la fumée, et s'enfonçant ou
s'éteignant dans la profondeur du tableau, donnent à la scène de l'étendue
et de la vigueur à la masse principale" (*Œ*, p. 596). Occasionally pictures by
Casanova seem to hark back to some Dutch or Flemish genre painter like
Wouwerman—mentioned by Diderot apropos of two pictures in the *Salon
de 1767* (*Œ*, p. 599)—or to look ahead to Meissonier.[29]

Diderot's indirect confrontations with Rosa's themes and manner in
Jacques-Philippe Loutherbourg (1740–1812) and especially Hubert Robert
(1733–1808) can be dealt with more briefly since the works by these two
artists that Diderot saw and described in his *Salons* are reminiscent of Vernet
and Casanova. Loutherbourg, it is worth pointing out, studied for a time

under Casanova (*Œ*, pp. 611, 632) and eventually moved to London, where, no doubt, his pre-romantic landscapes were even more popular than in Paris. (He was a member of the royal academies in both cities.) He exhibited at the Salon from 1763 until 1771, the year of his move to London. Especially from 1767 on, his subject matter overlaps that of Vernet and Casanova, not to mention Poussin (*Œ*, pp. 628–29). Despite some strictures, Diderot's criticism of Loutherbourg in his *Salon de 1767* bristles with familiar terms evocative of Rosa: "murailles ruinées," "fabrique voûtée," "vaisseau penché," "grand rocher," "horreurs de la tempête"—recalling the "horreur des Alpes" and "horreurs d'une mêlée" already noted—"mer orageuse," "ciel obscur," "masses escarpées, hérissées, inégales," "flots sombres et écumeux," "vaisseau battu de la tempête," etc. (*Œ*, pp. 621–25). In the same *Salon, Autre Paysage* (i.e., *Paysage avec château et chute d'eau*) is described in Rosaesque terms, for its "vieux château," "gros quartier de roche brute," "haute masse de roches couvertes d'arbustes," and "torrent," though the rather pastoral genre scene in the foreground inspires negative comparisons with Vernet and, revealingly, Poussin (*Œ*, pp. 625–30). Diderot might have pointed out that the "arbustes" fringing the "masse de roches" on the left are leaning as if lashed by the wind, like so much of Rosa's vegetation, and the rocks themselves, to our eyes, are highly suggestive of such works as *Paesaggio roccioso con figure* (S 245) and *Paesaggio con sant'Antonio abate e san Paolo eremita* (S 249), to mention just a few of the pictures that evince Rosa's obsession with massive, jagged boulders. It is a *Tempête* shown at the Salon of 1769 that finds Diderot enraptured by a Loutherbourg that appeared as the *Salon* was about to close: "C'était une *Tempête;* ah! mon ami, quelle tempête! Rien de plus beau que des rochers placés à la gauche, entre lesquels les flots allaient se briser en écumant; au milieu de ces eaux agitées, on voyait les deux pieds d'un malheureux qui se noyait attaché au débris du vaisseau, et l'on frémissait" (*Œ*, pp. 632–633). And, from here on, as often, Diderot focuses on the melodramatic and human content of the picture, so obviously similar to his beloved Vernet. The Rosaesque pictures Loutherbourg exhibited in 1771 do not, in general, keep Diderot long—of *Un paysage* (no. 102), for example, he says simply: "Fort bon." (*Œ*, p. 634)—and the pictures on which he dwells inspire a mixed reaction: of *Une bataille de cuirassiers contre les Turcs*, despite "beaucoup de chaleur" and "la couleur [. . .] belle et variée," Diderot pronounces the painter "un peu lourd et court jusque dans ses chevaux" (*Œ*, p. 635); but he is charmed by *Un naufrage*. Here again, however, he is more touched by the pathos of the scene ("Ce sujet est pathétique et plein de naturel; il parle à l'âme") than by the jagged rocks to which the survivors cling and the "fureur des flots" that caused their plight (*Œ*, p. 636).

As for Hubert Robert, we have already seen that Diderot was sensitive to "la poésie des ruines," that is, to Robert's favorite subject and the one that made him a favorite in the pre-romantic era, especially for his constantly recurring depictions of classical architecture in ruins. Robert spent nearly eleven years (1754–1765) in Italy, mostly in Rome; he also accompanied the abbé de Saint-Non to Naples in the spring of 1760 and made drawings that eventually appeared as engravings in Saint-Non's monumental *Voyage pittoresque de Naples et de Sicile* (1781–1786). Thus Robert had a long, close contact with the city where Rosa had spent most of his life as an artist and he had visited the city of Rosa's birth. The interaction between these two artists is not as great as that between Rosa and the other painters whom we have been examining for signs of Rosa's influence. Classical ruins are not a major theme in Rosa's work, even though they figure prominently in the background in several of his *Battles,* notably the well-known picture now in the Louvre (and in Paris since 1664). Moreover, the ruins in Rosa's pictures suggest the ferocity and destructiveness of war, while in Robert's they are the product of the slow attrition of time, with a mood Diderot describes as "une douce mélancolie" (Œ, p. 641). Perhaps it is Rosa's occasional suggestion of a certain *délabrement*, as in several of the early pictures in the Pitti—*Il Ponte* (S 39), for example—that is closest in mood to Robert. However, the architecture is not antique, and Rosa's leaden pallet is not Robert's. Robert first exhibited at the Salon of 1767 (he had been admitted to the Académie royale de peinture et de sculpture in July 1766, soon after his return from the long stay in Rome), and Diderot immediately took notice of him, devoting a good deal of space to his numerous *envois*—including some unfavorable comparisons with Vernet (Œ, pp. 638–39). Since, as already suggested, the Rosaesque elements in Robert's work are not to the fore—and Diderot could not have known that the French artist made a drawing of Rosa's *Mercury and The Dishonest Woodsman,*[30] no doubt while in Rome—the critic has little or no occasion to expostulate on such elements. But when he theorizes about what he himself called "la poésie des ruines," he conjures up many images that will remind us of Rosa:

> Les idées que les ruines réveillent en moi sont grandes. . . . Qu'est-ce que mon existence éphémère, en comparaison de celle de ce rocher qui s'affaisse, de ce vallon qui se creuse, de cette forêt qui chancelle, de ces masses suspendues au-dessus de ma tête et qui s'ébranlent? Je vois le marbre des tombeaux tomber en poussière, et je ne veux pas mourir! et j'envie un faible tissu de fibres et de chair, à une loi générale qui s'exécute sur le bronze! Un torrent entraîne les nations les unes sur les autres au fond d'un abîme commun; moi, moi seul, je prétends m'arrêter sur le bord et fendre le flot qui coule à mes pieds.
>   Si le lieu d'une ruine est périlleux, je frémis. (Œ, p. 644)

If this landscape, with its crumbling rock, deepening valley, trembling forest, looming crags, inspires the awe associated with the sublime rather than "la douce mélancolie," it is because Diderot's imagination has been transported from the ruins of man's constructions, located in history, to the world of nature, which is being imperceptibly destroyed by immeasurable ages. Whether Diderot has Rosa in mind or not does not matter; the world he imagines behind or beyond Robert's picturesque ruins is more like Rosa's than it is like Robert's. It is as if the critic wished the French artist were more like the Italian one.[31]

While Diderot's unwitting revelation of Rosa's presence in contemporary painting represents, as already acknowledged, a hidden, underground phenomenon, that presence made itself felt more openly in a small body of somewhat disparate documents. The abbé François Arnaud, coeditor with Jean-Baptiste Suard of the *Journal étranger*, in the issue for February–March 1760, reviewed Giovanni Gaetano Bottari's *Raccolta di lettere sulla pittura, scultura ed architettura* (1757–1773), which offered in its early volumes the text of twenty of Rosa's letters to his friend G. B. Ricciardi. Arnaud used the occasion to relate some of the standard anecdotes about Rosa, to offer, in a long footnote, a critical evaluation of his work, and to quote at length from a letter in which the artist issued a vehement declaration of artistic freedom. These extracts are the first publication in French from Rosa's correspondence. (Ricciardi had complained that the pictures Rosa painted for him contained too few human figures.) Arnaud is struck by the consistency of the artist's style or manner as both writer and painter: "On croit, en lisant ses lettres, voir ses tableaux et ses estampes: c'est la même fougue, la même bizarrerie, la même singularité."[32] In a letter of 1773, Suard made an interesting comparison between two tales of Diderot and Rosa's work: "Ce sont deux tableaux de Salvator Rosa dans une galerie peinte par Albane."[33] In 1776, Pierre-Jean-Baptiste Nougaret, in his *Anecdotes des beaux-arts*, reprints Rosa's letter to Ricciardi, which Arnaud had revealed to French readers, and similarly regales them with colorful anecdotes about Rosa and, in particular, the serio-comic atmosphere surrounding Rosa's deathbed.

Rosa did not fare even this well with the poets in the eighteenth century who produced didactic poems on the art of painting, after the manner of Charles Du Fresnoy's *De arte graphica* (1668), which Roger de Piles had rendered into French almost simultaneously. The abbé François-Marie de Marsy, in his *La Peinture* (1740), and Watelet, in his *L'Art de peindre* (1760), do not even mention Rosa. Only Antoine-Marin Lemierre finds a place for him in *La Peinture* (1769), by including a reference to "ce hardi Salvator."[34]

While French writing about Rosa had made clear from the beginning (i.e., Guillebaud, in 1647) that the painter was also a writer, direct access to Rosa's poetry seems to have remained limited in France long after the *Satire* had been published in Italy, around 1694. In fact, there has never been a complete French edition of Rosa's satires, either in Italian or in French translation. But both editions of Dezallier d'Argenville's crucial text about Rosa in his *Abrégé de la vie des plus fameux peintres* (1745, 1762), open with sentences that insist on Rosa's literary achievement. Dezallier's 1745 text begins, "Il est rare qu'un peintre se soit autant distingué dans les lettres que dans son art, on trouve l'un & l'autre dans *Salvator Rosa* ou *Salvatoriel* fils d'un arpenteur."[35] This sentence is repeated in 1762, but the author also provided some explicit information on Rosa's poetry, identifying the subjects of the six satires known at that time and quoting nine lines in Italian from *La Musica*. This brief passage would seem to be the first publication in France of a poetic text by Rosa.

From these humble beginnings, knowledge of Rosa's satires spread, but in halting fashion. As noted earlier, the Marquis Daignan d'Orbessan had included a translation of Rosa's first satire, *La Musica*, in his *Mélanges historiques, critiques, de physique, de littérature et de poésie* (1768), but, while this work was published in Paris and Toulouse, the learned magistrate lived and wrote in the Comté de Foix, far from the capital.[36] In 1784, a brief passage on Rosa's satiric poetry was included in the French translation of Girolamo Tiraboschi's *Storia della letteratura italiana*—the original appeared at Modena in 1772—and is rather pungent, though shaky, as biography: "Salvator Rosa, peintre & poëte Napolitain, avec un style négligé, avec beaucoup de traits obscenes, mais invectivant avec hardiesse & déclamant d'un ton vigoureux, est, quoique de fort loin, l'émule de Juvénal. Ce peintre poëte qui a écrit contre les poëtes & les peintres, & dont nous parlerons encore une fois, mourut à Naples l'an 1675."[37] French knowledge of Rosa's poetry, to judge by the published texts I have discovered, would make no more significant progress until, like so much of Rosa's life and work, they were brought to vivid life in Lady Morgan's epoch-making biography, published in both English and French in 1824.

If access to Rosa's poetic production was largely blocked until the publication of Lady Morgan's book, Frenchmen had, as we have seen, many ways of seeing and reacting to his work in the visual arts: there were paintings, drawings, and etchings in French collections, including the monarch's. But the expansion of tourism in the eighteenth century opened up many new opportunities for French art-lovers to view his work, since the favorite destination was Italy, the storehouse of a large number of Rosa's pictures then as now. Even though Italy declined as a source of significant artistic production (though one must not exaggerate: eighteenth-century Italy produced a number of artists who cannot be dismissed as insignificant), the accumulated wealth of earlier masterpieces and the even older remains of Roman civilization tempted ever more tourists to cross the Alps and do the Italian sections of the Grand Tour. These experiences led to an immense body of travel writing about Italy (too vast to sift in this study) that can be selectively sampled for evidence of Rosa's standing.

Except for the allusions to Rosa in the texts by le Père Nicaise examined earlier, I find no travel documents from the seventeenth century that reflect French contact with Rosa and his work. (Guillebaud never went to Italy.) André Félibien may have heard of Rosa during his Roman stay (1647–1649), but his writing on Rosa reveals no direct knowledge of either the man or the work. Several French painters, notably Jacques Courtois ("le Bourguignon") and two members of the Parrocel dynasty, clearly knew the artist or his work or both, but they left no literary record of their experience. Even Dezallier d'Argenville, who had traveled to Italy and encountered evidence of Rosa's reputation, relied primarily on the major Italian sources—Baldinucci, Pascoli, and De Dominici (Passeri's book was not published until 1772)—rather than on personal contact with Rosa's work, when he wrote his important texts of 1745 and 1762. His cousin Mariette probably supplied him information and critical assessments of Rosa's drawings and etchings. His museological entries on Rosa's paintings may, in some cases, reflect visits to Italian galleries such as the Pitti and to churches, but the information he provides could have been gleaned secondhand from his Italian literary sources, Baldinucci et al.[38]

However, French visitors to Italy could have enjoyed a rich experience of Rosa's work, especially in Rome and Florence. The accounts by French travelers to Italy show that, in a number of cases, they took advantage of the opportunity. The documents reveal a rising, if uneven, curve. Montesquieu, traveling in Italy between 1728 and 1729, makes no reference to Rosa but does mention a number of Italian artists close in time to Rosa: Reni, Domenichino, Bernini, Solimena, Guercino, Preti, Albani, Luca Giordano, Zuccari, and Maratti.[39] About a decade later, another French magistrate, the Président Charles de Brosses, takes note of Rosa's works in various churches and galleries in Genoa, Venice, Bologna, and Rome.[40] De Brosses's comments are, at best, succinct ("fort joli," "médiocre," "fort beau," "excellents"); more often than not, he simply names the subject or indicates the genre of a picture. At least he visited the church where Rosa is entombed and noted the bust of the painter. Charles Duclos, in 1767, almost entirely absorbed in papal politics, has no time for Rosa in his *Voyage en Italie* (not published until 1791). Rosa fared a little better with another more notorious French visitor to Italy, the Marquis de Sade, who was avoiding the French authorities in 1775–1776. He did not visit Rosa's tomb but did record his contact with some half a dozen Rosa pictures in Rome, as his *Voyage d'Italie* reveals. However, he provides no commentary or evaluation of any of them,[41] not even *The Murder of Abel* in the Palazzo Borghese, perhaps the picture now in the Galleria Doria Pamphili (S 191). That Sade was aroused by some of the art treasures to be seen in Italy is evident from his *Juliette ou les prosperités du vice:* in the Uffizi, the narrator lingers over Titian's *Venus,* the sculptured *Medici Venus, Caligula caressant sa sœur,* and two sculptures on suitably erotic subjects, a *Hermaphrodite* and a *Priape.*[42] It is clear that Sade drew on his Italian experience in the writing of *Juliette,* but Rosa, it appears, was not a very meaningful part of that experience: Sade's lengthy description of a volcanic landscape in the Appenines (VIII, 590–93) might well have included a reference to Rosa but did not. Nor did the passage about the brigand Brisa-Testa (IX, 206 ff). Sade's tastes in art do not have the flavor of pre-romanticism. It is particularly tantalizing that, in Naples, he devotes a curious passage of the *Voyage d'Italie* to Masaniello's revolt (XVI, 402–03) but makes no reference to the legend that Rosa took part in the uprising. Presumably he was unaware of Rosa's participation; in any case, he is more interested in the purely political and military aspects of that historical episode.

The Italian travel books were mostly published posthumously. They seem to have played the role that postcards or photographs do for modern tourists: they were proof of the authors' travel adventures and meant or, at least, allowed to circulate among their friends; certainly this is true of De Brosses's *Lettres.*[43] But another sort of travel writing flourished in the eighteenth century: guidebooks for tourists. While such books often dealt with practical matters such as food and lodging, they undertook, in many cases, to help tourists decide what monuments and works of art they should see and sometimes suggested why. This was particularly important for travelers to Italy, given the enormous number of tombs, ruins, churches, galleries, paintings, and statues with claims to the tourist's attention.

The painter Nicolas Cochin's *Voyage d'Italie ou recueil de notes sur les ouvrages de peinture ou de sculpture qu'on voit dans les principales villes d'Italie* (1756)[44] seems to represent a turning point. As Elisabeth Chevallier says: "Au tournant du demi-siècle, les amateurs voient enfin paraître le guide qui leur faisait défaut."[45] From the standpoint of the present study, it suffers from Cochin's decision to exclude Rome from his recueil—there was, he claimed, simply too much art in the Eternal City (I, viii). Still, Rosa makes a respectable showing in his guidebook intended for art-lovers, even if Cochin just barely mentions Rosa's *Assumption* (now in Notre-Dame) and *St. Paul the Hermit* in Milan and says nothing about his *Doubting Thomas*—or any other painting—in Viterbo. Florence had, and still has, one of the greatest numbers of Rosas, and so Cochin mentions a number of Rosas (or works attributed to Salvator Rosa):

Un beau Paysage de *Salvator Rosa,* d'une couleur vraie; & un autre petit tableau de deux figures, du même maître, touché de grande manière & avec beaucoup d'esprit. (II, 6; in the Uffizi)

Un grand Paysage, dit de *Salvator Rosa,* mais qui ne paroît point du tout en être. (II, 62; Pitti)

Deux Paysages, de *Salvator Rosa:* ils sont beaux, mais les figures n'en sont pas touchées avec esprit. (II, 71; Palazzo Corsini)

It is not always possible to identify the paintings mentioned by Cochin; the "autre petit tableau de deux figures," however, is certainly the *Paesaggio con due figure,* an oil sketch still in the Uffizi (S 54). Perhaps Cochin's most interesting reference to Rosa concerns a *Sacrifice d'Abraham* by Livio Meus, also in the Uffizi: "Ce tableau est fait, dit-on, pour imiter la manière de *Lanfranco,* mais il semble plutôt dans le goût de *Salvator Rosa.* Il est composé avec le caractère fier de ce peintre, c'est-à-dire de grand goût & avec beaucoup de feu" (I, 15). Cochin has other significant references to Rosas that he has seen:

Deux paysages, où sont des rochers, de *Salvator Rosa,* très-beaux, brossés librement, & de la plus belle facilité. (II, 154; Bologna, Palais Zambeccari)

Un petit tableau représentant des Soldats, par *Salvator Rosa.* Il est excellent. (III, 144; Venice, Palais Sagredo)

On voit aussi deux tableaux d'animaux, de M. *Roos* ou de *Salvator Rosa,* dont l'un, où est une chevre, est bien brossé: le petit fond en est très-beau. (III, 182; Vicenza, Palais de la justice)

Une petite Marine fort belle, de ce ton grisâtre coloré, du Salvator Rosa. (III, 229; Brescia, Casa Avogadri)

Un petit tableau fort beau, représentant des soldats, la mer & quelques rochers: il paroît de *Salvator Rosa.* (III, 230; Brescia, Casa Avogadri)

Today there are no paintings by Rosa in Bologna, Venice, Vicenza, or Brescia. But, with the possible exception of the animal paintings in Vicenza—and even Cochin says that they may be by "M. Roos"—the pictures may have been by Rosa but moved to other locations since the time of Cochin, or we could be dealing here with pictures "in the manner" of Rosa or pictures mistakenly attributed to Rosa, perhaps by Johann Melchior Roos (1659–1731), a landscapist and *peintre animalier.* But Bénézit and Thieme and Becker do not list any pictures by him in Vicenza.

Some years later, writing to a young artist (Pierre-Charles Jombert, prix de Rome, 1772)—the *Lettres à un jeune artiste peintre, pensionnaire à l'Académie royale de France à Rome*[46] remained unpublished until 1836— Cochin seeks to steer his young correspondent toward Rosa but uses even stronger language than in 1756: "vous serez effrayé de la fierté, du grand, du sublime, mêlé de quelque chose de barbare, que vous trouverez dans Salvator Rosa."[47]

From about midcentury, then, there exists a genre of travel writing with a different purpose from that of the books by Montesquieu, De Brosses, and Sade. One may say that, as early as Misson's well-known *Nouveau voyage d'Italie fait en l'année 1688* (1691), publishers had been aware of a market for touristic guidebooks to Italy. And Misson did contain the promise of things to come: "Il y a chez Misson . . . des développements qui doivent être considérés comme les premières analyses d'œuvres d'art figurant dans un guide de voyage" (Chevallier, p. 370). But Misson's often-reprinted book was replaced by Cochin, especially with regard to the attention it gives the visual arts. After Cochin, typical guidebooks incorporated the kind of information he had provided. According to Elisabeth Chevallier, the most important were those of the abbé Jérôme Richard and the astronomer Jérôme de Lalande. Richard's six-volume *Description historique et critique de l'Italie* appeared in Paris in 1766; Lalande's *Voyage d'un François en Italie,* in 1769. Rosa fared rather well with the abbé Richard's *Description.* In the "Discours préliminaire," Richard, writing on landscape, gave Rosa the second prize: "Claude Lorrain a parfaitement réussi dans ce genre, & tient le premier rang parmi les paysagistes. *Salvator Rosa* a représenté la nature brute & sauvage, mais d'un style noble & grand; il connoissoit les points de vûe les plus frappans des Apennins où il paroît qu'il avoit étudié la nature."[48] Volume III of Richard's work contains a "chronologie des peintres en Italie," in which, under the heading "École romaine," he provides a concise and rather favorable sketch of Rosa's work, introduced by a slightly erroneous date of birth and a correct date of death:

Ses tableaux de chevalet sont répandus dans toute l'Italie, où ils sont fort estimés. Il peignoit avec la plus grande vérité, & rendoit la nature telle qu'elle étoit. On a de lui d'excellens tableaux de batailles, de chasses, de paysages & d'animaux, qui étoient son vrai genre.[49] Son coloris est vigoureux; son dessein [*sic*] est quelquefois bizarre; mais tous ses tableaux ont un air original, qui ne permet pas que l'on ne s'y méprenne [. . .]. Salvator Rosa a gravé à l'eau-forte tous ses desseins, dont on trouve la collection chez ses héritiers à Rome. (III, xl)

Rather oddly, in his pages on Florence, Richard mentions not a single picture by Rosa. In Naples, the good abbé has a vague reference to Masaniello's revolt, but none to Rosa, Falcone, or the *Compagnia della morte* (IV, 101–05, 256). In Rome, however, he takes note of the tombs of Maratti and Salvator Rosa (VI, 344), "peintre de Rome & poëte distingué," and, more importantly, praises three pictures by Rosa: "une bataille de *Salvator Rosa,* l'un des meilleurs tableaux que j'aie vu [*sic*] de ce maître, & qui pourroit faire le pendant de celui de P. de Cortone, qui est au Capitole" (p. 75), "le meurtre d'Abel, très-grand tableau de *Salvator Rosa,* d'un pinceau fier & vigoureux" (p. 81), and "Job qui écoute les reproches des ses amis, tableau de belle expression & d'un pinceau vigoureux, par *Salvator Rosa.*"[50]

Lalande, in his *Voyage,* takes note of two pictures by Rosa in Milan: "Une Assomption que l'on dit de *Salvator Rosa,* c'est un tableau bien composé, bien dessiné, où il y a beaucoup d'expression; il est un peu gris & peu vigoureux" (the picture is now in Paris [S 156]), and *San Paolo eremita* (S 157), then in the Dominican church of La Vittoria and now in the Brera; but he pronounces it and a matching picture by Francesco Mola to be "deux grands & beaux paysages."[51]

A sort of climax to the discovery of Rosa by French travelers can be seen in the complicated history of the abbé de Saint-Non and his *Voyage pittoresque et description des royaumes de Naples et de Sicile* (1781–1786). Jean-Claude Richard, abbé de Saint-Non (1727–1791), was one of the most enlightened art-lovers of his time: his mother was descended from Bon Boullogne, and his sister was the wife of a certain Bergeret, another great "amateur." Saint-Non was a friend of Boucher, Hubert Robert, and especially Fragonard. Little hindered by his ecclesiastical duties, he went to Italy in 1759 for a two-year stay. With Robert he visited the monuments of Rome and made a trip to Naples. At the end of May 1761 he took Robert and Fragonard on an excursion to Tivoli. After his return to Paris, he conceived an ambitious plan for a huge illustrated publication to be entitled *Tableaux de la Suisse et de l'Italie.* The first two volumes, dealing with Switzerland, appeared in 1779 but did not enjoy much success.[52] Focusing on the Italian part of this enterprise, he became associated with Vivant Denon, who was in Naples as part of the French embassy staff in the years 1776–1785. In his leisure time, Denon worked to assemble the drawings of Italian scenes and accompanying texts needed for Saint-Non's great undertaking. As Wildenstein says: "le texte, quoique signé par Saint-Non, est rédigé sur place par le jeune Vivant Denon aidé de savants qui lui fournissent des 'mémoires' " (ibid.). The publication of the great work, beginning in 1781, triggered a quarrel between Saint-Non and his collaborator, which ultimately led to Denon's independent *Voyage en Sicile* (1786).[53] The importance of this complicated business for this account of Rosa's "fortune" lies in several revealing passages in the literary outcome, Denon's travel book. While still working for Saint-Non, Denon relates the disappointment that he and his team felt on arriving in a region near Salerno which they had been led to expect to be especially picturesque:

> Nous quittâmes la grande route pour prendre à gauche celle du monastère de la Trinità, fameux par ses archives et la singularité de son site, et où l'on dit que le Poussin et Salvator Rosa ont été chercher les modèles de ce genre, grand, noble et sévère, qui les caractérise. Nous n'y trouvâmes cependant rien qui ait pu plaire beaucoup à ces deux peintres célèbres de Paysage: l'on n'y voit qu'une nature sauvage sans des formes très heureuses, des roches pauvres, et des montagnes couvertes de taillis et de broussailles, qui n'inspirent et ne peignent point l'idée que l'on peut se faire *des belles horreurs de ce genre.*[54]

If he failed to find the Rosaesque landscape he sought near Salerno, Denon had a happier adventure in north central Sicily, but only after traversing a dreary tract interesting to scientists but not to lovers of art:

> Nous fîmes dix-huit milles sans trouver une maison ni un paysage supportable jusqu'à *Calatavuturo,* où le pays devient aussi grand et aussi sublime qu'il avoit été maussade jusques là. Montagnes escarpées, rochers suspendus, apperçus de la mer, grands vallons, vieux châteaux bâtis comme dans les contes des fées; tout y est grand, tout y est mystérieux et magnifique: on ne compose pas mieux. Il semble que Salvator Rosa ait arrangé tout cela, ou qu'il y soit venu peindre ses tableaux.[55]

Such passages suggest that for many sensitive, cultivated Frenchmen of the late eighteenth century, as for many of their English counterparts, Salvator Rosa and "sublime" landscape had become interchangeable.[56]

    Charles Blanc's *Le Trésor de la curiosité* (1857–1858) furnishes us a convenient survey of the Paris art market for the period that concerns us. Blanc's first reference to Rosa registers the sale of a landscape in the Madame de Verrue sale in 1737 (Blanc, I, 6). But it is in the last third of the century that Rosa's presence becomes noticeable. Blanc lists the following sales of works by Rosa for this period:

1767—Julienne: *Apollon et la Sibylle de Cumae* (Blanc, I, 137)

1772—Duc de Choiseul: *Paysage* (I, 198)

1775—Mariette: *L'Enfant prodigue* (I, 280)

1775—Marquis de Felino: *Paysage* (I, 309)

1776—Neyman: *Glaucus et Scylla* (I, 327)

1777—Randon de Boisset: *Tobie et l'ange* (I, 352)

1777—Prince de Conti: *Paysage* (I, 376)

1778—Charles Natoire: *Samuel* [sic] *chez la Pythonisse* (I, 425)

1778—Menageot et autres: *Paysage* (I, 427)

1779—De Péters: "deux paysages dans le goût de Salvator" (I, 451)

1779—Abbé de Juvigny: *Combat de Cavalerie allemande contre la Cavalerie turque* (I, 458)

1786—Page: "morceau burlesque: *Funérailles de Salvator*" (II, 109)

1795—Calonne: *Vue romantique d'un port dans la Calabre* (II, 170).

[Blanc borrows information to the effect that eight Rosas were traded in this sale (II, 167, 168).]

Blanc's tabulation calls for several comments. First, with a few exceptions, Rosa's pictures did not fetch unusually high prices. The *Apollon et la Sibylle de Cumae* was the highest-priced picture at the Julienne sale in 1767, bringing 12,012 livres. This was almost certainly the picture that had once belonged to Mazarin and is now in the Wallace collection; it was bought by the Earl of Ashburnham, who outbid Catherine the Great.[57] In 1775 Mariette's *L'Enfant prodigue*—previously owned by Horace Walpole—went to Catherine the Great and is in the Hermitage today. The landscape sold by the Prince de Conti in 1777 went for the relatively high price of 3,600 livres. The *Samuel chez la Pythonisse* in the Charles Natoire sale in 1778 cannot be the picture on this subject bought by Louis XIV before 1683 but a somewhat smaller version, now lost.[58] Finally, the use in 1795 of the expression *Vue romantique* and the rather high price for this picture are extremely suggestive of a change of climate, one that favored the emergence of a romantic Rosa, the landscapist.

A modern study of Parisian sales catalogues in the eighteenth century reinforces and, in some respects, amplifies Blanc's findings. In 1982 Daniel Wildenstein and Jean Adhémar, sifting a larger body of documents than Blanc, revealed that, of works by seventeenth-century Italian painters, Rosa's were most often listed in these catalogues after Guido Reni's and Luca Giordano's. Here are the figures for the numbers of paintings listed for the most frequently cited artists of this group: Reni—125; Giordano—95; Rosa—87; Locatelli—85; Albani—73; G. B. Castiglione—71; Guercino—64; F. Lauri—61; Maratta (sic)—59; Solimena—56; Feti—54; Domenichino—52; Mola—50.[59]

Rosa's works in media other than painting were also arousing the interest of French collectors in the second part of the eighteenth century. An *œuvre*—in this case a group of fifty prints—figured in the Edme Bouchardon sale in 1762, according to Blanc's *Trésor* (I, 109). In the Cayeux sale (1769), Blanc shows for Rosa "Son œuvre, et plusieurs morceaux d'après lui," sold for 130 livres (I, 158). In the second Mariette sale, an item listed by Blanc (I, 298) joins the *œuvres* of Pietro Testa and Rosa, bound together in a single volume which included 126 Rosas.[60]

As for Rosa's drawings, as we have seen, connoisseurs were already collecting them in the late seventeenth century. A fine set of ninety-six Rosa drawings was listed in Mariette's 1741 catalogue of Pierre Crozat's fabulous collection, said to have been the largest in Europe at the time.[61] Crozat spent several years in Rome negotiating the purchase of Queen Christina's paintings by Philippe, Duc d'Orléans, regent at the beginning of Louis XV's reign. Crozat successfully negotiated for the paintings with Prince Livio Odescalchi, who had bought them from the Queen's heir, Cardinal Decio Azzolino. For himself he bought from Prince Livio a large number of Rosa drawings (the Odescalchi family still owned some as recently as 1973), but it is possible that he purchased some from the Rosa heirs.[62] For the later eighteenth century there is evidence in Blanc's *Trésor* of the popularity of Rosa's drawings: in 1779, at the D'Argenville sale, a "dessin à la plume et lavé" that is described as "Un vieillard à genoux, les mains jointes, dans un paysage," went for forty-eight livres, one s[sou?] (Blanc, I, 442).

Clearly, Rosa was popular among French collectors in the eighteenth century. Were these French art-lovers following the lead of their English rivals, who in roughly the same years were avidly collecting Rosas? Or had Louis XIV and Mazarin set the fashion handed down to great nobles bearing such names as Conti, Rohan-Chabot, Choiseul, and Calonne, who, in their turn, served as tastemakers in the eyes of opulent financiers like Pierre Crozat or connoisseurs like Mariette? The taste for Rosa in France never reached such heights as it did in England; still, the French market for Rosa was strong. The Rosas hanging in the great royal and noble galleries or in collections of rich bourgeois were sometimes available to art-lovers; "stately homes," then as now admitted visitors; guidebooks to Paris, like that of the younger Dezallier d'Argenville[63] described the galleries and "cabinets" and, by implication, invited interested tourists to visit them. Despite this accessibility—which must not be exaggerated—of Rosa paintings in France at this time, Rosa the man had not yet become the stuff of fiction and legend, nor the object of serious critical and scholarly writing.

All in all, this study of Rosa's reception in French writing between the middle of the seventeenth century and the end of the eighteenth clearly reveals that he had indeed crossed the Alps.

CHAPTER TWO

Toward Romanticism

The legend of Rosa's participation in Masaniello's revolt seems not to have found any echo in revolutionary France.[1] But the words of Lévesque, quoted earlier, especially the expression "fierté sublime," and the reference in a 1795 sales catalogue to one of Rosa's landscapes as a *Vue romantique* (Blanc, *Trésor de la curiosité,* II, 170) show that Rosa's work was in tune with revolutionary times.

The most important influence the Revolution exerted on the French reception of Rosa was the result of the great surge of museological activity that it fostered. The years of tumult saw the nationalization of much of France's artistic patrimony, the confiscation of the royal collection, the creation of the Musée du Louvre, and the accumulation in Paris of huge quantities of statues and paintings "liberated" by revolutionary—and later Napoleonic—armies. Despite the background of violence and upheaval, a great organizational activity proceeded apace. One consequence was the publication of a great body of art writing. One might say that Napoleon, David, and Vivant Denon replicated the work of Louis XIV, Le Brun, and Colbert, and that art critics and art historians like C. P. Landon and Henri Laurent were the counterparts of Félibien and De Piles.

Rosa's works were not a prominent part of the booty brought to Paris during the revolutionary and imperial decades. I have been able to identify only two Rosas amid the plunder: an *Assumption* (S 156) taken from Santa Maria della Vittoria in Milan and *Madonna del Suffragio* (S 158), from San Giovanni alle Case.[2] Actually, Rosa's presence in France may even have been diminished during this period: it is likely that, even if the removal of the Orléans collection to England had little or no effect, some Rosas in other collections emigrated with their owners. Lady Morgan's catalogue (II, 308) indicates that the Marquis of Stafford's *Soothsayers* (S 167) had once belonged to the Duc de Choiseul.[3]

It was primarily the Rosas that had been in Paris all along that benefited from the outpouring of French art writing in the early years of the nineteenth century: The *Bataille héroïque* sent to Louis XIV in 1664, the *Saül et la Pythonisse*, which he acquired by 1683, and *Tobie et l'ange*, whose history is unclear—C. P. Landon speaks of it as coming from the "ancienne collection."[4] The *Assumption* brought from Milan toward the end of Napoleon's reign did not, however, go entirely unnoticed: C. P. Landon provided a very close description of it in his *Annales*.

The art critics and historians who set out to describe the treasures on view in Paris thanks to the museological work of the revolutionary and imperial regimes wrote in an unprecedented manner about the pictures they saw. The way seems to have been pointed by Robillard-Péronville and Pierre Laurent[5] in *Le Musée français*, a series published in fascicules beginning in 1803, with texts by Simon-Célestin Croze-Magnan, E. Q. Visconti, and T. B. Emeric-David. This sumptuous publication featured Rosa's *Tobie et l'ange* (*Tobie et Azarias*) in volume I. After quoting the biblical text that inspired the painting, the writer—probably Croze-Magnan—goes on to evaluate and criticize it at length:

> Il est difficile de rendre plus exactement la scène dont il est ici question, que ne l'a fait Salvator Rosa dans ce joli tableau. Il a su donner à ses figures une simplicité noble et gracieuse, soit dans leurs attitudes, soit dans leurs expressions. On croit entendre parler l'ange qui instruit Tobie de ce qu'il doit faire; et l'on remarque dans la tête du jeune homme la confiance et l'attention de la candeur et de l'ingénuité. Les poses sont naturelles et agréables, et les draperies jetées avec élégance et légèreté.
>
> Mais le peintre n'a-t-il pas eu tort de donner des ailes à Azarias, qui n'était pas encore reconnu par Tobie pour être un ange, mais seulement pour son guide et son compagnon de voyage? Cette inadvertence détruit tout l'intérêt de la vérité historique, et n'est pas excusable dans Salvator, qui se piquait de la plus scrupuleuse observation des convenances et du costume. Il prononce lui-même sa condamnation par ces vers de sa troisième satire, intitulée, la Peinture: Bisogna che i pittori siano eruditi, nelle scienze introdotti, e sappian bene le favole, l'istorie, i tempi, i riti. [Twelve more lines expand on this idea.]
>
> Quant au faire, ce tableau pourrait bien être regardé comme une esquisse avancée. Il est peint hardiment et à l'effet. Le paysage et le ciel sont négligés et très heurtés; mais telle était presque toujours la manière de Salvator, qui exécutait souvent avec incorrection, mais jamais sans enthousiasme.[6]

Then follows a French translation of the passage from Rosa's poem (plus the measurements of the picture). All in all, this is the first critique in French of a painting by Rosa clearly revealing direct knowledge of the picture. Most of the critical vocabulary is pallid and conventional: "joli tableau," "simplicité noble et gracieuse," "poses . . . naturelles et agréables," "draperies jetées avec élégance et légèreté." But the passage concerning Rosa's "faire" or "manière" is somewhat more vivid and reflective of pictorial reality: "une esquisse avancée," "peint hardiment et à l'effet," "le paysage et le ciel sont négligés et heurtés."

Ideologically—I refer to the various currents of art history and criticism circulating at the opening of the nineteenth century—one finds here an interesting convergence: standard classical emphasis on the rules, decorum, and *le costume,* a dash of Winckelmann despite Rosa's "incorrection" ("simplicité noble et gracieuse"); and a willingness to find beauty in his bold and passionate style ("hardiment . . . enthousiasme"). Perhaps more interesting are the emphasis on the painting's literary source, the Bible, and the appeal to Rosa's own satire on painting: both texts are quoted verbatim (and the fifteen lines in Italian are only the second such direct citation in a French context from Rosa's poetic works). The Rosa who emerges from this treatment is less pre-romantic than the one presented by Lévesque. This may be due in part to the fact that Robillard-Péronville and Laurent are limited to a specific picture, one with a biblical subject set in landscape, whereas Lévesque is generalizing, thinking of pictures in which a certain type of Rosa landscape is dominant. It is not surprising that, after the whirlwind of the Revolution and the restoration of order, Rosa should be presented as living in symbiosis with neoclassicism.

The most extended criticism of Rosa's work in the early years of the nineteenth century was made by Jean Joseph Taillasson (1745–1809) in his *Observations sur quelques grands peintres, dans lesquelles on cherche à fixer les caractères distinctifs de leur talent* (1807). It is also the most sympathetic. Taillasson was a pupil of Vien, a member of the Académie royale de peinture, and, according to Bénézit's brief sketch, "Ses œuvres sont froides et conventionnelles."[7] Perhaps so, but Taillasson wrote a poem on *Le Danger des règles dans les arts* (1785) and translated Ossian as well as Homer. The article on Taillasson in the *Biographie universelle* praises his *Observations* primarily for "l'impartialité bien rare à l'époque où l'auteur écrivait" (XL, 576). Be that as it may, Taillasson is quite sympathetic to Rosa's work (as for Rosa the man, Taillasson is content to quote Félibien: "C'étoit un homme imaginatif, qui faisoit facilement des vers, et d'une conversation aisée"[8]), and some idea of his esteem is conveyed by the fact that Rosa is one of the sixteen Italian artists considered—he treats forty-four in all—and that the chapter on Rosa is placed immediately after that on Claude Lorrain. Remarkable too is the fact that Taillasson's discussion of Rosa is nearly pure criticism, mixing general observations and discussions of particular pictures.

While all of the eight specific pictures on which Taillasson chooses to focus can be lumped together as history paintings, it is Rosa's landscapes that occupy the foreground. He begins with words reminiscent of Lévesque: "Une fierté sauvage, une bizarre, dure et brûlante énergie, une sorte de barbarie dans les pensées, et dans la manière de les rendre" (*Observations*, p. 20). These lines are apparently intended as a general introduction to Rosa's work, though Taillasson may have Rosa's landscapes uppermost in his mind's eye. But, after some brief remarks on the artist's drawing ("incorrect" but "plein de chaleur et de vie"), color ("souvent belle . . . pas toujours d'une grande recherche de tons," "forte et vigourouse"), and "lignes principales" ("contrastées hardiment, fortement, durement"), the critic passes to descriptive passages clearly focused on Rosa's land-scapes. First, he tells us, Rosa chooses only "les sites sauvages, piquans par une effrayante nouveauté; il ne peint jamais des plaines riantes, de riches vallons; il peint d'arides déserts, de tristes rochers; il choisit les plus affreux, et s'ils ne le sont pas, ils le deviennent par la manière dont il les rend" (pp. 20–21). This contrast with the idyllic landscapes of other painters is developed for a whole page, full of vivid details about Rosa's trees, including a curious comparison between Rosa's trees and storm-tossed ships with broken masts. The passage culminates in a striking contrast between Rosa's landscapes and Claude's. The former

> ressemblent toujours à ces lieux favorables aux assassinats, à ces chemins écartés de toute habitation, où l'on ne passe jamais la nuit, et que le jour on traverse avec rapidité, sur lesquels on trouve exposé [*sic*] des restes de fameux brigands, sur lesquels on vous dit: "là, un voyageur fut égorgé; là, son corps sanglant fut traîné et jeté dans les précipices." Combien sont différentes ces belles solitudes, peintes par Claude le Lorrain, où le voyageur charmé ne connoît d'autre crainte que celle de les quitter, dans lesquelles les troupeaux peuvent, en assurance, paître des herbes solitaires, et s'abreuver d'eaux limpides et pures; où tous les objets emprunts d'une teinte de bonheur, retracent la douce image des jardins d'Eden! (pp. 21–22)

If one remembers that Taillasson's chapter on Rosa comes immediately after the chapter on Claude, one is tempted to see in the two chapters at the least a diptych, and perhaps a deliberate effort to pit one landscapist against another. And one cannot say that Rosa is sacrificed to his French rival: Taillasson holds that Rosa's frightening and sinister landscapes—he does not use the word "sublime"—are on a par with Claude's *loci amœni.*

Although Taillasson seems to think first of landscape when he thinks of Rosa, he devotes considerable attention to Rosa's pictures on historical, religious, and mythological subjects. One is struck, indeed, by the fact that, while no individual picture is named in his passages on landscape, the critic mentions eight specific titles of this second sort. But his main point is that in both domains Rosa is the same. His brief descriptions of *Regulus* (i.e., *The Martyrdom of Atilius Regulus*) (S 113), *The Crucifixion of Polycrates* (S 213), *Saul and the Witch of Endor* (S 210), *Glaucus and Scylla* (S 193 or 194), insist on the painful or frightening elements in these pictures. Even when painting "des objets plus aimables," Rosa makes them other by his manner—his examples are *St. John the Baptist* (S 122 or 192) and *Plato's Academy* (an etching—S 15 [Was there once a painting on this subject?]): "les philosophes, le saint homme inspiré et les hommes simples qui l'écoutent ressemblent à des voleurs de grands chemins" (pp. 22–23).

Taillasson is probably the first French critic of Rosa to extract a philosophical message from the artist's work: "La vue de ses ouvrages fait réfléchir et rêver sombrement; et chez lui, la philosophie ne présente jamais que de dures vérités" (p. 23). Taillasson illustrates with a fine interpretation of *Democritus Meditating* (S 106; also an etching): "Au milieu de tombeaux solitaires et ruinés, il a peint Démocrite environné d'ossemens d'hommes et d'animaux de toute espèce, ensemble confondus. Le philosophe les regarde avec un rire amer, et, la tête appuyée sur sa main, il semble dire: 'hommes insensés, peut-on ne pas rire de vos innombrables projets, en voyant comment ils finissent?' " (p. 23). Taillasson was a pure product of the French academic tradition as it unfolded in the late eighteenth century, but here he seems to divine the romantic Rosa—not, as we would expect, in his landscapes, but in one of his historical pictures. Probably unaware of Dürer's *Melencolia I* (Dürer is not among the forty-four artists treated in the *Observations*) the critic has, nevertheless, sketched a portrait of Democritus that contains key analogies to Dürer's angel. And the Greek philosopher's "rire amer" foreshadows the romantic theme of sardonic laughter and Lady Morgan's use of the same expression.

This insightful view of Rosa's *Democritus* leads to the climax and suggests the conclusion of Taillasson's study of Rosa, constructed around an interpretation of the *Heroic Battle* (S 111), the grandiose battle picture in the Louvre. Though relegated to lesser locations for a good part of its life (the king let it be known in 1697 that he no longer wanted to display the picture at Versailles,[9] and we know that it spent a good part of the eighteenth century at the Luxembourg), by 1807, when Taillasson was writing, it was on view in the "Musée Napoléon," i.e., the Louvre. At that moment in history, the picture could draw on two deeply entrenched traditions: the French classical one, which had climaxed in the reign of "le grand monarque," and the neoclassical one, which emerged as the Revolution approached. It might also seem relevant in the age of Napoleon and his constant military campaigns. It is difficult to say why Taillasson gives such prominence to this picture in his discussion of Rosa, or just which aesthetic is guiding him. It is doubtful that he is motivated only by his belief that Rosa "a principalement excellé" in this genre ("c'est là qu'il se déploie avec aisance l'énergique et originale âpreté de son caractère" [p. 23]). But, in any case, here he gives us a remarkable interpretation of what he calls "un ouvrage admirable" (ibid.):

> une poésie de carnage anime la scène; les ruines solitaires d'un palais, une vaste et aride plaine, des montagnes sauvages, le ciel, tous les objets de ce tableau ont un aspect funeste, et semblent avoir été faits pour ne retentir que de cris funèbres.[10] La dureté de la couleur, la fierté de la manière de peindre font un accord parfait avec la vive et féroce expression des figures. La Discorde et la Rage triomphent au milieu des maux qu'elles font: la soif dévorante du sang embrase tous les combattans; et jamais, sur un théâtre de carnage, les blessures et la mort ne furent présentées plus terribles et plus affreuses. (pp. 23–24)

Taillasson, in praising this picture and in treating it at such length, may be reflecting the long-standing aesthetic preference for the heroic and the antique. But he seems also to transcend his classical and neoclassical predilections by refusing to fault the painter for the "dureté de [sa] couleur." Rather, he finds a unity of style and content: the harsh and unlovely color befits a picture in which men slaughter each other, in which Discord and Rage triumph, rather than some great military hero. These allegorical figures— Taillasson invents them himself; there are no such abstractions in the painting—may be a throwback to an earlier poetic tradition, but they are soon effaced by the grim reality of war: "la soif dévorante du sang . . . un théâtre de carnage . . . les blessures et la mort." We are not far from the new manner of depicting warfare devised by such painters as Gros and Géricault. And one catches a glimpse of such pictures as Delacroix's *Massacres de Scio* (1824).

Taillasson here turns briefly to Rosa's poetry, emphasizing the biting quality of his satires—"on sent bien que sa muse a dû s'abreuver d'amertume et de fiel" (p. 24)—and the "fact" that he wrote only satires ("elles sont trèsmordantes"), and then returns to more relevant topics. Seemingly dealing with the figures in his paintings and where earlier he had compared Rosa's landscapes to bandit-ridden regions, he now makes it clear that the artist actually painted such figures (as well as "guerriers ajustés d'une manière singulière, et nouvelle"—a link to his discussion of the Louvre *Battle*): "l'image des sbires, des contrebandiers et des voleurs" (ibid.). The passage closes, by a certain logic, with a quick reference to Rosa's etchings ("beaucoup d'esprit . . . ces bizarres héros" [ibid.]).

Taillasson's conclusion places Rosa in a context that resounds with motifs much more suggestive of the age to come than of the culture battered by the French Revolution. He opens with a general observation that condenses his view of the whole of the artist's work: "Ses ouvrages plaisent surtout par une teinte de merveilleux noir" (ibid.), and then provides an intriguing explanation: "les hommes aiment le merveilleux, de quelque couleur qu'il soit; ils courent çà et là, ils s'agitent, se tourmentent pour fuir l'ennui: ils se précipitent et vont étouffer pour voir une tragédie qui les déchire, quoique bien souvent ils n'y gagnent que de funestes idées" (ibid.). Taillasson seems to be aware of the *mal du siècle* and to have a premonition of Baudelairean ennui. In the visual arts, the experience is less painful than in tragic drama, where unity of tone and subject allow no relief. But in the museum there are contrasting experiences to be had: "les sanglans et féroces guerriers de Salvator Rosa peuvent s'enfuir devant un groupe des Amours de l'Albane" (p. 25). Taillasson's last words offer perhaps the most positive assessment to date of Rosa, at least in France: "Présenter aux hommes la nature, n'importe de quelle espèce, et la leur présenter d'une manière nouvelle, voilà ce qu'ils exigent absolument, à ce prix seul ils accordent une durable célébrité; et parce que Salvator Rosa a rempli ces conditions, il a une réputation que vainement on voudroit lui disputer" (ibid.). The requirement that artistic creations give pleasure is fundamental in Western aesthetics from Plato and Aristotle forward. But to suggest that artists should achieve this by offering a new picture of reality was not a common teaching in the France of Le Brun and Boileau. And what of "les bienséances," "le goût," "la vraisemblance," and "les règles"? Taillasson never evokes these cardinal principals. Rosa's draftsmanship may be "incorrect" but it is "plein de chaleur et de vie"; his color may be limited in range—or even "dur" (as in *Heroic Battle*)—but it is also "forte et vigoureuse" and "convient parfaitement au style général de ses tableaux" (p. 20). The "impartialité" for which Taillasson was praised by his biographers (in Michaud's *Biographie universelle*) allowed him to see beyond the norms and principles in which he had been raised and which he practiced in his own painting. One suspects that he is an art critic deserving of more attention. Though his pages on Rosa are little known and had little impact on the evolution of Rosa's fortune, they mark a step forward from the standpoint of this study.

Rosa figures in various books that reflect the museological development of France in the early decades of the century. Literarily, this development took the form of great collections like the ones produced by C. P. Landon and the team of Robillard-Péronville and Pierre Laurent. Landon's *Annales du Musée ou recueil complet de gravures d'après les anciennes écoles italienne, allemande, hollandaise, etc.,* was begun near the turn of the century and continued even after Landon's death. The first edition of the eight volumes covering the Italian School appeared in 1801–1805.[11] Landon includes three works by Rosa, plates 28–30 (pp. 43–46), which, using his titles, are *L'Ange Raphaël et le jeune Tobie, L'Ombre de Samuel apparaît à Saül,* and *La Vierge délivrant les âmes du Purgatoire;* the last named is the *Madonna del Suffragio* (S 158), taken from Milan and already mentioned. All three pictures were in the "Musée Napoléon" in the days of the empire.

Landon's readers, in addition to engravings of the three paintings by Charles Pierre Joseph Normand (*Tobie* and *La Vierge*) and Michel-Olivier Le Bas (*Saül*), were provided descriptions of the three pictures and a brief "vie et œuvres" tacked on at the end of the description of *Tobie;* embedded in it is a capsule criticism of Rosa's work. Both the biography and the criticism are standard fare and, ultimately, derived from Dezallier d'Argenville. One might at least note what Landon says of Rosa as a landscapist: "Doué d'un rare talent pour le paysage, il se plaisait à représenter des sites sauvages et romantiques" (p. 44). Some of Landon's remarks must date, in their published form, from the Restoration era or, possibly, from the very beginning of the July Monarchy (he died in 1826). But it is possible that they date from as early as 1816, because he mentions the return of the *Madonna del Suffragio* to Milan and refers to the *Paesaggio con soldati e cacciatori,* purchased in 1816. An early date—before 1824, in particular—would be more interesting than a later one as that would place his use of the word "romantiques" prior to the great debate on romanticism in Paris.

The major interest of Landon's pages on Rosa lies in the surprisingly minute character of his descriptions. Apropos of *Tobie,* Landon begins: "Salvator Rosa a choisi le moment où Raphaël ordonne au jeune Tobie de saisir le poisson qui menaçait de le dévorer, et d'en prendre le fiel, le cœur et le foie" (p. 43). But the critic immediately points out that "Le peintre s'est écarté, en plusieurs points, de l'exactitude historique," that is, from the biblical account. This bit of negative criticism gives way to a favorable assessment: "Au reste, ce tableau, ou plutôt cette esquisse, fait honneur au peintre. Le mouvement des figures est expressif et bien rendu. Le paysage, touché d'une manière large et savante, rappelle les productions capitales de Salvator, dans cette belle partie de la peinture" (ibid.). Landon's treatment of *L'Ombre de Samuel apparaît à Saül*[12] is similar, but begins with a summary of the biblical account (I, Samuel, 28). The description of the subject is prefaced with the observation that "Un sujet aussi pittoresque convenait parfaitement à l'imagination vive et féconde de Salvator Rosa," and leads to the following evaluation: "Toutes les parties du tableau concourent à l'effet que le peintre a voulu produire. Le dessin a quelque chose de sauvage et fier: le coloris est sombre, et, pour ainsi dire, mystérieux. L'exécution est ferme. Le seul reproche que l'on puisse faire à Salvator Rosa, c'est d'avoir donné des armes modernes à Saül et aux deux Israélites" (p. 45). In dealing with the *Madonna* (*La Vierge délivrant les âmes du Purgatoire*) from Milan, Landon is perplexed by the absence of a specific textual source in the Bible and the implications of Catholic doctrine concerning purgatory: "puisque le miracle de la résurrection générale n'est point encore arrivé, il semble assez difficile de justifier l'artiste d'avoir essayé de représenter un semblable sujet, qui réellement n'offre rien à l'art du peintre " (p. 46). But, he decides, no harm has been done: painters have always assumed the right to present God, angels, and demons in human guise. In his overall criticism of this picture, Landon is somewhat less enthusiastic than about the other two pictures by Rosa: "Ce morceau, l'un des plus capitaux de Salvator Rose, est bien composé et d'un bon dessin, mais il manque de noblesse; le coloris en est médiocre et dur: une teinte enfumée absorbe un grand nombre de détails que la touche ferme du peintre aurait pu rendre intéressans" (ibid.). Though surrounded by rather banal critical observations, Landon's descriptions have the merit of exactitude, inspired as they are by a careful look at the pictures—or, perhaps, at the engravings (as far as the literary theme is concerned). We have seen something similar in Taillasson's discussions of several of Rosa's pictures in 1807, and another and even more remarkable example of this sort of *explication de texte* is to be found in a document dating from about the same time, *Le Musée royal*, a sequel to *Le Musée français* of Robillard-Péronville and Pierre Laurent published by the latter's son Henri (1779–1844). The painting singled out is another of the Louvre's holdings, the *Saül et la Pythonisse*. As in the earlier series, it is difficult to assign responsibility for the "descriptions et notices littéraires." The catalogue of the Bibliothèque Nationale mentions E. Q. Visconti, F. Guizot, and Comte C. O. F. J. B. de Clerac. Whoever the author of the text that concerns me here may be, he follows closely the pattern we saw in the description of *Tobie et Azarias* in the earlier series. After quoting verbatim the biblical account of Saul's encounter with the Witch of Endor, the author launches his *explication:*

Il est clair, par ce passage, que Samuel, aperçu de la Pythonisse, est demeuré invisible pour Saül, auquel seulement il fait entendre sa voix; mais il paroît également que le peintre a négligé, ou plutôt omis à dessein cette circonstance qui ne pouvoit se rendre sans ôter à son tableau toute apparence de vérité, puisqu'il eût dû alors nous représenter Saül comme ne voyant pas ce qui est devant ses yeux, et parfaitement visible aux notres. Saül voit Samuel, car il le regarde. Prosterné à terre, il vient de lever la tête, non avec l'incertitude d'un homme qui cherche à démêler d'où vient le son qui l'a frappé, mais avec un saisissement attentif, et tel que le produit la vue d'un objet effrayant et connu. D'ailleurs Samuel n'a point encore parlé à Saül; il arrive, et, quoique entièrement sorti de terre, il monte, pour ainsi dire, enveloppé dans son manteau blanc. A l'expression de sa figure, on pressent déjà ces effrayantes paroles qu'il va prononcer sur Saül: Demain, vous et vos fils serez avec moi. Mais, comme pour annoncer à Saül sa réprobation, les premiers regards de Samuel sont fixés sur la Pythonisse, qui n'a point fini le travail de l'évocation, ainsi qu'on le voit par la violente contraction de ses traits et de ses membres, et par la branche de verveine qu'elle continue d'agiter de la main gauche au-dessus de la flamme placée sur un autel, tandis que de la main droite elle anime cette flamme en y jetant de nouveaux ingrédiens. Il y a donc lieu de croire que le peintre a saisi l'instant de l'apparition, et l'a voulu rendre egalement sensible aux deux principaux assistans: mais il semble qu'il ait cherché à conserver dans les serviteurs de Saül quelque chose de la circonstance indiquée par l'Ecriture; ils ne regardent point Samuel, qui, s'ils pouvoient le voir, devroit être certainement le principal objet de leur curiosité: placés à quelque distance, dans un lieu bas, au-dessus duquel ils ne se montrent qu'à mi-corps, mais d'où toute la scène se déploie devant eux, ils n'ont d'attention que pour la Pythonisse, et ne paroissent pas même apercevoir les spectres qui remplissent le fond du tableau, confondu dans la nuit et dans la fumée.[13]

The writer begins his conclusion with a mild criticism of Rosa's anachronistic armor and his depiction of monsters, i.e., the specters. On the latter point, he concedes: "A l'époque où peignoit Salvator Rosa, les idées de magie échauffoient les imaginations, et la peinture se plaisoit à inventer et à multiplier des monstres. Au moins ici Salvator Rosa les a placés dans un sujet auquel ils paroissent convenir, quoiqu'ils en interrompent un peu trop le religieux silence" (ibid.). But the final verdict on this picture is highly favorable: "Au reste on retrouve dans cette composition l'ardeur et la terrible énergie du peintre; sa couleur forte et sombre s'adapte admirablement au sujet, et contribue beaucoup à l'effet singulier et frappant de ce beau tableau" (ibid.).

While it is this final assessment of Rosa and his work that permits us to locate the critical view of Rosa on the unfurling map of writing about him, what is most remarkable about the passages quoted is the minute description-cum-interpretation of a specific painting: we get a foretaste of the iconological studies of a Panofsky, e.g., his famous interpretation of Poussin's "*Et in Arcadia ego.*" The point to make, in this context, is that Rosa's work is accorded serious and detailed attention. One might observe, too, that he is one of the nineteen artists (fourteen Italians, two Frenchmen, one Fleming, and two Dutchmen) vouchsafed a place in Laurent's "*Seconde Série. Histoire.*" (While Raphael and Poussin are given pride of place—in space—they are represented by three pictures each, whereas all the other artists are represented by one apiece.) Additionally, history painting continued to be the genre enjoying the greatest prestige in the opening decades of the nineteenth century, especially in France. Thus, all in all, Rosa is given a rather high place on Parnassus in the *Musée royal.*

Rosa's widely acknowledged pre-eminence as a landscape painter is not apparent, or barely so, in the documents that we have just been examining from this period. This seeming neglect of the major aspect of his work results from particular circumstances: aesthetically, the priority given to history painting and, incidentally, the fact that the authors and publishers of the *Musée français,* the *Musée royal,* and the *Annales du musée,* and even Taillasson chose to write about pictures that hung in the Louvre. Other documents reflect the fact that, for the cultivated public, Rosa was primarily a landscapist. In his *Dictionnaire des beaux-arts* (1806), A. L. Millin, who organized his book by genres and technical terms, treats Rosa only in the article "Paysage" (III, 107–138), where he appears as one of those who worked under Urban VIII (d. 1644):

> Les trois plus célèbres paysagistes qui parurent ensuite, furent Salvator ROSA, Claude GELLÉE, dit communément LE LORRAIN, et Gaspar DUGUET. . . . Le premier choisissoit le plus souvent ses scènes dans la nature sauvage: de sombres forêts, des roches escarpées, des précipices, des cavernes, des champs hérissés de ronces, des arbres tronqués, renversés ou tortueux, sont les objets qu'il peignoit de préférence. Rarement ses paysages sont animés d'une couleur vive. Comme il traitoit bien les petites figures, il en plaçoit dans presque tous ses tableaux, où l'on voit ordinairement des bergers, des marins, et surtout des soldats. (III, 116)

Millin reveals that, while Rosa deserves mention as one of the three most famous landscapists of his time, Claude Lorrain was the most significant of the three: "Un paysage de Dughet ou de Rosa se parcourt en bien moins de temps que ceux de Gellée, qui cependant sont resserrés dans un champ plus étroit" (III, 117).

Two writers who focused almost exclusively on landscape painting, Pierre-Henri de Valenciennes and Jean-Baptiste Deperthes, demonstrate considerable admiration for Rosa. In the "Réflexions et conseils à un élève, sur la peinture, et particulièrement sur le genre du paysage," which occupy nearly half of his *Eléments de perspective pratique* (1800), Valenciennes (1750–1819), called "le David du paysage" in his day, obviously knew both Rosa's work and the natural landscapes that he painted. Like Millin, Valenciennes treats his subject thematically. Apropos of rocks along the coast he writes:

> Nous en avons vu, dans l'Archipel et sur la côte d'Italie, qui ont des formes très-pittoresques dignes de l'attention du Peintre, sur-tout pour la vivacité et le contraste des couleurs. On en trouve qui sont de la plus grande beauté sur les côtes de Gênes et de Naples, à Sorrente, dans la Calabre, et autour de la Sicile. Salvator Rosa et [Joseph] Vernet les ont étudiées avec le plus grand soin: on peut s'en convaincre par leurs immortels ouvrages. (p. 494)

Of Rosa's marines en general, he says:

> Salvator Rosa a fait des Marines sur les côtes, avec la force et la hardiesse qui caractérisent son faire. Les rochers qui sont inclinés sur les eaux sont du plus grand style, ainsi que les arbres qu'il a disséminés sur le rivage et qui enrichissent ses compositions. Ses figures surtout sont parfaitement prononcées; et sa couleur argentine et ferme tout à la fois, lui assigne un des premiers rangs dans tous les genres de peinture qu'il a voulu essayer. (pp. 496–97)

One is a little surprised to see Rosa listed among the modern artists who excelled in hunting scenes.[14] More understandably, Valenciennes mentions Rosa as a painter of battles (and unlike several of the authors writing at about the same time, he implies that Rosa accurately rendered "la forme et l'usage des diverses machines et armures" of the various peoples who figure in such pictures).

Perhaps the most interesting reference to Rosa in Valenciennes's "Réflexions et conseils" occurs in a passage in which the writer, in a discussion of the right way to paint the different regions of Italy, arrives at Calabria:

> Cette contrée a été sûrement visitée et étudiée par le Poussin, Salvator Rosa et Vernet. C'est dans ce pays si riche de forme et de végétation, que ces grands hommes ont pris ces beaux rochers qu'on a tant de peine à rendre en peinture, et qu'ils ont si bien représentés. On assure que Salvator aimoit, de prédilection, ceux de Sorrente, sur le bord de la mer. Vernet ne les a pas négligés, comme on peut voir dans ses ouvrages. (p. 583)

As art criticism, this passage tells us little—the language is vague, if lauda-
tory. But Valenciennes's claim that Rosa knew, loved, and painted the rocky
coastlines of Calabria or those at Sorrento raises the question whether he
knew the legends about Rosa's wanderings in southern Italy. Elsewhere,
Valenciennes includes Rosa in a list of artists who, for him, symbolize Italy:
"la patrie des Titiens, des Salvator, des Both, des Stella, des Locatelli, etc."
who served foreign artists as a source of "cette chaleur de composition et
cette pureté de style qu'on ne trouve pas ailleurs."[15] Clearly, Valenciennes
admired Rosa but he neither mentions nor describes any specific pictures.

Valenciennes's pupil and imitator, Deperthes (1761–1833)—"peintre de
paysages, musicien et écrivain" according to Bénézit—makes a larger place
for Rosa in *his* book on landscape than had his teacher. In his *Histoire de
l'art du paysage, depuis la renaissance jusqu'au dix-huitième siècle* (1822),
Deperthes devotes over ten pages to Rosa: a biographical sketch and a discussion of the artist's "bizarre" and, we gather, wrong-headed ambition to be
considered a history painter and not a mere landscapist introduce the main
body of the section on Rosa. In essence, Deperthes is poised between recognition of Rosa's originality and emotive power, as seen especially in his landscapes but also in the Louvre's *Battle,* and disapproval of "ce qu'il offre de
défectueux." On the one hand, he singles out for praise two of Rosa's "belles
marines," "d'un ton clair et argentin,"[16] and *Les Augures* (a version of S 167
or 168): "il ne serait guère possible de se figurer une composition plus riche,
plus gracieuse et plus sagement ordonnée" (p. 254). On the other hand: "[L]a
verité de ton de couleur, dans les formes et dans la disposition des objets est
fréquemment sacrifiée à une exagération qui ne permet pas de douter que
l'artiste, au lieu de consulter la nature et de la prendre constamment pour
guide, n'ait mieux aimé suivre les caprices d'une imagination désordonnée"
(p. 256).

Deperthes opens his critical discussion with several vivid paragraphs that
stress Rosa's power to arouse emotion, and fear in particular, culminating in
a particularly elaborate evocation of the typical pre-romantic Rosa landscape
compared point by point with "une nature riante" (p. 250):

> Contemplez ces paysages dans leur ensemble, au premier aspect ils vous
> remueront fortement, examinez-les dans leurs moindres détails, vous y
> remarquerez cependant tous les objets qui tant de fois vous ont charmé
> dans la nature, et vous vous étonnerez que la main d'un homme qui vouloit
> en quelque sorte les embellir encore dans ses imitations, se soit plu à les
> déformer au gré de son caprice, en ne les présentant que sous le point de
> vue le plus défavorable. La voûte qui les domine ne brille point d'un bleu
> d'azur diversifié par des nuages d'or et de pourpre; un ciel âcre ou plombé

répand de toutes parts une lumière incertaine et blafarde, tantôt vigoureuse et tranchante avec la noirceur d'ombres fortement prononcées; les arbres plantés sur ce terrain n'y produisent point un ombrage favorable aux bergers et aux troupeaux; d'énormes troncs noueux, dépouillés en partie de leur écorce et de leurs branchages, élèvent audacieusement jusqu'aux nues leurs cimes battues par les vents et les tempêtes. Les eaux qui arrosent ces campagnes, n'y serpentent point dans de riantes prairies; elles ne s'y étendent point en nappes limpides entre des coteaux verdoyans; on les voit s'échapper de l'enfoncement caverneux d'une montagne inculte, se frayer un passage entre des quartiers de roches éboulées, et se précipiter en mugissant dans la profondeur d'un abîme ténébreux.

Au milieu de ces déserts, nulle sécurité pour l'ami de la retraite . . . il n'aperçoit aucune habitation, pas même au loin, qui le rassure par la perspective de lieux plus fréquentés. Si quelques êtres vivans animent de leur présence ces effrayantes solitudes, c'est un chasseur qui attendait sa proie au passage et qui vient de l'atteindre d'un plomb meurtrier, ou c'est un voyageur tremblant pour ses jours qui, précipitant sa marche, se flatte d'échapper à de sinistres présages; mais vain espoir: au détour d'un rocher environné de précipices, il tombe dans une embuscade, il va succomber sous le fer de vils assassins. (p. 252)

Deperthes goes on to concede that human nature grows weary of an unbroken series of "sensations douces et agréables" (p. 253) inspired by "smiling landscapes": satiety opens the way for Rosa's pictures, "à raison de la nouveauté des sujets et de leur bizarrerie," over and above "une vigueur de coloris et une fermeté d'exécution portées l'une et l'autre au plus haut degré d'énergie" (Ibid.).

Here Deperthes provides the reader a bit of relief by dwelling briefly on some pictures that diverge somewhat from Rosa's norm, i.e., the "belles marines," already mentioned, "qui n'offrent ni dans leur ordonnance la fougue habituelle de son imagination, ni dans le coloris ces teintes dures et ressenties qui rembrunissent encore la physionomie austère de ses paysages" (p. 254). But the critic, as if fascinated by the other Rosa, regarded perhaps as the *real* Rosa, turns to another specific painting, also in the Louvre like one of the "belles marines": *Bataille héroïque* (whose title he does not give):

De quelque côté que la vue se porte sur ce vaste théâtre de carnage et de désolation, elle n'aperçoit qu'une horrible mêlée d'hommes avides de sang, luttant corps à corps, et dont la férocité se peint sur les traits du vaincu avec une expression de rage qui ne le cède en rien à celle du vainqueur. En avant, le terrain est jonché de cadavres et de débris d'armes mutilées: tout près s'élève une colonnade en ruine; et non loin du champ de bataille, à l'extrémité d'une plaine dominée par des montagnes incultes, des vaisseaux embrasés dans une anse exhalent une épaisse fumée dont les tourbillons épars dans l'atmosphère étendent sur le lieu de la scène un voile funèbre qui semble n'intercepter la lumière du ciel que pour redoubler l'horreur de l'action. Invention pittoresque et poétique, exécution fière et brûlante, expressions vives et terribles, tout est réuni dans ce tableau, véritable chef-d'œuvre du peintre, et qui lui assure des droits à une renommée encore plus grande et plus durable que celle dont il peut être redevable à ses étonnans paysages. (pp. 254–255)

Deperthes, as if reminded suddenly that his subject is landscape after all, returns to that theme and summarizes Rosa's genius in that domain: His "génie abondant et nerveux" and his "conceptions naturellement vigoureuses et soutenues par une exécution ferme et hardie" nearly always powerfully affect the "spectateur." The spotlight is thrown briefly on his talent for painting rocks and—linking up with Rosa's great battle picture—on the human figures who enliven the scenery: "ce sont pour la plupart des guerriers revêtus de costumes extraordinaires, mais ajustés d'une manière piquante, et dont les attitudes et les traits ont quelque chose de sombre et farouche qui s'accorde parfaitement avec l'aspérité des paysages" (p. 256).

Thus Deperthes oscillates back and forth. He is drawn to the energy, power, and originality of Rosa, which he finds primarily in the painter's landscapes but also in the Louvre battle scene. He cannot resist the *frisson* of fear, even horror, inspired by Rosa's murky, threatening skies, blasted trees, angry rivers, jagged boulders, bleak mountains and wildernesses, travelers beset by assassins on a mountain road. The words "caprice," "bizarre," and "bizarrerie" will yield in the end to "exagération" and "imagination désordonnée." As he concludes, Deperthes falls back into the neoclassical attitudes from which he seemed at first to be escaping: the impartial viewer may recognize in Rosa "un grand paysagiste," but he will refuse to propose him as a model.

[I]l est de son devoir de signaler ces écarts comme une conséquence inévitable de l'oubli des principes, afin de faire sentir que le génie sans les règles est sujet à s'égarer, et que les œuvres de l'art, de quelque prestige qu'elle soient environnées, n'obtiennent jamais des succès unanimes et durables, à moins qu'elles ne soient avouées par la raison et qu'elles ne portent l'empreinte de la nature dans ce qu'elle offre de plus agréable ou de plus majestueux. (pp. 256–57)

The reader of Deperthes's treatise is, as it were, subjected to a slide lecture in which views from Rosa are shown side by side with views from Claude Lorrain. For the most part, the teacher talks about the former, obviously drawn to the Rosa landscapes in a sort of horrified fascination. Lightning flashes, trees are lashed by the wind, torrents rush down boulder-strewn canyons. Then "the rules," "reason," and "nature" reassert their claims, and the lecture ends with a *locus amœnus* à la Claude.

Approximately contemporary with Deperthes's treatise is an essay on Rosa by the very minor painter Charles-Louis (or Jacques)-François Lecarpentier (1744–1822). Older than most of the writers discussed in this part of the present study, Lecarpentier was a native of Normandy and became a professor at the École des Beaux-Arts in Rouen. His essay on Rosa seems to have been written toward the end of his life; it presents itself as *suite* to the author's *Galerie des peintres célèbres,* published in Paris in the year before his death.

The most important thing to say about Lecarpentier and Rosa is that the Frenchman is one of the Italian's most ardent admirers. He stresses Rosa's originality, his independence of schools, teachers, and influences (though he admits, at one point, that he may owe to Ribera "cette force de couleur, cette fermeté, la vigueur et l'effet qui se font admirer dans ses ouvrages" [p. 16]), and his unmistakably individual style. He bestows on him such epithets and qualifiers as "génie créateur," "vrai talent," "le peintre le plus singulier, et l'un des plus étonnans de l'École d'Italie," and "ce génie extraordinaire" (pp. 1–3). Lecarpentier also stresses Rosa's versatility: his "génie créateur s'empare de toutes les parties de la peinture" (p. 1); "Nouveau Protée, *Salvator* se transforma dans tous les genres de la peinture" (p. 2); "semblable à notre Sébastien Bourdon, [il] embrassa tous les genres de la peinture, l'histoire, les batailles, les paysages, les assemblées de soldats, de sorciers, de buveurs, de bohémiens; les rencontres des voleurs; rien ne peut être étranger à ce singulier génie" (p. 6). Lecarpentier summarizes the quality and character of Rosa's achievement in glowing terms:

> Il faut sur-tout admirer dans Salvator la finesse et la fermeté de sa touche, toujours sûre et savante; la richesse, la variété de ses pensées, la tournure singulière de son génie, le caractère et l'air de vérité qu'il sait donner à ses têtes; le goût exquis de son feuiller qui le place fort au-dessus de beaucoup d'habiles peintres de paysages, ainsi que la manière large et variée avec laquelle il traite les diverses écorces des arbres. (p. 4)

The individual major qualities of Rosa's work come through more clearly when Lecarpentier seeks to convey its affective side: "Les compositions de *Salvator,* quoique pleines de feu et d'enthousiasme, ont cependant une certaine teinte de mélancolie, et inspirent un sentiment de tristesse qui pénètre l'âme" (p. 2). And he adds: "Les figures dont il anime les compositions en augmentent encore l'effroi, par l'air sombre et farouche qu'il leur imprime" (p. 3).

While emphasizing Rosa's versatility and giving some slight though favorable attention to his drawings ("touchés avec esprit" [p. 5]) and etchings ("habile graveur" [ibid.]), Lecarpentier, who himself practiced *inter alia,* the genres of landscapes and marines (Bénézit, VIII, 392), focuses on Rosa as painter of battles, landscapes, and marines. Without mentioning the Louvre's *Battaglia eroica,* Lecarpentier captures its violence in vivid terms: "On y voit la fureur du soldat portée à l'excès, les combattans corps à corps se porter des coups effroyables; d'autres, enveloppés pêle-mêle dans des tourbillons de poussière et de fumée, vont se confondre avec les fonds, et laissent à peine appercevoir quelques faibles lumières à l'horison [*sic*]" (p. 2). Lecarpentier conveys the impact of Rosa's landscapes in a passage probably not inspired by any particular example:

> Qu'y a-t-il de plus imposant que ses paysages et la forme gigantesque de ses arbres, qui, souvent dépouillés d'une partie de leurs feuilles, présentent une tête altière aux vents les plus impétueux.
>
> Est-il rien de plus effrayant que ses immenses rochers, dont les masses ébranlées paraissent menacer d'une chûte prochaine l'homme assez téméraire pour y chercher un asile? À la vue des tableaux de Salvator, on se croit transporté dans les lieux romantiques et sauvages, séjour ordinaire des terribles nécromanciers. (Ibid.)

Rosa's marines, too, inspire a sense of the sublime—a word not used by Lecarpentier in his writing about Rosa: "Peint-il les 'plaines liquides de la mer,' soit qu'elles paraissent agitées par les fougueux Aquilons, soit qu'elles offrent une superficie calme et paisible, leur teinte sombre et noirâtre n'offre à l'imagination que l'idée d'un gouffre immense, dont elles dérobent l'énorme profondeur" (p. 3). As with Rosa's landscapes, one is left wondering whether Lecarpentier has any specific pictures in mind or is drawing on some undisclosed sources. He certainly visited the Louvre, which, curiously, he still calls "Le Musée-Napoléon" (p. 6), for he mentions "son beau tableau de bataille" and "celui de l'ombre de Samuel, evoquée par la pythonisse" (ibid.). Whatever else of Rosa's he saw in the Louvre is lumped together as "plusieurs autres sujets et beaux paysages du plus grand style, et de l'effet le plus vigoureux" (ibid.).

Lecarpentier shows to rather good effect as an art critic dealing with Rosa. As an art historian he is far less satisfying. While he gives correct information about Rosa's birthplace and date of death and refers to his discovery by Lanfranco, he tells his readers that Rosa was born in 1605 and he implies that the artist's studio in Naples became the center for that city's greatest scholars and artists (p. 4). Let us leave Lecarpentier by granting him credit for the enthusiasm, insight, and admiration he poured into his sketch of Rosa and for being one of the earliest of the artist's critics to call his landscapes "romantiques" as well as "sauvages."

Another, and greater, French artist of this period, Girodet, is significant here because he is a major artist and because he wrote art criticism in poetic form. Moreover, at least two of Girodet's own works—the drawing *Paysage avec serpent* and the painting *Le Torrent* (both now in the Musée Magnin in Dijon)—are in a Rosaesque vein. Girodet's poem *Le Peintre* was composed in the last years of the empire and the beginning of the Restoration but published posthumously in 1829.[17]

Like nearly every major French painter of this period, Girodet made the usual pilgrimage to Italy—he spent the years 1790–1795 in Rome—and was inspired by this experience to recount in his poem the southward journey of a young artist. For a number of lines we seem to be traversing a Rosa landscape:

> À peine il entrevoit ces pays fortunés
> Où le Rhône répand ses flots désordonnés,
> Et bientôt, du milieu des plaines opulentes,
> Il contemple, étonné, les Alpes imposantes
> Dont l'immense rideau se déploie à ses yeux:
> Leur pied presse l'enfer, leur tête fend les cieux.
> Là, d'énormes rochers, informe colonnade,
> Dont la fable eût construit le palais d'Encelade,[18]
> L'un sur l'autre entassés, défendaient les chemins
> Que Cybèle interdit à l'aigle des Romains.
> Emmanuel voulut,[19] et ces rocs indociles
> Devinrent, en s'ouvrant, l'heureux lieu des villes;
> Leur masse, leur hauteur et leur dure âpreté,
> Tout, par Emmanuel, fut à la fin dompté;
> Et ces hardis travaux d'un bienfaisant génie
> Unirent à jamais la France et l'Ausonie.
> Ô Guaspre! ô Salvator! où sont-ils vos pinceaux?
> Du peintre épouvanté de ces vastes tableaux,
> Tout frappe, tout absorbe et grandit la pensée.
> Immobile, sans voix, la poitrine oppressée,
> Il sent fléchir sous lui ses genoux chancelans;
> Il voit d'un œil troublé les objets vacillans;
> Accablé, mais ravi des beautés qu'il admire,
> Le seul cri de l'extase échappe à son délire.
> Altéré de la soif de sentir et de voir,

Moi-même, riche alors de jeunesse, d'espoir,
Et des illusions d'un avenir immense,
Quand je quittai le sol, le doux sol de la France,
À l'esprit imprévu de ces rocs menaçans,
Un désordre nouveau bouleversa mes sens;
Mes regards dévoraient les cieux et les abîmes,
Et mon âme nageait dans ces grandeurs sublimes. (pp. 58–59)

Girodet intended to treat landscape in the "Cinquième veillée" of an earlier and related poem, which exists only in fragmentary form.[20] So this Alpine scene and its "énormes roches," "rocs menaçans," "abîmes," and—to sum it all up—"grandeurs sublimes" are all we have to tell us what Girodet might have written, in a didactic vein, about landscape and Rosa's stature as a model for artists working in that genre. His admiration for the Italian artist is obvious—he puts him at least on the same level as the lesser Poussin (i.e., Gaspard Dughet).[21] Girodet's fellow artist François-Marius Granet (1775–1849) did a pen-and-ink and brown wash drawing in Rome in 1817 entitled *Salvator Rosa's House in Rome.*[22]

Another artist of this generation who paid tribute to Rosa directly or indirectly was Achille-Etna Michallon (1796–1822) in *La Mort de Roland* (1819). The art critic and art historian Pierre-Marie Gault de Saint-Germain (1756–1842) made the affinity between the two artists very clear:

The vast landscape of M. Michallon fixes the attention of the viewer by a character of grandeur and energy of which there exists no example in the [French] school. The somber wastelands of Salvator, the turmoil of the earth under the brush of that famous Neapolitan, offer nothing more fierce nor more appropriate to the episode from the poem of Roland with which the painter has enriched his picture.[23]

The leading writers who represent this period of transition and tumult yield a certain number of interesting references to Rosa, though fewer than one might hope or expect. I find no reference to Rosa in the voluminous work of Chateaubriand.[24] A list of great Italian artists in his *Voyage en Italie,* even though it occurs in a passage recounting his visit to Naples in January 1804, omits Rosa: "Michel-Ange, Pérugin, Raphaël, Jules Romain, Dominiquin, Titien, Caragio [*sic*]."[25] But Naples offers some hope of finding something for the *noble vicomte* to admire: "À Naples, au contraire, la chevalerie se mêle au caractère italien, et les prouesses aux émeutes populaires; Tancrède et le Tasse, Jeanne de Naples et le bon roi René, qui ne régna point, les Vêpres Siciliennes, Mazaniel et le dernier duc de Guise, voilà les Deux-Siciles" (ibid.). Chateaubriand does not refer to Masaniello's revolt in his vast tableau of revolutions, ancient and modern, the *Essai sur les Révolutions* (1797), but this fleeting reference to "Mazaniel" shows that he was aware of it. And an early text—roughly contemporary with the *Essai*—suggests that he knew the work of Rosa or some painter who painted in the tradition that Rosa helped to found. In a "Lettre" addressed to someone not yet identified and dated "Londres, 1795,"[26] Chateaubriand produces an essay to which he gave the title "Sur l'art du dessin dans les paysages."[27] Recommending "plein air" studies to the apprentice artist, he writes: "Qu'un jeune homme soit frappé de l'effet d'une cascade qui tombe de la cime d'un roc et dont l'eau bouillonne en s'enfuyant: le mouvement, le bruit, les jets de lumière, les masses d'ombres, les plantes échevelées, la neige de l'écume qui se forme au bas de la chute, les frais gazons qui bordent le cours de l'eau, tout se gravera dans sa mémoire."[28] Here, only the "frais gazons" come from the "smiling landscapes" in the Claudian tradition. Chateaubriand has already, a few lines earlier, made it clear that in teaching landscape painting, too much emphasis has been placed, at least by "maîtres ordinaires" and "amateurs comme nous," on technique, at the service of idealism: "[O]n ne nous apprend point à étudier les objets mêmes qui nous flattent si agréablement dans les tableaux de la nature; on ne nous fait point remarquer que ce qui nous charme dans ces tableaux, ce sont les harmonies et les oppositions des vieux bois et des bocages, des rochers arides et des prairies parées de toute la jeunesse des fleurs" (ibid.). This even-handed approach is misleading, for, as we have seen, in thinking of nature as the young artist will encounter it, there is more of Rosa (or "Gaspard Poussin") than of Claude. Chateaubriand, as Théophile Gautier said, with admittedly some exaggeration, "inventa la mélancolie moderne."[29] And so the young artist, after studying botany must "s'enfonce[r] dans la solitude" and "quitte[r] ces plaines déshonorées par le voisinage de nos villes" (p. 167). The kind of nature Chateaubriand's artist must imagine when he would represent "le grand" sounds—or, rather, looks—like a Rosa landscape: "des montagnes entassées jusqu'aux cieux, des torrents, des précipices, la mer agitée, des flots si vastes que nous ne les voyons que dans le vague de nos pensées, des vents, des tonnerres" (ibid.). One is tempted to see here a clear foreshadowing of the famous "vague des passions," especially if we add the opening sentence of the very next paragraph where Chateaubriand evokes "[le] penchant que l'homme a pour détruire" (ibid.) and develops the idea that "nous avons toutes les peines du monde à nous peindre le calme des flots, à moins que nous n'y mêlions des souvenirs de terreur" (p. 168). And, here, once again Chateaubriand could be thinking of Rosa, or perhaps of one of Joseph Vernet's seascapes, as he imagines the young artist who learns to subdue and organize the chaotic nature he had imagined in the light of his experience of nature as it really is:

> Que, rempli de ces folles idées du sublime, un paysagiste arrive pendant un orage au bord de la mer qu'il n'a jamais vue, il est tout étonné d'apercevoir des vagues qui s'enflent, s'approchent et se déroulent avec ordre et majesté l'une après l'autre, au lieu de ce choc et de ce bouleversement qu'il s'étoit représentés. Un bruit sourd, mêlé de quelques sons rauques et clairs entrecoupés de quelques courts silences, a succédé au tintamarre que notre peintre entendoit dans son cerveau. Partout des couleurs tranchantes, mais conservant des harmonies jusques dans leurs disparates. L'écume éblouissante des flots jaillit sur des rochers noirs; dans un horizon sombre roulent de vastes nuages, mais qui sont poussés du même côté: ce ne sont plus mille vents déchaînés qui se combattent, des couleurs brouillées, des cieux escaladés par les flots, la lumière épouvantant les morts à travers les abîmes creusés entre les vagues. (Ibid.)

At the highest stage of his artistic development, the young art student will create paintings in which some Rosaesque elements can still be identified as well as some suggestive of Poussin, Lorrain, or Hubert Robert:

> Tantôt il égarera les yeux de l'amateur sous des pins ou peut-être un tombeau couvert de lierre appellera en vain l'amitié; tantôt dans un vallon étroit, entouré de rochers nus, il placera les restes d'un vieux château; à travers les crevasses des tours on apercevra le tronc de l'arbre solitaire qui a envahi la demeure du bruit et des combats; le perce-pierre couvrira de ses croix blanches les débris écroulés, et les capillaires tapisseront les pans de murs encore debout. (Ibid)

"Smiling landscapes" are not to be ruled out entirely, "soit que l'image du bonheur convienne peu aux hommes, soit que l'art ne trouve que de foibles ressources dans la peinture des plaisirs champêtres, réduits pour la plupart à des danses et à des chants" (p. 165).

Many years later, in a poem dated 1822, the writer briefly evoked the Alpine landscape—"abîmes," "cimes," "ce vieux bois, où fuit une eau limpide," "remparts"—but saw it primarily as the rugged threshold of his marvelous Italian adventures.[30] In Italy itself, as we have seen, Chateaubriand seems not to have had any memorable encounter with Rosa's work. As in Diderot's art criticism, one might identify a subterranean and indirect influence of Rosa, or at the least an affinity. It was no doubt the great seventeenth-century French landscapists that would have come first to mind when he thought of landscape painting.

Chateaubriand's great contemporary Madame de Staël constructed a somewhat different *musée imaginaire* in *Corinne ou l'Italie* (1807). Technically, the painterly ideal elaborated in the novel is her heroine's, but there is no reason to think that Corinne and Germaine would not have shared the same taste in the visual arts. In Book VIII, "Les statues et les tableaux," Staël's heroine and the male protagonist, Oswald (Lord Nelvil), visit the chief artistic glories of Rome on display in the Vatican, in the Sistine Chapel, and in Canova's studio; the sculptures are all from antiquity, while the paintings (Michelangelo, Raphael, Domenichino) are all from the sixteenth and seventeenth centuries.[31]

Corinne then invites Oswald to see her own collection ("la galerie de tableaux que des artistes de mes amis m'ont composée" [p. 213]), which is on display at her country house at Tivoli. There are works by two Renaissance and seventeenth-century Italians, Titian and Albani;[32] by contemporary Frenchmen, David, Drouet (i.e., Drouais), Gérard, and Guérin; and by several artists either virtually forgotten (Rehberg, painter of a *Dido*) or difficult to identify (a scene from Tasso said to be in "la galerie de Florence" and a scene from *Macbeth* [Reynolds? Fuseli?]). Finally, we arrive before the picture that interests us most here. It corresponds, Corinne tells Oswald, to her preference for landscapes devoid of human figures: "Ce qui vaut le mieux, ce me semble, en ce genre, c'est la manière de Salvator Rosa, qui représente, comme vous le voyez dans ce tableau, un rocher, des torrens et des arbres sans un seul etre vivant, sans que seulement le vol d'un oiseau rappelle l'idée de la vie" (p. 222). Corinne concludes her comments on this untitled picture with some rather surprising words: "L'absence de l'homme au milieu de la terre excite des réflexions profondes. Que serait cette terre ainsi délaissée? Œuvre sans but, et cependant œuvre encore si belle, dont la mysterieuse impression ne s'adresseroit qu'à la Divinité !" (Ibid.) Do we have here an echo of Kantian ethics and aesthetics? Staël was one of the first French writers to encounter Kant's thought, and her friend and correspondent Charles de Villers was an important intermediary between the German philosopher and the French reading public. In any case, it is odd that Staël should believe that Rosa's landscapes contain no human figures—that cannot be said of a single one of them. This misunderstanding and the absence of any title for this Rosa landscape in Corinne's gallery suggest that she is relying on a vague, general impression of Rosa's work, based on dim memories of actual examples or even on textual sources. We have already seen that those who write about Rosa, even when they emphasize his landscapes, rarely mention specific pictures. Her rather brief, unadorned catalogue of natural objects— "un rocher, des torrens et des arbres"—reinforces this impression. From

Claude to Corot, the "paysage historique," while not officially recognized as a separate genre at the Paris Salons until 1817, was in fact there all along and represented a growing tendency; eventually French landscape painting would break entirely free of "history." Staël was probably unaware of the philosophical content of many of Rosa's works, not to mention his own stated preference for history painting. Still, however shaky her grasp of Rosa, Staël's brief evocation of his landscape "manner" and her accompanying reflections put her in the vanguard of theorists of landscape painting and foreshadow the Barbizon painters and the Impressionists.

Stendhal was nearly a generation younger than Chateaubriand and Staël, but, though he began to write seriously only after the beginning of the nineteenth century, he was formed by a world they would have still recognized. For one thing, he shared their love for things Italian and indeed outdid them in that respect. In the visual arts, he worshiped Correggio: "Pour Stendhal, le Corrège n'a pas été un peintre, mais la peinture même."[33]

It is in his *Histoire de la peinture en Italie* and related texts that the first references to Rosa appear in Stendhal's writing. The *Histoire*, originally conceived as a translation of Luigi Antonio Lanzi's *Storia pittorica dell'Italia*, was in gestation from 1811 to 1817, the year of its publication. At first glance, we have the impression that, unlike Madame de Staël, Stendhal saw and remembered several works by Rosa. His account of his visit to the Pitti in late September 1811 includes the notation: "Il y a des tableaux superbes. Une marine de Salvator Rosa m'a frappé."[34] When he speaks of "un paysage de Salvator Rosa" and "[le] beau paysage si frais de Salvator Rosa,"[35] also seen at the Pitti, he does not tell us precisely what Rosas he has seen. Clearer ideas emerge in the surprising context of a discussion of the Venetian school: he refers to Rosa's "tableaux si curieux où il présente des magiciens et des transformations."[36] And, as we shall see, he certainly saw the *Heroic Battle* in the Louvre.

Given that Lanzi's history of Italian painting provided at least the point of departure for Stendhal's *Histoire,* it is natural to wonder if the French author drew on the Italian when writing about the Rosas in the Pitti. To judge by the passages on Rosa in the French translation of Lanzi's book (1824), there are no specific references to such pictures.[37] Pending further evidence, we can assume that Stendhal had direct knowledge of a certain number of Rosa's work seen in Italy. And he obviously saw at least one Rosa in the Louvre.

Stendhal's encounter with Rosa was not, however, a determining or overwhelming experience. There are no extended passages devoted to Rosa anywhere in Stendhal's writing. Those that we do find are scattered from the *Histoire de la peinture en Italie* (1817) to the *Mémoires d'un touriste* (1838).

A few of these references convey a general idea of Stendhal's estimate of Rosa. In the *Histoire,* Rosa is included in a "Tableau chronologique des artistes les plus célèbres" (*OC*, XXVI, 275), and there is a similar reference in *Promenades dans Rome* (1829) (*OC*, VI, 249). The latter work also provides us an insight into Stendhal's ranking of Italian painters: Rosa is in the third rank, while Michelangelo, Raphael, Leonardo, Giorgione, Titian, Annibale Carracci, Reni, Domenichino, and Guercino are accorded places in the first rank. Elsewhere in *Promenades,* apropos of the *Martirio dei santi Cosma e Damiano* (S 252), in San Giovanni de' Fiorentini in Rome, he dubs Salvator Rosa "ce peintre original."[38] This is not a brilliant showing. It is worth recalling, however, that both the *Histoire* and the *Promenades* are heavily dependent on secondary sources—for example, the latter, purporting to be a guidebook based on a tour of Rome in 1828, was entirely composed in Paris, quarried out of Lalande and other authorities. One could conclude that Rosa's position in Stendhal's hierarchy suffers when the latter draws on other authorities.

A more favorable view of Rosa, however, emerges from passages in which Stendhal actually seems to be trying to characterize Rosa's work. Concerning the painting of battle scenes, he writes: "Il faut une imagination impétueuse et noire, un Jules Romain, un Salvator Rosa."[39] Twice Stendhal contrasts Claude Lorrain and Salvator Rosa: "le style paisible et charmant du Lorrain" versus "l'âme sévère et inflammée de Salvator Rosa"[40]; in a marginal note beside Claude's name and dates in a "liste des peintres italiens dont il faut regarder les ouvrages," the "air tranquille et serein," which the French painter achieved in his quest for ideal beauty, is set against Rosa's landscapes and their "physionomie atroce précisément le contraire."[41] Earlier in the same *Salon de 1824,* apropos of Sigalon's *Narcisse,* he had spoken of the "pinceau heurté de Salvator Rosa."[42] A rather different facet of Rosa's art, his color, is suggested when Stendhal writes of "la manière chargée d'ombres de ce peintre."[43]

This last quotation, touching briefly on Rosa's style, is meant to place the artist in a historical context. (Stendhal is speaking of the development of the Venetian school and, specifically, of Gregorio Lazzarini [1655–1730] and his alleged rejection of the Rosa style.) It raises the question of how much historical information Stendhal had absorbed about Rosa. The short answer is not much. He mentions several anecdotes involving Rosa.[44] He is aware of the location of several Rosas, but is not always speaking from firsthand experience. He mentions the tombs of Rosa and Carlo Maratti in Santa Maria degli Angeli in Rome, but, here too, the information is probably mere borrowing.[45] He claims to have seen a Rosa in Avignon,[46] but gives no title or any other particular. Perhaps symbolic is the entry for 3 August in *Promenades dans Rome,* in which the guide-narrator relates that, on arriving in Rome, he took lodgings in the house on the Via Gregoriana in which Rosa had once lived; unfortunately, he gives a wrong address.[47] Especially interesting is the discovery by Victor Del Litto that a book on the Masaniello episode by one Giovanni La Cecilia (1801–1880) was in Stendhal's baggage when he returned to Italy in 1839 after his three-year "leave."[48] In attempting to identify La Cecilia's book and, if possible, the specific edition Stendhal owned, I have discovered that such standard authorities as the catalogue of the Bibliothèque Nationale, the *Bibliographie de la France,* Pierre Larousse's *Grand Dictionnaire universel du XIXe siècle,* and the *Enciclopedia italiana* list only Italian editions (Livorno, 1847–1848; Naples, 1848) that date from several years after Stendhal's death, not to mention his trip to Civitavecchia in 1839. But an American database (OCLC) lists the following entry: Jean La Cecilia, *Masaniello ou la révolution de Naples en 1647.* Paris: Pagnerre, 1838. Thus the French edition allegedly found by the Papal officials who examined Stendhal's baggage in 1839 did exist. He must have bought it during his Parisian leave of absence.[49]

All in all, the harvest gathered in Stendhal's work so far is not plenteous. One can conclude that Stendhal saw and admired a certain number of Rosa's works and found something "original" and vivid in them ("imagination impétueuse et noire," "âme sévère et enflammée," "physionomie atroce," "pinceau heurté") despite his clear preference for Italian painters of the sixteenth and seventeenth centuries who, except for Michelangelo, have little in common with Rosa: the great idealizers from Raphael, Leonardo, and Correggio to Reni, Guercino, and Domenichino.

The *Salon de 1824* is a crucial document in the present account in several respects. For one thing, it brings us to the critical year in the history of French writing about Rosa, the year that saw the publication of Lady Morgan's book about Rosa. More directly relevant to our theme is the fact that Rosa figures in an important and revealing discussion by Stendhal about romanticism. (One might note that this document appeared in the gap between the two parts of Stendhal's pivotal contribution to the battle raging in Paris over romanticism, *Racine et Shakspeare* [*sic*] [1823, 1825].) The word "romantique" has already surfaced several times in this study, most notably in Le Tourneur's preface to his French translation of Shakespeare in 1776 and in Charles Blanc's entry in his *Trésor de la curiosité* (II, 170) on the Calonne sale in 1795: "Un paysage de Salvator Rosa: *Vue romantique d'un port dans la Calabre.*" In Stendhal's 1824 text, the critic singles out a painting by Rosa and gives clear proof that he has actually seen it, and, most important, he links the picture to the debate over romanticism, but not in the way we might expect. Because the passage in question, inspired by Horace Vernet's *Bataille de Montmirail,* represents a point of convergence for so many currents, it is worth citing in full:

> Un critique, grand ennemi du romantisme, affuble de l'étrange épithète de *shakspearien* le tableau de M. H. Vernet, tandis qu'il appelle *homériques* les tableaux de Raphaël et de David. Il est plus simple de dire: *J'appellerai romantique tout ce qui n'est pas excellent.* Par cet artifice fort simple, peu à peu le mot romantique deviendrait aux yeux du public le synonyme de mauvais.
>
> Ce qui est *romantique* en peinture, c'est la *Bataille de Montmirail,*[50] ce chef-d'œuvre de M. H. Vernet, où tout se trouve, même le *clair-obscur.* Ce qui est classique, c'est une bataille de Salvator Rosa, à peu près de même dimension, et que l'on peut voir à l'extrémité de la grande galerie du côté de la Seine. Le *romantique* dans tous les arts, c'est ce qui représente les hommes d'aujourd'hui, et non ceux de ces temps héroïques si loin de nous, et qui probablement n'ont jamais existé. Si l'on veut se donner la peine de comparer les deux batailles que je viens d'indiquer, et surtout *la quantité de plaisir* qu'elles font au spectateur, on pourra se former une idée nette de ce qu'est le romantique en peinture. Le classique, au contraire, ce sont les hommes entièrement nus qui remplissaient le tableau des Sabines.[51]

Rosa, then, becomes deeply, though briefly, involved in the great debate over romanticism, at its height in 1824. Stendhal restates the most trenchant and important ideas of his *Racine et Shakspeare,* most amusingly expressed in this oft-cited passage: "Le romanticisme [*sic*] est l'art de présenter aux peuples les œuvres littéraires qui, dans l'état actuel de leurs habitudes et de leurs croyances, sont susceptibles de leur donner le plus de plaisir possible. Le classicisme, au contraire, leur présente la littérature qui donnait le plus grand plaisir à leurs arrière-grands-pères."[52] But he surprises us by thrusting Rosa's battle picture in the Louvre back into the classical era, whereas the picture of Rosa that has been emerging from the texts so far examined is of a talented painter whose work is marred by irregularities and "defects" or, in the late eighteenth century, of a romantic artist *avant la lettre.* Stendhal's treatment of Rosa in the *Salon de 1824* tells us how far the discussion of romanticism has come by the end of the first quarter of the nineteenth century. After the "excesses" of the Revolution and the epic military campaigns of the Napoleonic era, a picture like Rosa's *Heroic Battle,* with its anonymous, leaderless warriors in antique armor may not stir the souls of most modern viewers. The classical architecture of the ruin to the right is still stylistically acceptable in 1824, but it lacks specificity, as do the all-purpose mountains in the distance. Vernet's picture, on the other hand, shows events that had taken place virtually on the doorsteps of Paris only ten years before. Because the battle fought at Montmirail in early 1814 was a great victory for Napoleon's army, it bestowed a relevance and an emotional impact that are an extraneous consideration for viewers of a later day, but it was obviously moving to Parisians of 1824.[53]

Stendhal's relegation of Rosa's picture to the ash heap of (art) history should come as something of a surprise to those who have followed the rising curve of the artist's fortune traced in this study. It may foreshadow his eventual decline, though I believe that that has more to do with the changes wrought in French landscape painting during the nineteenth century than with the history of battle-scene painting; for Stendhal and his contemporaries the genre was still a vital one, as his admiration for Vernet's picture reveals. Gros, Géricault, Delacroix, and Vernet himself would keep it alive, in various ways, for several more decades. The fact that Stendhal even bothers to invoke Rosa's picture is to be explained by the fact that the picture was in the Louvre and so easily available for viewing by those visiting the Salon exhibition. Moreover, its size was comparable to that of Vernet's picture ("à peu près de même dimension"). Finally, it may well be that, among the battle pictures then on view in the Louvre, Rosa's still enjoyed considerable favor. If Stendhal brings in David's *Sabines* at the very close of the passage we are examining, it is primarily because it had all those nudes—the nude being the norm in the representation of heroic human figures, especially in the post-Winckelmann era. Raphael's battle scenes were not accessible, being attached to the walls of a room in the Vatican. The line of French practitioners of battle painting—Courtois, the Parrocels, Van der Meulen—had died out. A famous picture by a popular artist, and one that was just steps away from where viewers admired not only the *Bataille de Montmirail* but Vernet's *Portrait en pied de M. le maréchal de Gouvion-Saint-Cyr*, made a convenient target and point of comparison.[54]

Despite Stendhal's preference for Vernet's battle scene over Rosa's, the popularity of the latter artist was about to receive a powerful boost from Lady Morgan's book, published in Paris and London in both French and English, in early 1824. Stendhal may have written off Rosa as "classic," but Lady Morgan found a way to fit Rosa into the context of a world still shaken by revolutionary tremors and about to know the full tide of romantic modernism. In Restoration France and beyond, the past was still a living force, a source of parallels with current events: the frequent references in painting and literature to Charles I, Cromwell, and the English revolution that coincided almost exactly with the revolt in Naples in 1647 provide a well-known example. Delacroix's *Bataille de Taillebourg* (1837) and Ingres's *Jeanne d'Arc* (1854) were meaningful to Frenchmen and Frenchwomen who had little use for the institutions of the thirteenth or the fifteenth century. Thanks to Lady Morgan, Salvator Rosa's pictures would hang for a while longer in the *musée imaginaire* of nineteenth-century France, and the man and his story would come to life in novels, plays, and poems. [55]

CHAPTER THREE

Enter Lady Morgan

Lady Morgan, the author of the book that attached Rosa and his work firmly to the rising romantic movement, was born Sydney Owenson in Dublin, probably in 1776.[1] She was the daughter of an Irish actor, Robert Owenson (originally MacOwen) and an English mother who died while Sydney was still a child. Despite her father's chronic financial difficulties, she struggled out of the typical situation of poor girls of her era by serving for a time as a governess. Literature seemed to offer a way up: a first volume of poems appeared in 1801; her first novel, in 1803. *The Wild Irish Girl, a National Tale* (1806) was a great success, and Sydney was henceforth championed by the liberal Catholic party in Ireland—titles like *Patriotic Sketches of Ireland* (1807) and *O'Donnel* (1814), another "national tale," are representative of this phase of her work.

Literary success brought social promotion and marriage. Sydney became a member of the Marquis of Abercorn's household, and in 1812 married Sir Thomas Charles Morgan, her patron's surgeon. The fall of Napoleon opened the continent to her, and she visited France in 1815. Perhaps in emulation of Madame de Staël's *De l'Allemagne*, first published in London in 1813, she produced the very popular but controversial *France* (1817). Four years later, having spent a year (1818–1819) in Italy, she brought out *Italy*, conceived in a similar spirit and also controversial—it was banned by the king of Sardinia, the emperor of Austria, and the pope (to whom she was presented while in Rome). These books and a number of her earlier writings on Irish themes gave Lady Morgan a prominent place in the liberal movement in western Europe; when in Paris, she moved among such French circles as those of Benjamin Constant and Lafayette. Byron called *Italy* "fearless and excellent."[2]

It is tempting to see Lady Morgan as Byron's partner in promoting local independence movements, and the publication in 1824 (the year of Byron's death) of *The Life and Times of Salvator Rosa* makes a nice coincidence. But Lady Morgan's book had been in gestation for some time. She tells us that early in life the collections of paintings at Kilkenny Castle "awakened a passion for [art's] noble powers which in after life broke forth in my life of *Salvator Rosa*, of all my works the most delightful to myself."[3]

Already, in *The Wild Irish Girl*, extolling Irish scenery for "the bold features of its varying landscape, the stupendous altitude of its 'cloud-capt' mountains, the impervious gloom of its deep embosomed glens, the savage desolation of its uncultivated heaths and boundless bogs," she pointed to Rosa as the ideal painter of such landscapes: "The glowing fancy of Claude Loraine [*sic*] would have dwelt enraptured on the paradisial charms of English landscape, the superior genius of Salvator Rosa would have reposed its eagle wing amidst those scenes of mysterious sublimity with which the wildly magnificent landscape of Ireland abounds."[4] Moreover, in the home of her friend, the Marquis of Abercorn, she could have seen two of the pictures she (II, 307) lists as being in the latter's collection in 1823: *Vanitas* (S 114) and *Natura morte emblematica* (S 115), which Rosa painted on a harpsichord case.

Her ambition to write a book about Rosa seems to have taken on concrete form during her travels in Italy as she researched her book about that country. In Rome, Lady Morgan frequented Bonapartist circles and met various members of Napoleon's family, including his uncle, Cardinal Fesch. The cardinal allowed her "to rummage about his palace and admire his gallery and his pontifical toilet—his pictures by Rafael, and his point laces."[5] In a long footnote in Lady Morgan's *Italy*[6] she tells us that she saw a portrait of Masaniello in the cardinal's collection. In Naples, the same passage reveals, the archbishop of Taranto "shewed us a most curious original picture of Massaniello [*sic*] and his good dame." The context is a discussion of the events of 1647 in Naples, "that well-known and formidable insurrection which has given the name and feats of an obscure young fisherman to posterity, and bequeathed to the people of Naples the threat, as often and so vainly used under the reiterated oppression of centuries" (III, 200). Having, in her footnote, mentioned the portrait of Masaniello seen in Naples, Lady Morgan refers back to her visit to Cardinal Fesch's palace.

Cardinal Fesche [*sic*] shewed us another original picture in Rome of this piscatory demagogue! He is dressed in his fisherman's simple and picturesque habit. I think, but I am not certain, that his Eminence told us the picture was done by Salvator Rosa. This is at least possible, as that true

Neapolitan spirit took an active part in Masaniello's revolt, and amused himself in the cave of the conspirators by drawing all their pictures by torchlight. [See *Vita di Salvator Rosa,* prefixed to his *Satires.*] (III, 200–01)

Lady Morgan had already admired some of Rosa's works in the Pitti in Florence: "Here too are some of Salvator Rosa's finest sea-pieces, with those calm skies and waters, and brilliant lights, so contrasted to the force, gloom, and energy of his Catiline conspiracy" (II, 132–33). But the Rosas admired in Florence roused no political reactions in the lady from Ireland. The alleged portrait of Masaniello in Rome, associated in her mind with the similar picture she had seen in Naples, was quite another matter: she turns automatically to the Spanish tyranny in the seventeenth century, replaced by that of Austria in the eighteenth (III, 201). Writing in the years when "the Metternichs and the Castlereaghs" (II, 132) ruled Europe, just a few years after the Bourbons regained possession of the Kingdom of Naples, she could easily see the relevance of Masaniello's revolt and of the life of Salvator Rosa to the post-revolutionary, post-Napoleonic world around her, torn between liberalism and reaction. A brief reference to Rosa in another passage in *Italy* takes on new meaning, seen in this light. Contemplating the wild landscape of the valley of the Nera that inspires her, she tells us that the rugged beauties of the scene "demand a Byron's pen, or a Salvator's pencil!" (II, 316). A revealing juxtaposition—sublime scenery ("the poetry of landscape"), England's notorious, rebellious poet, and Salvator Rosa.[7]

Lady Morgan published nothing of importance between *Italy* (1821) and her book on Rosa. We must suppose that she was cultivating the seed planted in Italy by her encounter with reminders of the artist's work and his life, especially his participation in Masaniello's revolt. It is clear that when she wrote *Italy,* she had read about this episode: as we have seen, she refers to a "*Vita di Salvator Rosa,* prefixed to his *Satires*" (III, 201). In Florence, at the Pitti, she admired several of Rosa's pictures; in Rome, Cardinal Fesch showed her a portrait of Masaniello thought to be by Rosa. We can assume that in various English, French, and Italian galleries she saw some of Rosa's works—those on view in the Louvre, for example. Even though originally conceived as a "romance,"[8] the book she proposed to write about Salvator Rosa would require a great deal more knowledge about the painter and his work than she could draw on when the project was conceived.

The years between *Italy* and *The Life and Times of Salvator Rosa* must have been largely devoted to research. Stevenson describes the process as follows: "All available books on the subject . . . were supplied by [her publisher] Colburn, and every English patron of art who owned a Salvator was solicited for information. Earls Darnley, Grosvenor, Cowper, and Milltown were among those who responded, and Caroline Lamb obtained copious notes from her brother, William Ponsonby" (p. 235). It would be more exact to say that while she did not consult "all available books on the subject," she did a remarkable piece of research, especially given the fact that she worked on the book far from Italy. She relied heavily on three of the fundamental Italian texts, the sketches of Rosa published in the eighteenth century by Passeri, Baldinucci, and Pascoli—there are dozens of references to these authors, often with supporting quotations in Italian in the footnotes. She had access to an edition of Rosa's *Satire* and often quoted from them; she consulted the biographical preface to her edition of these poems—indeed, her account of Rosa's participation in Masaniello's revolt seems to come from this source, not from De Dominici, whose name never appears in her text. She had access to twenty of Rosa's letters to his friend Giovanni Battista Ricciardi and reprinted them in an appendix, providing both the original Italian and a translation.[9] Another important source was Dr. Charles Burney's *General History of Music* (1776–1789), from which, unfortunately, she uncritically drew much irrelevant "information" for the lengthy passages about Rosa's supposed attainments as a musician. There are several score of other sources of information or, at least, literary quotations: Italian poets from Dante to Rosa; various Italian, French, and English critics, notably Joshua Reynolds, and art historians (Lanzi, Bellori, and Dezallier d'Argenville); great literary figures like Voltaire and Byron; the famous seventeenth-century English traveler John Evelyn; reference works like the *Encyclopædia Britannica*[10] and Matthew Pilkington's *Dictionary of Painters* (1770); Italians who associated with Rosa (Ricciardi, Lorenzo Lippi, and A. Abati). But it was the biographies of Baldinucci, Passeri, Pascoli, an edition of Rosa's poetry with a biographical sketch by Anton Maria Salvini, first published in 1770, and twenty letters from Rosa to Ricciardi, published by Bottari in the middle of the eighteenth century, that provided the bulk of the material she exploited. The absence of De Dominici's biography from the list of her sources and her reliance on Dr. Burney are the only serious flaws that can be laid to her research.

The book appeared almost simultaneously in London and Paris, in the latter city in both English and French. The title page of the French edition bears the date "Avril 1824," and lists a Belgian outlet for the book as well as the French publisher. Said to be the "2ᵐᵉ édition"—presumably the English original counted as the first—it was published by one Alexis Eymery (ca. 1795–ca.1880), of whom his biographer, J. Richardot, writes: "s'il est libéral, il ne fut point bonapartiste avant que le culte de l'Empereur devînt à la mode" (*DBF*, XIII, 345). Thus, fittingly, Lady Morgan's biography was published in France by a "liberal" with Bonapartist leanings. As for her translators, one was a certain Mademoiselle Adèle Sobry, who had already done the French version of Lady Morgan's *Italy;* given the dates of her publishing career—the years of the Restoration and July Monarchy—one can speculate that she was a daughter or granddaughter of the curious figure, Jean-François Sobry (1743–1820),[11] who managed to serve both the Revolution and Napoleon. Mademoiselle Sobry's literary activity seems to have been confined to making translations from English: in addition to five works of Lady Morgan, she translated works by E. G. Bulwer-Lytton, Disraeli, Mrs. Trollope, Washington Irving, and other British and American authors. As for the person named "Pierhuc" who shared the work of translating *The Life and Times of Salvator Rosa,* to the best of my knowledge he is otherwise unknown to history or bibliography.[12]

　In its French edition Lady Morgan's book is in two volumes, each something over 300 pages long. Eymery provides a brief "Avertissement du libraire-éditeur" that contains one especially perceptive sentence about the book he is offering to the public: "La politique, les mœurs et les arts présentent un ensemble parfait" (I, i). Lady Morgan's own preface, dated "Kilddare [*sic*] street, Dublin, 1er octobre 1823" (I, ix), in addition to the expected acknowledgments at the end, is noteworthy for its account of her efforts to begin her research while in Italy—efforts defeated by the fact that the only work recommended to her was the *Parnasso italiano,* "recueil fabriqué sous *l'approbation du Grand Inquisiteur du Saint Office*" (I, v). Actually, this experience spurred her into action, since the picture of Rosa provided by this "authorized" text conflicted with what she knew of Rosa's work: "Dès-lors, il me parut évident que la flétrissure imprimée sur la mémoire de l'un des plus grands peintres et du poëte le plus philosophe, avait pour cause, non les vices de l'individu, mais l'esprit d'indépendance, et les doctrines politiques du sincère ami de son pays" (I, vi). In broad outline, we see here the Rosa to whose life and work, both artistic and literary (even musical), Lady Morgan devoted herself. She admits that her enthusiasm for "les œuvres du patriote italien qui s'élève avec hardiesse au-dessus d'une époque de dégradation" exceeds even that for "le mérite extraordinaire de l'artiste" (I, iii). She goes on to place Rosa in history "entre Michel-Ange l'artiste patriote, et Filicaja,[13] le poète de la liberté" (I, vi). The reference we have already seen to the Inquisition and to Rosa as "l'artiste patriote" and to Filicaja as "le poëte de la liberté" leads on to a passage in which she tells us that her Italian friends could not help her with her research: "Plusieurs ont subi la persécution; la plupart ont sauvé leur vie par de périlleuses évasions et un exil où les poursuit l'indigence; quelques-uns, au moment où je trace ces lignes, passent, incertains du sort qui les attend, leurs plus belles années dans des donjons solitaires, où ils n'ont pour distraction que l'entretien des geôliers" (I, vii–viii).

Lady Morgan's Rosa is a historical figure very relevant to the Europe of 1823–1824, the Europe of Metternich and the Holy Alliance, and to the Italy of those same years, where Carbonari fomented revolution and laid the groundwork of the Risorgimento; where—closer to home—O'Connell and O'Connor stirred Irish unrest. No doubt it was because Rosa was so relevant, so timely, that Lady Morgan was drawn to him, and she never lost sight of this raison d'être for her biography. But she had to deal with the reality of Rosa's fame and popularity, primarily based on his work as an artist and, especially, as a painter. After all, it was his reputation as a painter that inspired his early biographies, and it was his career and achievement as a painter that these texts sought to document. Her solution was to emphasize as much as possible Rosa the man, the poet, and the thinker. One might say that this approach entailed exaggerating the value of Rosa's poetry: if the fame of Rosa the painter and etcher has dimmed considerably since the mid-nineteenth century, his present standing as a poet is only a faint shadow of what it was for Lady Morgan. Today his *Satire* are known only to specialists of his paintings and etchings and to a few other scholars. But as we study Lady Morgan's book, even if Rosa the artist is uppermost in our minds, we must remember her publisher's observation: "La politique, les mœurs et les arts présentent un ensemble parfait."

Lady Morgan opens her book with a broad sketch of Italian painting from the thirteenth through the sixteenth century. It is essentially a political or social history, emphasizing the preponderant, indeed oppressive, influence during the earlier period of the church, sole or nearly sole patron of the visual arts, which it used to inculcate orthodox beliefs and to combat potentially or actually subversive ideas, and thus to maintain power and wealth. Writers became courtiers and flunkies, while painters were richly rewarded for producing the murals, altarpieces, and reliquaries needed by the church. In northern Europe, the Reformation emphasized music (e.g., in Luther) at the expense of the visual arts. Philosophy, i.e., science, turned men's minds in still other directions and persisted despite persecution and the Inquisition. By the beginning of the seventeenth century, painters were reduced to being the *dependenti* of the princes of the church or hirelings of the Bourbons, the Stuarts, and the Habsburgs. Seemingly a digression, this picture is, in a sense, a *repoussoir* of Rosa's life, personality, and work. His struggle to assert his independence against the princely patrons, ecclesiastical and secular, who controlled Italy and its artistic and intellectual activity, is implicit in the panorama that Lady Morgan here unrolls before us.

Except for the conclusion and the various appendices, the story she has to tell from this point on is, by and large, straightforwardly chronological.[14] The sections devoted to Rosa's family origins, childhood, and education are those that show Lady Morgan at her myth-making best. As she had stated in her preface: "J'ai représenté Salvator tel que me l'ont montré les vraisemblances" (I, vi–vii). For lack of documents, she fleshes out the story of the artist's early life, giving a sentimentalized account of his schooling, complete with a digression denouncing the practice, still in force in Italy in her time, of confining infants in swaddling clothes ("ces horribles maillots" [I, 39, n.]). She imagines the child's "éducation orthodoxe" (I, 32),[15] his conflicts with parents and teachers, and the emergence of his artistic vocation. Fortunately, the book of nature lay open before him: "Rosa reçut ses premières inspirations en contemplant les magnifiques scènes du Vésuve et du Pausilipe" (I, 35). The harsh treatment of the Somascan fathers and their Scholastic educational system failed to crush his independent spirit or to turn him away from his artistic vocation; here and elsewhere, Lady Morgan stresses Rosa's classical learning, which he acquired during the earlier, more humanistic phase of his schooling amid the memories of Greek and Roman culture that hovered over Naples and its enchanted bay. This experience was crucial to the formation of the mature Rosa:

> Ce fut pendant ce temps de tranquillité et d'étude; ce temps où les passions encore endormies laissent l'imagination errer dans un monde idéal; où l'esprit jeune et pur reçoit avec plus d'empressement que de choix toutes les impressions de vertu et de grandeur humaine, que Salvator rassembla ce trésor d'érudition classique, et prit ce goût pour les anciens qui l'inspirèrent plus tard comme peintre et comme poëte. Il confiait alors à sa vaste mémoire ces antiques légendes qui donnèrent leur caractère à ses grands tableaux, à ses poëmes sérieux, caractère si fortement opposé à celui des productions plus légères de sa plume et de son pinceau, par lesquelles il est maintenant placé à la tête de l'école *romantique* d'Italie et jugé digne d'être associé à Shakspeare et à Biron.[16] (I, 47–48)

Before turning to Rosa's training as a painter, Lady Morgan develops a long digression (II, 55–66) on his alleged involvement in the musical life of his time. We have already seen that, like many others, she took seriously what Dr. Charles Burney had said on the subject in his well-known *A General History of Music* (1776–1789). Burney had extrapolated his account of Rosa as a musician from nuggets of authentic information. As the latest authority on the subject summarizes the situation in *The New Grove* (XVI, 192), "Although [Rosa] may have been an amateur musician, the traditional assertion that he composed music has been proved false." Lady Morgan, one imagines, could not resist the temptation to make Rosa out to be a master of three arts. How far she was willing to go is clear from her claim that "ses essais de composition musicale analysés par les doctes *arbitres* du goût dans les siècles futurs, seraient déclarés, non-seulement admirables pour un *dilettante,* mais, sous le rapport de la mélodie, supérieurs à la plupart des œuvres des maîtres de son temps" (I, 62). Here, Lady Morgan may be hiding behind the authority of Dr. Burney[17] and other "doctes *arbitres* du goût," but in another passage she boldly depicts the young Rosa as "l'un des plus brillans et des plus heureux donneurs de sérénades à Naples":

> Plusieurs de ces figures gracieuses et légères, qui échappèrent depuis à son pinceau fidèle ou à son rapide burin, avec leurs cheveux et leurs plumes flottantes au gré du vent, sont, à ce qu'on dit, des portraits de lui, tantôt caché sous un balcon, tantôt incliné sur la proue d'une félouque, chantant sur son luth les charmes ou les rigueurs de la Chloris du moment. (I, 65–66)

We are on more solid ground in the following pages, in which Rosa's biographer recounts his formal training as a painter. Discounting the statements of "plusieurs biographes" to the effect that he first studied under his uncle Paolo Greco, she focuses on his apprenticeship with his brother-in-law Francesco Fracanzano (whose name is always misspelled, sometimes as Francanziani, sometimes Francanzani[18]). But the young Rosa was more inspired by nature than by his teacher's lessons:

> [I]l passait ses journées à parcourir les scènes de ses courses enfantines, partant à l'aube du jour, chargé d'un portefeuille et d'une palette; et l'on dit que même alors, non-seulement il dessinait, mais qu'il peignait d'après nature, (dal naturale).[19] . . . En revenant de ses rudes mais utiles voyages à travers des solitudes inconnues, côtoyant des abîmes, gravissant des précipices où son génie entreprenant pouvait seul pénétrer; il trouvait un asile sous le toit de sa sœur. (I, 70–71)

According to Lady Morgan, Fracanzano, while he may have played a minor role in forming Rosa's talent, unlike his own parents, encouraged him in his painterly vocation.

But the book of nature was soon to be opened much wider than ever before and to lead Lady Morgan into what may be the most important of her inventions about Rosa. She describes the *giro* the budding painter undertook to complete his education. She portrays Rosa as rejecting the usual tour of study in the galleries, churches, and famous studios of Rome, Milan, Florence, and Venice, an experience that led only to the adoption of the manner of some *chef d'école:* "Dans sa manière d'agir fantasque et originale, laissant à des talens plus timides, à des sentimens moins exaltés que les siens, la *routine banale* des académies et des ateliers, il prit une direction que n'autorisait aucun précédent, et s'attacha à l'école où aucun maître ne donne des lois au génie entreprenant, où aucun élève n'est servilement astreint à en suivre: l'école de la nature!" (I, 73). For some ten pages (I, 74–84), Lady Morgan tracks Rosa through southern Italy. On his way out of Naples, he strode alongside the newly erected royal palace where, "sous des voûtes dorées, dormait à cette heure matinale le puissant et magnifique peintre de cour, Spagnoletto" (i.e., Ribera), attended by his servile "suivans" (I, 75). She imagines, too, that he passed near "la demeure somptueuse préparée dans le palais épiscopal . . . pour le grand et persécuté Dominiquin" (I, 76), whom, in her paranoid way, she depicts as dreaming that some other painter in Naples, e.g., Lanfranco or Ribera, might murder him. Rosa, fleeing "les vices et les crimes de *l'ordre social d'alors*" (Ibid.), "a parcouru les sites sublimes et sauvages de la *Basilicate*, de la *Pouille* et de la *Calabre*, la *Magna Græcia* des anciens" (I, 77). Lady Morgan points out that Rosa's biographers have given few concrete details of his *giro*, but she affirms that his landscape paintings, "composés de vues maritimes ou montagneuses, de roches empilées, de ruines antiques, paysages dont l'identité est toujours marquée par quelque trait caractéristique et authentique, aussi bien que par le costume et la physionomie des personnages composant ces charmans petits groupes connus sous le nom de ses *Figurine*" (I, 77), must reflect actual experience. Lady Morgan had not herself visited Magna Græcia, but she had the huge folios of the abbé de Saint-Non's *Voyage pittoresque du royaume de Naples et de Sicile* (1781–1786) and their magnificent engravings to guide her—she refers to the book several times (I, 79–81). It is very characteristic of Lady Morgan that she exploits this episode—after having virtually invented it—to reemphasize Rosa's classical erudition and the inspiration he drew from the visible memories of antiquity to be contemplated in southern Italy. But the ruins of Magna Græcia did not only provide figurative motifs: they accounted, at least in part, for the melancholy pervading Rosa's work: "Cependant tout ce qu'avaient perdu ces contrées jadis florissantes (le mouvement de leurs ports commerçans, la splendeur de leurs écoles de philosophie), était compensé aux yeux du jeune poëte-peintre, du philosophe adolescent, par la sublime dévastation, la grandeur mélancolique qui leur restaient" (I, 78). Lady Morgan links the painter's contacts with the ruins of Magna Græcia to his painting *Democritus* (S 106) but, typically, gives an autobiographical explanation of the deeper meaning of the picture: "Son Démocrite, c'était lui-même; et la morale de sa composition n'était que le résultat naturel de ses réflexions mélancoliques lorsqu'appuyé sur la tombe de l'affranchi de Saturninus, il traçait les ruines de Cannes, de cette cité dont les palais splendides, la population voluptueuse n'étaient plus représentées que par des monumens et des inscriptions funéraires" (I, 80). Similarly, the original inspiration for the painter's *Magicienne du Capitole,* i.e., *La Strega* (S 80), came to him as he wandered "au milieu d'objets si admirablement en harmonie avec ces images terribles" (I, 81).

The pages devoted to Rosa's *giro* culminate in an account of his wanderings in the wilder parts of southern Italy, "les montagnes des Abruzzes et de la Calabre (les plus sauvages et les plus élevés des monts Apennins) . . ." (Ibid.). She even supposes that he lingered longest in these regions, where the rugged scenery still revealed a human element that inspired the artist, inhabited as it was "par des êtres pleins de cette inquiète énergie, de cet esprit d'indépendance indomptable, attributs moraux des régions montagneuses" (I, 82).[20]

The climax of this exposure to nature was to come when the artist occasionally pushed into the highest mountains of the Abruzzi, "ces amphithéâtres de rochers fermés par des forêts de noirs sapins, baignées par des torrens écumeux, offrant souvent les traces des commotions de la nature, qui dans ces hautes régions ne connaît jamais le repos" (I, 83). Here Lady Morgan launches into an almost apocalyptic vision of Rosa's face to face encounter with a sublime landscape:

> Là, presqu'à la vue du hardi et solitaire étudiant, des collines comblaient des vallées; des vallées se transformaient en collines; des rivières changeaient leur cours; et des feux sortant tout à coup de la terre dispersaient la riche végétation que leur chaleur cachée avait produite. Là, au milieu des tremblemens de terre, des flammes volcaniques, dans une atmosphère d'éclairs et de tonnerres, ce Dante de la peinture a pu saisir les élémens de son fameux Purgatoire; car ce sont des phénomènes semblables, dont l'effet dévastateur et la reproduction mystérieuse sont hors de la portée et des intérêts humains, qui sans doute inspirèrent d'abord à l'homme sa foi craintive, et l'idée de son Dieu de colère! les tortures prolongées pour des siècles; et les feux du châtiment éternel! le purgatoire d'une église, et l'enfer de toutes deux! (I, 83–84)

Lady Morgan's account of Rosa's *giro* in southern Italy, though expressed in florid, even lurid language, is not entirely of her invention. Rosa's first biographer, Passeri, to cite words from the *résumé* of his chapter on Rosa, "Va in campagna a copiare i paesi più belli" (*Vite*, p. 478). Baldinucci has the young Rosa visiting "li contorni de Napoli, e suo porto, a disegnare vedute terrestri, e maritimi" (p. 438) and striking out on his own: "Fatto poi di se stesso scolare e maestro, gran parte del suo tempo incominciò ad impiegare in disegnare con grande accuratezza, fuori di Napoli, vedute di quelle colline" (Ibid.). Pascoli simply speaks of Rosa seeking out "le vedute più belle di quel bellissimo sito" (p. 64), presumably the Naples region.[21] In none of these founding texts is it a question of Rosa's wandering in Basilicata, Calabria, and the Abruzzi. But the claim that Rosa drew inspiration from scenes observed in some or all of those regions was already in the air when Saint-Non published his *Voyage pittoresque* in the 1780s: The narrative text prepared by Vivant Denon says that Rosa found inspiration in the landscape around La Cava. Denon, in his own *Voyage de Sicile*, makes a similar statement. As we have seen, Valenciennes, in his *Réflexions et conseils sur le genre du paysage* (1800), writes about Calabria as an inspiration for Rosa's landscape: "Cette contrée a été sûrement visitée et étudiée par le Poussin, Salvator Rosa et Vernet" (p. 583). Lady Morgan may have found the germ of her travelogue in the *Voyage pittoresque* of Saint-Non or, possibly, in some English source. In any case, whether she created this part of the Rosa legend or not, she gave it more space and more vivid form than any previous writer on Rosa.

One could say as much about her next major contribution to the Rosa legend. Her account of Rosa's travels leads directly into a highly developed narrative of Rosa's life among the bandits of the Abruzzi, complete with a dissertation on "La position sociale et politique des bandits" (I, 85). It will be recalled that a pre-romantic cult of the noble bandit or outlaw developed in the generation before Lady Morgan, thanks notably to Schiller's *Die Räuber* (1781). Having traveled in Italy, Lady Morgan may not have subscribed whole-heartedly to this myth: at one point she states that "leurs rangs étaient remplis, il est vrai par le rebut de la société, par des êtres nés hors de l'enceinte de la civilisation ou qui en avaient été rejetés pour leurs crimes," though there was a slight admixture of noblemen on the lam (I, 86–87). Still, concerning them, she uses such terms as "valeur" (I, 87) and "sévère grandeur de caractère, indifférente à toute humaine souffrance" (I, 89), as well as "passions plus sauvages que les élémens au milieu desquels elles étaient nourries" (ibid.). What matters is that, for Rosa, they were "des sujets bien dignes d'occuper l'attention d'un être accoutumé à observer les choses en philosophe et en poëte" (ibid.). Rather surprisingly, Lady Morgan compares the guerrilla war between the Abruzzi mountaineers and the Spanish and German troops in Rosa's time[22] and the clash of arms seen in one of Rosa's most famous paintings. In this warfare, she writes, "on pouvait discerner le caractère distinctif de ce grand et admirable tableau de bataille," i.e., the *Heroic Battle* in the Louvre. She goes on to describe for two pages an etching by Rosa inspired by a dramatic episode from his captivity among the bandits: it represents a young woman, the wife or mistress of the bandit chief, pleading for the life of a young prisoner, who, Lady Morgan is convinced, is Rosa himself.[23] This sort of interpretation clearly reflects the curiosity about the artist's life, which was growing ever more intense and which Lady Morgan was intent on fostering—and satisfying.

From this point on, Lady Morgan's account is rather straightforward and—leaving aside the Masaniello episode—unexceptionable, primarily because the documentation for Rosa's life and work is much more abundant and reliable for the post-Neapolitan phases of his career, thanks primarily to Baldinucci and Passeri. Both of these writers knew Rosa personally, the former in Florence and the latter in Rome. True, there are developments that will strike us as dubious or extraneous: on Scholastic philosophy (I, 57–59), the Barberinis and Pope Urban VIII (I, 137–41), the Flemish school of painting (I, 149–53), the *commedia dell'arte* (I, 203–09), the early history of opera (I, 247–50), European politics in the 1630s and 1640s (I, 279–86), Lorenzo Lippi and his *Malmantile raquistato* (II, 46–52), on the Pincio, the Villa Medici, and the Villa Borghese (II, 81–85), Marino and Marinism (II, 186–87), and Italian political satire (II, 189–90). Somewhat more germane than most of these digressions are appreciations of many of Rosa's major contemporaries and near contemporaries in Italian art: Caravaggio (I, 104–09) and Ribera (I, 109–12) were the leaders of the Neapolitan school from which Rosa sprang; Falcone (I, 128–29) was Rosa's teacher in the genre of battle pictures; Lanfranco (I, 117–20), it is generally agreed, "discovered" the young Rosa's work; Domenichino (I, 113–16), Lanfranco, and Guercino (I, 122–23) did major commissions in Naples; Bernini (I, 42–45) directly clashed with Rosa, who dared to ridicule him during the carnival of 1639; Claude Lorrain (I, 229–31) and Dughet (I, 231–32) competed in Rome with Rosa in the field of landscape; Dolce (II, 24) and Pietro da Cortona (II, 24–25) worked in Florence during Rosa's stay in Tuscany. Two of these artists emerge as *bêtes noires* in Lady Morgan's account: Ribera and Bernini. Both dominated the artistic scene in Naples and Rome respectively. Both are presented as self-serving schemers eager to drive out all rivals and maintain their own monopoly. Lady Morgan's picture of Ribera is particularly dark: first he is lumped with Correnzio and Caraccioli as one of "ces vrais bandits de la peinture." Then she spells out his villany:

> Son objet était de chasser de Naples tous les hommes à talens qui ne sortaient pas de son école; et soutenu par son crédit auprès du gouvernement et par le courage féroce de ses deux spadassins et de leurs suivans, il donna pleine carrière à ces noires passions qui dirigeaient son poignard contre la poitrine

de ses adversaires et conduisaient son pinceau à créer ces images des souffrances, des difformités humaines, ces tortures, ces agonies détaillées avec une si effrayante fidélité. (I, 110)

As for Bernini, "le tyran des arts" at Rome:

Il ne reconnaissait aucun mérite dans l'artiste qui ne courbait pas le genou devant le trône sur lequel la mode et la faveur l'avaient élevé; ses disciples étaient ses esclaves; et dans le nombre infini de ceux qui recherchaient sa protection, bien peu en tirèrent de vrais avantages. (I, 145)

These ruthless—and successful—schemers serve admirably as Lady Morgan's foils to the stiff-necked independence of Rosa, constantly stressed in her account. Already, in her preface, she sees him as towering over his decadent and servile compatriots, as the enemy of "les littérateurs vendus aux institutions que sa plume et son pinceau attaquèrent tour à tour si judicieusement et avec tant de hardiesse" (I, v). Later, she naturally incorporates into her account the anecdotes that show Rosa declining the invitation of princes, twitting cardinals, ridiculing the all-powerful Bernini, playing games with academies, and arguing with those who sought to dictate the themes and contents of his work.

In a way, all this is encapsulated in Lady Morgan's pages on Rosa's involvement in the Masaniello episode. As we have seen, she did not draw directly from the primary source of this legend, the art historian Bernardo De Dominici's biographically organized history of Neapolitan painting. De Dominici (1683–ca.1750) was a native of Naples and presumably drew on local sources and traditions. He was primarily responsible for putting into circulation the stories about Rosa's role in Masaniello's revolt. Lady Morgan drew, however, on the more summary account given in Salvini's preface to his edition of Rosa's satires; this text, we suppose, was digested from De Dominici. Lady Morgan, depending so heavily on Passeri, Baldinucci, and Pascoli, is at pains to explain why these authors say nothing about Rosa's alleged involvement in the events of July 1647 in Naples. Her reasoning is characteristic: "Passeri et Baldinucci passent sous silence cet événement des plus importans dans la vie de Salvator. Étant l'un et l'autre attachés à l'église ou à l'état, et vivant dans une crainte légitime de l'Inquisition, ils jugèrent sans doute que ce silence était ce qui vaudrait le mieux pour la mémoire de leur ami" (I, 300, note). As for Pascoli, who had no personal acquaintance with Rosa, as he lived a generation or so later, he speaks of Rosa's trip to Naples at the time of the rebellion "avec la réserve *convenable,* évitant soigneusement toute allusion politique" (I, 300, note)—Lady Morgan takes advantage of a vague reference in Pascoli (p. 67) to a seemingly nonpolitical trip Rosa made to Naples, arriving (says Lady Morgan) "dans les derniers jours de 1646" (I, 301, note).[24] Since the rebellion against the Spaniards broke out in July 1647, Rosa must have foreseen the troubles in his native city (while Pascoli has Rosa returning to Naples in order to show off his new affluence and to "fare da signore"). Lady Morgan states (I, 299) that Rosa, overcoming his earlier renunciation of his native city, "accourut à son secours au bruit des premiers efforts qu'elle fit pour recouvrer sa liberté. . . . À l'instant même il ferme sa maison, et part pour Naples, où il fut reçu avec distinction" (I, 299–300). She had already sketched a dramatic picture of Rosa as an *engagé* artist who frequented the torch-lit midnight gatherings of Masaniello and his followers:

> Au milieu de ces groupes si pittoresques, un homme paraissait les contempler non-seulement avec l'œil d'un poëte, mais avec celui d'un peintre: cet homme, pour lequel pas une forme, pas une teinte, pas un reflet de lumière n'étaient perdus, qui dessinait en donnant son avis, et étudiait en écoutant; cet homme dont le génie flexible saisissait les objets sous leurs aspects moral et matériel, et dont la plume et le pinceau auraient été également capables de léguer Masaniello à la postérité, quand l'étonnante destinée du capitaine du peuple ne lui eût pas assuré une place distinguée dans l'histoire,—cet homme était Salvator Rosa. (I, 298)

A footnote to this passage informs us that Rosa made several sketches of Masaniello and his fellow rebels and recounts her exposure, in Rome and Naples, to several portraits of Masaniello and of his wife "tirées par Salvator Rosa à la lueur des torches *col lume di torcia*" (Ibid.). A little later Lady Morgan recounts the formation of the *Compagnia della morte* by Rosa's friend Falcone and other young artists (I, 302). Falcone was elected captain "et Salvator Rosa, à son arrivée à Naples, fut enrôlé dans ce corps, dont il devint l'un des membres les plus distingués. . . . L'histoire rapporte précisément que Salvator était *'uno dei soldati più fidi di Masaniello'* l'un des plus fidèles soldats de Massaniello" (I, 302–03).

Here, for some pages, we lose sight of Rosa, as Lady Morgan relates the climactic phases of the Masaniello uprising. But she certainly has in mind the reputation of her hero when, in a long footnote (Ibid.), she denies the official accounts of the revolt—the only ones available, she says—that always accused "la Banda della Morte" of having committed *"orribili stragi*, un horrible carnage":

> Mais pendant le règne de Masaniello, il n'y eut point de carnage, excepté celui des bandits qui tombèrent victimes de leur propre trahison dans l'église

des Carmes. . . . [S]i la bande de Falcone (composée de jeunes gens artistes, etc.), sans armes régulières ni discipline, l'emporta sur les vétérans des troupes royales, et en fit un carnage, il n'y a rien en cela qui puisse noircir leur caractère. (I, 303)

Another revealing footnote to the narrative of the turbulence in Naples complains of the heavy hand of weak but oppressive governments threatened with revolution:

Dans aucun pays la police n'a été plus perverse qu'en Irlande. L'achat public que le gouvernement a fait des droits de la noblesse dans les *bourgs pourris,* comme il aurait acheté une propriété privée, à l'époque de l'union, démontre clairement le *but,* et l'histoire d'Irlande démontre les moyens de ce régime proconsulaire. (I, 304–05)

Such a comment explains some of Lady Morgan's interest in Rosa, her admiration for the "patriote italien" and for "l'esprit d'indépendance, et les doctrines politiques du sincère ami de son pays" (I, iii, vi).

Rosa, in Lady Morgan's account, reappears only after the insanity and murder of Masaniello and the crushing of the brief but violent rebellion he led. The lesson she draws, and which she presumes Rosa drew, from the Neapolitan experiment is one of dashed illusions: "Quelles qu'avaient pu être les espérances de Salvator Rosa et d'Aniello Falcone, elles finirent avec l'existence de Masaniello. L'idée que cet événement leur donna du caractère d'un peuple formé à l'école d'une dégradation politique, dissipa toutes les espérances qu'ils avaient fondées sur un patriotisme devenu chimérique" (II, 2–3). In a footnote to this passage, Lady Morgan evokes and quotes from Rosa's fourth satire, *La Guerra,* which she compares to Petrarch's invocation to Cola Rienzi: "Salvator apostrophe l'esprit et les vertus de Masaniello, avec une grande force de sentiment" (Ibid.). Rosa's retreat to Rome is quickly related: "Salvator Rosa retourna à Rome, le cœur flétri, lassé, ulcéré, 'Faint, weary, sore, embroised, grieved and brent [*sic*],' et plein d'une rage qu'il était hors de son pouvoir, et peut-être de son inclination, de dissimuler" (II, 4). Lady Morgan supposes that Rosa's bitter experience of revolution inspired the satire entitled *La Babilonia.* She analyzes, mostly by means of summary, this "églogue dramatique . . . sous une forme qui tient de l'allégorie" (II, 5), which she pronounces perhaps unequaled in Italian literature "sous le rapport de la hardiesse, de la verité, de la profondeur des sentiments, et de la force de l'expression" (II, 7).

The rest of Lady Morgan's narrative, as indicated, follows closely the events of the Tuscan and Roman years of Rosa, the best-known part of his life. We must point out that she places the section devoted to Rosa's experiences in Florence, at the Medici court, and at Volterra with the Maffei, in the period 1647–1657, whereas it would be more accurate to say 1640–1649. The few dated letters from Rosa to Ricciardi, from which she quotes, all bear dates that fall in the 1650s and 1660s, and so were of little help to her. As she points out (II, 19, note), Passeri gives only two dates in his whole account, those of Rosa's birth and death—she might have said the same of Pascoli. Perhaps the need to insert the Masaniello episode into Rosa's life unhinged her chronological framework. It is not reassuring that she takes to task "l'honnête Passeri, qui est un abrégé de la confusion et de la négligence des écrivains italiens du 17ᵉ siècle" for paying so little attention to dates (II, 19, note), especially since this is intended to support a statement by Lanzi to rebut Passeri's claim that Rosa went to Florence "immédiatement après sa sortie contre les théâtres privés de Bernini." As it happens, Passeri is close to the mark: it was during the carnival of 1639 that Rosa attacked Bernini, and he must have gone to Florence in the following year.[25] Moreover, Baldinucci, who knew Rosa in his Florentine years, twice says that the artist was in Florence in 1642—testimony that she ought to have taken seriously.

It would be easy to bog down in quibbling with Lady Morgan over details of historical and biographical fact. She had, as I will show later, important contributions to make to art history, apropos of Rosa and his work. But in the short run, it was the currency she gave to certain legends about Rosa—his wanderings in the Abruzzi, his captivity among bandits in those mountains, his participation in the Masaniello rebellion—that caught the fancy of her readers, notably certain poets, novelists, and dramatists. What they made out of Lady Morgan's imaginings will be treated later. For the present, let us try to delineate in broad strokes the portrait of the romantic artist she found in Rosa, bearing in mind that for her the artist and the man were almost inseparable.

Four salient and intimately related features of Rosa as man and artist (taking this latter term in a broad sense) emerge in Lady Morgan's treatment: nature, liberty, passion, and melancholy. The eighteen-year-old Rosa rejected the *route battue* and "la routine banale des academies et des ateliers" (ibid.) in favor of "l'école de la nature" (ibid.), and set out on his *giro:*

> Les pas de Salvator se dirigèrent d'abord vers les sauvages et magnifiques régions de son pays natal, que la culture n'avait pas encore outragées. Pleines de périls et de difficultés, elles auraient été considérées comme impénétrables par la médiocrité, mais elles offraient un attrait irrésistible à celui dont l'âme fière jouissait d'elle-même dans la solitude, où elle découvrait des combinaisons infinies du sublime et du terrible, si propre à satisfaire une imagination brûlante, active, incapable de goûter l'insipide

contrainte des formes de convention, une imagination pour laquelle la contemplation de l'homme "n'avait aucun délice," pour qui les ouvrages de
l'homme n'étaient pas un assez puissant stimulant. (I, 74)

In this passage Lady Morgan manages to fuse her major themes: The young
painter, bursting with the urge to escape artistic conventions, plunges into
uncultivated wilderness. There he faces danger and solitude amid scenes
both sublime and terrible. In later passages, the tone of youthful ardor is
muted; the artist becomes more philosophical as he finds in nature the moral
life and restless vitality of mankind, and these new insights are reflected in
the finer works of his maturity:

> Tout y était large, expressif de force, de grandeur. Dans un rocher, un marbre,
> un nuage, on voyait l'élévation de ses idées. Ses plus petites figures avaient
> quelque chose qui indiquait le caractère moral en accusant la forme phy-
> sique. Son chef de brigands se distingue toujours des misérables coquins
> ses suivans, moins par le costume que par ces traits caractéristiques que
> l'éducation imprime généralement sur l'homme et même sur la brute. Les
> feuilles légères de ses arbres qui semblent vibrer au souffle du vent, la
> hardiesse de ses mouvemens de terrains, ses groupes de figures toutes
> animées, déploient une vie, une activité, qui excitent des sentimens ana-
> logues à leur expression dans les spectateurs, et prouvent que la nature,
> dans les ouvrages de ce peintre comme dans les siens propres, n'est jamais
> en repos. (I, 101–02)

Lady Morgan claims, in a footnote to this passage, to have "sous les yeux" a
sketch by Rosa that illustrates her words about the brigand chief and his
separateness from his followers: "C'est une figure isolée, un chef de voleurs.
Il est seul près d'un rocher; ses cheveux flottent négligemment au gré du
vent, son visage porte les traces de cette pensive mélancolie, que les remords
turbulens des esprits vulgaires n'ont jamais produites" (I, 101, note). Taking
the two passages together, we find quite a remarkable ensemble of images:
wild nature; a haughty, lonely outcast; the fluttering foliage; the brigand's
hair floating in the wind; the animation exuded by the natural scene, the
"little figures," and the viewers of the picture; the brigand's pensive melancholy and the grosser feelings of lesser men.

Lady Morgan traces a darkening, deepening view of Rosa and his work
as she follows him to Rome, where he shuns the various "académies" then
dominating the art scene. He studied anatomy in the Sistine Chapel, "devant
les beautés gigantesques du jugement dernier" (I, 172): "S'il a suivi une école
autre que celle de la nature, ce fut celle de ce peintre son grand prototype,
qui, dans *ses trois parques* du palais Pitti, à Florence, rappelle si bien et les

trois *Weird sisters* de Shakspeare et la *Sorcière* de Salvator" (I, 172–73). In Rome, Rosa found himself, as a landscapist, in competition with Claude Lorrain and Gaspard Dughet, in whose works, according to Lady Morgan, "le monde terrestre est plongé dans un agréable repos" (I, 232), a "tranquille beauté," a source of joy to mankind (I, 233). Rosa challenged this reassuring view of nature:

> Son pinceau magique donna à tous les sujets la vie, le mouvement et une effrayante activité. Le *famoso pittore delle cose morali* ne pouvait séparer les scènes des acteurs. . . . Représentant la nature comme il l'avait vue dans ses puissantes régions qu'il avait le plus étudiées, il la peignit comme l'agent inévitable des souffrances, en mêlant toutes ses grandes opérations avec les passions et les intérêts de l'homme, qu'il montrait frappé de son tonnerre, enterré dans ses avalanches et entraîné dans ses tourbillons! (Ibid.)

Later, at Volterra, he shunned the pleasures of Florence and found refuge in the mountainous landscape, "quelquefois par accès de mélancolie, plus souvent pour étudier des paysages sous un autre point de vue que ceux qui s'étaient présentés à ses regards au milieu des terribles sublimités de l'Abruzzi" (II, 66):

> Des rocs, des montagnes, des torrens, des masses d'ombres, des perspectives brillantes, tout ce qui mérite le plus d'être peint et qui se trouve dans les pays les plus distans, la nature l'avait concentré là; et là Salvator s'était abandonné, même à l'excès, à son goût philosophique et à ces pensées spéculatives dont il forma dans la suite le tissu de ses compositions. (II, 67)

The fruit of the painter's confrontation with Tuscan nature was, in addition to "son grand tableau des Bacchanales et la plupart des paysages qu'il fit pour le palais Pitti" (ibid.), a picture that reflected not the natural scene but its historical associations: "C'était là enfin où Catilina avait combattu et succombé, et que Salvator, qui n'était pas lui-même étranger aux sombres détails des conjurations, jeta les premiers élémens et conçut la première idée du plus noble de tous ses ouvrages, sa *Conspiration de Catilina*" (ibid.).[26] It seems that Lady Morgan was wrong in her effort to link Rosa's *Catilina* to his experience of nature in the Tuscan hills, but it is characteristic of her insistence on the philosophical side of the artist and on the essential unity of his inspiration, rooted in nature, his own passions, and his literary culture.

Lady Morgan's presentation of Rosa as landscapist reaches one of its most vivid and revealing developments in the following passage:

> Le moindre de ses paysages était plein d'intérêt, et fait pour exciter les

sympathies humaines. Ses forêts sombres et profondes, où l'on ne voit de
teintes claires que sur l'écorce argentée du chêne entr'ouvert qui forme le
plan avancé, paraissent le refuge du formidable brigand dont la figure hardie
et insouciante, avec ses habits et ses armes bizarres, fixe les regards plus
que toutes les beautés agrestes qui l'entourent. La longue ligne du chemin
pierreux, taillé dans ces masses de rochers suspendues sur des abîmes, est
le défilé où le brave chevalier, marchant à quelque entreprise généreuse,
est surpris par les brigands sans pitié, ou par l'orage qui menace de
l'exterminer à chaque pas de son cheval effrayé. Le voyageur harassé, le
marin naufragé, sont des images qui touchent le cœur, et donnent au site
inanimé une action morale et intéressante. (I, 234)

This is a key passage in Lady Morgan's book because it shows that she was
subject to ideas about Rosa already in circulation, especially among his English admirers. Her words may reflect, too, her exposure to pictures painted
by imitators of Rosa exploiting the "bandits in a landscape" theme. Her catalogue of Rosa works lists, for example, "Deux paysages, sites de forêts avec
bandits" (II, 306), "Un paysage avec bandits" (II, 307), "Paysage—Site de
rochers, chute d'eau, un beau groupe de bandits sur le premier plan" (II,
309), and "Paysage avec bandits" (II, 311—twice). It is revealing that all
these pictures were, according to Lady Morgan, in English collections.[27] The
splintered foreground oak tree may well reflect Lady Morgan's viewing of an
authentic Rosa, either the *Mercury and the Dishonest Woodchopper,* which
she lists in her catalogue as *Mercure et le bûcheron* (S 145), then in Sir
Abraham Hume's collection (II, 307), or the *Grand Paysage avec figures* (S
239), which she could have seen in the Louvre (II, 313). But the noble knight
ambushed by brigands and the shipwrecked sailor may also be taken from
pictures that Lady Morgan actually saw but that are no longer attributed to
him, e.g., the *Tempête sur mer* she lists as being in the collection of "Le
Marquis Hastings" (II, 311). Lady Morgan's book on Rosa undoubtedly gave
new impetus to the themes taken up, for example, by the French painter
Adrien Guignet in the romantic era.

Lady Morgan develops the theme of Rosa in nature in a number of passages, e.g., the one devoted to his trip to Loreto (II, 119–21), in which she
draws on Rosa's letter to Ricciardi of May 13, 1642 (II, 225–27). But the
texts already quoted abundantly illustrate Lady Morgan's ideas on the subject. As for the theme of liberty, i.e., Salvator's ardent love of it, again numerous passages could be cited, in addition to some we have already seen in
which this theme emerges. The artist's "esprit d'indépendance" (I, vi) is already stressed in her preface, where he is also seen in political terms as a
precursor of Filicaja's "inspirations libérales" (ibid.). Sprinkled through the

book are such expressions as "sa farouche indépendance" (I, 181), "sa passion dominante, l'indépendance" (I, 187), "l'indépendance de ses principes" (I, 220), "cette indépendance de caractère" (I, 263), "ces opinions hardies" (II, 9), and "le républicanisme farouche de Salvator Rosa" (II, 21). Although Lady Morgan, promoter of Irish nationalism and the Risorgimento, wishes to see in Rosa a precursor of such movements and emphasizes his patriotism and his "fierce republicanism," Rosa the lover of liberty is mostly to be found in her account of his relationships with art patrons and clients. True, this form of libertarianism could be seen as, in part, a political gesture, since the leading sources of pensions and commissions occupied the upper ranks of the "power structure" of the Italy of his time. But Rosa was primarily interested in freedom of artistic expression, freedom to choose the subjects and the genres of his paintings. This side of Rosa had already been well exhibited in a letter in which Rosa, in a cantankerous mood, upbraided his friend Ricciardi for attempting to persuade the painter to include more figures in the pictures done for his friends:

> A un peintre de mon rang, d'un génie fécond comme l'est le mien, on doit laisser toute liberté d'agir, et ne lui tracer de mesure que pour les dimensions de son talent. . . . [I]l faut seconder le génie du peintre et croire fermement que chaque bagatelle qui vient de la main d'un artiste consommé est digne de l'attention du connaisseur, et surtout se rappeler qu'un seul vers d'Homère vaut mieux que tout un poëme de Cherile. (II, 236–37)

Here Rosa's egotism and grumpiness appear in a somewhat unattractive light, but his words, especially given the time and circumstances, are still a remarkable expression of artistic freedom. The artist's passionate plea, however, appears in the context of his private correspondence with a generous friend and patron.

Lady Morgan especially enjoys recounting the occasions on which Rosa declined the invitations of rulers, such as Mattei de' Medici, to join their courts:

> Mais la proposition portait en termes exprès d'entrer au service du prince, *portarsi a' servigi*; cette expression avait révolté le républicanisme farouche de Salvator, qui avait d'ailleurs si publiquement, et en tant d'occasions, fait profession d'indépendance et de simplicité de vie philosophique, qu'il regardait comme une dérogation aux convenances et à sa dignité personnelle de s'engager volontairement, comme les grands peintres du siècle, au service particulier de quelque souverain. (II, 21) [Here a footnote quotes six lines to the same effect from the satire *La Babilonia*.]

Later Rosa had to deal with the flattering invitation issued by Archduke Ferdinand of Austria and his Medici wife to work for them in Innsbruck: "Mais Salvator refusa péremptoirement, quoique respectueusement, un honneur qui, malgré toutes ses distinctions, était toujours à ses yeux une *dépendance*" (II, 109). In a footnote appearing in both Italian and French, Lady Morgan quotes the passage from Pascoli that served as her source, concluding with the words: "Il avait coutume de dire qu'il mettait sa liberté au-dessus de tous les honneurs et de toutes les richesses du monde, parce qu'elle était au-dessus de tout prix" (II, 109). Not unexpectedly, Lady Morgan drew on the fund of anecdotes accumulated by Rosa's early Italian biographers, which illustrated Rosa's rather high-handed way of dealing with potential patrons—for example, the fashionable doctor who tried to determine the subject of the picture he was thinking of ordering from Rosa (I, 267–68) and the Roman prince who expressed surprise at the price demanded. Hoping to get a better bargain, the prince kept returning to look at the picture, but each time he asked the "dernier prix," the painter raised the sum; finally, to show his anger, he grabbed the picture, stomped on it, and so destroyed it. "*Son excellence* fit une retraite cérémonieuse, et ne vint jamais depuis marchander avec Rosa" (I, 265). These anecdotes complete with dialogue, are given to illustrate Lady Morgan's claim that Rosa mounted a systematic attack against the patronage system:

> Se réservant ainsi la liberté de suivre les inspirations de son génie, et de reproduire son propre caractère dans toutes les modifications de son esprit supérieur et singulier; non moins indépendant à l'égard de ses relations pécuniaires qu'à l'égard de celles qui concernaient son art, il résolut de s'émanciper tout-à-fait de la domination du *patronnage;* "et que Dieu aide (disait Baldinucci) quiconque veut marchander avec lui."(I, 264)

Still, in his earlier years, Rosa had accepted princely invitations and patronage. Lady Morgan is at considerable pains to explain the artist's willingness to be at the beck and call of rulers or cardinals. First of all, at the beginning of his first extended stay in Rome, his "caractère inflexible" (I, 174), his refusal to "se soumettre à faire sa cour dans les antichambres" (ibid.), reduced him to penury. Thus, he very grudgingly accepted the invitation of friends to accompany them to Viterbo and enter the service of Cardinal Brancaccio, the bishop of that city. At Viterbo, says Lady Morgan, "L'infortuné peintre [était] pénétré de l'humiliation de sa position, et plein de cette amertume que l'injuste oubli fait toujours éprouver à un génie altier" (I, 176). When asked to paint a fresco in the episcopal palace, Rosa heeded local prejudice against sacred or profane history and produced "quelque chose d'entièrement poétique, *lo scherzo de' mostri marini*" (I, 178). When the cardinal, pleased with these "jeux des dieux marins," invited him to do an altarpiece for the Chiesa della morte and left him free to choose the subject of the picture, Rosa chose the "thème hardi et périlleux" (I, 178) of the incredulity of St. Thomas, only the second time (says Lady Morgan) that he treated a historical subject (I, 179). His morale lifted by these early successes, Rosa felt anew the stirring of his deep-seated aspiration for fame: "Mais sa farouche indépendance paraît s'être révoltée en ce moment contre l'obscure et humiliante position dans laquelle il s'engageait peu à peu en restant dans la maison du cardinal" (I, 181). Although, as we have seen, Rosa rejected the advances of Mattei de' Medici, he later overcame his scruples and accepted an invitation to go to the court of Gian Carlo de' Medici, "quoiqu'il préférât une liberté laborieuse au joug léger d'une pompe servile" (II, 21–22). Similarly, concerning Rosa's relationship to the Maffei, Lady Morgan emphasizes the artist's innate preference for his independence over "les chaînes dorées de la cour," and claims that the length of his stay with them was left to "le goût, l'idée et le caprice de l'hôte original" (II, 66). Thus, whether declining to enter the service of some powerful patron or reluctantly agreeing to do so, Rosa is always shown as fundamentally independent and, when he could get away with it, blunt, even outrageous, in voicing his demands for artistic freedom. Lady Morgan's Rosa foreshadows Rostand's Cyrano de Bergerac and the "tirade des non, merci," to mention just one dramatic treatment of the theme of the independent artist and one whose mixture of fact, exaggeration, and fiction is reminiscent of her somewhat fictionalized biography of Rosa.

Lady Morgan, though she is quite aware of Rosa's comic talents and devotes considerable space to his display of them as actor and *improvvisatore,* points again and again to the somber side of his nature and its expression in his work. His father's early death, his poverty and early struggles for success, the machinations of his enemies, the evils afflicting Italian society and culture, and the failure of Masaniello's revolt instilled a pessimism that she characterizes as "tristesse" (I, 101; II, 9), "mélancolie" (I, 101; II, 46, 66), "mélancolique originalité" (I, 123), "chagrin" (I, 156; II, 4), "sombre découragement" (II, 28), and, in a darker register, "amertume" (I, 167; II, 87), "bile" (II, 4), "mécontentement plein de malignité" (II, 5–6), "irascible"(II, 99), "atrabilaire" (II, 192), and "désespoir" (II, 5). Such terms are applied at times to a permanent feature of Rosa's personality, at times to temporary moods ("accès") or reactions to specific events. As for specific works exhibiting this darker Rosa, Lady Morgan chooses a rather random group: a "croquis" representing a bandit chieftain ("profonde tristesse morale . . . pensive mélancolie" [I, 101, note]); the early *Agar,* which had been responsible for Lanfranco's "discovery"of him ("mélancolique originalité" [I, 123]); Rosa's "Cantate" ("noir et profond chagrin" [I, 156]); the "rire amer" that she detected—and rightly so—in Rosa's portrayal of the "laughing philosopher" Democritus (I, 277); but especially the poem *La Babilonia* and two paintings similarly inspired by the Masaniello episode, *L'Umana Fragilità* and *La Fortuna*. The poem in question reflected his "bile" (II, 4), "le désespoir où il est de le [son pays] voir se régénérer" (II, 5); the feeling expressed by Tirreno is "un mécontentement plein de malignité tout-à-fait épique, mais produit par la plus exquise sensibilité, par l'évanouissement de toutes ses espérances, et l'inutilité de tous ses efforts, pour diminuer les souffrances du genre humain, et améliorer ses institutions" (II, 5–6). As for the two paintings said to have been inspired by such feelings, they forcefully express "ces opinions hardies, et cette triste expérience qui avaient troublé la tranquillité de sa vie, et répandu des nuages de tristesse sur ses jours les plus brillans" (II, 9). In *L'Umana Fragilità* the resplendent beauty, joy, and innocence of the central figures are deceptive, for in this picture "Salvator représentait les peines qui accompagnent l'existence, ainsi que la vanité de la vie" (II, 10). It is a little surprising that Lady Morgan does not find Rosa's melancholy in any specific landscape, but all in all, her perception of the somber side of Rosa and his work is well founded.

Although Lady Morgan tells us frankly in her preface that it was Rosa the man more than Rosa the artist who inspired her to write her biography (I, iii), and though her book often illustrates this statement, she reveals in many ways and at length that she admires his work enormously, often giving her reasons. Several times she calls him or his work "sublime" (I, v; I, 198; I, 277): she dubs him "l'un des plus grands paysagistes de l'école italienne" (II, 305); the words "chefs-d'œuvre" and "beau" are applied to a number of pictures. In her preface, she spells out, though in rather general terms, what qualities originally drew her to Rosa: "la teinte philosophique et les conceptions poétiques des principaux tableaux de Salvator Rosa," "la profondeur de sentiment," "la puissante intelligence," and "la sauvage et mélancolique imaginative" (I, iv). A little later she turns to Rosa the man: "Salvator Rosa devait être placé, dans la succession des âges, entre Michel-Ange l'artiste patriote, et Filicaja, le poëte de la liberté" (I, vi). These words, though prefatory, sound like a summing up, a settled opinion based on her total experience as Rosa's biographer. In her account of Rosa's death and burial, she provides what might be called Rosa's epitaph:

> Vers le soir du 15 mars 1673, tout ce qui restait de l'auteur du Régulus, du Catilina, du gai Formica, du spirituel Coviello! du plus élégant compositeur

et du plus grand peintre de son pays et de son siècle, Salvator Rosa, enfin,
fut porté au tombeau dans l'église de Santa-Maria degli Angioli alle Terme.
(II, 165)

Her final assessment of Rosa's achievement, under eight rubrics—Rosa as
painter, as engraver, as composer, as architect (!), as comic actor,
improvvisatore, and conversationalist, as prose writer, and as poet—is heavily
weighted in favor of the final category: Of about thirty pages forming this
chapter, nearly twenty are devoted to Rosa the poet, the author of the *Satire.*
Here, too, Lady Morgan's interest in the man as against the artist shows
through, for what she saw in Rosa's satires was their bold and vehement
denunciation of the political and social evils prevalent in the Italy of his time,
and of hers.

> Cette force, cette hardiesse et cette liberté avec lesquelles il énonça ses
> opinions, qu'on regarde toujours comme hétérodoxes dans la moderne Italie;
> l'honnêteté, la courageuse et l'incorruptible probité avec laquelle il déchirait
> la tyrannie et l'hypocrisie, quoique entouré de despotes et d'inquisiteurs,
> sont la plus forte preuve que l'on puisse donner de son courage; ses satires,
> qu'il dirigeait contre l'égoïsme des grands, et contre la bassesse du peuple,
> peuvent bien racheter ces fautes de style, ces expressions de mauvais goût,
> défauts très-condamnables, sans doute, mais qui provenaient plutôt encore
> de l'opposition qu'il rencontrait, que de la véhémence de son caractère, et
> de la fougue indomptable de sa bouillante imagination. (II, 195)

While it is necessary to recognize this aspect of Lady Morgan's interest in
Rosa as poet and satirist, the major emphasis here will be her treatment of
Rosa the visual artist and his work. One helpful approach is to identify those
works of Rosa that most aroused her enthusiasm and fixed her attention and,
if possible, to show why. But before doing so, it is necessary to ask which of
the paintings and etchings she admired she had actually seen. From her
account in *Italy* (1821), we know that at the Pitti she admired "some of Salvator
Rosa's finest sea-pieces" and his *Congiura di Catilina.*[28] The latter made a
strong impression on her; she notes the picture's "force, gloom, and energy."
Except for the dubious portrait of Masaniello that Cardinal Fesch showed
her, no other picture by Rosa is specifically mentioned in her book on Italy.

In the Louvre, she certainly saw the *Saul and the Witch of Endor* and
the great *Heroic Battle,* but her own catalogue of Rosa's painted work also
lists a *Grand paysage avec fig.* (S 239, no doubt); this is the picture acquired
by the Louvre in 1816), a *Marine* (unidentifiable), and *Tobie et l'ange* (S
226). In Great Britain, there were many Rosas, true and false, to be seen, but

it cannot be shown that she actually saw many of them. All the pictures in her catalogue were then in private collections. It is quite likely that her friend and former patron, the Marquis of Abercorn, would have gladly allowed her to see the two pictures in his possession (S 114 and S 115), which Rosa painted on a harpsichord case; in any case, though she mentions them (II, 54), they do not seem to have made a vivid impression. We can tell that she, by her own admission and her identification of documents at her disposal, took many of her descriptions of pictures, often verbatim, from books, from a letter addressed to her by Vivant Denon, and from passages in Rosa's letters. In the category of books, she refers to the three basic Italian biographies, to Salvini's preface to his edition of Rosa's *Satire,* to Mongez's *La Galerie de Florence,* to reference works like the biographical dictionaries by Pilkington and Bryan, and to Taillasson's *Observations.* She tells us of having before her as she writes engraved versions of the *Congiura di Catilina* and something called *Le Faux Alexandre,* and the etching *The Genius of Rosa.* Her description of *Democritus in Meditation* is probably based on Rosa's own etching of the picture. Her catalogue of Rosa's work lists several dozen reproductive engravings done by Goupy and others; to some of these she would have had fairly easy access. Her rather precise description of *Xenocrates and Phryne* (S 179) seems to be based on direct observation, but the presence of an engraved version by Boydell in her catalogue probably means that she saw the reproduction and not the painting. Or she might have depended on what Salerno, in 1975, called an "ample" description by Passeri.

Whether actually seen or not, the pictures she most admires are *Saul and the Witch of Endor, Job, Prometheus, Democritus in Meditation, The Death of Atilius Regulus,* the Louvre's *Heroic Battle, Jason,* and, especially, *Catiline's Conspiracy.*[29] The first four of these earned the epithet "sublime" (I, v; I, 198; I, 277). As we have seen, *The Death of Atilius Regulus* and *Catiline's Conspiracy* are included in what I have called her epitaph for Rosa; earlier in her account she had spoken of the "magnifiques horreurs du *Régulus* de Salvator" (I, 275). She called *Jason* "une de ses plus belles productions . . . tableau plein de feu, et de cette hardiesse d'idées et de pinceau qui fait les grands maîtres" (II, 125). The *Heroic Battle* is pronounced "ce magnifique ouvrage" (II, 91) and "ce tableau incomparable" (II, 206, note). But it is *Catiline's Conspiracy,* to which she devotes over four pages, that clearly emerges as her favorite. She describes it in detail and vividly, explores the hearts and minds of the principal actors, and calls it "[le] chef-d'œuvre de sa vie et de son génie (II, 125) and "ce magnifique tableau" (Ibid.). She emphasizes the tense drama of the moment Rosa has chosen to represent, encapsulated in the words "horrible," "terrible," "horreur," and "affreux" (II, 126–28).

As she says: "Tel est ce tableau, qui forme une page de l'histoire et qu'on ne peut jamais voir sans éprouver une vive émotion" (II, 128–29).[30]

Another measure of Lady Morgan as a critic of Rosa is to take note of her attempts to locate him in the pantheon of painters. We are told that, when first shown, *Prometheus* "prit place à côté des chefs-d'œuvre du Titien et de Léonard de Vinci, effaçant toutes les productions modernes dont il était entouré" (I, 186), and that the anatomy of the central figure is worthy of Michelangelo (I, 187, note). In her account of Rosa's triumph at the show given at San Giovanni Decollato in 1668, the names of his principal contemporaries are worked in: Lorrain, Poussin, Maratti, Pietro da Cortona, the Carracci, and Domenichino (II, 133–34)—even those of Leonardo and Raphael. But, as already suggested, her favorite term of comparison is Michelangelo. She relates how he studied, in the Sistine Chapel, "les beautés gigantesques du jugement dernier" (I, 172):

> C'est ce qu'il avait coutume d'appeler son école d'anatomie; et quoique enthousiaste du coloris de Titien, le génie de Michel Ange était le seul avec lequel le sien pouvait sympathiser. S'il a suivi une école autre que celle de la nature, ce fut celle de ce peintre son grand prototype, qui, dans ses *trois parques* du palais Pitti, à Florence, rappelle si bien et les trois *Weird Sisters* de Shakspeare et la *Sorcière* de Salvator. (I, 172–73)

The reference to Shakespeare's *Macbeth* opens another way to describe Lady Morgan's view of Rosa. Several other rather vague *rapprochements* with Shakespeare are developed in her discussion of Italian comedy (I, 201–02, 208), and in Rosa's "Incantazione," one of his short poems, she claims to find "de grands traits de ressemblance avec les conjurations de l'Hécate de Shakespeare" (II, 256), i.e., one of the witches in *Macbeth*. Milton's youthful complaints "rappellent tout-à-fait l'humeur fougueuse, le tempérament ardent de Salvator" (I, 53, note).[31] Perhaps her most striking phrase relates Rosa to the greatest of all Italian writers: "ce Dante de la peinture" (I, 83); the expression occurs in the vivid passage on Rosa's *giro* in "les plus hautes chaînes des *Abruzzes*." There is a less questionable comparison with Juvenal and Horace: "emporté par son caractère, il déploie par fois avec la force du premier, un peu trop de sa rudesse" (II, 192); but this appears in her treatment of Rosa's satires. Fittingly enough, perhaps the most interesting and effective of such *rapprochements* are those with Byron: Rosa is not only the Dante of painting, he is also "ce Biron de la peinture" (I, 257). Lines from the British poet are quoted in connection with Rosa's *Prometheus* (I, 186, note) and *Saul and the Witch of Endor* (II, 134–35). But one suspects a political motivation here, for Lady Morgan, in a passage in which Rosa the satirical poet is called "[le] poète de la liberté" (II, 201), also singles out "la force nerveuse, et l'âme libre et fière d'un Alfiéri" along with "la poësie pleine de hardiesse, d'imagination et de philosophie d'un Biron" (ibid.). Also in connection with Rosa's satires, there is an interesting comparison and contrast between Rosa and Machiavelli. The later poet, she says, had one advantage over the earlier one: he was less cynical about humanity: "il n'y riait point de l'espèce humaine, ne cherchant qu'à corriger ses folies en les mettant au grand jour" (II, 192).

What, finally, should we think of Lady Morgan as a critic of Rosa's work and, particularly, his painted work?[32] First, perhaps, we must suppose that she saw only a rather small number of pictures and drew largely on various literary sources for her descriptions of them and to a lesser extent on etched and engraved versions. Another handicap, perhaps even more important, was her self-proclaimed identification with Rosa the man—patriot, precursor of the Risorgimento, lover of liberty, bold critic of the powerful and the corrupt. One suspects, too, that Rosa's work as a satirical poet engaged her more than it deserved. Despite these hindrances, she created a Rosa after his own heart: his disdain for landscape is echoed by her failure to give any serious attention to any of his works in that genre. His ambition to be considered a history painter is paralleled by her enthusiasm for ten or so of his paintings on themes from Greek and Roman antiquity and the Bible. Rosa would have been deeply pleased by her fondness for the "philosophic" side of his work, what she calls its "teinte philosophique," even though the philosophical content of his work is not really spelled out. Perhaps even more pleasing would have been her *rapprochements* between the painter and such literary giants as Dante, Shakespeare, Milton, and Byron, as well as her spotlighting of the teacher-pupil relationship between Rosa and Michelangelo—she implies that Rosa was a worthy disciple. All in all, though perhaps not as deeply acquainted as we would like with Rosa's paintings and etchings, she was a Rosa enthusiast and empathized with several important aspects of his creativity.

Since its first publication, Lady Morgan's biography of Rosa has been criticized for the freedom with which she treated historical reality. To these and other contemporary reactions of her book we shall turn later. Before doing so, it is fitting to dwell on her serious accomplishments as biographer and art historian, mindful of her failings already displayed. First, as Michael Kitson has stated, her biography of Rosa "was the first full-length biography of a foreign artist in English."[33] She provided her readers with French and English translations of twenty of Rosa's letters—all that was then known of a correspondence now known to include several hundred letters. As Kitson points out: "She also prints a number of Rosa's letters to Ricciardi in English translation, *which has not been done since*" (ibid., emphasis mine). It is worth pointing out, too, that while she never refers to De Dominici's biography of Rosa—the ultimate source of her "information" about the artist's participation in Masaniello's uprising[34]—she evidently studied carefully the founding texts by Passeri, Baldinucci, and Pascoli, and judiciously assessed the former two to be "les principales autorités sur lesquelles se fonde tout ce qu'on a écrit de nos jours sur Salvator"(I, 124). Not that she doesn't criticize all three of her major Italian sources for their discreet or cowardly silence about Rosa's role in the Neapolitan rebellion (I, 299–300). In any case, her frequent references to Passeri, Baldinucci, and Pascoli showed her readers the right path to follow in their search for reliable information about Rosa. On the other hand, her trust in Dr. Charles Burney's account of Rosa as musician was misguided, but this had few serious consequences, as it dealt with the least important of the artistic pursuits attributed to Rosa. Her admiration for Rosa's poetry, excessive though it may seem to us today, led her to include extensive discussion of these texts, including long quotations. Thus, in effect, she inaugurated in France the serious treatment of Rosa as poet.

Finally, Lady Morgan's book provides a rather remarkable—remarkable for the time—catalogue of Rosa's work (II, 305–19).[35] She lists over 175 paintings with locations. For England, she provides 113 titles; for Italy, 55; for the rest of Europe, 10. Titles, however, are often merely generic and lump pictures together, e.g., *Deux paysages* in Brussels. She gives a certain amount of museological information: the *Jason and the Dragon* belonging to William Ponsonby (S 218) is traced through several sales and owners (I, 306), and she notes that Lord Townsend's *Belisarius* had been a gift of Frederick the Great (ibid.). Outside the catalogue proper, in the main body of her text, she devotes considerable space to the description and evaluation of many individual pictures. While not all of these are authentic, at least one that she mentions (II, 43) has recently emerged from oblivion: Rosa's portrait of himself as Pascariello.[36]

Admittedly, Lady Morgan's catalogue does not measure up to modern *catalogues raisonnés*. For one thing, she never gives the dimensions of the pictures listed or attempts to date them.[37] Most seriously, she deals inadequately with the problem of authenticity. In this respect and others, there is a huge gap between her catalogue and the best one available to modern students of Rosa. She faced a difficult situation: for a long time, Rosa's popularity was such that many copies, fakes, and imitations were put into circulation and foisted onto unsuspecting buyers, especially English. To her credit, Lady Morgan admits that her catalogue "ne peut être considéré que comme la base de recherches plus étendues pour ceux que le peintre intéressera assez pour désirer mieux connaître ses ouvrages" (II, 305). In fact, she prudently disavows responsibility for the "originalité" of all the pictures listed, since she has had to rely on the work of others and pictures are often moved.[38]

As already suggested, Lady Morgan's catalogue of Rosa's etchings is somewhat incomplete, listing eighty-seven items. But the *Figurine* are all lumped together: "Bandits, figures et autres caprices. Soixante pages, le titre compris" (II, 318). She probably had no opportunity to examine for herself a set of the *Figurine;* if she had, her list would have come to ninety-three items.[39] Her book ends with a useful catalogue of some thirty engravings done after Rosa by Goupy (eight items) and a dozen and a half other reproductive engravers.

The critical reaction to Lady Morgan's book was, to say the least, muted and mixed. I have found only two reviews. One, by Charles Nodier, appeared very shortly after its publication, on March 5, 1824, in *L'Oriflamme,* and one by Francesco Salfi (1759–1832) in the *Revue encyclopédique* some time during 1824. Neither of these reviews is a mere "notice"; Salfi's runs to thirteen pages, while Nodier's is somewhat shorter. Both reflect the political divisions of the Restoration: Nodier takes Lady Morgan to task for being an "écrivain de parti" and for having written "une sorte de Factum révolutionnaire" marked by "un ton d'âcreté et un esprit de dénigrement qui repousse la confiance"— not surprising comments when one notes that Nodier's review begins with a long passage proclaiming that literature and the arts have normally flowered under monarchs and even under despots. Even his observation that her book is fictionalized history has a political slant: "elle a senti que l'histoire, bien plus que le roman, offrait les ressources les plus étendues pour calomnier le présent avec le passé, et emprunter aux morts les plus illustres la gloire de leurs souvenirs, pour en poursuivre les vivans." Nodier is certainly right in detecting the polemic intentions barely hidden under the surface of Lady Morgan's biography, and one understands, given his own political attitude toward the post-revolutionary regime of throne and altar, why Nodier took a dim view of the 1647 Masaniello rebellion in Naples and Rosa's part in the violence it entailed:

> Il est facile d'imaginer tous les désordres auxquels dut se livrer la populace la plus corrompue de l'Europe, conduite par un homme sorti de ses rangs. Mazaniello [*sic*], pour inspirer plus de terreur, ne marchait qu'entouré d'une troupe d'hommes déterminés, portant le titre de compagnie de la Mort, et dont Salvator fut un des chefs. C'est avec leur appui que *le pêcheur d'Amalfi* fit massacrer les nobles et incendier leurs maisons. Cependant notre historien femelle nous peint ce ramas de bandits comme une réunion d'hommes à principes et à sentiments, et se faisant scrupule de verser le sang et de rien dérober; enfin, elle en fait de petits saints révolutionnaires.

The other legend Lady Morgan helped to spread—Rosa's involvement with the bandits of the mountains of southern Italy—is treated in similar vein: "Rencontré par des brigans qui désolaient ces contrées, il paraît qu'il s'enrôla dans une de leurs bandes, qui, s'il faut en croire Lady Morgan, étaient composées de brigands héroïques fort différens de leurs confrères de tous les pays." Thus Nodier senses that there is a fictional element in her biography—"il faut louer l'imagination de l'auteur"—but he does not question the two episodes that are now known to be false to history, perhaps because it serves his own political agenda to accept these legends as truth.

Nodier is not, however, incapable of finding virtues, both in Rosa himself and in his biographer's work. There is little criticism of the painter's work. Of Rosa's famous wanderings in the Abruzzi, Puglia, and Calabria, he observes that it was here "que le jeune enthousiaste puisa le modèle de cette nature âpre et souvent sublime qu'il a su reproduire avec tant de verité dans ses tableaux." Clearly, Nodier's Rosa was the painter of "sublime" landscapes; he mentions no specific works and no other genres. Rosa the man wrings some grudging admiration from him: "Doué d'un esprit vif et enjoué, que fécondait sans cesse l'imagination la plus brillante." Rosa, Nodier notes, taking Lady Morgan's critical views at face value, "se plaça au premier rang parmi les poëtes et les musiciens les plus distingués de son temps." Still, Rosa filled his life with "chagrin" and "amertume," and stirred up a strong reaction among his rivals "par son orgueil et la violence de son caractère." Nodier congratulates Lady Morgan for having revealed "quelques détails curieux" about Rosa and generously recognizes her talent, "qui se montre souvent avec éclat dans plusieurs scènes décrites avec autant de charme que d'éloquence." He closes with a brief but slashing attack on the translators for "travestying" the English text.

Salfi's review is a very different matter. He is grateful to Lady Morgan for her effort to rescue Rosa from oblivion among the Italians. And he shares her political and religious views. Apropos of the youthful Rosa's rebellion against Scholastic philosophy, which his teachers tried to inculcate in him, Salfi writes: "Les subtilités futiles et rebutantes de cette fausse institution ne firent, au contraire, que l'exciter plus vivement comme tant d'autres, à s'adonner encore plus aux lettres et aux beaux-arts, et surtout à la musique et à la poésie" (p. 109). But Salfi objects to Lady Morgan's depiction of seventeenth-century Italy—she exaggerates and distorts in her attacks on "le despotisme et la superstition du XVIIe siècle" (p. 112)—and to her picture of the Italy of Rosa's time as "le dernier refuge de cette barbare dialecte qui soutenait et décorait tous les sophismes théologiques et politiques, par lesquels on enchaînait le genre humain" (p. 113). Unlike Nodier, he is able to cite chapter and verse: the Medicis' treatment of Marchetti was much less harsh than she would have it (p. 112); the Neapolitan barons were not the "braves feudataires" she sees in them (ibid.). Most of Salfi's criticisms reflect his superior knowledge of Italy's literary history—as the continuator of Ginguené's *Histoire littéraire d'Italie* (he was responsible for volumes X through XIV) and author of two histories of Italian literature and a history of Italian comedy, he was in a strong position. Thus he questions her "injuste prévention" against Tiraboschi (p. 114), and her implication that fine libraries were rare in Italy (ibid.). Her treatment of the *canti carnescialeschi* "rassemble . . . en peu de mots bien des erreurs" (p. 115); she is mistaken in claiming that the *commedia dell'arte* died out before the eighteenth century; her account of seventeenth-century poetry, and especially of the role of the Accademia della Crusca vis-à-vis Marini, is wrong-headed (p. 116); Rosa was not a neglected figure, a *poète maudit,* so to speak—Salfi is able to mention nine writers, from Passeri to Lanzi, who had written about Rosa, and favorably at that.

Returning to Lady Morgan's account of Rosa's life, Salfi agrees with Nodier in focusing on the two fundamental legends for which she did so much to attach to his name. As for Rosa's life among the bandits and his adherence to their organization, though attested by some of his biographers, "cette bizarre tradition fut inventée et accréditée par ses rivaux ou peut-être par ses admirateurs, qui ne pouvaient pas comprendre comment il avait su retracer la physionomie de ces héros des montagnes" (p. 118). Lady Morgan's attempt to link Rosa with Campanella's conspiracy against the Spanish occupants is given short shrift: Salfi points out that it had died out long before Rosa's birth (ibid.). Concerning Rosa's adherence to Masaniello's revolt, Salfi differs with Lady Morgan about the outbreak of this rebellion: contrary to what she says, it came about suddenly and accidentally. Rosa did not hasten to Naples on learning of the uprising; rather, he was already in Naples, busily painting, having gone there the year before, "et, comme il était ami de Falcone, qui s'engagea dans cette révolution (lui et ses élèves formant la compagnie de la Mort), Rosa suivit la même impulsion, et combattit, comme ses autres concitoyens, pour l'indépendance de son pays; puis Masaniello ayant été trahi et assassiné, il retourna à Rome, tandis que Falcone se réfugia ailleurs" (p. 119). Thus Salfi, except for one historical detail—the date of Rosa's alleged trip to Naples—accepts the broad outlines of Lady Morgan's account. But there are nuances of difference: Salfi implies that Rosa merely fought *alongside* Falcone's infamous company; moreover, he was a freedom-fighter and not, as Nodier would have it, a terrorist.

Nearing the conclusion of his review, Salfi gives a brief but judicious appraisal of Lady Morgan's claims for Rosa as a musician (Salfi never refers to Dr. Burney by name): "Il fut d'abord musicien, ou plutôt grand amateur de musique; il en profita surtout pour rendre encore plus agréables ses improvisations et ses entretiens académiques" (p. 119). According to Salfi, he was a better actor than musician, especially in the role of Coviello/Formica (ibid.). As for his lyric poems, so highly praised by Lady Morgan: "les exemples rapportés par lady Morgan, et qu'elle aurait mieux fait de passer sous silence, prouvent tout le contraire de ce qu'elle avance, ou du moins font voir qu'elle sent tout autrement que les Italiens les plus capables d'apprécier leur poésie" (pp. 119–20). The satires of which Rosa was so proud

> conservent toujours quelques traces de son peu de goût et de son trop d'abandon. Soit l'impatience de sa verve, soit l'importance qu'il donnait à ses idées, il se livre quelquefois à une abondance qui le rend un peu trop familier, inégal, quelquefois même ennuyeux. . . . [S]es satires sont bien loin d'être supérieures et même égales à celles de l'Arioste, de Chiabrera et de plusieurs autres de ses devanciers. (p. 120)

Except for some derogatory final remarks about the translation and the inaccuracy of the quotations from Italian, Salfi's conclusion deals first with the question of whether Lady Morgan's biography is history or fiction, by admitting that "certains détails, certains épisodes, plusieurs tableaux, lui donnent, en effet, une couleur romanesque" (p. 121). His final summation is that the book "renferme des réflexions spirituelles et ingénieuses, des récits pleins de vivacité et d'intérêt, des souvenirs non moins agréables qu'utiles, et un amour très-noble pour l'indépendance de l'Italie et pour la civilisation des peuples, qualités qui rachètent souvent le tort de son peu d'exactitude" (ibid.). Thus Salfi judges Lady Morgan as an Italian patriot, as a literary historian, and as a fellow liberal. Rosa's work as painter and engraver are virtually ignored.

Except for the somewhat disparaging footnote in Pietro de Angelis' article on Rosa for the *Biographie universelle* in 1825, these two reviews represent, as far as I know, the total of the immediate critical reaction to Lady Morgan's biography, and neither is truly enthusiastic. It is a disappointing harvest at first glance. But to be reviewed by Nodier, an important member of the romantic school during its Restoration phase, and by a serious literary historian was a better fate, perhaps, than the controversial Anglo-Irish author might have expected. As noted earlier, these reviews, especially Salfi's, go well beyond the dimensions and seriousness of a "notice." While *L'Oriflamme* (1820–1825) played but a minor role in the cultural life of the Restoration—it had only about forty subscribers[40]—the *Revue encyclopédique* (1819–1833) was a major periodical; as Hatin says: "Ce recueil, justement estimé, . . . compte parmi ses rédacteurs les hommes les plus éminents de l'époque . . ." (ibid., II, 569).

If Lady Morgan was destined to lose this critical battle, she would ultimately win the war, if not on the terrain of criticism, then on that of literary creation. Her Rosa was the one accepted by the poets, novelists, and dramatists of the romantic era, even if they did not always draw directly on the material she provided. The French translation of her biography is the only important work on Rosa ever published in France. It is revealing that in 1975 Salerno (p. 82) does not include a single book or article in French on Rosa in his *Bibliografia essenziale*—understandably, it should be noted, he lists only the English version of her book. The same observation holds for the bibliography given at the end of Michael Kitson's introduction to *Salvator Rosa: Haywoood Gallery, London, 17 October–23 December 1973.*[41] France, then, might seem to have been hostile or indifferent to Rosa and his work. We have already seen considerable evidence to the contrary, visible in documents covering more than a century. The story of Rosa's reception during the three or four decades that followed the publication of Lady Morgan's book will lay the idea permanently to rest and show that, before beginning to fade in the second half of the nineteenth century, Salvator Rosa was a beacon in the French firmament.

CHAPTER FOUR

Lady Morgan's Legacy

Although Lady Morgan's book made several serious contributions to the body of knowledge about Rosa accumulating in France since the seventeenth century, the immediate and most visible impact of her book was that, as a modern Rosa specialist has said, "she immortalized the two best-known legends about him: that he spent part of his youth as a prisoner of the Neapolitan bandits (whom she represents as noble outlaws of a Robin Hood type), and that he returned to Naples in 1647 to take part in the revolt of the fisherman Masaniello, slipping into the city unobserved and, with his fellow artists, fighting by day and painting by night."[1] Her early reviewers had strong reactions to these claims. Nodier, to whom Lady Morgan and therefore Rosa were anathema from an ideological point, accepted both legends as fact; it served his political agenda to show that Rosa "conspira contre son prince" and was one of Masaniello's "partisans les plus fougueux."[2] As for his adherence to a band of bandits, Nodier writes sarcastically, "On ignore combien de temps il exerça cette honorable profession" (p. 4). Francesco Salfi, representing Enlightenment and liberalism, dismissed Lady Morgan's story about Rosa and the bandits as "cette bizarre tradition . . . inventée et accréditée par ses rivaux, ou peut-être même par ses admirateurs," in short, a "fable."[3] On the other hand, sympathizing with Italy's Risorgimento, Salfi accepts the core of Lady Morgan's account of Rosa and Masaniello but claims that Rosa was already in Naples, quietly painting, well before the outbreak of the uprising; he at once joined Falcone and his pupils in the *Compagnia della morte* in the revolt. Thus Salfi sees Rosa as a patriot and freedom fighter—there is no hint, in contrast to Nodier's account, of revolutionary "excesses."

It would be impossible in a monograph like this one to spell out all the variations in French writing of the romantic era on the fundamental themes developed by Lady Morgan. We will examine a sampling of relevant and, I hope, revealing texts. In the same year as her book, the French translation of abbé Luigi Antonio Lanzi's history of Italian painting—the original Italian version was published in its most complete form in 1809—summarizes the work of Falcone's band in words that would have pleased Nodier: "ils firent un horrible massacre."[4] Leaving aside Dezallier's brief, vague, and garbled account (1762), I have discovered only one text in French prior to Lady Morgan's that links Rosa and Masaniello, Count Grégoire Orloff's *Essai sur l'histoire de la peinture en Italie* (1823). The Russian senator (1777–1826) writes of Rosa, Falcone, and their band (without using the expression "Compagnie de la mort"): "Entourés d'une foule de factieux, ils commirent . . . les excès les plus funestes; et après avoir massacré sans pitié une foule d'Espagnols, ils s'enfuirent lorsqu'ils virent la tempête se calmer par la mort du chef de l'insurrection. . . . La vengeance les animait plus que l'amour de la patrie."[5] It so happens that Orloff had the help of Pietro de Angelis (1784–1859) (soon to be the author of the article on Rosa in the *Biographie universelle*) in writing his *Mémoires historiques, politiques et littéraires.* Since De Angelis mentions both De Dominici and Salvini as sources of information about Rosa (Michaud, XXXIX, 11–12), it is clear that Orloff had a channel to biographical accounts of Rosa that could provide him the "facts" about Rosa's involvement with Masaniello. I have found only one text that refers to Orloff, the above-mentioned *précis* (1828) of Meissner's biography: "Nous avons consulté les mémoires du duc de Modène, ceux du comte Orloff, publiés plus récemment" (*Masaniello,* p. 5). There is every indication, then, that Lady Morgan is the principal, if not the sole, source for French readers of the two legends she "immortalized."

Other than Lady Morgan's book, the only serious piece of scholarship about Rosa that projects more or less the same picture of him is De Angelis' article for Michaud's *Biographie universelle,* which is the very first entry in Vol. XXXIX. De Angelis omits any hint of the story about Rosa and the bandits; he does not even show the artist as wandering in the wilds of southern Italy. Thus he provides no biographical explanation of how Rosa the landscapist replaced the "heureux détails de la vie champêtre" painted by Claude Lorrain and Poussin with "des sites d'un aspect sauvage et lugubre."[6] De Angelis, a partisan of the Risorgimento, gives a rather full and sympathetic treatment of Rosa's involvement in Masaniello's revolution, though his account is devoid of torch-lit painting sessions (he is one of the writers who would have it that Rosa the painter happened to be in Naples before the outbreak of the revolt).[7] The *Compagnia della morte* is mentioned, along with the names of ten of the artists enrolled in it, but no details of their activities are given. As for Rosa, "il était d'un caractère ardent, impétueux et indépendant" (p. 7). De Angelis repeats the widespread myth that Rosa painted Masaniello's portrait, and he claims that the artist tried in vain to save the "nouveau tribun" with his advice. De Angelis, then, as far as the Masaniello legend is concerned, depicts a Rosa quite like Lady Morgan's, but there is rather clear proof that he did not draw solely on her book—e.g., the list of artists who joined Aniello in the *Compagnia della morte* has no counterpart in her biography.

In 1835 Francesco Salfi twice recapitulates his earlier version (1824) in his continuation of Ginguené's *Histoire littéraire d'Italie,* in Vol. XIII apropos of Rosa's satires (p. 306) and in Vol. XIV in a survey of Neapolitan painting (p. 377). But Salfi deals with the legend of Rosa among the brigands—he admires Rosa's artistry in painting such figures but takes a very dim view of the real-life models: "Aucun peintre n'a mieux saisi le caractère de ces hommes dégénérés qui semblent haïr la société et la vie, et ne se plaire qu'à porter partout le trouble et la destruction" (XIV, 373). He is cautious in his handling of the question of Rosa's contact with the outlaws. "L'expression et la vérité qu'il leur a données a fait débiter et croire qu'il avait connu et fréquenté les bandits de son temps" (XIV, 373–74), a statement laid at Lady Morgan's door in a footnote reference to her biography.

In the genre of serious journalistic writing about Rosa, two articles deserve some attention for their handling of the two basic legends—both, incidentally, specifically refer to Lady Morgan. In 1835, the now-forgotten Alexandre de Saint-Chéron firmly rejects the legend of Rosa amid the bandits (he avoids the question of Rosa's enrollment in their ranks), and for an interesting reason: "Les biographes contemporains de notre artiste, ont nié cette anecdote."[8] Saint-Chéron accepts the claim that Rosa took part in Masaniello's revolt but handles the subject in a rather neutral manner—the *Compagnia della morte* is mentioned, but there are no "excesses." As for Rosa, he "ne resta pas indifférent à cette lutte; il abandonna ses travaux, ses plaisirs, son faste, pour se ranger sous l'étendard de la *Compagnie de la Mort*" (p. 208). Thus Rosa appears "engagé," but whether in a good or an evil cause is not made clear.

About eight years later, in *La Chronique,* one Almire Gandonnière,[9] who begins his article with references to Lady Morgan (and to "une charmante nouvelle" of Alexandre Dumas, of which more later), eschews "l'histoire ainsi poétisée par de grands écrivains" and calls the bandit story "un bruit populaire propagé par l'envie et fortifié par le genre même de ses productions."[10] Moreover, "tous ses biographes sérieux, ses contemporains Baldunicci [*sic*], Pascoli, Passori [*sic*], l'abbé Salvini et autres, ont énergiquement repoussé cette calomnie" (p. 318). The Masaniello legend, on the other hand, is swallowed whole, complete with the detail of Rosa sketching portraits of the rebels by flickering torchlight (p. 322), one of the more colorful of Lady Morgan's embellishments. Gandonnière betrays strong sympathy for "Mazaniello" and his followers—they rebelled against "la tyrannie imbécile du vice-roi de Naples" (Ibid.)—but insists on the fickleness of the mob who swept "l'illustre pêcheur" to power only to throw his mutilated corpse into a moat a little later.

References to Lady Morgan's Rosa are scattered about in other forms of writing that may be loosely lumped together as journalistic. An interesting example is the collection of travel writing from 1837 published under the title *L'Italie pittoresque;* it contained contributions by Nodier, Dumas, Berlioz, Charles Didier, Roger de Beauvoir, and several lesser-known figures. Thus Beauvoir, describing a visit to the "musée de Naples" and generalizing about the Neapolitan school, evokes rather obliquely the legend of Rosa and Masaniello:

> À voir en effet ces émeutes populaires, ces torches de Masaniello courant après la révolte échevelée dans chacune de ces peintures; à voir le sévère Philippe II, hôte terrible de ce grand musée, on se demande pourquoi à l'entour d'eux, à l'entour de Titien, de Luca Giordano et de Salvator, l'œil ne rencontre que de maigres tableaux et de tristes toiles, ou encore des *Canaletti*, pages vénitiennes arrachées à leurs tranquilles lagunes.[11]

A little earlier, dilating on the relation between the Neapolitan landscape and its painter, he wrote, "Atrani, la patrie de Masaniello, a été créée en même temps pour le rude pinceau de Salvator" (p. 21). Jules de Norvins, similarly, makes an implicit link between Rosa and the brigands legend as he recounts his trip through the bandit-infested Abruzzi: "Dans l'Abruzzi les fusils sont longs, ils portent loin, et les assassins sont couchés dans les nids des vautours. À chaque pas je reconnaissais les tableaux de Salvator Rosa, qui, sans doute, avait parcouru seul avec son génie les sauvageries de cette épouvantable contrée" ("État romain," p. 48).

Louis Viardot, the prolific author of guides to European museums, though disappointed by the Rosas in the Museo degli studi at Naples,[12] takes the opportunity to mention the painter's troubled relationship with his native city: "Il en fut chassé trois fois; par la misère d'abord, puis par le dédain et la haine de ses confrères puis enfin par la chute du parti populaire et patriote, du parti de Mazaniello [*sic*], qu'il avait embrassé avec ferveur, sous son maître Aniello Falcone, chef de la *Compagnie de la Mort,* où s'étaient enrôlés la plupart des artistes."[13] Étienne Delécluze, in his three-part study of Rosa's satires in the *Revue de Paris* (1840), treats the legend of Rosa and the bandits with considerable skepticism. "Lady Morgan," he writes, "a écrit tout un roman sur cette prétendue circonstance de la vie de Salvator Rosa."[14] On the other hand, he includes a rather long paragraph about Rosa and Masaniello. Whatever his sympathies with the artist, Delécluze, best remembered as the pupil and biographer of the "regicide" Jacques-Louis David, regards Falcone's *Compagnia della morte* ("cette troupe furibonde") as blood-thirsty mobsters who violated the laws of sanctuary and slaughtered their enemies "sans miséricorde" and "sans pitié" (p. 321)—although at night, by torchlight, they complied with Masaniello's whims and painted portraits of him for distribution among the people (p. 321). Louise Colet, in her *L'Italie des Italiens* (1863), relates that when she was a child, her father, having mentioned the "place Masaniello,"[15] would use the occasion to give her a history lesson: "Mon père me faisait lire dans les Mémoires du duc de Guise le récit de l'insurrection du hardi pêcheur: il me montrait Salvator Rosa faisant le portrait du héros populaire d'Amalfi."[16] As we shall see, the portraits of Masaniello painted by Rosa were an integral part of the artist's biography for many writers—thanks largely to Lady Morgan.

Her bequest to French poetry of the romantic period is rather a mixed bag. Henri de Latouche seems to have produced the first French poem that reflects Lady Morgan's legendary Rosa, "Le dernier jour de Salvator Rosa," which appeared in the *Revue de Paris* of January 1830.[17] The aged, despairing artist laments his present decrepitude and sterility, so different from the "nobles destinées" of his youth:

> Jeune, le sol manquait devant ses pas errans:
> c'est lui qui, dans la soif d'échapper aux tyrans,
> des cités, des états méprisant les barrières,
> du plus haut Apennin gravissait les bruyères.
> Là, rapproché du ciel, implorant ses fléaux,
> des splendeurs de la foudre éclairant ses pinceaux,
> c'est lui qui descendait sous la vague entrouverte.
> Puis, cherchant des périls plus féconds pour sa perte
> que l'abîme des mers et le front d'un volcan,
> du bandit de l'Abruzze osait tenter le camp.
> Là, tranquille et captif, aux feux de l'incendie,
> aux lueurs du poignard, sa main jeune et hardie,
> ses crayons inspirés saisissaient, palpitans,
> soit le vol des coursiers, le choc des combattans;
> soit devant les vainqueurs les vierges alarmées;
> la mort sur son front même . . . Et ces bandes armées,

> jusque dans leur sommeil sur des rochers épars,
> s'étonnaient de servir à la splendeur des arts.

The poet manages to evoke, more briefly, the artist's link with Masaniello: Rosa wishes he had died earlier "contre l'Espagnol quand Naples surgissant, / du belliqueux pêcheur eut accepté le sang." Despite the essentially neo-classical style, here we encounter a romantic Rosa—his *giro* in the mountains, his captivity among the bandits of the Abruzzi and their inclusion in his work, his sympathy for Masaniello. The very landscapes, whether those of the bay of Naples ("la vague entrouverte," "l'abîme des mers et le front d'un volcan") or of Italy's central mountainous regions ("les bruyères du plus haut Apennin," "[les] splendeurs de la foudre"), continue those vivid ones already depicted in pre-romantic texts.

Our next exhibit, Auguste Barbier's "Chiaia," originally part of his collection of Italian-inspired poems, *Il Pianto* (1833), presents a younger but equally melancholy Rosa. Bitter and impatient, he engages in a dialogue with a fisherman plying his trade amid the natural splendors of the bay of Naples. The fisherman upbraids the artist for his defeatism and self-absorption. Salvator seems to recognize the force of the fisherman's entreaty to join the cause of the people, but, in the poem's conclusion, ultimately rejects it and prepares to leave Naples for Calabria:

> Adieu, Naples! Salut, terre de la Calabre!
> Ecueils toujours fumants où la vague se cabre,
> O vieux mont Gargano, sommet échevelé,
> Rocs cambrés et noircis, au poil long et mêlé,
> Nature vaste et chaude et féconde en ravages,
> O terre, ô bois, ô monts, ô désolés rivages!
> Recevez-moi parmi vos sombres habitants,
> Car je veux me mêler à leurs troupeaux errants;
> Je veux manger le pain de tout être qui pense,
> Goûter la liberté sur la montagne immense.[18]

It would be difficult to prove that Barbier drew on Lady Morgan for the material of this poem. His Rosa has not yet encountered the brigands of the Abruzzi or become involved in Masaniello's revolt; at most, he anticipates his wanderings in the mountains of southern Italy: "terre de la Calabre . . . Gargano, sommet échevelé / Rocs cambrés et noircis . . . Nature féconde en ravages," but the details, like those evoked by Latouche, are standard fare by 1833. Is Barbier foretelling Rosa's life among the bandits with his reference to the "sombres habitants" of the rugged landscape he evokes? Perhaps. Much more certain is Barbier's identification of Rosa with the cause of liberty. Rosa tells us early on that he wanders "comme un esclave" (p. 146), and the fisherman says his fate is shared by all Neapolitans: "Nous sommes, beaux enfants d'une mère féconde, / Sous le joug attelés comme nos taureaux blancs; / . . . souvent battus par la verge étrangère" (p. 147). He spells out the sufferings endured by his countrymen at the hands of their rulers, but, essentially optimistic, anticipates the triumph of liberty. The word "liberté" occurs six times in the second half of the poem.[19] Rosa, as shown by Barbier, is not yet the ardent champion of the people of Naples; the liberty he seeks is personal and individual. But, even if he has the last word, one senses that the fisherman's prediction of the eventual triumph of Liberty ("Car je sais qu'un beau jour, . . . / En mon golfe divin je ferai bonne pêche. / Aux rives de Chiaia, sur le sable argenté, / Dans mes larges filets viendra la Liberté" [p. 150].) has implications for the liberty-loving artist. Barbier's references to the basic legends are not direct, but his Rosa is made of much the same material as Lady Morgan's, perhaps the very same.

Another poet of this period, Aloysius Bertrand, though working in the form of the prose poem, wrote no surviving poem about Rosa despite his evident interest in the visual arts: the subtitle of *Gaspard de la nuit* refers to Rembrandt and Callot. In fact, "Salvator-Rosa" is one of a dozen artists, mostly members of the northern schools, whom Bertrand promises to deal with in his "études"—promises largely unfulfilled.[20] The manuscript of *Gaspard,* however, reveals an epigraph for "Les Deux Juifs," which has been scratched out: "La ruelle est étroite et ce sont des brigands / Qui pour vous poignarder ne mettraient pas de gants," followed by the words "Gaspard de la nuit, pièce inédite / Salvator Rosa, poème" (p. 396).[21] Unfortunately, Bertrand's poem about Rosa was never written, but—as the reference to brigands makes clear—if it had been written, it would have placed the poet among the heirs of Lady Morgan.

The writer to whom we now turn, Arthur de Gobineau, is not remembered as a poet; however, in 1965 an Italian scholar, Paolo Berselli Ambri, published the texts of three poems by Gobineau that had been in manuscript form. One of these, "Le Roman de Manfredine," begun in 1838 but left unfinished, is a long narrative in alexandrines in which Rosa plays a major role. The setting is Naples, and the action is tied to Masaniello and his revolt. The heroine is a descendant of the Normans who had once ruled Southern Italy and so, as Berselli Ambri observes, she "appartiene . . . al gruppo dei *calenders,* come per i suoi meriti, indipendentemente, è ovvio, della nobiltà di sangue, vi appartiene Salvator Rosa."[22] Thus Gobineau's Rosa is presented in a favorable light; moreover, he is secretly in love with the high-born

Manfredine, who joins the revolutionaries and even becomes involved in plotting against the Spanish occupant. Gobineau may paint a favorable picture of Rosa, but he is decidedly hostile to Masaniello: when the fisherman takes charge of the rebellion, Gobineau evokes the *Club des Jacobins* and "Le masque pustuleux du vendu Mirabeau" (p. 132). Rosa, acting as Masaniello's "mestre de camp," deals with the motley throng of those seeking to identify themselves with the new régime:

> On accourait en foule: artisan, gueux, valet,
> Lazzaroni, voleur, brigand de tout calibre,
> Chacun quittait sa paille et s'était rendu libre:
> Tout courait, tout venait protester en jurant
> Qu'il avait cent raisons de haïr le tyran.
> L'un demandant un grade, apportait pour mérite
> Le meurtre d'un soldat surpris dans sa guérite;
> L'autre, plus héroïque, étalait sur sa main
> Un haillon de velours souillé de sang humain.
> Il fallait de ces gens honorer la colère,
> Ou baisser le regard, et pour le moins se taire. (p. 144)

Rosa himself describes his fellow revolutionaries as "des rhéteurs ignorants / Des sots, des spadassins, des rhéteurs de taverne " (p. 148).

As far as the surviving text reveals, Gobineau wishes to present us with the paradoxical situation of the haughty countess who, perhaps out of boredom, perhaps to spite the Spanish governor who seeks her hand in marriage, joins the popular cause and does not shrink from violence—or from the thought of having "les mains sales," as contrasted with Rosa, who turns remorseful over the revolutionary bloodshed and his partial responsibility for it. Such an irenic Rosa is just as fictional as the Rosa of Masaniello's uprising. Thus we need not follow the twists and turns of Gobineau's plot, especially since the poem breaks off without a clear indication of the direction it is taking. The presentation of Rosa, in the surviving text, is so fictionalized that we cannot be sure what sources Gobineau drew on. We can surmise that the legend of Rosa's involvement in the Masaniello episode, at least in broad outline, had become common knowledge and been accepted as a fact by cultivated French readers by 1838. By then there was an abundance of possible sources for the Rosa of his narrative, who is consonant with the Rosa portrayed by Lady Morgan even if he is not demonstrably derived from her version of the *engagé* artist.

Gobineau presents Rosa primarily as the lover of Manfredine and an active partisan of Masaniello. Though his later fame as an artist no doubt accounts for his inclusion in the poem, the poet pays little attention to Rosa the artist—understandably, given the background of violence. Thus Gobineau has no descriptions of paintings done at night by torchlight. The earliest reference to Rosa's work leaves us wondering if Gobineau knew it either from personal observation or by reputation: "ton pinceau, Rosa, dont la riche couleur / Fait paraitre éclatants des objets sans valeur" (p. 146). Gobineau, we gather, is unaware of the numerous criticisms of Rosa's color as "terne . . . triste," etc., and he seems to think Rosa painted still lifes in the Dutch manner. He is on firmer ground when he calls Rosa "le peintre des brigands" (p. 149)—the only reference in the poem to the other founding legend put in circulation by Lady Morgan. The only other passage in which Gobineau, through his omniscient narrator, focuses on Rosa as an artist is not very revealing as art criticism:

> Et Salvator Rosa vit encor de nos jours
> Par son oeuvre admirée et qu'on cherche toujours.
> Ses tableaux embrunis de scènes émouvantes,
> Aux avides marchands échappant dans les ventes,
> Et le lord d'Angleterre et le riche hollandais
> En couvrent à poids d'or les murs de leurs palais.
> Il était jeune alors, sa puissance inconnue
> Ne touchait pas ainsi les hauteurs de la rue;
> Il aimait le terrible et son cœur plein de feu
> Accourait au devant des projets hasardeux. (p. 204)

In the poem's last allusion to Rosa, however, we rejoin Lady Morgan's legend: Rosa is "Un de ceux qui parlaient le mieux de liberté" (p. 205). Gobineau presumably is referring to Rosa's paintings, as there is nothing about the satires in the surviving text.

Gobineau seems to have understood that poetry was not his genre, thus the poem was left unfinished, and his poetic endeavors were not published until nearly a century after his death. Even if he had completed his poem and published it, it is doubtful it would have done much to further the knowledge and appreciation of Rosa—certainly not Rosa the artist—in the romantic era.

The remaining poetic texts to be examined will not detain us long. With one exception, their authors were as lackluster as Gobineau, and their poems about Rosa are forgotten. The Marquis de la Rochefoucauld-Liancourt[23] in his *Satire imitée de la 4me de Salvator Rosa*[24] recreates the dialogue between the artist and Timon of Athens in Rosa's fourth satire, *La Guerra*. But the Rosa of Lady Morgan appears only in the high-minded Marquis's prefatory biography of the painter-poet. His passage about Rosa and Masaniello is noteworthy, first, for several factual errors, then for its account of Rosa's role as a member of the *Compagnia della morte* (never explicitly named). La Rochefoucauld-Liancourt claims that the band was organized by "Salvator et son beau-frère Franzone [*sic*]" (p. 7). As for the band's activities: "C'était une véritable troupe d'assassins qui parcouraient les rues de Naples, tuant tous les Espagnols qu'ils rencontraient, allant les chercher dans les maisons où ils se cachaient, et n'en épargnant aucun" (ibid.). Rosa is seen as a somewhat reluctant participant: "il ne prit pas autant de plaisir à ces actes sanguinaires qu'aux représentations du carnaval de Rome" (ibid.). The Marquis, incidentally, calls the death of Masaniello "un heureux hasard" (ibid.). Some idea of the research which went into the poem may be gathered from the lines in which Salvator speaks of his life, his religion, and his role as creative artist:

> Je suis un simple fils d'une famille austère;
> Je n'ai plus de parents, et ne fus jamais père;
> Je vis seul avec Dieu, sans crainte et sans regret,
> Je n'ai que moi pour maître, et que moi pour sujet.
>
> Mais je suis un ami de la simple nature.
> Invoquant le Dieu fort et sa lumière pure,
> Je veux, sans offenser un seul concitoyen,
> Être censeur du mal et conseiller du bien. (p. 27)

The passage in *La Guerra* in which Rosa expresses sympathy with Masaniello's revolt is not linked directly either in the poet's resumé or in his running commentary, to the historical events, even though, as his preface reveals, La Rochefoucauld-Liancourt obviously knew something about the events of 1647. The reflection of Lady Morgan's Rosa is not only pale but distorted.

Similar criticism can be made of another imitation in French verse of Rosa's fourth satire, *Satire contre la guerre,* by the rather obscure Francisque Tapon Fougas. Here, at least, the reference to Masaniello and his uprising is incorporated into one of the quatrains and an accompanying explanatory footnote:

> Vois un pauvre pêcheur dictant aux puissants rois
> Toutes ses volontés, leur imposant ses lois,
> Ayant entre ses mains tout l'argent des gabelles,
> Qui demain du gibet gravira les échelles [1].

On sait que Salvator Rosa se trouva à Naples et joua un rôle dans le drame de Masaniello, rôle que ses détracteurs acharnés n'ont pas manqué de tourner autrement qu'à sa gloire.[25]

One can deduce from the list of his publications in the catalogue of the Bibliothèque Nationale and from the *postscriptum* to his imitation of *La Guerra* (pp. 30–32) that Tapon Fougas was a rather stormy petrel; for one thing, he was a partisan of the Risorgimento. Most pertinent is the account he gives in the *postscriptum* of the difficulties he encountered in publishing his imitations of Rosa.[26] As he says at the beginning of the *postscriptum*, "En vérité, les satires de Salvator Rosa ne sont pas nées sous une heureuse étoile!" (p. 30). Thus Rosa was able to stir controversy in the French-speaking world two centuries after his death: at least for the moment, the romantic Rosa of Lady Morgan was alive and well and relevant. As "son traducteur-imitateur" says: "ne dirait-on pas, en effet, que ces violentes sorties contre l'*Envie*, contre la *Musique,* contre la *Guerre* et contre tous les abus et tous les vices de son temps sont bien plutôt la satire vivante du nôtre, et que c'est encore plus le dix-neuvième siècle que le dix-septième que Salvator Rosa a fustigé de son vers immortel?" (p. 51).

Lady Morgan's Rosa enters romantic prose fiction more auspiciously, escorted by Alexandre Dumas père. In a two-part *feuilleton,* which appeared under the title "Salvator Rosa. Mœurs napolitaines" in *Le Courrier Français* March 28 and 29, 1843, and which later in the same year was absorbed into the full-length narrative of *Le Corricolo,*[27] Dumas relates a rather implausible story set in an equally implausible frame-tale. In one of his touristic rambles near Naples, Dumas is led by a young peasant named Salvator to his family's house. The handsome old grandfather reveals that his family, a dynasty of unsuccessful painters, owns three paintings that have been in their possession for two hundred years and which, despite the family's poverty, they refuse to sell, even to the Prince of Salerno.[28] The old man shows the visitor one of the pictures, a landscape in Rosa's wildest manner (the name Rosa has not yet been mentioned): "C'était à coup sûr un souvenir des Calabres ou des Abruzzes. Figurez-vous des rochers noirs dévastés, menaçants, suspendus comme un pont sur l'abîme: une plaine aride et maudite, éclairée par la lumière intermittente et livide d'un ciel orageux" (p. 467). Like Madame de Staël, Dumas supposes that there is no sign of human life in "cette scène de désolation et d'horreur" (ibid.). But there are gruesome human remains: "Des os fracturés, des lambeaux de chair humaine sont semés çà et là sur le sol" (ibid.). Impressed by this picture ("on dirait une page du Dante traduite en peinture" [ibid.]), the narrator presses his host to tell how his family came by these fine pictures. The old man's flashback narrative reveals that Rosa visited the house on three occasions and, each time, painted a picture and left it with his hosts as an expression of gratitude. On the first occasion, the nineteen-year-old traveler accepts the hospitality of these kindly peasants: he is on his way to Rome to seek his fortune and glory. The painting left behind is the landscape already mentioned. Salvator/Salvatoriello recounts his early life in some detail to his host, in terms that epitomize Lady Morgan's understanding of the painter: fleeing from an uncomprehending family and teachers, "je me sauvai au bout du monde, en Pouille, en Calabre, dans les Abruzzes, que sais-je? J'ai erré de vallée en vallée, de montagne en montagne; j'ai souffert le froid et la faim. Je suis tombé dans les mains des brigands qui m'ont forcé à être des leurs" (p. 472).[29] Twelve years later, in 1646, Rosa returns rich and famous and dressed accordingly. At first unrecognized by the peasant family, he pretends to be an avid collector and tries to buy the picture he had given his hosts on his earlier visit. They refuse to sell it, and soon Rosa reveals his true identity and informs his overjoyed hosts of his fame, fortune, and bitter struggles. This time, he leaves them a painting that Dumas relates to a specific work of Rosa: "C'était la reproduction fidèle, ou plutôt la conception première du célèbre tableau de la *Fortune*" (p. 477).[30] Rosa, who makes a point of having shed the pejorative nickname Salvatoriello for his real name, announces that he is on his way to Naples: "[J]'ai une mission sainte et belle à remplir . . . ma patrie m'a renié, je vais me venger de ma patrie! mais en brisant ses fers, en exterminant ses tyrans, en lui rendant la liberté!" (Ibid.).

The story, mimicking, as it were, the hero's movements, hastens to its conclusion: six months later, a disheveled Rosa appears at midnight and asks shelter. Once again, even though he is fleeing Naples after the failure of Masaniello—who is not named but called simply "un homme, un pêcheur" (p. 478)—the artist, before heading for Rome, leaves behind a painting done on the spot. It is very different from the two earlier pictures bestowed on his peasant hosts: "Ce n'était plus ni un site agreste et sauvage, ni une éblouissante satire: c'était une scène atroce, flagrante, épouvantable de destruction, de mort et de vengeance!" (Ibid.). In short, a battle scene. And, as in the landscape he had painted on the occasion of his first visit, Dumas adds some gruesome details that go somewhat beyond the fury of Rosa's battle pictures. Here, Dumas does not seem to be referring to a specific picture but encapsulating—with some exaggeration—the genre with which Rosa was commonly associated. It is likely that Dumas is relying to some extent on his memory of the *Battaglia eroica* in the Louvre, easily accessible to him throughout his life.

Though replete with coincidences and improbabilities, Dumas's "charmante nouvelle," as Almire Gandonnière had called it, effectively captures three facets of Rosa's work—his landscapes, his satirical paintings,[31] and his battle scenes, which are linked to key episodes of the artist's life: his wanderings in the Abruzzi, his early struggles and triumphs in Rome, and his participation in Masaniello's revolution.

Rosa's next appearance in romantic fiction occurs in Eugène de Mirecourt's *Masaniello*,[32] a brief adventure novel of the type that Dumas and his imitators had popularized during the July Monarchy. Rosa plays a subsidiary role in the plot, the main line of which involves an "amour impossible" between Masaniello and the imaginary Isabelle, daughter of the Spanish governor—a situation that is doubly fictional, in that Mirecourt has invented the character of Isabelle and, at the same time, overlooked the fact that the historical Masaniello was married (Lady Morgan has a brief passage on Masaniello's wife [I, 290]). Mirecourt's Masaniello not only is an eligible bachelor but had once dreamed of being a painter, like his friend Salvator Rosa. Though Rosa appears only episodically, Mirecourt intertwines the lives of the revolutionary fisherman and the painter at critical points; for example, Masaniello rescues Rosa from brigands who captured him while he is out painting in "nos montagnes" (p. 14). They do not realize that it is pointless to hold a poor artist for ransom. While being held a captive in the brigands' cave, Rosa, in a scene suggesting that Mirecourt was aware of Rosa's work in the *bambocciato* style as well as of the legend of his torch-lit nights of painting during his days in the *Compagnia della morte*, paints the portraits of several of the bandits.[33] The author even manages to work in a reference to Rosa as a painter of battle pictures: to one of the more prepossessing brigands, who wants to know how *he* will be depicted, the artist replies: "Je t'habillerai en reître et je te jetterai sur un cheval blanc dans une mêlée furieuse" (p. 15). In gratitude for Masaniello's intervention, Rosa eagerly joins Masaniello's cause: "Il ne sera pas dit que l'épée de Salvator Rosa dorme dans son fourreau de cuir, pendant qu'on se battra dans Naples au cri de liberté! . . . Liberté, liberté sainte! s'écria l'artiste, serait-il vrai que tu féconderas encore cette vieille terre napolitaine, que tant de révolutions ont déchirée?" (Ibid.). Rosa accepts the need for extreme measures, but Mirecourt avoids any specific reference to the *Compagnia della morte* and therefore its alleged excesses. Nor is there any reference to Aniello Falcone, the historical leader of the *Compagnia*. In Mirecourt's account, Rosa plays a leading role in the fighting: in Masaniello's words, pronounced before a great crowd of the people, "Je nomme chef de cette troupe Salvator Rosa, le premier de Naples par le génie, le grand peintre que vous connaissez tous" (p. 17). A little earlier, in fact, Rosa had cast himself as a major leader of the struggle: "Tu [Masaniello] commanderas les pêcheurs pendant la bataille;

moi je conduirai les lazzaroni" (p. 16). The climax of Rosa's career as a revolutionary comes after the defeat of the Spaniards: in another crowd scene, Masaniello has Rosa mount a podium in order to transcribe the triumphant fisherman's proclamation: "Le peintre mit un genou en terre, tira de sa poche les tablettes sur lesquelles il avait esquissé, la veille, les rudes physionomies des brigands du Vésuve, et Masaniello lui dicta trois décrets d'une voix brève et rapide" (p. 20). Though Rosa appears only episodically in Mirecourt's story,[34] the spotlight shines brightly on him at critical moments. And Mirecourt continues to emphasize his role and status as an artist. In any case, his Rosa is obviously one of the avatars of Lady Morgan's hero, even if the novelist has played a little more fast and loose with history than she had.

The debt to Lady Morgan (whom Mirecourt never mentions) is even more explicit in the novella "Salvator Rosa dans les Abruzzes," by one Adelphe Nouville, published in the *Bulletin de la Société des gens de lettres* in June 1855. Nouville developed a rather touching tale out of the two pages (I, 90–92) in which Lady Morgan extrapolates a "story" from one of Rosa's etchings. Bartsch had given a minimalist description of this print: "Cinq soldats s'entretenant ensemble. On remarque celui qui a la tête appuyée sur sa main gauche, laissant reposer l'autre sur son genou droit. Le chiffre est gravé à droite sur le bord du mur."[35] Lady Morgan had, I believe, looked at this *Figurina* more carefully than Bartsch: one of the five "soldiers" is a woman whose right index finger seems to rest on the head of the man sitting in the center foreground in a pose reminiscent of the angel in Dürer's *Melencolia I.* Lady Morgan—who saw the "soldiers" as armed bandits—concluded that the central male figure represented Rosa himself, in despair at being held captive by these bandits and evidently expecting the worst, while the female figure was the mistress or wife of the leader of the bandits, who was momentarily absent. Lady Morgan reads a poignant drama into this scene: the woman is intervening to save the young captive: "Elle plaide avec adresse pour la vie du jeune homme, en faisant remarquer avec un dédain affecté sa faiblesse et son peu d'importance; mais on voit qu'elle commande en même temps qu'elle cherche à persuader. . . . Le prisonnier sera sauvé; car jamais une cause sur laquelle une femme porte la toute-puissance de sa sensibilité n'a été perdue" (I, 91–92).

Though essentially fiction—a fiction, in fact, derived from another fiction (Lady Morgan's story of Rosa and the sympathetic bandit's wife), Nouville's story is grounded as well in the more solid parts of Lady Morgan's. But, since his tale catches Rosa at a fairly early moment, fact and fiction are blended. It is Lady Morgan's account of the childhood and adolescence of Rosa that is nearest to fiction; she may have simply incorporated into her biography parts of the novel she had originally intended to write. However, when Nouville reaches the central narrative, he launches into fiction pure and simple, creating a biography for the young woman—he calls her Imola Falcone—who will ultimately effect Rosa's escape. Nouville here creates, in fact, an interesting and sympathetic character. It is Imola who first discovers the young artist painting in the wilds of the Abruzzi, of which Nouville offers a long, vivid description: "Volcans éteints, villes détruites, ruines fantastiques," etc. (p. 142). She is rather the worse for wear, and her clothing and person show signs of violence and stress; moreover, the author sees her as a rather virile figure. But she has an artistic temperament, is impressed by the landscape Rosa is painting, and sees in him the romantic artist, a doomed genius: "la gloire t'a baisé au front; j'ai entendu dire autrefois par un poète que ce baiser-là doit être tôt ou tard payé fort cher. Jeunesse, bonne mine et du talent! . . . C'est dommage" (p. 143). When some of the brigands emerge from the rocks, she protects the handsome young painter from these trigger-happy outlaws. While waiting for Imola's husband, head of the band, to return and decide his fate, Rosa becomes friendly with two of the bandits, Giuseppe and Coviello, and learns that they are not only Robin Hoods, as we would expect: the former was once an artist, a student of Caravaggio, compelled to flee into the wilderness and join the bandits after having killed a young German painter; the latter, a "Musicien distingué, excellent professeur de luth" (p. 146), had fallen in love with one of his female students, a young aristocrat, and, having dared to declare his love, was dismissed and so forced, like Giuseppe, into a life of banditry. When Guido Falcone returns, he is disgusted to learn that the prisoner is a young artist: "—Un enfant! s'écria Guido Falcone; un artiste! un musicien! un peintre! nous avions bien besoin de cela!" (p. 147). Nouville is at his most effective in his handling of the triangle that has developed. Rosa becomes aware that Imola, in looking kindly upon him, is somewhat alienated from her husband: her marriage is strained because Guido, who had once rescued her from the lecherous viceroy whose *sbires* had abducted her, now totally absorbed in his conspiracies against the rulers of Naples, neglects his wife. Imola, feeling trapped in her life with Guido and struck by Rosa's love of freedom, tells him how to escape. At the emotional climax of the story, the young artist plants a burning kiss on her hand.

Nouville's tale is the most elaborate fiction derived from Lady Morgan's founding legend about Rosa and the bandits. It grows out of a fanciful passage in her book but turns the mere outline of a narrative into an effective story with believable characters—even Rosa, the hero, shown as less than heroic, when he first encounters the brigands; and Imola is truly interesting and complex: fundamentally loyal to her husband and the way of life into which he and the other bandits have been forced, she has fond memories of a happy, carefree girlhood amid the beauties of the bay of Naples, and, drawn to the brave, young artist who symbolizes freedom, she makes possible his escape. Her husband Guido is a standard "noble bandit" of Byronic mien: "Sur son visage intelligent outre la révélation mélancolique d'un esprit au-dessus du vulgaire aux prises avec des remords énergiques et turbulens, outre les restes fatigués d'une beauté virile dont Salvator lui-même a reproduit depuis et plusieurs fois le type grandiose et abrupte, on pouvait remarquer une extraordinaire expression de méfiance et d'anxiété" (p. 146). The two minor figures, Giuseppe and Coviello, though only broadly drawn, are both sympathetic and amusing, a sort of Don Quixote and Sancho Panza pair. Thus the world of brigands as created by Nouville is one in which Rosa is neither the only artist nor the only sympathetic character.

Since the events of Nouville's tale all take place while Rosa is still young, poor, and unknown, there can be no question of his involvement with Masaniello; the omniscient narrator refrains from referring to the episode. But, through Guido's conflict with the Spanish oppressors—first as rescuer of Imola and then as a participant in a recent plot which the Spaniards had suppressed "avec une cruauté proverbiale" (p. 146)—we get a foretaste of Masaniello's revolution. Guido's expected fate foreshadows that of the fisherman: "le jeune chef semblait comme entrevoir de loin les tortures affreuses qui l'attendaient dans le *carcere duro*" (ibid.).

There are two other fictions in which Rosa plays a role, but one not so closely modeled on Lady Morgan's original. Both are, like most of the texts we have been examining, by writers virtually forgotten to literary history. Joseph Méry's novel *L'Ame transmise*[36] is a rather implausible story set in Naples and Rome in the mid-seventeenth century. The action begins on May 10, 1646, and ends about twenty years later. In the earlier parts of the story, Rosa appears simply as the painter of the bridal portrait of a beautiful young woman. This picture resembles nothing ever painted by Rosa: "Ce n'était ni une belle femme, ni une jolie femme que son pinceau avait reproduite, c'était l'idéalisation de l'Ange, avec les formes de la vierge; une de ces figures qui ne rappellent aucun besoin, aucune infirmité, aucune misère de notre triste nature" (p. 68). Later, when the action of the plot moves to Rome, Raphael's *Transfiguration*—on which the narrator dilates for several lines—plays a small role in the story: the young protagonist, Léontio, enters San Pietro in Montorio and finds some inner peace as he contrasts the crazed boy in the foreground and "cette resplendissante atmosphère où flottent les élus du Seigneur, . . . ce nuage céleste et limpide" (p. 78). Minutes later he encounters a stranger sitting beneath the Acqua Paola. Magnificently dressed, his fingers bedecked with rubies and emeralds, he carries a sword with a vermeil sheath. As for the man himself: "Sa tête était plus remarquable que son costume de prince. Il y avait des muscles sur son visage pour tout exprimer; ses yeux flamboyaient de génie; ses lèvres avaient la contraction dédaigneuse de l'ironie perpétuelle; sa couronne de cheveux noirs donnait à sa physionomie un caractère sombre et menaçant" (ibid.). It is not necessary to cite Lady Morgan—the view of Rosa as misanthropic and melancholy was a familiar one. As for the rich costume, Pascoli had put in circulation an anecdote about Rosa that harmonizes with Méry's picture, and Lady Morgan (I, 300–01) had passed the story along (Dumas, we have seen, was also familiar with it—and there is every reason to believe that he drew directly on Lady Morgan and not on her source). The young man falls into conversation with the richly dressed man and discovers that it is Salvator Rosa to whom he is talking—the very person he wanted to see. For his part, Rosa is struck by the young man's face: it looks familiar; moreover, it interests him because it is "sérieux comme Satan" (p. 79). He quickly makes a sketch of Léontio's face and shows it to him: "Voilà ta tête, je vais la prêter à mon spectre de Samuel évoqué par la pythonisse d'Endor. Mon tableau représente le moment où tu sors du tombeau" (ibid.).

Rosa reappears at the dénouement, and we learn that he has played a *deus ex machina* role in the complicated plot, which is something of a detective story. In the final explanation, Rosa briefly mentions his life among the bandits in the Abruzzi. The Masaniello legend is evoked early on, but not with reference to Rosa (p. 72). Méry's novel or novella offers, then, only faint reflections of both the real Rosa and the one depicted by Lady Morgan. It is curious to see the author, on the one hand, inventing a totally imaginary and un-Rosa-like female portrait, and, on the other, referring to a very real picture, one that could be seen in the Louvre.[37]

Our last Rosa narrative is "Romuléo," which Charles Didier (1805–1864) included in the collection *Les Amours d'Italie*.[38] Set in Rome in modern times, Didier's story centers on an impecunious and unsuccessful painter who adores Rosa, especially his landscapes, and is apparently unaware that Rosa himself preferred other genres: "Il adorait les sites sauvages qu'il a peints de préférence à tous les autres, ses arbres tourmentés, ses ciels orageux, ses rochers abruptes, et jusqu'aux brigands qu'il a placés dans ses paysages, où ils sont si bien à leur place" (p. 484). Romuléo knows Rosa's satires by heart and recites long passages to the narrator and his friends with great vehemence. But, most of all, he admires Rosa for his life and specifically for having joined the bandits who arrested him in the mountains: "Romuléo appelait cela entendre la vie, et il soutenait que de notre temps, encore plus que de celui du grand artiste, la seule existence digne d'un homme indépendant était celle qu'il avait adoptée" (p. 415). The narrator concludes that, if there is such a thing as transmigration of souls, "Romuléo n'était autre que Salvator Rosa lui-même, revivant sous une autre forme et sous un autre nom" (ibid.). Romuléo even lives in an attic in what was once Rosa's house, at no. 33, Via Gregoriana. His paintings reveal a certain talent, but he follows too closely in Rosa's footsteps: "Lui aussi peignait des sites formidables, des natures tourmentées, le tout émaillé de bandits. Un de ses premiers tableaux, son premier peut-être, avait été naturellement Salvator Rosa arrêté par les brigands et s'enrégimentant dans la bande" (p. 486).

Essentially lazy, Romuléo, when he does occasionally paint, "reproduisait toujours la même pensée, un site sauvage et une scène de brigands" (p. 488). If he lacks Rosa's energy and his restless quest for original subjects, he shares his idol's antagonism toward the artistic establishment, e.g., the neoclassical Camuccini (David's Italian counterpart, so to speak), the academies, and in particular the Académie de France and the Academy of Saint Luke—Rosa, it will be recalled, waged a running war with the latter. Didier's portrait of Romuléo suggests a certain physical and temperamental resemblance with Rosa: "tout en lui accusait la force et l'agilité, mais il avait une mauvaise figure" (p. 487). He had thick sideburns and black eyes. When he was excited, his face took on a fierce expression. He seems to incarnate the Rosa of the *Satire,* the antagonist of Bernini, the painter of *La Fortuna,* though Didier does not draw these parallels. Didier goes well beyond modeling his Romuléo on Rosa by telling us that, as a child, Romuléo was said to have killed a younger brother with a hammer.

The heart of Didier's story lies precisely in his protagonist's imitation of what he imagines to have been Rosa's life. In secret, Romuléo is the head of a band of brigands, the Comitive du Dictateur, Romuléo himself being the dictator. Romuléo's band kidnaps the beautiful marquise Orséolo, known as "la belle Settimia," and the leader forces her to marry him—unlike Rosa, Romuléo seems to have been the marrying kind. The interaction of art and life is made evident in Romuléo's words to his beautiful captive:

> Ma première admiration fut Marco Sciarra [a legendary sixteenth-century bandit]; la seconde et celle de toute ma vie Salvator Rosa qui cumule la double gloire de l'artiste et de l'homme libre; car vous n'ignorez pas que lui aussi a fait dans son temps la libre vie des montagnes. Ce sont là j'espère des autorités. . . . Frustré de mon vivant par l'envie de l'une des deux gloires de Salvator Rosa [his success as a painter], je me suis rabattu sur la seconde, et celle-là je m'en flatte ne me fera pas défaut. (pp. 539–40)

Justifying his life, he foreshadows the Harry Lime of *The Third Man:* "Les cavernes des véritables brigands ne sont pas dans les montagnes, elles sont au milieu du monde, ou plutôt le monde n'est qu'un immense coupe-gorge" (p. 450).

The conclusion of Didier's story takes a turn away from the theme of Romuléo's emulation of Rosa's imagined life: the marriage is a happy one; Romuléo and the marquise return to Rome, and the couple is accepted by society. Romuléo settles into a conventional life: "Quoiqu'il ait gardé un faible pour Salvator Rosa, il n'en parle presque plus et répète, de peur de se compromettre et pour dire comme tout le monde, les lieux communs qui ont cours à Rome sur les tableaux consacrés" (p. 553). At story's end, Romuléo has become a member of the Academy of St. Luke.

Set in the nineteenth century, Didier's story, understandably, does not refer to the Masaniello-Rosa legend. Otherwise, this amusing novella is in the mainstream of the tradition left to French writers by Lady Morgan. But the story's denouement suggests a certain decadence of the tradition: by giving up his secret life in the mountains and his brigand ways, Romuléo ultimately deflates the legend. His adaptation to the real world reminds us of the way in which the anticlerical Homais of *Madame Bovary* compromises his principals, learns to live with the village *curé,* and is awarded the Legion of Honor at the end of Flaubert's novel (published just a few years earlier than "Romuléo"). The steam is being let out of the mythic Rosa bequeathed by Lady Morgan.

This realistic trend did not, apparently, envelop the versions of Rosa that appeared on the French stage in roughly the same period. Indeed, Rosa's *entrée en scène* had to wait until 1851.[39] The two operas presented in the late Restoration on the theme of Masaniello—Carafa's *Masaniello ou le pêcheur napolitain* (1827) and Auber's immensely successful *La Muette de Portici* (1828)—omit Rosa from the cast of characters.[40] The team of Charles Desnoyer and Gustave Albitte endeavored to repair this oversight in *Salvator Rosa, vaudeville en deux actes,* which premiered at the Ambigu-Comique on December 29, 1836. This play was, apparently, never published, which suggests that its production history was brief and inglorious.

Matters were quite different with Ferdinand Dugué's *Salvator Rosa, drame en cinq actes et sept tableaux,*[41] first presented at the important Théâtre de la Porte-Saint-Martin on July 19, 1851. It was a rather elaborate production, directed by Hippolyte Coignard and with music by Adolphe Vaillard, sets by Devoir, and costumes by Alfred Albert. The role of Masaniello was taken by Philibert Rouvière, an actor who impressed Baudelaire enough that he wrote two articles about him.[42] Salvator Rosa was played by Étienne-Marin Mélingue (1808–1875), a very popular actor who was especially successful in playing characters from Dumas, e.g., Dantès and D'Artagnan.[43]

The large cast of characters and the complications of the plot make for a play difficult to summarize. The focus here will be on the ways in which Dugué's Rosa conforms, or does not conform, to the model put in circulation by Lady Morgan, and on Dugué's treatment of the Masaniello legend and of history in general. First, there is the love triangle the playwright invents to supply the always-needed love interest. He imagines that the two (imaginary) sisters of Masaniello are both in love with Salvator Rosa; one of the sisters has been a successful actress in France under the stage name of Lucrezia (Rosa's long-time mistress, whom he notoriously married when he was at death's door, was named Lucrezia). Equally invented is the presence of Masaniello in Rome during two of the play's tableaux. There is a *Compagnie de la Mort* in Dugué's *drame*, but it is headed by a rogue nobleman, le Comte Coppola; the brigands have another band, led by one Pietromala. Ribera is given a rather large role in the action—he is held hostage at one point during the uprising in Naples. Dugué presents Ribera as leader of an oppressive pro-Spanish group of his disciples; of the three named, only Micco Spadero (Domenico Gargiulo [1612–1679]) can be certainly identified. In actuality Spadero was a fellow student of Aniello Falcone along with Rosa, not a pupil of Ribera. In Dugué, Ribera and Bernini are seen together in Rome, hatching evil against Rosa. At one point, Ribera offers the young painter his protection and is proudly rejected. Yet the two artists are not shown simply as bitter enemies: Ribera expresses his admiration for Rosa's achievement ("le sublime dans l'horrible" [p. 20]) and singles out as an example Rosa's *Ixion sur la roue*, a picture listed neither by Lady Morgan nor by the best modern catalogue of Rosa's work. Toward the end of the play, Rosa intervenes to rescue Ribera from an angry Neapolitan mob and arranges for him to return to Spain unharmed.

Since Rosa is the protagonist, it is understandable that Dugué expands Rosa's role in the Masaniello episode beyond Lady Morgan, who merely tells us that Rosa, on arriving in Naples, enlisted in the *Compagnia della morte*, "dont il devint l'un des membres les plus distingués" (I, 302). But Dugué's Rosa is a rather irenic figure who not only saves Ribera's life but goes about Naples during the uprising, sparing as many persons from revolutionary violence as he can. Ultimately, after Masaniello's death, Rosa feels remorse over his involvement in the revolt and addresses an angry speech to the mob: "L'artiste était devenu soldat, l'amour de mon pays m'avait fait oublier tout le reste, je m'étais battu comme un lion pour votre indépendance, mais vous n'êtes que des meurtriers, et vous me faites horreur!" (p. 94). He kills Pietromala, entrusts the two sisters who had been rivals for his love to Falcone, with whom they sail away, and, dauntless, remains behind in Naples to defend liberty to the death. As Rosa turns to go to Masaniello's funeral, the crowd shouts: "Vive Salvator!" (p. 95). One wonders if all of the audience understood that the Rosa of history survived to become the painter we know.

Still, Dugué's Rosa clearly is derived from Lady Morgan's biography. The two fundamental legends bulk large in his dramatization. Having experienced a *giro* (apparently five years long!) that closely resembles the one traced by Lady Morgan (I, 76–82), he knew the joy of freedom and learned to love wild nature: "pendant qu'une magnifique tempête déracinait les arbres, j'ai dessiné un Démocrite insultant à la vanité humaine au milieu des tombeaux en ruines!" (p. 9). A significant part of the play's action takes place against just such a backdrop: the stage directions for the third tableau specify: "Une gorge de montagnes dans les Abruzzes. Chaos de rochers. Torrent au fond" (p. 35). On the way to Rome, Rosa arrives in this rugged place and is so smitten by the scenery that he is tempted to stop and sketch the scene before him: "C'est très-sauvage, très-pittoresque, mais il y aurait besoin d'une figure humaine pour animer cette solitude.[44] (Il s'assied sur un bloc.) Par exemple, il faudrait là, sur cette roche, un pâtre, un bandit, n'importe?" (p. 37). Here Dugué achieves a quite amusing touch. As if in answer to Rosa's wishes, Pietromala begins to emerge from the rocks and creep up on the preoccupied artist, who, spotting Pietromala, shouts at him: "Ne bougez pas!" (p. 37). Some of the brigands are intrigued by Rosa's creativity. Coppola and his *Compagnie de la Mort*—also referred to as *Partisans Napolitains*—arrive on the scene as well, intending to kill Rosa; the artist has to deal with two bands of outlaws, whereas for Lady Morgan one had been enough. Though later seen as a bloodthirsty gang, here Pietromala's brigands momentarily appear sympathetic. Their leader proclaims that he and his followers are the equals of their noble allies: "vous n'êtes, dans nos montagnes, que des Bohémiens comme nous" (p. 41). When Pietromala, in turn, prepares to kill his captive, two of the band, impressed by his talents as artist and musician, try to have his life spared; one of them, ordered to shoot Rosa, manages to miss (in the event, it is Hermosa, arriving with a message from Masaniello, who saves the artist's life).

As we have seen, in his handling of the other major myth popularized by Lady Morgan, Dugué greatly develops her sketchy treatment of his role in the Masaniello revolt. For her, Rosa had been simply one of the "most distinguished" members of Falcone's *Compagnia*—how he distinguished himself we are not told. Rosa reappeared in her narrative after the death of Masaniello (II, 2–3), when he and Falcone felt obliged to flee Naples. Dugué tells us—without staging the acts in question—that Rosa and Falcone have been serving as guardian angels to those whose lives are in danger from the rebels. The playwright manages to bring Ribera and his followers back into the drama;

they are in the hands of the revolutionaries, and even Masaniello seeks to punish them. Rosa eventually manages to spare their lives and to send Ribera back to Spain. Later, as the people turn against Masaniello, Rosa makes plans to protect him from the fickle Neapolitans. (It is while Rosa is off stage that Masaniello dies at the hands of the mob—in the wings.) Now disgusted by the excesses of the very revolution he had helped to lead, Rosa denounces the rebels as murderers, kills Pietromala when attacked by him, produces evidence that the brigand chief had been in the pay of the Spaniards, and, after seeing that Masaniello's two sisters are safe, remains to fight on for liberty. The end of the play offers Rosa as a virtual apotheosis of the sublime, peace-loving artist, acclaimed by the crowd. For the moment, Rosa is virtually the uncrowned king of Naples, unfazed by the death of his predecessor, Masaniello.

If Dugué, in shifting the spotlight from Masaniello—the usual hero of stories, poems, and plays about the 1647 rebellion—has greatly enlarged Rosa's part in these events, there are other elements in his play that show him as dependent on Lady Morgan. Rosa's rivalries with Ribera and Bernini, the rather sinister presentation of Ribera, Rosa's proud independence from protectors, and his famous participation as Coviello in the Roman carnival are all derived from Lady Morgan's biography. Her frequently expressed hostility to the Inquisition is probably reflected in the scene in which Ribera tries to turn Rosa into a protégé. The plucky young artist not only rejects the great man's patronage but dares to attack Ribera's work: "Vos toiles sentent l'inquisition, l'Espagnol chez vous passe avant l'artiste" (p. 20).

Dugué's play was given a lavish production, and starred several of the most popular actors of the time. As we shall see in the next chapter, it was reviewed favorably and at length by Théophile Gautier. It was successful enough to be taken on tour in the provinces. The *Journal d'Alençon* of March 7, 1852, announced a performance of the play for that day—a tiny piece of evidence, perhaps, but suggestive. According to the catalogue of the Bibliothèque Nationale, the play was revived in 1856, presumably in Paris. That Dugué's *drame* found an echo in Baudelaire adds another dimension to the history of the play. Although he does not highlight Rouvière's performance as Masaniello—and does not mention it at all in his obituary article—Baudelaire remembered it. He admired Rouvière enought to write two brief articles about him, the only actor to be so honored. (Perhaps the fact that Rouvière was something of a painter influenced him.) What, then, are we to think of the claim advanced by Philippe Berthelot in 1901 in an article on Louis Ménard? Apropos of Baudelaire's scathing criticism of Ménard's *Prométhée délivré* (1843–1844), he writes: "Ménard ne lui rendit pas la pareille quand Baudelaire vint lui lire son drame *Masaniello* qui n'a jamais paru."[45] Given the absence of any other evidence of the existence of a drama by Baudelaire about Masaniello, I am inclined to think that Berthelot is referring to *Manoël,* the incomplete play Ernest Prarond developed from the text entitled *Idéolus,* which he and Baudelaire wrote in collaboration. Since Ménard and Baudelaire cannot have been on good terms after the appearance of the latter's hostile review of *Prométhée délivré* (*Le Corsaire-Satan,* February 3, 1846), it seems unlikely that, even if he had written a play about Masaniello, Baudelaire would have gone to see Ménard and have read his play to him. As for Salvator Rosa, we have no way of knowing how Baudelaire, if he had written a *Masaniello,* would have treated Rosa or even *if* he would have included a part for Rosa in his play.

The rest of Salvator Rosa's place in the history of French drama is quickly told. The *drame en cinq actes* by one Chardon, given at the Théâtre de Belleville in 1852, was apparently never published. The same can be said for the opera *Salvator Rosa,* with words by Edouard Plouvier and a certain Bergeron—the catalogue of the Bibliothèque Nationale does not list a *Salvator Rosa* among Plouvier's works, and *The New Grove* has no reference to any composer named Bergeron. As for the three-act *opéra comique Salvator Rosa,*[46] first performed at the Opéra-Comique April 30, 1861, with words by Eugène Grangé and Henri Trianon and music by one Duprato, little needs to be said. Supposedly set in Rome around 1640, the play is essentially a love story. The authors of the libretto apparently knew little more than that Rosa was a painter of unconventional life and that he once used the pseudonym Formica. At the end the artist yields his beloved to the man she really loves, announces, "Oui, je reprends ma vie nomade, ma vie d'artiste et de bohème!" (p. 61), and disdains glory and love: "fumée que tout cela!" (p. 62). The final chorus hails the hero—"Vive Salvator"—and sings:

> Quittant sans cesse
> Ville et maîtresse,
> Libre et content,
> Sans lourd bagage,
> Dans son voyage,
> On va chantant:
> Tra la la la la la !
> Quel sort vaut celui-là! (Ibid.)

A happy ending for the play but a rather sad conclusion to the history of Rosa as a character in French drama.[47]

Finally, Rosa became the subject of French painting in the romantic era.

As Patricia Condon writes: "Immensely popular from the thirties into the forties and fifties were subjects derived from the biographies of famous persons, especially scenes from the lives of artists."[48] Earlier, Francis Haskell traced this genre or theme into the last quarter of the eighteenth century,[49] citing John Hamilton Mortimer, "the English Rosa" (p. 57); for the nineteenth century, he mentions Adrien Guignet's *Salvator Rosa chez les brigands* (p. 72), discussed below. Rosa's life provided matter for at least one painting of this sort during the Restoration: Victor Hugo, reviewing an exposition of painting mounted in the cause of the Greeks in 1826, mentions— and praises highly—"deux très petits tableaux" by Louis Boulanger, one of which was a *Salvator Rosa pris par les brigands*. The theme and the date of this picture suggest that the artist knew, directly or indirectly, Lady Morgan's biography, published just two years earlier. Unfortunately, this picture seems to have disappeared: Aristide Marie's study of Boulanger, written a century after Hugo's review, mentions no such picture.[50] But, even though standard reference works, e.g., Thieme and Becker (XXXIV, 446) and *La Grande Encyclopédie* (VII, 659), state that Boulanger made his debut at the Salon of 1827, it is easier to believe that a painting about Rosa has been lost than to believe that in 1826 Hugo invented or imagined such a painting. In any case, Boulanger produced a *Mort de Salvator Rosa* or *Derniers Moments de Salvator Rosa,* known through a lithograph published in *L'Artiste* in 1844.[51] Lady Morgan's account of Rosa's death (II, 154–65) could easily have inspired Boulanger. Deathbed scenes of this sort were a subdivision of the genre we are discussing; Ingres's picture of the death of Leonardo "in the arms of François Ier" is perhaps the best-known example.[52]

Also in 1844, Adrien Guignet (1816–1854), the French painter of this period closest to Rosa in spirit,[53] produced *Salvator Rosa chez les brigands,* published in etched form in *L'Artiste* and now lost.[54] The history of Rosa as a subject in French painting ends, I believe, with another representation of Rosa among the brigands (*Salon de 1867,* no. 98) by the obscure Jean-Joseph Bellel (1816–1898). The Salon *livret* provides the following commentary: "Résolu de faire son *giro,* c'est-à-dire une tournée d'apprentissage, il s'enfonça dans le pays des Abbruzzes [*sic*], contrée montagneuse et sauvage, où il rencontra des figures étranges faites tout exprès pour animer un tel paysage."[55]

Scholars, critics, and biographers have offered other suggestions as to Rosa's influence on French painters of this period, but the *rapprochements* do not reflect Lady Morgan's legends about Rosa. Such is the case with Anna Klumpke's quotation of Rosa Bonheur's own words about her copies made from "les dessins de Salvator Rosa"[56] and Loÿs Delteil's account of how Charles

Meryon conceived a passion for etching and made copies "d'après les estampes de . . . Salvator Rosa" and others.[57] While Albert Boime, likewise, in his massive study of Couture, presents considerable detailed evidence of this artist's admiration for Rosa—the artist, the man, and the poet—and of the influences he absorbed from him, he does not refer to Lady Morgan or evoke directly her image of Rosa.[58]

The popularity impressionism eventually enjoyed should not blind us to the possibility that, long after the 1860s, genre scenes showing Rosa among the brigands or on his death-bed occasionally appeared among the large body of academic pictures that continued to appear in France for many more decades. There may even have been Rosaesque landscapes long after the Barbizon painters, Corot, and the impressionists transformed landscape painting. In painting as in literature, Lady Morgan's legacy may not have produced a single masterpiece during the decades leading up to this epoch-making development, but French romanticism's "imaginary museum"—if we take the expression to encompass all the images of Rosa, whether in poetry, fiction, drama, or the visual arts—did find a place for Rosa, symbolic of another revolution and another view of nature.

CHAPTER FIVE

Rosa and the Major Romantics

Lady Morgan's French romantic heirs were, for the most part, lesser noncanonical figures; except for Dumas, none of the major romantics devoted an entire, independent work to Rosa as presented in her book. Stendhal, as we have seen, was well aware of Rosa, but his references to Rosa mostly predate the publication of Lady Morgan's biography, and none of them reflect the legends about the artist that she was largely responsible for putting into circulation. In the crucial year of 1824—crucial to Rosa's "fortune" and crucial, too, in the history of the French romantic movement—Stendhal, reviewing that year's Salon, relegates Rosa to the classical past: "Ce qui est classique, c'est une bataille de Salvator Rosa."[1]

Lamartine shared with Dumas and Stendhal a rich experience of Italy, including long stays in Florence and Naples; the latter city and its bay, moreover, are the subject or the setting of a number of his poems and of the Graziella episode of *Les Confidences* (1849). But Lamartine was not nearly as drawn to the visual arts as either of these other two writers, especially Stendhal. He wrote only one piece of art criticism, and that rather late in life (1858–1859), an article on Léopold Robert's *Les Moissonneurs*, published in the *Cours familier de littérature* (*Entretiens* XXXVI and XXXVII); in it, he confessed: "S'il s'agissait de moi personnellement, j'avouerais que je préfère la musique à la peinture, sans doute parce que la nature m'aura doué d'une oreille plus sensible que le regard."[2] As C. W. Thompson observes: "A Florence il ne paraît pas s'être intéressé à la peinture entre 1825 et 1828, même s'il acheta quelques tableaux avant de rentrer en France" (ibid.). Still, the visual arts were by no means a closed book to Lamartine: he had personal contacts with a number of painters, including Chassériau, Couture, Huet, and Delaroche (ibid.); he had a definite set of preferred artists—Léopold

Robert, Ary Scheffer, Decaisne, Gudin, Gérard (ibid.); in 1828 or 1829, he bought some engravings of paintings by John Martin (p. 5). In 1811, on his way to Naples, according to *Les Confidences,* he lived for a time in Rosa's neighborhood in Rome, boarding with a painter.[3] On another occasion, in the Eternal City he met Lady Morgan's friend, the Duchess of Devonshire.

However, Lamartine seems not to have discovered Rosa as part of his encounter with Italian culture and the Italian landscape. There are no references to Rosa in *Graziella* or in the poems with Neapolitan themes and settings. Lamartine produced no *transpositions d'art* in the manner of Théophile Gautier.[4] But, still steeped in neoclassical aesthetics and familiar with the current of descriptive nature poetry that arose in the eighteenth century, Lamartine does present us with landscapes that may be seen as Rosas in literary form.

In "L'Isolement," the opening poem of *Méditations poétiques* (1820), a volume rather quickly accepted as the cornerstone of romantic poetry in France, the poet paints a twilight landscape suggestive of Rosa: "Ici, gronde le fleuve aux vagues écumantes. . . . ces monts couronnés de bois sombres."[5] This may be a somewhat softened version of Rosa—the poet himself calls the scene "ces doux tableaux"—but the very next poem in the volume, "L'Homme," addressed to the modern poet whom Lady Morgan recognized as a spiritual brother of Rosa, "ce Biron [*sic*] de la peinture,"[6] has the wildness of a Rosa landscape:

> Qui que tu sois, Byron, bon ou fatal génie,
> J'aime de tes concerts la sauvage harmonie
> Comme j'aime le bruit de la foudre et des vents
> Se mêlant dans l'orage à la voix des torrents!
> La nuit est ton séjour, l'horreur est ton domaine:
> L'aigle, roi des déserts, dédaigne ainsi la plaine;
> Il ne veut, comme toi, que des rocs escarpés
> Que l'hiver a blanchis, que la foudre a frappés;
> Des rivages couverts des débris du naufrage.
> . . . .
> Lui, des sommets d'Athos franchit l'horrible cime,
> Suspend aux flancs des monts son aire sur l'abîme,
> Et là, seul, entouré de membres palpitants,
> De rochers d'un sang noir sans cesse dégouttants,
> Trouvant sa volupté dans les cris de sa proie,
> Bercé par la tempête, il s'endort dans sa joie.
> . . . .
> Sur ces sommets noircis par d'éternels nuages,
> Sur ces flots sillonnés par d'éternels orages. (pp. 4–5, 7)

Even the mellifluous "Le Lac" contains its glimpses or "echoes" of Rosa-like landscape:

> Tu mugissais ainsi sous ces roches profondes,
> Ainsi tu te brisais sur leur flancs déchirés,
> . . . sombres abîmes.
> . . . .
> O lac! rochers muets! grottes! forêt obscure
> . . . tes orages
> . . . ces noirs sapins . . . ces rocs sauvages
> Qui pendent sur tes eaux. (pp. 38–39)

Another extended example of Rosaesque landscapes can be found in "La Solitude" (*Nouvelles Méditations poétiques* [1823]), whose lonely protagonist

> . . . aime à contempler ses [God's] plus hardis ouvrages,
> Ces monts, vainqueurs des vents, de la foudre et des âges,
> Il s'élance . . .
> Et porté par degrés jusqu'à ses sombres flancs,
> Sous ses pins immortels il s'enfonce à pas lents:
> Là, des torrents séchés le lit seul est sa route,
> Tantôt des rocs minés sur lui pendent en voûte,
> Et tantôt, sur leurs bords tout à coup suspendu,
> Il recule étonné; son regard éperdu
> Jouit avec horreur de cet effroi sublime,
> Et sous ses pieds, longtemps, voit tournoyer l'abîme!
> . . . .
> Le nuage, en grondant, parcourt en vain vos cimes,
> Le fleuve en vain grossi sillonne vos abîmes,
> La foudre frappe en vain votre front endurci;
> Votre front solennel, un moment obscurci,
> . . . .
> Et ces ruisseaux pleuvant de ces rocs suspendus,
> Et ces torrents grondant dans les granits fendus,
> Et ces pics où le temps a perdu sa victoire . . . (pp. 135–36, 138)

Stanzas XXIII and XXV of *Le Dernier Chant du pèlerinage d'Harold* offer Rosaesque elements: "ce rocher . . . creusé par les mers," "sommet chauve et sombre," "un tertre vert sur un pic suspendu," "L'Erymanthe . . . par un torrent fendu," "un gouffre vaste et sombre," "Des troncs déracinés en hérissaient les flancs," "gouffre sans repos," "abîme qui fume," "bords déchirés," "noir précipice," etc. (pp. 218, 222). The "paysage" of "La Chute du Rhin à Laüffen" (1830) exploits a similar vein. The sight of the falls of the

Rhine and perhaps even more the deafening roar of the furious waters—the whole spectacle encapsulated in the phrase "cette horreur sublime"—draw from the awe-struck poet "un cri de surprise et d'effroi" (p. 495), and inspires a vivid description replete with towering rocks, rushing waters, clouds of foam, and sound effects to match. The words "abîme," "gouffre," "rocher," "roc," "torrents," "flots," and "bords" catch the visual elements in the scene.

The Alpine scenery of *Jocelyn* (1836), not unexpectedly, provides similar passages, which it would be redundant to quote after what we have already seen in earlier works. Naturally, the snow, the "brouillard glacé," the "frimas glacés qui blanchissent ma tête" (p. 592), and other wintry details evoke images several removes from Rosa's more southerly climes, but some of the visual effects overlap: "les torrents / Hurlent d'horreur aux bords des gouffres dévorants, / Précipités du ciel sur le rocher qui fume," "les troncs des sapins," etc. (ibid.). The hero's first climb to the Grotte des Aigles (pp. 603–04, 605), the views he has there over the surrounding mountains (p. 607) and the grotto itself (pp. 608–09) give the poet many opportunities to call up a number of the motifs we have already isolated: "abîme," "horreur," "gouffre," "roc," "rochers," "cimes," "voûte," "pics glacés," "blocs," "quartiers," even if he sometimes grants his hero contact with more beneficent aspects of Alpine nature. The opening "Récit" of *La Chute d'un ange* (1838) casts the mountainous coast of Lebanon in similar terms: "Ces écueils mugissants," "Ces grands blocs dentelés, / Coups de hache au rocher qui montre ses blessures," "noirs ravins," "Le lit sec d'un torrent que le soleil calcine" (pp. 805–07)—at least this last detail, along with certain others, shows that, even if the landscape is adorned with the famous cedars of Lebanon, there are no verdant Alpine meadows here.[7]

That Rosa's presence can be suggested even if his name does not actually appear in such passages finds justification from several sources. In a passage in *Jocelyn* the diarist tells us that it was Ossian's poetry that drove him out into the wild, misty landscape:

Ossian! Ossian! lorsque plus jeune encore
Je rêvais des brouillards et des monts d'Inistore;
Quand, tes vers dans le cœur et ta harpe à la main,
Je m'enfonçais l'hiver dans des bois sans chemin,
Que j'écoutais siffler dans la bruyère grise,
Comme l'âme des morts, le souffle de la bise,
Que mes cheveux fouettaient mon front, que les torrents
Hurlant d'horreur aux bords des gouffrés dévorants
Précipités du ciel sur le rocher qui fume,
Jetaient jusqu'à mon front leurs cris et leur écume

Quand les troncs des sapins tremblaient comme un roseau
Et secouaient leur neige où planait le corbeau,
Et qu'un brouillard glacé, rasant ses pics sauvages,
Comme un fils de Morven me vêtissait d'orages. (p. 592)

In *Les Confidences,* Lamartine recreates what he calls "le moment d'Ossian" (*OC,* XXIX, 120) and the deep impression the poems of "ce Dante surnaturel" made on him as he lived at Milly, with its "gorges sauvages du Bugly," its "montagnes," "torrents," "cascades," and "ruines sous les rochers" (p. 116). A large part of the charm exerted by the Celtic bard stemmed from the landscapes he painted: "Ossian, ses sites et ses images correspondaient merveilleusement aussi à la nature des montagnes presque écossaises, à la saison de l'année et à la mélancolie des sites où je le lisais" (pp. 120–21). Further details, again, paint a somewhat more northerly scene than what we see in typical Rosa landscapes, but the long passage contains one of Lamartine's few direct references to the Italian: "Des érudits curieux ont prétendu et prétendent encore qu'il [Ossian] n'a jamais existé ni écrit, que ses poèmes sont une supercherie de Macpherson. J'aimerais autant dire que Salvator Rosa a inventé la nature!" (p. 121). Thus Lamartine associates in a revealing reminiscence Ossian, the landscapes he saw around him in youth, and Salvator Rosa, who here personifies for him the very idea of landscape painting.

In June 1838, some years before *Les Confidences,* Lamartine inscribed in the album kept by Hugo's young daughter Léopoldine a rather long poem which evokes Rosa in its second line:

Didine! si j'étais peintre, artiste, graveur,
    Salvator ou Carrache,
Si je savais tenir, moi poète rêveur
    Dont la plume s'arrache,

Le burin, le crayon, le pinceau; dans l'instant,
    De cette page blanche,
Je vous ferais un cadre, un tableau palpitant,
    Une divine planche.[8]

The picture imagined in the following stanzas is not suggestive of Rosa, except for the mysterious bird, "dans l'ombre, attentif et debout / Sur son roc solitaire..." (p. 43). Georgel finds the poet's allusions to Rosa and "Carrache" hard to explain: "Il semble bien que ces noms soient venus un peu au hasard sous sa plume" (p. 44). Still, given the relative scarcity of references to specific artists in Lamartine's work, this evocation of Rosa stands out. And it suggests that Lamartine, even if the "roc solitaire" is just another allusion to the Rosa landscape of convention, was at least dimly aware of the macabre side of Rosa's work. He may have remembered *Saül et la Pythonisse,* on view in the Louvre, or the Pitti's *Temptation of St. Anthony* and other *stregonerie.* It is noteworthy that, in his verse tragedy *Saül* (1817–1818), Lamartine included the very scene in which Saul consults the Witch of Endor, and, in fact, this passage figures in the *Nouvelles Méditations poétiques* (1823) under the title "L'apparition de l'ombre de Samuel à Saül. Fragment dramatique" (*OP,* p. 166). The dramatic form of *Saül* precludes a textual reference to Rosa but it may well be that the well-known picture in the Louvre caught his eye and even, conceivably, became the initial inspiration for his play; as the editor of the *Œuvres poétiques* observes, Lamartine was often in Paris during the period when *Saül* was in gestation. Moreover, as the editor of the critical edition of *Saül* points out, Alfieri's play on the same subject has no consultation with the Witch of Endor.[9]

If there is an overt presence of Rosa in Lamartine's *imaginaire,* it is quantitatively small. But there is a large, if subterranean presence in many passages evoking mountainous scenery dear to Lamartine, scenes he could contemplate at Milly. Such "doux tableaux" are frequently evoked, sometimes briefly, sometimes at considerable length. Along with the more Alpine scenery of *Jocelyn,* the falls of the Rhine, the rocky coast of Lebanon, and the sunlit beauties of Naples and its bay, they are an important part of the poetic decor of his work.

Vigny's relationship with the visual arts is similar to Lamartine's: he wrote no art criticism; he transposed no paintings into words, even if several of his best-known poems, notably "Moïse," "La Colère de Samson," and "La Mort du loup," open with rather painterly descriptive passages, and even if in two manifesto-like poems, "La Maison du berger" and "L'Esprit pur," he sees his poems as "tableaux."[10] But Vigny's childhood and youth were mostly spent in Paris, which gave him access to the world of the visual arts earlier than Lamartine enjoyed it. And he grew up under the wing of a mother who was an amateur painter; indeed, in Vigny's perhaps overindulgent eyes, she was a fine artist.[11] After studying drawing in Girodet's studio, Vigny became something of a draftsman and, as Lamartine relates, liked to show his sketches to friends.[12] He retained a deep admiration for his teacher, whom he called "le Raphaël de notre âge"[13] and "le poétique auteur d'*Atala* et d'*Endymion.*"[14] He dedicated the poem "La Beauté idéale" (1825) to the "manes" of Girodet. Girodet's prize-winning *Scène de déluge* (1806), along with Poussin's picture on the same subject, played a role in Vigny's poem "Le Déluge." In later years he came to have an enormous admiration for Ingres, "le grand-maître raphaëlesque de notre temps"[15] and in 1831–1832 he pressured his friend Brizeux to arrange to have him invited to the great man's studio (pp. 76, 189). Behind both Girodet and Ingres we sense the spirit of Raphael, who was, indeed, Vigny's great admiration among artists of the past.[16] Given that he also admired Flaxman,[17] the total impression left by the list of Vigny's favorite artists is that he strongly favored "la ligne" over "la couleur." Raphael, Flaxman, Girodet, Ingres—a line of idealizing creators, a current of neoclassical sensibility. Yet, in an often-cited sentence from his *Journal* which indeed pays tribute to Raphael, Vigny shows that his "Neo-Classicism" was not entirely conventional and rigid: "Si j'étais peintre, je voudrais être un Raphaël noir, forme angélique, couleur sombre" (*OC* [Pléiade(1965)], II, 1001).

We can, thanks to this brief and pregnant credo, understand how the boy Vigny could be struck by Rosa's somber and almost sinister depiction of *Saul and the Witch of Endor*. And we have not only his memories from late in life, as recorded in the *Mémoires inédits*, to prove it; a passage in the early poem, "Le Trappiste," seems to corroborate his recollection, though in rather unspecific language:

> Tel un mort, évoqué par de magiques voix,
> Envoyé du sépulcre, apparaît pour les Rois,
> Marche, prédit, menace, et retourne à la tombe,
> Dont la pierre éternelle en gémissant retombe.[18]

Another early poem, "Le Cor," may have been partly inspired by Michallon's *La Mort de Roland* (1817), with its Rosaesque landscape setting.

The only other text in the body of Vigny's work that refers to Rosa does so directly but also rather mysteriously. In one of the "Notes sans dates" published along with the *Mémoires inédits*, Vigny thinks of Rosa in relation to his own study of the soldier's fate, *Servitude et grandeur militaires* (1835):

> *Salvator Rosa*
>   Que chaque soldat avait dix ou douze duels corps à corps dans une bataille. On sortait couvert de cicatrices.
>   La guerre de Crimée a renouvelé ces combats à l'arme blanche.[19]

It is not certain that Lamartine saw and remembered Rosa's huge battle piece in the Louvre, but we cannot doubt that Vigny did—and that his memory of the picture stayed with him for a long time. The reference to the Crimean War (1854–1856) provides a *terminus ante quem* for this passage.[20] As a former soldier and as the author of *Servitude et grandeur militaires*, Vigny would naturally be drawn to scenes of battle, though his thought focused on the response of heroic individuals to the dilemmas and challenges of duty rather than on scenes of conflict. Still, the pessimism exuded by Rosa's huge picture in the Louvre would easily have found an echo in the more somber recesses of the poet's soul.

One who writes on the relationship between Vigny and Salvator Rosa must regret that the author of *Daphné* and of the *Poèmes philosophiques*[21] was unacquainted with the philosophical part of Rosa's work,[22] his paintings of such ancient philosophers as Democritus, Diogenes, Empedocles, Heraclitus, Protagoras, Pythagoras, and Xenocrates—to mention only the best known. Rosa's depiction of such tragic figures from the Bible and classical antiquity as Abel, Job, Prometheus, Atilius Regulus, and Belisarius would have appealed to the poet who proclaimed, in "La Maison du berger": "J'aime la majesté des souffrances humaines." Both Rosa and Vigny admired the fortitude many of these philosophers and leaders exhibited in reaction to their suffering. This is evident in Rosa's choice of subjects; Vigny explicitly recommended "stoïque fierté" in "La Mort du loup." Rosa's etching of Plato's Academy, his paintings of assemblies of philosophers, and his individual, sometimes anonymous philosophers would have appealed to Vigny, and, despite Vigny's distancing of himself from Catholicism, he might well have been drawn to Rosa's vivid scenes of martyrdom (Saints Bartholomew, Cosmas, Damian, and Lawrence) or even to his austere hermits (Anthony, Anthony the Abbot, Paul the Hermit) living in "sainte solitude." Many of Rosa's pictures on such subjects achieve in painting something akin to what Vigny sought to do in his "poèmes," i.e., to represent a philosophic thought in epic or dramatic form.[23] Vigny the "philosophical poet" within the romantic movement and Rosa the painter of the allegories *Vanitas* and *Humana Fragilitas*—in addition to numerous pictures on such themes—are, sad to say, only a *rendez-vous manqué*. But not one of the pictures in question was accessible to Vigny,[24] and so he had no opportunity to hang a few of Rosa's philosophic paintings on the walls of his *tour d'ivoire*. Still, Vigny had seen several of Rosa's paintings in the Louvre, and as a result, several images of Rosa's creation were securely lodged in his *musée imaginaire*. We are left to wish that the author of *Servitude et grandeur militaires* had seen Rosa's *Belisario* or *Cincinnato chiamato dalla fattoria*.[25]

References to Salvator Rosa are not numerous in the immense and multifarious work of Victor Hugo. Rosa is not among the artists in the poem catalogue of "Les Mages" (*Les Contemplations*, 1856), nor is he among the "points culminants" exalted in *William Shakespeare* (1864), to mention two texts that provide catalogues of major figures in his *musée imaginaire*. On the other hand, the texts containing references to Rosa are major ones: the preface to *Cromwell* (1827), *Notre-Dame de Paris* (1831), *Le Rhin* (1842), *Les Misérables* (1863), and *William Shakespeare.* True, these references are brief, occasionally fleeting, but they make clear that Hugo knew at least two works by Rosa and that he was impressed by them. And, unlike Lamartine and Vigny, Hugo had a deep, intimate, and life-long involvement with the visual arts; for one thing, he was an original artist himself, whose drawings attracted critical attention as early as 1837 (select reproductions began to be published in 1863 in a volume with a prefatory essay by Théophile Gautier). Baudelaire expressed admiration for them in his *Salon de 1859,* and later writers from Verhaeren and Huysmans to Claudel and Breton followed suit.[26]

Like the young Vigny, the young Victor Hugo had the good fortune, despite stays in Italy and Spain, to spend much of his early life in Paris and so was able to view the Parisian art world from early on. Thus, as we have seen, he had a glimpse of the now-lost *Salvator Rosa pris par les brigands,* one of "deux petits chefs-d'œuvre" his friend Louis Boulanger showed at the *Exhibition de tableaux au profit des Grecs,* which opened May 17, 1826. Young Hugo saw the exhibition as a chance to review "La nouvelle école de peinture."[27] Boulanger's picture, unfortunately, is not described, nor does Hugo refer to Lady Morgan's "myth." The "myth" had found a home in Hugo's capacious memory, whether derived directly from Lady Morgan or from some other source it is impossible to say. Seeing Boulanger's episode from Rosa's wilderness years may have been the writer's first contact with Rosa. More likely, he had already seen pictures by Rosa in the Louvre by the time he wrote his article about Boulanger and "la nouvelle école de peinture."

In the following year, the preface to his drama *Cromwell*—the best known of French romantic manifestoes—provides the first direct reference to Rosa in Hugo's works. In footnote II, Hugo illustrates his theories about the grotesque with examples from the visual arts: "Les orgies de Callot, la *Tentation* de Salvator Rosa avec son épouvantable démon, sa *Mêlée* avec toutes ses formes repoussantes de mort et de carnage, le *Triboulet* de Bonifacio, le mendiant rongé de vermine de Murillo,[28] les ciselures où Benvenuto Cellini fait rire de si hideuses figures dans les arabesques et les acanthes, sont des choses laides selon la nature, belles selon l'art" (*OC,* III, 51). Clearly, Hugo, by late 1827, had seen the huge battle scene in the Louvre, and he seems never to have forgotten "ses formes repoussantes de mort et de carnage"— as we shall see in discussing *Notre-Dame de Paris* and *Les Misérables.* The "antique" architectural background of the battle is ignored; it is the human clash dominating the foreground that has stuck in the writer's mind. As for Rosa's "*Tentation . . .* avec son épouvantable démon," Hugo must have seen the engraving by J.-B. Wicar and his assistants, reproduced in the four-volume set of plates published under the title *La Galerie de Florence* between 1789 and 1807[29] or perhaps elsewhere. Understandably, Hugo is interested in the huge, looming figure of the demon and not in the cowering saint. Hugo, then, is selective in his recall of these images, and Rosa has become associated in his mind with violence and horror.

Rosa next appears in *Notre-Dame de Paris* (1831), in a brief reference that makes a curious *rapprochement* or, rather, a sort of fusion of Rosa and Flemish painting. In the episode in which Quasimodo wins a contest for the ugliest grimace (Livre premier, ch. V), Hugo works his way past several works of art—e.g., "ces cauchemars pétrifiés sous la main de Germain Pilon" (*OC*, IV, 51)—on his way to the climax of the riotous scene: "L'orgie devenait de plus en plus flamande. Teniers n'en donnerait qu'une bien imparfaite idée.[30] Qu'on se figure en bacchanale la bataille de Salvator Rosa" (ibid.). As C. W. Thompson says, "This progression of artistic references strongly suggests that only the confused mass of interlocked bodies and grimacing faces in the lower half of Rosa's painting came near to corresponding in Hugo's imagination with the tumult he wished to describe" (p. 122), which confirms what we saw in Hugo's earlier reference to Rosa's *Heroic Battle*, the exclusive focus on the writhing foreground. It is noteworthy that the context for this passage involves Quasimodo, one of the supreme incarnations of Hugo's aesthetics of the grotesque. Where Stendhal, in 1824, had seen Rosa's battle scene as classical, Hugo easily absorbs the same picture—and its creator—into the core of his romantic program.

About a decade later, in *Le Rhin* (1842)—in a passage not included in the original edition—Hugo refers to Rosa in a vivid evocation of the childhood vision summoned up by the words "Forêt-Noire":

> Je me figurais une forêt prodigieuse, impénétrable, effrayante, une futaie pleine de ténèbres avec des profondeurs brumeuses, des sentiers étroits cheminant à une herbe épaisse peuplée de reptiles invisibles, sous des arbres géants; partout des racines tortueuses sortant à demi de terre comme des poignées de serpents; de sinistres branchages épineux, des fouillis de sarments hideux se découpant comme des filets d'encre sur le ciel livide et y traçant çà et là l'inextricable paraphe du démon; des silhouettes immobiles de chats-huants perchées dans ces réseaux noirs; des yeux de braise flambant dans l'ombre comme des trous au mur de l'enfer; tantôt forêt lugubre d'Albert Dürer, tantôt forêt sinistre de Salvator Rosa; tantôt des bruits affreux, tantôt un silence horrible; les râles des chouettes, les huées des hiboux ou la morne taciturnité du sépulcre; le jour, une vague lueur; la nuit, une obscurité effroyable, avec quelques étoiles pareilles à des prunelles

effarées, dans les intervalles des arbres ou un blanc rayon de pleine lune au bout des branches. Du reste, les arbres de cette forêt de mes rêves n'étaient ni des sapins, ni des ormes, ni des chênes; c'étaient des arbres. (*OC*, VI, 819)

There may be more of Dürer than of Rosa in this nightmare forest scene, even though the two artists are seemingly put on the same level and the elements derived from their works are thoroughly intertwined. The "chouettes" and "hiboux," however, may refer explicitly to figures in the spooky background of *Saul*. But there is even more of Hugo himself bodied forth from his extravagant imagination. Certainly, it would be difficult, even leaving aside the sound effects, to find a picture by Rosa that comes close to Hugo's vision, and even more difficult to identify any such picture by Rosa that Hugo could actually have seen. The macabre subject of the *Temptation of St. Anthony*—known through Wicar's engraving—and the sinister creatures in the background of *Saül et la Pythonisse* may have been conflated with the prevailing notion of Rosa as the painter of wild, somber landscapes. The only Rosa landscapes accessible to Hugo, i.e., in the Louvre, *Tobias and the Angel* (S 226) and *Landscape with Soldiers and Hunters* (S 129), especially the former, simply do not match the nightmarish forest Hugo claims to have seen in his childhood dreams.[31]

   Le Rhin concludes with an immense panorama of human progress, which, according to Hugo, began in earnest at the beginning of the seventeenth century with the appearance of a number of great scientists, philosophers, artists, writers, and political leaders. Hugo's list of these great men puts Rosa in illustrious company: the other artists mentioned are Guido Reni, Poussin, Ribera, Van Dyck, Rubens, and Rembrandt; among the writers are "le jeune Corneille et le vieux Shakespeare" (*OC*, VI, 498). The name of "le jeune Salvator Rosa" appears between those of "le jeune Rembrandt" and "le jeune Milton," which leaves us wondering if Hugo means Rosa the painter or Rosa the satiric poet. In the absence, so far, of any evidence that Hugo was aware of Rosa as a fellow poet, whose *Satire* could be seen as foreshadowing his own *Châtiments*, it seems most likely that it is the painter and not the poet whom Hugo has in mind. But if so, what aspect of Rosa's painted work entitles him to a place in this pantheon? Perhaps, simply, the greatness of his achievement—after all, not one of the other artists mentioned contributed directly to the advancement of freedom of expression, and some of the names on Hugo's list, e.g., Wallenstein and "le jeune Richelieu," might be seen as enemies of this kind of progress.[32] Hugo pays Rosa a great compliment, but we cannot be sure just why.

Until we reach *Les Misérables* (1862) there is just one reference to Rosa, occurring in the never-used manuscript fragments associated with *Châtiments* in connection with a projected poem dealing with the Franco-British alliance during the Crimean War. The manuscripts show Hugo toying with the following combinations:[33]

This tantalizing little text shows that, somewhere along the way, an echo of Lady Morgan's Rosa had lodged in Hugo's consciousness, perhaps derived from his encounter with Louis Boulanger's painting of *Salvator Rosa pris par les brigands* (1826) or from one of the many texts that, between 1824 and the mid-1850s, drew on her biography of Rosa. One wonders just how Hugo would have linked Rosa's wanderings in the Abruzzi with the Crimean War or the alliance between France and England.

Some ten years later, in the long, vivid account of the Battle of Waterloo, which constitutes an immense epic within the novel *Les Misérables*, Hugo arrives at "un intervalle obscur" in the fighting. The novelist thinks once again of Rosa's battle picture at the end of a swirling vision of uniforms of different armies: "des tableaux, non des lignes stratégiques; ce qu'il faut à Salvator Rosa, non ce qu'il faut à Gribeauval [the great authority on artillery]" (*OC*, XI, 264). Hugo pushes on to some general observations about battles and refers to two other painters: "Pour peindre une bataille, il faut de ces puissants qui aient du chaos dans le pinceau; Rembrandt vaut mieux que Vandermeulen, Vandermeulen, exact à midi, ment à trois heures" (ibid.). Since Rembrandt was not a painter of battle scenes, one wonders why, in this context, Hugo mentions him as a contrast to Vandermeulen. The violence and confusion of Rosa's battle would seem to be a fitting reference. But Hugo had an immense admiration for Rembrandt. According to Judith Gautier, he proclaimed: "[J]'aurais voulu être, j'aurais dû être un second Rembrandt."[34] And, besides, he had already dropped Rosa's name once in this passage, no mean compliment. In the chapter entitled "Le fond de la question," Hugo, distinguishing "l'émeute" from "l'insurrection," makes a brief allusion to Masaniello: "L'émeute, c'est Mazaniello [*sic*]; l'insurrection, c'est Spartacus" (*OC*, XI, 745). But Rosa's legendary participation in Masaniello's uprising is never mentioned by Hugo.[35]

The story of Hugo and Rosa seems to end in another key work from this period. In the "Fragments réservés," which grew out of *William Shakespeare* (1864), the section entitled "Le Goût" defends the literary exploitation of the grotesque and the trivial as practiced by great artists: "Le calembour quand il est d'Eschyle . . . les sauvageries quand Shakespeare les fait . . . la charogne quand le vautour et Salvator Rosa la rongent" (*OC*, XII, 418). Hugo probably evokes a vulture here because he again remembers the gruesome, birdlike creature who hovers over the saint in Rosa's *Temptation of St. Anthony*. Hugo is reverting to one of his primordial images of Rosa: the artist of the grotesque. The reference is brief, if vivid. Perhaps what matters most here is that Hugo puts Rosa in the company of Aeschylus and Shakespeare and, it must be said, many others, some of whom are not of the same caliber. But Aeschylus and Shakespeare are the supreme heroes, the supreme geniuses, of Hugo's book, the towering precursors of the third Aeschylus for whom the world is being made ready and who is perhaps already in the world. Hugo pays more honor to Phidias, Michelangelo, Rembrandt, and Piranesi (p. 247) than to other visual artists evoked in *William Shakespeare;* even Dürer is only one of twenty-nine great Germans, outclassed by Beethoven but still enjoying a rather special place (p. 191).

A half dozen or so references to Rosa will seem but a small tribute from when one considers the gigantic bulk of Hugo's work and the many artists, writers, and other cultural heroes to whom he pays homage (leaving aside the countless kind remarks showered on those who approached him with sufficient deference). But several of the references to Rosa are intensely vivid, and most appear in major works or in related documents: the preface to *Cromwell, Notre-Dame de Paris, Le Rhin, Châtiments, Les Misérables, William Shakespeare*. Hugo's pantheon of great geniuses is large and commodious; many artists jostle each other for places there. Rosa's place may be modest but it is permanent. And he earned it through the impact of just two works, one seen at the Louvre, the other in an engraved version.

Alfred de Musset, the youngest of the four romantic poets canonized in French literary history for a century or more, never mentions Rosa or his work, despite a profound involvement with Italy, Italian literature, and Italian painting. His tale "Le Fils du Titien" and his play *André del Sarto* are set in the world of Italian Renaissance art. *Lorenzaccio* evokes that same world through the episodic appearance of a young art student, Tebaldeo. As for art criticism, Musset reviewed one Salon,[36] reviewed the "Exposition au Luxembourg au profit des blessés,"[37] an exhibition built around two of Gros's famous episodes from Napoleon's Egyptian campaign, and left the fragmentary article "Sur Raphaël et Rubens." Looking at these and other works, and at Musset's works in general, we find that he often refers to Raphael,

Michelangelo, Titian, and Rubens,[38] and occasionally to Giorgione and Correggio, an exceedingly conventional set of preferences, one that seems to limit Italian art to the giants of the sixteenth century.[39] In a nutshell, for Musset Italian art died with Michelangelo: "L'art avec lui tomba" (*La Coupe et les lèvres*, "Dédicace").[40] Such a view of the history of Italian painting obviously left no place for Rosa.

With Gérard de Nerval we encounter a similar situation—a writer with many ties to things Italian, as shown by his brief but telling glimpses of the bay of Naples. He visited the region twice (autumn of 1834 and late November 1843) but evinced no real interest in Rosa. However, he was at least aware of Rosa's existence: a manuscript variant of his article "Les poésies de Henri Heine"[41] reveals that Nerval's list of three marine painters, who are compared—unfavorably—to Heine's *Nord-See*, originally included the name of Rosa along with those of Backhuysen and Joseph Vernet; in the definitive text, Rosa has been replaced by Van de Velde, i.e., Willem Van de Velde the Younger (1633–1707).[42]

In the work of another member of Musset's generation, Théophile Gautier, Rosa's star is clearly on the ascendant. For Gautier, who seriously studied painting for a while, the visual arts were a constant preoccupation—according to the Goncourts, he proclaimed himself to be a man "pour qui le monde visible existe."[43] In his poetry, he carried *ekphrasis* to a new level in the pieces he called "transpositions d'art." Perhaps most important of all, Gautier, who lived mostly by journalism, was probably the most prolific French art critic of the nineteenth century; he wrote over 350 articles reviewing the Paris Salons and a few other comprehensive shows devoted to contemporary art, and much else besides—over 700 articles. The largest number of references to Rosa by any French author studied here is to be found in the works of Gautier. In the large body of his production, which is still difficult to access because it was never published in volume form, there are certainly numerous references as yet undiscovered. Yet Gautier never devoted a whole poem, a whole piece of fiction, or a whole article to Rosa. This is understandable in part because Gautier, as a *salonnier* and journalist living by his pen, wrote primarily about the art of his own time.

The place and importance of Rosa in Gautier's *musée imaginaire* are perhaps best revealed in his guide to a very specific museum, the Louvre. The Salon carré, he says, contains "la plus glorieuse réunion de peintres qui puisse se voir au monde":

> Léonard de Vinci, Pérugin, Raphaël, André del Sarto, Corrège, Sébastien del Piombo, Giorgione, Paul Véronèse, Titien, Tintoret, Guerchin, le Guide, Francia, Ghirlandajo, Van Eyck, Antonello de Messine, Murillo, Ribera,

Rembrandt, Rubens, Van Dyck, Claude Lorrain, Poussin, Le Sueur, Jouvenet, Philippe de Champagne [*sic*], Rigaud, Gaspar Netscher, Metsu, Ostade, Gérard Dow, et quelques autres encore dont les noms formeraient litanie; il n'y manque que Velásquez.[44]

Today, Gautier might draw up a rather different list of the most glorious old masters to be seen in the Louvre, and in the context of the present study, the absence of Rosa attracts attention, even if one cannot quarrel with Gautier's complaint about the absence of Velásquez. But Rosa does appear elsewhere in Gautier's guide to the Louvre: he devotes nearly two pages to three pictures by Rosa on display in the Grande Galerie: *La Pythonisse d'Endor, Une bataille,* and *Paysage,*[45] to use his titles. As we shall see, he gives rather vivid and enthusiastic descriptions of these works, especially of the first two. To draw on the title of another of Gautier's longer works of art criticism, Rosa is not one of the gods or demi-gods of sixteenth- and seventeenth-century European painting.[46]

In more concrete terms, what does Rosa represent for Gautier? First, he is the painter of the three pictures in the Louvre just mentioned—they are the only paintings by Rosa he ever specifically mentions. His description of *La Pythonisse* expatiates on the macabre and fantastic character of the picture (*Guide*, pp. 110–11); in describing *Une bataille,* he stresses the violence, perceptively observing that Rosa was not depicting a particular victory or defeat: "C'est la bataille en elle-même, personnifiée pour ainsi dire" (p. 111). Similarly, *Paysage* "contient toute la poétique du genre," i.e., landscape (p. 112). Though *Paysage* is less fully described than the other two pictures, Gautier seems to see it as more representative of Rosa than the others, for he introduces the passage on *Paysage* with a general observation: "Salvator Rosa, le premier, a introduit dans l'art ce que nous entendons par *pittoresque,* élément tout à fait inconnu des anciens maîtres: un aspect singulier de la nature, un effet d'ombre ou de soleil inattendu, une configuration sinistre de rocher, un entassement de nuages farouches" (pp. 111–12).

Although Gautier often cites other aspects of Rosa's work, especially Rosa as a painter of battles, it would appear that he found the essence of Rosa in his "picturesque" landscapes. Certainly, this is the Rosa we meet in two passages of Gautier's early poetry, his earliest references to Rosa. In *Albertus* (1832) his protagonist, a young painter, is clearly a disciple of Rosa, as stanza LXXXI reveals:

Albertus travaillait.—C'était un paysage.
Salvator eût signé cette toile sauvage.
Au premier plan des rocs,—au second les donjons
D'un château dentelant de ses flèches aiguës

Un ciel ensanglanté, semé d'îles de nues.
Les grands chênes pliaient comme de faibles joncs,
Les feuilles tournoyaient en l'air; l'herbe flétrie,
Comme les flots hurlants d'une mer en furie,
Ondait sous la rafale; et de nombreux éclairs
De reflets rougeoyants incendiaient les cimes
Des pins échevelés, penchés sur les abîmes
    Comme sur le puits des enfers.[47]

Even if Albertus has exaggerated somewhat luridly—the whirling leaves, the lightning flashes—and has introduced elements more suggestive of Victor Hugo's drawings—the lacy profile of a medieval chateau against a vivid sunset—we recognize nonetheless some of the stock motifs of Rosa's landscapes: rocks, bent trees, blasted pines. And the expression "toile sauvage," encapsulating the whole, includes the adjective we have often seen applied to Rosa's landscapes, more often, probably, than any other.

In "Thébaïde," a poem first published in 1837, the poet yearns for a solitude à la Salvator Rosa:

J'aimerais que ce fût dans une roche creuse,
Au penchant d'une côte escarpée et pierreuse,
Comme dans les tableaux de Salvator Rosa,
Où le pied d'un vivant jamais ne se posa;
Sous un ciel vert zébré de grands nuages fauves,
Dans des terrains galeux, clairsemés d'arbres chauves,
Avec un horizon sans couronne d'azur,
Bornant de tous côtés le regard comme un mur,
Et, dans les roseaux secs, près d'une eau noire et plate,
Quelque maigre héron debout sur une patte.
Sur la caverne, un pin, ainsi qu'un spectre en deuil
Qui tend ses bras voilés au-dessus d'un cercueil,
Tendrait ses bras en pleurs; et du haut de la voûte
Un maigre filet d'eau, suintant goutte à goutte,
Marquerait par sa chute aux sons intermittants
Le battement égal que fait le cœur du temps.[48]

Gautier need not be held to account for this veering away somewhat from a generic Rosa landscape, with such details as the lurid sunset, the heron standing on one leg, and the thin stream of water: this is not the "transposition" of any specific painting by Rosa, certainly not of the one Rosa landscape Gautier undoubtedly saw—the Louvre's *Paysage*, with its cluster of dubious human figures. In fact, it may be that Gautier's elimination of the human element from the landscape ("Où le pied d'un vivant jamais ne se posa") reflects a literary tradition; Madame de Staël's re-creation of a Rosa landscape in *Corinne* excludes all human and animal life: "un rocher, des torrens et des arbres, sans un seul être vivant, sans que seulement le vol d'un oiseau rappelle l'idée de la vie."[49]

These two passages from Gautier's early poetry are his nearest approaches to "transposition d'art" in verse involving Rosa. But the passages on three Rosas in his guide to the Louvre should be put on view here, too, since they are vivid word pictures describing works of art. First, scorning Albani and "ses éternelles redites mythologiques," Gautier directs us to *La Pythonisse d'Endor,*

> un tableau romantique avant le romantisme. La Pythonisse, vieille stryge bizarrement éclairée par le feu du trépied qu'elle attise, évoque l'ombre de Samuel, qui apparaît avec son visage spectral à moitié englouti dans une draperie sinistre, semblable à un suaire. Rien de plus terrible et de plus lugubre que ce fantôme, arraché au tombeau par les formules de la nécromancie. Saül, prosterné, ose à peine l'interroger, et les deux gardes qui l'accompagnaient se reculent pâles d'épouvante. Au fond, à travers l'ombre, grouillent hideusement des formes fantastiques, têtes de cheval décharnées, squelettes à ailes de chauves-souris, hibous [*sic*] aux prunelles d'une vague phosphorescence, tout le personnel des rondes du sabbat maintenu dans une gamme sourde, éteinte, confuse, qui, par son indécision même, augmente encore la terreur, car on pressent plus qu'on ne veut. (*Guide,* pp. 110–11)

Here Gautier produces an ode in prose to the grotesque, the macabre, and the fantastic, encapsulated in such words as "bizarrement," "spectral," "sinistre," "suaire," "terrible," "lugubre," "épouvante," "grouillent hideuse-ment des formes fantastiques," and "terreur," not to mention the words that refer to loathsome objects actually seen in the painting. Gautier probably never saw any of Rosa's major *stregonerie*—for example, the one now in the National Gallery in London (S 78) and already at Althorp House in 1761.[50] But Gautier's fondness for this strain in romanticism can be traced a least as far back as *Albertus* (1832) and had its sources of inspiration in that subschool of romanticism, the "école frénétique," perhaps best illustrated by several tales by Nodier, passages in Hugo's preface to *Cromwell,* or certain of the same writer's early poems, e.g., "La Ronde du sabbat" (*Les Orientales*). His use of the label "romantique" for this picture is fully justified, especially since it makes clear that Rosa's romanticism predates the term and the movement.

Gautier's prose transposition of *Une bataille* is not only vivid—we would expect that from this "magicien ès lettres françaises" (as Baudelaire called him)—but also insightful:

> *Une Bataille* est une page d'une rare énergie et d'une beauté étrange. La lutte ne se passe à aucune époque désignée et ne se rapporte à aucun fait historique. C'est la bataille en elle-même, personnifiée pour ainsi dire. Près d'un portique aux colonnes de marbre roussâtre, des cavaliers s'attaquent avec un acharnement, une furie et une impétuosité incroyables. Ils se hachent, se transpercent, se tailladent, se martèlent, se renversent de leurs chevaux aux larges croupes, employant tout un arsenal d'armes antiques, barbares et féroces. Au fond, pour gagner les montagnes, la déroute galope éperdument, et sur la mêlée sanglante se roule un ciel aux nuages menaçants, où l'orage semble continuer les discordes de la terre. (p. 111)

Here, Gautier applies no label, makes no effort to place the picture in literary or art history; he paints a word picture and extracts the painting's meaning. Gautier was well aware of Rosa's importance as a painter of battles; in several passages of his art criticism he places Rosa in the line of those who excelled in this genre, from Falcone and Bourguignon to Gros and Horace Vernet. Here he perceives that Rosa painted "la bataille en elle-même" and not a specific battle, unlike Van der Meulen, Gros, or Vernet.

The passage already mentioned in which Gautier hails Rosa as the inventor of the *pittoresque* in painting leads into his third "transposition d'art" in prose: "Le cadre de Salvator Rosa que le musée possède et qu'indique le simple titre de *Paysage,* contient toute la poétique du genre: ciel orageux, torrent aux eaux noires, arbres à demi déracinés, roches aux déchirures convulsives, figures sinistres, qui semblent apostées pour un guet-apens, et, somme toute, effet piquant dont on dit: Quelle belle décoration cela ferait pour un théâtre!" (p. 112). Of Gautier's "transposition," we can say at least that it is vivid and accurate, unless we wish to quibble over his interpretation of the human figures—"picturesque" perhaps but not necessarily "sinister." This picture (S 239), whose authenticity has been questioned even by Salerno himself, is not one of Rosa's best, but Gautier manages to extract from it some key motifs of Rosa landscapes. At least by the time he wrote this passage, in 1867, Gautier knew the Rosa legends put in circulation by Lady Morgan. After all, he had reviewed Dugué's drama *Salvator Rosa* in 1851, but nowhere in Gautier's own poetry or fiction does he exploit these legends. In writing about *Paysage* he shows a vague awareness of the Rosa of legend but concentrates on the landscape and makes no effort to place Rosa in the painting.

The large number of references to Rosa in Gautier's work would seem to make him the painter's major French champion. The closest he came to producing a complete text about Rosa was his review of Dugué's 1851 drama, *Salvator Rosa,* already examined at length. This review is mostly a résumé of the play, much of which offers, as we have seen, imaginary episodes in Rosa's life, usually derived from Lady Morgan's biography. Consequently, it is Rosa the man and not the painter who emerges from Gautier's pages. But Gautier the art critic and former art student is also involved in the composition of the review. First of all, he observes that Rosa's life and work justify Dugué's choice of subject: "Son génie, ses talents variés, sa vie aventureuse, la part qu'il prit aux événements politiques de Naples, semblent devoir fournir de nombreux éléments aux combinaisons scéniques."[51] Gautier also observes that, as far as he knows, no dramatist had yet treated the subject, and he mentions E. T. A. Hoffmann's "nouvelle charmante," but without giving its title (p. 246). Gautier reveals some general knowledge of Rosa's personality, calling him an "esprit libre, capricieux et fantasque" (p. 242) and "ce génie aventureux, à la fois peintre, poëte, musicien, acteur et soldat—un vrai descendant de Benvenuto Cellini pour le talent et le caprice" (p. 250). He sympathizes with his fellow poet-painter, the Rosa who, for lack of proper shelter or lodging, uses his paint box as a pillow and his manuscript poem as bolster (p. 246). Despite the dramatic form of the text, something of Rosa's work is conveyed to the readers of Gautier's review: the opening scene revolves around a painting by Rosa, *Agar dans le désert,* which is not described, however. Later, as we have seen, the dramatist presents an amusing and colorful episode in which Rosa is so taken with the "site . . . si sauvagement pittoresque" that he interrupts his journey to Rome in order to sketch it. Gautier describes the stage-set as "un âpre site de montagnes, des éboulements de roches, un torrent noir qui tombe dans un gouffre, quelques sapins demi-foudroyés étendant vers le ciel leurs rameaux suppliants: une réminiscence de ce sombre paysage de Salvator qu'on voit au Musée, un lieu fait à plaisir pour les assassinats" (pp. 248–49). Gautier virtually describes the drawing Rosa produces: "un léger crayon de ces roches férocement difformes, de ces arbres égorgés dont les tenailles rouges ont l'air de plaies saignantes, de ces nuages monstrueux, gros de tonnerres, dont il fera plus tard un de ses chefs-d'œuvre" (p. 249), presumably the landscape in the Louvre evoked a few lines earlier.

The passages studied so far convey nearly all of the various facets of Rosa's life and work that caught Gautier's serious attention and inspired his admiration. But there is one body of references not yet exploited that significantly enriches this picture—the numerous comparisons and other *rapprochements* Gautier establishes between Rosa and other painters. Some of these, the most straightforward, place him in the tradition of battle painters, of whom Gautier cites a long line in several reviews: Italian masters of the Renaissance (Leonardo, Raphael, Michelangelo); Italian, French, Flemish, and Dutch painters of the seventeenth and eighteenth centuries (Falcone, Bourguignon, Le Brun, Wouwerman, Van der Meulen, Parrocel, Casanova); and modern French chroniclers of France's military adventures from the Revolution to the conquest of Algeria (Gérard, Girodet, Gros, Decamps, Carle and Horace Vernet).[52] Clearly, Gautier regarded Rosa as a major and original practitioner of this genre.

Sometimes, in making such *rapprochements,* Gautier wants to distinguish one of the contemporary specialists in battle painting. We are told that Horace Vernet "ne ressemble ni à Raphaël . . . ni à Lebrun . . . ni à Salvator Rosa, ni au Bourguignon, ni à Van der Meulen, ni à Gros."[53] And Decamps's *Bataille des Cimbres* surpasses Rosa in its depiction of rocky, desolate, and arid scenery, though here it is Bourguignon's "mêlées" that are evoked as counterparts to Decamps's battle.[54]

Gautier is not content to make facile comparisons and contrasts between Rosa and other painters of battle scenes. As we have seen, he goes to the heart of the picture in the Louvre: "C'est la bataille elle-même, personnifiée pour ainsi dire" (*Guide,* p. 111). Elsewhere, he expands on this insight: "la célèbre bataille de Salvator Rosa n'a rien d'historique: c'est un combat imaginaire d'ennemis inconnus où le peintre a mis toute sa férocité et toute sa sauvagerie."[55] Two years later, apropos of Bénédict Masson's *Bataille de Trasimène,* Gautier compares the modern painter to Rosa, not because of the historical accuracy of Masson's picture, but because of his striving for "l'effet, la couleur, le pittoresque, le ragoût" (*Exposition de 1859,* p. 72). The colorful description of Masson might have been written about Rosa's *Bataille:* "Il a entrechoqué, culbuté, piétiné, taillé en pièces tout ce monde hurlant et grimaçant avec beaucoup de feu, d'énergie, de mouvement et de férocité. Sa toile rugit, se crispe, saigne et représente bien le fourmillement d'une bataille." In the same Salon, in François Nicolas Chifflart's "très-beau" *Faust au combat,* Faust and Mephistopheles, "montés sur des chevaux fantastiques, soufflant le feu par les naseaux, échevelés, cabrés, des gerbes d'étincelles aux sabots, traversent au vol une mêlée à la Salvator Rosa, et sèment la mort à droite et à gauche" (pp. 281–82). Gautier, though primarily interested in "le monde visible," intuited the painter-philosopher in Rosa—his battle pictures are comments on war and its horror and ferocity.

Gautier's Rosa is also an important landscape painter as well as a major painter of battles. In texts already examined, we have seen that he identifies such standard features of Rosa landscapes as mountains, forests, torrents,[56] somber skies, and bent trees but also adds touches of his own that exaggerate the wildness and melancholy of "typical" Rosa landscapes: stagnant waters, flashes of lightning, whirling leaves, "weeping" pines, and an absence of human figures. What Rosa landscapes did he know other than the Louvre's *Paysage* acquired in 1816 (S 239)? One of Gautier's letters provides a possible candidate. In 1837 he wrote to Eugène Piot, then embarked on a trip to Holland: "Si tu rencontres un Everdingen, fais-m'en deux pages de description, c'est un maître dans le goût de Salvator Rosa, j'ai vu une cascade de lui à la vente d'Erard—magnifique."[57] As for Rosa waterfalls, could Gautier have seen, in some form or other, the impressive *Grotta con cascata* (S 70) then— and now—in the Pitti?

A third motif appearing in Gautier's writing about Rosa is that of brigands and other humans suggestive of violence and disorder. Gautier was certainly aware of the legend of Rosa's alleged encounters with Italy's notorious outlaws and shared the widespread tendency to see brigands in the armed male figures who people some of Rosa's landscapes—it was not necessary to have read Lady Morgan's biography. Recounting an 1849 visit to the Louvre, Gautier points out in Rosa "le peintre des solitudes et des brigands"[58] even as he expresses regret that the Louvre did not display Rosa's "grande bataille" in the Salon carré. But it is in his remarks about certain pictures of Adrien Guignet that Gautier most clearly highlights this aspect of Rosa's work. In 1846 he writes that Guignet's *L'Orgie des condottieri* "pour l'énergie, la vigueur, et la sauvagerie, rappelle heureusement Salvator Rosa."[59] When he adds, "le désordre le plus affreux, mais le plus pittoresque règne dans la caverne," he seems still to be thinking of Rosa, who, as Gautier believed, invented the picturesque in painting.

A much more famous painting leads Gautier to propose a rather surprising *rapprochement*: of Rembrandt's (so-called) *Night Watch,* he writes, "Ces bons Hollandais ont pris sous son pinceau des moustaches en croc, des barbes en feuilles d'artichaut, des sourcils crispés, des tournures de hanches, des allures cambrées et des façons de matamores. Jamais condottieri, lansquenets, stradeots, n'eurent la mine plus rébarbative; les brigands de Salvator Rosa ont l'air d'honnêtes gens à côté de ces dignes miliciens."[60]

Gautier's evident interest in the picturesque figures of outlaws and other unruly types helps us to understand one of his most frequent *rapprochements,* that between Rosa and Jacques Callot. Reviewing Dumanoir and Dennery's *Don César de Bazan* in 1844, Gautier loosely links the two artists in his praise of the great actor Frédéric Lemaître: "Il saura substituer à la figure indécise, mollement charbonnée par le fabricant, une silhouette vivante, digne de Salvator Rosa ou de Callot."[61] The following year, the resemblance between the two artists is much more vividly limned in a passage from the *Voyage en Espagne,* which captures a group of dancing Gypsies seen in Granada: "La sauvagerie d'attitude, l'accoutrement étrange et la couleur extraordinaire de ce groupe, en eussent fait un excellent motif de tableau pour Callot ou Salvator Rosa."[62] Many years later, marveling at the "science des noms" displayed in Hugo's *La Légende des siècles,* Gautier develops an elaborate comparison worthy of the inventor of the *transposition d'art:* "Les rimes se renvoient, comme des raquettes un volant, les noms bizarres de ces forbans, écume de la mer, échappés de chiourme venant de tous les pays, et il suffit d'un nom pour dessiner de pied en cap un de ces coquins pittoresques campés comme des esquisses de Salvator Rosa ou des eaux-fortes de Callot."[63] Gautier must have seen some of Rosa's *Figurine,* but, rather troublingly, he distinguishes between the "esquisses" of Rosa and Callot's etchings, as if unaware that the Rosa works are also etchings. Yet a few years earlier, Gautier had made it clear that he was quite aware of Rosa as etcher: in an essay on etching from 1863, "Un mot sur l'eau-forte," Gautier provides a quick history of the medium as practiced by the great painters, with Rosa heading the list: "Salvator Rosa, entre un tableau et une mascarade, a égratigné le vernis noir au bout de son poignard, et y a dessiné, avec sa crânerie caractéristique, des brigands et des soldats."[64] It is revealing that the next name on Gautier's list is that of Callot, who, he says, "a fait mordre par l'acide tout ce monde fourmillant de bohémiens, de vagabonds et de masques" (ibid.). Gautier, then, knew that Rosa had made etchings and that Rosa and Callot had treated similar subjects and were stylistically akin to one another: "brigands . . . soldats . . . vagabonds . . . masques / égratigné le vernis noir du bout de son poignard . . . crânerie . . . a fait mordre par l'acide." His insight is confirmed by the foremost modern authority on Rosa's etchings: Richard W. Wallace clearly places Callot among the most important influences exerted on Rosa's etchings (also mentioned are such artists as Liagno, Bosse, della Bella) and specifically notes that, in one group, Rosa "experimented with the long, vertical, parallel modeling and contour lines that are characteristic of the etchings of Jacques Callot."[65]

We have already seen Gautier's revealing, if surprising, *rapprochement* between Rosa and Rembrandt's *Night Watch.* A resemblance or affinity between Rosa and Rembrandt is also implied in a sentence already quoted from Gautier's 1869 article on Adrien Guignet in which he links the names of Rembrandt, Rosa, and Decamps.[66] Gautier leaves us wondering just what Rosa shares with Rembrandt, whereas, in the previous quotation, we may suspect the critic of a bit of overwriting: most observers have tended to see Rosa's mysterious figures as bandits and brigands. Unfortunately, Gautier did not see fit to relate Rosa to Rembrandt on stylistic grounds by pointing to the two artists' common heritage from Caravaggio.

Gautier shows to better effect in a passage from the *Voyage en Espagne* (1845) devoted to one of Goya's *Caprichos:* "Plus loin, c'est *el coco,* croque-mitaine, qui vient effrayer les petits enfants et qui en effraierait bien d'autres, car après l'ombre de Samuel dans le tableau de la *Pythonisse d'Endor,* par Salvator Rosa, nous ne connaissons rien de plus terrible que cet épouvantail."[67] This is Gautier's reaction to the third in the series, "Que viene el Coco," in which the hooded figure of the bogeyman looming up on the right is certainly reminiscent of Rosa's ghostly figure of Samuel, also dominating the right-hand side of the picture. One could point to important differences between the two images, e.g., the fact that, in Goya, the face of the hooded figure is hidden from the viewer. But Gautier is on firm ground in seeing an affinity between Goya and Rosa as painters of the grotesque and the lugubrious—an aspect of the romantic aesthetic on which he often drew himself.[68]

With Goya, we reach virtually to Gautier's own era. As we have seen, he makes *rapprochements* between Rosa and several other artists of his own time or close to it: Girodet, Gérard, Gros, Decamps, and Horace Vernet, to mention the best known. We can logically complete this survey of Gautier's references to Rosa by dwelling briefly on several artists who were his exact contemporaries. In the fourth installment of his "Salon de 1846" (*La Presse,* April 3, 1846), he reviews several paintings by Adrien Guignet; of one he writes (in a passage already seen in part):

> *L'Orgie des condottieri,* pour l'énergie, la vigueur, et la sauvagerie, rappelle heureusement Salvator Rosa. Le désordre le plus affreux mais le plus pittoresque, règne dans la caverne. La table,—un simple quartier de roc,—est toute rouge de vin où il se mêle peut-être bien un peu de sang, et les bandits y dorment sur leurs bras croisés, ivres morts, épuisés de débauches et de querelles. Dans un coin sombre frissonne un groupe pâle de captives nues, qui espère qu'on les a peut-être oubliées.

Since Guignet was the nearest thing to a disciple of Salvator Rosa in the nineteenth century and was known as such, this *rapprochement* comes as no surprise, but it is vivid, and Gautier's description is like a small *transposition d'art* without the framework of verse. In a similar vein is his word-picture inspired by Gustave Doré's drawings of the Alps:

> Rien de plus primitif, de plus solitaire et de plus grandiose que cette cime de montagnes aux anfractuosités drapées d'un éternel manteau de neige où le soleil couchant, déjà disparu pour la vallée ou la plaine, laisse encore une mince frange rose; le torrent qui roule sur les assises d'un gigantesque escalier de granit, avec des ressauts, des bouillonnements et des fumées d'écume sous la lueur livide d'un ciel d'orage a l'âpreté farouche d'un Salvator Rosa.[69]

Even though he had seen few Rosas, Gautier would recognize that certain elements in this picture could not be traced to the Italian, whose mountains were rocky enough but did not reach far enough north to be covered with eternal snows. But the adjectives "primitif," "solitaire" (again the motif of landscapes without human figures), "grandiose"; the craggy rocks, the seething torrent, and the stormy sky can be justified. And "l'âpreté farouche d'un Salvator Rosa" captures well the emotional tonality of many of Rosa's pictures, the side of him usually called "sauvage."

Gautier probably referred to Rosa more often than any other French writer of the nineteenth century—or of any century. That record can be explained in part as a function of the sheer quantity of his art writing. But the many references to Rosa would not suffice alone to justify regarding Gautier as the most important French writer about Rosa. He never wrote a whole poem or a whole article about him. He produced no full-fledged *transposition d'art* of a picture by Rosa. But he left several fine verbal transcriptions of specific works by Rosa and several passages that capture the major aspects of Rosa's work: its "sauvagerie," its pre-romantic romanticism, its "âpreté farouche," the artist's mastery of several genres, especially battle scenes and landscapes that contain "sinister" and "picturesque" bandits or, sometimes, are uninhabited or seeming so. Gautier does not display much specific art historical information about Rosa—leaving aside his acceptance of the legends made current by Lady Morgan—but he has a good idea of Rosa's place in the history of painting. He knew something about Rosa the man and his temperament. Rightly or wrongly, moreover, he had a high opinion of Rosa: he may not have placed him among gods or even the demi-gods of painting, but he wished that Rosa's oft-cited *Battle* might hang in the "Salon sacré," i.e., the Salon carré, alongside works by Leonardo, Perugino, Raphael, del Sarto, Veronese, Titian, Tintoretto, et al. Except for Lady Morgan, Rosa had no more ardent and expert promoter in France than Gautier.

Four great French authors of the romantic era who were long treated, in literary history, as apart from or only tangentially related to the romantic school—Balzac, George Sand, Sainte-Beuve, and Michelet—were all quite aware of Rosa's work and reacted to it strongly, if infrequently. Balzac, reacting in late March 1839 to Stendhal's *La Chartreuse de Parme,* had expressed his envy of and admiration for the famous episode recounting the hero's participation in the Battle of Waterloo: "C'est fait comme Borgognone et Vouvermans [*sic*], Salvator Rosa et Walter Scott."[70] The compliment, aimed primarily at Stendhal, spills over onto Rosa as well as Scott and the other painters of battles. Like so many others, Balzac was impressed by the big *Battle* in the Louvre. The comparison with Walter Scott is unique in the

French writing about Rosa. We cannot tell if he has any specific work or works by Scott in mind; virtually all of Scott's novels had been translated into French by 1839, and there is massive evidence of Balzac's interest in Scott and of the latter's influence on him. What is interesting in this text is the link implied between the visual arts and literature. Unfortunately, Balzac does nothing to spell out this relationship.

Other references to Rosa in Balzac's works yield uneven results. In *La Vendetta* (1830), Servin, the art instructor, proclaims that the portrait of the heroine, Ginevra di Piombo, is drawing of the mysterious *proscrit*, Luigi di Porta—she is well on the way to falling in love with him—"est un chef-d'œuvre digne de Salvator Rosa!"[71] The image Ginevra is creating is never described; moreover, a page or so earlier Luigi's countenance is said to be "aussi gracieuse que celle de l'Endymion, chef-d'œuvre de Girodet" (p. 1052). It is difficult to see much in common between Salvator Rosa's "sauvagerie" and "rudesse" and the languid, rather effeminate picture by Girodet; perhaps it is the word *proscrit* that has triggered a reference to Rosa. Balzac, in another early work, *Les Chouans* (1829), has a phrase on Rosa that undercuts this *rapprochement* between Rosa and Girodet: the contrast between the heroine's joy as she appears in splendid wedding attire and the "terreur si profonde empreinte sur tous les traits qu'il semblait aux convives voir dans ces deux figures un tableau bizarre où l'extravagant pinceau de Salvator Rosa aurait représenté la vie et la mort se tenant par la main" (VIII, 1206). At least here, there is something precise; Balzac may have actually looked carefully at the Rosa paintings in the Louvre and drawn some conclusions about the painter's brush work or manner. Or could he have recalled Stendhal's phrase, "le pinceau heurté de Salvator Rosa," in his *Salon de 1824*?[72]

In *La Peau de chagrin* (1831), Balzac's hero, Raphael, empathizes with the pictures in the extraordinary antique shop he visits after an evening of disastrous gambling: "Il grelottait en voyant une tombée de neige de Mieris, ou se battait en regardant un combat de Salvator Rosa"[73]; long before reading *La Chartreuse de Parme*, Balzac knew that Rosa was a painter of battles—knowledge acquired, no doubt, in the Louvre.

Therefore, Balzac knew and admired Rosa's *Battle,* and he made an interesting three-way *rapprochement* involving Rosa, Stendhal, and Walter Scott. But his idea of Rosa's work is unclear. And, if he knew anything about Rosa's life and personality, he does not reveal it in his writings.

George Sand gives us more substantial fare, even if she makes no reference to Rosa in her dozen novels set wholly or partly in Italy, even in *Le Piccinino* (1847) with its handsome young brigand hero and its rocky, volcanic landscapes.[74] Annarosa Poli, in her study of Sand's Italianism, suggests that as early as 1824 she was initiated into things Italian by an article on Canova by Henri de Latouche, in which he compares "l'apathie condamnable de Canova à l'ardeur d'un Michel-Ange ou d'un Salvator Rosa."[75] A few years later, in Auguste Barbier's *Il Pianto* (1833), Sand found "des portraits poétiques des artistes italiens qu'elle admirait le plus: Cimarosa, Salvator Rosa, Michel-Ange, Masaccio" (p. 41). On April 22, 1855, in Rome she visited Rosa's tomb, as her *Agenda memento 1855* reveals (p. 7). On May 1 of the same year, after visiting the Pitti, she jots down in the *carnet:* "de beaux Raphaëls, des Paul Véronese, des Titiens, un superbe portrait par Salvator Rosa" (p. 291). However, writing to Delacroix on July 27 about her recent Italian trip, she describes her awe ("Une stupeur, une terreur, un enthousiasme") at the ceiling of the Sistine chapel, totally overshadowing "les Ghirlandaio, les Albane, les Salvator et tutti quanti, mais non pas Mr Titien et autres vénitiens que l'on retrouve à Florence, ni les Rubens et les Van Dyck que l'on retrouve à Gênes."[76] Both of these references to Rosa leave us a little perplexed: there is no portrait by Rosa currently in the Pitti and nothing by him among the murals of the Sistine Chapel. But the latter reference to Rosa seems to be intended to lump him with some lesser Italian painters of the Renaissance and baroque eras, whether their works appear on the walls of the Sistine Chapel—like the one by Ghirlandaio—or not—like Albani and Rosa. No clear idea of Sand's image of Rosa emerges; we only surmise that he is distinctly inferior to Michelangelo and even to Titian, Rubens, and Van Dyck. If not flattering to Rosa, her ranking of him behind Michelangelo and company would probably be accepted by the vast majority of critics and art lovers.

Two other passing references to Rosa show Sand to be aware of his principal claim to fame and popularity—his landscapes—and of the character of the most popular of these works. On October 31, 1859, writing to Victor Borie, she acknowledges, "[J]'ai une prédilection pour les sites déchirés, et c'est pour ce goût-là que je pardonne à Salvador [*sic*] Rosa tout ce qu'on lui reproche."[77] A similar idea of what Rosa's landscapes meant for Sand emerges in a passage from *Lupo Liverani* (1868): "Un site Salvator Rosa, dans des rochers abrupts, au bord de la mer.—Le soleil vient de se coucher—Peu à peu la nuit vient et la lune se montre."[78] Jagged rocks are everywhere in Rosa, often beside the sea; there are a few sunsets, e.g., in *Marino del porto* (S 43), which Sand could have seen in the Pitti in Florence, and Rosa's skies are often rather somber even when the scene depicted is seen by daylight. I am unable, however, to spot a single moon shining anywhere in Rosa's work. Sand's idea of Rosa landscapes is the conventional one; one would like to know what catalogue of "reproaches" she had in mind in the letter to Victor Borie. Perhaps she was conscious that the "dramatic," grandiloquent style of landscape was yielding to the more realistic manner of Huet, Corot, and the Barbizon painters.

Curiously, it is Sand's earliest reference to Rosa that proves to be most interesting. Writing to Emile Regnault on April 12, 1831, evidently reacting to the recent publication of Hugo's *Notre-Dame de Paris,* she waxes lyrical over what she probably thought of as "her" local Gothic cathedral, Saint-Etienne in Bourges, only about thirty miles from her beloved Nohant:

> C'est le romantique du romantisme, au lieu que Notre-Dame en est le classique. Notre-Dame, c'est parmi les monuments gothiques ce que Chateaubriand est parmi les écrivains, et S-Etienne, ce que Victor Hugo est parmi les poètes, ou bien c'est Byron et Hoffman [*sic*], Raphaël et Salvator, Rossini et Weber, Planat et Odry. . . . Notre-Dame est un tout sublime, où, comme dit fort bien Victor Hugo, le génie de l'architecture corrige à tout instant le caprice de l'artiste. A S-Etienne, l'architecte a été envahi au contraire par le génie de l'artiste, toutes les règles ont été violées et les rêveries bizarres, sauvages et magnifiques de l'imagination ont été jetées à pleines mains sur de grandes murailles sévères, ouvrage d'une autre génération qui jure à tout instant à côté des découpures sarrasines et qui pourtant donne à l'ensemble un caractère étrange de force imposante et de rudesse antique.[79]

We do not need to judge Sand's elaborate schema contrasting two Gothic cathedrals as representing two faces of romanticism, incarnated in French literature by Chateaubriand and Hugo, by Byron and Hoffmann in foreign literature, Rossini and Weber in music, and Planat and Odry as actors. The crucial point for this study is that Sand squarely places Rosa in a line of artists that extends from Raphael, the classicist, to Rosa, the romantic. Her insight is worthy of Théophile Gautier's perceptive formulation, "romantique avant le romantisme."[80] Moreover, she spells out her idea of romanticism in vivid terms: "caprice," "toutes les règles ont été violées," "rêveries bizarres, sauvages et magnifiques," "découpures sarrasines,"[81] "étranges," and "rudesse antique." One cannot miss the adjective "sauvage," perhaps the one most often used to characterize Rosa's work. And it is noteworthy that, in this romantic phase of her artistic and emotional life, Sand chooses Rosa to incarnate romanticism in painting, and probably in landscape painting in particular. And whatever defects she may have been aware of later and however she may have ranked him against the great masters of Italian and Flemish painting, in 1831 she sees him as a worthy foil to the "divine" Raphael and as deserving mention alongside such great names as Chateaubriand, Hugo, Byron, Hoffmann, Rossini, and Weber. Sand is not a major player in the story of Rosa's reception in France, but her role is worth telling.[82]

Sainte-Beuve offers less grist to our mill. Revealingly, his few references to Rosa date from the years when the critic was still close to the mainstream of romanticism though also moving away from it. In an article on Senancour (*Revue de Paris,* January 1832), he describes that author's "génie du paysage" in painterly terms: "une peinture originale et grave, qui ne se rapporte à aucun maître, quelque chose d'intermédiaire entre les prés verdoyants de Ruysdaël et les blanchâtres escarpements de Salvator Rosa."[83] It is likely that Sainte-Beuve has in mind the landscape in the Louvre, which does indeed display areas of whitish rock but is not devoid of vegetation. Sainte-Beuve's idea of Rosa landscapes, as expressed here, is valid as far as it goes. But, given especially that this seems to be his only reference to what was, after all, the Rosa subject matter par excellence for his eighteenth- and nineteenth-century viewers, we would have to conclude that Rosa the painter meant little to Sainte-Beuve.

Reviewing Auguste Barbier's *Il Pianto* the following year, he did not find a direct opening for an evaluation or description of Rosa's painted work: it is in a political role that the young Rosa appears, in the third part, "Chiaia." Sainte-Beuve calls this part of Barbier's poem "un mâle dialogue entre un pêcheur sans nom, qui sera Masaniello si l'on veut, et Salvator Rosa; les espérances de liberté n'ont jamais parlé un plus poétique langage."[84] The critic goes on to quote sixteen lines in which the fisherman glorifies "le peuple" and reprimands the artist for standing aloof from their struggles. Here Sainte-Beuve calls Rosa "le génie mécontent, sinistre et découragé" (p. 238). A little further on, the critic reveals that he is aware not only of Rosa's bitter, satirical side but also of the legend of Rosa's wanderings in the wilderness. But Sainte-Beuve presents these as an evasion, a form of selfishness: a certain type of modern poet, "au lieu de répondre d'une lyre sympathique à l'appel fraternel des hommes, et farouche, inutile, manquant de foi au lendemain, s'enfuit comme Salvator Rosa dans les montagnes" (ibid., p. 239). Here Sainte-Beuve misreads Barbier's poem: the poet gives the last word in the debate between fisherman and artist to the latter, whose escape to the woods and mountains of Calabria is presented as a move toward freedom for the artist intellectual as well as a gesture of solidarity with the rest of humanity:

> O terre, ô bois, ô désolés rivages!
> Recevez-moi parmi vos sombres habitants,
> Car je veux me mêler à leurs troupeaux errants;
> Je veux manger le pain de tout être qui pense,
> Goûter la liberté sur la montagne immense.

Sainte-Beuve's misinterpretation does little for the understanding of Rosa in

France but sheds light on the critic, who, in the early 1830s, was tugged in various directions as he dealt with his snarled relationship with Hugo, distanced himself from militant romanticism, and flirted with Saint-Simonisme and Lamennais's liberal Catholicism. When he calls Rosa "le génie mécontent, sinistre et découragé" and twists the meaning of Barbier's poem, he may, all unaware, be revealing his own confusion and turmoil.

While Sainte-Beuve may have seen the Rosa landscape in the Louvre, with Michelet we have evidence of a closer contact with the painter's work and a more impassioned reaction. His earliest reference to Rosa (1825), however, reveals only that he was aware that Rosa was a leading Italian artist and poet in the age of Louis XIV: as painter, Rosa is listed along with Reni, Albani, Lanfranco, Domenichino, Guercino, and Bernini; as poet, he is lumped with Marino and Tassoni.[85]

In his *Journal* the historian records a number of direct encounters with Rosa's work or what he took to be such. In Florence, on April 1, 1830, he reacted strongly to two pictures by Rosa in the Pitti: "*Bataille* furieuse de Salvator Rosa; il fallait avoir toutes les furies dans l'âme. Son *Catilina*, l'œil perçant, est terrible: l'homme qui reçoit la coupe a une cuirasse de fer et une chevelure brune comme l'airain."[86]

Two weeks later, in Rome, on the point of leaving for Bologna, Michelet sketches with a broad brush the migration ("progrès") from southern idealism to northern materialism: "Rome est le véritable centre: équilibre, orthodoxie, philosophie de médiateur. . . . En peinture, la partie la plus matérielle, le coloris, réussit à Venise, la grâce en Lombardie (Bologne mixte), le dessin à Florence, l'esprit à Naples (Salvator Rosa): dessin vague, coloris nul" (ibid., I, 67). Michelet could have seen a number of Rosa's works in Rome (though not in the Vatican). But, whatever he saw in Rome or elsewhere, one is surprised to see Rosa as the representative of "l'esprit" on the basis of his "dessin vague" and, more justifiably, "coloris nul." Michelet's association of Rosa with the Neapolitan school could be questioned, but it does show that the historian knew at least one fundamental biographical fact about Rosa.

On August 14, 1841, on the ceiling frescoes in the Chapelle de la Trinité at Fontainebleau, he was taken by "un sauvage et un fol triste, dans le goût de Salvator Rosa" (ibid., I, 365). These two figures were parts of the elaborate decorating scheme carried out by Martin Fréminet (1564–1619), "peintre du Roi" under Henri IV. The *rapprochement* between Fréminet and Rosa does little credit to Michelet's feeling for Fréminet's Italianism; modern art historians cite a number of names, especially that of Michelangelo, but never that of Rosa. Granted, they are seeking actual influences, not mere affinities.[87]

Several other references to Rosa in Michelet's *Journal* only whet our appetite. What work or works of Rosa did he see at the Royal Library on December 19, 1843, or later that same day, *chez* "M. Belloc" (*Journal*, I, 543)?[88] Or in the Musée de Rouen on September 13, 1848?[89] On December 23, 1849, he showed "la Guerre," i.e., Rosa's *Battle*, to Athénaïs (II, 81). Two other references to Rosa in the *Journal* (I, 365; II 328) do not record direct contacts between the historian and authentic works by Rosa.[90] Some idea of Michelet's regard for Rosa's work is conveyed when, on August 30, 1846, he expresses regret that "tant de Rembrandt, tous les Salvator" in the Schamps collection in Antwerp have been sold off to England (I, 648). There is not a single reference to Rosa, however, in the twelve volumes of Michelet's correspondence.

We have already seen that Michelet was stirred by two of Rosa's battle paintings, one in the Pitti in Florence and one in the Louvre. Two further texts, both dealing with the horrors of the Thirty Years' War, also attest to his interest in this aspect of Rosa's work; since the picture in the Louvre was accessible to him for many years and since he made a special visit there on at least one occasion to see the picture in his beloved's company, it was probably this picture that was most clearly present in his mind. The briefer and less vivid of the two texts appears in a section of the *Histoire de France* on "Richelieu et la Fronde" (1858). In a passage on Wallenstein, "un joueur" who "spécula sur la fureur du temps, celle du jeu" and who "laissa le soldat jouer tout, la vie, l'honneur, le sang. C'est ce que vous voyez dans les noirs et fumeux tableaux de Valentin, de Salvator."[91] This is the only time, I believe, that critics have made a *rapprochement* between Rosa and Valentin, e.g., the latter's name never appears in Gautier's long lists of painters of battle scenes.[92] But it is Michelet's characterization of these pictures—"noirs et fumeux," "sombres," "ténébreuses"—that matters most: Rosa's leaden skies and smokey clashes of men and arms are well captured in these words.

Over a decade earlier Michelet had unleashed an even more vivid and vehement tirade against the Thirty Years' War, "cette vilaine guerre, la plus laide qui fut jamais, . . . artificielle et mécanique . . . un combat de machines ou de fantômes":[93] "Nulle histoire ne ferait comprendre ce phénomène abominable, s'il n'en restait quelque image dans les peintures maudites de ce damné Salvator" (pp. 76–77). In a note designed to explain this epithet, Michelet writes: "Le mot est dur, j'y ai regret. Si ce grand artiste peint si cruellement la guerre, c'est qu'il eut sans doute plus de cœur qu'aucun des contemporains, et qu'il sentit mieux l'horreur de cette terrible époque" (p. 7). Did Michelet believe that Rosa had actually witnessed the horrors of the Thirty Years' War? We have no evidence that he ever witnessed any war. But Michelet knew that war was a favorite subject for Rosa, and he was moved by the two specific pictures of his that treated that theme. He knew, too, that Rosa was a poet, and he may well have read the pages devoted to his poetry in Salfi's *Histoire littéraire de l'Italie* (Vol. XIII, 1835) or Delécluze's articles on Rosa's satires in the *Revue de Paris* (1840). The vehemence of his words—"les peintures maudites de ce damné Salvator"—expresses the indignation aroused by the "phénomène abominable" of war and its horrors. Historian and painter were responding in like manner to the same calamity, vibrating on the same wavelength.

Michelet's few references to Rosa's works show that his estimate of the artist wavered. Nothing indicates that Rosa was one of his favorite artists. He never wrote at length on any work by Rosa and nothing even faintly comparable to his elaborate interpretation of Dürer's *Melencolia I* in the *Histoire de France*.[94] His writings do not reveal much knowledge of Rosa's life or his place in art history. But he had a passionate reaction to at least two of Rosa's pictures: "*Bataille* furieuse," "peintures maudites," "ce damné Salvator." On several occasions, then, the historian-critic, in writing about Rosa, answered Baudelaire's call for criticism to be "partiale, passionnée, politique."[95]

Edgar Quinet, who was Michelet's friend, fellow historian, and comrade in arms in the ideological wars of the early 1840s, referred to Rosa only once, as far as I know. In *Allemagne et Italie: Philosophie et poésie* (1839), generalizing rather too facilely about the people of Naples, e.g., "Ce peuple-même se chauffe au soleil,"[96] Quinet is forced to admit that Neapolitans are not all the same: "Cependant, du sein de ce sibarisme [*sic*] mendiant, quand une âme vient à s'éveiller par hasard, elle s'exalte dans le spiritualisme ou s'arme d'une énergie sans bornes. Pythagore et son école, Saint Thomas d'Aquin, Vico, Spagnoletto, Salvator Rosa, ce furent là d'étranges lazzaronis" (pp. 202–03).

Of the major French writers of the romantic generation (those born ca. 1790–1820), all except Musset knew Rosa's work and reacted to it in writing. Reflections of Rosa appear in various genres: poetry, fiction, history, criticism, correspondence, and *journaux intimes*. Rosa may not have been a major preoccupation for any of these writers, but the quantity of their references to him and his work, though quite variable from author to author, demonstrates that the Italian artist was a standard reference in this period. Moreover, a fairly consistent view of him and his work prevails: Rosa is a romantic artist *avant la lettre*, especially in his landscapes. Several of the paintings by Rosa on display in the Louvre, only one of which was a landscape, also contributed to the elaboration of this view, or set of views. Perhaps because of the paucity of his paintings to be seen in Paris, Rosa did not become one of those "beacons" of the world of painting hailed by Baudelaire, but his name deserves to be mentioned along with several artists of the past who won a place in the *musée imaginaire* of the most creative writers of the romantic era, worthy to join the giants of the Italian Renaissance and France's own Grand Siècle—Dürer, Rembrandt, Piranesi, Goya, John Martin—not perhaps in the Grande Galerie but in smaller, less conspicuous rooms.

CHAPTER SIX

Criticism, Scholarship, and Journalism, 1824–ca. 1860

We have seen the gradual emergence of Rosa and his work from a sort of literary penumbra in the long period between the first reference in French to him (1647) and the publication of Lady Morgan's biography (1824). Before about 1800, with few exceptions, discussions of Rosa were brief and occurred in various forms of expository prose: biographical dictionaries, encyclopedias, art history, art criticism, treatises on painting, and travel writing. During the Restoration (1814/1815–1830) the landscape was markedly changed, largely as a result of the great cultural shift that brought romanticism to the fore in literature, music, and the visual arts. As far as Rosa is concerned, Lady Morgan's book should be seen as the proximate cause of this change: it turned Rosa into an embodiment of romanticism by furnishing poets, dramatists, and fiction writers with a wealth of information and, perhaps more important, some attractive misinformation about Rosa the artist and the man, linking him to leading romantic themes and figures. In the decades of high romanticism, Rosa became the subject of poems, plays, and fiction and engaged the attention and the admiration of nearly all the literary figures whose works came to form the canon of French romantic writing.

In addition to the essential contribution of Lady Morgan's biography of Rosa, the Restoration years were marked by a quickening tempo of romantic events and trends: the appearance of the major young romantic poets, in painting the outburst of vigor and color in Géricault and Delacroix, the 1824 debate over romanticism, the rumblings of a musical upheaval in the early work of Berlioz, the "Battle of *Hernani*," the rise of a Bohemian subculture among young artists and intellectuals. What these developments meant for the reception of Rosa and the shaping of his image during the romantic period proper has been abundantly shown in the preceding chapter. Abundantly, but not completely. A study of numerous references to Rosa and his work in the writings of scholars, critics, and journalists working in a number of prose genres will complete this account of Rosa's "glory years" in France. Despite the difficulty of classifying many of the texts involved, a generic approach will be applied.

The genres to be examined first are those linked to Rosa's status as a practitioner of the visual arts, that is, art criticism and art history. The criticism of Rosa's work appears scattered through various sorts of writing, as had much art criticism from Vasari on. Rosa was subjected to critical assessment in two histories of Italian art that appeared in France just before and in the same year as Lady Morgan's biography. In his *Essai sur l'histoire de la peinture en Italie*,[1] the Russian senator Count Gregory Orloff (1777–1826) mixes nuggets of criticism with his account of Rosa's life and work. Rosa is pronounced, along with Aniello Falcone, "l'honneur de son école" (II, 367); he is primarily a landscapist (ibid.); his later landscapes are "sombres et terribles" (II, 368). Orloff summarizes his view of Rosa in these terms: "La fierté, l'énergie, une mélancolie sombre et altière guidaient les crayons de ce peintre. Il dessina avec grandeur. Son coloris est souvent pur, et sa touche est toujours mâle et pleine de génie" (ibid.). The Count is aware of several of Rosa's history paintings (*Catiline's Conspiracy*, the Louvre *Battle*, *The Rescue of Moses*, *Mercury and the Peasant*, and *Jonah*), some of which he could have seen in Italy; but he does not judge or characterize them (ibid.).

In 1824, a French translation by Madame Armande Dieudé of Luigi Lanzi's respected *Storia pittorica dell'Italia*[2] was published in Paris as *Histoire de la peinture en Italie*.[3] Lanzi (1732–1810), curator for antiquities at the Uffizi in the latter decades of the eighteenth century, had, we can assume, much direct observation of Rosa's works in Florence; the few pictures he mentions, however, are mostly elsewhere. Like Orloff and so many others, Lanzi emphasizes Rosa's landscapes, whose somber character, according to Lanzi, is an effect of Caravaggio's influence:

> [I]l semble dans les paysages s'être fait une maxime de les représenter sans choix, ou plutôt de choisir ce qu'il y trouvait de moins souriant. Les *forêts sauvages* décrites par Dante, les rochers, les précipices, les cavernes, des champs couverts de débris, sont les scènes qu'il se plaît le plus à présenter aux yeux. Les arbres, ou coupés, ou déracinés, ou difformes, sont ceux qu'il retrace le plus fréquemment ; et loin de répandre dans l'espace aucun des effets de l'astre qui vivifie la terre, il est rare qu'il y introduise une certaine vivacité de couleur. . . . ce style nouveau plaît par la sévérité, ainsi que le vin flatte le palais par son âpreté. (II, 238–39)

Lanzi notes the frequency and popularity of Rosa's "little figures" and speaks of Rosa's work in other genres ("marines," "sujets d'histoire," "scènes de sorcellerie," "tableaux d'autel," "sujets profanes" [ibid.]; he offers the following capsule description of Rosa's manner: "dans toutes ses compositions son style n'est jamais choisi, ni toujours correct, mais animé, facile, savant quant à l'emploi des couleurs, et régulier dans l'harmonie" (II, 238).

In the year following Lady Morgan's biography appeared in Vol. XXXIX of Michaud's *Biographie universelle, ancienne et moderne,*[4] with an article on Rosa as the first entry, twenty-three columns long. The author, Pietro de Angelis, like Rosa, was a native of Naples.[5] As an Italian by birth, a Neapolitan, and a partisan of the Risorgimento, De Angelis was temperamentally well fitted to write on Rosa; moreover, he had done research for Count Orloff's *Mémoires historiques, politiques et littéraires sur le Royaume de Naples* (Paris, 1819–1821). The bulk of De Angelis's text, as one might expect in an article in the *Biographie universelle,* deals with the life of Rosa and certainly draws on Lady Morgan's biography, which he calls "le roman plutôt que l'histoire de ce peintre" (p. 12).[6]

De Angelis's criticism of Rosa's work takes the form of generalizations about the nature of his genius and observations, sometimes quite detailed, on specific pictures. Rosa's very first works, he says, "avaient déjà cette vigueur qui est empreinte dans tous ses ouvrages" (p. 2), and the young Rosa developed a rapidity of execution "qui était d'accord avec la fougue de son imagination et l'impatience de son caractère; ses compositions, pleines de verve et d'énergie, décelaient l'originalité de son talent" (ibid.). De Angelis develops at some length the theme of Rosa's independence and originality, especially in his landscapes:

> Génie neuf et indépendant, il dédaigna de suivre les traces des autres: à une époque où la peinture comptait très-peu de modèles, et offrait un très-grand nombre d'imitateurs, il sut imprimer à son style un cachet tellement original, que les yeux les moins exercés sont en état de le reconnaître. Il dépouilla la nature de tous ses ornements; il écarta de ses tableaux ces beaux chênes, ces riches péristyles, ces brillants épisodes de la mythologie, ces heureux détails de la vie champêtre, que la riante imagination du Lorrain et des Poussins avait introduits dans leurs compositions. Il les remplace par quelques vieux troncs sillonnés par la foudre, combattant contre la fureur des autans, se brisant sous les coups redoublés de la tempête; par d'arides déserts, de tristes rochers, des sites d'un aspect sauvage et lugubre, qui jètent l'ame dans la plus profonde rêverie. (pp. 3–4)

Later De Angelis, after relating the "terrible catastrophe" (p. 7) of Masaniello's failure, lumps together some half dozen of Rosa's history paintings as evidence of this change of character: "On y entrevoit ce profond mépris, cette vive indignation contre les vices des hommes et les crimes des sociétés" (ibid.). The pictures in question are briefly characterized in such a way as to underscore the pessimism at their core. For example: "C'est Démocrite, insultant à la vanité humaine au milieu des tombeaux ruinés" (ibid.).[7] In a similar passage (p. 10) three of Rosa's history paintings—*Pythagoras Emerges from the Underworld* (S 165), *Catiline's Conspiracy* (S 180), and *The Martyrdom of Saints Cosmas and Damian* (S 252)—are briefly characterized. A long description (ibid.) of the famous *Saul and the Witch of Endor* (S 210) turns out to be lifted from C. P. Landon's *Annales du Musée;* the quotation fills up a column of De Angelis's text.[8] For De Angelis, "Ce tableau marque la maturité du talent de Salvator Rosa, et le plus grand développement de son génie" (p. 10), a judgment suggesting that De Angelis, aesthetically as well as politically, was in tune with his times.

Critically, the core of De Angelis's article is a long description of the "fameuse bataille" (S 111) in the Louvre, which impressed so many viewers in the early nineteenth century.[9]

> Le moment choisi par Salvator Rosa, est celui où la victoire est disputée avec le plus d'acharnement; c'est une poignée de braves, que la mort a épargnés, et que les chances du combat amènent dans un endroit solitaire. La valeur et la vengeance animent ces guerriers, pour qui le trépas est moins à craindre qu'une défaite: ils occupent le devant de la scène, jonché d'armes et de cadavres. Les vainqueurs sont mêlés aux vaincus; les mourants se confondent avec les morts: le désordre est partout, la confusion nulle part. Le peintre a disposé ses groupes avec intelligence; et chaque figure est placée de manière à pouvoir se remuer facilement: elles déploient une vie et une activité extraordinaires. Les plans éloignés retracent la fin de l'action, dont chaque épisode est une partie essentielle du sujet. D'un côté, sont dressées les tentes des vainqueurs; de l'autre, on voit fuir les débris de l'armée: la mort plane partout; et le soldat dans sa fureur, ne respecte ni le temple des dieux, ni les paisibles demeures des bergers. L'incendie d'une flotte qu'on voit brûler dans le lointain, ajoute à l'horreur de cette scène: ce qui n'a pu tomber sous le fer est dévoré par les flammes; et le vent disperse du même souffle les cendres des chaumières et celles des vaisseaux. (p. 9)

This passage deserves to be seen alongside similarly detailed descriptions we have found in the writings of Taillasson, the authors of *Le Musée français*, and C. P. Landon. Such passages are noteworthy for their concreteness and specificity, at odds with so much critical writing of this and the surrounding periods. De Angelis's contribution is interesting for its emphasis on the well-organized structure he claims to see in Rosa's picture, along with the violence that is plain for all to see. One cannot say that he supplies any *interpretation* of the picture, except for what emerges from this somewhat surprising juxtaposition of order and violence. De Angelis is a little more pithy, if conventional, in a brief comment on Rosa's *Satires:* "En général, on peut dire que Salvator a écrit ses Satires comme il a peint ses tableaux, se montrant plus occupé de la force du dessin que de la beauté du coloris" (p. 8). Here De Angelis seems rather even-handed, not eager to make Rosa a partisan of either "le dessin" or "la couleur." At least he refrains from criticizing Rosa's *coloris* as "terne," "froid," etc.

If De Angelis is a respectable critic of Rosa's work, one cannot say that he is remarkable. But, placed as it was in one of the most important reference works produced in France in the nineteenth century, one that is still in wide use, his evaluation of Rosa assumes a great importance.

In 1826 Francesco Salfi, who in 1824 had subjected Lady Morgan's biography to a long but somewhat negative review in the *Revue encyclopédique*, devoted over two pages to Rosa's satires in his *Résumé de l'histoire de la littérature italienne.*[10] Despite some reservations—e.g., Rosa "brilla dans les satires plutôt par son talent que par son art" (II, 29)—Salfi gives a generally enthusiastic assessment of the *Satire,* inspired mostly by his admiration for Rosa's bold, frank denunciations of the tyranny and corruption of Italy's rulers, secular and especially clerical. Only one "fact" about Rosa's life is specifically mentioned: his participation in Masaniello's revolt (II, 30), an act of which Salfi clearly approved. Rosa the man and the poet are one: "Ses satires sont la preuve incontestable de sa manière de penser. Il les écrivit en homme libre, ou, du moins, comme s'il n'écrivait pas en Italie" (ibid.). Salfi's climax is a ringing endorsement of Rosa's poems: "De toutes les satires italiennes celles de Salvator Rosa furent les seules avec lesquelles se familiarisa la multitude. . . . A cet égard on peut les regarder comme plus nationales et plus utiles que les autres" (II, 31).

Salfi, in 1824, may have found fault with many details of Lady Morgan's treatment of Rosa, but two years later, writing on the subject of Rosa's poetry, he was essentially in agreement with her and, as such, one of Rosa's most ardent partisans.

Rosa gets slight and slighting treatment in the huge *Traité complet de la peinture* of the very academic Jacques-Nicolas Paillot de Montabert (1771–1849).[11] The only connected passage on Rosa is a very brief historical and biographical résumé (I, 579). In chapter 495 ("On néglige la justesse de coloris parce qu'elle a été négligée par des peintres très-célèbres"), after lashing out at the "lazzis de la palette des peintres rejetons des écoles venitiennes," denouncing them as "triviales extravagances," Paillot cites Rosa's "couleur terne et aride" (VIII, 24–25), presumably as an example of great painters who neglected "la justesse de coloris." In chapter 552, Paillot, offering some general considerations on landscape, comments on the recent creation of a prize for the best "paysage héroïque." He cites Claude, Ruysdael, Karel Dujardin, Paul Brill, and Rosa as proof that a landscape can be beautiful without being heroic (VIII, 394). A few pages later, Rosa is again cited along with "les Poussin," Claude Lorrain, Titian, and several others as evidence that one need not travel to the ends of the earth to paint good landscapes (VIII, 402). Paillot had been a pupil of David and, in his *Traité*, promoted a rather severe neoclassicism. It is a little surprising that he treats Rosa rather gently, perhaps because Rosa eschewed the risqué and the erotic.

An even more negative view of Rosa is met in the guidebook/travelogue of a certain Antoine-Claude-Pasquin, *dit* Valery (1789–1847), *Voyages historiques et litteraires en Italie*,[12] a work that had three editions. In Florence at the Pitti, Valery finds the *Conjuration de Catilina* "beaucoup trop vantée et qui n'a rien de romain ni d'antique" (III, 148). A *Christ chassant les vendeurs du temple* in Genoa—no such picture appears in Salerno's catalogue—is "très vanté, un de ces éternels chefs-d'œuvre de Salvator Rosa, des galeries d'Italie, chefs-d'œuvre qui ne sont le plus souvent, comme celui-ci, que des ouvrages fort ordinaires" (V, 53). The *Mort d'Abel* in the Galleria Doria-Pamphili is, similarly, "vantée, quoique maniérée de composition et de couleur" (IV, 152). Valery seems to purse his lips in Viterbo: "On vante à l'église de la Mort le *S. Thomas mettant le doigt dans la plaie du Sauveur*, de Salvator Rosa" (IV, 251). But occasionally Valery unbends. The *San Torpè* in Pisa "a sa hardiesse" (III, 208). *The Martyrdom of Saints Cosmas and Damian* gets a mixed review: "il y a de la verve d'exécution et une certaine chaleur de coloris, mais il n'est qu'une preuve de plus que l'artiste manquait d'études et qu'il ne savait dessiner" (IV, 16). But before the tomb of Rosa in Santa Maria degli angeli, Valery pronounces the epitaph "exagérée" because it puts Rosa on a par with the greatest painters and poets of all time (IV, 110). Negative views of Rosa have been held since the beginning of the literature on him; the attitudes that gave rise to such views could usually be linked to neoclassical tradition and convention. With the forgotten Valery we seem to be dealing not with the exponent of a certain aesthetic or defender of the rules but with a *blasé* traveler. In any case, the seeds of Rosa's decline are planted, even if Valery is not typical of the countless authors of travel books about Italy.

Before 1830 serious art writing was rather rare in the periodical press. With the coming of the July Monarchy, greater press freedom (which suffered a setback, however, a few years later) encouraged the creation of many new newspapers and reviews. An outstanding product of this development was *L'Artiste,* founded in 1831. It would have a long life and publish works by illustrious writers, e.g., Gautier and Baudelaire, to mention just two.

It was in *L'Artiste* for May 31, 1835, (vol. IX, 18ᵉ livraison) that a certain Alexandre de Saint-Chéron (fl. 1833–1873) published what I believe to be the first article about Rosa to appear in any French periodical.[13] It is primarily a "life and works" of the artist, with emphasis on the life. The elements are arranged in chronological order. Saint-Chéron tips his hat to Lady Morgan's "roman en deux volumes" (p. 205): "Tout en consultant le travail de cette dame, nous nous défierons de son imagination et de sa crédulité, et nous rectifierons ses erreurs par le témoignage des biographes contemporains de notre artiste" (ibid.).[14]

Saint-Chéron's principal theme, in his treatment of Rosa, is perhaps the insistence on the relationship between the artist's life and the character of his work: "Presque tous les grands artistes ont eu une existence agitée et originale, et celle de Salvator Rosa fut particulièrement romanesque, dramatique, remplie d'accidens bizarres ou extraordinaires, et nul n'a mieux empreint ses créations des variétés et des impressions de son existence" (ibid.). His very choice of subjects reveals "la sombre mélancolie, l'amertume, l'indignation qui emplissait son âme" (p. 208). The "combinaisons infinies du sublime et du terrible" of the wild landscapes he encountered in his early wanderings "contribuèrent à donner à ses paysages cet aspect sombre et dévasté" (p. 206). After the failure of Masaniello's revolt, Rosa produced two of his most beautiful works: "A peine de retour à Rome, le cœur flétri, ulcéré, Salvator se remit à ses travaux, et à composer sous l'influence des sentiments qui l'agitaient" (p. 208). The two pictures in question were *Humana Fragilitas* and *La Fortuna,* both highly satirical in their allegory. In his *Job,* Rosa powerfully expressed his own struggles and disappointments: "Ce sujet convenait à l'âme triste et dégoûtée de Salvator, dont l'orgueil insatiable n'était jamais satisfait de sa position. Dans cette peinture, Job paraît aussi fatigué des remontrances de ses amis que tourmenté de ses propres afflictions" (p. 209).

One curious motif, in Saint-Chéron's criticism, and one of the first to emerge, is his perception of the intellectual and ideological underpinning of Rosa's work: he finds it essentially postreligious: "son inspiration fut étrangère à l'inspiration toute religieuse des âges précédens" (p. 205). For Rosa lived at a time when the Reformation had undermined Europe's religious faith: "elle avait affaibli ou ruiné ses croyances; préparé les esprits à des habitudes toutes philosophiques; engendré cet état moral de doute, d'inquiétude, d'indépendance individuelle, sombre et sauvage, dont les effets sont encore sensibles sous nos yeux" (ibid.). Perhaps alone of these little-known art critics, Saint-Chéron sees Rosa as modern: "il est presque un artiste contemporain dans l'originalité, l'allure, la direction de ses pensées et de son talent; il y a en lui du Byron pour l'orgueil, ses colères contre l'ordre social, son scepticisme, cette tristesse amère, maudissante, qui ressemble à la révolte de Satan" (p. 209).[15] It is quite striking that Saint-Chéron pays much greater attention to Rosa's secular work on classical subjects than to his pictures on Christian themes: he has a respectful appreciation (p. 207) of the *Madonna del suffragio* (S 158) and shows real enthusiasm for the early *L'Incredulità de san Tommaso* (S 10): "Ce tableau d'histoire . . . manifestait déjà les hautes qualités de son pinceau, la puissance d'invention et la facilité de composition" (p. 206).[16]

It is difficult to tell exactly which of Rosa's pictures Saint-Chéron had actually seen. A good many are described in such a way as to suggest that he had seen them: *Agar*—the picture Lanfranco admired when he "discovered" Rosa—*L'Incrédulité de saint Thomas*, a *Prométhée*, *Une sorcière*, *L'Enfant prodigue*, *La Mort de Régulus*, *Humana fragilitas*, *Fortuna*, *Bacchanales*, *Job*, *Jason*, the *Conpiration de Catilina*, and *Saül et la Sorcière d'Endor*. The last named he saw in the Louvre; indeed, he twice complains about the un-fortunate placing of the picture by the museum authorities. He certainly saw the big *Battle* picture in the Louvre but does not describe it. He simply calls it "une *Bataille* très-renommée" and adds later that it is too well known to need description.[17] Though he has certainly seen some pictures by Rosa, Saint-Chéron rarely dwells on technical questions: apropos of the *Prométhée*, typically, he mingles comment on the "expression" and Rosa's mastery of anatomy (p. 207). The *Conspiration de Catilina* is treated similarly: "La variété et l'énergie des têtes, l'habileté des poses, l'art qui préside à l'arrangement des groupes, tout justifie l'enthousiasme qu'excita cette peinture" (p. 209). A number of pictures are simply pronounced masterpieces: "un des chefs-d'œuvre de Salvator Rosa" (p. 209); "une des plus belles compositions de Salvator" (p. 207).

In a long passage near the end of his article Saint-Chéron sums up "les principaux traits du génie de Salvator":

> [I]l fut doué d'une imagination vive, pleine de chaleur et d'entraînement, d'une conception mâle, rapide, d'une exécution facile, d'une verve bouillante qui animait les détails comme l'ensemble. Les critiques contemporains lui reprochaient de l'exagération dans le dessin, des chairs peu naturelles, des attitudes communes, des airs de tête toujours dédaigneux. Ces reproches vont trop loin, et ils ont cependant quelque chose de vrai; en effet, le dessin de Salvator n'est pas toujours correct, mais il ne manque jamais d'aisance et de grandeur; on pourrait souhaiter plus d'élégance dans ses figures, mais non pas plus d'originalité, plus de vie. Salvator présentait une de ces

bizarreries qui se retrouvent souvent dans les hommes de génie, c'est qu'il dédaignait précisément ce qui constituait son plus beau talent, l'art de peindre le paysage. . . . Toutefois, Salvator n'en a pas moins réussi à devenir un des plus grands paysagistes de la peinture. (p. 210)

The summit of Saint-Chéron's achievement may be the lines that follow here:

S'il est une étude piquante à faire pour le plaisir des contrastes, c'est de comparer les paysages de Salvator, de Claude Lorrain et de Ruysdaël. Chez l'un, la nature n'apparaît que dans un magnifique désordre, avec des torrens qui se brisent contre des rochers, avec des montagnes, des arbres frappés de la foudre; il vous laisse une impression de tristesse, de solitude et d'effroi. Chez le Lorrain, c'est la création en fête, parée, noyée dans des flots de lumière; elle invite à la joie, au bonheur, à l'amour; chez Ruysdael, c'est une nature calme, sans éclat, un peu voilée, comme le ciel de la Hollande. (p. 210)

Saint-Chéron may not have been the best qualified person to introduce Rosa into the columns of such a review as *L'Artiste*, but there are nuggets of criticism scattered amid the boilerplate of his prose. He is only a critic by fits and starts. Some of his art history is dubious, and he is probably disingenuous in claiming to rise above Lady Morgan's "roman." But his Rosa is a philosophical artist who shuns baroque and rococo frivolities in favor of a painting inspired by melancholy, pride, and indignation.

In the same year (1835) Rosa debuted in the periodical press, Francesco Salfi, in his continuation of Ginguené's ambitious *Histoire littéraire d'Italie*,[18] offered two passages on Rosa, about twenty pages in Vol. XIII on Rosa as satirical poet and four pages in Vol. XIV on Rosa as painter. (The two volumes appeared about six months apart.) Understandably, since he is writing a history of Italian literature, Salfi inserts the biography of Rosa in the longer discussion: it is fairly standard stuff, but with some emphasis on the artist's education and the impact of his writing on his experience. Concerning Rosa and his part in Masaniello's uprising, he writes: "Rosa ne demeura pas étranger à cet événement; il défendit l'épée à la main l'indépendance de son pays, et immortalisa par ses vers et son pinceau ce jeune pêcheur qui, devenu en peu de jours le chef de tout le peuple napolitain, fut successivement trahi, assassiné et déifié" (XIII, 306).

The same view of Rosa as satirist emerges here as in his briefer treatment, his 1826 *Résumé de l'histoire de la littérature italienne*. The imperfections in the *Satire* are spelled out, however, in more detail: "Le style de Rosa est ordinairement inégal, quelquefois trop familier, même ignoble. L'auteur se laisse entraîner par sa verve, et adopte sans aucun choix tout ce qu'elle lui suggère. Il écrit comme un improvisateur qui n'a ni le temps, ni la patience de se corriger" (XIII, 309). Then there are "ces fougues monotones et fatigantes," an excess of erudition, a tendency to wander from his main subject (ibid.).

Still, Salfi admires Rosa the satirist and the artist, and for much the same reasons as those given in the *Résumé* of 1826: "Ce qui surtout le distingue, c'est qu'il imprime à toutes ces productions son caractère original et indépendant. Il retraçait la nature physique et morale, dans ses tableaux et dans ses vers, d'après ses propres observations. Ennemi déclaré de l'*imitation*, il s'indignait de toute espèce d'entraves, et faisait tous ses efforts pour briser celles des autres" (XIII, 308). In a long passage from *La Pittura,* given both in French and in Italian, Rosa proclaims his love of frankness and his devotion to the common good (XIII, 308–09).

A little more than half of Salfi's treatment of Rosa's satires is a rather straightforward résumé of the six satires. Only apropos of the fourth, *La Guerra,* does he rise above the pedestrian: "Le sujet en est vraiment trop grave pour se prêter au piquant du genre satirique; mais l'auteur nous en dédommage par les grandes vérités qu'il expose, vérités qui, si elles sont maintenant trop communes, étaient de son temps rares et hardies" (XIII, 316). Again, it is Salfi's sympathy for Rosa as partisan of Masaniello and his revolt that inspires him:

> Il parle de cet événement avec tout l'intérêt d'un homme qui y a figuré; et si quelques biographes avaient mieux examiné cet endroit de sa satire, ils ne se seraient pas donné tant de peine pour prouver qu'il était resté étranger à la révolte de Masaniello, comme s'il eût été contraire à son caractère d'y prendre part. (XIII, 317)

Salfi's pages on Rosa's satires are not only largely flattering to the poet; they are the most thorough discussion of them between Lady Morgan's book and a series of articles by Delécluze in 1840.

No such claim can be made for the four pages on Rosa as painter in Vol. XIV of the *Histoire littéraire d'Italie,* but they are deserving of a careful examination, even if Salfi is primarily a literary historian. He begins with high praise, calling Rosa "un peintre qui, par la variété de ses talens et l'originalité de son génie, a mérité plus que tout autre l'admiration de la posterité" (XIV, 371). Salfi emphasizes Rosa's deliberate quest for original subjects in his history paintings (XIV, 371–72). In Salfi's eyes, Rosa brought "la force d'Eschyle" (XIV, 372) to his very first history painting, his *Prométhée* (presumably S 8), and in general made a rather subversive use of Greek mythology: "[il] fit voir à ses contemporains comment elle peut servir à exprimer les grandes vérités qu'il serait dangereux d'exprimer autrement" (ibid.).

Except for a rather ambiguous remark about Rosa's color—"On le trouve, dans ses paysages et ses marines, coloriste encore plus étonnant que dans ses tableaux d'histoire" (XIV, 373)—Salfi barely mentions questions of style and technique: the subject matter and the emotional impact of Rosa's work monopolize his commentary. In his pictures "l'on reconnaît la superiorité de son esprit et de son caractère" (XIV, 371); these works are admirable "par la grandeur de ses compositions, dont il ne voulut emprunter les sujets à personne, par le mouvement expressif de ses figures, et par la hardiesse et la force de sa pensée" (XIV, 371–72). Salfi mentions seventeen pictures by name, mostly without giving any details or any evaluation. From those over which he pauses a moment he draws moral and philosophical lessons: in *L'Incredulità de san Tommaso* Rosa expressed "toute la sagesse de la pensée qui ne cède qu'au témoignage des sens et à l'évidence de l'observation" (XIV, 372). The flames that should consume the martyred saints Cosmas and Damian "[les] respectent" and "s'élancent contre les bourreaux" (ibid.). From *Pindar and Pan* we learn that "le génie et l'enthousiasme ne peuvent être communiqués que par la contemplation de la nature" (XIV, 373). The symbolic meaning of "la *Fragilité humaine*" and "la *Fortune*" is spelled out (ibid.). Rosa's battle scenes reveal "les suites funestes du despotisme et de la guerre" (XIV, 374).

Salfi is aware of the various facets of Rosa's work; indeed, he calls him "ce peintre encyclopédique" (XIV, 374) and specifies that Rosa painted history pictures, religious pictures, battles, marines, and, of course, landscapes. He devotes a rather standard passage to Rosa's work in this latter genre, beginning: "Il y présente ce que la nature a de plus sauvage et de plus horrible" (XIV, 373). This topic leads naturally on to some remarks about the "petites figures" Rosa placed in his landscapes: "A ces scènes de désordre physique, il en joignit de perversité morale. Aucun peintre n'a mieux saisi le caractère de ces hommes dégénérés qui semblent haïr la société et la vie, et ne se plaire qu'à porter partout le trouble et la destruction" (ibid.). Salfi is noncommittal on Lady Morgan's claim that Rosa lived among the bandits (ibid., note 1). The substantive part of Salfi's criticism ends with the claim that just as Rosa, the painter of battle pictures, vied with Falcone ("qu'on consultait alors comme un oracle dans ce genre de composition") and Cerquozzi, similarly "il s'était placé, par ses paysages, à côté du Lorrain et du Poussin" (XIV, 374). Even if we interpret this latter name as a reference to the lesser Poussin, i.e., Gaspard Dughet, this is high praise. In the early nineteenth century as in the seventeenth and eighteenth, Claude Lorrain generally enjoyed the highest reputation among all landscape painters.[19]

One senses that Salfi's contact with Rosa's work must have been, for the most part, indirect. He never gives the impression of transmitting to his reader the experience of lingering over any particular picture. Perhaps, in part because he is not a practitioner of the visual arts or an art critic, Salfi almost entirely ignores questions of style and technique; this omission confers the advantage of not forcing him into the traditional discussion of "faults" and infringements of the rules. Salfi sees primarily in Rosa a reflection of his own political and religious leanings as a partisan of the Risorgimento and an heir of the *philosophes* and the Enlightenment. He admires Rosa for his gritty courage in his struggles against the artists, e.g., Ribera in Naples and Bernini in Rome, who each dominated the art world of his time and place, and for his criticism of the powers that were. The Rosa we see here is, then, a counterpart of the Rosa Salfi presented in his twenty pages in Vol. XIII on Rosa the satiric poet, and he is of a piece with the man and the artist projected in Lady Morgan's biography, but, though he knew her book, he may be writing largely independent of her influence.

About midway through the period that saw Rosa being warmly received in France on several levels, he became the object of a violent attack, the most sustained he was to undergo prior to Ruskin's. This onslaught came in the form of three articles on Rosa's *Satire* by the critic Etienne-Jean Delécluze (1781–1863), published in the *Revue de Paris* August 30, September 27, and October 25, 1840. Delécluze, a pupil and follower of Jacques-Louis David, is probably best known for his biography of his teacher, *Louis David, son école et son temps* (1855). Though generally faithful to David's legacy and example, Delécluze was not without a tincture of romanticism. He was part of the politically liberal group clustered around the periodical *Le Globe* during the Restoration, which included Stendhal, Mérimée, Sainte-Beuve, and Viollet-le-Duc (Delécluze's nephew), and he took a certain interest in Shakespeare's Italian sources. But in his critical and historical writings, most of which originated as articles in the *Journal des Débats*—to which he contributed for over forty years (1822–1863)—and other leading periodicals, he staunchly defended neoclassicism and inveighed against "la bourrasque romantique." Delécluze exhibited in the Salons from 1808 to 1814, but turned to literature and became a prolific author of journalistic criticism. Early on, things and persons Italian loomed large among his interests; his first article in the *Débats* (November 25, 1822) was on Canova, and he was the first writer in France to translate Dante's *La vita nuova* and *Canzoni*.[20] Before writing on Rosa's satires, Delécluze translated most of Ariosto's satires in the *Revue de Paris* in six installments appearing between July 14 and October

29, 1839. Thus Delécluze brought impressive credentials to the study (and translation) of Rosa's satires.

He also brought to the subject, almost undiluted, his hostility to romanticism. Except for a few concessions in Rosa's favor, his articles are a forceful, sometimes virulent attack, not only on the *Satire* but on Rosa the man and his work, graphic as well as literary. Moreover, Delécluze targets, beyond Rosa, romanticism itself and especially what he took to be the romantic concept of the man of genius; it is as if Rosa and his satires served as a pretext for the more general attack.

Using one of Salvini's editions of the *Satire*, Delécluze works his way through the six satires in three installments, the first of which is titled *La Musica*, the second *La Poesia* and *La Pittura*, and the third *La Guerra, La Babilonia*, and *L'Invidia*. The three texts occupy over fifty-five pages of closely-printed matter, perhaps 30,000 words, enough to compose a small book (and indeed there was a *tirage à part*, as often happened with Delécluze's articles, even with single articles).

Delécluze's first article[21] opens with some generalities that place Rosa in the context of the encyclopedic tendency that characterized the Italian genius from Dante to the beginning of the seventeenth century. He cites a number of well-known examples, Leonardo, Michelangelo, etc., but tips us off that Rosa is in for some criticism: "Quoique placé à une distance incommensurable de ces grands hommes, cependant Salvator Rosa, peintre et graveur habile, homme d'esprit faisant des vers, comédien renommé et musicien pétulant et agréable, servira à fortifier la proposition que j'ai avancée" (I, 318). Rosa, in fact, has enjoyed an inflated reputation and is "parmi les artistes du second ordre, peut-être faudrait-il dire du troisième ordre" (I, 318–19). Still, "il avait de l'invention et de la verve" (I, 319) and so deserves our attention. Delécluze then undertakes a biographical sketch, about three pages long, based, he tells us, on "une vie très prolixe écrite par Baldinucci, ami intime et admirateur passionné de Salvator Rosa" (I, 318–19). Delécluze dismisses Lady Morgan's stories about Rosa's wanderings in the Abruzzi and Calabria and, specifically, the anecdote of his capture by brigands: her book is "tout un roman" and "cette anecdote peu vraisemblable n'est nullement prouvée" (I, 320). On the other hand, he fully accepts the legend of Rosa's participation in Masaniello's uprising—not, it would appear, on the strength of Lady Morgan's testimony but probably because the story appears in the introduction to Salvini's edition of the *Satire*, which he tells us he used (II, 273).[22] As he concludes his biography, Delécluze briefly strikes what will become a *leitmotiv:* despite his pretense of philosophic scorn for human weakness, Rosa's conduct reveals a very flawed man. Delécluze concludes his introduction to Rosa with some general remarks about the *Satires,* described as "ouvrages très imparfaits sous le rapport de l'invention, entachés de mauvais goût, mais où l'auteur s'est peint, ainsi que son siècle, souvent avec exagération et toujours avec énergie" (I, 324). Delécluze's view of the satires, of Rosa's artistic production, and of his claim to a lofty philosophical position has, thus, been made clear.

The structure of Delécluze's first article is surprising. Since Rosa's first satire is about music, Delécluze yields, not for the last time, to the temptation to digress, introducing a history of music, especially of vocal music, and most particularly of opera (I, 324–27). Over two pages of Rosa's diatribe against the vocal music of his time are quoted verbatim. The satire, taken as a whole, is characterized as "hérissée d'allusions aux personnages de l'antiquité, ordinairement déclamatoire, entachée de mauvais goût et parfois d'obscénités" (I, 329). Delécluze then allows that the poem's conclusion, a diatribe against the exorbitant popularity of the performers of his time, is "écrit avec une certaine verve d'expression basse et populacière" (ibid.). But the contrast between Rosa's actual life and his "exagérations puritaines" (ibid.), "ton solennel," and "sainte et pieuse colère" (I, 329–30) opens the way again for Delécluze's accusation of hypocrisy: "celui qui l'a écrit fut pendant toute sa vie, par instinct ainsi que par habitude, un baladin déterminé, un grimacier célèbre, en un mot un véritable farceur" (I, 330); moreover, "il était ouvertement épicurien" and wrote "sous la même influence à demi-hypocrite qui fit écrire Horace, Sénèque, Martial et Pétrone" (ibid.). Finally, Rosa's satire reflects a gloomy, uneasy inner life and contains not one "éclair véritable de gaieté: quand il veut être grave, il est gourmé; s'il cherche à plaisanter, il devient grossier et obscène" (ibid.).

At this point, Delécluze turns his article over to another author in order to reveal, by way of contrast, the deficiencies in Rosa. After a brief introduction, he quotes for over seven pages from Benedetto Marcello's satirical brochure, *Il teatro alla moda.*[23] In conclusion, Delécluze fires a final salvo: "Près de cette satire légère, mais ferme et tracée avec tant de naturel, celle de Salvator Rosa, enfarinée d'érudition et laissant percer l'humeur jalouse de l'auteur à travers le vernis de stoïcisme dont elle est recouverte, ne gagne pas à la comparaison" (I, 337).

This first article, despite its warped structure and lengthy digressions, sounds the major themes of Delécluze's complaints against Rosa. Before spelling these out, it needs to be said that here and there he finds something good in Rosa's poems. *La Pittura* "offre des détails curieux" (II, 261) and is "écrite parfois avec verve" (II, 264). A certain passage of the same poem is a "morceau curieux et écrit avec verve" (ibid.). The long episode involving Buffamalco and a talking monkey, to which Delécluze devotes three pages, is "l'un des plus piquans [morceaux] de Salvator Rosa, de verve brutale mais spirituelle" (II, 268–69). Rosa's verses, in the passage from *La Guerra* on Masaniello's revolt, are "pleins de passion" (III, 266), and a brief pessimistic outburst wins his approval: "Ces paroles, écrites par la même main qui n'épargna pas les soldats espagnols dans les rues de Naples, ne sont pas sans portée; aussi ne peut-on les lire sans émotion" (III, 269). But one feature of *La Poesia* wrings a major admission from Delécluze: Rosa's assault on "l'école italienne" (II, 259):

> Salvator Rosa prit courageusement une tout autre manière, et, s'attaquant à des choses vraies, réelles, dont il faisait un choix en observant le monde, aux bergers imaginaires introduits dans les poèmes à la mode, il substitua des hommes véritables et mit de côté le jargon de la galanterie pour reprendre un langage, sinon plus simple, au moins plus vrai. Considérées sous ce point de vue, les poésies, et surtout les satires de Salvator Rosa, malgré leurs défauts, ont une qualité franche qui les distingue des ouvrages écrits vers le même temps en Italie. La plupart des poètes alors composaient de fantaisie; Salvator travailla d'après nature. Comme poète, c'est là son mérite, et c'en est un considérable. (II, 259)[24]

These positive notes, however, are nearly drowned out by the negative ones.[25] In addition to what we have already seen in discussing Delécluze's treatment of *La Musica,* one may note the following apropos of *La Poesia:* "une fausse gravité dont on est rarement dupe, et qui rend la lecture de ses satires particulièrement fatigante" (II, 257); "aucune vue générale sur la littérature, ni même le moindre détail sur les poètes du temps ou sur leurs écrits. Les remarques, les critiques de Salvator sont si vagues, et cet homme s'attache à des défauts si mesquins . . . que ce bavardage littéraire n'excite aucun intérêt. Cette satire . . . n'est guère qu'un sermon ennuyeux" (II, 258). *La Pittura* arouses the following reactions: "Le défaut du plan, la bizarrerie de certaines inventions et la recherche des petits détails, ôtent toute majesté et toute profondeur à cette production," which should have been shorter; the critic complains of "la profusion des énigmes mythologiques" (II, 261). Rosa is "assommant" when he resorts to Antiquity (II, 261); a passage that is "curieux et écrit avec verve" lacks "délicatesse" and "goût" (ibid.); apropos of *La Babilonia,* it offers Rosa a "sujet fécond mais terrible" (III, 270), but when he has a good target in sight, injustice, Rosa fails. The passage in question "manque de précision, de clarté, et est surchargé au contraire d'une suite de métaphores aussi mal choisies que pauvrement exprimées" (III, 272).

Much of Rosa's sixth satire, *L'Invidia,* is quoted verbatim, with little or no comment except for the poet-speaker's portrait of "le prince des calomniateurs" being denounced as "obscène" (III, 274). The critic focuses, however, on "un fort long apologue par lequel il [Rosa] démontre que le miel tiré de la *rose* devient le mets favori des dieux" (III, 276). In Delécluze's eyes, "Jamais la fatuité d'un rimeur médiocre ne s'est montrée plus audacieuse et plus ridicule à la fois" (III, 277).

Brief assessments of Rosa as painter, musician, and poet lead into Delécluze's final attack, directed at Rosa the would-be philosopher and Rosa the man. "Comme peintre coloriste, il n'est qu'un successeur de la faible école des Carraches, ce qui ne le place pas très haut dans la hiérarchie pittoresque [. . .]. Salvator Rosa est un peintre de troisième ou quatrième ordre" (III, 278). As a musician, Rosa enjoyed some success, but his talent in this genre was "secondaire, se combinant avec celui de comédien, qui . . . était la faculté brillante de l'artiste napolitain" (ibid.). As for Rosa the writer, Delécluze declines to repeat "le genre de mérite et les grossiers défauts de Rosa considéré comme écrivain," except to concede, once again, that Rosa at least treated reality and developed "un style précis" that contrasted favorably with the "locutions inintelligibles et recherchées" in vogue in his time (ibid.).

The remaining seven pages of Delécluze's third article are devoted to demolishing "les étranges prétentions de cet homme à passer pour un profond philosophe, pour un austère moraliste et un inébranlable stoïcien" (ibid.); this is to be effected by an examination of Rosa's life in the light of these claims. First, that life was anything but austere: in Florence he enjoyed the generous patronage of the Grand Duke and turned his home into an academy that was, according to Baldinucci, "l'habitation de la joie, le marché de l'allégresse" (III, 278), frequented by a horde of glitterati, who came to "ooh!" and "ah!" over Rosa's performances and share his lavish meals (III, 279–80). This adulation bestowed on Rosa by his sycophantic admirers leads Delécluze into a lengthy development on Rosa's vanity (III, 280–82)—perhaps the human flaw most often singled out by Delécluze.[26] Other labels attached to Rosa's personality and character are "bizarrerie" (III, 284) and jealousy (I, 337; II, 270). But, as already suggested, it was Rosa's claim to be a philosopher and moralist, and an austere moralist of Stoic mold, that galled Delécluze the most. For Delécluze, this was all a charade, "cette comédie," "cynisme affecté" (III, 282). The approach of death, however, led to the collapse of "tout l'échafaudage de philosophie qu'avait élevé Salvator Rosa" (III, 282): "Le baladin ainsi que le philosophe s'évanouirent, et il ne resta plus en lui qu'un malade maussade et hargneux, quand la crainte de la mort ne lui faisait pas exprimer son désespoir par des plaintes et des lamentations frénétiques, car jamais homme n'a montré plus de faiblesse aux approches de sa fin" (III, 283). His grudging, deathbed marriage to his longtime mistress Lucrezia, the mother of his two sons, was the result not of charity and paternal feeling but of fear of eternal damnation (ibid.).

In the last two pages of his article, Deléluze recapitulates many of the points already made. The one he seems most eager to leave with his readers is that Rosa has had a nefarious influence as "l'original de ces hommes de *génie* auxquels il a servi de modèle depuis le XVIIe siecle" (III, 277). Though the words "romantique" and "romantisme" are not used, one cannot doubt that the pupil of David has these concepts in mind when he speaks "de ces artistes et poètes à talens faciles, de ces écrivains ou de ces peintres dédaigneux des grands principes des arts, qui hasardent tout sans crainte, qui n'ont d'autres règles que leur gôut, d'autre boussole que leur fantaisie" (ibid.). In this passage and in the final pages of his article, Delécluze affirms that this very unbridled individualism ill served Rosa the artist: "c'est précisément lorsque *le prodigieux génie* de Salvator Rosa a usé pleinement de son indépendance et de sa liberté, qu'il a donné naissance aux productions les plus faibles" (III, 278).[27] In the later passage (III, 284), he explains why "certains esprits faux" allotted Rosa—"cet habile peintre de paysage"—such a high rank: "C'est parce que son génie, c'est-à-dire son caractère, ses dispositions naturelles, le portaient à ne suivre aucune loi consentie, mais à vivre, à agir, à parler et à peindre, au contraire, selon sa propre fantaisie" (III, 284). Here Delécluze emerges in his role as teacher—he wrote a piece titled *Précis d'un traité de peinture contenant les principes du dessin, du modelé et du coloris, et leur application à l'imitation des objets et à la composition* (1828)—and warns of the danger for the art student "non seulement de les [les tableaux de Rosa] imiter, mais même de les voir" (III, 285). The example set by much greater artists—Dante, Petrarch, Ariosto, Tasso, Leonardo, Raphael, Michelangelo, Poussin, Lesueur, Claude, Milton, Pascal, Corneille, Bossuet, Molière, Racine—refutes the claims of Rosa's admirers and imitators: "Non, il n'est pas vrai . . . que le caractère d'un *homme de génie* . . . soit l'extravagance, le dévergondage dans les idées et la conduite" (ibid.).

Delécluze's last lines fold together, by way of contrast, the true artist and Rosa, the would-be artist and the man:

> L'homme qui se sent un vrai mérite est avant tout simple; il attend patiemment que ses vertus ou ses talens se développent, et c'est le propre du charlatan vaniteux de se donner beaucoup de peine pour faire croire qu'il possède un mérite qu'il n'a pas. Se vanter de ne pas craindre la mort,

comme l'a fait Salvator Rosa dans son tableau, *spretor mortis,*[28] et mourir en pleurant et en criant d'effroi, cela suffit pour faire apprécier la valeur d'un homme. (ibid.)

While Rosa's satires are, despite some wandering of his attention, Delécluze's main subject, Rosa's paintings and engravings are not entirely neglected: as we have already seen, in his first article, Delécluze ranked Rosa "parmi les artistes du second ordre, peut-être faudrait-il dire du troisième ordre" (I, 318). In his third article, Delécluze demotes him: "En somme, Salvator Rosa est un peintre de troisième ou quatrième ordre" (III, 278). He concedes only that Rosa was a "peintre et graveur habile" (I, 318) and, more specifically, "habile peintre de paysage" (III, 284), "un habile paysagiste" though inferior to Titian, Poussin, Claude, and even "Guaspre Poussin," who produced "quelques bons tableaux de paysage" (ibid.). Sometimes Delécluze criticizes Rosa's style and technique: he calls him a "coloriste faible et dessinateur barbare" (III, 285) and denounces "l'incorrection du dessin des personnages dans les compositions de Salvator Rosa" (ibid.). Few individual works are mentioned and only one is described: Rosa's etching *Le Génie de Salvator Rosa,* "composition, d'ailleurs fort médiocre" (II, 273). This work and two of Rosa's paintings, *Catiline's Conspiracy* (S 180) and *Diogenes and Alexander* (S 68),[29] provoke Delécluze's fundamental attack, already stated several times elsewhere, on "toutes ses compositions mythologiques, historiques et allégoriques, [qui] sont triviales et gourmées quant à l'expression, et au-dessus de toute critique sous le rapport du dessin."[30] Delécluze is, at least, consistent with himself: at the heart of his negative view of Rosa is a dislike of the artist's pretentions to being a philosopher or a philosophic painter and poet. The words "prétention" and "prétentieuse" echo Delécluze's frequent references to Rosa's vanity. Thus Rosa the artist and the man, as seen by Delécluze, are all of a piece.

The importance of Delécluze's articles is difficult to gauge. Can we say that their negative criticism helped to bring about the decline in Rosa's reputation and popularity as a painter? Probably not, given that the main object of Delécluze's criticism is Rosa's satires; the negative views of Rosa's paintings and etchings are incidental to that subject, even if consistent with it. Did Delécluze, at least, arouse interest in Rosa's satires? There is no evidence to that effect, but he did put copious extracts from them on display in one of the leading literary reviews of the romantic period. In his own way, then, Delécluze served Rosa's cause.

After Delécluze's pages on Rosa, no major critical documents appear for about a decade and a half. But scattered references to Rosa surface, in the periodical press, in guidebooks and travel narratives, and in fiction. Ludovic Vitet, reviewing Paul Delaroche's vast mural in the Salle des prix at the Ecole des Beaux-Arts,[31] conveys a rather low opinion of Rosa in a passage concerning notable omissions from among the roster of artists depicted. He does not criticize the painter for the absence of Guido Reni and Guercino, and "je lui pardonne également de n'avoir pas admis Salvator Rosa" (p. 947). He feels a little more strongly that Tintoretto should have been included and strongly objects to the exclusion of Leon Battista Alberti; perhaps for patriotic reasons, he complains about the absence of Jean Cousin and Philippe de Champagne (sic) (p. 948).

In the 1840s, Louis Viardot (1800–1883) (husband of the famous singer Pauline Viardot, née Garcia) produced a number of museum guides, the fruit of his extensive travels across Europe. Viardot sometimes lists pictures by Rosa that have either disappeared, have been transferred to other museums and collections, or have been attributed to other artists (or have perhaps been reduced to the status of copies). Thus in Madrid, of the four pictures mentioned, only "sa grande *Marine,* représentant la ville et le golfe de Salerne"[32] corresponds to a picture now listed by Salerno (1975) as being in the Prado; the "vaste *Paysage,* où on voit saint Jérôme étudier et prier" (ibid.) could be a copy of a picture now in Rome (S 135). Viardot mentions seven Rosas in Vienna that are difficult to match with Salerno's pictures in that city.[33] According to Viardot, in the Hague there are "quelques bons paysages de Salvator Rosa."[34] And so on, through London, Munich, Dresden, Rome, and Naples. Occasionally he finds himself gazing at an authentic Rosa. No doubt the museums of Europe contained many mislabeled pictures; the current examination of Rembrandt's *œuvre* reminds us that works attributed to a major painter sometimes turn out to be works wholly or partly by his pupils, imitations, out-and-out copies, or works more or less in his manner. Still, Viardot had, in addition to a high opinion of "cet artiste si original, si varié, si fécond" (*Italie,* p. 298),[35] a rather good idea of Rosa, gleaned from books, no doubt, as well as from direct contact with some authentic Rosas or plausible imitations. The *Landscape with St. Jerome* in Madrid ("ce paysage magnifique" [*Espagne,* p. 71]) inspires a typical divagation on Rosa, especially as seen in his landscapes: "Rien ne convient mieux à son imagination sombre et bizarre, que la représentation du désert, de la nature sauvage, de ces contrées incultes, abandonnées, où les ronces croissent au bord des flaques d'eau, et qui n'ont pour ornements qu'un roc stérile, un tronc brûlé par la foudre" (ibid.). The six Rosas seen in Munich, all landscapes—two of them authentic—inspire a similar passage, for they are "dans la manière qui convenait le mieux à son humeur sombre et bizarre, à son pinceau hardi et capricieux, une nature inculte, stérile, sauvage " (*Allemagne,* p. 118).[36] An alleged Rosa, *Tempête sur mer,* in Dresden is "traitée avec la sombre énergie particulière à son talent" (p. 285). Several of the expressions used in the above passages reappear verbatim in the passage in which Viardot admits that Naples' Museo degli studi has only "quelques imitations de ses élèves, plus ou moins heureuses mais restées toujours loin du maître" (*Italie,* p. 299).

In the Pitti in Florence, Viardot faced a better selection of Rosa's works— eleven pictures, he says. (And there is every reason to believe that all the works he saw were authentic.) Here the guide admired a self-portrait (presumably S 36, now in the Uffizi), "fort bien d'accord avec le caractère, le talent et la vie de cet étrange artiste" (p. 197). Viardot is also enthusiastic about "une grande *Bataille,* excellente par la composition et les détails," and "deux magnifiques *Marines,* les plus vastes, je crois, et peut-être les plus belles qu'il ait jamais peintes" (ibid.). Curiously, he finds "sa célèbre *Conjuration de Catilina*" (S 180) overrated: seeing it "confirme bien l'opinion que des demi-figures ne suffisent jamais à rendre clairement un sujet quelque peu compliqué. Le manque de clarté est, en effet, le défaut capital de cette œuvre de Salvator, qui le rachète d'ailleurs, autant que possible, par de rares et brillants mérites d'exécution" (*Italie,* p. 197). Three unidentified Rosas in the Marquis of Westminster's collection[37] Viardot finds "horriblement sombres" and their subjects "à peine explicables" (*Angleterre,* p. 140). But, as we have seen, Viardot sometimes used "sombre" in a rather positive way, speaking of the artist's "imagination sombre et bizarre," coupling this expression with "son pinceau hardi et capricieux" (*Espagne,* p. 71; *Italie,* p. 299); elsewhere, it is Rosa's "humeur sombre" that is linked to the same expression (*Allemagne,* p. 118).

Viardot was aware that Rosa practiced several genres: he specifies "l'histoire, le paysage, les marines et les batailles" (*Espagne,* p. 71). As we have seen, he provided fairly standard characterizations of Rosa's landscapes (ibid.; *France,* p. 87). Two of Rosa's battle scenes are briefly characterized as "ces mêlées confuses et sanglantes . . . ces mers bouleversées" (*Allemagne,* p. 118), expressions recycled elsewhere (ibid., p. 222; *Espagne,* p. 71; *Italie,* p. 299; *France,* p. 87). It is Rosa as history painter who disappoints Viardot. We have seen how his somewhat negative reaction to the *Conspiracy of Catiline* in the Pitti in Florence, "ce tableau fameux, et trop fameux peut-être" (*Italie,* p. 197), illustrative of his major flaw, "manque de clarté" (ibid.). In Paris, where he was similarly presented with works of undoubted authenticity, Viardot is even more outspoken. While the *Landscape with Soldiers and Hunters* acquired in 1816 (S 239) wins his admiration (*France,* p. 87), the two most famous Rosas in the Louvre are roundly criticized; both illustrate

Rosa's ineptitude in history painting. The Neapolitan resembled Caravaggio "par sa vie aventureuse, son caractère mobile et emporté qui réagissait sur son talent" (ibid.), but failed to measure up to the earlier artist when he attempted "la haute histoire":

> [P]arce que, sans avoir un style beaucoup plus noble, il ne put acquérir ni autant de clarté dans la composition, ni autant de rigueur dans le rendu des objets et des personnages. Si on ôtait, par exemple, à son *Apparition de l'ombre de Samuel* le titre qu'elle porte, on n'empêcherait point pour cela, tout en masquant le défaut de noblesse, de sainteté, de style propre, que ce ne fût une composition très-confuse et de très-faible exécution. Salvator, il faut l'avouer contre l'orgueilleuse opinion qu'il avait de lui-même, a pleinement échoué dans tous les sujets historiques, même ceux qui ont joué d'une célébrité temporaire, comme la *Conjuration de Catilina* du palais Pitti. (p. 86)

The Louvre's huge battle scene (S 111) is subjected to similar criticism (p. 87): "Ce mot d'antique, et les nécessités d'arrangement qu'il entraîne, l'ont évidemment déconcerté et refroidi, sans lui enlever son plus habituel défaut, la confusion" (ibid.).[38]

Like his contemporary Gustav Friedrich Waagen (1794–1868), Viardot visited many of the great museums and galleries of Europe and described a vast number of pictures. But he was more of a popularizer than a professional art critic or art historian. For one thing, his interests were broader— he was a translator of Spanish and Russian literature, editor with Pierre Leroux and George Sand of the *Revue indépendante,* and director of the Théâtre-Italien for a time. The guidebooks he wrote are the by-product of his travels with Pauline Viardot on her concert and opera tours. They are quite readable and, while sketchy as serious art history, convey effectively the leading traits and qualities of the artists he discusses. His low opinion of several of Rosa's history paintings foreshadows the decline of Rosa's fame in the second half of the nineteenth century. But, writing in the 1840s, Viardot has the merit of insisting on those parts of Rosa's work that for a century or so before had been his claim to fame. He wished that the Louvre had one of Rosa's marines to serve as a pendant to its *Landscape,* "pour qu'on y trouvât le novateur, intronisant, après les classiques Poussin et Claude, le romantisme dans la représentation de la nature" (*France,* p. 87). All in all, Viardot was a reliable guide to the Rosas in the major museums of Europe.

Paul de Musset (1804–1880) was, if anything, even more of an Italophile than his more famous brother Alfred. Many of his writings, whether in the form of fiction or of travel books, reflect his rich Italian experience. But

Rosa, as painter, does not generally show to advantage in Musset's references to him. In *Course en voiturin* (1845), when Musset visits Rome's "Palais Doria," "un *Saint Jean prêchant dans le désert,* par Salvator Rosa," the work is mentioned without comment (II, 104). But earlier, in Genoa, when he visits "la Galerie D °°°"—presumably "D" means Doria-Pamphili—he is surprised to come upon "un tableau couvert de blanc d'Espagne dont on ne voyait que le cadre" (I, 33)! When a servant explains that "il signore Marchese" is responsible for veiling the picture, the servant then crosses himself and states that he would not want to have the picture in his room. The narrator agrees and, on asking the name of the painter, learns that the picture is by Rosa: "— Bonté divine! un Salvator Rosa. Le signor marquis a bien du courage d'oser braver un bandit comme celui-là" (I, 34). Here, for the first time, Musset indulges in his *ad hominem* criticism of Rosa: the painter is a bandit (and, as we shall see, a bloodthirsty rebel). This spills over into the subjects of the paintings by Rosa that Musset sees in Italian galeries: the Caravaggios, Rosas, and Riberas in the Galerie D°°° all represent "des sujets sinistres" (I, 33).

In the Pitti in Florence, however, Rosa gets a favorable nod: "Les tableaux les plus remarquables de la première salle sont le *Mariage de sainte Catherine* du Titien et deux superbes marines de Salvator Rosa."[39] But, in the room containing Raphael's *Leo X* and Michelangelo's *Three Fates,* Musset seems unimpressed by "deux batailles de Salvator Rosa, dont les acteurs ressemblent assez à deux armées de brigands" (pp. 43–44). In Naples, Musset says nothing about Rosa the painter: it is Aniello Falcone and Rosa's alleged role in the revolt of 1647 that inspire in him a condemnation of the people of Naples in general ("inconstant et frivole" [p. 343]) and the *Compagnia della morte* in particular: "Au lieu d'apprivoiser les lazares et de réprimer leurs excès, les compagnons de la Mort semèrent l'épouvante" (ibid.). Musset in a later passage reveals a standard idea of Rosa's landscapes: "Le bourg de la Cava, situé au pied du mont Fenestra, dans une vallée d'un aspect sauvage, rappelle autant que les Abruzzes les lieux aimés de Salvator Rosa" (pp. 420–21).

In the novel *Livia* (1852), Musset has a rather vehement passage in which a stranger accosts the narrator in the Palazzo Doria in Genoa:

> L'étranger me montrait un Saint Jean prêchant dans le désert.
>
> —Vous devinez de reste, poursuivit-il, de qui est cet ouvrage. Ce Saint Jean a la mine d'un voleur, et c'est dans les Abbruzzes [*sic*] qu'il prêche. Salvator Rosa n'a jamais su représenter autre chose que son propre visage et les précipices où il détroussait les passants. Saint-Jean, Prométhée ou Catilina c'est toujours lui-même, et ce qui prouve qu'il était assez amoureux de sa personne pour n'avoir d'autre idéal que sa face crépue et couleur de réglisse.[40]

The painting in question cannot be identified; it may have been a copy of one of the two treatments (S 120 and S 122) of the subject, one of which is now in Glasgow, the other in St. Louis. The emphasis on Rosa's depiction of faces introduces a new and surprising motif into Rosa criticism, accusing the artist of an obsession with his own likeness—an accusation that would make more sense if addressed to Dürer, Rembrandt, or Van Gogh. It must be borne in mind that, although this reproach is spoken by a fictional character, it does seem to reflect Musset's own view, which may be rooted in a dislike for Rosa the man, seen as a bloody-minded revolutionary and a highway robber. Such a view of Rosa suggests the ebbing of the tide of romanticism—and the persistence of Lady Morgan's founding myths.

Charles Didier (1805–1864) was, if anything, an even more ardent lover of people and things Italian than Paul de Musset. And we have already shown that, in his story "Romuléo" (1859), he, too, was thoroughly acquainted with the romantic Salvator Rosa of Lady Morgan: his protagonist is a modern incarnation and, at the same time, a caricature of the painter. The story bathes in a post-romantic irony, reflective of the author's disillusionment in later life. But in several of his earlier works, the standard romantic view of Rosa flickers forth. Curiously, there is no reference to Rosa in Didier's *Rome souterraine* (1833), his most famous book, even though it contains a sharp passage on "la satire du peuple romain"[41] and refers occasionally to great Roman painters of the past (I, 40–41, 214, 249–50). However, a few years later in *La Campagne de Rome* (1842), on a hunting trip in the Maremma, his party encounters "un spectacle aussi pittoresque qu'inattendu,"[42] a score of shepherds clad in goatskins and armed with rifles: "Il ne manquait à leur ceinture de cuir que des pistolets et des poignards pour représenter fidèlement une des comitives calabraises où s'inspira le génie farouche de Salvator Rosa" (ibid.). On the southern borders of the Campania, the traveler comes within view of scenery that inspires a vivid description suggestive of early Rosa seascapes, with their rocky coastal outcroppings (S 52), natural bridges (S 70), and landscapes dominated by massive bridges (S39): "[T]outes les îles . . . de l'archipel napolitain se succèdent les unes aux autres comme les piles de quelque pont gigantesque jeté sur les mers par les mains puissantes, inconnues, qui élevèrent les murs cyclopéens des montagnes" (p. 290). The scene also inspires some critical reflection involving Rosa:

> Tel est, mon cher ami, le panorama merveilleux qui se développe autour de nous; quelque effort qu'on fasse, les mots ne traduisent pas plus la nature, qu'un squelette ne donne l'idée de la beauté; c'est à peine si l'artiste qui réunirait en lui Claude Lorrain et Salvator Rosa, l'homme du repos et l'homme du mouvement,[43] réussirait avec la ligne et la couleur à vous

présenter une pâle et confuse image de ce paysage . . . j'allais dire sublime, mais c'est un mot dont on a tant usé et abusé dans ces derniers temps qu'il faut le laisser reposer pendant deux générations au moins avant de pouvoir décemment l'employer. (p. 291)

In Didier's novel *Raccolta: mœurs siciliennes et calabraises* (1844), the narrator seeks refuge near Cape Spartivento on the southern tip of Calabria and finds himself on a high, exposed peak, facing a ruggedly awe-inspiring landscape in which one senses the echo of René on Etna as well as a re-minder of Rosa:

Derrière moi s'élevait un vaste amphithéâtre de montagnes; à mes pieds s'ouvrait, comme un abîme, une vallée longue, immense, sans habitations, sans culture, et si démesurément profonde que mon œil effrayé refusait d'aller au fond. Les flancs en étaient tout hérissés de sapins, ou de rochers à pics fracturés, noircis par les siècles et les orages; elle était là muette, solitaire, inculte comme aux premiers jours de la création; il y avait en elle quelque chose de primitif, de vierge; l'homme ne s'y sentait pas. Un chevreuil broutait paisiblement au soleil; un aigle planait en silence pardessus les abîmes; encadrée entre deux montagnes, la mer bleuissait au loin. Jamais scène plus fière, plus mâle, plus austère, plus poétique ne tomba du pinceau de Salvator Rosa.[44]

If the broken boulders and other "sublime" features of this scene are standard in evocations of Rosa landscapes, we must note that the insistence on the ab-sence of man strikes a less banal note, one that Madame de Staël and a few others had struck before. Didier's wanderings in Italy in the late 1820s had taken him into remote spots rarely frequented by tourists; he had direct knowl-edge of the kinds of landscape that, rightly or wrongly, had become associated with Rosa. His Rosa, in these early works, was encountered in nature, not merely recollected from museums. He had also, we must not forget, been encountered, directly or indirectly, in Lady Morgan's biography.

In 1844 the Belgian author Adolphe Siret (1818–1888)[45] produced *Dictionnaire historique des peintres de toutes les écoles depuis les temps les plus reculés jusqu'à nos jours,*[46] which was republished at least five times. The section on Rosa provides the reader with a potted biography (according to which, Rosa "fut partisan de Masaniello" and joined the *Compagnia della morte*), a list of Rosa's paintings (with location), and a critique of Rosa's work, which is mostly favorable to the artist:

Manière tout originale et qu'aucun artiste n'a réussi à bien imiter; sans briller par le dessin des figures, elles sont toujours bien conçues et bien posées dans ses paysages dont elles augmentent l'effet; touche large, heurtée et fière; couleur toujours sévère et parfois monotone, sans être jamais désagréable à l'œil; sites grands, sauvages et empreints du caractère sombre de l'auteur; ses premiers tableaux mêmes se ressentent déjà de cette vigueur qu'il déploya par la suite à un aussi haut degré; il se fit une manière expéditive, d'accord avec la fougue de son imagination et l'impatience de son caractère; composition pleine de verve et d'énergie. De tous les genres, c'était celui des batailles qu'il préférait; il pouvait y déployer à son aise l'originalité âpre et mélancolique de son esprit; la chaleur de ses inventions, la fermeté de son pinceau, la disposition savante de ses groupes lui assignent un rang supérieur parmi ses rivaux; génie neuf et indépendant, il sut imprimer à ses œuvres un cachet particulier qu'il est difficile de méconnaître, et dédaigna toujours de suivre les traces des autres; il dépouilla la nature de tous ses ornements, écarta de ses tableaux ces beaux arbres, ces riches péristyles, ces brillants épisodes de la vie champêtre qui font le charme des ouvrages de Claude Lorrain et du Poussin. (p. 419)

Here follows a standard description of the typical "sauvage" landscape by Rosa that concludes: "Personne mieux que lui n'a réussi à troubler l'air, à agiter et à éclairer les eaux, à représenter le désordre majestueux qui rend la nature plus imposante et plus animée." Siret has succeeded in creating in compact form an unexceptionable Rosa, presumably composed of the materials found in the works of earlier art critics and art historians. Those who consulted his reference work were not misled, but they might be left wondering what—except for his landscapes—an actual picture by Rosa looked like.

The greatest French art critic practicing in this period treats Rosa only briefly and in passing. In the Salons of 1845 and 1846, Baudelaire reveals his awareness of the affinity between Rosa and the work of Adrien Guignet (1816–1854). In both texts[47] he sees Guignet as oscillating between the influence of Decamps and Rosa. In the *Salon de 1846* the picture in question is unquestionably Rosaesque, especially in subject matter: *Les Condottières après un pillage.* But Baudelaire provides no assessment of Rosa or any description of his work. (Nearly twenty years later, in his catalogue of Prosper Crabbe's collection, Baudelaire again reveals that he knows the Rosa of romantic legend: apropos of an unidentifiable *Crucifixion,* he calls the soldiers carrying out Jesus' punishment "terribles bandits à la Salvator" [*OC,* II, 963].) Since he mentions that the actor Philibert Rouvière played the role of Masaniello in Ferdinand Dugué's *Salvator Rosa* (1851), it is possible that Baudelaire had seen this play. [48]

Similarly, another major art critic of this period, Théophile Thoré (1807–1869), has only incidental references to Rosa in his *Salon de 1846,*[49] where he includes Rosa in a list of Italian painters who still made Italy illustrious in the time of Vouet; the others are Annibale Carracci, Domenichino, Guercino, and Caravaggio (p. 158). Elsewhere in the same work, attempting to establish affinities between Decamps and the great national schools of the past, he finds only minor reflections in Decamps of the Flemish, Dutch, and Spanish Schools: "[I]l est plutôt Italien, de l'école napolitaine, avec Salvator Rosa, et presque Vénitien pour la fermeté de la pâte et la splendeur du coloris" (pp. 107–08). He is aware that Rosa did rocky landscapes: "Salvator Rosa a fait des rochers; il s'est arrêté au pied des montagnes" (p. 137)—here he is making the point that no painter can fully represent nature. Almost inevitably, given the accessibility and renown of Rosa's *Battaglia eroica,* he evokes Rosa apropos of a modern painter of battles, but only to emphasize differences: "Il ne faut cependant point attendre de M. Horace Vernet des mêlées furieuses comme dans les batailles de Salvator, ou du Bourguignon, mais des épisodes dramatiques, vivement saisis et spirituellement exprimés" (p. 184). One would wish for a greater, more vivid presence of Rosa in the work of one of the most important critics of the midcentury. But, as in the case of Baudelaire, we are faced with the fact that, in reviewing the Salons, such critics were necessarily focusing on contemporary art. Moreover, when Thoré turned his attention to the past, he generally wrote about Dutch art; after all, he virtually invented Vermeer.

A younger *salonnier* with similar interests was Eugène Fromentin, who published a *Salon de 1845* in an obscure provincial paper. Before turning to the pictures on display at the Salon, Fromentin delivers himself of some general observations about the modern French School and the place in it of genre painting:

> Nous pouvons, à bon droit, nous flatter d'avoir, sinon créé, au moins ressuscité la peinture *de genre.* Nous avons fait plus: en associant dans une même école, la plus vaste et la mieux constituée qui se soit jamais vue, la naïve et joviale bonhomie des Flamands, les périphrases galantes de Watteau et de Boucher, la franchise brutale de Zurbaran, de Ribera et de Murillo, l'âpre rudesse de Salvator, en ravivant, en fécondant l'un par l'autre tant de germes épars, nous avons transformé *le genre.*[50]

In his later masterwork, *Les Maîtres d'autrefois* (1876), though Flemish and Dutch painting is his subject, Fromentin will evoke Rosa and his battle scenes—no doubt, the one in the Louvre is uppermost, perhaps alone, in his mind—apropos of "deux grandes pages" in the Hague, one by Berchem and the other by Wouwerman: "Il y a du Salvator Rosa, moins le style, dans ces simulacres d'escarmouches ou de grandes batailles, dont on ne connaît ni la cause, ni le moment, ni le théâtre, ni bien nettement non plus les partis aux prises" (ibid., p. 672). Fromentin clearly had little interest in Rosa, but he has put his finger on a crucial aspect of the Neapolitan's depiction of battle: Rosa is never celebrating a particular victory or glorifying some man on horseback; he is laying bare the horror of war.

The next important document is from the pen of the art critic and art historian Charles Blanc (1813–1882), a prolific writer, twice *directeur de l'administration des Beaux-Arts,* holder of a chair of aesthetics created for him at the Collège de France, and a member of the Académie Française. Blanc's massive *Trésor de la curiosité* (1857–1858) has already provided information to this study about the sales of works by Rosa in the art market of the eighteenth and nineteenth centuries. Now we turn to the fascicule on Rosa that appears in the gigantic *Histoire des peintres de toutes les écoles,* whose 631 fascicules appeared from 1849 to 1876. The fascicule on Rosa— sixteen pages long—seems to have been published in 1856.[51]

Blanc's section on Rosa devotes more space to art history than to art criticism; most of the text, in fact, is biography à la Vasari, drawn from Baldinucci and others. As a critic of Rosa's work, Blanc sends a rather mixed message. On the positive side, Rosa's marine landscapes were "vraiment sublimes," but Blanc adds: "quand il s'abstenait d' y représenter des figures humaines" (p. 4); his talent is marked by "variété" (ibid.); even his earliest pictures, though "de grossières ébauches," are "fièrement peintes, enlevées à la hâte, et marquées au coin d'une imagination échauffée et bizarre" (p. 3); the *Agar,* which led to Lanfranco's discovery of the young and unknown artist,[52] is characterized as "cette peinture libre, fière, brossée à l'effet," and Blanc seems to share Lanfranco's admiration for "l'énergie et la chaleur du pinceau" of Rosa (p. 4). Some unidentifiable landscapes painted after Rosa settled in Rome are "magnifiques" (p. 14).

These brief quotations reveal that Blanc's preference goes to Rosa's marines and landscapes. On the basis of a picture seen in a private collection in Paris,[53] Blanc waxes enthusiastic:

> [I]l est impossible d'imaginer rien de plus saisissant, de plus lugubre. On n'y voit d'abord que des rochers amoncelés en amphithéâtre au bord de la mer et battus par des vagues noires sous un ciel funèbre. Aucune créature vivante, aucun navire: seulement, en y regardant bien on croit apercevoir des crevasses, des lambeaux de voiles, des cordages, un mât brisé, les restes d'un naufrage déjà ancien et dont les vestiges ont à moitié disparu. On ne peut considérer ce tableau sans éprouver un frisson. Non, jamais un peintre ne sut dégager du spectacle de la nature une poésie plus pénétrante. (p. 4)

Here, Blanc strikes one of the most noteworthy themes of his criticism of

Rosa by emphasizing the intermingling of the man and his work: "Mais que dis-je: elle est dans le cœur du peintre, cette poésie, plutôt que dans les aspects de la nature. Pour découvrir les paysages et les marines de Salvator, il fallait avoir ses tristesses, son amertume, son âme exaltée, remplie de fiel et de génie" (ibid.).[54]

In Blanc's eyes, Rosa was a pioneer and an original, indeed a precursor, in his landscapes and marines, earning himself a place beside the most prestigious practitioners of these genres:

> De même que Poussin, Claude et le Guaspre avaient inventé les heureuses campagnes de l'Arcadie, et ouvert aux yeux du poète les perspectives lumineuses d'un horizon paisible et sans fin, de même Salvator avait découvert dans la nature de nouveaux aspects, répondant aux cordes les plus sensibles du cœur humain. Je veux parler de la tristesse amère de ses paysages, de ses marines désolées, si bien faites pour inspirer le sentiment de la terreur. Par ce côté, Salvator était un novateur, lui aussi; il inaugurait le romantisme en Italie. De nos jours, quels sont les hommes qui vont au Louvre admirer ce *Paysage pris dans les Abruzzes* [S 239], dont la nudité est si affreuse et le caractère si sublime? Ce sont précisément les romantiques de notre âge, ceux qui trouvent la nature toujours belle, même dans ses horreurs; ce sont les prôneurs de la fantaisie individuelle, les contempteurs des règles apprises et des beautés convenues. Et, il faut l'avouer, tant qu'ils se renferment dans le domaine du paysage, les partisans de Salvator Rosa n'ont pas moins raison que les admirateurs de Claude. Il y a bien des manières d'idéaliser la nature, pourvu qu'on la regarde avec les yeux d'un poète. (p. 10)

Blanc also admired Rosa as a painter of battles: "c'était un genre où le peintre excellait, pouvant y déployer toutes ses qualités distinctives, une verve entraînante, l'énergie des mouvements et des expressions, et la touche la plus vaillante qui fut jamais" (p. 12). The critic may have seen several of Rosa's battle pictures, in the Pitti, for example. But what is certain is that he saw the *Battaglia eroica* (S 111) in the Louvre, "sa grande *Bataille* . . . qui peut passer pour le chef-d'œuvre du genre" (p. 14). After quoting from Rosa's own letter to Ricciardi (August 17, 1652) about his commission from Cardinal Corsini, Blanc launches into a paragraph of sustained praise:

> Ce qui est merveilleux dans cette *Bataille*, c'est la forte unité du tableau. La composition, le coloris, la touche, tout concourt à une sorte d'harmonie funèbre. Jamais on n'imagina une mêlée plus horrible d'hommes et de chevaux, de combattants furieux, de mourants écrasés, de cadavres en lambeaux. Les figures n'y sont pas idéales, comme celles de Raphaël dans la *Bataille*

de Constantin; elles sont d'une réalité effrayante: on les sent palpiter et frémir, on les entend hurler de rage. Partout la vue ne rencontre que des images de désolation: ici c'est une colonnade en ruines; là-bas ce sont des navires en feu au pied des falaises les plus sauvages, et la fumée de l'incendie obscurcit encore un ciel déjà sinistre. La couleur est chaude, l'exécution fière et brûlante; les coups de pinceau du maître sont aussi violents que des coups d'épée, et il semble qu'enivré de la poésie des batailles, il ait respiré avec plaisir l'odeur du carnage. (ibid.)

Along with Blanc's sympathetic evocations of Rosa's marines and landscapes, this is the high point of the painter's relationship with his critic. It comes as something of a surprise after the highly negative remarks, early in his essay, about Rosa as history painter. Perhaps, since this battle picture does not even pretend to be about some particular battle recorded in history, either sacred or profane, or in mythology, Blanc sees the picture as belonging to some other genre, a sort of human landscape, as it were.

Even in his sympathetic characterizations of Rosa's marines and landscapes, Blanc hints at reservations and suggests limits to Rosa's genius. For example, Rosa's marines are sublime when the painter refrains from representing human figures. Already, on the sixth page of his essay—he is dealing with the Rosa who has already been to Viterbo[55]—he severely criticizes a *Prométhée déchiré par le vautour.*[56] Blanc provides a vivid description of the picture, but not because he admires "cette grande figure que Salvator croyait, dans sa vanité, digne de Michel Ange,[57] mais qui n'est en somme, qu'une étude académique dont le sentiment est vulgaire, dont les formes sont courtes et sans noblesse" (p. 6). Blanc explains that "Prométhée doit être beau jusque dans son désespoir" (ibid.).

We are prepared, then, for Blanc's denigrations of Rosa's history paintings: "Salvator y laisse voir un côté vulgaire, non-seulement dans la forme humaine, mais dans le geste qui est théâtral, et dans l'expression qui est forcée" (p. 10). Two pictures are cited as proof, *The Prodigal Son* (S 127) and the Louvre's *Pythonisse d'Endor* (S 210).[58] Of the former, Blanc writes: "Son *Enfant prodigue*, au lieu d'être un fils dégradé, avili par la misère, et devenu rustique par la condition à laquelle ses débauches l'ont réduit, est un personnage d'une trivialité native, incapable de nous inspirer l'intérêt qu'éveille en nous la belle parabole de l'Ecriture" (p. 10). The Prodigal's "distinction primitive" should have been still visible: "Les souillures d'une âme qui se souvient tout à coup de sa pureté première, eussent été si bien exprimées par l'altération des formes dans un corps prématurément usé et vieilli, mais où les prestiges de la beauté ancienne eussent reparu!" As for the *Pythonisse d'Endor,* "en dépit d'un certain grandiose dans les lignes et d'un clair obscur bien entendu, [elle] présente aussi de la banalité dans les draperies, des gestes insignifiants à côté d'une pantomime violente, des expressions outrées qui touchent à la grimace et une sorte de solennité d'emprunt qui est comme le prélude de notre moderne mélodrame" (ibid.). Blanc had been sympathetic, to say the least, to the romanticism of Rosa's landscapes, but, here, in comparing the *Pythonisse* to "our modern melodrama," Blanc is parting company with most romantic criticism. His disdain for melodrama smacks of neoclassic huffiness. Blanc, incidentally, seems unaware of one group of Rosa's paintings, his *stregonerie* or scenes of witchcraft, which contain elements akin to the "spooky" animals hovering in the background of this picture. One would like to have his reaction to such a picture as the *Streghe e incantesimi* (S 78), then at Althorp House and now at the National Gallery in London. In still another genre, he gives the impression of having seen *Humana Fragilitas* (S 116) and *La Fortuna* (S 126) but dismisses the latter as "cette allégorie d'ailleurs assez lourde" (p. 12).

Rosa's portrayals of Pythagoras (either S 164 or 166 and S 165) give Blanc the opportunity to note Rosa's predilection for novel subjects ("données toutes nouvelles" [p. 15]), but he is not impressed by Rosa's quest for novelty. The public success of these pictures was misleading: it encouraged Rosa to think of himself as "un peintre de figures héroïques" (ibid.). This misconception of his talents produced a sense of strain and artifice: "La recherche du style eut fait perdre à Salvator ses qualités natives, son originalité, sa valeur. Il était de ces artistes que l'on ne peut châtier sans les amoindrir, et dont le génie abrupt et sauvage devait être incivilisable" (ibid.).

Nearing his conclusion, Blanc speaks highly of Rosa's etchings, earlier called "ses jolies eaux-fortes" (p. 5):

> Elles sont pleines de génie, ces eaux-fortes; la pointe en est libre et légère. Les figures en sont maniérées et dessinées de pratique, mais élégantes, expressives et originales. Le paysage en est toujours excellent. Le peintre graveur se plaisait à y indiquer avec esprit des jardins enchantés comme ceux d'Armide, des arbres à demi-dépouillés, des troncs noueux, et ces mélancoliques bouleaux dont on croit sentir le frémissement dans l'estampe du *Saint-Guillaume, ermite*.[59] (p. 15)

Perhaps Blanc, himself trained as an engraver, was sensitive to the charm of Rosa's etchings out of fellow feeling. His praise is justified but warped in emphasis: he gives short shrift to the bulk of Rosa's etchings—the sixty *Figurine*. He shows that he is aware of their existence in his "Recherches et indications" but calls them simply "Un livre de *Soldats,* de *bandits* et autres figures en soixante feuilles" (p. 16).

In the last sentences of the main body of his text, Blanc returns to the very balanced view revealed in the quotations above taken as a whole. Characteristically, Rosa the man is juxtaposed with the artist:

> Capable de haines vigoureuses, Salvator était chaleureux et fidèle dans ses amitiés. Il aima passionnément sa patrie; mais il la voulait libre, et il l'abandonna quand il la vit asservie et dégradée. Il montra ainsi, au milieu d'une société en décadence, quelques-unes des vertus antiques, et s'il ne lui fut pas donné, comme peintre, de s'élever au-dessus de l'art dégénéré et corrompu de son temps, il sut du moins y laisser une trace profonde dans ces paysages sublimes où il a pressenti et devancé l'art de l'avenir. (p. 16)

Rosa's reception by journalistic critics in France reached an ambiguous climax in three articles published in *L'Artiste* in 1864–1865. The author was the now-forgotten Charles Coligny (1823–1874),[60] whose articles form, forty years later, a sort of bookend matching Lady Morgan's biography, a late outcropping of romanticism. His enthusiasm for Rosa is equal to hers and, like hers, stems from political roots: for Coligny, Rosa is romantic, democratic, liberal, revolutionary, an ardent patriot who took up arms for the people of Naples. Comparisons between Rosa and Byron, it might be noted, appear several times in the writings of both the Irish nationalist and the future Communard. Moreover, as we shall see, Coligny borrowed several passages from Lady Morgan's book, to which he refers once.

Coligny first took up the cause of Rosa in an article published in the September 1, 1864, *L'Artiste* under the title "Le génie de Salvator." His second contribution, "Michel-Ange et Salvator Rosa," appeared on August 1, 1865; on August 15 came "Les gravures de Salvator Rosa," the briefest of the three texts.[61] Aside from the encomiastic treatment of Rosa—both the man and the work—what is most striking about Coligny's criticism is the extremely broad brush with which he paints and the extraordinary number of *rapprochements* and comparisons between Rosa and an almost incredible variety of artists, poets, philosophers, and even musicians. Chronologically, his references range from Homer to his own day. On the first page of the longest of the three, "Michel-Ange," he manages to work in the names of Raphael, Titian, Shakespeare, Montaigne, Leonardo, Correggio, Daniel da Volterra, Fidenza, Haydn, Boccherini, Ingres, Delacroix, Rubens, Van Dyck, and Delaroche. Taken as a whole, this article offers a vast, if miniaturized, fresco of art in the Renaissance and seventeenth century. Coligny prefers being pinnacled dim to dealing with the nitty-gritty of collecting and museology; only the article "Gravures" is something of an exception, focusing on a specific genre. He is aware of the broad outlines of Rosa's life, but gives few dates. He is able, thanks to Lady Morgan, to quote a few passages from Rosa's letters to Ricciardi ("Génie," p. 100; "Gravures," pp. 82, 83). He is aware that Rosa painted battle scenes, landscapes, and history paintings. He mentions by name a number of individual works by Rosa; indeed, he provides ("Gravures," p. 83) a long list of his paintings that have been engraved by various engravers, but this list is taken word for word from Lady Morgan (II, 320–21), with some reshuffling of the order in which the titles are given. Coligny never mentions any of the pictures in the Louvre, except for a fleeting reference to *Saül*. The painting *La Fortuna* (S 126) ("Michel-Ange," p. 54) and the etching *Le Génie de Salvator Rosa* ("Gravures,"p. 83) are described in great detail, but both of these descriptions are slightly reworked versions of passages from Lady Morgan's biography (II, 11–12, 16; II, 114–16). In short, Coligny's criticism of Rosa's work is based on little or no contact with his paintings and etchings and relies heavily on Lady Morgan.

Such slight acquaintance with Rosa's work was no hindrance to Coligny's admiration for Rosa. In "Génie" (p. 97) he boldly proclaims him "le dernier grand peintre de l'Italie." As a landscapist, "Salvator Rosa a jeté les fondements d'un nouveau poëme épique" (p. 98). The same essay concludes: "Salvator Rosa est un de ces Christophe Colomb qui disent: il faut que je découvre un monde ou que je périsse!" (p. 100) The very title of Coligny's second article, "Michel-Ange et Salvator Rosa," prepares us for an extended comparison and contrast between the two artists, and the critic often obliges, e.g.,

> Michel-Ange a fait voir Moïse; Salvator a fait voir Prométhée. L'un a refait la Bible; l'autre a refait la tragédie grecque, qui est l'expression de la liberté dans la patrie d'Eschyle et de Sophocle. Michel-Ange est comme un Père de l'Eglise; Salvator est un vrai fils de la Philosophie. Dans les artistes et dans les hommes, tous deux sont des originaux. Salvator est romantique et patriote; Michel-Ange est patriote et apocalyptique. Michel-Ange est un homme-monument; Salvator est un homme-drame. (p. 50)

Both, says Coligny, were involved in the bloody events of their respective times: "Les deux peintres furent deux héros, deux héros malheureux des armes à la main; ils ne sauvèrent pas Florence, ils ne sauvèrent pas Naples. Mais s'ils ne furent pas vainqueurs, ils ne furent pas esclaves" (ibid.).

Two pages later, Coligny develops another elaborate, ringing *rapprochement* of the two artists:

> Michel-Ange et Salvator ont le génie hautain, audacieux, indépendant de tout, libre de tout. Le vieux maître a l'esprit plus sublime et plus sourd; le nouveau maître a l'esprit plus philosophique et plus clair. L'âme de Michel-

Ange parle sans cesse à la mort; l'âme de Salvator parle sans cesse à la vie.
Tous les deux ont une fierté sans pareille, dans la vie comme dans l'art. Raphaël
reprochait à Michel-Ange de marcher toujours seul comme le bourreau;
Salvator Rosa s'était fait une solitude farouche au milieu de sa société. . . . Il
ne fut jamais homme de génie par paresse; il n'était pas napolitain pour être
lazzarone; le hasard ne le poussa pas; son humeur ne fut jamais cynique.
Ainsi l'aurait aimé le noble et profond Michel-Ange. (p. 52)

Coligny's *rapprochement* of Michelangelo and Rosa reaches out and enve-
lopes other great creators, e.g., Dante: "Comme Michel-Ange, il [Rosa] avait
lu et il adorait Dante. Il a fait un tableau du *Purgatoire*.[62] Comme Beethoven
et comme Michel-Ange, Salvator Rosa dédaigne les routes communes; sa
muse sauvage et libre se complaît dans les fureurs et dans les désordres des
plus grandes passions. On dirait que leur génie, à tous les trois, et je nomme
Byron pour faire le quatrième, s'est trouvé à l'étroit dans le cercle ordinaire
des sentiments humains" (ibid.).

Occasionally, Coligny comes down to earth and at least mentions specific works of art. Several references show that he is aware that Rosa painted
a *Prometheus,* but his most precise observation of the picture seems to be
borrowed: "L'anatomie du Prométhée a été proclamée digne de Michel-Ange"
("Michel-Ange," p. 53); Lady Morgan, as we have seen, had written:
"L'anatomie de cette figure est digne de Michel-Ange" (I, 187). There are
several references to a *Purgatory,* but no details are provided. He notes Rosa's
fondness for painting certain Greek philosophers: "Ce Pythagore, qui montre
l'homme libre même devant son créateur, lui a servi d'étude favorite, et il a
peint et gravé Pythagore. Ce Diogène jetant sa coupe lui a souri, et il est
revenu quatre fois à Diogène. Démocrite, qui crée une philosophie ironique
et céleste, lui inspire de l'enthousiasme, et il revient trois fois saluer
Démocrite"[63] ("Génie," p. 98). He believes that Rosa painted a *Christ Driving the Money-Changers from the Temple* and a *Christ Holding a Globe*
("Génie," p. 98), probably because Lady Morgan lists two such pictures in
her catalogue (II, 312, 317).

Coligny's way of characterizing Rosa's work normally lacks precision:
"énergie" ("Génie," p. 97), "imagination" (p. 98), "passion" (ibid.), "sa muse
sauvage et libre" ("Michel-Ange," p. 52), "le peintre fougueux" ("Gravures,"
p. 82), "ses inspirations sombres et philosophiques" ("Michel-Ange," p. 52);
Rosa's etchings have "la souplesse et l'expression d'une langue" (ibid.). These
blurry images beome a little sharper when Coligny speaks of "ses têtes
sauvages et féroces, ses paysages noirs et pittoresques" (ibid.) and "les têtes
pleines de vie et d'expression" ("Gravures," p. 83). Virtually the only time
Coligny raises a technical point is his reference to "l'intelligence du clair-

obscur" (ibid.) revealed in Rosa's etchings; the source of this observation, for once, is *not* to be found in Lady Morgan. Another passage suggests, but through negative assertions, the character of Rosa's work: "sa peinture n'affectait pas des traits hermaphrodites, des mélodies de lignes, des subtilités de couleur, une palette calculée sur la fugue plus que sur le contre-point. . . . Salvator Rosa ne s'est pas occupé si Caravage exagérait ses ombres, et Barroche le brillant de ses couleurs" ("Génie," p. 98). It is difficult to say what Coligny means when he says, "Ses plans sont libres et capricieux, mais la nature les ordonne profondément" (ibid.).

Rosa virtually disappears from view in several long digressions. In "Génie," Coligny launches into a diatribe, which takes up about a third of the article, against several great writers of antiquity whom, according to the critic, Rosa detested or who were the ultimate cause of the church's persecution of the artist: Aristotle (the source of Scholasticism and the Inquisition), Cicero ("encore un persécuteur, un courtisan, un homme de ce juste milieu, qui est souvent le milieu mauvais et le milieu injuste" ["Génie," p. 99]), and Horace ("le véritable courtisan . . . le vrai flatteur et le vrai pourceau d'Epicure" [ibid.]). From this outburst we learn that "Une seule *satire* de Salvator vaut la *poétique* d'Aristote" (ibid.); that Rosa was a Stoic, not an Epicurean;[64] and that he was incapable of toadying to the great and powerful, unlike Cicero, Horace, Fuscus, and Pollio.

About a fourth of "Michel-Ange" is given over to a sweeping panorama of art and culture in the Renaissance and the seventeenth century: "Le mouvement commence à Cimabue et finit par Salvator" ("Michel-Ange," p. 51). The critic works in historical sketches of painting and even, to some extent, sculpture in Italy, France, the Low Countries, and Spain—Germany gets short shrift (two lines on Dürer). Various relationships, mostly rather tenuous, between Rosa and artists from these countries surface occasionally; e.g., in Claude Lorrain, "la création est en fête, est parée, est noyée dans des flots de lumière, invite à la joie, au bonheur, à l'amour: chez Salvator, la nature n'apparaît que dans un magnifique désordre" ("Michel-Ange," p. 52).[65] Salvator was the only painter in Rome with whom Velásquez could have gotten along: the Spanish painter "connaissait les passions de l'homme comme Salvator la morale des passions et la passion de la morale" (ibid.). Among his Italian contemporaries, Rosa preferred Domenichino to Guido Reni and defended Albani even against his friend Ricciardi ("Michel-Ange," p. 51).

Coligny shows to best advantage, perhaps, in his emphasis on the philosophical side of Rosa, though, like Lady Morgan, he does little to spell out the philosophical content of Rosa's work. He calls Rosa "un vrai fils de la Philosophie" ("Michel-Ange," p. 49). In the fifteenth and sixteenth centuries, Poliziano and Michelangelo were still imbued with Christianity: "ce n'était pas encore l'heure d'être philosophe comme Salvator Rosa" (ibid., p. 54). Rosa eschewed religious art after the manner of Titian and Correggio: "la religion lui aurait fait fausse route, il prit la philosophie ("Génie," p. 98).[66] Coligny buttresses this view with passages that emphasize Rosa's fondness for portraying Greek philosophers, but only certain Greek philosophers (Aristotle, obviously, was not one of them): "Ce Pythagore, qui montre l'homme libre même devant son créateur, . . . Diogène jetant sa coupe, . . . Démocrite, qui crée une philosophie ironique et céleste" ("Génie," p. 98).[67]

Coligny finds another Greek element in Rosa. He often refers to Rosa's *Prometeo,* of which he may have seen an engraved version; it is possible, however, that he extrapolated his ideas from Lady Morgan's biography. For one thing, she quotes a long, vivid description of the picture, taken from Mongez's *Galerie de Florence.* In any case, he develops an affinity between Rosa and the principal source of the Prometheus motif, Aeschylus. Rosa "sympathisait avec Prométhée contre Jupiter" ("Génie," p. 98). "Michel-Ange a fait voir Moïse; Salvator a fait voir Prométhée. L'un a refait la Bible; l'autre a refait la tragédie grecque, qui est l'expression de la liberté dans la patrie d'Eschyle et de Sophocle" ("Michel-Ange," p. 50). "Salvator ne fera pas son Prométhée comme l'artiste florentin [Michelangelo] a fait son législateur hébreu" (ibid., p. 53). "Eschyle était son poëte, comme Prométhée son héros. . . . Eschyle avait le sentiment de sa dignité et de son indépendance" (ibid., p. 55).[68]

Coligny is not content to label Rosa a philosopher; he wishes to see in the artist and poet a moralist: "c'est aux hommes comme Salvator à être l'écho des concerts de l'homme, à être les peintres des douleurs et des choses sociales, *pittore delle cose morali*" ("Génie," p. 97). Rosa is "le peintre et le satiriste des causes morales" ("Michel-Ange," p. 48); even in his depiction of nature, "il était le peintre des choses morales" ("Michel-Ange," p. 53; see also p. 54).[69] Coligny's Rosa is, in a modern sense, a humanist: "Il a toutes les désillusions de soixante siècles, mais il a toutes les espérances des siècles futurs. Sa fine et nerveuse organisation lui donne les émotions du passé, les malaises du présent, les joies de l'avenir. Il est homme" (ibid.). A little surprisingly, Coligny's Rosa is also something of a scientist: he masters the disorder of nature (ibid., p. 52): "Comme Léonard, Salvator entra dans le cercle de la philosophie naturelle et de la philosophie morale" (ibid., p. 53). In a passage eulogizing Peiresc, according to Coligny, "un esprit animé comme Rosa avait dû tout de suite se nourrir de toute cette science, de toute cette littéraure, de toute cette philosophie" (ibid., p. 54).

If there is a core to Coligny's view of Rosa the man, the artist, and the writer, it is in the idea of freedom. This manifests itself, at the lowest level, in his pride: "Salvator a le génie altier, il est toujours prêt à se peindre lui-même en poëte superbe au front puissant" ("Génie," p. 98). "Le romantique Salvator n'était pas l'homme de la modestie, mais il était l'homme de la liberté" ("Michel-Ange," p. 53). But this pride is not, for Coligny, mere egotism or vanity: like Michelangelo, he has "le génie hautain, audacieux, indépendant de tout, libre de tout" ("Michel-Ange," p. 52). This claim has a political ring when Coligny uses the words "libéral" and "libéralisme" in speaking of Rosa, who "représente l'homme libéral de son siècle" ("Génie," p. 97). Elsewhere, Coligny writes, "Salvator, le Napolitain libéral et militant, avait un culte pour Dante, le patriarche révolutionnaire de la poésie italienne" ("Génie," p. 100). Coligny twice refers to Rosa's participation in Masaniello's uprising. As a militant supporter of Masaniello, Rosa was a precursor of the Risorgimento, the Italian emancipation from foreign occupation: "A Naples, le patriotisme dicte à Salvator Rosa ce qu'il a dicté dans Florence à Michel-Ange" ("Michel-Ange," p. 50). Coligny's emphasis on Rosa's freedom of spirit reaches a peak of truculence when he writes:

> Pour être le peintre de la liberté, de la philosophie et de la terreur, fallait-il qu'il poignardât le grand duc de Florence, comme il avait voulu poignarder le vice-roi de Naples? J'affirme seulement que si le pape Urbain VIII, Innocent X ou Clément IX, lui eût lancé un coup de bâton comme Jules II à Michel-Ange, le peintre des batailles aurait fait voler toutes les échelles du Vatican sur le dos du Saint-Père. (ibid., p. 53)

The artist's liberalism expressed itself in his art as well and in particular in his refusal to be of any school: "Salvator ne se rattache à la grande tradition des écoles; il est le libéral du XVIIᵉ siècle" (ibid., p. 49); "Salvator n'était d'aucune école; qui dit école dit limite" (ibid., p. 52). Coligny identifies Rosa as an enemy of such institutions as the Accademia della Crusca ("Génie," p. 100), of Marinismo ("Michel-Ange," p. 55), and Versailles classicism ("Génie," p. 98). Rosa rejected the tutelage of Ribera ("Michel-Ange," p. 52), who persecuted him (ibid., p. 50), and satirized the "arts serviles du cavalier Bernin" (ibid., p. 53; see also "Génie," p. 98). Not only was he of no school—he had no disciples or imitators (ibid.; "Michel-Ange," p. 54; "Gravures," pp. 83, 84).

In Coligny's three articles there are still other *rapprochements* that could be pointed out, many other great names that could be dropped, and several other motifs that could be pursued, but the foregoing pages suffice to reveal the lineaments of his Salvator Rosa, perhaps at too great a length given the obscurity of the writer. But Coligny's cluster of articles about Rosa constitutes one of the most enthusiastic assessments of Rosa ever written directly in French, matching Lady Morgan's biography. He did not draw on her for the material of poems, fictions, and plays about Rosa, as did the authors treated in chapter 4. Rather, he sought to match her sweeping generalizations about Rosa the artist, the man, the militant, the thinker. Then, too, the twenty-five columns in *L'Artiste* form one of the most substantial tributes to Rosa in French, the equivalent perhaps of sixty or seventy pages of an ordinary book. In this respect, they belong with Delécluze's series of articles on Rosa's satires and Blanc's fascicule on Rosa in the *Histoire des peintres de toutes les écoles*. Whatever the weaknesses of Coligny's texts as art criticism or art history, they are the last vivid expression of the romantic vision of Rosa, a glowing romantic sunset before the darkness begins to gather about Rosa and his work.

CHAPTER SEVEN

A Fading Beacon

The story of Salvator Rosa's "fortune" in French literature from about 1860 to the present is not the story of a total eclipse but of a gradual waning, a perceptible loss of popularity and prestige. To my knowledge, a passing reference to him by Colette in *La Maison de Claudine* (1922) is his only appearance in the literary work of a major French writer; in the early section entitled "Le sauvage," Sido thinks wistfully of the familiar objects left behind when she married; among them is "le grand Salvator Rosa légué par mon père."[1] His life and work during this long period become grist for the mills of scholars, critics, compilers of and contributors to reference works, even authors of children's books, rather than a source of inspiration to poets, novelists, and dramatists. Yet paintings by Rosa remained on view in the Louvre's Grande Galerie, as attested in the catalogue of that museum's holdings compiled by Georges Lafenestre and Eugène Richtenberger toward the end of the nineteenth century.[2] Moreover, by virtue of the Duc d'Aumale's donation in 1886 to the Institut de France of the Musée Condé at Chantilly, a number of Rosas became, in effect, the property of the French nation and were soon made accessible to the public, forming the largest body of his work in France. This collection had been put together by Henry, Duc d'Aumale (1822–1897), son of King Louis-Philippe. He had acquired his Rosas from his father-in-law, Prince Leopoldo of Salerno, in 1854.[3] The Duke's treasure was slow in being discovered; the article on Rosa in *La Grande Encyclopédie* (XXVIII, pp. 928–29), published in 1900, makes no mention of the Rosas at Chantilly and, in fact, locates three of them in Naples. Perhaps these pictures attracted little attention simply because they were not in Paris. In any case, their addition to the national patrimony seems to have done little for Rosa's fame.

Curiously, however, at the beginning of this long fading of Rosa from the French consciousness, two poets paid tribute to him in the prominent magazine *L'Artiste*. In the issue for June 15, 1862, appeared "Salvator Rosa," five quatrains by Léon Dierx (1838–1912), a future Parnassian and Mallarmé's successor as "Prince des poètes."[4] The poem's first two quatrains question the artist about the source of his inspiration:

> Qu'avais-tu dans l'esprit, maître à la brosse ardente,
> Pour que, sous ton pinceau, la nature en fureur
> Semble jeter au ciel une insulte stridente,
> Ou frémir dans l'effroi de sa sinistre horreur?
>
> Pourquoi dédaignais-tu les calmes paysages
> Dans la lumière au loin ourlant leurs horizons,
> Les lacs d'azur limpide, et sur de frais visages
> L'ombre du vert printemps qui fleurit les gazons?[5]

The answer to this question is a little surprising, coming from a poet on the verge of joining the Parnassian group of "les Impassibles":

> Il te fallait à toi l'atmosphère d'orage,
> Quelque ravin bien noir où mugisse un torrent
> Qui boit et revomit l'écume de sa rage,
> Quelque fauve bandit sur des rochers errant.
>
> L'ouragan qui s'abat sur tes arbres d'automne
> Rugissait, n'est-ce pas? dans ton âme de fer.
> Tu ne te plaisais pas au bonheur monotone,
> Mais aux transports fougueux déchaînés par l'enfer.
>
> Ce sont tes passions qui hurlent sur tes toiles;
> Toi-même, tu t'es peint dans ces lieux dévastés,
> Dans ces chênes tordant, sous la nuit sans étoiles,
> Sur l'abîme béant leurs troncs décapités.

Budding Parnassian or not, Dierx creates a highly romantic Rosa, painter of highly romantic landscapes, and evokes, in addition to bandits, many of the landscape features often highlighted in the writing about Rosa for about a century—features, by the way, that are largely lacking in the one Rosa landscape Dierx definitely could have seen in the Louvre, *Paesaggio con soldati e cacciatori* (S 239). Rather than creating the *transposition d'art* of a particular painting, the poet may be simply reflecting the well-established literary and critical image of Rosa's landscapes, including storms—though not one of his landscapes literally depicts a storm. Dierx does not include any biographical details, but he seems aware of Rosa's reputation as a proud and truculent personality: "maître à la brosse ardente," "insulte stridente," "âme de fer," "transports fougueux."

The other Rosa-inspired poem from this period appeared in *L'Artiste* for May 15, 1864. The author, Ernest d'Hervilly (1837–1911), was Dierx's almost exact contemporary and, like him, became a member of the Parnasse.[6] In fact, the well-known poem by Gabriel Marc, "L'entresol du Parnasse," evoking a gathering of Alphonse Lemerre's authors, couples the names of the two in a single line of its group portrait: "Voici Dierx et D'Hervilly."[7] But, while Dierx went on to become "le Prince des poètes," D'Hervilly turned to comedy and humorous fiction.

In 1864, however, he is still a potential Parnassian. His poem on Salvator Rosa is one of the most elaborate *transpositions d'art* ever attempted; it makes D'Hervilly, at this stage of his poetic evolution, a faithful disciple of Théophile Gautier.[8] But it is in sharp contrast to Dierx's in several respects: it is much longer (twenty-six quatrains as against five) and it is inspired by a specific painting, the *Battaglia eroica* in the Louvre. Entitled "Une bataille de Salvator Rosa," it is dedicated to the Comte de Nieuwerkerke, *surintendant des beaux-arts* during the Second Empire. The poem looks hard and close at Rosa's huge picture, first in a rather sweeping view that occupies the first eight stanzas, then in greater detail, in stanzas 13–24. Like Dierx, D'Hervilly addresses the painter, asking for the source of his inspiration:

> Sombre Napolitain, peintre à l'âme de fer,
> Qui donc t'avait gonflé le cœur de tant de haines,
> Et te faisait couvrir ta palette d'enfer
>   Du carmin sinistre des veines?

> Qui donc haïssais-tu, grand Salvator Rosa?
> Quel infâme insulteur de ta farouche étoile,
> Quel ennemi, quel peuple, injuste et dur, brisa
>   Ta main sur ce billot de toile?

> Qui sont-ils ces mourants que tu fais, que tu tords,
> Et, que ta brosse, à terre, achève par centaines?
> Qui sont-ils?—Vengeais-tu, longuement, sans remords,
>   Proscrit, des misères lointaines?

> Rude amant de l'horreur, quels crânes, quels vaisseaux,
> Ouvrais-tu de tes traits? quelle âme était frappée?

> Dis, qui donc perçais-tu de tes coups de pinceaux,
>   Qui sont comme des coups d'épée?

Thus, like Dierx, D'Hervilly traces the strong emotion conveyed by Rosa's picture to the artist's biography and his inner life.

But D'Hervilly is dealing with a furious battle, not with landscape, however stormy and gloomy ("nature en fureur"). His real theme is the horror of war, encapsulated in various epithets—"combat horrible," "noir massacre, incessant, effroyable! / Un énorme carnage, une tûrie, un long / Egorgement impitoyable," "Mêlée épouvantable"—but even more in a series of sharply focused details like the following:

> Horreur! là, sur le dos de son cheval, cloué,
> Un homme, en pleins poumons percé d'un coup de lance,
> Expire en selle, et , comme un ruban dénoué,
>   Son bras impuissant se balance!

And so through six more stanzas that prove that, faithful to the tradition of the *transposition d'art* as established by Théophile Gautier, especially in "Melancholia," his long poetic disquisition on Dürer's *Melencolia I,* D'Hervilly has examined the painting with extraordinary care, perhaps with more care than any other observer. The heaping up of the gory and gruesome incidents depicted may seem excessive; perhaps a greater poet would have found a more economical way to exploit Rosa's painting as material for a denunciation of the horrors of war. But D'Hervilly's accumulation is effective in its own way, perhaps especially in a stanza near the end:

> Partout de grands débris!—et la Destruction,
> Marchant à pleins talons sur des cadavres roides,
> Sent à ses pieds brûlants l'inerte succion
>   De cent lèvres à jamais froides.

But D'Hervilly does not forget the artist who provided him the matter of his poem. After a stanza stressing the utter futility of this particular battle, he ends with a prediction for the distant future:

> Mais un homme naîtra, marqué par l'Art au front,
> Poussière de guerriers, sans noms comme sans taille,
> Et grâce à lui, héros d'un jour, vos os auront
>   L'honneur de vivre en sa Bataille!

D'Hervilly the poet is virtually forgotten today—the *National Union Catalog* does not indicate the presence of a single volume of his poetry in American libraries. But his careful description of Rosa's *Battaglia eroica* deserves to be remembered here, not only for its vivid evocation of war's bloody-minded destructiveness but for its tribute to Rosa, perhaps the most eloquent ever bestowed on him by any French poet.

These poems by two future Parnassians should probably be seen, along with Charles Coligny's three articles on Rosa in *L'Artiste* in 1864–1865, as the last flare-up of Rosa's fading beacon. Not that the flame dies out completely. There are substantial articles on Rosa in major reference works of the late nineteenth century: in 1863, by Ernest Breton in Dr. Hoefer's *Nouvelle Biographie générale* (XLIII, 622–26)[9]; in 1875, in Pierre Larousse's *Grand Dictionnaire universel du XIXe siècle* (XIV, 149–50)[10]; in 1900 by Eugène Plouchart (1868–1934) in *La Grande Encyclopédie* (XXVIII, 928–29).[11] It is discouraging to observe that in all three of these standard reference works errors of fact are copied and legends prolonged: all three articles repeat the story of Rosa's participation in Masaniello's uprising. All three emphasize the biography of the artist. Breton, writing in a compilation explicitly biographical in nature, provides no general description or assessment of Rosa's work. The author of the article in Larousse's *Grand Dictionnaire universel* offers, in addition to quotations from De Angelis and Viardot, seven lines of his own devising: "Le caractère de la peinture de Salvator Rosa est une sorte de grandeur sauvage, d'âpreté et d'orageuse mélancolie; sa touche est large, énergique et fière; son coloris est plein de vigueur et d'éclat; il excellait à peindre les scènes violentes, les batailles, les brigands, les paysages sévères, les scènes à effet." Plouchart's judgment is more nuanced:

> Son originalité a été son paysage et ses batailles. Il a créé le paysage historique, repris plus tard par Hubert Robert; ses *Batailles*, "des égorgements dans le bitume," sont des mêlées tragiques, un peu confuses, où l'outrance des expressions et des attitudes est visible. Néanmoins il compose avec adresse et s'applique à donner l'illusion du mouvement. L'on retrouve dans ses toiles, surtout dans les scènes historiques, les traces d'un effort constant dans un style élevé, que gâtent un peu son dessin pléthorique et la lourdeur de sa palette.

All three articles refer briefly to Rosa's etchings; all, citing Dr. Burney, credit the story of Rosa as a composer of music; all provide fairly long lists of Rosa's paintings, with locations. These lists, however, differ markedly from one another and often bear little relation to the most authoritative catalogues available today, those of Salerno: for example, in 1863 Breton's catalogue lists about thirty-five pictures, whereas, Salerno in 1975 lists 264; Breton locates

five Rosas in Nantes, whereas none in that city figure in Salerno. To conclude: these three otherwise reputable reference works conveyed much misinformation or inadequate information to those who consulted the articles
on Salvator Rosa. Examination of these texts furnishes a cautionary tale to
the readers of encyclopedias and biographical dictionaries.[12]

A look at the articles on Rosa in the four editions of Emmanuel Bénézit's
*Dictionnaire critique et documentaire des peintres, sculpteurs, dessinateurs
et graveurs de tous les pays,* which first appeared in 1911–1924 in a three-
volume format, will reinforce this point. Most revealing is that the tale of
Rosa and Masaniello, though long since discredited, appears in all four articles, including that in the 1999 edition.[13] While the Masaniello legend remained a constant feature of the articles in Bénézit, we can observe a revealing
change in the general assessment of Rosa that concludes the main body of
the article. In the first edition the sentence is: " Artiste vraiment remarquable
dans ses marines, ses paysages et ses batailles, il manifesta toute sa vie le
désir de se faire une réputation de peintre d'histoire sans que cette prétention
se justifiât" (III, 658). This appears unchanged in 1954 in the second edition
(VII, 347–48). In the third edition (1976), "Marguerite Bénézit" adds: "La
critique moderne a beaucoup plus retenu de son œuvre les paysages pré-
romantiques, avec décors de ruines antiques, allusions littéraires, évocations
de sorcelleries et de nécromancie, qui devaient influencer Magnasco et Marco
Ricci" (IX, 85). This text reappears in the fourth edition unchanged (XI, 900).

Evidence of a relative decline in Rosa's fortunes in France after about
1860 can be found in several rather disparate fields. The revival of Dugué's
Salvator Rosa at the Théâtre de la Porte-Saint-Martin, noted by *Le Nain
Jaune* for July 25, 1866, is the only evidence I have discovered of Rosa's
presence in the French theater in the latter part of the nineteenth century.
In Hippolyte Taine's *Voyage en Italie,* published in the same year, there is
only a passing reference to Rosa, and this despite the fact that Taine devotes
many pages to the works of art encountered in Italy. In a passage that, rather
revealingly, treats landscape as a late, decadent product of artistic development, Taine writes:

> Peut-être le paysage n'est-il que le dernier moment de la peinture, celui
> qui clôt une grande époque et convient aux âmes fatiguées. . . . Du moins il
> en est ainsi en Italie; si l'art du paysage s'y développe, c'est à la fin, au
> temps des arcadiens et des académies pastorales; il occupe déjà la plus grande
> partie des toiles de l'Albane; il remplit toutes celles de Canaletti, le dernier
> des Vénitians, Zucarelli, Tempesta, Salvator, sont des paysagistes. Au
> contraire, du temps de Michel-Ange et même de Vasari, on dédaignait les

arbres, les fabriques; tout ce qui n'est pas le corps humain semblait accessoire. (I, 262)

There is a passage on brigands (I, 81–82), but it does not refer to Rosa. There are several mountainous landscapes; indeed, the book ends as Taine passes through the Alps; out the train window he sees, *inter alia,* "les troncs mourants, les cadavres d'arbres mutilés" (II, 437), but he does not mention Rosa. Visiting Santa Maria degli Angeli in Rome, he takes no note of Rosa's tomb (I, 294–95). For Taine, the four greatest creators were Dante, Shakespeare, Beethoven, and the Michelangelo of the Sistine Chapel murals (I, 217); it is understandable that Rosa would not make this list. But a serious art critic visiting Rome, Florence, and Naples might well have found a place for Rosa in, say, his list of Neapolitan painters (I, 44). Taine's book was reprinted many times; it was perhaps the most popular *Voyage en Italie* published in France in the late nineteenth and early twentieth centuries (the copy I have consulted, allegedly the eighteenth edition, was probably published in the 1920s). Rosa's almost total absence from Taine's book is at least symptomatic.

Rosa, one might say, took refuge in children's literature, much of it published in the provinces! In 1868, the prolific Frédéric Koenig (pseudonym of Just-Jean-Etienne Roy [1790–1870]) published *La Jeunesse de Salvator Rosa.* It was the product of the Catholic publishing house of Mame, in Tours, and was part of their Bibliothèque de la jeunesse chrétienne. One hundred thirty-nine pages long, Koenig's book was reprinted half a dozen times up to 1884. The year before, one Victor Delcroix published *Salvator Rosa, peintre célèbre*—sixty-three pages long—in Rouen, chez Mégard; it formed part of the Bibliothèque morale de la jeunesse. The final, rather pitiful, book in this series is René Samoy's *Un enfant peintre et musicien,* published in 1925 by Larousse in the collection *Les Livres roses pour la jeunesse;* it is just twenty-eight pages long. The material for these pious biographies was no doubt to be found in Lady Morgan's seminal work, but MM. Koenig, Delcroix, and Samoy must have consulted it in a very selective way. Rosa married Lucrezia on his deathbed and died a pious Catholic; he lies buried in Santa Maria degli Angeli. But the still-living Rosa outraged the Pope with such pictures as *La Fortuna* and such satiric poems as *L'Invidia.*

Rosa is granted a page—and one illustration (the Louvre *Battle*)—in Paul Mantz's *Chefs-d'œuvre de la peinture italienne.*[14] Mantz's three paragraphs on Rosa are about half biography—he devotes six lines to the Masaniello story (but says nothing about alleged wanderings in the Abruzzi, Rosa's life among the bandits, and the like)—and half criticism. The writer grants Rosa "une originalité très-accentuée," but reveals a somewhat surprising preference for the "marines d'un très-grand aspect" in the Pitti, over "ces paysages où il entasse, sous un ciel d'orage, des rochers et des troncs d'arbres frappés de la foudre"; these latter are "des inventions artificielles et qui, violentes par l'intention, restent froides parce qu'elles ne sont pas empruntées à la nature." Mantz then focuses on the Louvre's *Battle*, "une preuve éclatante" of Rosa's talent for this genre. His final judgment, however, is mixed: "Ce tableau est un des meilleurs de l'artiste: l'exécution est pleine de verve, le pinceau y montre une dextérité amusante. Ce n'est pas sans dessein que nous employons ce mot: la *Bataille* de Salvator, en effet, n'est pas très-sérieuse, et ce qui y manque le plus, c'est le sentiment de la tragédie." All in all, Mantz's is a curious assessment. His downgrading of Rosa's landscapes as artificial and unnatural might be understandable if the critic revealed awareness of what was happening to landscape painting in France in 1870. Perhaps even more surprising is his emphasis on "dextérité amusante" and lack of tragic feeling in the one painting he actually describes.

The art critic and fine-arts administrator A.-F. Gruyer published a handsome catalogue of the Musée Condé's holdings at the end of the century: *La Peinture au château de Chantilly;* Rosa is treated in the first volume, *Les Ecoles étrangères* (1896). Gruyer ascribes thirteen paintings to Rosa—more than for any other painter treated in this volume—five of which are not accepted by Luigi Salerno in his 1975 catalogue, the most authoritative to date. In a brief "notice" preceding the catalogue entries, Gruyer commits several minor historical mistakes and, more seriously, devotes one sixth of the space to the Masaniello episode and Rosa's alleged part in it. The subject of each painting is soberly described, some critical comments are usually appended, and some misinformation about the provenance of the pictures is provided— all thirteen are traced to the Prince of Salerno's collection; Gruyer claims that four of the pictures were once in a chapel of Santa Maria del Popolo in Rome (the church in question was actually Santa Maria di Santomonte).

It is Gruyer's criticisms of the paintings that are of most interest now, as they reveal the erosion of Rosa's reputation in the latter part of the nineteenth century. Gruyer has much admiration for Rosa as landscapist: the three *Petits paysages* (S 148, S 149, and S 241) still accepted as from the hand of Rosa by Salerno are all praised, especially *Marina* (S 149): "Parmi les innombrables paysages qu'a peints Salvator Rosa, celui-là est un des plus calmes, un de ceux qui présentent les plus belles clartés, où les lignes se balancent avec le plus d'harmonie, dont les tons chantent avec le plus de douceur" (p. 159). The five biblically inspired pictures get very harsh treatment, e.g., of the *Resurrezione di Lazzaro* (S 175) he writes: "Le Christ est vulgaire, Lazare l'est davantage, et c'est parmi les comparses qu'il faut chercher pour y trouver peut-être un reste de noblesse" (pp. 154–55).

One of these pictures on religious themes receives perhaps the most interesting of Gruyer's criticisms: *L'Angelo lascia la casa di Tobia* (S 178):

> On ne peut se défendre d'y reconnaître l'accent de sincerité qui ennoblit la trivialité des figures, non plus que la fougue qui les anime et qui est de bon aloi. C'est toujours dans ce que la nature offre de violent et de vulgaire que Salvator Rosa va chercher ses modèles. Aucun peintre ne s'est plus mêlé au bas peuple. Malgré les vicissitudes qui l'ont tantôt élevé très haut, tantôt précipité très bas, il n'a jamais cessé d'être le peintre des pêcheurs et des *lazzaroni*. Son Daniel et son Jérémie sortaient tout à l'heure des cloaques de Basso-Porto; voici maintenant son Tobie qui vient de débarquer à la Mergellina. (p. 154)

It is not necessary to pierce Gruyer's references to Basso-Porto and La Mergellina to grasp that, although he grudgingly acknowledges the "accent de sincérité qui ennoblit la trivialité des figures" and "la fougue qui les anime," Gruyer intends Rosa no compliment in crowning him "le peintre des pêcheurs et des *lazzaroni*." This criticism, even if unnecessarily harsh and ill-founded, is original with Gruyer. At the same time, Rosa's landscapes retain their charm for him.

French scholarship on Rosa has not been very important in the period we are considering, which saw the emergence of art history as a serious field of work. There is not a single work by a French writer in Luigi Salerno's "bibliografia essenziale" in his fundamental monograph of 1975. In 1898, Fernand Engerand (1867–1938) published an article on the Louvre's *Heroic Battle* in *La Chronique des arts et de la curiosité*. A few years later, Rosa did not fare well in the folio-sized volume on painting in Louis Gonse's *Les Chefs-d'œuvre des musées de France*. The only reference to Rosa occurs in a passage devoted to the Musée départemental des Vosges in Epinal, in which Gonse praises the Rosa landscape (S 259) in this museum but expresses a preference for the museum's Claude Lorrain; the latter is reproduced in a small black and white, but this honor is not granted to the picture by Rosa.[15] Three years later, the obscure E. E. Hamy—his name does not appear in the catalogue of the Bibliothèque Nationale—published an article in *L'Art* on an alleged Salvator Rosa in the Musée de Boulogne-sur Mer; no list or catalogue of Rosa's work that I have seen includes any painting in that location. An article by a major Italian Rosa specialist, Leandro Ozzola, appeared in the April 1911 issue of the *Gazette des Beaux-Arts:* "L'œuvre de Salvator

Rosa" (pp. 279–90). Ozzola's text is more of an "appreciation" of Rosa than art history, but, writing in the leading French art historical journal, he gives his French readers the benefit of his considerable expertise, getting into questions of authenticity, of pictures by "Rosa" in French museums, and ending by rejecting a dozen of them. (It is suggestive that this article is the only one devoted exclusively to Rosa during the first century of the *Gazette*— a fact revealed by the index published in 1968.)

Rosa's stock seems hardly to have risen in the nearly nine decades of French scholarship since Ozzola's article. He is not mentioned in the pair of articles on "L'art romain du XVIIe siècle" by Marcel Reymond in the prestigious *Revue des deux mondes* in 1912 (March 15, pp. 388–421; May 15, pp. 386–405). Reymond may have purposefully excluded Rosa because he considered him a member of the Neapolitan school; if so, he did not bother to explain this decision. Similarly, in 1918, Louis Bréhier omits any reference to Rosa in his iconographical study, *L'Art chrétien*[16]; this may be the result of Rosa's reputation for anticlericalism, but it overlooks the fact that Rosa painted about seventy pictures on religious themes. Elie Faure's massive *Histoire de l'art,* whose section on modern art was first published in 1920, rather curiously, mentions "les batailles et les paysages romantiques de Salvator Rosa" in a passage on painting on the eve of the French Revolution.[17] In the multiple-volume *Histoire de l'art en Europe,* directed by André Michel and published between 1905 and 1928, Rosa is not well served by the author (André Pératé) of the chapter on "La peinture italienne au XVIIe siècle."[18] While many of the facts are unexceptionable, we are told—as so often before—about the artist's "courses vagabondes dans les montagnes des Abruzzes, la fréquentation des moines et des bandits calabrais," "sa musique," and "la folle et généreuse aventure" of his role in the Masaniello revolt. Pératé focuses on the three pictures from the Louvre that are illustrated, praising the *Landscape* as perhaps the best example of Rosa's "paysages d'une âpreté romantique," and the *Battle* for "une vraie splendeur de décor héroïque." Before returning—for good—to the biography of Rosa, Pératé delivers himself of his final critical judgment:

> Il est moins heureux dans les compositions d'histoire ou de piété, malgré une certaine imagination triste et macabre dont il les anime parfois. S'il se souvient trop exactement de la gravure de Dürer lorsqu'il peint l'*Enfant prodigue,* il sait rendre l'horreur théâtrale d'une apparition de spectre dans sa *Pythonisse d'Endor.* Son *Tobie et l'ange* de Chantilly a quelque chose de rembranesque; mais il y a bien de la vulgarité dans les trois autres tableaux de la même collection, le *Daniel,* le *Jérémie,* le *Lazare,* qui proviennent, comme celui-là, de Sainte-Marie-du-Peuple, à Rome.

Though disappointing in several respects, Pérate's pages on Rosa have the merit of introducing Rosa's work at the Musée Condé to the readers of André Michel's huge and ambitious history of European art.

The chapter on the Italian Schools of the sixteenth, seventeenth, and eighteenth centuries supplied by Gabriel Rouchès to the relevant volume of Jean Guiffrey's *La Peinture au Musée du Louvre* follows a well-worn path— like Gonse, Rouchès confines himself to one picture, the Louvre's great *Battle* scene—Rouchès's paragraphs on Rosa, whom he calls "ce Napolitain, le plus Napolitain de tous par son caractère," "cet autodidacte, ce magnifique improvisateur," provides some valuable information about the history of this picture (especially in the eighteenth century), but is primarily concerned with bringing out Rosa's place in the history of battle painting.[19] First, he insists on Rosa's originality vis-à-vis his predecessors in this genre (Raphael, Giulio Romano, and Pietro da Cortona) whose works he could have seen in Rome: "il donne à ses groupes de combattants une fougue et une violence par lesquelles parle sa nature ardente et enfiévrée" (ibid.). Likewise, with respect to the background, Rosa, though borrowing from the Bolognese masters and Poussin, "modifie le caractère du paysage" (ibid.):

> Il associe la nature à ses sentiments. Il donne à ses grands rochers, aux nuages qui les entourent, un aspect tragique qui accentue l'œuvre de destruction accomplie par le temps et par les hommes: le temps qui ruine les plus beaux édifices et les hommes féroces qui s'égorgent, tuent les animaux, brûlent les navires, anéantissent des vies et des richesses. Ce lyrisme pessimiste apporte un élément nouveau dans l'art si complexe du XVIIe siècle et constitue, pour une part, l'originalité de Salvator Rosa.

An article by Lucien Rudiauf that I have not been able to consult, "Delacroix et Salvator Rosa" (no. 23, 1943, pp. 11–15), published in the Belgian periodical *Apollo,* posits the influence of the Italian painter's *Temptation of Christ* at Chantilly on the French artist's Saint-Sulpice mural depicting Jacob's struggle with the angel; the two works are shown in illustration. The American art historian Wylie Sypher mentions Rosa some half a dozen times in an article in English, "Baroque Altarpiece. The Picturesque."[20] Sypher's emphasis is on eighteenth-century English art and Rosa is cited primarily as an influence on the rise of the picturesque, which he sees as a prolongation, in attenuated form, of the baroque. Perhaps his phrase, "The tumultuous sullen landscapes of Salvator Rosa" (p. 40) is worth citing. Louis Hautecœur, covering the same period in the *Histoire générale de l'art* by Eugène Pittard and others, mentions Rosa only as one of the "tenebrosi," i.e., the painters influenced by Caravaggio,[21] but vouchsafes a paragraph or so to the leading members of the Bolognese school and even to Lanfranco. Rosa figures in Léon Reni-Mel's article, "De la peinture militaire et historique," a lecture given at the Sorbonne in 1954 and published the following year in the *Revue Historique de l'Armée* (T. XI, pp. 139–50); I have not seen this text but it is almost certain that, like so many French art critics and historians before him, Reni-Mel illustrates his account by citing the *Heroic Battle* in the Louvre. In 1959, Antoine Schnapper, in "Quelques œuvres de Joseph Parrocel,"[22] discussed the influence of Rosa on the eighteenth-century French artist but mentioned other influences as well.

The second half of the 1950s saw a massive updating of Bréhier's study of Christian iconography, Louis Réau's *Iconographie de l'art chrétien.*[23] In 1918, it will be recalled, Bréhier did not have a single reference to any work by Rosa. Réau was better informed or more diligent, or both: still, among the hundreds, perhaps thousands, of works catalogued, only six are by Rosa: four Old Testament subjects, one from the New Testament, and one from the lives of the saints.[24] Given the abundance—rarely noted—of Rosa's paintings on religious themes, it is disappointing that Réau saw fit to list so few works by Rosa; it would appear that a thorough study of this aspect of his work is in order.

The decade or so leading up to the tercentenary of Rosa's death offers slim pickings. Victor-Lucien Tapié omits Rosa altogether from his little manual, *Le Baroque,* in the popular "Que sais-je?" collection (Paris: Presses universitaires de France, 1961). In the following year, as we have seen, Georges Wildenstein, a propos of the abbé Nicaise, unearthed a tidbit of biographical information that showed that, in Rome, Nicaise and Rosa were neighbors and that the former provided a thumbnail sketch of the painter emphasizing his eccentricity and calling attention to the artist's satires.[25] Germain Bazin, in *Baroque and Rococo,* devoted five lines of text and one illustration (S 43) to Rosa; from his text we learn: "Salvator Rosa . . . , who was by turns a revolutionary, a bandit, a strolling player, and a writer of plays, harmonized his life with the romanticism of his art. His innovation was to paint wild landscapes, which later influenced Gaspard Dughet in Rome."[26] Four years later, in his study of the baroque, Bazin, apparently after some serious digging, disavowed the legends he had credited in 1964 as "fables which Ozzola had already utterly discredited as early as 1908" and provided several judicious paragraphs on Rosa's works and life.[27] A tidbit of art historical information emerges in a brief 1969 article by Alessandro Parronchi, published in the *Revue de l'art* (no. 5, pp. 43–45), involving a drawing "attribué à Salvator Rosa" in the Uffizi that represents a satyr's head.

In 1973 the tercentenary of Rosa's death went uncelebrated in France—

no exposition was devoted to him, and not a single article was published about him. And this while Italian, British, and American scholars and curators produced major evidence of Rosa's vitality. The best that France could muster was a review by one R. Hurel of Giampiero Bozzolato's contribution to the tercentenary, his catalogue of Rosa's etchings: *Le incisione di Salvator Rosa: catalogo generale*.[28] In 1975, Anthony Blunt found the occasion to mention Rosa and Dughet as sources of inspiration to English theoreticians of the picturesque.[29] In the following year in the same periodical, Marie-Nicole Boisclair, knowingly or not, deprived Rosa of the importance Germain Bazin had attributed to him in 1964 as an influence on Dughet: "Plus que Salvator Rosa, Titien aurait pu initier le Guaspre à l'art des coups de vent."[30]

After a gap of nearly two decades in art historical writing about Rosa, the acquisition, by the Musée des Beaux-Arts in Caen, of a hitherto unknown version of *Glauco e Scilla* occasioned a perceptive and enthusiastic assessment of Rosa by Alain Tapié.[31] Tapié's most interesting insight is into Rosa's individual way of dealing with historical and mythological subjects, his special blend of baroque and classicism:

> Toujours l'ésotérisme d'un sujet, l'expressionnisme d'une scène, l'esprit d'expérience et la virtuosité ludique dans le traitement de la valeur et de la couleur l'emportent sur la convention et le genre et font de Salvator Rosa un peintre singulier, poète avant tout. . . . L'exubérance naturaliste se glisse dans le paysage classique, l'obscurantisme magique fleurit au milieu des allégories les plus avérées. L'attrait pour une nature prolifique, envahissante, vient comme décadrer, déséquilibrer les sujets religieux les plus stables, les plus attendus.

More conventionally, Tapié points to Rosa's "mélancolie ardente si bien traduite par ce jaune marron" and the "agitation inquiétante qui correspond très précisément à des obsessions philosophiques et allégoriques. . . ." His brief, ostensibly museological piece stands out in the post-romantic decades for its rather surprising rehabilitation of a side of Rosa's production frequently ignored or denigrated, usually in favor of his landscapes.

Two of the most recent contributions by French art historians or art historians writing in French deal with Rosa's relationship with the two Poussins: Mario Chiarini's "Gaspard Dughet: ses liens avec ses contemporains et les paysagistes nordiques italianisants de la génération suivante"[32] and Michel Hilaire's "Le paysage français sous l'influence de Poussin et de Salvator Rosa."[33]

The most recent appearance of Rosa in French art history is in a similar context: Maria Teresa Caracciolo's "Adriaen van der Cabel et le mythe visuel de l'Italie."[34] Van der Cabel was one of the many Northern artists who, over several generations, traveled in Italy and interacted with the art and the landscape of that country but, according to Caracciolo, never surrendered to their blandishments or to the Counter-Reformation ambiance:

> Enfermés dans leur "bande," souvent marginalisés par leur fidélité à la religion réformée, les peintres du Nord opposaient au système de pensée issu du Concile de Trente, comme à ses formes officielles d'expression, une résistance de l'esprit qui trouva un écho, dans les années 1630, dans l'attitude de Salvator Rosa. Celui-ci fut, comme Poussin, un adepte de la pensée "stoïcienne"; il fut aussi attentif aux courants contemporains du Quiétisme, et devint l'un des grands innovateurs dans le domaine du paysage, auquel il rendit sa dimension sauvage et insoumise, animée d'un sentiment panique, d'inspiration païenne. (ibid., p. 95)

While this attempt to link the ebullient and free-thinking Rosa with quietism comes as something of a shock,[35] Caracciolo is on firm ground in regard to the Stoic strain in Rosa's art and sensibility. She offers an interesting new facet to Rosa by suggesting that it may have been Rosa who turned van der Cabel's attention toward the work of Giovan Benedetto Castiglione (p. 96). Finally, she holds that, after settling in Lyon around 1670, the Dutch artist achieved in his landscapes a synthesis "entre la tradition des premiers italianisants, la vision de Poussin, régie par un ordre intérieur, celle de Claude Lorrain, arcadienne et lyrique, et celles de Gaspard Dughet et de Salvator Rosa, pittoresques et romantiques avant la lettre" (ibid.). In her English abstract (p. 108), Rosa's influence on van der Cabel is even more strongly emphasized: "Under the influence of Italian masters such as Salvator Rosa and Castiglione, van der Cabel changed his typically Nordic, meticulous and polished style to the broader, more open manner."

The story of Rosa's appearances in literary history is soon told. In 1866, Gustave Lanier, in his brief *Les Grands Ecrivains de l'Italie*,[36] includes Rosa in a list of Italy's great writers, painters, and musicians (p.1) but does not mention him in his treatment of seventeenth-century literature. The eminent Italianist, Henri Hauvette (1865–1935), devoted about half a page to Rosa in his *Littérature italienne,* first published in 1906 and several times reprinted. Hauvette, in his chapter on Marinismo, hands down a rather mixed sentence on the poet and his satires: Rosa stands alone "par sa nature ardente et sa vive imagination,"[37] and his first three satires have the merit of treating subjects familiar to him and about which he felt deeply. Then the historian turns toward the negative and the personal: "Mais il est long et diffus; sa verve compense mal l'insuffisance de sa culture littéraire. Ce pittoresque personnage est encore un déséquilibré: il s'est fait l'apôtre des idées les plus nobles, le défenseur de la vertu et de la religion, sans s'apercevoir que sa vie privée démentait tous les beaux principes énoncés dans ses vers." Moreover, thanks to modern criticism, we now know that he does not deserve the "auréole" he had worn because of his alleged role in Masaniello's revolt. If Hauvette seems a little prudish, at least he has the honor of being the first French writer aware of Cesareo's revelation in 1892 of the truth about Rosa's whereabouts in July 1647. The only other reference to Rosa that I have found in French literary histories of Italy, in Marie-France Tristan Baron's chapter on the period of the Counter-Reformation and the baroque in a textbook, agrees with Hauvette in distinguishing Rosa from the Marinists' "bizarreries conceptistes," but sees in his work a tentative "retour au classicisme" that Hauvette had not recognized.[38]

In 1946, Pierre Du Colombier (1889–1975), a prolific and versatile art historian, included four extracts from Rosa's writings in the anthology *Les Plus Beaux Ecrits des grands artistes;*[39] Rosa is one of the fifty-seven authors represented in the volume and one of six "Baroques et classiques." In a brief prefatory "notice" (p. 103), Du Colombier offers a digest that finds space for several of Lady Morgan's legends. As for Rosa the writer, the anthologist provides Rosa's *Cantata* (the Italian text of which Lady Morgan had included) as given by Delécluze in his articles on Rosa in the *Revue de Paris* in 1840, and three of Rosa's letters to Ricciardi (Letters IX, XIII, and XIV in Lady Morgan).[40] The *Cantata*, "cynique, débraillée," rather surprisingly, reminds Du Colombier of Spain's picaresque literature—he has in mind Cervantes's "El coloquio de los perros"—more than of "la poésie regulière de l'Italie." But it also suggests "un tableau des *tenebrosi* de l'école napolitaine, avec ses filous et ses ruffians." Rosa's letter of May 13, 1662, written after his trip to Loreto, is included because "le sentiment du paysage qui se fait jour . . . paraît d'un siècle et demi en avance" (p. 105). The angry letter of June 6, 1664, perhaps the most famous of all Rosa's letters, similarly looks ahead according to Du Colombier: "Salvator Rosa ne revendique point les droits du génie avec moins d'ombrageuse impatience que ne feront les grands romantiques" (p. 106). In the letter of January 2, 1665, full of the artist's money worries, "Salvator Rosa garde au moins, dans son âpre humeur, la supériorité de l'homme qui dépense plus aisément encore qu'il ne gagne" (p. 108).

If we look for Rosa in the sumptuous "coffee-table books" published in France and in French since the Second World War, it would appear that Rosa has little or nothing to say to the postwar generations. He is in the index to the volume on seventeenth-century painting in Skira's collection, "Les

Grands Siècles de la peinture," but the actual reference to him is *introuvable*.[41] In René Huyghe's *Art Treasures of the Louvre*,[42] Rosa is entirely absent from the paragraph devoted to seventeenth-century Italian painting: mentioned are Annibale Carracci, Reni, Domenichino, and Guercino (p. 24). A decade later, Huyghe's successor at the Louvre, Germain Bazin, makes no place for Rosa in a text that is clearly overshadowed by the handsome illustrations; the only Italian painter who makes an appearance in what Bazin calls "the Golden Century of Painting" is Caravaggio.[43] The most recent books I am aware of that belong to this genre—neither of which I have been able to consult—the collective volume *Louvre. Portrait of a Museum*[44] and Anne Sefrioui's *500 Chefs-d'œuvre du Louvre*,[45] one suspects, continue the current trend.

Rosa seems never to have been honored in France with any sort of "one-man show." But his works have been shown, along with those of other artists, in a number of expositions put on in various French museums in recent decades. The first of the series for which I have found evidence was entitled "Dessins romains du XVIIᵉ siècle," and displayed two of his drawings—both related to the painting *The Death of Atilius Regulus*—at the Louvre's Cabinet des dessins, apparently in early 1960.[46]

The tercentenary of Rosa's death, as already noted, was not marked in France by any special manifestation and, certainly, by no show devoted exclusively to him. Logically, he ought to have been included in the show at the Cabinet des dessins, "Le dessin italien sous la Contre-réforme," which ran from the late spring until early autumn of that year, but the reviews and announcements that I have found do not mention his name.[47]

Rosa's etchings appeared alongside those of Altdorfer, Bosse, Callot, Dürer, Van Dyck, Claude Lorrain, and Rembrandt in the exposition "Maîtres de l'eau-forte des XVIᵉ et XVIIᵉ siècles," mounted at the Louvre with works drawn from the Edmond de Rothschild collection.[48] Four works by Rosa appear in Pierrette Jean-Richard's catalogue (pp. 105–09). We might note that in her "notice" on Rosa, Jean-Richard calls Rosa a "musicien."

At the Grand Palais during the summer of 1983, a show, given earlier at the Royal Academy of Arts in London and at the National Gallery in Washington, was devoted to "Painting in Naples 1606–1705: Caravaggio to Giordano"; the catalogue, by Clovis Whitfield and Jane Martineau, published under the same title, features seven works by Rosa, all from Italian and English collections or galleries (see pp. 233–38). The summer of 1988 saw another exposition at the Cabinet des dessins on seventeenth-century drawing in Rome, but I have not seen proof in print that Rosa was included—the only native Italian artists mentioned in a brief announcement in the *Gazette des Beaux-Arts*[49] are Bernini, Carracci, Mola, Maratti, and Sacchi. The Grand

Palais was the setting, in the autumn of that same year, for the show "Seicento: le siècle de Caravage dans les collections françaises"; nos. 135 and 136 were works by Rosa from museums in Strasbourg (S 170) and Epinal (S 259).[50] In the spring of 1989, "La gravure italienne du Seicento" was shown at the Musée de la Chartreuse in Douai; according to the brief anonymous report in the *Gazette des Beaux-Arts*[51] Rosa was one of the Roman artists represented. I have not been able to determine if Rosa's work figured in the exposition "Le Paysage en Europe: du XVIᵉ au XVIIIᵉ siècle" held at the Cabinet des dessins in the winter and early spring of 1990.[52] Whether drawings by Rosa figured in the show "La Rome baroque de Maratti à Piranèse," put on by the Département des arts graphiques of the Louvre the following year, is not clear to me.[53]

For the most recent exposition potentially involving Rosa, the news is better: he makes a modest showing in the exposition "Le paysage et la question du sublime," sponsored by the Association Rhône-Alpes des conservateurs and the Musée de Valence in 1997. Drawing on museums in the Rhône-Alpes region, the exposition could not present any authentic picture by Rosa—Salerno's catalogue lists no Rosas at any museum in the region—but includes a *Paysage rocheux avec quatre personnages* lent by the Musée des Beaux-Arts in Lyon and said to be from Rosa's studio.[54] This picture, prominently featuring a lightning-struck tree, is shown in color, and used to illustrate one of the many aspects of the sublime: "Vers le sublime de la violence figée," an idea spelled out in a paragraph of interpretation accompanying the reproduction and at greater length in the "Catalogue des œuvres exposées" (p. 232):

> Tout se passe comme si—à l'insu du peintre?—l'ordre minéral esquissait l'ordre animal sans parvenir à l'accomplir. Dans sa banalisation, la violence se trouve désamorcée. (p. 36)

> Une lecture de gauche à droite du tableau fait ainsi apparaître une tension particulière: nous partons de l'arcadie, pays calme et serein, pour accéder, crescendo, au sombre domaine de Thanatos, messager de la mort. (p. 232)

More standard nuggets of art history are scattered through the texts composing the volume, pointing to Rosa's influence on, or affinity with, Alessandro Magnasco, the little-known Leonardo Coccorante, and the German imitator of Rosa, Christian-Wilhelm Dietrich (pp. 222, 205, 209). And some texts collected by John Grand-Carteret in *La Montagne à travers les âges* (1903–1904) are cited to illustrate and reinforce Jean Starobinski's claim that "le souvenir des tableaux pittoresques, à la Salvator Rosa, a joué un rôle important dans la découverte de la montagne."[55] Marcel Destor's brief "notice" on Rosa, though flawed by its claim that the painter was "également poète, *musicien* et graveur" (p. 231, my emphasis) is interesting for its periodization of Rosa's artistic development:

> A ses débuts, il exécute quelques scènes de bataille dans le goût du Napolitain Aniello Falcone (1607–1656). Il s'oriente ensuite vers la bambochade. . . . Au réalisme de ses débuts succède une période d'idéalisation classique dans le sillage de Nicolas Poussin. Rosa explore par ailleurs dans ses paysages les mêmes voies que Claude Lorrain dans sa recherche d'une beauté supérieure de la nature. Suit une dernière phase "visionnaire," dans laquelle la recherche n'est plus orientée vers une forme de beauté idéale, de perfection, mais plutôt vers l'expression d'une certaine solennité, d'une certaine majesté, qui peut aller jusqu'à devenir interpretation de quelques visions terribles et saisissantes. Rosa fut en somme un romantique avant la lettre. (ibid.)

A concluding sentence works in a place for Rosa's *stregonerie* (which date from his years in Florence), expressive of "une forme d'idéal artistique fondé sur la puissance de la 'laideur morale.' " In addition to subjecting Rosa's work— or at least one work inspired by Rosa's teaching—to some rather trendy analysis, this catalogue and its text take Rosa to the end of the twentieth century and leave him there alive and well, if no longer the towering figure of two centuries earlier.

A more encouraging sign of Rosa's durability is that, in a recent reorganization of its holdings in Italian painting of the seventeenth and eighteenth centuries, the Louvre has bestowed the name "Salle Salvator Rosa" on a large room—formerly the "Salle Van Dyck"—now devoted to painting in Rome, Naples, and Genoa in the seventeenth century.[56] Three Rosas are on display there: *Heroic Battle, Saul and the Witch of Endor* (newly restored), and *Landscape with Soldiers and Hunters.*

Conclusion

The story told in this study of Salvator Rosa's reception in French literature is, in its grand lines, one of rise and decline. It cannot be a coincidence that this trajectory parallels that of French romanticism. To describe and fully explain Rosa's rise and decline would require an exploration of the larger phenomenon, too daunting a task to undertake here. It must suffice to cite key moments and developments that reveal the parallelism at work. Several paintings by Rosa and some of his etchings reached France while the artist was still living and found homes in the most prestigious collections, those of Louis XIV and Mazarin. Their critical reception, however, was mixed in the few French texts from the classical period that mention the artist. André Félibien's statement (1679) is representative when it calls Rosa's manner "bizarre & extraordinaire" (Roger de Piles does not treat Rosa at all). An early emblematic moment occurs in 1776 when Pierre Le Tourneur, in the preface to his translation of Shakespeare into French, applies the word "romantique" to "Les tableaux de Salvator Rosa" as well as to alpine scenery and English gardens. In the same period, later to be labeled "pre-romantic," the greatest French art critic of the century, Diderot, showed a deep sympathy for the paintings of several contemporary artists; his vivid descriptions, especially of their landscapes revealed that Rosa's influence, direct or indirect, was alive and well.

Pierre-Charles Lévesque, in his and Claude-Henri Watelet's *Dictionnaire des beaux-arts* (1788–1791), does not apply the epithet "romantique" to Rosa's work, and still speaks of the painter's "conceptions bizarres et capricieuses" and calls him "un barbare," but adds: "mais qui étonne, qui effraie par sa fierté sublime." Twice he uses the word "sauvage," an adjective destined to dominate descriptions of Rosa's works, especially his landscapes, for a long time. Clearly, Rosa's reputation, by the end of the eighteenth century, is likely to benefit from the turbulence of the Revolutionary era. A 1795 sale catalogue labels a landscape by Rosa as "Vue romantique."

The legend of Rosa's participation in the 1647 uprising in Naples led by the fisherman Masaniello seems to have been mentioned only off-handedly and only once in France in the eighteenth century. I have found no texts from the period of the Revolution referring to Masaniello's uprising or Rosa's alleged part in it. But the political upheaval had a huge impact on the world of the visual arts through the nationalization of royal and other collections and the confiscation of art treasures in countries occupied by French armies during the decades of revolutionary and imperial wars. This development produced or fostered a large body of museological writing in which attention was focused on the Rosa paintings on view in Paris and, in particular, in the Louvre. The huge *Heroic Battle* given to Louis XIV and the depiction of Saul's encounter with the Witch of Endor especially, were the subject of searching analysis and detailed description. If we turn to major writers of this period, we find that, while Chateaubriand never mentioned Rosa, he clearly revealed, in several texts, a sensitivity to the kind of scenery popularized by Rosa and his imitators. Madame de Staël and Stendhal revealed, however, awareness and understanding of Rosa's work; the former, in *Corinne*, includes an unspecified Rosa landscape, in her heroine's private collection, thus introducing Rosa as a theme and reference in French imaginative literature.

But it was the publication in the crucial year of 1824 of Lady Morgan's biography of Rosa that brought him and his work into the mainstream of the romantic movement. A French translation of her book was published in Paris almost simultaneously with the English version, which appeared in Paris as well as in London. *La Vie et le siècle de Salvator Rosa* is the most important document in the history of Rosa's reception in France. It projected an image of Rosa perfectly in accord with the liberal minds of Restoration romanticism with its glorification of the artist as an independent creator and *engagé* activist. Rosa's alleged part in Masaniello's revolt and his supposed adventures among Italy's mountaineer bandits became firmly fixed as features of the Rosa persona. His imagined wanderings in the Abruzzi were seen as the inspiration for the typical Rosa landscapes, with their rocky crags, boulders, turbulent streams, storm-lashed trees, lightning-struck tree trunks, and brooding skies.

In Lady Morgan's biography, Rosa the man, the poet, the musician—she swallowed whole the account put into circulation by the English musicologist Dr. Burney—the political activist, and the thinker were all highlighted with vibrant sympathy. Her admiration for Rosa's work, both in the visual arts and in poetry, knew no bounds, and she compared him favorably to

Michelangelo, Dante, and Byron. Moreover, although her work was some-times dismissed as too close to fiction, Lady Morgan made available to French readers the results of her considerable research among the most reliable Italian sources of biographical information about Rosa and, unfortunately, some less trustworthy documents. She also published what was then known of Rosa's correspondence—twenty of his letters to his friend Ricciardi—and provided a long catalogue of Rosa's work, one that would not satisfy modern specialists—it included many works of doubtful or indeed non-existent au-thenticity and also has many gaps, especially for pictures not in Great Brit-ain. Even with these flaws, it was a valuable document.

It was the vivid image of Rosa the man and political militant, the parti-san of Masaniello, the wanderer in the Abruzzi, the friend and perhaps ac-complice of bandits, that represented Lady Morgan's primary contribution. This image was reflected most concretely in poems, fictions, and dramas mostly by lesser-known writers. Perhaps the peak of this trend as reached in Ferdinand Dugué's *drame, Salvator Rosa,* which received an elaborate five-act production at the Théâtre de la Porte-Saint-Martin in 1851. Nearly all of the major French romantics—Musset is the major exception—at the very least revealed an awareness of Rosa's work or life or both, though none pro-duced a whole work devoted to Rosa, unless one counts a novella by Dumas. Lamartine once expressed the ambition to be "Salvator ou Carrache" and, without direct reference to Rosa, painted a number of Rosaesque landscapes in his poetry. It is possible that a scene in his tragedy *Saül* was inspired by the picture in the Louvre representing Saul's consultation of the Witch of Endor. Vigny, who aspired to be a "poète philosophe," was unaware of the philo-sophic side of Rosa—he had no access to the works that reflected it—but clearly knew the *Battle* in the Louvre. Victor Hugo, too, knew this picture and at least one other and had a place for Rosa in a vast panorama of Euro-pean culture he sketched in *Le Rhin* (1842). But he may have gotten closest to the subject, first, in his ringing preface to *Cromwell* (1827), in which Rosa's *Temptation of St. Anthony* and *Heroic Battle* are linked to Hugo's glorifica-tion of the grotesque and later, in a passage of *Le Rhin*, excluded from the original edition, devoted to an evocation of the Black Forest as once seen in his childish imagination, "tantôt forêt lugubre d'Albert Dürer, tantôt forêt sinistre de Salvator Rosa." And Rosa makes vivid if brief appearances in such major texts as *Les Misérables* and *William Shakespeare*. Rosa figures little or not at all in the work in such important figures as Balzac, Musset, Bertrand, Nerval, Sand, and Michelet but, for all except Musset, there is evidence for their knowledge of his work and of the legends about the man. Only Dumas, among major romantic authors, produced a complete work inspired by Rosa, a novella entitled "Salvator Rosa. Mœurs napolitaines," which was soon absorbed into the novel, *Le Corricolo* (1843).

Théophile Gautier is a special case, the result in part of the sheer abundance of his art criticism. As a poet, he allotted Rosa only partial appearances in two early poems, *Albertus* and "Thébaïde": the passages in question are vivid descriptions of the typical "savage" Rosa landscape. He never composed a full-fledged *transposition d'art* based on a specific painting. There are, however, fine prose *transpositions* of three of Rosa's paintings in the Louvre, and his comments on two of these pictures are insightful: the *Battle* "est la bataille en elle-même"; *Saul and the Witch of Endor* is "un tableau romantique avant le romantisme." Trained as an artist, Gautier evolved into a very important art critic; if we sift his writings in that genre, we find many references to Rosa. While he does not rank him among the "gods" and "demigods" of painting, he obviously has a high opinion of him and a sound idea of Rosa's place in the history of painting and his kinship with other artists; emphasis is on Rosa as a landscapist and painter of battle pictures. All in all, Gautier is, after Lady Morgan, Rosa's principal champion in France.

Rosa's presence, then, in French literature of the romantic era is considerable. An examination of the work of lesser figures only confirms this claim. Henri de Latouche and Auguste Barbier devoted substantial poems to him. Rosa plays a large and sympathetic role in an extensive narrative poem by Gobineau, "Le roman de Manfredine," which the author did not complete and never published. Two future Parnassians, in the early 1860s, devoted poems to Rosa: Léon Dierx evoked the typical Rosa landscape; Ernest d'Hervilly produced a remarkably detailed *transposition d'art* of the *Battle* in the Louvre. We should note that both of these texts appeared originally in *L'Artiste,* further evidence that Rosa was a well-known artist in literary circles.

In prose fiction, except for the already mentioned tale by Dumas, Rosa did not fare as well as in poetry and drama. Joseph Méry's *L'Ame transmise* (1837) and Eugène de Mirecourt's *Masaniello* (1851) assign Rosa only a subsidiary or episodic role. More interesting are the rather affecting tale "Salvator Rosa dans les Abruzzes" (1855) by the forgotten Adelphe Nouville and Charles Didier's novella, "Romuléo" (1859). Nouville developed a surprisingly effective work from an anecdote in Lady Morgan's biography inspired by one of Rosa's etchings. Didier created a colorful modern Italian, half painter half bandit, clearly derived from the same biography. But it was, as already indicated, Ferdinand Dugué, whose *drame Salvator Rosa* (1851) most effectively turned the color and drama of Rosa's life into a work of literature. In contrast, the *opéra comique Salvator Rosa* by Eugène Grangé and Henri Trianon (1861) is a slight and trivial piece.

Discussions of Rosa in other literary genres are numerous and various: articles in reference works such as Michaud's *Biographie universelle* (1825), museum guide-books like those of Louis Viardot in the 1840s, or works of art history and literary history: notably, Rosa is given a fascicule (1856) in Charles Blanc's immense *Histoire des peintres de toutes les écoles,* a sort of consecration but one to be judged in proper proportion by considering that Blanc allotted certain artists several fascicules. Moreover, Blanc is decidedly negative about Rosa's history paintings and his quest for novel subjects. A unique feature of Blanc's *Histoire* is that it provides a number of engraved illustrations, eight for Rosa (three of them represent the three best-known Rosas in the Louvre). He concludes his chapter on Rosa with a certain amount of museological information on Rosa's etchings and drawings, on the location of his paintings, on sale prices drawn from the period 1767–1809, and reproductions of Rosa's signatures.

On a somewhat lower level, there is the phenomenon of Rosa's appearance in literary periodicals like *L'Artiste* and the *Revue de Paris*: an article in the former review by the little-known Alexandre de Saint-Chéron (1835), who hailed Rosa as a modern artist, inaugurates the series, continued by Etienne-Jean Delécluze's mostly negative study of Rosa's *Satire* in the latter (1840) and the little-known Almire Gandonnière, who showed himself a true heir of Lady Morgan in an encomiastic article on Rosa in the less important *La Chronique.* A cluster of three articles by the militant Charles Coligny in *L'Artiste* in 1864–1865 closes this chapter in the story of Rosa's reception, a last flare-up, so to speak, of the beacon originally set ablaze by Lady Morgan. Delécluze's study, in three installments, deserves special attention because, at the height of romanticism—a decade after *Hernani*—we encounter the first important onslaught against Rosa. Delécluze attacks not only the *Satire,* his ostensible subject, but Rosa the man, accused of hypocrisy, the alleged philosopher-painter, and most of Rosa's painted work—only the landscapes find favor in his sight. In a way, Delécluze, student and biographer of David, appears a mere hold-over from neoclassicism. But, in the event, he foresaw and helped to prepare Rosa's decline, albeit unwittingly. Developments in the field of painting, the rise of Realism à la Courbet, and, especially, of new modes of landscape painting with the emergence of the Barbizon School and Impressionism were more likely the underlying cause. One can say that the tide begins to turn against Rosa starting in 1840; it picks up power in the 1850s with Charles Blanc's reservations; it swirls around somewhat confusedly in the 1860s but then goes out for good. The translation of three of Rosa's *Satire* by the utterly obscure Tapon Fougas had no effect even at this critical juncture; equally in the century and a third since the last poems inspired by

Rosa's work (Dierx and D'Hervilly) and the last articles about Rosa in a literary review (Coligny), not a single really important work on Rosa has been published in France. The nation's acquisition of important paintings by Rosa (housed in the Musée Condé at Chantilly since the 1880s) was little noticed or exploited. The tercentenary of Rosa's death in 1973 was marked by no manifestation in France. Rosa has never been given a one-man show in that country. References to Rosa can be found in various works of art history, in reference works, in a few early "coffee-table" books and manuals, in histories of Italian literature.

The first reference to Rosa appeared over three and a half centuries ago (1647). Serious information about the man and his work, drawn from the most reliable of Italian sources, began to seep into French writing in the middle of the eighteenth century, thanks primarily to Dezallier d'Argenville and his *Abrégé de la vie des plus fameux peintres* (1745; revised edition 1762). The upsurge of the pre-romantic sensibility opened the way for Rosa, directly or indirectly, to enter the stream of French culture. Lady Morgan's biography completed this work, turning Rosa into something of a cultural hero, a romantic artist, the independent genius, the militant, a precursor of revolution and liberalism. Romantic writers, major and minor, with only a few exceptions, paid various forms of tribute to Rosa. As artist, Rosa was nearly always seen as a landscapist; a certain idea of the typical Rosa landscape, usually characterized as "sauvage," emerged, curiously without being based on specific pictures. Sharp attention, when it was focused on Rosa's work, nearly always turned to two or three pictures on display in the Louvre, especially the huge *Battle,* donated to Louis XIV, and the *Saul and the Witch of Endor* acquired by the royal collection in roughly the same period. Serious art writers were often aware of Rosa's etchings and even his drawings, and wrote admiringly about them as early as the eighteenth century, but these works had little literary impact.

One is tempted to conclude that France was not "Rosa country," in contrast to his native land, where the bulk of his painted work is to be seen and where criticism and scholarship about him continue to thrive, or even to England, where he was once immensely popular and where his works—both authentic and otherwise—hung in many private collections at the time of Lady Morgan's biography *cum* catalogue. In modern Great Britain, scholarship on Rosa has been noteworthy. Thanks perhaps to the migration of many Rosas from British to American collections, American scholarship on Rosa has outshone that of the French, e.g., in the catalogues of Rosa's etchings and drawings by Richard Wallace and Michael Mahoney, respectively. As for Rosa the poet, while several of his satires were translated by three minor writers, no edition of them has ever been published in France. Lady Morgan extolled them, but the important critic and scholar Delécluze sharply criticized them in a series of articles in 1840.

And yet the present study has turned up scores of French references to Rosa in many different literary genres, including works of poetry, fiction, and theater. Rosa attracted the attention and, often, the admiration of major literary figures like Diderot, Staël, Stendhal, Lamartine, Hugo, Balzac, Sand, Dumas, Michelet, and especially Gautier. Enthusiastic articles about Rosa appeared in leading literary reviews from the 1830s to the 1860s. A five-act drama by the otherwise obscure Ferdinand Dugué received an elaborate production in 1851 with two of Paris's finest actors in leading roles. After about 1865, references to Rosa appear episodically in French art writing.

In the late seventeenth century Louis XIV had the huge *Battle*, Cardinal Corsini's gift, relegated to storage. Thanks to the Revolution and Napoleon, this picture and several others by Rosa were given prominent exposure in the Louvre. At the end of the twentieth century, in the refurbishing of that museum, a room devoted to seventeenth-century Italian painting has been re-named in honor of Salvator Rosa. He never became, either for critics or for the general public, one of the supreme artists like those whom Baudelaire hailed as beacons. But, while the glow of his achievement has faded, it has not disappeared and seems to be guaranteed a permanent, if relatively modest, place in France's richly furnished *musée imaginaire.*

Notes

Introduction

1. The picture is now in the Terra Museum of American Art in Chicago. On its history and interpretation, see William Kloss, *Samuel F. B. Morse* (New York: Harry N. Abrams, 1988), especially pp. 126–35.

2. *Italian Landscape in Eighteenth-Century England: A Study Chiefly of the Influence of Claude Lorrain and Salvator Rosa on English Taste, 1700–1800* (New York: Oxford University Press, 1925).

3. *Bandits in a Landscape: A Study of Romantic Painting from Caravaggio to Delacroix* (London and New York: The Studio, 1937).

4. I base this surmise on the findings of the late W. T. Bandy, who discovered that the early Russian and Spanish translators of Poe used Baudelaire's translations as their base text, not the English originals. See W. T. Bandy, "Were the Russians the First to Translate Poe?," *American Literature*, XXXI (January 1960): pp. 479–80.

1. Crossing the Alps

1. Cited by Jacques Thuillier, "Textes du XVIIe siècle oubliés ou peu connus concernant les arts," *Dix-Septième Siècle*, XXXV (1983): pp. 125–40 (131). As Guillebaud (1585–1667), a learned Feuillant, apparently never went to Italy, he must have heard of Rosa through a French artist who had made the trip or from Italian artists working in Paris.

2. I speculate that the picture was a gift from the French authorities to Sir Robert Walpole, the eminent politician and statesman, father of Horace Walpole, perhaps at a time—for example, in the period ca. 1725–1730—of rapprochement between France and England. The senior Walpole had a fine collection, housed mostly at his splendid estate, Houghton, in Norfolk. A modern authority on Horace Walpole states that there were four Rosas at Houghton (Martin Kallick, *Horace Walpole* [New York: Twayne, 1971], p. 67). The Walpole collection undoubtedly included *The Prodigal Son* (S 127); see J. H. Plumb, *Sir Robert Walpole: the King's Minister* (London: The

Cresset Press, 1960), p. 86, as well as Salerno's 1975 catalogue. I have not been able to consult Horace Walpole's *Aedes Walpolianae* (1747), which contains a description, and perhaps a history, of his father's collection.

3. Le Comte de Cosnac (Gabriel-Jules), *Les Richesses du palais Mazarin* (Paris: Librairie Renouard, H. Loones, successeur, 1884), p. 338.

4. This picture would leave for England after a little more than a century (see the article by R. A. Cecil, "*Apollo and the Sibyl of Cumae* by Salvator Rosa," *Apollo*, no. 816 [June 1965]: pp. 464–69). It had probably been inherited by Mazarin's principal heirs, his niece Hortense Mancini and her husband, the Duc de Mazarin; at the time of the Julienne sale (1767), it was bid for by Catherine the Great but went to the Earl of Ashburnham, fetching the highest price in the first part of the sale.

5. In his recent *Salvator Rosa. His Life and Times* (New Haven and London: Yale University Press, 1995) p. 217, Jonathan Scott states that the French ambassador to the Vatican, Créquy, "bought one large painting and two smaller ones when he was in Rome and ordered another after his return to Paris," but provides no specific titles or documentation.

6. *Catalogue de livres d'estampes et de figures en taille douce* (Paris: Frédéric Léonard, 1666), p. 31.

7. I cite the modern reprint (Geneva: Minkoff, 1972).

8. *Entretiens sur les vies et sur les ouvrages des plus excellens peintres anciens et modernes* (Trévoux: Impr. de SAS, 1725), IV, p. 178. I cite the modern reprint (Farnborough: Gregg Press, 1967).

9. This letter to Carrel (September 22, 1700) was published in October 1703, in the *Nouvelles de la République des lettres*—see "J. P. Bellori," *Archives de l'art français*, I (1851), pp. 36–37. As for "l'ouvrage qui paraîtra bien tôt," it may be his translation of Bellori's *Catalogue of Pictures in the Vatican*—but, when he died in 1696, Bellori still had not sent Nicaise a copy of this text, published in Rome in 1695. It appears that Nicaise eventually obtained a copy of Bellori's book and translated it but did not live to see this work into print—he died on October 20, 1701. A manuscript was reported to be in existence by the abbé Philibert Papillon in his *Bibliothèque des auteurs de Bourgogne* (Dijon, 1742—but Papillon is spoken of on the title page as "feu M. l'abbé Papillon"). See *Archives de l'art français* I (January 15, 1851): pp. 35–36.

10. On the vexed question of the publication dates of De Dominici's three volumes, I follow those given by F. Bologna in the *Dizionario biografico degli Italiani* (XXX, 623).

11. *Archives de l'art français* IV (1853–1854): pp. 231–32.

12. I cite the 1792 edition as reprinted by Minkoff (Geneva, 1972). The title of the original edition is slightly different.

13. The Marquis Anne-Marie Daignan d'Orbessan (le Président d'Orbessan) (1709–1796), included a translation of Rosa's *La Musica* in his *Mélanges historiques, critiques, de physique, de littérature et de poésie* (Paris, 1768). Otherwise Michaud's claim that Rosa's satires were translated into French seems to be unfounded.

14. The place of publication "Amsterdam" in the earlier editions is false; see Limentani's supplementary bibliography.

15. Pierre-Jean Mariette, *Description sommaire des dessins des plus grands maistres d'Italie, des Pays-Bas et de France, du cabinet de feu M. Crozat* (Paris: Pierre-Jean Mariette, 1741 [Geneva: Minkoff, 1973], p. 15.

16. Is Dezallier telescoping the names of Masaniello and Aniello Falcone?

17. The author of this article is Lévesque—Watelet had died in 1786.

18. I have used the reprint by Slatkine (Geneva, 1972).

19. *Œuvres esthétiques,* ed. Paul Vernière (Garnier, 1959), p. 261; hereafter abbreviated as *Œ*.

20. Two of them, however—*Democritus and Protagoras* and *Apollo and the Cumaean Sibyl*—left France in the eighteenth century for England.

21. Toronto: University of Toronto Press, 1972.

22. *Shakespeare traduit de l'Anglois* (Paris: Vve Duchesne, 1776), I, cxviii-cxix, note 1.

23. *Œuvres esthétiques,* ed. Paul Vernière (Paris: Garnier, 1959), p. 261.

24. Francesco Casanova (1727–1802) was a brother of the famous amorist, Giacomo (Jacques) Casanova.

25. In the latter part of the seventeenth century, however, Rosa had attracted the occasional French pupil, e.g., Charles-Antoine Hérault (1644–1718), Noël Coypel's brother-in-law, who went to Rome in 1672 to study with Poussin and Rosa (Poussin, however, was already dead when Hérault arrived, in late January 1673, and Rosa was seriously ill and a few months away from death. See Henry Lapauze, *Histoire de l'Académie de France à Rome* [Paris: Plon, 1924], I, p. 39). Baldinucci states that Jacques Courtois, "le Bourguignon" (1621–1676), learned from and imitated Rosa's battle scenes via personal contact (Baldinucci, V, p. 441). And Rosa's influence, direct or indirect, can be felt in the battle pictures of two members of the Parrocel dynasty, Joseph (1646–1704), known as "Parrocel des batailles," and his son Charles (1688–1752); several of the latter's etched "Études de soldats" are said by Robert-Dumesnil (*Le Peintre-graveur français* [Paris: F. de Nobele, 1967], II, pp. 215–17) to be "dans le goût de Salvator Rosa."

26. The picture is now in a private collection. Passages not quoted from the *Œuvres esthétiques* are taken from the critical edition of the *Salons* by Jean Seznec and Jean Adhémar (Oxford: Clarendon Press, 1957–1967; 4 vols.).

27. In 1745, Vernet was commissioned by the Earl of Milltown to make a copy of Rosa's *Death of Atilius Regulus;* the copy is now in the National Gallery of Ireland, in Dublin (see Michael Wynn, "A Copy by Joseph Vernet of Salvator Rosa's *Atilius Regulus,*" *BM*, CXIII [September 1971]: p. 543). The picture was then in the Galleria Colonna. The following year, the Marquis de Villette commissioned Vernet to do a set of eight paintings, two of which were to be "dans le goust de Salvator Rosa avec des rochers, cascades, troncs d'arbres et quelques soldats avec des cuiraces" (L. Lagrange, *Les Vernet. Joseph Vernet et la peinture au XVIIIe siècle* [Paris, 1864], quoted by Philip Conisbee in "Salvator Rosa and Claude-Joseph Vernet," *BM*, CXV [December 1973]: p. 790. Conisbee's article is a judicious study of the affinity between the two artists and of the likely influence of the Italian painter on the French one. He points out that Vernet still had in his studio at the time of his death copies of two landscapes by Rosa.)

28. Jane Turner, ed., *The Dictionary of Art*, V (1996), pp. 907–8; Bénézit (1999) III, p. 315.

29. There are a few pictures by Rosa in the same vein—or, at least, parts of pictures: the lower right-hand corner of *Il Ponte* (S 39) or the central group in *Paesaggio con viaggiatori che chiedono la strada* (S 37). Such pictures and certain others serve to remind us of links between Rosa and certain northern artists—Brill, Van Laer, and, perhaps, in a different vein, Elsheimer—but it is likely that French painters of the eighteenth century would have gone to the principal source, the *fons et origo*, of such pictorial traditions, the Dutch and Flemish painters of genre scenes.

30. The picture (S 145) was in the Colonna collection in Rome in the eighteenth century and has been in the National Gallery in London since 1837. The drawing is in Valence.

31. As for Diderot's two great contemporaries, Voltaire offers just one rather non-committal reference to Rosa (*Correspondance*, ed. Theodore Besterman [Paris: Gallimard/Bibliothèque de la Pléiade, 1975–1993], VI, p. 361) and Rousseau, apparently, none.

32. *Journal étranger*, February–March 1760 (reprinted in Suard and Arnaud's *Variétés littéraires* [1804] II, p. 376; I quote from the Slatkine reprint of 1969).

33. Gabriel Bonno, ed., *Correspondance de Suard avec la Marquise de Bayreuth* (University of California Publications in Modern Philology, XVIII, p. 153.)

34. *Œuvres choisies de Lemierre* (Paris: Lecointe, 1829), II, p. 55.

35. *Abrégé* (1745), p. 350; the sentence is slightly different in 1762, but the meaning is unaltered (II, p. 273).

36. Michaud's *Biographie universelle* accords him a brief notice, but *La Grande Encyclopédie* has no entry on him and there is no reference to him in *Critical Bibliography of French Literature: The Eighteenth Century*, edited by George R. Havens and Donald F. Bond (1951). However, there is an entry on him in the *Dictionnaire de biographie française* (IX, pp. 1495–96), where his dates are given as 1709–1796.

37. Tiraboschi, *Histoire de la littérature d'Italie* abrégée par Antoine Landi. T. V (Berne, 1784), pp. 235–236. Tiraboschi's other reference to Rosa—much longer, curiously, than the passage just quoted—deals with Rosa's life and his painted work (V, p. 269; note on p. 313).

38. For Naples he mentions a *Saint Nicholas of Bari* and a *Saint Francis Xavier Preaching to the Japanese* which are, obviously, not by Rosa. As for the landscape said to be in Düsseldorf, it may be the *Gideon's Soldiers* (S 258), now in Munich.

39. Montesquieu, *OC* (Pléiade), I, pp. 664, 697, 709, 719, 722, 741, 771–77, 790.

40. Frédéric d'Agay, ed., *Lettres d'Italie du président de Brosses* (Paris: Mercure de France, 1986), I, pp. 111, 229, 278; II, pp. 64, 335, 351, 364, 383, 384, 388.

41. Sade, *OC,* T. XVI (Paris: Cercle du livre précieux, 1977): pp. 310, 334, 339, 341, 342, 343.

42. *OC,* T. IX (1967): pp. 22–24.

43. René Michéa, "Autour des *Lettres familières* du Président de Brosses," *RHLF* XLII (January–March 1935): pp. 63–71. Michéa shows De Brosses tinkering with the text of his letters and lending copies to various people.

44. Cochin's original title was *Voyage pittoresque d'Italie;* from 1758 on, the book was retitled. I quote from the 1972 reprint (Geneva: Minkoff) of the 1758 edition of the *Voyage* and from the original 1836 edition of the *Lettres* discussed later; page and volume numbers are those of the original.

45. "Les guides d'Italie et la vulgarisation de la critique d'art au XVIIIe siècle," *RLC*, XLV (July–September 1971): pp. 366–91 (p. 373).

46. Paris: aux bureaux du *Journal des Beaux-Arts*, 1836.

47. *Lettres*, p. 33. Cochin's list of artists suggested as models or at least as worthy of study by the young man in Rome is fairly conventional: Raphael's name leads all the rest; Michelangelo, however, is denigrated.

48. I quote from the "new edition," *Description historique et critique de l'Italie* (Paris: Saillant, Desaint, J. M. Coru de la Goibrie, 1769), I, lxxxvi.

49. Richard is probably conflating Rosa and one or more of the German dynasty of *animaliers* named Roos.

50. Ibid., p. 106. The pictures in question are S 154 (now in Cleveland), S 191 (still in the Galleria Doria Pamphili), and S 222 (now in the Uffizi).

51. Lalande, *Voyage en Italie* (Paris: Veuve Desaint, 1786; 2nd ed.), I, p. 432.

52. Georges Wildenstein, "L'abbé de Saint-Non artiste et mécène," *GBA,* no. 1090 (November 1959): p. 231.

53. See Judith Nowinski, *Baron Dominique Vivant Denon (1747–1825): Hedonist and Scholar in a Period of Transition* (Madison, NJ: Fairleigh Dickinson University Press, 1970), pp. 46–50.

54. Quoted by Elisabeth and Raymond Chevallier, *Iter Italicum: les voyageurs français à la découverte de l'Italie* (Paris: Les Belles Lettres; Geneva: Slatkine; Moncalieri: Centro interuniversitario di ricerche sul "Viaggio in Italia," 1984), p. 81. It is likely that "le Poussin" here means Gaspard Dughet, and not his brother-in-law Nicolas Poussin.

55. Dominique Vivant Denon, *Voyage en Sicile* (Paris: Le Promeneur, 1993), p. 60.

56. At about the same time, the English Patrick Brydone wrote, in his popular *Tour through Sicily and Malta* (1773), of the inspiration that Poussin (Gaspard Poussin?) and Rosa found in the scenery near Naples: "C'est l'étude de ce paysage enchanteur et romanesque qui a formé nos plus grands maîtres de paysage: ç'a été l'école du Poussin et de Salvator Rosa, surtout ce dernier, qui composa ses morceaux les plus célèbres sur les rochers escarpés et sourcilleux qui bordent cette côte; c'est sans doute la contemplation journalière de ces grands spectacles qui remplit leurs esprits de cette multitude d'idées, qu'ils ont fait passer avec tant d'élégance dans leurs peintures" (quoted by E. and R. Chevallier, *Iter Italicum,* p. 89, note 32). Note that "Poussin" and Rosa are here treated as great masters of landscape, without reference to Claude Lorrain. The latter's prestige remained enormous, but another school of landscape painting had found a place for itself in the *musée imaginaire* of the late eighteenth century.

57. This is probably the *Paysage et figures* catalogued by Lady Morgan, said to be in the collection of "Le comte de Ashburnam" (II, p. 308).

58. We might note a piece of negative evidence: when the magnificent Orléans

collection was sold off in the revolutionary period by Philippe Égalité, only one Rosa figured in the transaction. Lady Morgan (II, p. 309), states that a *Moïse sauvé des eaux* owned by the Duke of Buckingham had been bought from the "galerie d'Orléans" for 2,500. Salerno seems to confirm her claim: he places a *Ritrovamento di Mosè* (S 129, now in the Detroit Institute of Arts) in the collection of the Marquis of Buckingham in the early nineteenth century.

59. Daniel Wildenstein and Jean Adhémar, "Les tableaux italiens dans les catalogues de ventes parisiennes du XVIIIᵉ siècle," *GBA,* nos. 1362–1363–1364 (July–August–September 1982): pp. 1–78; on Rosa, see pp. 44–45.

60. This rather high figure may indicate that the Rosa *œuvre* contained duplicates or "morceaux d'après lui."

61. Pierre-Jean Mariette, *Description sommaire des desseins des grands maîtres d'Italie, des Pays-Bas et de France, du cabinet de feu M. Crozat. Avec des réflexions sur la maniere de dessiner des principaux peintres* (Paris: Pierre-Jean Mariette, 1741).

62. On these matters see Michael Mahoney, *The Drawings of Salvator Rosa* (New York and London: Garland Publishing, 1977), pp. 14–30.

63. Antoine-Nicolas Dezallier d'Argenville, *Voyage pittoresque de Paris* (Paris: De Bure l'aîné, 1749; republished several times).

2. Toward Romanticism

1. A biography of Masaniello by August-Gottlieb Meissner (1753–1807), originally published in 1784, appeared in a French translation in 1789. Meissner does not mention Rosa. Madame de Staël, incidentally, in one of the manuscripts of *De l'Allemagne,* briefly treats Meissner and mentions his *Masaniello;* she had a copy of the original German edition in her library at Coppet (*De l'Allemagne,* ed. Comtesse de Pange [Paris: Hachette, 1958–1960], III, p. 322).

2. The *Assumption* is still in Paris, in Notre-Dame; the *Madonna del Suffragio* was eventually returned to Milan and assigned to the Brera.

3. Salerno (1975) gives a slightly different account of the picture's history, but his words "dal 1793 nella raccolta Stafford" are especially suggestive. (Lady Morgan's 1824 evidence [II, p. 309] tracing the *Finding of Moses* [S 129] to the Orléans collection is not beyond question.)

4. *Annales du Musée,* VII, 43 (second edition, 1832).

5. The obscure Robillard-Péronville (d. 1809) seems to have functioned only as financial sponsor of the project. Pierre Laurent (1739–1809) was an engraver.

6. Robillard-Péronville et al., *Le Musée français* (Paris: Imprimerie de L.-E. Herhan, 1803–1807), I, no. 17.

7. For a recent reappraisal of Taillasson as art critic, see Edouard Pommier, "J. J. Taillasson, *Observations sur quelques grands peintres,*" pp. 273–291 in *Seicento: la peinture italienne du XVIIe siècle et la France* (Paris: La Documentation française, 1990).

8. This comes from a very brief "vie et œuvres" (p. 329) separate from the main essay on Rosa.

9. Note taken in the Louvre's research department.

10. It is noteworthy that, here as in the *Democritus*, Taillasson "hears" something in the painting.

11. The present study is based on the second edition of these volumes (1823–1835); Rosa appears in Volume VII (1832).

12. *Annales*, Tome IX, no. 18 (1805).

13. Henri Laurent, *Le Musée royal* (Paris: Imprimerie de P. Didot, 1816–1818), Seconde série. Histoire, no. 15. This collection appeared over about ten years, concluding in 1827.

14. Like Cochin, he may have here conflated Rosa with one of the Roos family.

15. I, pp. 596–597. Valenciennes's list of artists is rather puzzling—two of the artists named, Both and Stella (Jan-Dirksz Both and Jacques Stella), were not Italians but did spend considerable time in Italy.

16. One of these, rather puzzlingly, is said to be in the Louvre.

17. *Œuvres posthumes de Girodet-Trioson, peintre d'histoire . . .* , ed. P. A. Coupin (Paris: Jules Renouard, 1829), Vol. I.

18. The giant Enceladus was defeated by the Olympian gods and, according to Virgil, lived under Etna and caused its tremblings.

19. A reference to the construction of the "passage des échelles"—completed in 1670—by Duc Charles Emmanuel II of Savoy (1634–1675).

20. See pp. 405–407 of Coupin's edition of the *Œuvres posthumes*. The passage on "marines" was completed; in it Girodet evokes a shipwreck scene by Vernet—without reference to Rosa.

21. In the "Discours préliminaire," Girodet, making the point that from the Greeks on, many painters have also been writers, refers to Rosa's satires, "trop cyniques sans doute, mais pleines de feu, et où l'on ne saurait méconnaître le cachet du poète" (*Œuvres posthumes*, I, 9).

22. See Richard Kendall, "Letter from Aix-en Provence. 'More Lasting than Bronze,'" *Apollo*, no. 348 (February 1991): pp. 132–133.

23. Quoted by Peter Galassi, *Corot in Italy: Open-Air Painting and the Classical Landscape Tradition* (New Haven & London: Yale University Press, 1991), p. 60. On Michallon, see Blandine Lesage, "Achille-Etna Michallon (1796–1822). Catalogue de l'œuvre peint," *GBA*, no. 1575 (October 1997): pp. 101–142.

24. For a recent cluster of articles on Chateaubriand and painting, see *Société Chateaubriand, Bulletin* 38 (1996).

25. *OC* (Paris: Garnier frères, 1859–1861), VI, p. 295. A few days earlier, visiting the Galerie Doria, he takes note of a "grand paysage" by Gaspard Poussin (VI, p. 290). The context for this list is curious: Chateaubriand appends the comment: "mais, dans tout cela, pas un chevalier, rien de l'Europe transalpine" (VI, p. 295).

26. The editors of the most recent edition of Chateaubriand's correspondence point out that, in 1795, the author was living in Beccles (Suffolk) and not in London; they are inclined to accept the date as correct, and the address as wrong.

27. *OC*, III, pp. 165–169; *Correspondance générale*, ed. Béatrice d'Andlau et al. (Paris: Gallimard, 1977) I, pp. 69–73.

28. *OC*, III, p. 166.

29. *Histoire du romantisme* (Paris: Gustave Charpentier, 1874), p. 4.

30. "Les Alpes ou l'Italie," *OC*, III, pp. 568–569.

31. *Corinne ou l'Italie*, ed. Claudine Herrmann (Paris: Des femmes, 1979), I, pp. 204–9.

32. These works are now attributed to Murillo and Allori.

33. Philippe Berthier, *Stendhal et ses peintres italiens* (Geneva: Droz, 1977), p. 131. Rosa is not mentioned in Berthier's book.

34. *Journal; OC*, ed. Victor Del Litto and Ernest Abravanel (Geneva: Edito-Service S.A., 1967–1974), XXX, p. 302.

35. *OC*, XXVI, p. 98; XLIV, p. 116.

36. *Mélanges; OC*, XLVII, p. 207. In Stendhal's time, most of Rosa's *stregonerie* were on view in Florence.

37. See Lanzi, *Histoire de la peinture en Italie* (Paris: H. Seguin, 1824), II, pp. 237–239.

38. *OC*, VII, p. 341; cf. the expression "d'un esprit original" which occurs in an anecdote about Rosa's visit to Bologna (*Mélanges; OC*, XLVIII, p. 375).

39. *Histoire; OC*, XXVI, p. 232.

40. Ibid., *OC*, XXVII, p. 225.

41. *Salon de 1824; OC*, XLVII, p. 274.

42. *OC*, XLVII, p. 35.

43. *Mélanges; OC*, XLVIII, p. 214.

44. *Mélanges; OC*, XLVII, pp. 327–28; XLVIII, p. 179, p. 375.

45. *Promenades; OC*, VII, p. 290.

46. *Mémoires d'un touriste; OC*, XV, p. 286.

47. *OC*, VI, p. 16. On the critical point of Rosa's alleged participation in Masaniello's revolt, Stendhal has nothing to say, even though he mentions this historical incident several times (*Rome, Naples et Florence; OC*, XIV, p. 27; *Promenades; OC*, VII, p. 351; *Mémoires d'un touriste; OC*, XVI, p. 391; *Mélanges; OC*, XLVIII, p. 300).

48. See *OC*, XLIX, p. 188; and a note on p. 401.

49. The article on La Cecilia in the *Enciclopedia italiana* (XX, p. 342) is the only source of information about La Cecilia's rather interesting life that I have been able to locate. La Cecilia, a *carbonaro* and a follower of Mazzini, spent many years in French exile during the July Monarchy and must have written his *Masaniello* while in France. Apparently the events of 1848 made it possible for him to publish his book in Italy.

50. A reproduction, in black and white, of Vernet's picture is provided in David Wakefield's *Stendhal: The Promise of Happiness* (Bedford [Bedfordshire]: The Newstead Press, 1984), p. 172. The picture is now in the National Gallery in London; a copy by Henri Scheffer is at Versailles, according to P. Larousse (XI, p. 519), but Bénézit does not show one.

51. *OC*, XLVII, p. 81; "*Sabines*," of course refers to David's famous picture.

52. *OC*, XXXVII, p. 39.

53. Vernet's painting benefited, in Stendhal's eyes, from the fact that, along with

several dozen of his works, it was denied a place in the Salon of 1822 by the Restoration authorities as being too explicit in its glorification of Napoleon. The Duc d'Orléans (the future Louis-Philippe) bought it and so was responsible for the fact that it ultimately entered the National Gallery in London (no. 2965 in the *Illustrated General Catalogue* [London: The National Gallery, 1923], p. 778).

54. Between 1822 and 1824, Vernet and the régime had patched up their differences: Vernet had half a dozen pictures in the *Salon de 1824;* among them, in addition to the portrait of Napoleon's marshal, was one of the Duc d'Angoulême, Charles X's dauphin.

55. It is worth mentioning that Théodore Géricault died just on the eve of the Lady Morgan era, on January 26, 1824, leaving copies he had made, many of them around 1814 according to Lorenz Eitner, *Géricault. His Life and Work* (London: Orbis Publishing, 1983), pp. 57–58. Rosa is one of the fourteen Italian painters whom Géricault copied (ibid., p. 329, note 36): the inventory of the artist's estate included "cinq tableaux esquisses, copies d'apres Salvatorose [*sic*], Schidonne, Caravage, Mola et Lesueur (Michel le Pesant, "Documents inédits sur Géricault," *Revue de l'Art*, no. 31 [1976]: p. 80). Eitner, in his study of the catalogue of the estate sale later in 1824. ("The Sale of Géricault's Studio in 1824," *GBA*, no. 1081[February 1959]: pp. 115–26) had not been able to identify any specific work by Rosa—or, in fact, most of the "Plus de cinquante autres copies d'après Raphael, . . ." etc. (ibid., p. 126). According to F.-H. Lem ("Comment j'ai rendu un Géricault au Louvre," *Connaissance des arts*, no. 131 [January 1963]: p. 69) a now-lost copy of Rosa's great battle scene in the Louvre lies behind an oil sketch *Bataille de Thermopyles*, which had been found in the museum's réserves: "On note immédiatement de grandes analogies de composition, d'atmosphère, dans le choix du site, dans la répartition des groupes de figure [*sic*] à travers le paysage, dans un certain 'sfumato' qui emporte en un même mouvement lyrique les combattants, la poussière qui naît de leur mêlée et les éléments du site, rochers, accidents de terrain, ciel nuageux" (ibid.). For Lem, Géricault copied Rosa's battle because it was "une page hautement significative où se trouvaient en puissance les solutions d'un grand tableau de bataille" (ibid.), not merely another copy of an old master done for pedagogical purposes.

3. Enter Lady Morgan

1. For a useful brief introduction to Lady Morgan's life and work, see Kathleen Reuter Chamberlain, "Sydney Owenson, Lady Morgan (25 December 1776 ?—6 April 1859)," pp. 216–222 in Bradford K. Mudge, ed., *British Romantic Novelists, 1789–1832 (Dictionary of Literary Biography,* vol. 116) (Detroit: Gale Research, 1992).

2. Leslie A. Marchand, ed., *Byron's Letters and Journals* (Cambridge: The Belknap Press of Harvard University Press, 1973–1982), VIII, p. 189.

3. Mary Campbell, *Lady Morgan: The Life and Times of Sydney Owenson* (London, Sydney, Wellington: Pandora, 1988), p. 33.

4. Miss Owenson, *The Wild Irish Girl, a National Tale* (London: Richard Phillips, 1808 [4ᵗʰ ed.]) I, pp. 52–53.

5. Lionel Stevenson, *The Wild Irish Girl: The Life of Sydney Owenson, Lady Morgan (1776–1859)* (New York: Russell & Russell, 1936), p. 217.

6. London: H. Colburn, 1824 (III, pp. 200–01).

7. Lady Morgan reverts to being just a tourist in one other passage where Rosa is mentioned: she includes a reference to his house at no. 33, via Gregoriana, in a catalogue of Roman places of interest to lovers of painting (II, p. 437). (She cannot resist, however, closing the paragraph as follows: "The rooms in the Quirinal, where Lawrence painted Pope Pius the Seventh's and Cardinal Gonsalvi's splendid portraits, will be sought for by future inquirers in interesting topography, when such anomalies in society as Popes and Cardinals shall live only in the pages of that history their deeds darkened" [ibid.].)

8. Stevenson, *The Wild Irish Girl*, p. 234.

9. As we have seen, Giovanni Gaetano Bottari had published twenty of Rosa's letters in volumes I and II of his *Raccolta di lettere sulla pittura, scultura ed architettura da' piu celebri personaggi dei secoli XV, XVI e XVII* (Rome, 1754–1773).

10. I have not been able to determine which edition of the *Britannica* she consulted, but it could not have been the first (1768–1771), which contains no article on Rosa; four other editions had appeared by 1817.

11. See Michaud, *Biographie universelle*, XXXIX, pp. 511–12.

12. The names of Sobry and Pierhuc do not appear on the title-page—only in the *Bibliographie de la France*.

13. Vincenzo da Filicaja (1642–1707), a native of Florence. He resisted the current of Marinism. He was most famous for odes celebrating the Christian victory over the Turks in 1683.

14. Her chronology does not, however, always match that proposed by modern authorities, who have many more documents, e.g., letters by Rosa, to consult than she did.

15. Rather typically, Lady Morgan lingers for several pages of chapter 2 over the stultifying effects of Scholastic philosophy and, digressing within her digression, denounces Kant, "ce grand prêtre de la métaphysique subtile." She manages to enlist Napoleon in her brief campaign against "Les faux raffinements de cette philosophie" (I, p. 54).

16. In the early nineteenth century Shakespeare's name was often spelled by French writers as Lady Morgan—or her translator—does (cf. Stendhal's famous *Racine et Shakspeare*), and Byron's name was similarly misspelled, by assimilation with the name of a great noble French family. Lady Morgan's French translators rather consistently followed these practices throughout their version of her book.

17. For Burney's own statements about Rosa as musician, see his *The Present State of Music in France and Italy* (1771) and *A General History of Music* (1776–1789). I have consulted Percy A. Scholes' edition of the former work (London and New York: Oxford University Press, 1959)—see pp. 214–15, 217, 221, 223, 225—and Frank Mercer's edition of the latter (New York: Dover Publications, n.d.)—see pp. II, 620–28.

18. Baldinucci (p. 439) spells it "Francenzano"; Passeri gives the correct spelling (but gives his first name as "Ciccio"); Pascoli calls him "Francesco Francanzano" (p. 63), but omits any reference to a family relationship; De Dominici writes "Francesco Francanzano" (p. 215). Clearly, Lady Morgan drew her spelling of this artist's name from some other source.

19. A footnote indicates that this is a quotation from Passeri.

20. Lady Morgan works in a long footnote on the conspiracy supposedly organized by "le célèbre Tomaso [*sic*] Campanella, auteur de plusieurs ouvrages philosophiques," and various other individuals in Calabria, including several bishops, 1,500 bandits, and about 300 monks. The government in Naples, she says, discovered the plot and executed its leaders "dans les tortures les plus cruelles et les plus prolongées" (ibid.). The plot in which Campanella was involved, which led to his long imprisonment, took place in 1599. Lady Morgan may have confused this incident with a plot organized in the 1630s by Campanella's follower Tommaso Pignatelli.

21. De Dominici embroiders on these spare accounts: he would have it that, accompanied by his young pupil, Marzio Masturzo, Rosa undertook boating trips "per disegnare massimament le vedute della bella riviera di Posilippo, e quelle verso Pozzuoli, quasi tanti esemplari prodotti dalla natura" (p. 215).

22. Her reference to Spanish and especially German troops would probably have had a contemporary ring to French readers in 1824, just a few years after the Allied occupation following the fall of Napoleon.

23. The etching in question is one of the *Figurine* (Bartsch, no. 61). There is not the slightest justification for Lady Morgan's reading of this print as autobiographical. It is related to his painting *Paesaggio con soldati* (S 162).

24. Characteristically, Pascoli gives no date for this episode; in fact, the only dates he gives in his biographical sketch are those of Rosa's birth and death. One can deduce from his narrative only that this trip to Naples came *after* Salvator Rosa's return to Rome following the Viterbo period.

25. Luigi Salerno, *Salvator Rosa* (Milan: Edizioni per il Club del libro, 1963), p. 93. Leaving aside dates for events after Rosa's death, Baldinucci's record is a little spotty: he gives 1671 as the date of Rosa's death (p. 464).

26. Lady Morgan here seems to have been misled by the fact that one version of the *Congiura di Catilina* is in the Pitti (the other is also in Florence—see Salerno 1975, p. 99). She overlooks what Rosa himself tells us in a letter which she herself reproduces (II, pp. 232–33) of September 8, 1663, that the picture whose subject he says he took from Sallust, has recently been displayed in the annual Pantheon exhibition (Salerno 1963, p. 98); in other words, it was painted in Rome.

27. One suspects that we are facing here a situation like the one in the old joke to the effect that Corot painted two thousand pictures, of which three thousand are in the United States.

28. Lady Morgan, *Italy* (London: Henry Colburn, 1824), II, pp. 132–33.

29. Rather surprisingly, not a single picture dominated by landscape figures in this list. However, there is a long and vivid passage (I, pp. 232–34) paying a general

tribute to works in this genre. In her treatment, *Baccanale* (S 83), which mingles mythology and landscape in approximately equal amounts, is said to be "plein d'images poétiques" and "d'un effet extraordinaire" (II, pp. 44–45).

30. In a very long footnote, she quotes the high praise of Vivant Denon, who had provided her a copy of his own engraved version, and some fifteen lines from Passeri, who calls the picture "mirabile" (II, p. 129). The vividness of her description is probably due to her direct observation of the engraving rather than to her recollection of having seen the painting in the Pitti.

31. See the similar, rather vague comparison at I, p. 136.

32. She devotes little time and space to Rosa's etchings—perhaps she saw few of them—and says almost nothing about his drawings (I, p. 153, p. 176), but these were inaccessible to her.

33. *Salvator Rosa. Hayward Gallery, London, 17 October-23 December 1973* (London: Arts Council, 1973), p. 16.

34. The brief "life and works" which prefaced a number of Anton Maria Salvini's editions of the *Satire* from 1770 on was her immediate source for many of the colorful details of that episode.

35. Her treatment of Rosa's etchings, however, had already been surpassed a few years earlier by Bartsch's in his *Le Peintre-graveur.* And she provides no list or catalogue of Rosa's drawings.

36. See Jonathan Scott, *Salvator Rosa: His Life and Times* (New Haven and London: Yale University Press, 1995), p. 60.

37. Some information of this sort appears, however, in the main body, e.g., I, pp. 275–76, and II, 13.

38. She tells us, notably, that the Duchess of Devonshire, whom she had met in Rome, has been her source of information for pictures there. Her Roman informant was Elizabeth Cavendish (1758–1824), wife of the fifth Duke of Devonshire; she had settled in Rome toward the end of her life and generously patronized the arts and the archeological digs in the Forum.

39. See Richard W. Wallace, *The Etchings of Salvator Rosa* (Princeton: Princeton University Press, 1978).

40. Eugène Hatin, however, indicates that it was one of a half dozen or so "ultra" periodicals that Villèle's régime "amortissait" for a sum given variously as from 300,000 to 426,714 francs (*Bibliographie historique et critique de la presse périodique* [Paris: Firmin Didot, 1866], II, pp. 352–53). For a more recent discussion, see Michel Vivier, "Victor Hugo et Charles Nodier collaborateurs de *L'Oriflamme* (1823–1824)," *RHLF,* LVIII (July-September 1958): pp. 297–323; on Nodier's review, see pp. 306–08.

41. (London: Arts Council, 1973), pp. 17–18.

4. *Lady Morgan's Legacy*

1. Michael Kitson, "Introduction," *Salvator Rosa. Hayward Gallery, London, 17 October–23 December 1973* (London: Arts Council, 1973), p. 16.

2. *L'Oriflamme*, March 5, 1824, pp. 3–4.

3. *Revue encyclopédique*, XXII (1824), p. 118.

4. *Histoire de la peinture en Italie* (Paris: H. Seguin; Fufart, 1824), II, p. 415. The French translator was a Madame Armande Dieudé. Tiraboschi, whose history of Italian literature appeared in French in 1784, had said nothing about bandits or Masaniello; see *Histoire de la littérature d'Italie* (Berne, 1784), V, pp. 235–36, 269, 313. A. G. Meissner, Masaniello's German biographer—his book was published in Leipzig, also in 1784; French translations appeared in 1789 and 1821—makes no mention of Rosa or of the *Compagnia della morte* in his rather detailed account of Masaniello's uprising, nor does the *précis* of Meissner published by "M.C.L." in 1828: *Masaniello, histoire du soulèvement de Naples en 1647* (Paris: Chez les marchands de nouveautés). I am indebted to Prof. Lawrence M. Porter for his examination of Meissner's biography.

5. *Essai sur l'histoire de la peinture en Italie* (Paris and London: Bossange, 1823), II, p. 369. Orloff mentions Rosa in other works about the cultural life in Italy but without referring to the two legends about Rosa that concern us here; see his *Mémoires historiques, politiques et littéraires sur le royaume de Naples* (Paris: Chassériau et Hécart, 1819–1821), IV, p. 376, and *Essai sur l'histoire de la musique en Italie* (Paris: P. Dufort; Chassériau, 1822), I, p. 241–42.

6. *Biographie universelle*, XXXIX (1825), p. 4.

7. He retells an anecdote from Pascoli, who claims that Rosa had gone to Naples to show off his new wealth; Lady Morgan (I, pp. 300–301) repeated the story.

8. "Salvator Rosa," *L'Artiste*, IX (May 31, 1835), 18ᵉ livraison, p. 206.

9. On Gandonnière see Baudelaire, *OC* (Pléiade [1975–1976]) II, p. 996 and p. 1542, and Nerval, *Œuvres* (Pléiade [1960]), I, pp. 956, 958–59, 985, and accompanying notes.

10. *La Chronique*, 2ᵉ année, t. II (March–July 1843), p. 318.

11. "Musées d'Italie," 2ᵉ livraison, p. 22.

12. Viardot says there are two Rosas in the museum, a *Jesus Disputing with the Doctors* and a *Parable of the Beam and the Straw.* These are S 187 and S 108.

13. *Les Musées d'Italie* (3ᵉ éd.; Paris: L. Hachette, 1859), p. 298.

14. *Revue de Paris*, August 30, 1840, p. 320.

15. Perhaps, in Colet's time, there was a Place Masaniello in Aix-en-Provence; it seems that there is no such square in that city now.

16. Cited by A. Aruta Stampacchia in *Louise Colet e l'Italia* (Geneva: Slatkine, 1990), p. 131, n. 46.

17. It was republished as "Vieillesse de Salvator Rosa" in Latouche's 1844 collection, *Adieux, poésies* (Paris: Impr. de Lacour et Maistrasse), pp. 354–57.

18. *Poésies de Auguste Barbier, Iambes et poèmes* (Paris: Alphonse Lemerre, 1898), p. 155.

19. The poet's four uses of the word "peuple" deserve comment, too. Salvator twice speaks disdainfully of the people; the fisherman more than balances the artist's words with a veritable hymn to them:

Du peuple il faut toujours, poète! qu'on espère,
Car le peuple, après tout, c'est de la bonne terre,

. . . .

C'est le genou de Dieu, c'est le divin appui:
Aussi, malheur! malheur à qui pèse sur lui! (p. 152)

20. Bertrand, *Œuvres complètes,* ed. Helen Hart Poggenburg (Paris: Honoré Champion, 2000), p. 205.

21. In an unpublished manuscript recently acquired by the Bibliothèque Nationale, *Œuvres posthumes d'Alcofribas,* Bertrand juxtaposes references to "le crayon de Callot" and "le pinceau de Salvator Rosa" (p. 432).

22. *Poemi inediti di Arthur de Gobineau* (Florence: Leo S. Olschki, 1965), p. 51.

23. Frédéric-Gaëtan de La Rochefoucauld-Liancourt (1779–1863).

24. Paris: Typ. Morris et Comp. (1857).

25. F. Tapon Fougas, *Satire contre la guerre imitée de Salvator Rosa (1656–1659)* (Geneva: les principaux libraires, 1866), p. 6.

26. Tapon Fougas indicates that the printing of his *L'Envie* and *La Guerre* was suspended by the Belgian authorities on August 11, 1866, and that the latter was published in Geneva. He acknowledges having "adouci dans nos vers les crudités de l'original" (p. 31, note).

27. I am indebted to Professor Claude Schopp for much detailed information about the pre-original publication history of *Le Corricolo.* Here I use the modern edition prepared by Jean-Noël Schifano (Paris: Desjonquères, 1984).

28. Leopoldo, Prince of Salerno, was the father-in-law of one of Louis-Philippe's sons, the Duc d'Aumale. Dumas, in early life, was on good terms with the Orléans royals; later, he joined in Garibaldi's overthrow of the Bourbons at Naples. As we shall see in chapter 7, some of the Rosas now in the Musée Condé were acquired by the Duc d'Aumale after the death of his father-in-law.

29. Rosa's account of his childhood and youth are even more obviously clearly derived from Lady Morgan; this is especially clear from the following detail: "au lieu de réciter mes psaumes, je volais tout le charbon qui me tombait sous la main pour tracer des paysages sur les murs des cellules, ou dessiner le profil de mon révérend précepteur. Dieu seul peut savoir ce que mes chefs-d'œuvre m'ont coûté de calottes" (p. 147). Cf. Lady Morgan (I, p. 36): "Avec de simples morceaux de charbon, il couvrait ces vieux parois de la representation de ses paysages favoris." It must be noted that Lady Morgan cites a half dozen lines from Baldinucci as the source of this passage; theoretically, Dumas could have consulted Baldinucci.

30. Dumas's dependence here on Lady Morgan is especially evident: her catalogue of Rosa's work must be the source of the observation that Dumas's interlocutor makes, "c'est le véritable original de Salvator; celui qui est en Angleterre n'est qu'une copie" (p. 177). (It is now in the J. Paul Getty Museum.) This "copy," as Lady Morgan notes (II, 306), was in her time in the collection of the Duke of Beaufort, where it remained until 1959 (Salerno, 1963). Dumas describes the painting (p. 177) in words evidently adapted from Lady Morgan's (II, pp. 11–12).

31. Dumas even manages to work in a parallel with Rosa's satires in verse: the artist, on his second visit, originally intended to recite one of his satires in order to express his disillusionment with Rome, but decides, instead, to paint the "conception première" of *La Fortuna*.

32. Paris: G. Havard, 1851. There were six republications of the text between 1851 and 1869.

33. Mirecourt is faithful to the legend when, as we shall see, he refers to Rosa's painting such portraits *during* the revolution.

34. In his only other appearance, Rosa, while working on a mural in a church, warns Masaniello that Isabelle may be an agent of her father, the Spanish governor.

35. Bartsch, *Le Peintre-graveur*, XX, p. 286, no. 61.

36. Originally published as part of *Scènes de la vie italienne* (Brussels, 1837). I cite from the 1853 edition; Méry republished the book in 1856 as *Les Amants du Vésuve* (Paris: Librairie nouvelle).

37. In a later novel, *Monsieur Auguste* (1859), Méry writes of his young protagonist, named Octave: "La figure du jeune homme aurait exigé le pinceau d'un Salvator Rosa de salon; elle était effrayante et superbe." (I cite a later edition [Paris, Michel Lévy, 1871], p. 5. I am indebted to Graham M. Robb for this information.)

38. Paris: L. Hachette, 1859.

39. There is evidence that Rosa's life had inspired Italian playwrights as early as 1822; see Silvio D'Amico, ed., *Enciclopedia dello spettacolo* (Rome: Le Maschere, 1954–1968), Index, p. 800.

40. On the Masaniello theme in French opera, see Jean R. Mongrédien, "Variations sur un thème: Masaniello. Du héros de l'histoire à celui de *La Muette de Portici*," *Jahrbuch für Opern-Forschung*, I (1985): pp. 90–121.

41. Paris: Michel Lévy, 1851. Dugué (1816–1913) was a prolific author of poetry, novels, and especially theater; most of his plays are identified by the catalogue of the Bibliothèque Nationale as *drames*, mostly in five acts.

42. *OC* (Pléiade, 1975–1976), II, pp. 60–65, 241–43; elsewhere, he likened Rouvière to Frédérick Lemaître (II, p. 811). See also his implied praise of Rouvière in his review of the Exposition universelle of 1855 (II, p. 593). In twice passing in review Rouvière's career, Baudelaire just barely mentions, once, the actor's performance as Masaniello (II, p. 63). I will treat later the claim that Baudelaire wrote a drama entitled *Masaniello*.

43. On Mélingue, see Pierre Larousse, *Grand Dictionnaire universel du XIXᵉ siècle*, X, 1775. (Mélingue, it might be noted, was a sculptor as well as an actor, and two of his sons became painters of historical and literary subjects.)

44. Madame de Staël, it will be recalled, had praised a Rosa landscape without human figures in Corinne's collection.

45. "Louis Ménard," *Revue de Paris*, June 1, 1901; quoted by Claude Pichois in *Baudelaire*, *OC* (Pléiade, 1975–1976), II, p. 1114, note 1 to p. 63.

46. Paris: Michel Lévy, 1861.

47. The opera *Salvator Rosa* by the Brazilian composer Carlos Gomes (1836–1896), with a libretto by Antonio Ghislanzoni, premiered in Genoa on March 21, 1874, and was performed in Milan the same year, but was never performed in France.

48. "Historical Subjects," in *The Art of the July Monarchy: France 1830 to 1848* (Columbia, Mo., and London: University of Missouri Press, 1990), p. 95. Condon refers to pictures on Giotto, Dürer, and Ribera in the Salon of 1839.

49. "The Old Masters in Nineteenth-Century French Painting," *The Art Quarterly*, XXXIV, no. 1 (1971): pp. 55–85.

50. Aristide Marie, *Le Peintre poète Louis Boulanger* (Paris: H. Floury, 1925).

51. A reduction of this lithograph is reproduced in Aristide Marie's book on Boulanger (p. 53).

52. In their *Granet peintre de Rome* (Aix-en Provence: Association des amis du Musée Granet, 1992), p. 187, Isabelle Néto Daguerre and Denis Coutagne introduce into their discussion a drawing by Granet entitled *Salvator Rosa au lit de sa mort épouse sa maîtresse dont il avait eu plusieurs enfants* and provide a small reproduction but do not mention a date.

53. On Guignet, see Jacques Thuillier, "Adrien Guignet perdu et retrouvé," in the catalogue by Sylvain Laveissière, *Adrien Guignet, peintre: 1816–1854* (Autun: Musée Rolin, 1978), pp. 5–9; and Laveissière's "Chronologie," pp. 11–16.

54. For a reproduction, see the above-mentioned article by Haskell (p. 72, Fig. 19).

55. Masaniello was also a theme for French artists in this period. According to Pierre Larousse's *Grand Dictionnaire universel du XIXᵉ siècle* (X, p. 1295), there were two *Funérailles de Masaniello,* one by S. Massé (Salon de 1834) and one by Alexandre Fragonard (Salon de 1842), and a *Masaniello renversant les bureaux de la gabelle et brûlant les emblèmes de l'Inquisition* by Vivone (sic: Visone, i.e., Giuseppe or Joseph Visone, who was a native of Naples) (Salon de 1837). Larousse also mentions statues of Masaniello by Dantan aîné (Salon de 1833) and Jean Schey (Salon de 1840); I do not find the former listed in the *livret* for the Salon of 1833. In a later generation, François-Nicolas Chifflart (1825–1901) painted a *Masaniello,* now in the Musée des Beaux-Arts in Arras. More pertinently, according to Bénézit (III, p. 588), Chifflart also produced fifteen drawings entitled *Salvator Rosa et les brigands* now in the Victoria and Albert Museum. In his catalogue of the 1972 exposition in Saint-Omer, *François-Nicolas Chifflart 1825–1901* (Liévin: Imprimerie artésienne, 1972), Pierre Georgel provides a reproduction of *Masaniello* and also mentions an etching, *Salvator et les brigands,* published by the Société des Aquafortistes in 1863; the drawings in London are probably related to this etching.

56. Anna Klumpke, *Rosa Bonheur: sa vie, son œuvre* (Paris: Ernest Flammarion, 1908), p. 165.

57. Loÿs Delteil, *Le Peintre-graveur illustré (XIXe et XXe siècles),* tome second: *Charles Meryon* (Paris: Chez l'auteur, 1907), ca. p. 11. (This book is not paginated.)

58. Albert Boime, *Thomas Couture and the Eclectic Vision* (New Haven and London: Yale University Press, 1980). See especially pp. 311–13 and 354–55. Couture himself, according to Boime (pp. 80–81), detected the influence of Rosa on Decamps.

5. Rosa and the Major Romantics

1. Stendhal, *OC*, ed. Victor Del Litto and Ernest Abravanel (Geneva: Edito-Services S.A., 1967–1974), XLVII, p. 81. Stendhal, no doubt, has in mind the Louvre's *Battaglia eroica* with its classical architectural motif, vaguely antique armor, and remoteness from contemporary life.

2. Quoted by C. W. Thompson, "John Martin et l'image de la ville moderne chez Vigny et Lamartine," *RLC*, XLV (January–March 1971): p. 9.

3. Lamartine, *OC* (Paris: Chez l'auteur, 1863), XXIX, p. 143.

4. It should be observed, however, that, in a note he added to *Jocelyn* (1836), apropos of the passage entitled "Les Laboureurs," Lamartine states that Robert's *Les Moissonneurs* "est évidemment le type de ce morceau." (See Mary Ellen Birkett, "Lamartine and the 'Poetic' Painting of Léopold Robert," *Symposium*, XXXIII [Winter 1979]: p. 311, note 7. For a sensitive general study of Lamartine's art of landscape description, see Birkett's *Lamartine and the Poetics of Landscape* [Lexington, KY: French Forum, 1982].)

5. Lamartine, *Œuvres poétiques*, ed. Marius-François Guyard (Paris: Gallimard/Bibliothèque de la Pléiade, 1965), p. 3.

6. Lady Morgan, I, p. 257; see also I, p. 188, and II, pp. 134, 201.

7. Brief passages revealing similar images can be found in "Immortalité" (p. 17), "Ode"(p. 30), "Le Génie" (p. 55), "L'Ange" (p. 153), "Milly ou la terre natale" (p. 393), "La Marseillaise de la paix" (p. 1174), "Ressouvenir du Lac Léman" (pp. 1177–78), "A Lucy L . . ." (p. 1186), "Cantique sur le torrent de Tuisy près de Belley" (pp. 1496–99).

8. *L'Album de Léopoldine Hugo*, ed. Pierre Georgel (Villequier: Musée Victor Hugo, 1967), p. 42.

9. Jean Des Cognets, ed., *Saül* (Paris: Hachette/STFM, 1918), pp.viii, 47.

10. See Jacques-Philippe Saint-Gérand, "Où donc est la Beauté que rêve le poète?," *Association des Amis d'Alfred de Vigny*, XIII (1993–1994): pp. 8–20, especially pp. 19–20. On Vigny's visual imagery, see François Germain, *L'Imagination d'Alfred de Vigny* (Paris: José Corti, 1961), especially pp. 148–50, 155. In summary, Germain writes that Vigny was "Ni décorateur, ni peintre au sens où l'était Chateaubriand" (p. 155).

11. See the episode involving her copy of Mignard's portrait of Madame de Sévigné (Vigny, *Mémoires inédits. Fragments et projets*, ed. Jean Sangnier [Paris: Gallimard, 1958], p. 50; see also François Germain's rather skeptical comment (op. cit., p. 438).

12. Germain, op. cit., p. 250, note 4.

13. Vigny, *Correspondance*, ed. Madeleine Ambrière (Paris: Presses universitaires de France, 1989–1997), I, p. 176.

14. *Mémoires inédits*, p. 50.

15. *Correspondance*, II, p. 189.

16. Among contemporary artists, Vigny corresponded with Louis Boulanger, David d'Angers (who did a medallion portrait of the poet), Achille Devéria, Delaroche, Tony Johannot, and Jules Ziegler.

17. See the *Mémoires inédits,* p. 53.

18. *OC,* ed. François Germain and André Jarry (Paris: Gallimard/Bibliothèque de la Pléiade, 1986), p. 89.

19. *Mémoires inédits,* p. 350.

20. I am assuming that Vigny's encounter with Rosa's painting took place early in his life, like that with *Saul and the Witch of Endor.*

21. Vigny's preferred title for this collection may have been *Les Destinées* but, at one time, *Poèmes philosophiques,* his eventual subtitle, was considered as a title for the volume. For a recent discussion of this question, see the introduction to Paul Viallaneix's edition of *Les Destinées: Poèmes philosophiques* (Paris: Imprimerie nationale, 1983).

22. Nearly a fifth of Rosa's painted work could be described as "philosophical."

23. Preface to the 1837 edition of *Poèmes antiques et modernes.*

24. It cannot entirely be ruled out that he could have seen an engraved version of one or more of Rosa's "philosophical" paintings.

25. The strong affinity between the two creators also raises the question of why Rosa was never drawn to the tragic history of Julian the Apostate: Julian's dramatic death would seem to be a subject ready-made for Rosa, the painter of battle scenes, of ancient philosophers, and of notable Greek and Roman victims of fate and of persecution. But on reflection we remember that, bold as he was in satirizing ecclesiastical corruption, Rosa was aware that he lived in the capital of Catholicism, which had seized on Julian as the archetypal apostate. On artistic grounds, too, there is a difficulty: Rosa's battle pictures never deal with the triumphs or defeats of individual leaders—they are about war in general. Another *rendez-vous manqué* is worth pointing out: Vigny's references to Juvenal in the *Journal d'un poète* (*OC,* II, pp. 1119, 1191, 1292, 1296, 1302, 1319, 1336) suggest that he saw himself as an heir to the great Roman satirical poet, as did Rosa. But Vigny seems to have been totally unaware of Rosa's satires.

26. For an account of Hugo's career as artist and the reception of his work, see Pierre Georgel, "Histoire d'un 'peintre malgré lui': Victor Hugo, ses dessins et les autres," in Hugo's *OC,* ed. Jean Massin (Paris: Club français du livre, 1967–1970), XVIII, pp. 13–80; see also other essays included in the critical apparatus of this edition by Théophile Gautier (ibid., pp. 1–11), Pierre Georgel (V, pp. i–xx), Gaëtan Picon (XVII, pp. i–xvi), Jean Massin (ibid., pp. i–xv), and Tony James (XV, pp. xxvii–xlviii). From the rest of the abundant scholarly writing on Hugo and the visual arts, one might select J.-B. Barrère, "Victor Hugo et les arts plastiques," *RLC,* XXX (1950): pp. 180–208, reprinted in his *Victor Hugo à l'œuvre: le poète en exil et en voyage* (Paris: Klincksieck, 1966), pp. 247–79; and C. W. Thompson, *Victor Hugo and the Graphic Arts (1820–1833)* (Geneva: Droz, 1970). The above-mentioned edition of Hugo's complete works devotes the final three volumes to his paintings and drawings.

27. The text of Hugo's article, apparently not published at the time of composition, is now found in *OC,* II, pp. 983–86.

28. It is interesting to compare Hugo's attitude with that of Vigny, who disliked

the realism of Murillo's *Petit Pouilleux;* see the *Journal d'un poète* in his *OC,* ed. F. Baldensperger (Paris: Gallimard/Bibliothèque de la Pléiade, 1965), II, p. 1099.

29. Authorities differ as to the publication date of the final volume; I follow Bénézit's account (XIV, p. 588). The general editor was Antoine Mongez.

30. Perhaps today we would expect Hugo to refer, rather, to the crowded, tumultuous canvases of Pieter Brueghel.

31. In "Lettre XXXVIII," which describes the "Effroyable tumulte!" of the falls of the Rhine (*OC,* VI, p. 479), Hugo, rather surprisingly, evokes Poussin, but only because there are "de petits endroits paisibles au milieu de cette chose pleine d'épouvante."

32. And why is William of Orange, who died in 1583, included at all?

33. *Œuvres poétiques,* ed. Pierre Albouy (Paris: Gallimard/Bibliothèque de la Pléiade, 1964–1967), II, p. 261.

34. *Mémoires de Madame Judith,* quoted in *OC,* XVIII, p. 53.

35. In *L'Année terrible,* Masaniello's name occurs in a catalogue of victims of tyranny; here, too, there is no reference to Rosa (*OC,* XV, pp. 21–25; see also pp. 119–20). Of course, Rosa deserves much less than Masaniello to be seen as a victim of tyranny.

36. "Salon de 1836," *RDM,* April 15, 1836.

37. *Le Temps,* October 27, 1830; January 1, 1831.

38. *Œuvres complètes en prose,* ed. Maurice Allem and Paul-Courant (Paris: Gallimard/Bibliothèque de la Pléiade, 1960), pp. 981–82.

39. In the "Salon de 1836," he mentions a half dozen now-obscure Italian painters who were once celebrated and successful; to the extent that I can identify them under the (dis)guise of the names that Musset has given them, they all come from the same period as his great favorites, except for Arpino, i.e., Giuseppe Cesare, il Cavaliere d'Arpino, who died in 1640.

40. He probably did not know that Titian outlived Michelangelo by a number of years.

41. *RDM,* July 15 and September 15, 1848 (*OC,* ed. Claude Pichois et al. [Paris: Gallimard/Bibliothèque de la Pléiade], I [1989], pp. 1121–32).

42. Willem Van de Velde the Elder (ca. 1611–1693) was also a painter of marines, but was less famous than his son.

43. Edmond and Jules de Goncourt, *Journal: mémoires de la vie littéraire.* Vol. I: *1851–1863,* ed. Robert Ricatte (Paris: Fasquelle; Flammarion, 1956), p. 343 (May 1, 1857).

44. *Guide de l'amateur au musée du Louvre* (Paris: G. Charpentier, 1882), p. 25. (We must remember that Gautier is here listing the old masters represented in a very specific place, and, in fact, in 1849, he wrote that he wished Rosa's "grande bataille" were on display in the "*Salon sacré.*") "Etudes sur les musées," *La Presse,* February 10, 1849; reprinted in *Tableaux à la plume,* in *OC* (Slatkine), II (1978), p. 27.

45. No doubt the picture (S 239) acquired in 1816.

46. See *Les Dieux et les demi-dieux de la peinture* (1863), a collaborative effort.

To be exact, the divinities are Fra Angelico, Leonardo, Michelangelo, Raphael, Correggio, Titian, Rubens, Holbein, Hemling (sic), Veronese, Rembrandt, Van Dyck, Poussin, Le Sueur, Velásquez, Murillo, David, Prud'hon, Reynolds, and Hogarth; Gautier himself wrote the sections on Leonardo, Murillo, Velásquez, Hogarth, and Correggio.

47. *Poésies complètes,* ed. René Jasinski (Paris: A. G. Nizet, 1970), I, p. 167.

48. II, pp. 65–66; in the following eight lines, the poet strays farther and farther from Rosa, imagining himself being covered with ivy and turning into a tree.

49. *Corinne,* ed. Claudine Herrmann (Paris: Des femmes, 1979), I, p. 222.

50. With one exception, all the other pictures in this series (S 72, 74–77, 80, 82) are in Florence and Rome, several in private collections. But Gautier might have seen the engraved versions of two of Rosa's more macabre works.

51. *Histoire de l'art dramatique en France depuis vingt-cinq ans,* 6ᵉ série (Paris: Hetzel, 1859), pp. 245–46.

52. "Horace Vernet," *Le Moniteur,* July 24, 1864 (OC [Slatkine], IX, pp. 313–14); "Salon de 1857. XIX," *L'Artiste,* November 7, 1857, pp. 147–48; *Exposition de 1859,* ed. Wolfgang Drost and Ulrike Henninger (Heidelberg: Carl Winter, 1972), pp. 72, 82.

53. "Horace Vernet," *Le Moniteur,* July 24, 1864 (OC [Slatkine], IX, 313).

54. *La France industrielle,* no. 1 (April 1834), p. 19; cited by Michael Clifford Spencer, *The Art Criticism of Théophile Gautier* (Geneva: Droz, 1969), p. 106.

55. "Salon de 1857. XIX," *L'Artiste,* November 7, 1857.

56. There may be more torrents in the writing about Rosa's landscapes than in the pictures themselves.

57. *Correspondance générale,* ed. Claudine Lacoste-Veysseyre et al. (Geneva: Droz, 1985), I, 97. The Dutch painter in question is Allart van Everdingen (1621–1675), who painted many pictures featuring waterfalls.

58. *La Presse,* February 10, 1849; reprinted in *Tableaux à la plume* and in *OC* (Slatkine), II, p. 27.

59. "Salon de 1846," *La Presse,* April 13, 1846; quoted by Karen Dana Sorenson, "Théophile Gautier's *Salon de 1846:* A Critical Edition" (unpublished Ph.D. dissertation, Vanderbilt University, 1992), p. 143.

60. "Un tour en Belgique et en Hollande," in *Caprices et zigzags* and in *OC* (Slatkine), V, p. 95. In 1869, Gautier recalled that five of Guignet's pictures were noticed in the Salon of 1840 "pour l'originalité de la composition, la chaude enérgie de la couleur, la férocité de la touche et l'accent étrange du talent. Le jeune artiste semblait avoir fondu dans sa manière Rembrandt, Salvator Rosa, Decamps, mais en y ajoutant sa propre personnalité" ("Adrien Guignet," *Le Magasin pittoresque,* January 1869; *Tableaux à la plume* (OC [Slatkine], II, p. 254). This formulation implies that the three artists mentioned are different from each other in fundamental ways, but their fusion in Guignet's work nevertheless suggests some compatibility, the capacity to blend.

61. *Histoire de l'art dramatique en France . . . ,* 3ᵉ série (Paris: Hetzel, 1859), p. 244.

62. *OC* (Slatkine), I (1978), p. 120.

63. *Les Progrès de la poésie française depuis 1830, OC* (Slatkine), XI, p. 395.

64. *Tableaux à la plume* (*OC* [Slatkine]), II, p. 233. Several recent Rosa specialists, led by A. Petrucci ("Salvator Rosa acquafortista," *Bollettino d'arte*, XXVIII [1934–35]: p. 28) and especially Mario Rotili (*Salvator Rosa incisore* [Naples: Società Editrice Napoletana, 1974], p. 7) give *L'Artiste*, 1857, VIIe série, as the source of this anecdote; but I have not been able to locate it in any other text than "Un mot sur l'eau-forte." Richard W. Wallace, in *The Etchings of Salvator Rosa* (Princeton U. Press, 1979), p. 105, recapitulates Petrucci and Rotili.

65. Wallace, p. 30; see also pp. 20, 21 (fig. 6), 22, 26, 28, and 35.

66. See note 61, *supra.*

67. *OC* (Slatkine), I, p. 120.

68. e.g., in *Albertus,* stanzas VII-XII, CVIII-CXII. Goya's famous "Black Paintings" were not acquired by the Prado until 1881; Gautier mentions only three oil paintings as being owned by the museum at the time of his visit, one of which, the *Dos de mayo,* was in fact relegated to the antichamber. Gautier's knowledge of Goya's grotesque side was based largely on his acquaintance with the *Caprichos* and other works on paper.

69. *Moniteur universel,* March 9, 1864; cited in Gautier, *Correspondance générale,* T. VII (Geneva: Droz, 1993), p. 100.

70. *Correspondance,* ed. Roger Pierrot (Paris: Garnier, 1960–1968), III, p. 584. In Balzac's long review of the *Chartreuse* in his *Revue parisienne* of September 25, 1840 (in *OC,* ed. Marcel Bouteron and Henri Longnon [Paris: Louis Conard, 1912–1940], XL, p. 401), there is no counterpart to this passage.

71. *La Comédie humaine,* ed. P. G. Castex (Paris: Gallimard/Bibliothèque de la Pléiade: 1976–1981), I, p. 1053.

72. *OC,* ed. Victor Del Litto and Ernest Abravanel, XVII (1972), p. 35.

73. *La Comédie humaine,* X, p. 72

74. *Le Piccinino* (Paris: J. Hetzel, 1859), pp. 38, 52, 62, 67.

75. Annarosa Poli, *L'Italie dans la vie et dans l'œuvre de George Sand* (Paris: Armand Colin, 1960), p. 22; see also pp. 24–25.

76. *Correspondance,* ed. Georges Lubin (Paris: Garnier), XIII (1978), p. 267.

77. *Correspondance,* XV (1981), p. 545.

78. Cited by Maria Grazia Profeti in her *"Lupo Liverani / El condenado por desconfiado:* lessemi attanti vs. sememe attanti," pp. 1193–1216 in Elio Mosele, ed., *George Sand et son temps. Hommage à Annarosa Poli* (Geneva: Slatkine; [Moncalieri] Centro interuniversitario di ricerche sul "Viaggio in Italia," 1994), p. 1196.

79. *Correspondance,* I, p. 836.

80. See p. 143, *supra.*

81. See Paul Frankl, *The Gothic: Literary Sources and Interpretations through the Centuries* (Princeton: Princeton University Press, 1960), pp. 376–77, on the alleged "Saracen" origins of Gothic architecture.

82. One might say that Sand's "pastoral" novels of the 1840s show her evolving

new ideas about nature in a way that parallels the evolution of landscape painting itself in the work of Corot, Millet, and the Barbizon school.

83. *Portraits contemporains* (Paris: Celmann-Lévy, 1870), I, p. 167.

84. *Portraits contemporains*, II, p. 237.

85. *Tableau chronologique de l'histoire moderne*, in *OC*, ed. Paul Viallaneix (Paris: Flammarion, 1971–), I, pp. 142–43. The same information is repeated verbatim in the *Précis de l'histoire moderne* (1828), in *OC*, II, pp. 183–84.

86. *Journal*, ed. Paul Viallaneix and Claude Digeon (Paris: Gallimard, 1959–1976), I, p. 60. There are currently two Rosa battle scenes (S 88 and S 89) in the Pitti; as the latter was formerly in the Uffizi, the picture Michelet saw was presumably S 88. The *Catilina* in the Pitti is now considered a copy of a picture in the Casa Martella, also in Florence (S 180).

87. On Fréminet, see Sylvie Béguin, *L'Ecole de Fontainebleau. Le Maniérisme à la cour de France* (Paris: Gauthier-Seghers, 1960), pp. 132–36; Guillaume Janneau, *La Peinture française au XVIIe siècle* (Geneva: Pierre Cailler, 1965), pp. 20–21; and Alain Mérot, *French Painting in the Seventeenth Century* (New Haven and London: Yale University Press, 1995), pp. 47–49, 60. None of the illustrations in these works helps in identifying the "sauvage" and the "fol triste" singled out by Michelet. It seems that most of the space in the frescoes is taken up by scenes from the Old Testament and the life of Christ; as Béguin says: "leurs sujets mettent en concordance l'Ancien et le Nouveau Testament, alternant avec des figures allégoriques ou sacrées" (p. 135).

88. Jean-Hilaire Belloc (1786–1866) painted a portrait of Michelet in 1844–1845. He was married to Louise Swanton Belloc (1796–1881); the prolific English writer Hilaire Belloc (1870–1953) was their grandson. Madame Belloc was herself a prolific author and translator, e.g., of *Uncle Tom's Cabin*.

89. Ibid., I, p. 701; there are no Rosas in Rouen now, according to Salerno's 1975 catalogue.

90. The *Brebis attachée et mourante* mentioned in the entry for November 7, 1863 (II, 228) is probably the work of one of the half dozen *peintres animaliers* named Roos, whose name was often Italianized to Rosa. It should be noted that Michelet himself questioned the attribution to Rosa.

91. *OC*, IX (1982), p. 253; the manuscript shows two variants for the crucial phrase "noirs et fumeux tableaux": "sombres peintures" and "ténébreuses peintures" (p. 611).

92. See *supra*, p. 146.

93. *Du prêtre, de la femme, de la famille* (Paris: Comptoir des imprimeurs unis, 1845), p. 76.

94. See James S. Patty, *Dürer in French Letters* (Paris: Honoré Champion; Geneva: Slatkine, 1989), pp. 237–43, 301–2. On the general question of Michelet and the visual arts, see Jean Pommier, *Michelet interprète de la figure humaine* (London: The Athlone Press, 1961).

95. "Salon de 1846," *OC* (Pléiade), II (1976), p. 418.

96. Paris and Leipzig: Desforges et Cie, 1839.

6. Criticism, Scholarship, and Journalism, 1824–ca. 1860

1. Paris: Bossange, 1823.

2. The Italian original had appeared in Florence in 1792 and was republished several times.

3. H. Seguin; Fufart.

4. Paris: L. G. Michaud, 1825.

5. An ardent supporter of King Joachim Murat, whose sons he tutored, De Angelis was forced into exile by Murat's fall and took refuge in Paris. In 1826 he went to Buenos Aires, became deeply involved in Argentine politics, wrote abundantly on Argentine history, and compiled a seven-volume *Colección de obras y documentos relativos a la historia antigua y moderna de las provincias del Río de la Plata* (Buenos Aires, 1836–1837).

6. De Angelis eschews the stories about Rosa's alleged wanderings in the Abruzzi and encounters with bandits, but accepts the legend of his participation in Masaniello's revolt. A bibliographical note at the end of his article refers to Baldinucci and Passeri ("auteurs contemporains") and to Pascoli, Salvini, and De Dominicis (sic). The musical compositions and lyric poetry published by Dr. Burney are dismissed as "bien faibles sous tous les rapports" (p. 12).

7. The pictures are, in addition to the *Democritus* (S 106), *Prometheus* (S 8 or 109), *Socrates Drinking the Hemlock* (Salerno lists no such picture), *The Death of Atilius Regulus* (S 113), *Legend of the Founding of Thebes* (*Cadmus Sowing Serpent's Teeth*) (S 152), *Fragilità umana* (*Humana Fragilitas*) (S 116), *Justice Abandoning the Earth* (S 67/159?), *La Fortuna* (S 126).

8. De Angelis omits Landon's criticism of Rosa's anachronistic armor.

9. De Angelis is in error in saying that this picture arrived in Versailles in 1652, the year of its creation; he seems to have been misled by the letter given in Lady Morgan's biography in which Rosa speaks of the commission he has received from the papal nuncio, Corsini, to paint a battle picture for the King of France (II, pp. 206–10); the letter is dated August 17, 1652. Lady Morgan was apparently unaware of the actual date of the picture's delivery to Louis XIV.

10. Paris: Janet, 1826; 2 vols.

11. Paris: Bossange, 1828–1829; 9 vols.

12. Paris, 1831–1833; 5 vols.

13. There were, as we have seen, at least two reviews of Lady Morgan's biography. See chapter 3.

14. I have identified only one place where Saint-Chéron clearly departs from the Rosa of Lady Morgan's novel: he rejects—without referring to her—the story which claimed that Rosa had lived with bandits in the Abruzzi: "Les biographes, contemporains de notre artiste, ont nié cette anecdote" (p. 206). (I find no reference to Baldinucci and Passeri, the only two biographers of Rosa who can be called his contemporaries.) On the other hand, the story of Rosa's participation in Masaniello's revolt is swallowed whole.

15. Near the end of his article, Saint-Chéron dubs Rosa "ce génie tout byronien"

(p. 210). One suspects, once again, that Saint-Chéron has profited from his knowledge of Lady Morgan's biography, even while dismissing it as a "roman."

16. He mentions only in passing "son *Enfant prodigue*" (p. 207), "deux *Saint Jean*" (p. 209), and "son *Triomphe de saint Georges sur le dragon*" (ibid.).

17. In a museological conclusion, Saint-Chéron briefly deals with the general question of the location of Rosa's works; he is quite explicit in listing five pictures then in the Louvre: "la *Grande Bataille*, la *Sorcière d'Endor*, un grand paysage, une marine, et un petit tableau qui représente *l'ange et Tobie*" (p. 210).

18. Ginguené's history (Paris: L.-G. Michaud) began appearing in 1811; Ginguené, who died in 1816, was able to complete nine volumes. Francesco Saverio Salfi (1759–1832) took up the work after Ginguené's death; volumes X–XIV appeared posthumously in 1834–1835. On Salfi see Carlo Nardi, *La vita e le opere di Francesco Saverio Salfi (1759–1832)* (Genoa: Libreria editrice moderna; Rome: Arti grafiche Ugo Pinnerò, 1925).

19. We should note that Salfi does not mention any Rosa landscape by name—a phenomenon we have encountered before.

20. For a recent assessment of Delécluze's Italianism, see Gian Paolo Marchi, "Studi danteschi di Etienne-Claude [*sic*] Delécluze: appunti critici con una lettera inedita di Alessandro Manzoni," *Lettere italiane,* no. 50 (1998): pp. 237–47, but, especially, Robert Baschet, *E.-J. Delécluze, témoin de son temps (1781–1863)* (Paris: Boivin, 1942), chapters 4–6.

21. References to Delécluze's three articles will be indicated in the following discussion by roman numerals representing them in their chronological order of publication.

22. Delécluze mentions three biographers of Rosa—Baldinucci, Passeri, and Bellori (who wrote nothing on Rosa)—but, like Lady Morgan herself, seems not to have read De Dominici, the real source of these stories.

23. Delécluze gives 1733 as the original date of publication (I, p. 330); *The New Grove* gives the approximate date as 1720. Marcello (1686–1739) was most famous for "settings in cantata style of the first 50 psalms in Italian paraphrases" (*The New Grove,* X, p. 649).

24. See also III, p. 270.

25. Delécluze seems to see Rosa as courageous for daring to criticize Innocent X's powerful and corrupt sister-in-law, Olimpia Maldachini (III, p. 272).

26. A sampling: "excessivement vaniteux" (I, p. 322); "cette vie vaniteuse" (I, p. 324); "vanité insupportable" (II, p. 260); "Une vanité et un égoïsme excessifs" (II, p. 269); "intraitable vanité" (II, p. 271).

27. Cf. Paul Valéry: "L'art vit de contrainte et meurt de liberté."

28. This phrase comes from the Latin distych accompanying the etching *Le Génie de Salvator Rosa.*

29. Delécluze could have seen the former picture in Florence; the latter, now in the Spencer collection at Althorp, was in the Earl of Carlisle's collection in Lady Morgan's day (II, p. 311). (Lady Morgan's translator places it in "Castle Homard" [*sic!*].)

30. See similar passages in I, p. 323 ("ses compositions philosophiques et allégoriques, si prétentieuses, si obscures, et toujours si triviales"); II, p. 257 ("Salvator Rosa a porté jusqu'au ridicule la prétention de se montrer profond philosophe et moraliste austère"); III, p. 285 ("ses compositions peintes, historiques, philosophiques ou allégoriques . . . l'obscurité prétentieuse, l'enflure et la lourdeur").

31. *RDM*, December 15, 1841, pp. 937–54.

32. *Les Musées d'Espagne*, p. 71. I have been unable to consult the early editions of Viardot's guides and have had to rely on later ones, all of which are described as "much enlarged." All bear the subtitle: *guide et memento de l'artiste et du voyageur.* After the initial references indicated in the endnotes, I refer to the various volumes parenthetically as *Allemagne, Angleterre, Espagne*, and *France;* the first of these was published by Paulin et le Chevalier in 1852; the three last-named by Hachette in 1859–1860.)

33. *Les Musées d'Allemagne*, pp. 221–22, 235, 240, 285.

34. *Les Musées d'Angleterre, de Belgique, de Hollande et de Russie*, p. 266.

35. Discussing the Neapolitan School, Viardot calls Rosa "le plus original et le plus grand de tous," but admits that he was a Neapolitan painter only by birth (*Espagne*, p. 70).

36. See a similar passage, inspired by the Louvre landscape (S 234) (*France*, p. 87).

37. Lady Morgan's catalogue opens with two pictures belonging to "Le comte Grosvenor," i.e., *Les Deux* (sic: *Trois) Maries au tombeau du Christ* and *Portrait de Salvator écrivant des vers;* the former can be identified as S 206, the latter as S 103, which Salerno (1975) calls *Ritratto di poeta.* Both are now in the Ringling Museum of Art in Sarasota.

38. Elsewhere, Viardot, apropos of the Marquis de Westminster's "horribly somber" landscapes, voices another criticism of Rosa: "Salvator n'est réellement grand que dans ses petits tableaux de chevalet" (*Angleterre*, p. 170).

39. *Voyage pittoresque en Italie: partie méridionale et en Sicile* (Paris: Morizot, 1872) p. 42; the original edition was published in 1855.

40. *Livia* (Paris: L. de Potter, 1852), I, pp. 17–18.

41. *Rome souterraine* (Paris: Paulin, 1848), I, pp. 122–23.

42. *La Campagne de Rome* (Paris: Jules Labitte, 1842), p. 171.

43. Didier's use here of the word "mouvement" probably reflects the earlier conflict between classicists and romantics, often characterized as "hommes de la résistance" and "hommes du mouvement." The immediately following reference to "la ligne et la couleur" is an even clearer evocation of that conflict.

44. *Raccolta: mœurs siciliennes et calabraises* (Paris: Hippolyte Souverain, 1844), II, pp. 78–79.

45. On Siret, see *La Grande Encyclopédie*, XXX, p. 76, and Pierre Larousse, *Grand Dictionnaire universel du XIXe siècle*, XIV, p. 707.

46. Brussels: Périchon, 1844.

47. *OC* (Pléiade), II, pp. 387, 478.

48. Whether this experience inspired him to plan a drama to be entitled *Masaniello,*

as Philippe Berthelot claimed in a 1901 article about Louis Ménard, was discussed in chapter 4. (See Claude Pichois's note, *OC*, II, p. 1114.)

49. Paris: Alliance des arts, 1846.

50. *OC*, ed. Guy Sagnes (Paris: Gallimard/Bibliothèque de la Pléiade, 1984), p. 890.

51. See the *Bibliographie de la France* for that year, p. 472, no. 3904; since the Rosa fascicule is the last to be listed, presumably it had appeared shortly before the framing of the text of entry no. 3904. For a recent view of Blanc, see Claire Barbillon's introduction to the reprint of his *Grammaire des arts du dessin* (Paris: Ecole nationale supérieure des Beaux-Arts, 2000).

52. According to Salerno (1975), neither of the two extant treatments of this theme (S 20, S 21) can be identified with the picture bought by Lanfranco.

53. One has to wonder just what picture Blanc had seen. There are several Rosas rather close to his description—S 26, S 48, S 64—but all contain human figures, small to be sure.

54. Cf. these words near the end of Blanc's study: "Dans l'art comme dans la vie, Salvator Rosa eut une physionomie bien tranchée, un caractère. Orgueilleux à l'excès, il dut à une haute opinion de lui-même la hardiesse de ses pensées, la fierté de sa manière, la fougue et l'éclat de son incorrigible talent. Elégant comme ses figures, il paraissait fait pour le monde. . . . [S]on âme reparaissait aussi âpre que ces rochers" (p. 16). (The words "orgueil," "fier," "vanité," and related expressions recur in Blanc's text; see especially pp. 6, 8, 10, 14 ("farouche"). Blanc also brings out admirable character traits: independence (p. 6, p. 15), love of liberty, both for himself and for his country (p. 6, p. 16) nobility ("âme généreuse et grande," p. 14), devotion to friends (ibid.), occasionally contrasting it with the artist's wit and gaiety in company (p. 12).

55. Blanc's chronology is defective here; he has Rosa returning to Naples after the Viterbo episode.

56. It is difficult to say which of the surviving representations of the theme is in question here, the very early lost painting known through an engraving, S 8[1], or S 109. Since Blanc refers to the beating of the vulture's wings and to a flaming volcano, the image seems closer to the later picture, now in Rome and perhaps identical with a picture owned by Rosa's friend, Carlo de' Rossi.

57. Cf. Lady Morgan: "L'anatomie de cette figure est digne de Michel-Ange" (I, p. 187).

58. The former picture had been in the Hermitage in St. Petersburg since the late eighteenth century, as Blanc well knew; perhaps he saw it there. In any case, his essay, despite his dislike for the picture, includes a large engraved version of it, done by J. Gauchard, presumably Félix-Jean Gauchard (1825–1872).

59. This etching, engraved by one Sargent (perhaps Louis Sargent [b. 1828]), is one of the eight illustrations included with Blanc's monograph.

60. There is a brief notice in the *Dictionnaire de biographie française* (IX, p. 222), from which it appears that Coligny was *secrétaire de rédaction* at *L'Artiste* from 1859 to 1870; that he prepared a book on *La Chanson française*, published posthumously

(1876); and that he led a disorderly, bohemian life, and became involved in The Commune. He may have written the highly favorable review of Tristan Corbière's *Les Amours jaunes* in *L'Artiste,* November 1, 1873. (See David Baguley, ed., *A Critical Bibliography of French Literature,* Vol. V: *The Nineteenth Century* [Syracuse: Syracuse University Press, 1994], II, p. 1173, no. 10254.)

61. These texts will be referred to as "Génie," "Michel-Ange," and "Gravures."

62. Probably a reference to the *Madonna del suffragio* (S 158) in Milan; Lady Morgan calls this picture *Le Purgatoire* (II, p. 318).

63. These statistics could have been gleaned from Lady Morgan's catalogue.

64. Elsewhere—"Michel-Ange," p. 53—Coligny allows that both Leonardo and Rosa were Epicureans, but not of the vulgar type.

65. Here, and perhaps elsewhere, Coligny has borrowed, with only slight changes from Saint-Chéron's article on Rosa published in *L'Artiste* thirty years earlier (see p. 167, *supra*).

66. In these passages, the words "philosophie" and "philosophe" have their Enlightenment meaning.

67. On Rosa's *Pythagoras*, see also "Michel-Ange," p. 53.

68. As we have seen, Coligny, like Lady Morgan (I, p. 187), finds the influence of Michelangelo in the anatomy of Rosa's *Prometheus;* see "Michel-Ange," p. 53.

69. Coligny undoubtedly drew on Lady Morgan in these passages, adopting a phrase she used at least three times (I, pp. 115, 233, 246): *famoso pittore delle cose morali.* She, in turn, was drawing on Baldinucci (V, pp. 455–56), who was quoting from an ode by Jacopo Salviati dedicated to Rosa. Salviati was probably "Salviati, Jacopo, duca," the author of *Fiori dell'orto di Gessemani e del Calvario; sonetti* (Florence, 1667), according to *The National Union Catalog of Pre-1956 Imprints* (Vol. 517, p. 176). The title page of the 1824 London edition of Lady Morgan's biography bears as an epigraph: "Famoso pittore delle cose morali. *Il Duca di Salviati.*"

7. A Fading Beacon

1. Colette, *Œuvres,* ed. Claude Pichois et al. (Paris: Gallimard/Bibliothèque de la Pléiade, 1986), II, p. 972.

2. I have consulted the English translation first published in 1893: *The National Museum of the Louvre* (Paris: Librairies-Imprimeries réunies, n.d.), pp. 114–15, where four pictures are listed.

3. According to Henry Lemonnier, "Les origines du Musée Condé," *GBA,* no. 754 (February 1925): p. 62, the seventy paintings of the Salerno collection constituted "les assises du futur Musée Condé."

4. The text, rather heavily revised, was republished in Dierx's *Poèmes et poésies* in 1864; my citations are taken from his *Œuvres complètes* (Paris: Alphonse Lemerre, n.d. [1894]), I, pp. 21–22.

5. Dierx does not, in this stanza, specifically evoke the landscapes of Claude Lorrain, so often contrasted with Rosa's by virtue of their warm, calm atmosphere,

but he is close to doing so—except perhaps for the evocation of the play of shadow on "fresh faces": the faces of Claude's human figures are unobtrusive.

6. D'Hervilly, unlike Dierx, contributed only to the second and third collections of *Le Parnasse contemporain* (1869–1871 and 1876).

7. The full text (eight stanzas) is given by Catulle Mendès in *La Légende du Parnasse contemporain* (Brussels: Auguste Brancart, 1884), pp. 242–45.

8. In fact, D'Hervilly, in *L'Artiste* for November 15, 1863 (p. 216), published a *transposition d'art*, "La Kermesse de Rubens," dedicated to Gautier.

9. Breton (1812–1875), described by Bénézit as "dessinateur et archéologue," draws heavily on Lady Morgan's biography, but in the brief bibliography at the end of his article calls her "Lady Montague"!

10. This article is anonymous; it quotes from "M. Breton," from the article by De Angelis in Michaud's *Biographie universelle* (a paragraph of generally enthusiastic praise for Rosa's work), and from Louis Viardot's rather negative assessment of Rosa as a history painter in *Les Musées de France*, pp. 86–87.

11. Like the anonymous writer in the *Grand Dictionnaire universel*, Plouchart quotes a passage from Ernest Breton's 1863 article—on Rosa's antics during the carnival of 1639—and also gives 1663 as the date of Rosa's return from Florence to Rome.

12. Larousse's *Grande Encyclopédie* (1971–1978) does not have a separate article on Rosa; the index reveals that he is mentioned half a dozen times in the articles on "baroque," "genre (peinture de)," "Italie," and "Naples."

13. These articles are all signed by Marguerite Bénézit, whose relationship to Emmanuel Bénézit I have not been able to determine. Emmanuel Bénézit (1854–1920) died before the appearance of the third volume of the first edition; even if Marguerite Bénézit was his daughter, it is difficult to believe that she herself was fully responsible for texts that go from 1924 to 1999.

14. Paris: Firmin-Didot, 1870, pp. 250–51. Mantz (1821–1895), like Charles Blanc, was an administrator of fine arts, and contributed heavily to Blanc's *Gazette des Beaux-Arts* and his huge *Histoire des peintres de toutes les écoles*.

15. Louis Gonse, *Les Chefs-d'œuvre des musées de France*, T. I (Paris: L.-H. May, 1900), p.127.

16. I have consulted the second (revised) edition (Paris: H. Laurens, 1928).

17. *Œuvres complètes* (Paris: Jean-Jacques Pauvert, 1964), II, p. 133. Faure's only other reference to Rosa, as far as I have discovered, simply mentions him in relating an anecdote involving an alleged encounter between Velásquez and Rosa, included in an article on the former artist published in 1903 (ibid., III, p. 886).

18. Paris: Armand Colin, 1921 (T. VI, première partie), pp. 115–117. However, this massive publication does offer three black-and-white illustrations of Rosa's work, all three being from the Louvre's collection: *Landscape with Hunters and Soldiers*, *Saul and the Witch of Endor*, and *Heroic Battle*.

19. Jean Guiffrey, ed., *La Peinture au Musée du Louvre* (Paris: L'Illustration, 1929), II, p. 62.

20. *GBA,* 6ᵉ série, vol. 27 (January 1945): pp. 39–58. From 1942 to 1948, the *Gazette*'s headquarters were in New York.

21. Paris: Flammarion, 1951, II, p. 154.

22. *La Revue des arts,* IX (1959): pp. 163–76.

23. Paris: Presses universitaires de France, 1955–59; three volumes in six tomes.

24. The pictures in question are: *Cain and Abel* (S 191), *Moses Saved from the Waters* (S 129), *Saul and the Witch of Endor* (S 210), *Jonah Preaching to the Ninivites* (S 155), *The Prodigal Son* (S 127), and *The Martyrdom of St. Bartholomew* (S 105) (Réau, II, pp. i, 97, 181, 252, 418; II, pp. ii, 335; III, pp. i, 183).

25. "Note sur l'abbé Nicaise et quelques-uns de ses amis romains," *GBA,* no. 1127 (December 1962): pp. 565–68.

26. *Baroque and Rococo* (New York: Frederick A. Praeger, 1964), pp. 45–46.

27. *The Baroque. Principles, Styles, Modes, Themes* (Greenwich, CT: New York Graphic Society, 1968), pp. 214–15; his remarks are illustrated by a reproduction of a version of *Scena di stregonerie* (S 72).

28. Padua: Edizioni 1+1, 1973; Hurel's review, which I have not been able to examine, appeared in *Nouvelles de l'Estampe* (no. 14 [1974]: pp. 17–21; illustrated).

29. "Des origines de la critique et de l'histoire de l'art en Angleterre," *Revue de l'Art,* no. 30 (1975): pp. 5–16 (p. 12).

30. "Gaspard Dughet: une chronologie révisée," *Revue de l'art,* no. 34 (1976): pp. 29–56 (p. 30).

31. *Revue du Louvre et des musées de France,* XLIV (April 1994): pp. 67–68. A small reproduction in color accompanies the text.

32. In Catherine Legrand et al., eds., *Le Paysage en Europe du XVIe au XVIIIᵉ siècle* (Paris: *Réunion des musées nationaux, 1994* [1995 according to *Les Livres disponibles*]), pp. 105–18.

33. *Estampille: l'Objet d'art,* no. 288 (February 1995): pp. 54–69.

34. In *GBA,* no. 1573 (February 2000): pp. 93–108.

35. However, Richard W. Wallace, *The Etchings of Salvator Rosa* (Princeton: Princeton University Press, 1970, pp. 44–45) plausibly identifies a strain of quietism in connection with several of Rosa's works.

36. Paris: Georges Kugelmann, 1866.

37. *Littérature italienne* (Paris: Armand Colin, 1906), p. 310.

38. In Christian Bec, ed., *Précis de littérature italienne* (Paris: Presses universitaires de France, 1982), p. 199.

39. Paris: La Colombe, 1946, pp. 103–08.

40. In his "notice," Du Colombier speaks somewhat slightingly of Rosa's satires but admits their "saveur indéniable."

41. Jacques Dupont and François Mathey, *The Great Centuries of Painting. The Seventeenth Century. The New Developments in Art Form: Caravaggio to Vermeer,* trans. S. J. C. Harrison (Geneva, Paris, and New York: Skira, 1951).

42. New York: Harry N. Abrams, 1961 (but originally published in 1951).

43. Germain Bazin, *The Loom of Art* (New York: Simon and Schuster, 1962).

44. New York: Steward, Tabori, & Chang, 1997; published in Paris the same year by Robert Laffont.

45. Paris: Editions Scala, 1999.

46. See Walther Vitzthum, "Seicento Drawings at the Cabinet des dessins," *BM*, CII (January 1960): pp. 75–76; Rosa is one of the five artists whose works are illustrated.

47. See the *Revue du Louvre*, 1973, no. 2, pp. 141–42, and the GBA, no. 1250 (March 1973): "La Chronique des arts," p. 20.

48. See the review by Marcelle Elgrishi-Gautrot in *Nouvelles de l'Estampe*, no. 51 (May–June 1980): p. 28.

49. No. 1431 (April 1988): "La Chronique des arts," p. 2.

50. The catalogue was published in Paris by the Réunion des musées nationaux. A review by F. S. in the *GBA* (no. 1440 [January 1989]: "La Chronique des arts," pp. 1–2) does not mention Rosa by name.

51. Nos. 1444–45 (May–June 1989): "La Chronique des arts," p. 7.

52. The show was organized by Catherine Legrand, Jean-François Méjanès, and Emmanuel Starcky and the catalogue published by the Réunion des musées nationaux.

53. See the brief anonymous review in the *GBA*, no. 1467 (April 1991): "La Chronique des arts," p. 1.

54. Chrystèle Burgard and Baldine Saint Girons, eds., *Le Paysage et la question du sublime* (Paris: Réunion des musées nationaux, 1997), p. 36.

55. The quotation is taken from Starobinski's *L'Invention de la liberté*, 1709–1789 (Lausanne: Skira, 1964), p. 160.

56. See Stéphane Loire, "La peinture italienne (XVIIe-XVIIIe siècles)," *La Revue du Louvre*, XLIX (June 1999): pp. 19–20.

Bibliography

Agay, Frédéric d', ed. *Lettres d'Italie du président de Brosses* (Le Temps retrouvé). Paris: Mercure de France, 1986.

Baldinucci, Filippo. *Notizie dei professori del disegno da Cimabue in qua*. Vol. V. Florence: V. Batelli e Compagni, 1847.

Balzac, Honoré de. *La Comédie humaine*. Ed. P. G. Castex et al. Paris: Gallimard/Bibliothèque de la Pléiade, 1976–1981. 12 vols.

Barbier, Auguste. *Poésies de Auguste Barbier, Iambes et poèmes*. Paris: Alphonse Lemerre, 1898.

Bartsch, Adam, *Le Peintre-graveur*. Vol. XX. Vienna: Imprimerie de J. V. Degen, 1820.

Baudelaire, Charles. *Œuvres complètes*. Ed. Claude Pichois. Paris: Gallimard/Bibliothèque de la Pléiade, 1975–1976. 2 vols.

Bertrand, Aloysius. *Œuvres complètes*. (Textes de littérature moderne et contemporaine, 32). Ed. Helen Hart Poggenburg. Paris: Honoré Champion, 2000.

Blanc, Charles. *Histoire des peintres de toutes les écoles*. Fascicule 176: *Salvator Rosa*. Paris: Vve J. Renouard, 1856.

———. *Le Trésor de la curiosité*. Paris: Vve J. Renouard, 1857–1858. 2 vols.

Breton, Ernest. "Rosa, Salvator." Cols. 622-26 in Dr Hoefer, ed., *Nouvelle Biographie générale*. T. XLII. Paris : Firmin Didot, 1863.

Burgard, Chrystèle, and Baldine Saint Girons, eds., *Le Paysage et la question du sublime*. Paris: Réunion des musées nationaux, 1997.

Chateaubriand, François René, Vicomte de. *Œuvres complètes*. Paris: Garnier frères, 1859–1861. 12 vols.

Chevallier, Elisabeth. "Les guides d'Italie et la vulgarisation de la critique d'art au XVIIIe siècle." *Revue de littérature comparée*, XLV(July–September 1971): 366–91.

Cochin, Nicolas. *Lettres à un jeune artiste peintre, pensionnaire à l'Académie royale de France à Rome.* Paris: aux bureaux du "Journal des beaux-arts," 1836.

———. *Voyage d'Italie ou recueil de notes sur les ouvrages de peinture ou de sculpture qu'on voit dans les principales villes d'Italie.* (Sources de l'histoire de l'art au XVIIIe siècle). Geneva: Minkoff, 1972.

Coligny, Charles. "Le génie de Salvator Rosa." *L'Artiste*, September 1, 1864, pp. 97–100.

———. "Les gravures de Salvator Rosa." *L'Artiste*, August 15, 1865, pp. 49–55.

———. "Michel-Ange et Salvator Rosa." *L'Artiste*, August 1, 1865, pp. 82–84.

Conisbee, Philip. "Salvator Rosa and Claude-Joseph Vernet." *Burlington Magazine*, CXV (December 1973): 789–94.

Cosnac, Gabriel Jules, Comte de. *Les Richesses du Palais Mazarin.* Paris: Librairie Renouard, H. Loones, successeur, 1884.

Coupin, P. A., ed. *Œuvres posthumes de Girodet-Trioson, peintre d'histoire*, Vol. I. Paris: Jules Renouard, 1829.

Daignan d'Orbessan, Anne-Marie, Marquis. *Mélanges historiques, critiques, de physique, de littérature et de poésie.* Paris: Merlin, 1768.

De Angelis, Pietro. "Rosa (Salvator)." Pp. 1–12 in *Biographie universelle ancienne et moderne*. T. XXXIX. Paris: L. G. Michaud, 1825.

———. "Rosa (Salvator)." Pp. 453–59 in Louis-Gabriel Michaud, ed., *Biographie universelle ancienne et moderne*. T. XXXVI. Paris: Ch. Delagrave et Cie, ca. 1870.

De Dominici, Bernardo. *Vite de' pittori, scultori ed architetti napolitani.* Vol. III. Bologna: Forni, n.d. (1971).

Delécluze, Etienne-Jean. "Les satires de Salvator Rosa." *Revue de Paris*, August 30, 1840, pp. 318–37; September 27, 1840, pp. 257–73; October 25, 1840, pp. 265–83.

Denon, Dominique Vivant. *Voyage en Sicile.* Paris: Le Promeneur, 1993.

Deperthes, Jean-Baptiste. *Histoire de l'art du paysage, depuis la renaissance jusqu'au dix-huitième siècle.* Paris: Le Normant, 1822.

Dezallier d'Argenville, Antoine-Joseph. *Abrégé de la vie des plus fameux peintres.* T. II. Geneva: Minkoff Reprints, 1972.

———. *Abrégé de la vie des plus fameux peintres.* T. I. Paris: De Bure l'aîné, 1745.

———. "Lettre sur le choix d'un cabinet curieux." *Mercure de France*, June 1727, pp. 1295–1319.

Diderot, Denis. *Œuvres esthétiques.* Ed. Paul Vernière. Paris: Garnier, 1959.

———. *Salons.* Ed. Jean Seznec and Jean Adhémar. Oxford: Voltaire Foundation, 1957–1965. 4 vols.

Didier, Charles. *La Campagne de Rome.* Paris: Jules Labitte, 1842.

———. *Raccolta: mœurs siciliennes et calabraises.* Paris: Hippolyte Souverain, 1844. 2 vols.

———. "Romuléo." Pp. 483-557 in *Les Amours d'Italie.* Paris: L. Hachette, 1859.

Dugué, Ferdinand. *Salvator Rosa, drame en cinq actes et sept tableaux.* Paris: Michel Lévy, 1851.

Dumas, Alexandre. *Le Corricolo*. Ed. Jean-Noël Schifano. Paris: Desjonquères, 1984.

Eichner, Hans, ed. *"Romantic" and its Cognates: The European History of a Word*. Toronto: University of Toronto Press, 1972.

Félibien, André. *Entretiens sur les vies et sur les ouvrages des plus excellens peintres anciens et modernes*. Farnborough (Hants.): Gregg Press, 1967.

_____. *Noms des peintres les plus célèbres et les plus connus anciens et modernes*. (Sources de l'histoire de l'art au XVIIIᵉ siècle) Geneva: Minkoff, 1972.

Fromentin, Eugène. *Œuvres complètes*. Ed. Guy Sagnes. Paris: Gallimard/ Bibliothèque de la Pléiade, 1984.

Gandonnière, Almire. "Salvator Rosa." *La Chronique: revue universelle*, 2e année, t. II (ca. March–July 1843): 318–24.

Gautier, Théophile. *Correspondance générale*. Ed. Claudine Lacoste-Veysseyre et al. Geneva: Droz, 1985–2000. 12 vols.

_____. *Exposition de 1859*. Ed. Wolfgang Drost and Ulrike Henninger. Heidelberg: Carl Winter, 1972.

_____. *Histoire de l'art dramatique en France depuis vingt-cinq ans*. 3ᵉ Série and 6ᵉ Série. Paris: Hetzel, 1859.

_____. *Œuvres complètes*. Geneva: Slatkine, 1978. 11 vols.

_____. *Poésies complètes*. Ed. René Jasinski. Paris: A.-G. Nizet, 1970.

Georgel, Pierre, ed. *L'Album de Léopoldine Hugo*. Villequier: Musée Victor Hugo, 1967.

Germain, François. *L'Imagination d'Alfred de Vigny*. Paris: José Corti, 1961.

Gobineau, Arthur, Comte de. *Poemi inediti di Arthur de Gobineau*. Ed. Paolo Berselli Ambri. (Biblioteca dell'*Archivum Romanicum*, Serie I. Storia-letteratura-paleografia. Vol. 75) Florence: Leo S. Olschki, 1965.

Goncourt, Edmond and Jules de. *Journal: Mémoires de la vie littéraire*. Vol. I: *1851–1853*. Ed. Robert Ricatte. Paris: Fasquelle-Flammarion, 1956.

Grangé, Eugène, and Henri Trianon. *Salvator Rosa, opéra comique*. Paris: Michel Lévy, 1861.

Gruyer, A.-F. *La Peinture au château de Chantilly*. Vol. I: *Les Ecoles étrangères*. Paris: E. Plon, Nourrit et Cⁱᵉ, 1896.

Hatin, Eugène. *Bibliographie historique et critique de la presse périodique*. T. II. Paris: Firmin Didot. 1866.

Hugo, Victor. *Œuvres complètes*. Ed. Jean Massin. Paris: Club français du livre, 1967–1970. 18 vols. in 36 tomes.

Kitson, Michael, et al. *Salvator Rosa, Hayward Gallery, London, 17 October–23 December 1973*. London: Arts Council, 1973.

Kloss, William. *Samuel F. B. Morse*. New York: Harry N. Abrams, 1988.

Lacombe, Jacques. *Dictionnaire portatif des beaux-arts*. Paris: Jean-Th. Herissant, 1753.

Lalande, Jérôme de. *Voyage en Italie*. T. I. Paris: Veuve Desaint, 1786.

Lamartine, Alphonse de. *Œuvres complètes*. Paris: Chez l'auteur, 1860–1866. 41 vols.

_____. *Œuvres poétiques*. Ed. Marius-François Guyard. Paris: Gallimard/ Bibliothèque de la Pléiade, 1965.

_____. *Saül*. Ed. Jean Des Cognets. Paris: Hachette/STFM, 1918.

Landon, C. P. *Annales du Musée ou recueil complet des gravures d'après les anciennes écoles italienne, allemande, hollandaise, etc.* Paris: Pillet aîné, 1832.

Lanier, Gustave. *Les Grands Ecrivains de l'Italie*. Paris: Georges Kugelmann, 1866.

Lanzi, Luigi Antonio. *Histoire de la peinture en Italie, depuis la Renaissance des Beaux-Arts, jusque vers la fin du XVIIIe siècle*. T. II. Trans. Mme Armande Dieudé. Paris: H. Seguin; Fufart, 1824.

La Rochefoucauld-Liancourt, Frédéric-Gaëtan, Marquis de. *Satire imitée de la 4me de Salvator Rosa*. Typ. Morris et comp., 1857.

Larousse, Pierre. "Salvator Rosa." Pp. 149–54 in Pierre Larousse, *Grand Dictionnaire universel du XIXᵉ siècle*. T. XIV. Paris: Pierre Larousse, 1875.

Latouche, Henri de. *Adieux, poésies*. Paris: Impr. de Lacour et Maistrasse, 1844.

Laurent, Henri. *Le Musée royal*. Seconde série: *Histoire*. Paris: Imprimerie de P. Didot l'aîné, 1816–1818.

Laveissière, Sylvain. *Adrien Guignet, peintre: 1816–1854*. Autun: Musée Rolin, 1978.

Lecarpentier, Charles-Louis-François. *Galerie des peintres célèbres*. Paris: Treuttel et Wurtz, 1821. 2 vols.

Le Comte, Florent. *Cabinet de singularitez, d'architecture, peinture, sculpture et gravure*. Paris: Estienne Picart; Nicolas le Clerc, 1699–1700. 3 vols.

Lem, F.-H. "Comment j'ai rendu un Géricault au Louvre." *Connaissance des Arts*, no. 131 (January 1963): 66–71.

Lemierre, Antoine-Marin. *Œuvres choisies de Lemierre*. T. II. Paris: Lecointe, 1829.

Le Tourneur, Pierre. "Introduction." *Shakespeare traduit de l'Anglois*. T. I. Paris: Vve Duchesne, 1776.

Limentani, Uberto. *Bibliografia della vita e delle opere di Salvator Rosa*. Florence: Amor di libro, 1955.

_____. "Salvator Rosa. Nuovi studi e ricerche." *Italian Studies*, IX (1954): 52–55.

_____. "Salvator Rosa: supplemento alla bibliografia." *Forum Italicum*, VII, no. 2 (1973): 268–79.

Loire, Stéphane. "La peinture italienne (XVIIᵉ-XVIIIᵉ siècles)." *La Revue du Louvre*, XLIX (June 1999): 19–20.

Mahoney, Michael. *The Drawings of Salvator Rosa*. New York and London: Garland Publishing, 1977.

Mariette, Pierre-Jean. *Description sommaire des desseins des grands maîtres d'Italie, des Pays-Bas et de France, du cabinet de feu M. Crozat*. Paris: Pierre-Jean Mariette, 1741; reprint, Geneva: Minkoff, 1973.

Marolles, Michel de. *Catalogue de livres d'estampes et de figures en taille douce*. Paris: Frédéric Léonard, 1666.

Méry, Joseph. *L'Ame transmise*. Lagny: Impr. de Vialat. 1853.

Michelet, Jules. *Du prêtre, de la femme, de la famille*. Paris: Comptoir des imprimeurs unis, 1845.

_____. *Journal*. Ed. Paul Viallaneix and Claude Digeon. Paris: Gallimard, 1959–1976. 4 vols.

_____ . *Œuvres complètes*. T. I, II et IX. Ed. Paul Viallaneix. Paris: Flammarion, 1971–1982.

Millin, A.-L. *Dictionnaire des beaux-arts*. T. III. Paris: Impr. de Crapelet-Desray, 1806.

Mirecourt, Eugène de. *Masaniello*. Paris: G. Havard, 1851.

Montesquieu, Charles-Louis de Secondat, Baron de la Brède et de. *Œuvres complètes*. T. I. Ed. Roger Caillois. Paris: Gallimard/Bibliothèque de la Pléiade, 1949.

Morgan, Sydney Owenson, Lady. *The Life and Times of Salvator Rosa*. London: Henry Colburn, 1824. 2 vols.

_____. *Mémoires sur la vie et le siècle de Salvator Rosa*. Paris: Alexis Eymery; Brussels: Brunet et Cᵉ, April 1824. 2 vols.

_____. *The Wild Irish Girl, a National Tale*. London: Richard Phillips, 1808.

Musset, Alfred de. *Œuvres complètes en prose*. Ed. Maurice Allem and Paul-Courant. Paris: Gallimard/Bibliothèque de la Pléiade, 1960.

Musset, Paul de. *Course en voiturin*. Paris: Victor Magen, 1845. 2 vols.

_____. *Livia*. Paris: L. de Potter, 1852. 3 vols.

_____. *Voyage pittoresque en Italie: partie méridionale et en Sicile*. Paris: Morizat, 1872.

Nerval, Gérard de. *Œuvres complètes*. T. I. Ed. Claude Pichois et al. Paris: Gallimard/Bibliothèque de la Pléiade, 1989.

Nodier, Charles. "Variétés. Mémoires sur la vie et le siècle de Salvator Rosa, par Lady Morgan." *L'Oriflamme*, March 5, 1824, pp. 3–4.

Nouville, Adelphe. "Salvator Rosa dans les Abruzzes." *Bulletin de la Société des gens de lettres*, X (June 1855): 141–49.

Orloff, le Comte Grégoire. *Essai sur l'histoire de la peinture en Italie depuis les temps les plus anciens jusqu'à nos jours*. T. II. Paris: Galerie de Bossange père; London: Martin Bossange et Cᵉ, 1823.

Paillot de Montabert, Jacques-Nicolas. *Traité complet de la peinture*. Paris: Bossange, 1828–1829. 9 vols.

Pascoli, Lione. *Vite de' pittori, scultori ed architetti moderni*. Vol. I. Rome: A. de' Rossi, 1730.

Passeri, Giambattista. *Vite de' pittori, scultori ed architetti che hanno lavorato in Roma, morti dal 1641 fino al 1673*. Rome: Gregorio Settari, 1772.

Plouchart, Eugène. "Rosa (Salvator)." Pp. 928–29 in *La Grande Encyclopédie*, T. XXVIII. Paris: Société anonyme de la Grande Encyclopédie, n.d. (1900).

Poli, Annarosa. *L'Italie dans la vie et dans l'œuvre de George Sand*. Paris: Armand Colin, 1960.

Profeti, Maria Grazia. "Lupo Liverani/El condenado por desconfiado: lessemi attanti vs. sememe attanti." Pp. 1193–1216 in Elio Mosele, ed., *George Sand et son temps. Hommage à Annarosa Poli*. Geneva: Slatkine; [Moncalieri] Centro interuniversitario di ricerche sul "Viaggio in Italia," 1994.

Richard, Jérome, abbé. *Description historique et critique de l'Italie*. Paris: Saillant, Desaint, J. M. Coru de la Goibrie, 1769. 6 vols.

Robillard-Péronville and Pierre Laurent. *Le Musée français*. T. I. Paris: Imprimerie de L.-E. Herhan, 1803.

Sade, Donatien-Alphonse-François, Marquis de. *Œuvres complètes*. T. IX et XVI. Paris: Cercle du livre précieux, 1967, 1977.

Saint-Chéron, Alexandre de. "Salvator Rosa." *L'Artiste*, IX, 18ᵉ livraison (May 31, 1835): 205–10.

Sainte-Beuve, Charles-Augustin. *Portraits contemporains*. Paris: Calmann-Lévy, 1870. 5 vols.

Saint-Gérand, Jacques-Philippe. "Où donc est la Beauté que rêve le poète?" *Association des Amis d'Alfred de Vigny*, XIII (1993–1994): 8–20.

Saint-Non, Jean-Claude Richard de. *Voyage pittoresque à Naples et en Sicile*. Paris: Dufour, 1829. 4 vols.

Salerno, Luigi, ed. *L'Opera completa di Salvator Rosa* (Classici dell'Arte). Milan: Rizzoli, 1975.

———. *Salvator Rosa*. Milan: Edizioni per il Club del libro, 1963.

Salfi, Francesco. Review of Lady Morgan. *Revue encyclopédique*, XXII (1824): 109–21.

Sand, George. *Correspondance*. Ed. Georges Lubin. Paris: Garnier, 1964–1991. 25 vols.

———. *Il Piccinino*. Paris: J. Hetzel, 1859.

Scott, Jonathan. *Salvator Rosa. His Life and Times*. New Haven and London: Yale University Press, 1995.

Siret, Adolphe. *Dictionnaire historique des peintres de toutes les écoles depuis les temps les plus reculés jusqu'à nos jours*. Brussels: Périchon, 1844.

Staël-Holstein, Germaine de, Baronne. *Corinne ou l'Italie*. Ed. Claudine Herrmann. Paris: Des femmes, 1979.

Stendhal (pseud. of Marie Henri Beyle) *Œuvres complètes*. Ed. Victor Del Litto and Ernest Abravanel. Geneva: Edito-Service S.A., 1967–1974. 50 vols.

Stevenson, Lionel. *The Wild Irish Girl: The Life of Sydney Owenson, Lady Morgan (1776–1859)*. New York: Russell & Russell, 1936.

Suard, Jean-Baptiste, and François Arnaud. *Variétés littéraires*. Geneva: Slatkine Reprints, 1969.

Taillasson, Jean Joseph. *Observations sur quelques grands peintres, dans lesquelles on cherche à fixer les caractères distinctifs de leur talent*. Paris: Chez l'auteur, à la Sorbonne, 1807.

Tapon Fougas, Francisque. *Satire contre la guerre imitée de Salvator Rosa (1656–1659)*. Geneva: les principaux libraires, 1866.

Thompson, C. W. "John Martin et l'image de la ville moderne chez Vigny et Lamartine." *Revue de littérature comparée*, XLV (January–March, 1971): 5–17.

_____ . *Victor Hugo and the Graphic Arts (1820–1833)*. Geneva: Droz, 1970.

Thuillier, Jacques. "Textes du XVIIᵉ siècle oubliés ou peu connus concernant les arts." *Dix-Septième Siècle*, XXXV (1983): 125–40.

Tiraboschi, Girolamo. *Histoire de la littérature d'Italie* abrégée par Antoine Landi. T. V. Berne, 1784.

Valenciennes, Pierre-Henri de. *Eléments de perspective pratique, suivi de Réflexions et conseils sur le genre du paysage*. Paris: Desenne, an VIII (1800).

Viardot, Louis. *Les Musées d'Allemagne: guide et memento de l'artiste et du voyageur*. Paris: Paulin et Le Chevalier, 1852.

_____. *Les Musées d'Angleterre, de Belgique, de Hollande et de Russie: guide et memento de l'artiste et du voyageur*. Paris: L. Hachette, 1860.

_____. *Les Musées d'Espagne: guide et memento de l'artiste et du voyageur*. Paris: L. Hachette, 1860.

_____. *Les Musées d'Italie: guide et memento de l'artiste et du voyageur*. Paris: L. Hachette, 1859

_____. *Les Musées de France, Paris: guide et memento de l'artiste et du voyageur*. Paris: L. Hachette, 1860.

Vigny, Alfred de. *Correspondance*. T. I–II. Ed. Madeleine Ambrière. Paris: Presses universitaires de France, 1989–1991.

_____. *Mémoires inédits. Fragments et projets*. Ed. Jean Sangnier. Paris: Gallimard, 1958.

_____. *Œuvres complètes*. T. I. Ed. François Germain and André Jarry. Paris: Gallimard/Bibliothèque de la Pléiade, 1986.

_____. *Œuvres complètes*. T. II. Ed. Fernand Baldensperger. Paris: Gallimard/Bibliothèque de la Pléiade, 1965.

Vivier, Michel. "Hugo et Nodier collaborateurs de *L'Oriflamme*." *Revue d'histoire littéraire de la France*, LVIII, no. 3 (July–September 1958): 297–323.

Wallace, Richard W. *The Etchings of Salvator Rosa*. Princeton: Princeton University Press, 1979.

Watelet, Claude-Henri, and Pierre-Charles Lévesque. *Dictionnaire des arts de peinture, sculpture et gravure*. T. IV. Geneva: Minkoff, 1972.

Wildenstein, Daniel, and Jean Adhémar. "Les tableaux italiens dans les catalogues de ventes parisiennes du XVIIIᵉ siècle." *Gazette des Beaux-Arts*, nos. 1362–1363–1364 (July–August–September 1982): 1–78.

Wildenstein, Georges. "L'abbé de Saint-Non artiste et mécène." *Gazette des Beaux-Arts*, no. 1090 (November 1959): 225–44.

Index

Bikinis,
Bell-bottoms
&
Little Black
Dresses

Kate Mulvey

Bikinis, Bell-bottoms & Little Black Dresses

70 GREAT FASHION CLASSICS

MERRELL

LONDON · NEW YORK

Contents

Introduction

What exactly is a fashion classic, an icon of style? The terms refer to a groundbreaking garment, something amazing that has come into our lives and on to the popular landscape. The ladylike shift, raunchy hot pants, the jaunty trilby hat, the slinky halter-neck dress, the shocking itsy-bitsy bikini, Coco Chanel's revolutionary little black dress: whether through clever design features or specific capabilities, or simply because they have captured the imagination, these garments have all made their mark on how we dress. They are the 'big hitters', the outfits that have shocked, inspired or delighted, and they have all helped to define the mood of their times.

What makes something in vogue? Why were baggy dungarees and skintight leggings (neither of them necessarily the most complimentary of fashions) the apex of cool one minute and cast into the wilderness the next, only to be reinvented as the ultimate in hip ten or twenty years later? These questions and more are answered in *Bikinis, Bell-bottoms and Little Black Dresses*, which traces the history of the 70 most influential, iconic garments of the last 100 years. In these pages are the super stiletto, the preppy loafer and the Vivienne Westwood mini-crini. Some of the garments listed in this book evoke a sense of adventure and derring-do: the trench coat, for example, is not just a beige mac, it is also a short cut to macho cool. The trench is the coat that won the war, the coat that defined an era of Hollywood private eyes, and it is now a mainstream fashion item and stylish unisex cover-up. Other items of clothing were originally so revolutionary and spectacular that they were bound to endure for decades. One such is the

miniskirt, which not only swept away the stuffy fashions of the 1950s, but also gave women a new sexual freedom; it is still able to shock today.

This book explains and explores the evolution of these 70 exciting pieces of clothing. Each entry traces the development of a garment through the decades, relating why and when it was in vogue, who wore it, and the changes and improvements it has undergone right through to the present day. For example, the straight chemise dress of the 1920s prepared the way for the shift dress; the short-lived hobble skirt of the early twentieth century became the pencil skirt; and the practical polo-neck jumper was swiped from French fishermen, only to become an enduring unisex classic.

Miniskirts and minidresses, the quintessential youth styles of the 1960s, can these days be dressed-down basics for a hip look (opposite), or sleek, high-fashion items, as shown by the Halston dress of 2000 below.

The point is, fashion is ever-changing and evolving. Clothes that once were old-fashioned and utilitarian are transformed into style 'must-haves' or elegant classics. Jeans, originally the cheap garb of railway workers, can now cost hundreds of pounds; today's designer T-shirts are descended from a humble piece of men's underwear; and the luscious cashmere hoodie originated from the ordinary sweat-absorbing sports top. As the reader will uncover in this book, clothes all have an individual history and their own fascinating tale; many have borrowed from the military, the sports field or workwear, and carry with them echoes of the conflict of the battlefield or the sweat of the athletics track.

After the Second World War, subcultural groups appropriated utilitarian clothes and used them to convey their messages. As seen with the Mods' military parka, the hippies' ethnic kaftan and the grunge

Dedicated followers of fashion: two young men model the new styles at London's International Men's and Boys' Wear Exhibition of 1973. Both wear trousers by Monte Cristo; Tuty (far left) sports a checked brown-and-cream sweater and cardigan by John Craig, Richard a diamond-patterned jumper by Azzura.

kids' Dr. Martens bovver boots, the authenticity of the 'real thing' gives the item an attitude, a drama and an aura of cool. This, in turn, inspires the designers who refine the original and send it down the catwalk as a high-fashion garment. Chic versions of plainer originals have included Claire McCardell's stylish 1940s Popover wrap dress, taken from the domestic house dress; Yves Saint Laurent's sexed-up safari jacket; and Marc Jacobs's reworking of the workaday plaid shirt. This book includes the most innovative fashion designers of the twentieth and early twenty-first centuries – among them Christian Dior, Coco Chanel, Calvin Klein, Roy Halston, Norma Kamali and Alexander McQueen – and their iconic designs.

The personalities who made these items into the next must-haves are also featured here. Celebrities, fashion models and actors have all influenced the way we dress:

Marilyn Monroe, a sex symbol for generations of men worldwide, in the provocative bedroom scene from the comedy film *The Seven Year Itch* (1955). The slip was once exclusively an item of lingerie, but today its modern incarnation is a staple of many a fashionable woman's wardrobe.

think of Jacqueline Kennedy and the shift dress, Steve McQueen and the desert boot or Audrey Hepburn and the ballet pump. Marilyn Monroe, Humphrey Bogart, Kurt Cobain, Liam Gallagher … these are the stars that made certain clothes cool. As this book shows, time and time again the silver screen has been inextricably linked to the rise of a style icon: such films as *Rebel Without a Cause* (1955), *Funny Face* (1957), *Bonnie and Clyde* (1967) and *Annie Hall* (1977) had a considerable impact on popular style. Television, mass media and celebrity endorsements also contribute to turning the ordinary into the glamorous and exciting.

The past 100 years have seen an accelerated rate of change and innovation in all areas of life. The emancipation of women, world events, technological developments and shifts in social attitudes

The American rapper Missy Elliott in a slinky pale tracksuit in 2005. It was in the 1980s that rap artists first sparked a global trend for sportswear as fashion.

have all had a major impact on fashion. From Chanel's revolution of womenswear, Saint Laurent's iconic trouser suit for women and the invention of Lycra to the emergence of street style, all these innovations go hand in hand with the social and cultural changes of the times.

Conversely, *Bikinis, Bell-bottoms and Little Black Dresses* gives an insight into how modern technology, mass marketing and ready-to-wear allow fashions to filter down near-instantaneously from the catwalk to the high street. Once-expensive items, such as silken parkas, leopard-print trainers and reworked pea coats, are soon available at a fraction of the price. Today everyone can be cool, and the evolution of various garments is complete. Or is it? Each entry concludes with where that item stands today, but there is no knowing what changes we will see in the coming decades.

Two bright and breezy smock dresses by Michèle Rosier for the French label Pierre d'Alby from 1967. Other designers who created clothing for the label, which was established in 1958 by Zyga Pianko, include Daniel Hechter, Agnès Troublé (agnès b.) and Nicole Farhi.

1. Little black dress

Simple, elegant and coolly stylish, the 'little black dress' (LBD) is a timeless classic. An international fashion icon since the early twentieth century, the LBD has undergone many changes in form and mood, but its allure has never waned. Today, whether it is dressed up with pearls and strappy sandals or cut short and skimpy and paired with tough-girl biker boots, the LBD can still hold centre stage on any occasion.

The little black dress started life in the 1920s. Before then, wearing black was inconceivable for a proper lady: black dresses were worn by domestic servants and the bereaved only. Then Coco Chanel came along and reinvented the way women dressed. When American *Vogue* first featured the French designer's modern dress in 1926, a new fashion aesthetic was born. Chanel's calf-length garment, made from the simple serge of the lady's-maid dress, was loose-fitting, had long sleeves and subtle diagonal detailing, and came in one colour only: black. It was an instant success with society belles. The first 'put-it-on-and-forget-about-it' dress, it became a symbol of the era's modern woman and presaged a new kind of dressing.

By the 1940s, wartime restrictions were making the LBD increasingly popular: a sleeveless or short-sleeved black sheath dress was both versatile and frugal, and a little black dress had the power to make any woman look elegant without great expense. In 1944 *Vogue* declared that 'ten out of ten women have one'. After the war Christian Dior's groundbreaking New Look called for hemlines to drop and skirts to become fuller; the LBD conformed, and by the end of the decade New Look black dresses with softly rounded shoulders, tiny waistlines and padded hips were a staple of cocktail evenings and dinner parties.

Against the backdrop of 1950s sexual conservatism, the LBD returned to its roots as a symbol of the rebellious woman. Hollywood silver-screen femmes fatales and fallen women were often portrayed in low-cut black halter-style dresses that clung daringly to their bodies. In 1946 Rita Hayworth had famously flaunted her curves and va-va-voom in a slinky, floor-length strapless black dress in the film noir *Gilda*, but it is the simple black dress

Still fresh after all these years: a 1950s incarnation of the sleeveless little black dress, modelled by the American songstress Dinah Shore (opposite), and the iconic design worn by a gamine Audrey Hepburn (left) in *Breakfast at Tiffany's* (1961).

Little black dress

with a feathery hem worn by Audrey Hepburn in the romantic comedy *Breakfast at Tiffany's* (1961) that has become the most iconic LBD. Designed by Hubert de Givenchy, and accessorized with pearls and oversized dark glasses, it epitomized cool, understated elegance. After the American first lady and fashion icon Jacqueline Kennedy was photographed in a little black shift in the early 1960s, the style became an emblem of cultivated chic.

The LBD spun its magic once again in the power-dressing 1980s. Expensive-looking styles, worn with sheer stockings and high-heeled, almond-toed court shoes, became the hallmark of the modern businesswoman in and out of the boardroom. Particularly popular were Claude Montana's versions in leather and Azzedine Alaïa's tiny black spandex dresses, as were Jean Paul Gaultier's black corset dresses. Today, with dressed-up glamour back on the catwalks, the LBD is back in vogue. Versatile, flattering and still as beguiling as ever, the little black dress is a tried-and-trusted classic, the sure-fire solution on those occasions when one can't decide what to wear.

Long, short, sleeveless or off the shoulder, the little black dress has remained a fashion staple through the decades.

2. Bell-bottoms

They were immortalized in the song 'Bell Bottom Blues' recorded by Derek and the Dominos in 1970, and have been loved by hippies, funksters and glam rockers. Bell-bottom trousers, one of the twentieth century's most flamboyant fashions, can be traced back to uniforms of the US Navy in the early nineteenth century. Cut into a bell shape from knee to ankle, these trousers were easy to roll up so that they did not become waterlogged when sailors were swabbing the decks, and could be removed over boots.

Only in the mid-1960s did the bell-bottom cross the line from standard naval issue to fashion wear, when trousers that clung to the thigh and flared gently from the mid-calf became popular with both men and women. Pioneered by the British designers John Michael and John Stephen as a reaction to the skinny drainpipes of the Teddy boys, they heralded a more fluid aesthetic. Worn with thinly ribbed jumpers or collarless Nehru shirts and pointed, elastic-sided Chelsea boots, not only were these trousers the epitome of cool, but also they paved the way for the 'anti-fashion', looser flared style of the late 1960s counterculture movement.

Californian hippies rejected chirpy, tidy designs in favour of a more natural style, and by the 1967 'Summer of Love', on the streets of San Francisco's Haight-Ashbury district thousands could be seen wearing tie-dyed T-shirts and scruffy flared trousers (dubbed 'hipsters' because they were worn low on the waist and tight on the hips). This tribal style was co-opted by such big brands as Halston, Dior and Yves Saint Laurent, and then filtered down into mainstream fashion. By 1969 the 'beautiful people' who hung out at trendy

Gently flaring 'boot-cut' bell-bottom jeans emerged in the mid-1990s. As this photograph shows, boots are not mandatory.

Bell-bottoms

clubs and venues, such as Andy Warhol's Factory in New York, could be spotted wearing brightly coloured, slinky hipsters in crushed velvet, accessorized with ruffled blouses and low-slung belts. Soon wide-legged, flared jeans and trousers were worn by everybody and with everything. Men teamed polyester bell-bottoms with suit jackets; women partnered high-waisted pale denim flares with a tight T-shirt and platform shoes. Popular fabrics included heavy crêpes, woollen jersey knits and crisp cottons.

In the 1970s, as fashion became more outrageous and experimental, sexy

tight-fitting bell-bottoms that drew attention to the area around the crotch ushered in a new camp aesthetic. Extra-tight satin trousers, pioneered by funk-music stars James Brown and Sly and the Family Stone, and promoted in such films as *Shaft* (1971) and *Super Fly* (1972), paved the way for the fashion fantasies of the disco look of gold lamé flares, embellished with rhinestones and worn with sparkly waistcoats and leotards.

Since that iconic era, fashion's love affair with bell-bottoms has ebbed and flowed. The version that resurfaced in the mid-1990s proved remarkably flattering: the new flare, described as 'boot cut', was cut slim on the thigh, softly fanning out over the foot. More recently, in 2011, Marc Jacobs, Derek Lam and Gucci all showed bell-bottoms on the catwalks, and retro flares have been spotted on the likes of the model Claudia Schiffer and the actresses January Jones and Mila Kunis, all of whom looked glossy and glamorous. Bell-bottoms, it seems, are here to stay.

In the mid-1960s Cher (above) was among those who went for the casual and simple California look, in which fitted tops exaggerated the large flare of the trouser.

Early fashion bell-bottoms, such as the ones shown opposite from 1966, emphasized a boyish silhouette.

In the late 1960s the blues and rock singer Janis Joplin worked the bell-bottom look with tailored flares and kitten heels.

3. Ballet pump

The comfortable ballerina flat has become a key item of footwear of the twenty-first century. The modern version – soft, low-cut at the front and with a proper lace tie, a stick-on bow and a flat heel for support – is a classic fashion chameleon that can bring a feminine touch to jeans or downplay the girliness of a summer dress.

Today's ballerina flat is a descendant of the soft ballet shoe of the mid-eighteenth century. While ballet shoes had been around since the 1680s, some twenty years after the French king Louis XIV had established the Académie Nationale de Danse, they had heels and buckles. It wasn't until a few decades later, when a French dancer named Marie Camargo removed the heels to help her technique, that the soft, flat ballet shoe was born.

In 1944 ballet shoes crossed over from the stage on to the street. The American designer Claire McCardell commissioned the New York ballet-slipper firm Capezio to make a rugged version for outdoor wear, under the name 'ballerinas', making ballet flats a fashion item. McCardell was looking for a simple shoe to complement her range of revolutionary casual dresses in breezy calico and gingham, and chanced on the idea of the ballet shoe because it was exempt from wartime leather restrictions. Light, comfortable and flexible with a hint of girlie appeal, the new ballerinas proved to be an astounding commercial success.

By the early 1950s ballerina flats had become a quintessential ingredient of the emerging 'teenager' style, and young women would often wear them with fitted shirts and capri pants or circle skirts. Not only did the shoes symbolize post-war women's freedom and comfort, but also they were the perfect footwear for the

Teenage kicks in the 1950s: ballet pumps were the ideal footwear for practising steps and twirls.

The classic ballet pump, cut low at the front and with a little bow, is a speciality of the Menorcan firm Pretty Ballerina, which has been producing this type of shoe since 1918.

fast-moving steps of the jitterbug and rock 'n' roll dances of the time. But it was the actress Audrey Hepburn who catapulted them on to the must-have lists of the international glitterati. In such films as *Roman Holiday* (1953), *Sabrina* (1954) and *Funny Face* (1957), dressed in neat outfits of white shirts, black turtleneck sweaters and ballerinas – designed by her favourite designer, Hubert de Givenchy – she created a new, streamlined model of chic that paved the way for the pared-down style of the early 1960s. The look was appropriated by other actresses, in particular Brigitte Bardot, who asked the French ballet-shoe company Repetto to make her a street-sturdy pair in crimson for her appearance in Roger Vadim's controversial film *And God Created Woman* (1956), giving ballet flats an added sex-kitten appeal.

Ballet flats resurfaced briefly in the mid-1990s with the British shoe designer Emma Pope's quirky velvet brocade slippers. A decade later, in 2005, ballerinas were revitalized by such gamine celebrities as Kate Moss and Sienna Miller, who wore them out on the town with black tights and cut-off shorts. Since then ballet flats have become a staple of modern footwear, worn by women of all ages and all types. They were a preferred choice of footwear for the stylish Carla Bruni-Sarkozy during her husband's presidency of France, at state events both at home and abroad. From the likes of the two-tone satin ballerinas produced by Stella McCartney to workaday foldable models that fit in handbags, these graceful flats can take a woman straight from a work meeting to the school gate to pick up her children, allowing her to run for the bus in between.

4. Jumpsuit

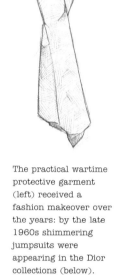

A sexy alternative to the maxi dress or an aesthetic faux pas? The jumpsuit, that all-in-one top-and-trousers that covers the entire body, is one of the most contradictory pieces of fashion. As a figure-hugging garment, it can create a strong, streamlined silhouette that looks glamorous and elegant; yet it can easily be quite unflattering. Despite this, since it entered the fashion vocabulary some sixty years ago, it has repeatedly come back into style.

The jumpsuit started out in the United Kingdom during the Second World War as a purely functional item, a feminine equivalent of workmen's overalls. When the sirens blared out in warning of an impending bombing raid, women reached for their Utility 'siren suit' and threw it on over their clothes before making their way to dirty underground shelters; even

the princesses Elizabeth and Margaret had their own. With its zipped front and wide trouser legs, the siren suit was not only practical but also warm. The aristocratic Elsa Schiaparelli produced beautiful versions in silk with large slouch pockets and hoods, and Digby Morton – a founding member of the Incorporated Society of London Fashion Designers, and among those selected by the British government to create Utility clothing – showed zipped and hooded siren suits in tartan Viyella.

By the 1960s the jumpsuit was no longer a protective piece of clothing but a high-end fashion item. When in 1965 Diana Rigg high-kicked her way to victory over baddies as the spy Emma Peel in the television series *The Avengers*, dressed in a tight leather jumpsuit by John Bates (who often designed under the name Jean Varon), her outfit sparked a trend that

The practical wartime protective garment (left) received a fashion makeover over the years: by the late 1960s shimmering jumpsuits were appearing in the Dior collections (below).

André Courrèges
adopted the sexy
halter-neck style
for his white 'bunny'
jumpsuit of 1969.

would last for more than two decades. Lithe young women took to sexy, shocking wet-look all-in-ones, accessorized with transparent plastic macs and calf-length boots. After a teenage Twiggy modelled Betsey Johnson's skintight leather jumpsuit with zips all the way down the legs in *Vogue* in 1966, the garment sold out immediately. Other notable versions included André Courrèges's 'space age' jumpsuits, featuring cut-out holes and paired with helmet-style hats, and futuristic designs by Pierre Cardin.

The fashion for jumpsuits continued into the 1970s. The luxury jumpsuit with wide trousers and halter-neck top, a sure-fire route to instant glamour, was appropriate for evening wear. For dances, dinners and parties, all-in-ones in such sensuous fabrics as gold and silver lamé, embellished with appliqué or sequins, were worn with high-heeled strappy sandals and the fashionable turban. Tight on the bottom and loose around the leg, these seductive garments granted freedom of movement and were designed to showcase the new keep-fit body ideal. Stretchy Lycra jumpsuits were popular with the trendy crowd at New York's Studio 54 nightclub; in particular, Norma Kamali's backless jersey jumpsuits encapsulated the wit and glamour of the 1970s New York scene and were shown to advantage by such celebrities and leggy models as Jerry Hall and Bianca Jagger.

The jumpsuit adapted to the fashionable silhouette throughout the 1980s, gaining shoulder pads, a nipped-in waist and more loosely fitting trousers. Thierry Mugler's diamanté-studded white cotton gaberdine jumpsuit, with its wide shoulders, represented the hard glamour

of the decade. Also the height of fashion were jumpsuits in femme-fatale leathers and bright pink parachute silk.

Today the jumpsuit is a chic option once again. Edgy yet practical, sexy yet emancipated, the 'onesie' has been reworked to skim the body in a flattering way. From a sleek black Yves Saint Laurent halter-neck version in silk crêpe to Baby Phat's denim jumpsuit and Vanessa Bruno's all-in-one with spaghetti straps and cropped leg, there is a jumpsuit style to suit anyone, and you don't have to be a six-foot model to wear one.

The American actress Rashida Jones in 2007 in a jumpsuit by the cult New York label Ruffian, established by the designers Brian Wolk and Claude Morais.

5. Plaid shirt

Comfortable, hard-wearing and quintessentially all-American, the chunky checked shirt is the opposite of sexy, and more about laid-back cool. Worn tucked into cut-off shorts or cinched over leggings, this versatile top can be the ultimate in feminine rough-and-ready chic, retaining echoes of its heritage as the functional flannel shirt worn by hard-toiling frontiersmen and hulking woodsmen in late nineteenth-century America. The shirt's warmth and durability later made it a favourite with hunters and railway workers, too. Mail-order catalogues of the 1920s featured a huge selection of checked 'lumberjack' shirts for male workwear.

The growth of leisure time in post-war America created a new casualness in dress, giving rise to a wide range of sports-style men's shirts. Smart plaid shirts, in Indian madras, Aertex and Viyella, were produced by such companies as Hathaway, Brooks Brothers and J. Press. Advertisements in *Esquire*, *Apparel Arts* and other publications showed handsome models in plaids and chinos, fishing or camping in spectacular scenery; by the mid-1950s smart plaid shirts teamed with corduroy or drip-dry trousers had become an essential part of the weekend wardrobe and the ultimate in college-boy chic. Women had the option of elegant tailored checked shirts to wear with slacks and ballet pumps, heralding the beginning of a casual unisex style that has endured through the decades.

In the late 1950s groups of young people in rumpled lumberjack shirts, tatty jeans and torn sweaters populated the jazz cafes of San Francisco and New York's Greenwich Village. These were the freewheeling beat poets, writers and disaffected college youth, who wore their

Double-dating at an American diner in 1953: smart plaid shirts and wholesome soda drinks.

Plaid shirt

sloppy uniform as a signifier of societal protest. For them, the plaid shirt was a badge of working-class authenticity, and a sartorial distancing from 'straight' society. The image of the cropped plaid shirt of the 1970s was very different: as the keep-fit body became fashionable, tops and jumpers were cut short to show off a toned midriff. Jean- and bell-bottom-clad young women knotted their plaid shirts under the bust.

The casual, brightly coloured flannel plaid shirt made a comeback in the 1980s, when it would be worn over a clashing striped T-shirt and with a pair of leggings. Flannel plaid shirts worn with tatty jeans, dirty trainers and beanie hats were the building blocks of countercultural chic in the early 1990s. This low-budget look was the anti-fashion choice of the Seattle grunge bands, such as Nirvana and Pearl Jam; their grunge-kid fans took to wearing

Casual chic: a 1940s ensemble of plaid shirt and shorts (opposite) from the Korday label; left, part of the debut collection from the Material Girl label (launched by Madonna and her daughter Lourdes) in 2010, featuring lace insets below the shoulders.

second-hand plaid shirts with ragged jumpers and combat trousers as an antidote to high fashion. In 1992 the look was taken to the runway in Marc Jacobs's Grunge collection for the Perry Ellis brand. Featuring luxurious but rumpled silk plaid shirts and cashmere thermals, the collection shocked the fashion press but struck a chord with other high-end designers; the upmarket plaid was born. Today the lumberjack is still in vogue, with vintage-style plaids a feature of recent collections by Isabel Marant, Marc Jacobs and Roberto Cavalli. Whether she wears it loose, over a T-shirt and shorts (à la Lindsay Lohan and Rihanna), or tightly fitted, with skinny jeans (Elle Macpherson, Charlize Theron), every woman, it seems, is expressing her inner lumberjack.

Tied in a knot, cropped, tucked in or left open over a T-shirt, the 'lumberjack' shirt was a staple of the 1990s grunge movement.

6. Denim jacket

The cowboy essential taken up by such icons as Steve McQueen has undergone many design changes through the decades.

Bleached, cropped, oversized, classic … in any of its many forms, the denim jacket is a unisex fashion staple. The jacket that started out in the United States as rugged workwear has been revamped and repackaged to such an extent that it can now be worn to the office, out to dinner and on to the red carpet all in the same day.

The jean jacket dates back to the late nineteenth century, and followed the first blue jeans as utilitarian outdoor wear for agricultural workers, ranch hands and workmen. The hard-wearing Levi Strauss 506 'pleat-front blouse' was launched in 1905; it was so popular that a cheaper version, the 213, was produced for the impoverished dust-bowl farmers and the hard-working, hard-drinking cowboys of the early twentieth century. The denim jacket crossed over into leisurewear when, along with blue jeans, it was mythologized in the 'all singing, all dancing' cowboy films of the 1930s and 1940s. Crooner Bing Crosby was a huge fan of top-to-toe denim, and wore his Levi 506 jacket on and off stage, further boosting its popularity.

In 1932 a garment that would revolutionize the jean jacket was launched by the jeanswear company Lee. The firm's Slim 101J jacket, aimed at cowboys, was shorter and slimmer than the Levi Strauss pleated garment, and it became the blueprint for the classic denim jacket as it is known today. Lee followed this with the Storm Rider 101LJ, blanket-lined for extra warmth and with a corduroy collar; it was instantly recognizable, and its effortless, masculine appeal made it iconic. In the 1950s and 1960s it was worn by such tough-but-tender film anti-heroes as Paul Newman (who wore a

Storm Rider with a pair of faded jeans and a studied air of indifference in the western *Hud*, released in 1963) and Steve McQueen (who gave the denim jacket a shot of rebel chic when he wore it out on the town), and the denim jacket went on to cover the backs of outsiders and 'bad boys'. Splattered with engine oil and covered in badges and insignia, it became the prized garment of biker gangs; Mods wore denim jackets with smart trousers and Ben Sherman shirts (a label established in 1965 specifically to compete with the American shirts the Mods had taken to); and the skinheads gave the jacket a tough edge when they teamed it with bovver boots and a two-finger salute to conventional society in the late 1960s.

It wasn't until the mid-1970s that the denim jacket lost its rebellious edge and became an integral part of the casual weekend wardrobe – so much so that pairing blue jeans with a denim jacket ('double denim') became a fashion statement. In what was arguably one of the greatest fashion faux pas of that decade, women wore hip-length or cropped denim jackets with flared jeans. The band Status Quo made double denim synonymous with dodgy, head-banging rock fans, yet this questionable fashion choice reappeared in the mid-1980s.

Today the denim jacket has made a comeback, and it was featured in the 2011 fashion shows by such design houses as Balmain, Gucci and Dolce & Gabbana. The type that is most popular with celebrities and 'ordinary' women alike is a faded retro denim jacket loaded with authenticity and cowboy associations, which can toughen up a light summer dress or give an ordinary outfit a hint of rock-chick appeal. The dependable denim jacket is a sartorial cure-all that will not be fading away any time soon.

A young woman in denim jacket poses outside the Ritz in London.

Rihanna may be one of the bestselling singers of all time, but dress-down denim jacket and cut-off shorts were her choice of attire on a visit in London in 2012.

7. Slip dress

Underwear-as-outerwear is one of fashion's more playful offerings, and there is nothing more beguiling than the slip dress. Unstructured, clingy and light as a feather, it is the definition of girlie simplicity. With its thin spaghetti straps and its lacy edges, this slinky descendant of the petticoat also carries with it a sense of semi-nakedness that draws attention to the body, giving it powerful sex appeal. Adored by aspiring starlets, mega movie stars and any woman who dares to bare in the name of style, the slip dress can be show-stoppingly erotic.

The slip dates back to the 1920s, when the streamlined 'flapper' dresses of the age required feminine undergarments in order to hang properly. These new-style chemises – highly decorative, deliberately sensual and often transparent – were the forerunner of today's fashion slip. Made of rayon ('artificial silk'), crêpe de Chine or silk tricot, they were smooth and soft to the touch, and were considered to be the height of luxury. Cut from fine chiffon, and embellished with black lace on the bodice and hem, the near-invisible, intimate slip was an added touch of glamour when worn under a diaphanous beaded party dress or a kimono-style wrap.

The slip continued to be worn in the 1930s and 1940s, changing its shape and hemline as the fashions of the day required. During the 1950s, however, as American regulations regarding advertising were relaxed, the language of lingerie was changed forever. In 1958 the US company Maidenform promoted its bras and slips on television for the first time. *Vogue* and the other glossies showed beautiful women in their underclothes, bringing the intimacy of lingerie into the public domain. The slip took on a sexy image in the bedroom thanks to the silver screen: curvaceous slip-clad stars (think, for example, of Elizabeth Taylor in *Cat on a Hot Tin Roof*, 1958, or *Butterfield 8*, 1960; and Janet Leigh in *Psycho*, also 1960) sparked demand for similar styles in boutiques and shopping malls all over America.

The slip moved out of the bedroom and into the fashion arena in the 1990s with the advent of the waif look and a desire

Slip dress

The screen siren Elizabeth Taylor and her fitted slip turn up the heat in the emotional drama *Butterfield 8* (1960).

for a more feminine style of dress. Skinny, androgynous-looking models sashayed down the catwalk in flimsy, sheer slip dresses that were the antidote to the 1980s power suit. Such designers as Thierry Mugler, Dolce & Gabbana and Jean Paul Gaultier gave us silken slip dresses in black, leopard print or pretty pinks that harked back to the 1950s undergarment. At once flirty, flimsy and purposefully provocative, they were a new take on feminine chic. Of particular note were Collette Dinnigan's sweet-as-candy slip dresses in light pink, peach and cream of 1998, and, the following year, John Galliano's collection of bias-cut silk slip dresses, which sold like hot cakes. Distressed camisoles and slips were the preferred look of such idiosyncratic 'grunge' figures as the American Courtney Love; in London in 1993, a nineteen-year-old pre-global-superstardom Kate Moss

daringly wore a totally transparent full-length slip dress for the Elle Model Agency Look of the Year party.

Today the slip dress is part of any fashionable woman's wardrobe, and a constant feature on the catwalks. Whether teamed with dainty kitten heels and a cardigan, or dressed down with a denim jacket and biker boots, the slip will never lose its aura of boudoir chic.

The French actress Virginie Ledoyen (above) shows off the rumpled look in a delicate bias-cut slip dress in 1997; the version shown left is more tailored and dress-like, but retains the classic lace trim.

8. Bikini

The radical design of the tiny 1940s bikini has had an enduring impact. These four triangles of fabric that strategically conceal and reveal the erotic zones of the female body made sunbathing sexy and fun.

Two-piece swimsuits came into fashion towards the end of the 1930s, when stretch fabrics and the newly invented nylon allowed them to be quite sophisticated. The bottom half, which always covered the navel, was elasticized in the manner of a foundation garment, while the substantial bra top provided uplift. By the 1940s take-up of the two-piece was increasing, and it was popularized in Hollywood movies. The first bikini, a reduced two-piece, was unveiled in 1946 at the Molitor swimming pool in Paris. It was designed by Louis Réard, a former car engineer; he named it after the South Pacific atoll in which the atomic bomb tests were being conducted because he predicted that the costume (which according to his firm 'wasn't a bikini unless it could be pulled through a wedding ring') would be 'highly explosive'. After catwalk models had refused to wear his creation on grounds of indecency, Réard turned to the dancer Micheline Bernardini to parade it. Pictures of her were flashed around the world, shocking polite society.

The new swimming costume was banned in such countries as Spain, Portugal and Italy. It failed to take off in the United States, where women thought it lacking in decency; as late as 1957, *Modern Girl* magazine was commenting that 'It is hardly necessary to waste words over the so-called bikini since it is inconceivable that any girl with tact and decency would ever wear such a thing'. But the bikini was an immediate sensation at Cannes and other French resorts, and was worn

Bikini-clad Bond girl Ursula Andress steps out from the sea in *Dr No* (1962); her bikini was created by the costume designer Tessa Prendergast. A survey conducted by Channel 4 in 2003 put this scene at the top of the '100 Greatest Sexy Moments'.

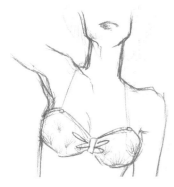

mostly by French starlets and Hollywood screen sirens; in 1955 Jayne Mansfield even attended a ball wearing nothing but a leopard-print bikini, and the British actress Diana Dors shocked onlookers – and the world's press – when she wore a mink bikini at the Venice Film Festival. Other landmarks in the evolution of the bikini include Brigitte Bardot on the beach in *And God Created Woman* (1956), and Ursula Andress emerging dripping from the sea in a white bikini, complete with belt buckle and scabbard, in the Bond film *Dr No* (1962). These seminal moments helped to promote the bikini and increase sales.

By the 1960s, with the emergence of youth culture, the bikini was finally deemed 'safe', and it featured heavily in a rash of squeaky-clean teen movies with such titles as *Beach Party* (1963) and *Bikini Beach* (1964). In 1964 *Sports*

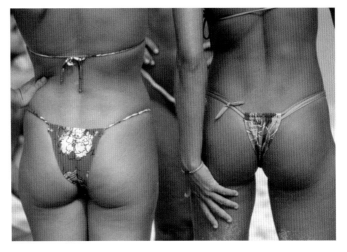

Illustrated magazine published its first swimsuit issue (now an annual event), and *Vogue* and *Harper's Bazaar* featured a slew of bikini-clad models in structured bra tops and hip-hugging briefs. The bikini became ever smaller, heralding the string bikini or 'tanga', an assemblage of tiny triangles of cloth held together with ties at the hip and neck. But it was to get skimpier still, and in the early 1980s the thong bikini – little more than a small triangle of material at the front and a narrow strip reaching round to the waistband at the back, dividing the buttocks – was taken up by women willing to put modesty aside in pursuit of the all-over tan.

Since then, bikinis have covered up. Sports bikinis with racer-back tops and short briefs resulted from the fitness craze of the late 1980s; other versions include the 'tankini', a two-piece that provides almost as much coverage as a one-piece, and more recently cropped 'boy shorts'. Today the bikini is a staple of swimwear fashion, and an essential part of any beach wardrobe.

In the 1980s the minimal 'tanga' bikini design (as seen on the beach at Ipanema, Brazil, above) maximized tanning, while the new athletic look inspired fashion houses to design the more conservative 'tankini' (left).

9. Leather trousers

Sleek and attention-grabbing, leather trousers have been an emblem of cool since the 1960s, when such controversial rock stars as Jim Morrison, Lou Reed and Jimi Hendrix popularized the look. The lure of leather is undeniable when it is worn super-tight; but, for women, when leather trousers are teamed with a crisp white shirt and a pair of ballet flats, they offer an unconventional combination of ladylike and sexy.

While the Texan cowboys of the 1870s wore a form of leather trousers, their chaps covered their legs and buckled on over trousers but had no seat and were not joined at the crotch. It was only when the motorcycle was invented in the late nineteenth century that riders took to wearing full leather trousers to protect the lower body. By the early 1950s these had become the signature garment of rabble-rousing biker gangs, worn with a matching black leather jacket and biker boots, and were associated with motorcycle toughs and 'bad boys'. With only a slight toning down of the look, leather trousers were enthusiastically taken up later in the decade by such young rock 'n' roll stars as Gene Vincent and Eddie Cochran.

Women got in on the act in the early 1970s. The trailblazing rock chicks Suzi Quatro and Chrissie Hynde, eager to distance themselves from the dolly-bird image of female singers, regularly wore black leather trousers as a symbol of empowerment. With the heritage of tight, hip-hugging leather trousers now firmly established in music, they also became standard wear for head-banging heavy rockers (worn, if not bare-chested, then with a scruffy T-shirt), while punk rockers preferred them paint-splattered, slashed or studded, as a symbol of alienation.

By the end of the decade leather trousers had trickled down from the street and were being reinterpreted as high-fashion items. The French designers Claude Montana and Thierry Mugler had the most impact on leather fashion, and their unstructured, loose leather trousers brought glamour to the look. Teamed with wide-shouldered leather jackets and high-heeled black court shoes, their creations

Jean Paul Gaultier constrasts tough, sleek leather trousers with a soft crushed-velvet top in a ready-to-wear collection of 2000.

Leather trousers

In the 2010s, the leather-trouser style of choice is a grown-up luxe alternative to the skinny jean: from Isabel Marant's cropped red leather variant, to the contemporary take on rock-chick chic by Yves Saint Laurent, super-tight shiny black trousers are the look of the moment. Sexy and shapely, they look good dressed down with a grey mottled marl sweatshirt and high-top sneakers for day, or dressed up with a pair of stilettos for evening.

Left: The model and socialite Poppy Delevingne keeps the leather-chic style simple at London Fashion Week in February 2012.

Below: Jim Morrison of the Doors on stage in 1968.

produced an uncompromising silhouette that symbolized the post-feminist woman. Expensive, luxurious and sensual, leather was the new status symbol, especially such designer items as Calvin Klein's neutral-coloured trousers (to be paired with a camel-toned jumper), Oscar de la Renta's diamanté-trimmed versions or Gianni Versace's bright blue femme-fatale leather jodhpurs – all from the very late 1970s and early 1980s. The leather fetish gear of the Goth and Perv subcultures led to a trend for high-glam versions in the early 1990s. These were encapsulated by Versace's Bondage collection of 1992, which featured rhinestone-encrusted leather trousers, and Mugler's slashed 'second-skin' leather leggings.

10. Shirtwaister

Shirtwaister

The shirtwaister, with its (usually) button-down front and no-nonsense utilitarian style, is an archetypal American fashion. A staple among 1950s housewives and career girls alike, plus the occasional sultry Hollywood actress, it is still a conservative classic, its elegant, practical chic earning it a place of honour in any woman's wardrobe.

The original shirtwaister – a plain cotton dress with buttons down the front, based on the design of a man's shirt – started its career in the United States in the early twentieth century as a nurse's uniform. Trim and smart, it went on to dress the new working women of the

1920s, who were taking up jobs in schools and offices after the First World War. In the following decade the cotton 'shirtmaker frock' was sold as a dress for golf and tennis, but its easy-to-wear simplicity soon brought it into the fashion mainstream.

By the early 1940s the *Ladies' Home Journal* and *Good Housekeeping* featured advertisements for 'classic shirtwaists' for both day and evening, and at all price points. Under the Traina-Norell label, the quintessential American designer brand of the 1940s, Norman Norell contributed elegant daytime shirtwaisters with wide shoulders and narrow skirts. Glamorous, full-skirted versions, with nipped-in waists and rounded shoulders, exploded on to the fashion scene in 1947 with Christian Dior's New Look, which reworked the shirtwaister into an haute-couture item that was hailed as the 'new femininity' by *Harper's Bazaar*.

This image of a young woman modelling a shirtwaister in Glen tartan wool in the late 1930s illustrates the longevity of the style.

The British-American actress Julianne Moore, photographed in 2007, shows a contemporary take on the genre.

Page 35: The well-dressed 1950s woman's travelling outfit, as snapped by the *Vogue* photographer Frances McLaughlin-Gill (designer unknown).

The 1970s American shirtwaister, a staple of the modern woman's capsule wardrobe, had an air of casual luxury that made it suitable for all occasions. Shown below is a dress by the American designer Gene Berk.

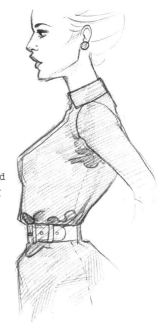

Indeed, the shirtwaister, more than any other garment, revealed the fashion priorities of the 1950s. Throughout that decade, the emphasis was on conformity and marriage, and such magazines as *Vogue* and *Women's Wear Daily* reinforced these notions with articles on how to dress appropriately and on how to 'look pretty for your husband'. The shirtwaister dress was often cited, as not only was it demure and respectable, but also it could be worn at any time of day. The 1950s incarnation – often produced in that era's boldly patterned fabrics, or in such lively colours as emerald, candy-pink and coral – featured either a straight or a full skirt, three-quarter-length sleeves and feminine, soft shoulders. This was identikit fashion: a nation of women was influenced by such iconic American TV sitcom mums as Donna Reed (*The Donna Reed Show*), Lucille Ball (*I Love Lucy*) and Barbara Billingsley (*Leave It to Beaver*) in their hallmark shirtwaisters.

The shirtwaist dress was reinterpreted for the busy working woman in the early 1970s, when such American designers as Calvin Klein, Roy Halston and Ralph Lauren created realistic, wearable clothes in which women could both run for the bus and go out for dinner. The classic button-through shirtwaister was unpretentious, easy to wear and determined to be 'real'. Worn either cinched or loose, with a few buttons left undone at the bottom to reveal tanned legs, and paired with strappy sandals or pumps, it had a crisp, minimalist feel that defined the 'natural woman' of the 1970s and was the epitome of all-American sexy.

Since those glory days the shirtwaister has come back into fashion every time the 1950s look is parodied on the catwalk. Donna Karan gave us 1950s-style,

wasp-waisted shirtwaisters in 2007, and in 2010 Lauren, Diane von Furstenberg and Tory Burch were among the designers that referenced America's fashion roots with reworked versions in bright silver and gold, glammed up with high stilettos. Whatever its style, the shirtwaister remains the epitome of simplified, restrained chic that showcases the woman, not the dress.

11. Flip-flop

Today's flip-flop has its roots in the Japanese *zori*, illustrated opposite in an eighteenth-century woodblock print by Kitagawa Utamaro.

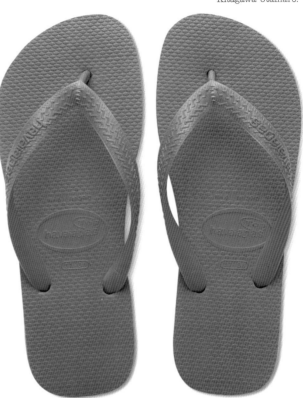

Flip-flops, the ultimate signifier of carefree summer living, are these days also among the coolest urban footwear around; so much so that in 2009 the actress Halle Berry elected to attend a red-carpet premiere in a simple black pair. Essentially just a sole attached to the foot by a two-pronged strap that is anchored between the toes, the flip-flop is one of the oldest forms of footwear. Variations of this most basic of sandals could be found in ancient African, Eastern and Egyptian cultures, where they were made from papyrus, rice straw, rawhide or other materials, depending on the region. The oldest surviving examples of such footwear, dating from around 1500 BC and made from papyrus, are on display in the British Museum in London. The precursor to the modern flip-flop, however, was the Japanese *zori*, a woven-soled item of footwear that was brought to the West by American soldiers returning from the Second World War.

The first mass-produced rubber versions are often said to have been manufactured in post-war New Zealand, and were known as 'Jandals', an abbreviation of 'Japanese sandals'. By the mid-1950s flip-flops had begun to be worn on the beaches of California; they soon became available from every dime store in every American town. Away from the beach, the flip-flop formed part of the new casual fashion for comfortable, practical attire. Young people took to wearing theirs with summer skirts, shorts or capri pants for picnics and other outings. Later the beatniks took it up as their sandal of choice: worn with jeans and a T-shirt, the eminently affordable flip-flop was the perfect anti-establishment piece of footwear.

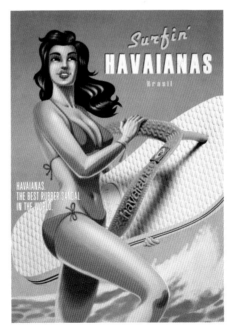

The Brazilian Havaiana flip-flop has become a cult item on the beach, in the city and, since 2003, even at the Academy Awards ceremony, at which each nominee receives an exclusive model of the sandal.

Flip-flop

Flat sandals complemented the new mini fashions of the 1960s, and jewel-encrusted leather flip-flops were a popular style. Upmarket New Yorkers and leggy models could now wear them with fashionable pyjama-style trousers, floaty minidresses and patterned leggings. At the other end of the fashion scale, 'flower power' and the 'hippy trail' introduced the leather version of the flip-flop – the 'Jesus sandal', a V-strap sandal imported from such countries as Mexico and India that became part of the hippy uniform of jeans and cheesecloth shirts. As ethnic fashions

carried over into the 1970s, such designers as Yohji Yamamoto and Issey Miyake introduced reworked Japanese clothing to a Western audience. Their multicoloured Japanese *zori* were particularly popular with the fashion crowd, and accessorized the era's sarongs and kaftans.

By the early twenty-first century a new brand of flip-flop had burst on to the international fashion scene. Havaianas – produced since the 1960s in Brazil, where they are worn by almost everyone of almost any class – popped up in the boutiques of New York, London and other cities around the world; it is now estimated that some 50,000 Havaianas are sold every day. Clearly Jennifer Aniston, possibly Hollywood's most stalwart flip-flop wearer, is not alone in her choice of off-duty footwear. They come in rubber or leather; are coloured gold, silver, or a myriad of other hues, plain or adorned with sparkling sequins or artificial flowers; and can be paired with shorts, smart trousers or floaty summer dresses. Small wonder that flip-flops are now the coolest way to remain comfortable in the urban jungle.

California cool from top to toe: Jamie Lee Curtis in 1983, laid back in beach-lifestyle footwear.

Gwen Stefani in 1998, before the singer recorded her solo albums away from the group No Doubt, in platform flip-flops at the MTV Video Music Awards in Los Angeles.

12. Pea coat

It is difficult to think of any coat that has had such enduring appeal as the naval pea coat. With its clean lines, its sharp, masculine style and its associations with maritime bravura, the dark, double-breasted woollen jacket has influenced fashion and popular style since the beginning of the twentieth century. Worn by rebels, hipsters, rock stars and style icons across the decades, it is the ultimate smart-casual jacket while also carrying a touch of nautical glamour.

The British Royal Navy developed the pea coat (also known as the pea jacket) in the mid-nineteenth century, from the warm reefer jacket worn on deck by previous generations of seamen when rigging and reefing (adjusting the sails). It became standard naval issue in 1857. A few years later it was taken up by the United States Navy, and its hip-length, double-breasted

The double-breasted, gold-button pea coat was a standard item of casual chic for the sailing set of the mid-1960s. Here a version by the label Claret is modelled by a Miss Katherine Ellis, a student at the American liberal-arts college of Bryn Mawr in Pennsylvania. Her friend, a David Felsen, wears a similar jacket.

M21 model became the quintessential navy outerwear: thick, dark navy-blue woollen cloth, with slash pockets, broad lapels and large, shiny buttons.

The pea coat came into its own in the movies. One early appearance was in *The Frisco Kid* (1935), in which James Cagney wore the jacket in his role as an Irish hoodlum, bringing an aura of proletarian chic to this functional garment. It went on to appear in a slew of naval films, and its appeal was further enhanced after heart-throb Steve McQueen wore a model provided by Alpha Industries, a supplier to the American defence forces, in the war film *The Sand Pebbles* (1966).

The garment's ruggedness made the pea coat a favourite with the American beatniks of the 1950s, who expressed both their disdain for shiny materialism and their search for a new vision by

Mind that sailor! Paulette Goddard suffers the attentions of a pea coat-wearing mariner in the film *Anna Lucasta* (1949).

Pea coat

complementing the jacket with jeans and striped Breton tops or black polo necks. But pea coats really got 'with it' in the early 1960s, when such new British bands as the Rolling Stones, the Kinks and the Beatles – all soon to become megastars – teamed them with sexy narrow trousers and Chelsea boots. Pop singers had become the new style leaders; any outfit they adopted immediately became a fashion trend, and top-end designers took up their styles. In particular, Yves Saint Laurent, whose popularity rested partly on his appropriation of such utilitarian garments as the safari jacket, glorified the pea coat in luxurious fabrics and created a new fashion template for the upmarket woman. The pea coat featured in his ready-to-wear boutique, Rive Gauche in Paris (set up in the mid-1960s), alongside long denim skirts and lace-up boots. In the United States, style icon Jacqueline Kennedy's habit of wearing her pea coat over a polo-neck sweater gave it a dash of Ivy League glamour.

By the middle of the 1960s, reefer detailing was everywhere in fashion. From jackets with big gold buttons to double-breasted, mini nautical coats and the fitted pea coats by the British label Foale and Tuffin, navy chic was a dominant look of the decade. Since that time, the pea coat for women has reappeared with every androgynous trend, and in 2011 pea coats – now more glamorous and sexy – were once again big news on the catwalks. Labels as diverse as Marc Jacobs, Yves Saint Laurent and Ralph Lauren have brought us tailored pea jackets in lambswool or cashmere, in pale pink, in cream and (still) in classic navy. Always easy to wear, the pea coat is the ultimate in comfort cool.

Two young models look shipshape and stylish in 1965 in tailored, full-length woollen pea coats (designer unknown).

Opposite: The American artist Howard Chandler Christy presented an alluring image of the pea coat in one of his Navy recruitment posters during the First World War.

I WANT YOU

for THE NAVY

Howard Chandler Christy 1917.

13. Trouser suit

The evolution of the trouser suit, as worn by women, has articulated female aspirations for almost the past hundred years. While today the trouser suit (a pair of trousers and a matching or coordinating coat or jacket) is a mainstay in many a woman's wardrobe, this set of tailored garments was once considered to be utterly scandalous. In Paris, a rule was introduced in late 1799 banning women

Marlene Dietrich in 1933. She was by then a Hollywood star, and broke the boundaries of gender style by adopting a man's suit as her signature style. She caused a stir, but the look was declared an instant trend by stylists.

from dressing 'like a man' unless they received permission from the city's main police station; this was amended in 1892 to permit trouser-wearing for women 'holding the reins of a horse', and again in 1909 for women 'on a bicycle or holding it by the handlebars'. Only in 2011 were steps taken to repeal the ban altogether.

By the 1920s women in the United Kingdom and United States had won the right to vote, and some flaunted their emancipation in what was thought of as extreme ways. These proto-feminists adopted tailored men's suits, including waistcoats, and the very short, slicked-down Eton crop hairstyle.

Only with the hijacking of men's tailoring by Yves Saint Laurent in 1966, when he introduced the sleek, streamlined outfit he dubbed *le smoking*, did the tailored women's trouser suit enter the fashion mainstream. While trousers had been worn for some time as sport and lounge wear, his was an altogether different concept, one that not only transformed the way women dressed but also put them on equal sartorial footing with men. Forget

The three-piece woman's trouser suit by Yves Saint Laurent (pictured here in 1967) brought the style into the fashion mainstream.

bra-burning, it was the mannish trouser suit that knocked the dolly bird off her gilded perch and became the first real article of 'power dressing'.

It had taken a Frenchman to start the revolution, but it was American designers who went on to popularize the look. By the early 1970s the gender-bender trouser suit had become the symbol of the woman who 'wanted it all', and battalions of pinstripe-suited women strode across that decade's landscape with a copy of Germaine Greer's revolutionary book *The Female Eunuch* (1970) under their arm. Calvin Klein, Roy Halston, Ralph Lauren and Bill Blass reworked the men's classics as part of their mix-and-match wardrobes for 'real working women'. Lauren launched a sharply tailored tweed suit; Klein produced grey flannel day suits that were smart, businesslike and sexy. The glamorous heroines of such popular TV series as *Charlie's Angels* helped to promote the look when they wore their pinstriped suits on screen, and the leggy clothes horses Jerry Hall and Veruschka inspired legions of fans when they modelled the suits in *Vogue*, *Nova* and a slew of other magazines. One of the biggest influences was Diane Keaton in Woody Allen's film *Annie Hall* (1977). Her kooky outfits of loose masculine trousers teamed with a man's shirt and tie, waistcoat and jacket helped to promote this new unisex fashion.

The 1980s trouser suit was not so much an outfit as a weapon. Huge shoulder pads, oversized men's-style jackets, peg-top gathered trousers and brogues made an assertive statement. Giorgio Armani, Donna Karan and Gianni Versace created simply tailored mannish suits in soft tweeds and fashionable plaid fabrics that

The supermodel Elle MacPherson in a classically tailored white three-piece suit in 2012. The flowing trousers give the outfit a luxurious tone.

were sometimes accessorized with braces, ties and cufflinks. In particular, Armani's beautifully made trousers and draped tailored jackets in luxury fabrics signified businesslike chic while also projecting a new kind of androgynous sensuality.

Today, while the classic trouser suit is still one of the professional woman's favourite ensembles, there are new reworked versions in feminine styles and bright colours. From Dolce & Gabbana's white edgy cuts with cleavage-hugging jackets, to the sultry look of the black tux worn with needle-thin stilettos (think of Angelina Jolie on the red carpet), the modern trouser suit is for the kick-ass woman who wants to walk tall and look sexy at the same time.

14. Hot pants

'Is bad taste a bad thing?' asked *Vogue* in 1971, as fashion became ever more outrageous. Despite stiff competition from platform boots and bell-bottom trousers, it was hot pants, the shortest of shorts, that proved to be one of the decade's most flamboyant and shocking garments. These petite shorts have flirted with fashion's edgier side ever since their 1970s glory days, reappearing every time the catwalk ramps up the shock factor.

Short shorts date from the 1930s, as seaside pursuits and other sporting activities became popular and beachwear a serious matter. Often in white, they became beachwear essentials. Jean Patou's swimsuit shorts in crêpe de Chine, worn with rubber sandals, were the apogee of

chic on the boardwalks of the Venice Lido and other fashionable European resorts. A decade later the two-piece playsuit, with its midriff-revealing top and tiny shorts, appeared as fashion wear. Crisp cotton shorts by such American brands as Koret, Jantzen and Cole of California became an integral part of the weekend wardrobe, to be slipped on for barbecues and beach parties. They were cute rather than overtly sexy, but they certainly showed an expanse of leg. Such 1940s pin-ups and starlets as Betty Grable (whose legs are said to have been insured by her studio for $1 million) and Marilyn Monroe often teamed them with little jumpers and wedge sandals.

Tight, bottom-skimming shorts first emerged on the European fashion scene in 1970. The mini had been pronounced dead, and the calf-length midi skirt was being promoted in its stead. Yet fashion still liked to shock, and whether it was a backlash against the midi silhouettes or a follow-on from the late 1960s micro-mini, the craze for teeny shorts exploded on to the streets. By 1971 the style had reached mainstream America, where *Women's Wear Daily* coined the term 'hot pants'. These figure-revealing, fun and sexy micro-shorts were the new fashion sensation. Young women wore them with skinny-ribbed tank tops or halter tops, teamed with coloured tights and platform boots. The less daring could opt for offering only a glimpse of their shorts through slit dresses and skirts. This option, however, was never taken up by the actress Catherine Bach in the long-running American television series *The Dukes of Hazzard* (1979–85); her cut-off denim hot pants became so familiar that they were affectionately known as 'Daisy Dukes', after the name of the character

Left: Tight, bottom-skimming hot pants emerged in the early 1970s as an alternative to the miniskirt.

Catherine Bach in the early 1980s, wearing her 'Daisy Duke' denim hot pants, in a promotional image for the television series *The Dukes of Hazzard*.

she played in the series. At about the same time, the disco era brought in a fashion for wearing satin hot pants and tight T-shirts.

In the early 1970s couture designers and upmarket labels offered this unabashedly sexy new style to the international set of 'beautiful people': Yves Saint Laurent paired superbly cut hot pants with boleros, Krizia produced cotton jersey versions, and Katharine Hamnett went for appliquéd hot pants with matching waistcoats.

After disappearing from view for a short while, hot pants returned in the mid-1990s thanks to 'girl power' and such pop groups as the Spice Girls, whose raunchy stage outfits were copied by a generation of young women. But perhaps the most notorious hot pants of recent times have been the gold lamé pair that appeared to have been spray-painted on to Kylie Minogue in the video for her single 'Spinning Around' (2000). Today thighs are on full display again, as hot pants, and in particular cut-off shorts, have come striding back into fashion. When Beyoncé headlined the Glastonbury music festival in 2011, she wore black hot pants that were so short they were covered by her jacket; Kate Moss pairs hers with wellington boots and a gold quilted Chanel

bomber jacket; and young women of all sorts wear cropped shorts with black tights and ballet pumps. Whatever the style, whether dressed down with flats or worn with high strappy sandals, hot pants have lost none of their flirt appeal.

More luxurious fabrics characterize high-couture hot pants, as seen here in Sonja Rykiel's collection for Spring/Summer 1997.

15. Black leather jacket

Rebellion was in the air when a youthful Marlon Brando rode into the American consciousness in 1953 in *The Wild One*. As Johnny, a mixed-up, angry young man with a penchant for outfits of white T-shirt, battered jeans and black leather jacket (by Perfecto Brand, made by the American company Schott), Brando was the epitome of macho cool and brooding magnetism. He was also the leader of a motorcycle gang, and at the time these gangs were seen as a threat to the social order. The film caused alarm (it was banned in the United Kingdom until 1967) but the black leather jacket, with its hard sheen and aura of menace, became the symbol of disaffected youth, going on to influence teenagers throughout the 1950s and beyond.

In common with many iconic items of street wear, the Perfecto jacket had its roots in the military. It was issued to American bomber pilots in the Second World War, because of its durability and protective qualities. After the war it was taken up by members of biker gangs, who were notorious for their drinking and rabble-rousing, and this gave the jacket its anarchic reputation. The black leather jacket has been the emblem of 'bad boys' ever since.

In the 1960s hell-raising gangs of Rockers, greasers (so named because of their slicked-back hairstyles) and Hells Angels bikers all made the black leather jacket their own. Their jackets were covered in badges, insignia and chains, and were accompanied by filthy jeans splattered with engine oil, and military helmets or peaked leather caps, as they terrorized towns and relished their reputation as outlaws. Meanwhile, members of the American organization the Black Panther Party, part

The emergence of punk in the late 1970s brought a celebration of rebellion. Such bands as the Clash, shown here in a photograph from 1984, used their black leather jackets as a tribal street uniform.

Black leather jacket

of the Black Power movement, wore it with their signature black berets to convey a confrontational image of radical protest.

Punk street style emphasized leather in the late 1970s. Along with metal studs and safety pins, bondage trousers and dirty T-shirts emblazoned with the shocking word 'sex', the black leather jacket epitomized punk's aggressive anarchy and no-hope attitude. In the early 1980s gay men took the biker look and made it into a lifestyle: from the Village People pop group (named after New York's bohemian Greenwich Village district) to the streets of the Castro district in San Francisco, moustached bikers with leather

jackets, tight leather trousers and black policemen's caps walked arm in arm, in defiance of 'straight' society.

The black leather jacket was finally given a wider audience when it became the uniform of rock musicians who wanted to be taken seriously. From Jim Morrison, Lou Reed and Bob Dylan to members of the Clash with their sod-you snarls, the jacket brought the finishing touch to the look of defiance. But despite a brief moment on the fashion runway in 1960, when Yves Saint Laurent became the first designer to use the black leather jacket, in his Beat collection, it was only in the 1980s that the black leather jacket finally lost its link with the motorcycle toughs and became a luxury fashion item. Leather was everywhere, and such designers as Katharine Hamnett, Azzedine Alaïa, Thierry Mugler and Gianni Versace sent down the runway blouson-style black jackets with shoulder pads and studs. The black leather jacket had been reborn, and women teamed it with baggy leather trousers and high court shoes.

Today the black leather jacket is worn by young and old alike. Tailored, classic or even fur-lined, it may no longer be the icon of the outsider, but it is still capable of suggesting an aura of defiant cool.

Opposite: The macho cool of a young Marlon Brando in *The Wild One* (1953) cemented the black leather jacket as an anti-mainstream icon of rebellion throughout youth culture.

Giorgio Armani's blouson-style cropped jacket of 1983 paid homage to the American pilot's jacket of the Second World War.

16. Breton top

Thanks to Coco Chanel, who swiped the striped motif from French fishermen in the early twentieth century, the Breton top was introduced as a fashion item. Its fresh, timeless look makes it ideal for lazy summer days, and its understated style, combining casual and classy in equal measure, has maintained it as a major style icon through the decades.

The top was formalized by the French navy, which in 1858 issued to its sailors a long-sleeved shirt made of strong, closely woven cotton, with blue and white stripes (twenty-one of each) and featuring a classic horizontal boat neck. Known as a *marinière* or *matelot*, the top soon became popular with fishermen in the Brittany region (hence its name in English), who wore it for its protective qualities and comfort.

In 1917 the nautical *marinière* made the transformation from workwear to fashion garment, when Chanel introduced it in her shop in the prestigious beach resort of Deauville in Normandy. With its mannish shape and simple elegance, the Breton top – which Chanel designed to be paired with her white yachting trousers – went on to become one of the key looks of the following decade, and a chic fashion item for the modern woman. By the mid-1920s Chanel's Breton-and-trouser combination had been taken up eagerly by European socialites as beachwear in such fashionable Mediterranean resorts as Antibes or Venice's Lido. Maritime themes continued to be popular throughout the 1930s, when striped nautical-style tops by such designers as Jean Patou were worn with shorts and white ankle socks for daytime leisurewear and resort wear.

Hollywood stars popularized the Breton top – for both men and women – during

A timeless classic of understated bohemian chic: Brigitte Bardot (opposite, top) in a traditional Breton top in 1956 on the set of *Her Bridal Night* (also known as *The Bride is Much Too Beautiful*); a crisp American take on the style, from 1966 (opposite, bottom).

The Breton top has undergone subtle redesigns but the essence remains the same. Jean Paul Gaultier uses it as his signature look, here seen in a more low-key incarnation on the French model Morgane, a face of Gaultier campaigns.

the 1950s. Marilyn Monroe, for example, was often photographed looking relaxed and sultry in a stripy T-shirt and jeans. It was still big with the French Riviera set, and was a distinct presence at the bars and cafes in Saint Tropez and other resorts: Brigitte Bardot wore hers with capri pants and ballet flats; Pablo Picasso practically lived in them. Away from the beach, French New Wave cinema took to the look, as epitomized by the elfin Jean Seberg in *Breathless* (1960) and the fiesty Jeanne Moreau in *Jules and Jim* (1962). Parisian existentialists gave it a whiff of countercultural angst, the Breton stripes standing out from the otherwise all-black outfits they favoured.

In the mid-1960s Yves Saint Laurent showed simple navy striped tees, kick-starting an urban trend for all things nautical. Partnered with his pea coat,

black jersey slacks and large sunglasses, the Breton was a key component of the emerging gamine style and a favourite of such international 'It Girls' as the American heiress Edie Sedgwick, who starred in several of Andy Warhol's films.

By the 1970s the seafaring top had slipped below the fashion radar, but it resurfaced briefly in the 1980s, often teamed with ripped jeans and smart blue blazers. Today the Breton stripe has reached the status of a must-have item; it has even become a sort of personal signature style for Jean Paul Gaultier. A staple of the high street, it has also made an appearance in collections from such diverse designers as Jil Sander, Marc Jacobs, Stella McCartney and Vivienne Westwood. Ultra-wearable, flattering and inexpensive, the Breton top remains a key element of any summer wardrobe.

17. Oxford bags

Ludicrous gimmick or landmark fashion style? The high-waisted, wide-legged trousers known as Oxford bags may have started out as a rebellious student prank in the 1920s, but they went on to become a trend that would influence menswear for the next three decades, and they are still swirling around the ankles of fashion-aware women today.

In 1924 a group of male students at the University of Oxford began wearing broad, pleated trousers as a form of rebellion against a ban on wearing 'knickers' (knickerbockers, or golf trousers) to lectures; as the hems of these 'bags' spanned anything from 58 cm to more than 1 m (22–40 in.), they could be slipped on easily over the forbidden knickers. The trousers were so extreme that they made newspaper headlines. Fashionable aesthetes would stroll up and down the streets of London and the boulevards of Paris in wide trousers and hip-hugging jackets, a floppy hat worn dipped over one eye.

The fad crossed the Atlantic after John Wanamaker of New York introduced 'bags' to the United States in 1925, and the fashion for wide-legged trousers lasted until blue jeans took over as the trousers of choice for young people in the early 1950s. Indeed, throughout the 1930s, the broad-shouldered suit with baggy trousers was the height of male elegance and the mark of the serious modern man. The trousers were often very high-waisted, giving the wearer a tall, erect appearance. The pairing of wide, cuffed trousers with a V-neck sweater became standard informal dress for such stars as James Stewart and Fred Astaire, who turned it into a signature look of casual elegance. Women also got in on the act. Coco Chanel,

whose clothes transformed womenswear with their blend of comfort and chic, developed baggy sailor-style 'yachting' trousers as part of her line in the 1920s, and Marlene Dietrich scandalized 1930s society when she wore wide-legged trouser suits as daywear.

Wide, spacious trousers were reclaimed in the 1960s by Britain's Northern Soul youth scene, in which in clubs across northern England an impressively energetic dance style was developed, along with fashions to match. In such places as the Wigan Casino and the Twisted Wheel in Manchester, boys dressed in 'baggies' – trousers that flared from the waist rather than the knees – pirouetted and stomped to an uptempo, Detroit-influenced beat.

The width of these Oxford bags, worn by a fashionable American college student in 1926, came in at 91.5 cm (36 in.).

The craze was short-lived, but wide-legged trousers and jeans re-emerged in the acid-house rave scene of the 1990s. As had been the case in Northern Soul clubs, all-night dancing required the comfort of extremely baggy trousers, only this time they were in fluorescent colours.

High fashion had restyled Oxford bags in the early 1970s. These new 'baggies' were simple and unstructured, yet had a modern, aspirational feel. Pleated, tailored tweed trousers by Yves Saint Laurent, Bill Gibb and the Stirling Cooper label were particularly popular, partnered with shirts and V-neck jumpers. For a laid-back

The reality-television star Kim Kardashian pictured in 2012 wearing Oxford bags in Beverly Hills. The wide-legged trouser is becoming a fashionable alternative to the skinny-jeans trend of recent years.

style, midriff-showing halter-neck tops or tied blouses were teamed with striped Oxford bags. High-profile fans of the style included Bianca Jagger, Jerry Hall and Farrah Fawcett.

Towards the end of the first decade of the twenty-first century, for the first time in years, wide, baggy trousers were again featured on the catwalk, offered by New York's hipper designer labels (such as Tory Burch, Marc Jacobs and Phillip Lim) as well as more traditional names. Chloé, for example, produced high-waisted caramel-toned versions, while Yves Saint Laurent's black Oxford bags made women's legs look endless. A response to the skinny-jeaned rock-chick look of the previous two decades, the trend for baggy trousers was a welcome development for any woman who wanted to look chic and classic without having to starve herself.

Oxford bags were a feature of the glam-rock scene of the 1970s. Such bands as the Bay City Rollers (whose guitarist Eric Faulkner is shown left, in 1977) pushed trouser-leg width to new limits.

18. Pyjama trousers

You can wear them with a comfy pair of fluffy slippers, or, as many women through the decades have found equally appropriate, high black stiletto heels and a slick of red lipstick. Pyjama trousers can be more than simply items of nightwear or outfits in which to eat breakfast at home. Since the 1920s, when the floaty pyjama escaped from the bedroom and wafted into the sophisticated salons of Paris and London, fashionable daywear versions have repeatedly appeared on the fashion catwalks. The garment's just-rolled-out-of-bed sex appeal has been a hit with artists (Pablo Picasso regularly wore white silk PJs), society gals and Hollywood sirens, and has ensured its continuing popularity.

Pyjamas entered the Western clothing lexicon after British colonialists of the eighteenth and nineteenth centuries discovered the loose, lightweight drawstring trousers worn in South and West Asia, and took up the style as nightwear. By the early twentieth century the pyjama had replaced the nightshirt as the norm for bedtime attire, but soon avant-garde fashion designers were plundering the bedroom and appropriating pyjamas as women's fashion wear. In early-1920s Paris, Edward Molyneux and Paul Poiret created brightly coloured models in silk or crêpe satin, trimmed in lace, for evening and lounge wear. These were a modern equivalent of the loosely structured tea gown of the previous decade, but far more daring and utterly scandalous. With their relaxed silhouette and decadent appeal, daytime pyjamas were a deliberate fashion statement against the restrictive clothes of the pre-war era. Greta Garbo and Marlene Dietrich were early adopters of the style.

Pyjama trousers were also taken up as beachwear at the chic resorts of the South of France and the Venice Lido. Coco Chanel pioneered the fashion for highly colourful beach pyjamas in jersey wool, which she sold at her shop in Deauville, Normandy. They were controversial at first, but by the end of the 1920s pyjamas worn with backless tops, wide-brimmed hats and espadrilles were popular beach attire for

An outfit of short-sleeved, jersey wrap-look top with matching pyjama trousers, from 1939 (designer unknown).

Pyjama trousers

A colourful take on
the pyjama trouser
by Los Angeles-
based Eduardo Lucero
from 2006.

fashionable women. The trousers remained
on the beach scene throughout the 1930s,
and were also the ideal garment in which
to play golf or tennis.

The Second World War put paid to such
carefree lifestyles, but fashion woke up to
the pyjama again in the 1960s, courtesy
of the Roman designer Irene Galitzine. At
a time when dress codes were becoming
increasingly informal, she introduced wide,
fluid trousers for at-home leisure: 'I don't
care for clothes that you have to think
about after you've put them on', she said.
Galitzine's creations, christened 'palazzo
pyjamas' by *Vogue* editor Diana Vreeland,
were both slim and flattering, and their
graphic prints and ornate embroidery
made them appropriate for both day and
evening. Also in Italy, Emilio Pucci produced
luxury casual silk jersey palazzos, with
their signature swirling patterns in blues,
oranges and reds.

Partnered with silky tops, halter necks
or tunics, palazzo pants continued to be
popular during the 1970s, both in the
United States and Europe. Roy Halston was
particularly known for his satin and crêpe
'pant suits', worn by his celebrity clientele,
and Yves Saint Laurent designed silk
pyjamas accessorized with cummerbunds
and stiletto sandals. Pyjamas then slithered
off the fashion compass, only to make
a comeback in the late noughties when
such high-end labels as Céline, Stella
McCartney and Louis Vuitton showed
their interpretations of the look. From
silk striped versions by Phoebe Philo to
colourful prints at Marni, the pyjama suit
still carries with it a hint of naughtiness.
After all, when a girl stands on a street
corner in her jim-jams, most people are
going to look twice.

A colourful take on
the pyjama trouser
by Los Angeles-
based Eduardo Lucero
from 2006.

19. Polo shirt

Male aspirational driving and dressing, 1970s-style.

With its classic, sleek lines and connotations of Old World money, the polo shirt references Ivy League style. Worn by such disparate groups as preppy Americans, 1960s Mods and middle-class urban men as a weekend alternative to the office suit, the polo is halfway between a proper shirt and a T-shirt, and, as such, the perfect piece of smart-casual wear.

The polo shirt dates back to 1926, when French tennis champion René Lacoste, nicknamed 'le Crocodile' for his tenacity (hence the brand logo), began wearing a short-sleeved, white cotton jersey shirt that he had designed for his own use. It became an instant classic, and in 1929 Lacoste teamed up with one of the country's largest knitwear manufacturers, André Gillier. Together they produced an innovative piqué cotton jersey tennis shirt with short sleeves and a three-button placket (it became known as a polo shirt after it was adopted by polo players in the 1930s). It was not launched in the United States until the early 1950s, but within a few years the Lacoste polo shirt had become the American Ivy League shirt of choice. At once relaxed, comfortable and elegant, it could be worn with a pair of Bermuda shorts during summer holidays at the beach, or with chinos and a crew-neck jumper in the winter. The polo shirt was an easy-to-wear garment, loved by men and women alike.

Others followed Lacoste's lead. In 1952 the British tennis star Fred Perry launched his own version, which he promoted across the UK and the United States. It was this shirt that was taken up in 1960s Britain by the Mods, who loved its smart-casual appeal. They wore it buttoned to the neck, often partnered with immaculate trousers or jeans and a double-vented, three-buttoned jacket. The 'Fred', as it was nicknamed, became an iconic item of working-class subcultural groups, not all of which were interested in looking 'smart': skinheads, who had a reputation for aggression and violence, teamed their Freds with turned-up jeans, braces and steel-capped boots.

Polo shirt

In the United States the traditional polo shirt was reworked as a higher-end fashion item. In 1972 Ralph Lauren launched his 'mesh shirt' as a prominent part of his Polo range, and other companies produced their own versions of the crisp white polo shirt, to be styled with fashionable wide-legged trousers and cardigans.

By the mid-1980s the polo shirt, and in particular the Polo Ralph Lauren model, had become a visual metaphor for the upwardly mobile yuppie, and also one of the most popular unisex fashions of the decade. In the UK, the Fred Perry polo shirt returned to prominence as an icon of the Two Tone ska revival of the early 1980s. Such bands as Madness, the Specials and the Selecter partnered their Freds with shiny silver two-tone suits and pork-pie hats as they played their jogging ska rhythms.

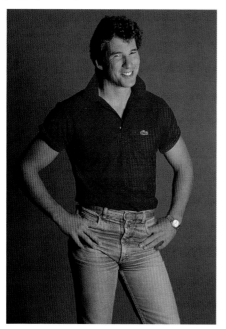

Although the polo shirt had fallen out of fashion by the 1990s, and had become the preserve of the ageing preppy and off-duty banker, high-end fashion designers have recently restyled it as a cult item, most notably for women. Towards the end of the first decade of the twenty-first century, Ralph Lauren introduced a new range of slim-fit polo shirts; Adidas and Tommy Hilfiger have produced cute versions in sugar-candy colours for the feminine tomboy. Today, whether it is cropped, as favoured by Miu Miu and Marc Jacobs, or the original Lacoste, the polo shirt is once again the ultimate in Ivy League chic, and a must-have for any woman who wants to work the preppy sportswear trend.

René Lacoste's white shirt is now produced in a rainbow of bright colours, as seen left on Richard Gere in 1985, and above at the Lacoste collection show of 2006.

Opposite: The American tennis player Helen Jacobs in 1935, looking smart and fresh in a fine white monogrammed polo shirt and roomy white trousers.

20. Wedge shoe

When the Italian shoe designer Salvatore Ferragamo introduced a shoe with a wedge heel – a built-up heel that merged with the sole in a solid triangle – in 1936, it was a revolutionary new style that offered both lift and greater stability than a spike-shaped heel. Thanks to Ferragamo's experiments with cork, the shoe was also lightweight. From his wedge-shaped mules to his evening sandals with embellished cork soles and satin uppers, his flamboyant creations were soon filling the pages of the world's top fashion magazines. In 1938 *Harper's Bazaar* declared: 'Whereas French women only wear orthopaedic sandals in the house or on the beach, Italian women have literally gone mad about the wedge.'

By the early 1940s a large percentage of American women owned a pair of wedge shoes. Models fabricated in wood, cork, raffia, string, linen and various other fabrics were the answer to wartime shortages of leather, and the wedge, with its chunky heel, was the perfect complement to the boxy suits of the era. Ferragamo continued to produce extravagant creations, such as his 'invisible' sandal of 1947, which had a curved sculptural wedge and a clear nylon upper. But with new dress styles the wedge gradually fell out of fashion, and by the end of the decade women were returning to narrow heels, signalling the arrival of the stiletto.

Wedges were revitalized in the 1970s. Although they were the less popular sister of the era's ubiquitous platform shoe, one particular style took America and Britain by storm: the super-comfortable, no-nonsense Kork-Ease wedge from New York. With its signature flesh-coloured

The invention of the wedge heel (an early style from about 1938 is shown opposite, top) heralded a new style for the 1940s. The shoes gave a touch of chic to later resort wear, as seen on a poolside Marilyn Monroe in 1950 (opposite, bottom).

platform sole, criss-cross vampy straps and 15-cm (6-in.) wedge, it became one of the most desired shoe styles of the decade.

Since then the wedge has gone in and out of fashion more frequently than even the miniskirt. The current crop features high, sculptural wedge sandals that, paired with skinny jeans, minidresses or full skirts, are perfect for chic summer dressing in the city. Of particular note

is the trainer-look 'high-top' wedge, a trend started in 2010 by Isabel Marant and Chloé that was soon followed by the high street. In the United Kingdom, *The Times* called them 'sensible but properly high fashion'; after years of vertiginous high heels, designers had finally managed to combine height with comfort. Other successful new styles include the wedge desert boot, the lace-up wedge boot and the flamboyant leopard-skin gladiator wedge sandal. As long as comfort is a key factor in fashion, the wedge will be around. Continually reinvented and restyled, it is a win-win choice, whether worn to the office, at a party or on a beachside promenade.

Still a firm favourite, the wedge has been revived as a chic celebrity favourite. Above, a floral platform pair graces the pedicured feet of the American actress Kirsten Dunst in 2012.

An early (1942–44) cork and textile wedge by Salvatore Ferragamo (left, top); and the BK52 wedge platform of 2012 by the cult French shoe designer Pierre Hardy.

21. City shorts

When it comes to men's knees, the dilemma of whether or not to bare them can be tricky; after all, some eighty years after shorts were introduced on the tennis court, where and how a man should wear them are still divisive issues. Calves can be said to have become liberated in the 1940s, when men started donning above-the-knee trousers for the beach, and today 'city shorts' have evolved into a practical daywear option. It is unlikely that we will see them in the boardroom or the courtroom in the near future, but they have nevertheless come a long way from their humble beginnings.

In the late nineteenth and early twentieth centuries, shorts were almost exclusively the preserve of young boys until they were considered to be old enough to wear proper trousers. Short trousers were thus associated with boyish pranks

The American jazz bandleader Lionel Hampton plays it cool in suit jacket and shorts at a concert in New York in 1953.

and scraped knees, and were sartorially unacceptable for the patriarchal male. When the British tennis champion Bunny Austin stepped on to the court in a pair of tailored short trousers in 1932 instead of the customary long trousers, he both caused a stir and sowed the seeds of a new casual fashion.

The trend for shorts quickly took off, especially with the rich and famous, who took to this groundbreaking summer wear when soaking up the sun in the popular American resorts of Palm Springs and Palm Beach, and in Nassau in the Bahamas. These new 'Bermuda' shorts, which had been appropriated from the armed forces serving in the tropics, were roomy, pleated and worn with the cuff turned up, about 7.5 cm (3 in.) above the knee, and would be teamed with loafers and a shantung jacket. Essentially a pair of trousers

A more casual modern take on city shorts is displayed by the chat-show host David Letterman, pictured standing alongside the comedian and television presenter Johnny Carson in 1988.

with the legs cut off, Bermudas were the progenitor of long 'city' shorts.

Resort fashions filtered down to the mainstream thanks to Hollywood and such magazines as *Life*, which featured images of Rock Hudson, Bing Crosby, Bob Hope and other stars unwinding at their beachside homes in their lightweight Bermudas. The growth of leisure pursuits during the late 1940s encouraged men to enlarge their wardrobe beyond the suit and tie. The casual look was further reinforced by newly established men's magazines in the United States, such as *Esquire* and *Apparel Arts*. These ran features on the vogue for a tanned, athletic body and showed handsome, rugged men in shorts and sunglasses looking sporty and relaxed.

By the late 1950s, the growing popularity of tailored shorts led to some manufacturers introducing shorter sports jackets, which offered casual styling and a balance of length that would complement the look. The classic American style was epitomized by the flat-fronted shorts produced by the J. Press company, in checks, stripes or plain colours, partnered with a three-buttoned polo shirt and slip-on topsider boat shoes (preferably by Sperry).

Since then, smart shorts have become an acceptable part of the male wardrobe. During the 1960s in New York, as fashions relaxed, men wore their Bermudas with a short-sleeved cotton shirt, long socks and brogues as a summer alternative to the city suit. The tailored short has continued to evolve. Today, for Louis Vuitton, Comme des Garçons, Giorgio Armani and other fashion houses, the city short – crisp, smart, slim and tailored – is an update on the classic American preppy look, and a cool, office-appropriate way to beat the heat.

Heavier, darker fabrics can transform shorts into garments that are more formally urban yet remain airy.

22. Blue jeans

Blue jeans are possibly the most iconic garment of the twentieth century. What started out as practical garb for the dust-bowl farmers and railway workers of early twentieth-century America became the symbol of the teenage rebel, the Woodstock generation and the glamorous crowd at New York's Studio 54 nightclub.

Jeans were launched in 1873 by Jacob Davis and Levi Strauss in San Francisco, after they had been asked to create a hard-wearing product for California miners and railway men. They came upon the idea of using copper rivets to strengthen the top corners of the front pockets, then added a leather back patch, lot numbers and back pockets. The archetypal Levi's 501 was launched in the 1890s.

In the 1930s the movies glamorized denim, with romantic, action-packed cowboy films featuring such handsome stars as John Wayne, Gene Autry and Gary Cooper. The crossover into leisurewear followed swiftly, after Levi Strauss & Co. started using the cowboy as its corporate icon in the late 1930s. In 1935 the firm created the first jeans for women, and in the 1940s charming images of a young Marilyn Monroe in blue jeans and a tight sweater sent sales rocketing.

Thanks to Hollywood, by the 1950s jeans had became a youth fashion item. Worn by such rebellious icons as Marlon Brando in *The Wild One* (1953) and James Dean in *Rebel Without a Cause* (1955), the rough-and-ready workwear jeans came to represent sex and danger. Society was smart, squeaky-clean and aspirational; Dean and his followers were scruffy, downbeat and unkempt. Exciting new rock 'n' roll stars, such as Elvis Presley and Eddie Cochran, further boosted

Left: A publicity still for the musical film *West Side Story* (1961) shows that, in an urban context, jeans were seen as the emblem of anti-establishment youth.

Opposite: Bruce 'the Boss' Springsteen in 1988, true to his American sartorial roots a few years after the release of his album *Born in the USA*.

Blue jeans

the exciting image of blue jeans, and they became a powerful unisex item, worn by teenagers of all social classes. Indeed, by the late 1960s, frayed blue jeans, sometimes customized with paint, embroidery or appliqué, had become a badge of defiance against mainstream society worldwide. Reeking of working-class authenticity, jeans were the uniform of anti-establishment hippies and glamorous young rock stars.

Jeans had achieved worldwide democratic status by the 1970s. High-waisted, faded, flared jeans were particularly popular at the time, paired with high platform shoes. Even the American president, Jimmy Carter, wore jeans. Calvin Klein became the first fashion designer to put blue jeans on the runway, in 1976: sophisticated and slim-fitting, his take was far removed from the earlier faded bell-bottoms. The socialite

Gloria Vanderbilt introduced her jeans in 1978; similar in style to Klein's, but featuring a monogrammed rear pocket, they were the first 'signature' jeans, and were promoted using her glamour and celebrity. Soon the market was flooded with such upmarket brands as Joseph, Jordache, Guess and Giorgio Armani, all vying for a piece of the lucrative denim market.

By the late 1980s vintage Levi's 501s had become popular as a backlash against the rampant materialism of the decade. Seen as simple and authentic, they were teamed with denim jackets and loafers, echoing the mid-twentieth-century style. During the following decade, flattering 'boot-cut' jeans and jeans cut low on the hip were the popular styles for women, with such 'luxury denim' labels as 7 for all Mankind, Earl and True Religion dominating the market. Today jeans come in many colours and styles, from skinny, boot-cut and tailored to dirty-wash guerrilla, and it appears certain that this ubiquitous garment will continue to be reinterpreted by every generation.

A model in a pair of button-front Levis for Gals jeans in 1972.

The *Twilight Saga* star Kristen Stewart wears a pair of ultra-hip figure-hugging jeans by 7 for all Mankind while out and about in Los Angeles in 2011.

23. Tracksuit

Once upon a time, the tracksuit was solely a functional, sweat-absorbing and protective outfit for the sports track, field or pitch. But for some time now it has constituted not only a unisex dress-down uniform, but also a glamorous yet wearable fashion displayed on the catwalk and at parties. The tracksuit – which in the 1920s consisted of a thick fleecy cotton pullover and matching sweat pants – has transcended sports and the gym to become a slouchy everyday alternative to jeans.

The tracksuit evolved into a coveted item of leisurewear in the 1970s, as the craze for fitness and jogging took off. *Vogue* fashion shoots re-imagined workout classes populated by beautiful models in leotards and tracksuits, and soon the velour towelling leisure suit had moved out of the keep-fit class and into the newly opened New York superclub Studio 54.

The world of marketing caught on to the trend, as seen in 1977 in a promotion for Virginia Slims cigarettes featuring the scarlet Ginny Jogger fleece tracksuit, and the tag line 'Run in it. Bicycle in it. Play tennis in it. Or just sit around looking smashing in it.'

Active wear had embarked on its road to high fashion by the 1980s. The sweats collection of the American designer Norma Kamali, with jogging suits cut in grey sweat shirting, was affordable, practical and perfect for a busy woman's wardrobe. Helen Robinson of London shop PX, a favourite on the New Romantics fashion and music scene, created partly padded cotton sweats to be teamed with cotton jersey polo necks; and Vivienne Westwood and Liza Bruce produced tracksuits and cycling shorts in high-voltage fluorescent colours. Such looks appealed to young

The rapper Da Brat rocks the mid-1990s street-style tracksuit look associated with the hip-hop scene.

Early tracksuits were the preserve of athletes. Left, the American swimmer Martha Norelius, a competitor in the 1924 and 1928 Olympic Games, models a late-1920s suit.

Tracksuit

women, who appreciated the merging of comfort and show-stopping novelty. Rap artists of the time, such as the members of Run DMC, who wore shiny Adidas tracksuits festooned with gold chains as their street-style uniform, also played a significant role in sparking a global sportswear fashion trend. The birth of logo mania saw the tarting-up of the tracksuit, with a price tag to match. Chanel, Calvin Klein and Moschino all splashed their names over sweatshirts and tracksuits, and designer sportswear became the new way to flaunt one's status.

Little wonder, then, that the fashion industry muscled in on the sportswear action and launched its own brands. In 1993 Ralph Lauren opened a sports emporium on New York's Madison Avenue; Prada Sport, DKNY Active and TSE Cashmere followed, with exciting and innovative sporty fashion separates that were sophisticated enough for both daywear and parties. By the turn of the millennium, fashion designers had teamed up with well-known sports brands to create cutting-edge ranges of clothing. Of particular note was the collaboration between Yohji Yamamoto and Adidas that created the Y-3 sportswear label, and Stella McCartney's own girlie separates for Adidas.

In 2003 the fashion buzz was all about the new brand Juicy Couture and its luxury tracksuits, which were produced in such feminine colours as baby-pink, blue and plum. Bum-hugging, flattering and sexy, the Juicy Couture outfit became the dress-down uniform of many celebrities: devotees included Paris Hilton, Geri Halliwell and Jennifer Lopez (who even designed her own version).

Today's fashion designers have continued to borrow sports styles, and to adopt innovative technology and materials to create designer joggers that are smart, chic and comfortable. From grey marl versions by Isabel Marant and Alexander Wang's black chiffon tracksuit, to Christopher Kane's joggers embellished with eyelets and mirrors, hanging out has never been so glamorous.

The American actress
Jamie Lee Curtis was
one of the countless
people who adopted
the tracksuit as their
leisurewear of choice
in the 1980s.

24. Smock

Unstructured, loose and billowing, the smock can hide a thousand sins. With its upper part often gathered in smocking and its lower part falling straight to the hip, this style of dress creates a free-flowing silhouette that emphasizes the underlying femininity of the wearer. Yet while today's fashion smocks are sweet and demure, their background is as the functional overgarment of the pre-industrial peasant.

In the early eighteenth century, at the dawn of the United Kingdom's Industrial Revolution, the smock was a long shirt-like garment, made of heavy linen or wool, that was worn by rural workers and farmers over their clothes to keep them clean. With people increasingly moving to work in urban centres, this type of garment gradually died out as rural and home-made clothing was ousted by clothes more fitting for the town. Later in the century, the

A colourful smock nightdress of 1966 by Fernando Sanchez for the New York lingerie company Warner's.

smock was the badge of the struggling artist, such as the Impressionist painters Paul Cézanne and Vincent van Gogh.

The smock entered the fashion scene in the early 1970s, as romance and retro became the buzzwords of the post-Woodstock generation. Designers were on a quest for nostalgia and, in an effort to create a new look, they plundered the dressing-up box of the past. In a kaleidoscope of brilliant colour and design, ethnic kaftans, gypsy tops and cheesecloth smocks were partnered with striped tights, tapestry coats and platform sandals. In 1972 *Vogue* declared that 'the most wearable dress this year is the gaily coloured smock'; in fact, the full-sleeved smock dress – in cotton peasant prints or plain calico for the summer, and matt jersey or woollen cloth for the winter – remained one of the key looks throughout

An American smock tunic from 1944 (designer unknown).

Below: The smock
defined the 1970s
post-hippy look, as
seen here in an
elaborate yet subdued
example from 1975.

The American
television personality
Kristin Cavallari
wearing a smock
dress at a media
event in 2012.

the decade. Colourful high-waisted smock dresses by Kenzo Takada (Kenzo) were particularly popular. The designer Bill Gibb introduced flamboyant, voluminous baby-doll smock dresses in marble-patterned silk. Gibb continued to produce smocks that were masterpieces of embroidery and imaginative reworkings of the hippy collage, with slashed sleeves, satin and prints all clashing in the same dress. Also all the rage were Biba's retro-chic nylon smocks with pretty floral patterns and gathered cuffs. By the mid-1970s, large 'tent' dresses and loose smock dresses

were found in most of the major collections. Jean Muir, Calvin Klein, Yves Saint Laurent and Sonia Rykiel were among the many designers who produced soft, unstructured smocks intended to be worn with thick-soled sandals or boots.

The smock remained popular throughout the early 1980s as fashion continued in a flamboyant vein. Women dressed as swashbuckling pirates or demure peasants in Wendy Dagworthy's simple farmer's smocks; floral-printed smocks were worn over trousers or short skirts; and Saint Laurent's off-the-shoulder evening smock in silk satin crêpe was the stuff of dreams. By the middle of the decade, however, power dressing had put paid to romanticism in fashion, and it was not until the twenty-first century that the smock was reworked as a major trend. In 2010 the neo-Lolita look was everywhere, offered by mainstream labels and such high-end names as Stella McCartney alike. Today the smock dress is the last word in versatility, worn over leggings or skinny jeans, or on its own paired with wedges or ballet pumps. Simply cut and comfortable to wear, it is the ultimate slip-it-on-and-forget-about-it dress.

25. Bovver boot

The singer Gwen Stefani loves them. The actress Drew Barrymore and the model Alexa Chung wear them with cut-off shorts and miniskirts, while Johnny Depp and Kate Winslet have been photographed looking particularly cutting-edge in theirs. Bovver boots, a generic term for the functional footwear originally produced by the Dr. Martens brand to keep workmen comfortable, and which later became synonymous with skinheads and punk rockers, have survived as a fashionable item and iconic brand of youth subculture for some fifty years.

The origins of this distinctive footwear lie in Germany. When in 1945 Klaus Märtens, a doctor in the German army, injured his ankle while skiing, he found that his standard-issue army boots were uncomfortable, and came up with the idea of using soles of air-impregnated rubber to offer comfort and support. His boots were particularly popular with German housewives during the late 1940s, but it was in 1958 that the Dr. Martens (Doc Martens, or DMs) we have come to know were born, when a Northampton-based shoe manufacturer called Bill Griggs bought the rights to make them in Britain and began adapting the design; he trademarked the cushioned rubber sole under the name AirWair. The classic eight-eyelet 1460 boot, launched in 1960 (and still part of the DM range), was aimed at people who were on their feet for long hours, such as police officers and postal workers.

The boots began to gain international standing after the guitarist of the Who, Pete Townshend, wore them on stage in the mid-1960s, when the band was enjoying great chart success. Years later he would refer to the boots in his song

'Uniforms' (1982): 'It don't matter where you're from, what matters is your uniform. Wear your braces round your seat, Doctor Martens on your feet.' Since those early days many other bands, from the Sex Pistols, the Clash and Madness to the Spice Girls, have given Dr. Martens their seal of approval.

By the late 1960s the heavy black boots were being adopted by the skinhead

Dr. Martens bovver boots were once synonymous with skinhead violence and anti-fashion statement. Today they come in a rich variety of colours and designs, and have been adopted by a new generation of fashion trailblazers.

movement; 'bovver boys' partnered DMs with short trousers, donkey jackets, shaven heads and lots of attitude. Skinheads were prone to kicking people in fights, so the boots soon became associated with violence and aggression. Photographs in the British press of football hooligans putting the steel-toe-capped boot in made headlines, but also increased DMs' kudos among young people, and for the next two decades they became the essential anti-fashion badge for disaffected youth.

Safety pin-wearing punks took up bovver boots in the late 1970s, customizing them with paint and teaming them with ripped-leather trousers and Mohican haircuts to create their distinctive style. Teenage boot-wearing rebellion continued in the 1990s with grunge and indie kids, who favoured deliberately downbeat styles as a protest against the vulgar consumerism of the age, and teamed their DMs with baggy jumpers, combat trousers and army jackets. Often the girls would decorate their boots with painted-on patterns and wear them with floaty dresses or miniskirts and striped tights.

Today, in common with many previously cult fashions, the appeal of the bovver boot has widened to take in the general population. The previously sober DM is now available in a variety of bright colours, from pink and lilac to gold and silver. Achingly hip young women have kicked off their high heels and opted for the comfort and tomboy chic of a pair of patent bovver boots, paired with a sequined or light and airy dress, skinny jeans or cigarette trousers.

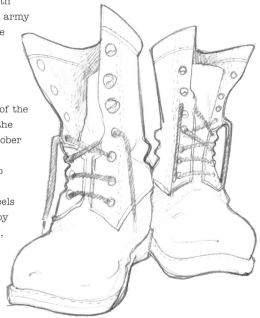

26. Nehru jacket

In the 1960s a new generation of teenagers and young adults began to deconstruct the dress codes of their era, and to find new ways to express themselves through their attire. The Nehru jacket, the West's first collarless tailored garment for men, became an archetypal item of 'with it' dressing. With its smooth, sleek front, it was a smart alternative to the suit and tie, and it helped to pave the way for the smart-casual looks that proliferate today.

The jacket was developed in the 1940s in India, where it was worn by government officials who did not wish to adopt the Western suit but wanted a more practical garment than the traditional *achkan*, a knee-length coat. Newspaper images of Jawaharlal Nehru, the first prime minister of independent India, meeting international leaders and celebrities brought the new shorter style to the attention of the West, but the fashion version of the Indian 'Nehru jacket' was introduced by the French designer Pierre Cardin in the early 1960s. He removed

from the standard business suit its collar, cuffs and lapels, in the process creating one of the most modern and revolutionary style images of the decade.

The look became globally famous after the British tailor Dougie Millings, who made stage outfits for the Beatles, dressed the band in a reworked version of Cardin's Nehru jacket, accessorized with matching tapered trousers and pointed Chelsea boots. The Beatles' landmark performance at Shea Stadium, New York, in 1965, at the height of Beatlemania, led to a surge in sales of the jacket, and it became known as the 'Beatles jacket'. This new look emphasized a boyish figure, rather than following the traditional broad-shouldered ideal of the 1940s and 1950s. It may seem unremarkable today, but was one of the key shifts in male style that lasted throughout the decade and beyond.

Oleg Cassini, who made his name as a Hollywood costumier in the 1940s and became the exclusive couturier to Jacqueline Kennedy during her husband's presidency in the early 1960s, further developed the concept of the sophisticated man of the world with his own version of the Nehru jacket in 1966. A smart Nehru, often partnered with a polo-neck top

The Nehru jacket is named after Jawaharlal Nehru, the first prime minister of independent India, pictured below in 1947. In the West, the late-1960s interest in mysticism and the East made it the sartorial choice of the discerning man (above).

Below: The American
actress Joan Allen in
a sober but striking
top influenced by the
Nehru jacket, in 1998.

rather than a button-down shirt, and
a scarf in place of a tie – and sometimes
with a gold medallion – became the
wardrobe choice for any style-conscious
male. It was also popular with the
counterculture musicians of the time:
wearers included members of the Doors,
the Mamas & the Papas, the Byrds and
Procol Harum.

The Nehru was a central element of
the James Bond films of the 1960s. From
its introduction by the eponymous mad
scientist in *Dr No* (1962), the jacket
became the uniform of any self-respecting
Bond villain – the most famous being evil
mastermind Ernst Stavro Blofeld, who
appeared in several of the films with his

signature grey collarless jacket and
white Persian cat.

The Nehru was reinterpreted for
women in the 1980s, tapping into the
mood for power dressing and neat
silhouettes. The fashionable cropped
Nehru jacket was fitted neatly at the
waist, cut slightly over the hips, and
worn over trousers or short skirts.
Giorgio Armani, the pioneer of
understated tailoring, created feminine,
softly tailored Nehru jackets in neutral
colours; women who preferred a more
opulent style could opt for the
embroidered silk versions produced by
the British designer Scott Crolla.

Today the Nehru jacket is a classic that
transcends the vagaries of fashion. Worn
by both men and women, it is loved for
its clean, minimalist aesthetic and slick-
but-not-showy statement. For women,
whether it is worn with jeans, tapered
trousers or a skirt, it is the quintessential
smart-casual garment that guarantees
they will blend in at any social occasion.

Mike Myers and
his Mini-Me (Verne
Troyer) channel the
Nehru-jacket look in
the spoof James Bond
film *Austin Powers:
The Spy Who Shagged
Me* (1999).

27. Miniskirt

Without a doubt, one of the most enduring
images of popular style is the miniskirt.
The thigh-baring garment made its
appearance in the early 1960s as a
sartorial emblem of freedom for young
women. In a departure from girdles and
restrictive pencil skirts, at last clothes
were being designed in which women could
walk freely. Since that time the miniskirt
has never really gone off the fashion radar.

In 1961, inspired by the Mods' sharp
suits and neat tailoring, the designer Mary
Quant started to create simple, clean-cut
miniskirts in bold colours for her shop,
Bazaar, in London's Knightsbridge. Quant's
miniskirt was regarded as outrageous and
daring, and, for all who wore it, was an
instant signifier of youthful trendiness.
Older people railed against its overt sex
appeal, but teenagers loved it. By the
following year, the 'happening' London
areas around Carnaby Street and the
King's Road were the stamping ground
of modern young women with huge doe
eyes, geometric haircuts by Vidal Sassoon,
skinny-ribbed jumpers and miniskirts,
in what became known as the Chelsea
Look. Short skirts necessitated new
undergarments, and with tights – a newly
available alternative to stockings – the look
was complete. Paris couture, too, decided
that it was time to expose the legs. Marc
Bohan (for Dior) and André Courrèges
were the first to show miniskirts;
Courrèges's simple A-line miniskirts with
boxy jackets in heavy wool crêpe became
a much-copied look of the decade. Yves
Saint Laurent followed this lead, and from
1965 sold his casual miniskirts in his
ready-to-wear boutique, Rive Gauche.

The miniskirt grew shorter and shorter,
becoming a symbol of the sexual revolution

and the most famous of the youth fashions.
Every woman tried some version of it;
miniskirts were available in all sorts of
materials, including fur, PVC, crochet knit
and even chain mail. 'Legs are it', *Vogue*
declared in 1966, as the mini dominated the
collections. By 1968 the bottom-skimming
micro mini was in, but two years later
fashion had gone ethnic, the 1960s bubble
had burst and hemlines fell to the floor.

The fashion designer
Mary Quant, a
trailblazer of the
miniskirt and British
youth style, adjusts
one of her creations
on a model in 1967.

Miniskirt

Miniskirts resurfaced in the late 1970s as an integral part of the outsider punk aesthetic, reincarnated in black leather, PVC and leopard print, and worn with ripped fishnet tights in a deliberately trashy and cheap look. The short skirt also became part of the 1980s power-dressing outfit: tight-fitting and often made of stretchy Lycra or wool, it was incorporated into business suits for women, and worn with cropped jackets with padded shoulders and high-heeled court shoes. This was not a teenage fad, but an assertive statement by the new professional woman, in control of her career and her life. In the 1990s the miniskirt went on to

become part of the 'girl power' uniform, as worn by the girl-group the Spice Girls, who accessorized it with cropped T-shirts and colourful platform boots.

As the super-slim, body-con look became the rage in the early years of the new century, the crotch-skimming micro mini made a spectacular comeback. Today the miniskirt regularly pops up on the catwalks, in every colour, style and fabric imaginable, from Stella McCartney's hanky-sized silk version to Marc Jacobs's denim miniskirts in gold lamé and neon colours. The tiniest of skirts are still to be found predominantly on teenagers and young women, but these days even more 'mature' women can regard the miniskirt as an essential part of their everyday wardrobe.

Madonna, superstar in the making, performing in 1985 in an artfully distressed outfit typical of her style at the time; more than twenty-five years later, the tough-but-tender look (left) is still fresh.

28. Crop top

A model in a crop top
and skirt on the banks
of the Seine in Paris
in 1946.

Free-spirited, youthful but also potentially one of fashion's cruellest styles, the crop top can be either a sexy show-stopper or an unmitigated sartorial disaster. Flesh is bared, and with midriff on show, it best suits the woman who is either very young or very fit. Yet since the 1940s, when starlets posed in bare-waisted two-piece playsuits, the cropped top has liberated stomachs the world over and made a daring fashion statement that is still popular today.

The crop top can be traced back to the 1920s and 1930s, when midriff-baring swimming costumes were introduced by the likes of the French designer Jean Patou and the American swimwear firm Jantzen. It was only in the 1940s, however, that mainstream American fashion took to tops that exposed the stomach. The playsuit, with its midriff-revealing top and tiny shorts, was just the thing for the beach and barbecue parties, and heralded a new relaxed resort style. Such Californian firms as Jantzen and Koret, and the New York-based designer Tina Leser, cleverly fused the exotic design of Hawaiian fabrics with quintessential Americana style to produce brightly patterned 'play' clothes that epitomized the casual look in the country's growing leisurewear market. Particularly popular for the weekend wardrobe in 1946 were Claire McCardell's cropped tops, designed to be worn with matching high-waisted skirts or shorts.

These flattering and sexy designs carried on throughout the 1950s, when cropped blouses and jumpers with three-quarter-length sleeves were often teamed with high-waisted capri pants and ballet flats. In the 1960s the navel came on show for the first time, with clinging resort-style

Crop top

Opposite: The 2003 catwalk collection of the Baby Phat label brought a more tailored couture style for the crop top.

trouser outfits that paired short tops and hipster flares. Emilio Pucci dressed celebrities in his brightly coloured pyjama suits with slinky trousers and long-sleeved, stomach-revealing tops, while crop tops and skirts by the London designer John Bates (who worked under the name Jean Varon) were a hit with young modelly types. In the 1970s the combination of halter-neck tops and hip-hugging jeans was particularly popular, as were blouses that tied under the bust, paired with tiny hot pants and knee-high boots.

As an emphasis on fitness developed in the 1980s, the loose-fitting cropped T-shirt became fashionable daywear. Young women showed off their gym-toned bodies in midriff-revealing vest tops and tees worn with cycling shorts and flouncy rah-rah skirts. Such films as *Fame* (1980), in which students at a New York school for the performing arts took to the streets in their cropped T-shirts and tracksuit bottoms, further popularized the look. In 1983, when Madonna gyrated in a mesh crop top in her video for 'Lucky Star', she not only caused controversy but also influenced a generation of teenagers (see also photograph p. 80).

By the 1990s the navel could not be avoided, as the crop-top-and-drop-jean pairing flooded the streets. Fans of the midriff (which on many people now featured navel rings) included such young celebrities as Drew Barrymore, Britney Spears, Gwen Stefani and the Spice Girls. Today the crop is back, but sophistication is the theme: Alexander Wang, Prada and Missoni have all showed this trend with high-waisted trousers and pencil skirts, revealing only hints of flesh. This once daring fashion has finally covered up – a bit.

The cropped T-shirt worn by the American actress Heather Locklear, pictured above in about 1980, epitomized the gym-influenced look of that decade.

29. Leotard

Fashion's love affair with the toned body is seemingly never-ending. That streamlined second skin, the leotard, was once the preserve of trapeze artists and school gyms, but it has been a major element of fashion since it entered the mainstream in the 1970s. Clinging to the bodies of disco-goers and businesswomen alike, the leotard has made its way through the decades, resurfacing every time 'skintight' fashions hit the catwalks.

The leotard made its first appearance in the mid-nineteenth century, when the French gymnast Jules Léotard pioneered the flying trapeze. To show off his figure he wore a close-fitting garment that was gusseted between the legs and cut low at the neck. It soon became traditional wear for modern dancers and entered the sportswear lexicon.

During the 1940s, a new easy-going way of life was developing in the United States and, along with it, a more casual approach to everyday clothes. The designer Claire McCardell chose the leotard as the basis of a revolutionary 'build your own' wardrobe of mix-and-match separates. Her leotard, launched in 1942, was an all-in-one jersey knit with long sleeves and legs, and could be worn under skirts, tunics or her famous Popover dress. These 'funny tights', as they were dubbed by *Life* magazine, were one of the most talked-about designs of the time, yet proved too radical for McCardell's mid-market clientele.

It wasn't until several decades later, with the advent of the fitness craze, that the leotard entered the fashion mainstream. In 1970s gyms women 'went for the burn' in brightly coloured leotards, footless tights and leg warmers. Now made of stretchy nylon and Lycra, the leotard became not only practical but also sexy. The shiny garment, popularized by Jane Fonda in her famous workout videos, soon became the basis of a new fitness fashion. With the explosion of disco in the mid-1970s, neon-coloured, rhinestone-covered leotards were suitable night-life attire, teamed with sparkly leggings and strappy sandals.

Opposite, bottom:
Brigitte Bardot as a
sexy young French
nightclub singer on
the set of the British
comedy film *Doctor
at Sea* (1955).

In the 1970s, leotards
and body suits stepped
out of the dance studio
and the gym. This
fine chequerboard-
patterned Angora
turtleneck body
suit, produced by
Chadbourn, provided
a sleeker alternative
to the shirt when
worn with a jacket.

The 'fit body' ideal continued throughout the decade, and in 1978 Norma Kamali presented a range of 'body wear' based on the leotard-and-leggings combination. By the mid-1980s, cling was everywhere, and leotards formed the basis of many fashionable looks, usually worn under ripped jeans or with tights and a rah-rah skirt; the look was completed with a twisted headband and a bum bag. Vivienne Westwood presented a sports collection featuring a fluorescent 'body suit' worn over black leggings, and Azzedine Alaïa designed jersey leotards that could be worn under his tight-fitting skirts.

In 1985 Donna Karan introduced a stretch body suit that formed the basis of a capsule wardrobe for the modern woman. This no-fuss garment was the ultimate in sexy wearability, and gave a sinuous silhouette. It could be teamed with a short skirt and a cropped jacket, and took the wearer from morning through to late evening. In the 1990s a brief flirtation with the thong body soon proved too uncomfortable for the average wearer, and the leotard returned to the dance studio.

The body has now reared its Lycra head again. In leopard-skin pattern or studded with sequins, it was everywhere on the catwalks in 2011. Whether worn as a show-stopping outfit with tights and skyscraper stilettos, or paired with a miniskirt or trousers, the leotard, with its smooth lines and figure-hugging glamour, should be around for a long time yet.

Functional but sexy
aerobic outfits of
the 1980s.

30. Stiletto

No footwear style is as sexy as the elegantly tapered stiletto. The shoe was launched in Italy (where *stiletto* is the name given to a small dagger) in the mid-1950s. It was a revolutionary idea; the high, thin heel created a completely new silhouette, altering how women moved and dressed, and it also helped to usher in an era of smouldering sex appeal.

While there is some ambiguity over who invented the stiletto, it was in 1955, when the French shoe designer Roger Vivier introduced the controversial *talon aiguille* ('needle heel') while working for the couturier Christian Dior, that the stiletto gained international recognition. Stilettos replaced the thick heels of the 1940s, and were a sign that fashion wanted to celebrate full-on femininity. After years of drab wartime fashions, young women tottered down the streets in

pointy stiletto shoes, cantilevered bras and tight-fitting tops and pencil skirts. The trend for stiletto heels swept Europe and the United States in the late 1950s, and at one stage the high-street versions were worn by virtually the entire female population.

The 1950s screen goddesses couldn't get enough of the stiletto: Elizabeth Taylor, Sophia Loren and Jayne Mansfield (who is said to have owned some 200 pairs) all wore them, to devastating impact. No one understood the shoe's effect better than Marilyn Monroe, who went so far as to have one heel made shorter than the other so as to emphasize her famous wiggle. While the man on the street loved the new fashion, not everyone was happy: doctors advised against wearing stilettos, warning that they would cause bunions, hammer toes and prematurely curved spines, and

Stiletto

officials banned them from public buildings as the heels dented and pierced floors. Yet nothing could stop the stiletto, and by the end of the decade the shoes came with such an extremely pointed toe that women often had to buy them one or two sizes too big in order to accommodate their toes.

Since the 1950s the stiletto has been in and out of fashion, but has never lost the power to seduce. As 'power dressing' took centre stage in the mid-1980s, the shoe style joined the shoulder pad and the designer business suit as a symbol of female ambition. High heels and short, sexy clothes were the uniform of the woman who wanted to get ahead. Not only did stilettos make her taller, but also they gave her authority in the boardroom and a sexual edge in the bar.

The super-stiletto clickety-clacked on to the fashion stage in the mid-noughties, with gravity-defying Jimmy Choo and Manolo Blahnik shoes. Sharply pointed and darkly sexy, these were the antithesis of the good-girl kitten heel and the slouchy flat, and women learned to totter on icicle-thin heels so high that the shoes became more akin to fetish objects than to functional footwear. As Alexandra Shulman, the editor of the British edition of *Vogue*, asserted in 2005, 'If God had intended us to wear flats, he wouldn't have invented Manolos'. And, according to stiletto-loving Madonna, they are 'better than sex'. The high stiletto taps into every woman's desire to dress up and be glamorous. After all, what other shoe has the power to lengthen and slim a woman's legs, emphasize her buttocks and bust, and give her an unmistakable va va voom, all in the click of a heel?

31. Tartan trousers

They are loud and colourful, utterly distinctive, and the roll-out garment for when one wants to make a splash or get a bit of attention. Whether they are in subdued browns and creams or in loud reds and greens, tartan (plaid) trousers carry with them connotations of burly Scottish Highlanders, punk-rock bands and wacky creative types. Their appeal lies in their paradox: at once classic and bohemian, traditional and rebellious, sexy and restrained, tartan trousers are a shocking delight.

In Scotland, tight-fitting, hose-like tartan 'trews' date back to the sixteenth century, when they were worn as a warmer alternative to the kilt during the severe Scottish winter. Tartan migrated from the Highlands and on to the fashion map in the 1930s thanks to the Prince of Wales's love of chequered trousers, which made tartan desirable and popular. Photographs of him wearing tartan lounge suits on the French Riviera (both before acceding the throne as Edward VIII and after his abdication in 1936) put tartan on the map, and it wasn't long before plaid became a favoured choice for men's casual wear.

By the 1950s American Ivy Leaguers had embraced the fashion for tartan trousers. Flat-fronted, in wool or thick cotton Oxford cloth, they were the epitome of relaxed preppy chic, paired with classic button-down shirts or Lacoste polo shirts. For women, fashionable daytime wear included tapered trousers in various tartans, partnered with a casual polo-neck sweater and loafers; this sartorial breakaway from the formal suit presaged the emerging casual style that became more widespread as the decade came to a close.

Tartan slacks continued to be popular for women throughout the 1960s. Yves Saint Laurent, a lover of plaid, created beautifully styled trousers for his Parisian prêt-à-porter boutique, Rive Gauche. In contrast to this ladylike look, as tight hip-huggers, tartan became a welcome fashion statement for the rich hippy and glamorous pop star. By the early 1970s, it was a catwalk mainstay. Mannish

The Duke of Windsor, as Edward VIII became after his abdication of the British throne in 1936, models his plaid golfing trousers at his villa near Paris in 1967.

Tartan trousers

trouser suits; wide, calf-length gaucho trousers; spacious Oxford bags: these flamboyant garments made their wearers stand out from the crowd, but were also comfortable and easy to wear. Punks took the look on with a dose of anarchy and sartorial subversion in the late

1970s, when Vivienne Westwood's bondage tartans – ripped, torn and festooned with chains and straps – gave the noble and traditional fabric an outrageous and provocative spin.

Highland mania has returned to hit fashion intermittently, with the early years of the twenty-first century seeing novel technicolour tartan trousers by cutting-edge designers. Junya Watanabe's collection of tartan jodpurs with bondage chains (2006) combined classic plaid with punk overtones, and a few years later Alexander McQueen – another devotee of tartan – created daring bumster trousers in his red-and-black McQueen tartan. More recently, red plaid jeans in particular have featured strongly in many collections. It's not a subtle look, but whatever the style or colour combination, a pair of tartan trousers remains an exciting everyday fashion.

The punk aesthetic of late 1970s/early 1980s Britain was still being emulated by this young Spanish man in 1991.

Opposite: Gwen Jenkins, fashion assistant at *Glamour* magazine in 1971, exits a New York taxi in a red plaid gaucho suit by Cacharel.

Left: Budding fashion icon Kate Moss models plaid trousers from Gianni Versace's spring collection in 1995.

32. Parka

Whether it is worn over a slinky dress and high heels or with a thick jumper, trousers and trainers, the roomy, hooded parka is a modern unisex classic. Cut slightly longer and looser than its close relation the anorak, it is not yet smart enough to be suitable as mainstream workwear, but the parka as we know it today has come a long way from its ancient beginnings.

The parka was developed in prehistoric times by the Inuit people of Canada's Arctic region, who needed outerwear that would provide protection against the brutal weather conditions. It was traditionally made from caribou pelts and sealskin, and had wide shoulders that granted the wearer great freedom of movement. It was this ability for allowing the carrying out of complex tasks and counteracting extremely cold temperatures that led the United States Army to adopt and adapt the original Inuit parka. Its M1951 fishtail parka – in heavy white or olive-green cotton cloth, with detachable mohair or alpaca lining and a hood that could be neatly folded into the jacket, and cut longer at the back so that it could be tied around the upper legs – was introduced in 1951 to help American soldiers facing severe conditions during the Korean War.

A decade later, the fishtail parka had become a symbol of rebellious British youth. While young Americans were listening to rock 'n' roll on jukeboxes, a small group of British teenagers was zooming around towns on Italian Lambretta motor scooters and dancing to soul music, ska and rhythm and blues. The Mods ('moderns') favoured sharp tailoring; they took to the big green military parkas available at army surplus stores because they were warm and ideal

Top: This photograph from 1928 shows Inuit women of Alaska in their warm, roomy outerwear, the precursor to the American parka.

Above: The practical military parka crossed into British fashion in the 1960s when Mods adopted it to protect their clothes from the elements.

Below: Yesterday's
army-surplus
bargain has evolved;
today, the comfy
parka is a desirable
winter classic.

for protecting their immaculate suits – and also eminently affordable. By 1964, media images of gangs of parka-wearing Mods clashing violently with Rockers in Brighton and other British seaside towns ensured the coat's status as a cult piece of clothing.

The Mod style and the fishtail parka lived on in a series of revivals, most notably in the late 1970s. Spurred on by such bands as the Jam and the Who, and by the Mod movie *Quadrophenia* (1979), young British devotees adopted the Mods' sartorial style, and would hang around on street corners in their smart Ben Sherman shirts and big green parkas festooned with pin badges and colourful patches. The original army parka enjoyed a brief resurgence of street credibility in the late 1990s. Images of Liam Gallagher from the band Oasis swaggering about the stage in a slouchy parka, and the model Kate Moss wearing hers over slinky minidresses and high heels, became synonymous with the Cool Britannia movement.

The parka has earned its status as a desirable fashion item and a key winter classic. From Miuccia Prada's fluorescent orange creations and Alexander Wang's slouchy silk-look parkas, fur-lined and belted at the waist, to the toned-down high-street versions in greys, blues and sludgy greens, the genius of this no-fuss overcoat is its rare ability to combine warmth, street cred and ease of movement.

The 1990s Britpop movement saw a resurgence in the Mod look, popularized by Liam Gallagher, lead singer of Oasis. He is pictured above in 1999.

33. Harem trousers

The French actress
Anouk Aimée in
1965, wearing harem
trousers by Glans that
balloon at mid-calf
into tight 'cuffs'.

Baggy, slouchy, tapered and with the crotch halfway down to the knee, harem trousers are hardly the sexiest of garments. On the plus side, they are immensely comfortable and can hide a multitude of sins, and are a great summer look when teamed with a simple vest top and gladiator sandals.

While harem trousers were worn nearly 2000 years ago in western and south-western Asia, in Europe it wasn't until the early twentieth century that they began to make fashion sense. In 1911 the innovative French designer Paul Poiret broke new sartorial ground with his dramatic 'harem skirts', billowing pantaloons cut to give the illusion of a skirt. Fashionable women loved this free-flowing style that allowed them to walk freely and dance to the new craze, the tango. While the harem-skirt fad didn't last long, it paved the way for the looser pyjama styles of the following decade.

Harem trousers were revived as high-fashion items in the mid-1960s, when interest in Eastern cultures and exotica led to a reworking of traditional ethnic clothing. A fusillade of Eastern, gypsy, Indian and African themes were shown side by side on the catwalk: slim-fitting, gently tapered harem trousers in sumptuous silks or velvets were paired with silk shirts and tucked into knee-length boots; gold lamé versions by Yves Saint Laurent were worn as evening wear, with matching satin coats and strappy high-heeled sandals. Embellished fabrics, beading and intricate embroidery were popular, as was printed silk. This anarchic mishmash of ethnic styles was the mark of the rich hippy: such luminaries as the Beatles and Bianca Jagger projected an air of moneyed exotica in their colourful ethnic-inspired garments.

A flowing jersey blouse and harem trousers (taken in at the knee) from Scott Barrie, 1974. Barrie was one of the first African-American designers to make his mark on fashion.

The former Doctor Who companion Freema Agyeman on the set of the television series *The Carrie Diaries* in New York in 2012.

Fantasy and Middle Eastern dress continued to dominate the European catwalks in the 1970s, and striped cotton harem trousers teamed with tunics and turbans made an appearance. Particularly popular were Issey Miyake's linen jumpsuits with harem trousers, and cropped linen 'gaucho' trousers and tunics by Bill Gibb for Baccarat. Saint Laurent's Moroccan-style ready-to-wear collection offered beautiful harem trousers, along with silk belts, bright purple tunics and high-heeled golden sandals. This new romantic style was characterized by layering, and knitted tank tops, ponchos, shawls and fringed suede bags all added to the look.

Harem trousers faded away in the late 1970s as the controversial creativity of punk took over, heralding a new brutalism in fashion. They made a brief but spectacular comeback in the late 1980s, when fashion fell for 'Hammer pants', named after the rapper MC Hammer, who was a big advocate of the baggy-crotch trousers that facilitated his feverish dance routines. The new style – which was much more voluminous around the thigh than earlier versions – was partnered with tight Lycra sports tops, shoulder-padded jackets and high-top trainers.

The dropped crotch has been revitalized for the twenty-first century, taking in such diverse styles as Balenciaga's relatively tame, skinny jean–harem hybrid in brown gaberdine, and Mango's harem shorts of 2009 with the leg holes hovering in line with the hem. While the harem style may never be popular with every woman, it has reintroduced a baggy silhouette into the fashion lexicon.

Menswear innovator: the rapper MC Hammer (left) in 1990, in his signature 'Hammer pants'.

34. Sneaker

When the sneaker was launched in the early twentieth century, no one could have envisaged its meteoric rise to ubiquity. Yet these canvas-upper, soft rubber-soled shoes have been worn as street wear by everyone from 1950s teenagers to contemporary pop icons. Mick Jagger even got married (to Bianca, in 1971) in a pair.

Rubber-soled canvas shoes known as plimsolls, intended for use as beachwear, were produced in the United Kingdom from the 1830s, but sturdier, thicker-soled canvas footwear developed in the United States at the turn of the twentieth century to cater for the new leisure sporting activities on offer. Keds, a forerunner of the modern sneaker, were launched in the USA in 1916 (and are still going strong). The following year the Converse All Star basketball boot made its first appearance.

The American basketball player Wilt 'The Stilt' Chamberlain, pictured here in 1958 in a pair of red Converse All Star sneakers. He is the only player to have scored 100 points in a single NBA game, a feat he achieved in 1962 while wearing a pair of white high-top All Stars.

The shoe took off in 1921, when Converse hired the basketball star Charles 'Chuck' Taylor to promote it, and two years later his signature began to appear on every ankle patch. It was the first time an athlete had endorsed a sports shoe, and its wide availability and youthful styling added to its appeal and popularity.

Ever since then, America has been in love with the sneaker, and in particular with the iconic Converse (known to Americans as 'Chuckies' or 'Cons'), which is now as much a part of US folklore as apple pie and baseball. The sneaker became part of the 1930s collegiate uniform and the laid-back footwear of the Californian beach look. The Converse – available only in black until 1947, when a white pair was introduced – and hundreds of similar styles by other companies went on to become the preferred footwear of the rebellious

No self-respecting rock star would be without a pair of sneakers. Left, American punk icons the Ramones show off the look in 1978.

Every Converse All Star since 1923 has featured the signature of the basketball player Charles 'Chuck' Taylor, who helped to develop the shoe. Today's models come in a myriad of colours and patterns.

teenager of the 1950s. Inspired by such stars as James Dean, who wore white sneakers in *Rebel Without a Cause* (1955), and Elvis Presley, who swivelled his hips in a pair of scruffy Jack Purcells (designed by the eponymous Canadian badminton champion in the mid-1930s), young people embraced the sneaker's air of effortless cool. Boys would team them with jeans and bomber jackets, and girls with calf-length pedal pushers and ankle socks.

A new contender in the sneaker wars emerged from California in 1966, when the newly established Van Doren Rubber Company started to make deck shoes that it sold direct to the public. When the skateboarding craze hit southern California in the following decade, Vans, with their thicker sole and padded sides, became the skaters' shoe of choice. Sneakers also became part of the mid-1970s New York punk look, with such bands as the Ramones and Blondie teaming theirs with ripped jeans, black leather jackets and lots of attitude.

The sneaker has been through many revivals, the most notable being the trend for fluorescent-coloured trainers in the 1980s; today the classic American sneaker is undergoing a renaissance. Limited-edition, highly collectable Americana is the name of the game. For the sneaker snob, a pair of beaten-up black or white Chuck Taylor originals, or a pair of vintage Vans slip-ons, have become must-have purchases. For the rest of us, the sneaker, with its sleek simplicity and the vast number of bright colours, patterns and variations available, has become a quintessential part of today's casual urban uniform.

35. Beaded dress

The point of the beaded dress is its 'wow' factor. Its ability to startle, dazzle and shine makes it the perfect look for any woman who isn't afraid to make a statement. Deliberately decorative and ornate, the beaded dress is less about function – it is heavy and the beads can snag – than about luxury, parties and glamour.

The idea of using beads as surface embellishment on garments dates back millennia. Women in ancient Egypt would regularly add beading to their clothes as decorative devices, and often wore beaded net dresses over plain tunics; sixteenth-century Venetian women used precious glass beads as decoration on their sumptuous dresses. But it wasn't until the twentieth century, and in particular after the First World War, that dresses entirely covered in beads entered the fashion mainstream. A hallmark of the prosperous 'roaring Twenties', the beaded shift dress became a symbol of youthful sex appeal. Scandalously short (at or just below the knee), loose and sleeveless, these dresses heralded a new awareness of the body. Arms were bare, legs and backs were exposed for the first time, and diaphanous fabrics created an illusion of nudity. Beading was used to emphasize the transparent materials and to catch the light, highlighting the risqué nature of the outfits. In the 1920s world of dancing and fancy-dress parties, these glittering shift dresses were said to be so dazzling that the nightclubs hardly needed lighting.

The beaded dress of the 1920s was a short-lived craze, killed off by the stock-market crash of 1929. A more serious era followed, and the Great Depression had Americans running to the moving pictures to escape into a world of lavish film-style

The elegant silhouette of the long-line 1920s beaded dress ushered in a new era of exoticism in fashion. The tulle and jet-beaded dress shown below was designed by Jean Patou in about 1928.

Beaded dress

glamour and fashion. Throughout Hollywood's golden era of the 1930s through to the 1950s, the cinema featured luxurious beaded costumes in shimmering silk and satin, which could take costumiers up to seven weeks to cover in beading. The gowns became ever more spectacular. Gold and silver lamé, festooned with an array of sequins and beads, helped to maintain the appeal of such stars as Jean Harlow, Marilyn Monroe and Veronica Lake.

By the 1960s British 'dolly birds' and models had taken over in the glamour stakes, and these young women embraced the new mini fashions. The beaded dress obliged, with sparkling mini shifts in bright pinks and blues. As fashion became more playful and fun, designers applied beading to a wider range of clothing, such as brightly coloured dress tops with matching sparkly leggings that shimmered and twinkled around the body.

The beaded dress has continued to sparkle throughout the decades. It makes the perfect Academy Awards dress: Renée Zellweger, Naomi Watts and Charlize Theron are just some of today's celebrities to have dazzled on the red carpet. In 1988 Cher won applause and gasps of admiration when she wore a daring, transparent beaded dress by designer Bob Mackie to pick up her Oscar for best actress in the romantic comedy *Moonstruck* (1987). It was provocative, but put her back in the limelight. Today there is a beaded dress to suit everyone. Whether as a Swarovski-encrusted gown worn for its old-school glamour, a brightly coloured diaphanous beaded shift by the British designer Matthew Williamson or a high-street version, the beaded dress is a party classic that never fails to shine.

36. Swimming costume

Swimming costume

Page 101: The evolution of the swimming costume has transformed a practical item of sportswear into a bold and sexy poolside statement.

The evolution of women's bathing costumes has closely mirrored trends in mainstream fashion and in society's attitudes to modesty, from the Victorian body-covering crinoline suit to the high-tech Speedo, and from the woollen French *maillot de bain* to the daring monokini (designed in 1963 by Rudi Gernreich to leave the breasts exposed). While today we can lounge by the pool in a barely-there halter-neck swimming costume, early bathing suits of the 1890s were essentially voluminous full-skirted dresses with matching ankle-length bloomers, made of woollen flannel. The prototype for the modern swimsuit dates from 1913 in the United States, when the Portland Knitting Company (later renamed Jantzen Knitting Mills) introduced a rib-stitch bathing costume for the male rowers of the Portland Rowing Club in Oregon. By the 1920s, as fashions became more sporty and relaxed, the active modern woman was offered woollen suits that were very similar to those worn by men – a shocking development, as they bared women's legs for the first time. Such European designers as Jean Patou and Elsa Schiaparelli responded by embellishing their *maillots* with brightly coloured, art deco-inspired motifs and designs. In the 1930s, the growing popularity of sunbathing inspired suits that were cut low at the back and had cut-outs at the side; most costumes incorporated short skirts to cover the thighs. The new concept of the 'beach wardrobe' also included a range of playsuits and overgarments.

The introduction of latex-based fabrics allowed the swimming costume to cling to every curve and heralded the glamorous styles of the 1940s and 1950s. Beachwear really came into its own thanks to

Hollywood. Such young starlets as Rita Hayworth, Betty Grable and Marilyn Monroe posed in fashionable swimwear, helping to make the swimsuit synonymous with feminine beauty, and by the mid-1940s the message was clear: glamour had hit the beach and everyone could take part. Soon showgirl-style swimming costumes in gold and silver lamé, with built-in boning and copious amounts of

shirring and draping, filtered down into
the average woman's beach wardrobe.
Exaggerated femininity was the hallmark
of the 1950s, both in fashion generally
and on the beach. The major American
swimwear companies, such as Cole of
California and Catalina, which had been
driving changes in swimwear styles and
technology since the 1920s, produced
swimming costumes cut like evening
gowns, with boning and the waist nipped
in, and decorated with beads and sequins;
also a part of the scene were animal
prints and exotic Hawaiian prints.

As the 1960s approached, the mood
changed and the fashion for the deep tan
and the skimpy bikini all but obliterated
the one-piece swimming costume. Yet the
swimsuit made a triumphant return in
the 1970s and 1980s, when the new ideal
of the fit, sculpted body led swimwear
manufacturers to produce stretchy suits
cut high on the thigh. Racer-style one-piece
'tank' suits with cross-back shapes allowed
women to dive straight in without fear
of their bikini bottoms slipping off, and
these suits not only bared more skin than
earlier types of one-piece, but also were
extremely light. Such new fabrics as Lycra
allowed for super-light, metallic-coloured
'skinsuits' that could double as dancewear
in the evenings.

Beachwear has remained an important
part of most wardrobes. Today there is
a wide variety of styles to choose from,
from streamlined athletic styles in
high-tech fabrics, to the retro styles of
the 1930s and 1940s with visible boning
and underwires, and glamorous pieces
with strategic cut-aways and metallic
finishes. Dressing up for the pool or the
beach has never been easier or more fun.

Design innovation
and fabric technology
have given designers
plenty of scope
for adventurous
interpretations of the
classic *maillot de bain*.

37. Wrap dress

of domesticity. Simplicity patterns of the 1930s show brightly coloured house dresses with heart-shaped pockets that were uncomplicated to make.

During the Second World War, as necessity became fashion's buzzword, such American designers as Claire McCardell created casual designs that were stylish enough to be worn in the city. McCardell's famous Popover dress of 1942, a wrap-front denim dress that featured a quilted pocket and a detachable oven mitt, was essentially a stylish remodelling of the humble house dress; it sold for only $6.95 and was an instant success. The Popover soon became available in other materials, such as cotton gingham, silk and corduroy, and women queued up to buy it.

The wrap dress blazed back on to the fashion scene as a symbol of women's liberation in the early 1970s, when women

Diane von Furstenberg's signature look, the wrap dress, shown as part of her ready-to-wear line of 1973. Its success put the designer on the cover of *Newsweek*, which called her 'the most marketable woman since Coco Chanel'.

'Feel like a woman, wear a dress', declared the American advertisement in 1973. The dress in question was no ordinary one, but the Diane von Furstenberg wrap dress. Since this figure-hugging jersey garment burst on to the New York fashion scene some forty years ago, it has become one of the bestselling dresses ever thanks to its synthesis of practicality and sex appeal.

The concept of the wrap dress can be traced back to the 1920s, when the 'house dress' was introduced in the United States as a simple dress in which to perform household chores. It was loose-fitting and easy to slip on, with two front panels that crossed over each other and tied at the back, and it could be worn on its own or over other clothes. Usually made of patterned, easily washable fabric, and embellished with appliqué or trimmed with rickrack, it was the ultimate symbol

The doyenne of the wrap dress, Diane von Furstenberg (top), and her sister Alexandra model late-1990s versions of her design.

Easy to wear and flattering yet practical, the wrap dress can be dressed down for casual wear, or up for a more formal look.

were emerging as a new force in the workplace and wanted clothes in which they could be comfortable at work. Slinky jersey dresses cut slightly above the knee, set off by shoes with ankle straps, became popular, as did the soft draped jersey dresses pioneered by the American designers Geoffrey Beene and Roy Halston. These unstructured yet body-hugging dresses came in many forms, but none was as famous as the Diane von Furstenberg wrap dress, launched in 1972. Simple and cut to flatter, this drip-dry cotton jersey dress clung to the body but flared at the bottom, and was both elegant and sexy. It was the ultimate go-anywhere dress. The prominent feminist Gloria Steinem was a keen supporter, and the dress became a national phenomenon. By 1975 Von Furstenberg was producing 15,000 dresses a week, and in 1980 Dolly Parton referenced the designer in her song 'Working Girl': 'Cause she must dress in comfort for the job she must perform … She's elegant and stylish … Designer clothes by Halston and Diane von Furstenberg … She goes so many places and she does so many things, 'cause she's a working girl.'

The wrap dress went into a fashion slump in the 1980s and 1990s, only to rise again in 1997 when Von Furstenberg relaunched her classic design, and it re-emerged as the quintessential sleek and sexy dress of the decade. Today the no-fuss wrap dress can still cut the sartorial mustard. Produced by such high-end labels as Issa and the high street alike, in styles ranging from leopard-print through ruffled chiffon to plain and simple, the wrap dress still manages to provide grown-up chic for any woman.

38. Poncho

An early-1920s image showing an Andean man in a poncho on a busy street.

Whether knitted or woven, plain or patterned, the poncho is the bohemian alternative to the coat or the jacket. A loose-fitting and easy-to-wear overgarment that consists essentially of a single piece of fabric with an opening in the centre for the head, it can also be surprisingly glamorous. Today's ponchos, from multicoloured fringed 'ethnic' versions to sparkly evening models, are less about the pot-smoking hippies of yore and more about serious style, and their one-size-fits-all convenience makes them a handy year-round cover-up, being equally at home over a light summer dress or a chunky polo neck in the winter.

The poncho originates from the Andean region of South America – brightly decorated woven examples dating from 200 BC are among the treasures of Peru's National Museum of Archaeology,

Anthropology and History – and made its way north up to Mexico. The concept was adopted by the military during the American Civil War (1861–65) as a way to keep soldiers and their equipment dry. The poncho's fashion debut came via the spaghetti western films of the mid-1960s, notably *A Fistful of Dollars* (1964) and *For a Few Dollars More* (1965), starring a mean- and moody-looking Clint Eastwood as the enigmatic, poncho-wearing 'Man with No Name'. Meanwhile, the countercultural hippies were 'turning on' to all kinds of ethnic dress. Kaftans and multicoloured ponchos with leather fringing, teamed with patchwork jeans and love beads, were the regalia of the San Francisco 'peace and love' community.

In common with many other types of anti-fashion dressing, the downbeat hippy look was hijacked by the fashion mainstream, and by the end of the 1960s ethnic-inspired ponchos were seen in most collections. The catwalk was buried in an avalanche of tie-dyed cotton dresses, embellished fabrics from India and Greece, brightly coloured ponchos, beaded headwraps and Native American headbands. Ponchos were everywhere, in a myriad of styles, from Pucci's

The drummer Ringo Starr in a Mexican poncho during a visit to Copenhagen in 1970, after the Beatles split.

Below: Classic with a twist from Alexander McQueen's Autumn/ Winter 2005–06 ready-to-wear collection.

brightly patterned chiffon versions to fringed styles by Emmanuelle Khanh. Away from the catwalk, fringed, woollen or crocheted ponchos, worn over granny dresses, jeans or long skirts, were popular with hippies, celebrities and the average woman alike.

The poncho stuck around in the early 1970s as ethnic-inspired clothes remained at the forefront of fashion. Such flamboyant designers as Bill Gibb showed beautiful multi-patterned full-length ponchos with drawstring necks; other bold and dramatic creations were Missoni's signature zigzag multicoloured knits and Kaffe Fassett's Indian-inspired versions. For women's daywear, woollen poncho dresses could be partnered with tights and boots, and Pauline Trigère's taupe silk poncho frock was particularly elegant for the evening.

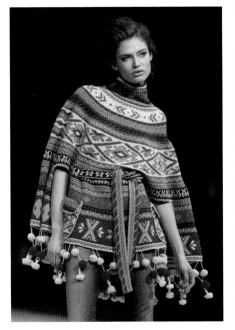

Relegated to the frumpy end of fashion in the late 1970s, the poncho was resurrected briefly around 2005 at the height of boho mania. The cutting-edge designers Alexander McQueen and Dolce & Gabbana showed many-hued Navajo-inspired ponchos, as well as gauzy summer versions. Such boho-look standard-bearers as Kate Moss, Keira Knightley and Sienna Miller were all papped working the trend. More recently the poncho has become fashion news again, with designer versions including creations by Alexander Wang, Hermès and Chloé. Thrown over a pair of skinny jeans for a lean silhouette, or cut-off shorts and wellies for a summer boho look, the poncho is the perfect cover-up for any woman with a touch of the hippy spirit.

A light summer poncho from the American label St. John in 2006.

39. Go-go boot

Nancy Sinatra sang a song about them; the leggy models Twiggy and Veruschka wore them with cut-away minidresses; men loved to see them on women's legs. 'Go-go' boots – simple, low-heeled yet sexy and smart – romped across the 1960s landscape and became one of the quintessential symbols of the sexual revolution. They were also among the first women's fashion boots of the twentieth century.

While boots had been a popular style of women's footwear in the nineteenth century, they were not recognized as a potential high-fashion item until the early 1960s, when a new style of footwear was needed to balance out the shorter hemlines. The fashion boot drew attention to the legs and accentuated the sleek new silhouette of the A-line minidress. In 1962 a variation of the Chelsea boot with a flat heel was being worn under jersey

trousers, but it wasn't until 1964 that the go-go boot stepped provocatively on to the fashion scene. That year André Courrèges shocked and delighted the fashion world when he sent his models down the catwalk in white geometric-cut dresses (the Moon Girl collection) accessorized with calf-height boots made of white plastic. Low-heeled and with a squared-off toe, his 'space-age' boots projected a modern, steamlined and unabashedly sexy look, and signalled the beginning of a trend that was to last until the end of the decade.

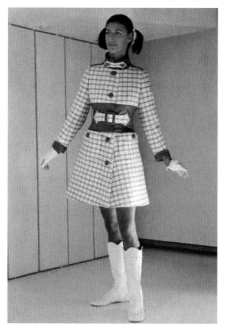

With his radical designs, Courrèges had created an 'anything goes' philosophy, and other designers were quick to follow. In 1965 Mary Quant launched a range of shiny, wet-look boots that came in a number of bright colours and had a zip round the ankle as well as down the length of the leg, so that they could also be worn as

André Courrèges boots and coat from 1968 (left). Courrèges had popularized the low-heeled go-go boot (opposite) in the mid-1960s.

Opposite: Elvis Presley
and a go-go-booted
Nancy Sinatra in the
musical action film
Speedway (1968).

ankle boots. Balenciaga produced a low, flat, brown patent-leather boot, and Roger Vivier (who had popularized the stiletto heel a decade earlier) made one in black with clear plastic sides. Manufacturers started mass-producing cheap copies in 'way-out' colours and materials, and these were extremely popular with teenagers, who wore them both on the street and to the discotheque. Go-go boots expressed the pop culture of the 1960s, and were popularized by dancers on the American television shows *Hullabaloo* and *Shindig*; sales skyrocketed after Nancy Sinatra wore a pair of sexy go-go boots to promote her single 'These Boots Are Made for Walking' on the *Ed Sullivan Show* in 1966. With the rising hemlines of the end of the 1960s the boots got higher, and such designers as Yves Saint Laurent made thigh-high boots intended to be worn with the tiniest of dresses.

In common with most of the fashion trends of the 1960s, by the beginning of the following decade go-go boots had petered out, their style not being compatible with the era's maxi dress and ethnic fashions. But they stomped back to their rebellious roots in the 1980s, when such street-conscious female rappers as Salt-N-Pepa wore flat, brightly coloured calf-length boots partnered with shiny leggings, big gold chains and lots of attitude. Flat-heeled mid-calf boots were revitalized in the early 2000s, as hemlines once again climbed up the thigh. Among the most popular of the new-style go-go boots has been the chunky, square-toed, go-with-everything mid-calf biker boot, which makes legs look long and slim whether it is worn with skinny jeans or a flouncy dress. Today, some fifty years after it kicked off the swinging 1960s, the go-go boot may have lost its air of rebellion, but it has retained all its appeal.

Go-go girl! The classic shimmy of the go-go dancer of the late 1960s.

40. Hoodie

The sports drama film *Rocky* (1976), starring Sylvester Stallone, brought boxing chic and the grey hoodie into mainstream fashion.

It is just a sweatshirt with a hood and sometimes a zip front. Yet the hoodie is at once a signifier of the outcast, a high-fashion item and an everyday unisex garment, and it manages to make a statement despite its utilitarian design.

It could be argued that the original 'hoodies' were the hooded robes or tunics worn by medieval monks. But the first zipped-up, hooded sweatshirt was produced in the 1930s by the American clothing manufacturer Champion, which conceived the top as protective cold-weather wear for labourers and athletes. The hoodie's take-up by football players and track athletes imbued it with a sort of sporty glamour, and it soon crossed over from being a purely functional item to serving as general casual wear. The great Sears Roebuck mail-order catalogues of the time offered hooded sweatshirts for $1, with the strapline 'keep warm for winter sports'. By the mid-1940s, in common with many other items of sports clothing, the hoodie was becoming part of the preppy uniform of university students and fashionable young men.

In 1942 the American designer Claire McCardell created the first fashion hoodie for women. Her Superman range of soft jersey knit hoodies was initially designed as part of her own personal ski ensemble; the simple tops were modern and practical yet also elegant, and they gave women a new fashion template. Later McCardell incorporated hoods into her other lines, and soon her hooded tops in grey jersey with side buttons were sold with matching skirts and culottes; hoods even featured in beachwear and wedding gowns.

The hoodie was granted the status of a subcultural icon with the film *Rocky* (1976). Jogging through the urban

The hoodie has become a staple of street wear across youth cultures. Here, the actors Kate Mara and Max Minghella opt for a his-and-hers look in 2012.

landscape in his grey, sweat-stained hooded top, the working-class Rocky Bilboa (Sylvester Stallone) represented rugged masculinity and the drive to win against the odds. Rocky was tough, sexy and successful, and so was his hoodie. By the end of the 1970s the hooded sweatshirt, with its us-against-the-world profile, was being taken up by the New York black hip-hop subculture as a garment of defiance. Such individual performers and groups as Grandmaster Flash, Eric B. & Rakim and Public Enemy wore brightly coloured hooded sweat tops with tracksuit bottoms and flashy gold jewellery. As hip-hop music gained momentum in the 1980s, its distinctive style was adopted as a mainstream youth fashion statement, and kids everywhere zipped up to look cool.

As with so many other subcultural trends, it wasn't long before the hoodie

Hoodie

was appropriated by high fashion and appeared on the catwalk. In the mid-1980s Azzedine Alaïa was among the designers who caught the mood of the time, launching hooded tops and dresses in his signature stretch jersey. Valentino presented cashmere hooded cardigan jackets, and Yves Saint Laurent featured velvet hooded coats. By the late 1990s hip hop's rising popularity had inspired such clothes-makers as Tommy Hilfiger, Calvin Klein, Versace and Ralph Lauren to create the status hoodie: expensive, beautifully cut and glamorous fashion items made of shiny, silky materials or soft cotton. Today the posh hoodie is everywhere on the catwalks, from Gareth Pugh and Stella McCartney to Marc Jacobs. Whether it is sequined, in leopard print or of the softest cashmere, the grown-up hoodie is a fashion essential in every woman's wardrobe.

In 1998 the American designer Stephen Sprouse paired a short-sleeved hoodie with one of his colourful graphic-print dresses.

The street-hoodie look has been associated with hiding the identity of troublemakers, leading some shops and organizations to ban hooded clothing on their premises.

41. Trench coat

There is something intrinsically glamorous and mysterious about the trench coat. When worn tightly belted with the collar turned up, this double-breasted garment has a cachet shared by few other pieces of clothing. Although it began as part of the military uniform, the trench coat became an icon of the twentieth-century wardrobe, its no-nonsense attitude glamorized by appearances on the silver screen and wrapping almost anyone in an aura of drama and derring-do.

In 1914, Thomas Burberry submitted to the United Kingdom's War Office a design for an officer's raincoat, using his own patented waterproof cotton gaberdine fabric, and he became an official outfitter to the British Army. Burberry's lightweight beige coat gained popularity with the armed forces during the First World War, when it could be worn in the rain-sodden trenches as an alternative to the heavy woollen coat, giving rise to the name 'trench' coat. The firm's original, Trench 21, was lined with woollen cloth and belted. It had wrist straps, a storm flap across the back for extra protection, and D-rings at the front and rear on which the officers hung map cases. The company is still best known for its trench coats.

After the war the trench coat crossed over from the battlefield on to the streets, when returning veterans were reluctant to sacrifice the comfort and practicality of military clothes. By the 1930s it had become a stylish garment for both men and women. Movies and actors have a way of elevating ordinary pieces of clothing to cult status, and in this the trench coat is no exception: screen siren Greta Garbo helped to boost the popularity of the coat when she famously wore hers

Jacqueline Kennedy Onassis (below), as she became after her marriage to the shipping magnate Aristotle Onassis, in a 1970s take on the classic trench.

Trench coat

over a man's trouser suit, with her trademark beret tilted on one side or a matching waterproof hat. Hollywood continued to do much to promote the coat in the 1940s and 1950s. Humphrey Bogart modelled the Trench 21 as it made its film debut in *Casablanca* (1942); loaded with authenticity and a certain heroic sex appeal, it thereafter became intrinsically connected with the hard-boiled, wisecracking, world-weary private detectives of the film noir movies of the period, such as *The Big Sleep* (1946), also starring Bogart, and *Out of the Past* (1947), starring Robert Mitchum.

Women, too, loved the trench, which became popular with actresses and style icons in the 1960s. The look was exemplified by Audrey Hepburn, who belted hers tightly and accessorized it with a pair of feminine low stilettos in

the film *Breakfast at Tiffany's* (1961). By the 1970s the trench had become a mainstream womenswear fashion item, complementing the mannish tailoring and trouser suits that became popular in the early part of the decade. Such American designers as Roy Halston and Calvin Klein included slimmed-down versions as part of their mix-and-match classics, and trench-coat detailing, such as epaulettes and ties on the sleeves, became an integral part of the 1970s look.

Since then, the trench coat has been a classic item of both menswear and womenswear, and it is still as popular as ever. Whether it is the traditional British trench or a slinky, silky revamped version, this coat is an elegant, classic cover-up that balances practicality and style. Its neutrality and simplicity are sure to make it the apogee of chic for years to come.

Variations in the classic trench colours and materials have included this mid-1960s neon tangerine version by Claret.

Opposite: The 1940s film-noir movement saw the glamorization of the street detective in his trenchcoat and fedora, as played by Humphrey Bogart.

Melanie Griffith works the trench look in *Working Girl* (1988), co-starring Harrison Ford.

42. Edwardian blouse

In the early years of the twentieth century, fashionable women in high-neck white blouses were a common sight in the United Kingdom and the United States, partly owing to the influence of the 'Gibson Girl', the character created by the American illustrator Charles Dana Gibson in 1890. With her hair piled into a loose chignon, and wearing a starched, high-neck blouse and a flowing skirt, the Gibson Girl personified the modern young woman. Beautiful, independent and focused on personal fulfilment, she was the ultimate in contemporary grace.

The Gibson Girl's new clothing style created the fashion for the 'Edwardian' blouse: white, close-fitting, front-buttoned with a lace-edged yoke and leg-of-mutton sleeves, and featuring tucks and pleats in the bodice. By today's standards the blouse may seem prim, but the style was extremely modern for the time. Forward-thinking women of the Edwardian period took up the fashion as a rejection of the overly fussy and frilly dresses of the period; this new, more practical style was adopted by working women, such as office workers and teachers, and worn for the new pursuits of cycling and rowing, which required freedom of movement.

The high-neck blouse came back into favour when retro dressing became fashionable in the early 1970s. Women were wearing pin-tucked blouses, lace petticoats and other clothes from the turn of the century, a time they felt had been simpler. The British designer Laura Ashley, in particular, found popularity with her nostalgic designs. Her conservative and demure high-neck blouses, in plain white

In this image from the late nineteenth century, a young American woman by the name of Joblina Howland embodies the charms of the 'Gibson Girl' of Charles Dana Gibson's illustrations. Her high-neck shirt was a revolution in women's fashion.

In the United Kingdom, a brief revival in the frilly high collar took place in the early 1980s, after the style was worn by Lady Diana Spencer in the period prior to her wedding to the Prince of Wales. The look became typical of the 'Sloane Ranger' style.

and floral prints inspired by the styles of
the nineteenth century, became part of the
smart hippy aesthetic.

While nostalgic dressing gave way
to disco wear and punk style, the Laura
Ashley Edwardian blouse kept on going.
In the early 1980s it was a staple of the
sartorially conservative style of the upper-
class Sloane Rangers (so called because
they lived near Sloane Square, London),
who wore it with sensible navy-blue skirts
and rows of pearls, and dressed it down
with a hard-wearing waxed Barbour jacket
(because such women also often had
homes in the country, or regularly visited
friends and family there). But it was
super-Sloane Lady Diana Spencer who
put the high-neck blouse firmly on the
fashion map. After the press carried
pictures of Prince Charles's fiancée smiling
bashfully in a ruffled blouse peeping out
from under a demure jacket in 1981,
white Edwardian blouses took off. Such
design houses as Valentino, Moschino and
even Chanel produced ruffled high-neck
blouses intended to be worn under peplum
jackets with gathered knee-length skirts.
This overdone and fussy style was quickly
nudged out of the spotlight by the brightly
coloured 'power jackets' and Lycra
miniskirts of the mid-1980s.

In the early twenty-first century the
ruffled high-neck blouse came back into
fashion and the Sloane look was given
an update. Laura Ashley and Paul Smith
produced floral and pin-tuck blouses, and
in 2005 there was even embroidery in
Burberry's and Dolce & Gabbana's new
collections. This time round, though, the
blouses were updated with an injection
of colour and small floral designs. Paired
with camel A-line skirts or long, narrow

trousers that elongated the legs, they were
part of the new ladylike chic. By the end
of the new century's first decade, for the
neo-Edwardian lady sweet ruffles and ties
were very much mixed with a touch of street
appeal: high-neck blouses were rocking in
black and dark purple, or in diaphanous
chiffon, and were paired not with prim morals
and bloomers, but with denim miniskirts,
lurex leggings and vertiginous heels.

43. Leggings

Dance classes and aerobics, popularized by videos by Jane Fonda and other stars, and by such venues as the New York Dance Center, became more than just exercise; they were also fun and sexy. When disco music rose to popularity in the mid-1970s, the dance-based look entered the fashion mainstream. Dance floors were packed with women strutting their stuff in leotards and sparkly leggings teamed with strappy golden sandals or stilettos.

All-American (left): an ensemble of star-covered leggings, vest top and blouse by Marc Jacobs, 1985.

Jane Fonda strikes a pose for the cover of *Jane Fonda's Workout Book* (1982).

Fashion can be a cruel affair. After all, what could be worse than a must-have trend that is so unforgiving, it can make even the slimmest of women look as if their legs are wrapped in cling film? Yet despite being one of fashion's trickiest style challenges, leggings, the stretchy cotton brother of the trouser, have survived and thrived in the decades since they appeared as dancewear in the 1970s.

The medieval version of leggings, known as hose, consisted of two separate woollen tubes – one for each leg – worn under a tunic, primarily for warmth. Leggings entered the fashion lexicon as the enthusiasm for keep-fit gained momentum in the 1970s, and women all over the globe 'went for the burn' dressed in leotards and stretchy cotton footless tights.

Camouflage-look leopard-print leggings were shown by the American designer Betsey Johnson in 2011.

By the beginning of the 1980s, sports clothing had become acceptable as general street wear, and leotards and leggings worn with trainers and dance pumps were seen on every street corner. Norma Kamali's 'sweats' collections, with leggings and jogging suits cut in brightly coloured cotton and grey flannel, inspired a myriad of copycat designs. Thanks to the wider adoption of Lycra in daywear fabrics, stretch was given a dose of sex appeal. In London, the label Body Map, established in 1982 by Stevie Stewart and David Holah immediately after their graduation from college, charmed fashion editors and trendsters with its 'second-skin' fashion, which featured stretchy dresses worn over brightly coloured leggings and footless tights. Vivienne Westwood's Hypnos collection with padded blouson jackets, black leggings and triple-tongued baseball shoes (1984) created an androgynous, figure-hugging silhouette.

The feel-good dance film *Flashdance* (1983) and the long-running Broadway musical *A Chorus Line* (premiered in 1975) did much to promote the gym-styled street look, in which leggings in a variety of colours and patterns were worn with off-the-shoulder baggy T-shirts and leg warmers. A young Madonna, with mussed-up hair, a cropped top and ripped leggings worn under a miniskirt, epitomized the street-urchin look of the mid-1980s.

Today leggings are a key trend on the catwalks. From Nicolas Ghesquière's gold-plated leggings for Balenciaga – ensationally displayed in 2007 by Beyoncé at the prestigious BET awards in Los Angeles – to laser-cut leather leggings from Rodarte, stretchy footless tights are now produced by a slew of premium brands. Away from the thigh one-upmanship of ultra-toned stars, the fashion for wearing capri-length leggings under dresses and floaty kaftans is the ultimate in early-summer dressing and gives a fresh twist to any classic outfit.

44. T-shirt

Walk down any street anywhere in the world, and you will see men and women dressed in T-shirts. Whether it is cut loose and baggy, cropped to the midriff or skintight, and whether it is paired with skinny jeans or a smart skirt, the humble T-shirt is a quintessential piece of unisex leisurewear. In common with blue jeans, this plain, originally unglamorous garment has managed through the decades to cross all sorts of social and stylistic boundaries, having been variously a symbol of the rock 'n' roll generation, a visual shorthand for anti-materialism and, especially in the 1980s, a status symbol.

The modern tee began life as an undergarment issued to American soldiers in the late nineteenth century. It embarked on its journey into the public consciousness during the Second World War, when American newsreels and such magazines

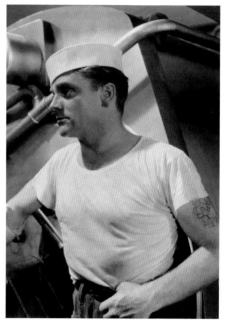

The T-shirt started out as an undergarment for US forces in the late nineteenth century. Here James Cagney sports a classic white model in the romantic comedy film *Here Comes the Navy* (1934).

as *Life* showed images of soldiers stripped down to their white T-shirts in order to keep cool. By 1948 the hugely successful Sears mail-order catalogue was advertising white T-shirts for all the family as smart holiday wear, yet despite making inroads into beach apparel the tee remained socially unacceptable as urban daywear.

The white T-shirt dipped its toe into the fashion pool in the 1950s as a symbol of teenage angst and rebellion, given a new street cred by a host of young Hollywood actors. Marlon Brando imbued it with dangerous sex appeal in *A Streetcar Named Desire* (1951), and James Dean became a teen icon with his outfit of white T-shirt, unkempt jeans and sneakers in *Rebel Without a Cause* (1955). The tee remained central to the outsider hippy look of the 1960s, for both men and women; colourfully tie-dyed or printed with peace-and-love

The tee has long been employed as a vehicle to communicate slogans and identity. Left, the British designer Katharine Hamnett (centre) in one of her T-shirts alongside the model Jodie Kidd in 2003; opposite, the American actress Jessica Alba in a Rolling Stones T-shirt in 2012.

motifs, it was teamed with scruffy jeans, beaded necklaces and long hair.

Mainstream women's fashion caught up with the T-shirt in the mid-1960s. Particularly chic was the striped long-sleeved tee, paired with capri pants or short flared trousers. In Paris, Yves Saint Laurent offered nautical T-shirts in his newly established ready-to-wear boutique, Rive Gauche, introducing the notion of the luxury tee. Despite this, throughout the 1970s the T-shirt remained standard unisex leisurewear, the ultimate in egalitarian chic and often used as a means of personal expression. Wearers could proclaim their political beliefs through images of the Latin American revolutionary Che Guevara or anti-war slogans; but the message could equally be a corny joke or a picture of teen heart-throb Donny Osmond. Stylistic variations of the time included the

cap sleeve; the scoop and V-neck; and the oversized women's T-shirt of the disco era, worn tied at the side, over leotards and sparkly leggings.

Sloganeering T-shirts continued into the 1980s. High-profile examples included 'Frankie Says Relax', produced as a marketing tool for the band Frankie Goes to Hollywood, whose debut single 'Relax' (1983) had been banned by the BBC because of its 'overtly sexual' nature; and Katharine Hamnett's Choose Life collection of 1984, featuring such politically controversial statements as '58 per cent don't want Pershing' (a reference to plans to site the American missile in Europe). But the 1980s will be remembered as a time when fashion went dressy, and this period also saw the rise of the luxury T-shirt, with such international designers as Ralph Lauren, Giorgio Armani and Calvin Klein offering expensive plain tees with their logos emblazoned across the chest. Worn under a beautifully cut jacket, the new designer T-shirt looked effortlessly chic and glamorous.

Since then, the appeal of the T-shirt has never waned. Away from the world of high fashion, the casual style and affordability of the T-shirt make it the ideal functional garment for today's fast-paced lifestyle.

Self-promotion from Diesel, one of countless fashion firms to have used the T-shirt to advertise their brands.

45. Platform shoe

In fashion, some of the most successful and popular designs have been among the least practical to wear. One such is the platform shoe, which began life as the *chopine* – a shoe mounted on a wide cork stilt – worn by the aristocratic ladies of sixteenth-century Venice to keep the hems of their long dresses out of the mud. *Chopines* soon became a fashion item in their own right, soaring up to 22 cm (9 in.) in height. Often servants would be required to help balance the wearer, meaning that only the very wealthiest could afford to wear them.

The development of the modern platform shoe (now often defined as having a sole at least 7 cm/3 in. thick) is usually credited to the French shoe designer Roger Vivier, of stiletto-heel fame, in the mid-1930s. When Vivier sent his creation to the American shoemaker

B. Delman, Delman was unimpressed, and it took the avant-garde designer Elsa Schiaparelli to see the potential of such a shoe. In 1939 she helped to launch the fashion for platforms when she showed them as part of her collection. Fashionable women swiftly adopted the look (which was also pioneered by Salvatore Ferragamo), and throughout the 1940s flamboyant platform sandals and shoes abounded. Footwear with high platforms in silver and gold, embellished with Chinese motifs or studded with brass and jewels, were revolutionary and sexy; above all, their thick soles made the high heels more comfortable. The singer and film star Carmen Miranda – who was only about 1.5 m (5 ft) tall – rarely wore any other type of shoe. By the mid-1940s most women in Europe and America owned at least one pair of platforms, usually soled

The petite actress and songstress Carmen Miranda pictured in 1948 in an early example of the height-boosting, skyscraping platform shoe.

Ultra-platform shoes on the streets of Japan in 2002.

Platform shoe

The 5.5-cm (2¼ in.) platform of Christian Louboutin's Daffodile range of 2012 gives the shoes a heel height of about 16 cm (6¼ in.).

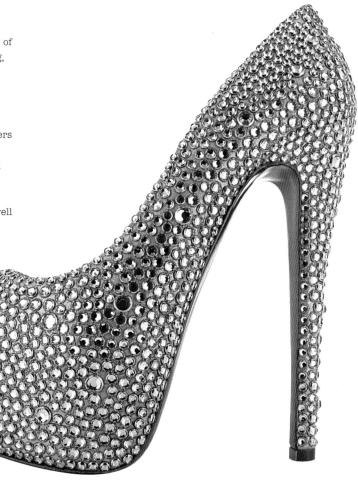

in cork because of the wartime shortage of wood and leather. They elongated the leg, and their bulky form complemented the boxy wartime silhouette.

The platform fell from favour in the late 1940s as the stiletto shoe teetered on to the fashion scene, but shoe designers have always striven to defy practicality, and in the late 1960s a platform revival took footwear to dizzying heights. The platform came in hundreds of versions, from a 1940s-style peep-toe that went well with chintzy retro summer dresses, to zipped suede boots. When Barbara Hulanicki designed a high skintight leather boot with a 12.5-cm (5-in.) heel for Biba, her London boutique, in 1968, the style was so popular that some 75,000 pairs were sold in just a few months. At their apogee in the mid-1970s, platform soles were usually 5 cm (2 in.) thick and heels 13 cm (5 in.) high. Thanks to the influence of such glam-rock stars as David Bowie, Gary Glitter and Elton John, who sported ridiculous spangly platforms covered in glitter or appliquéd leather stripes, the style became universal for men, too.

Platforms made the headlines again in 1993, after a vertiginously high pair by the idiosyncratic designer Vivienne Westwood sent the model Naomi Campbell crashing to the catwalk. Westwood's wooden platforms that laced up the leg, and towering black versions lined with studs, were extreme statement shoes. Today, the super-platform is coveted by the fashion cognoscenti. The French shoe designer Christian Louboutin should take some of the blame, with his toweringly high platform shoes that have become favourites with celebrities. Noted fans of the ultra-platform include the actress Gwyneth Paltrow and the singer Gwen Stefani; where the celebrities go, the high street follows, and today the super-platform is a global bestseller.

46. Turban

A soft and striking head covering that carries overtones of Eastern promise, the turban is one of fashion's more exotic offerings. Essentially a draped hat inspired by the headdresses worn by Muslim and Sikh men, it consists of fabric that is twisted and wrapped around the head. When it was introduced as a women's accessory in the early twentieth century, few would hve banked on its long-term survival.

While the history of the turban goes back thousands of years (it is mentioned in the Old Testament), it didn't enter the fashion vocabulary until 1910, when the French designer Paul Poiret shocked society with his 'maharaja' turban hat. Inspired by Sergei Diaghilev's innovative Ballets Russes and a love of all things oriental, Poiret's tightly swathed, often brightly coloured and ornate hats were intended to be teamed with his flamboyant

Marie Prevost in *The Godless Girl* (1929), the last silent film directed by the American film-maker Cecil B. DeMille.

harem pants, fluid silken pyjama trousers or kaftan-style dresses. The turban continued to be popular throughout the 1920s, and it paved the way for the close-fitting cloche hat that became the symbol of the liberated flapper. It remained beloved by 1930s Hollywood stars, including Gloria Swanson, Greta Garbo and the Polish-born Pola Negri, who offset her heavily kohled eyes with metallic-look turbans; in France, the designer Coco Chanel teamed hers with yachting trousers and a row of pearls.

The turban was revitalized during the Second World War, first as a practical necessity and then as one of the most popular styles of headwear. At a time when materials were in short supply, the turban was simple and chic, and allowed women to look groomed and smart all day and into the evening. The 1940s turban came in many styles: down-to-earth,

The turban's combination of style and practicality made such headwear essential for Second World War munitions workers in their drive to keep their hair clean and safe from becoming entangled in machinery. Less workaday versions could be worn in the evening.

Turban

Opposite: A composite image of the actress Susan Shaw wearing a variety of evening turbans in 1943. Such glossy styles could dress up drab wartime clothing.

Left: A model wears a crocheted boho turban backstage at Dolce & Gabbana's Autumn/ Winter 2004–05 collection in Milan.

inexpensive turbans were ideal as head coverings for British and American female factory workers, while flamboyant versions lifted wartime spirits and brightened up the drab fashions of the day. In Hollywood, Carmen Miranda's exuberant fruit-bedecked turbans almost stole the show in such riotous comedies as *That Night in Rio* (1941).

By the 1950s, pastel-toned turbans that coordinated with the era's fashionable outfits were the epitome of femininity and looked sophisticated with the slimline silhouette of the day. Exquisite turbans by the milliner Paulette Marchand were stylish and chic; her practical *chapeau mou* ('soft hat') remained a fashion staple throughout the decade. In the United States, John Fredericks and the French-born designer

Lilly Daché produced beautiful turbans that flattered rather than dominated any outfit.

As hats became less popular during the 1960s – a trend hastened by the advent of such short haircuts as the bob and the urchin cut – the turban disappeared from view. It was taken up again in the early 1970s as fashion went on a fantasy trip. Ultra-glamorous, theatrical clothing, such as flowing kaftans, silk jersey gowns and satin pyjama trousers, lent themselves to the draped simplicity of the turban. In the United Kingdom, Bill Gibb's spectacular patterned dresses were offset by flamboyant silk turbans; in France, Roland Klein created black turbans with matching jumpsuits, and Yves Saint Laurent produced evening silk ensembles with matching turbans that were a hit with the glitterati and the jet set.

While the turban fell under the radar during the 1980s and 1990s, it resurfaced as a cool fashion item in the twenty-first century. From shiny, metallic-look headdresses – such as the gold one worn by Kate Moss to accessorize a Marc Jacobs gold lamé dress at the Metropolitan Museum's Costume Institute Gala in New York in 2009 – to pretty pastel shades that partner Indian silks or printed dresses, the turban is a stylish accessory that lends a note of glamour to any outfit.

Pastel dresses and turbans designed in 1949 by Joset Walker. The French-born designer made her career in the United States.

47. Shift

The shift dress is a celebration of understated elegance and classic chic, especially when it is accessorized with a simple row of pearls and perhaps a cardigan. Its clean lines give it a sharp, smart appearance that is universally flattering and appropriate for any occasion. This deliberately simple garment is one of the greatest fashion revolutions of the past 100 years, and one of the first modern styles for women that is still seen today.

In the early twentieth century, as both fashion and the female body freed themselves from the constraints of the hourglass corset, ease of movement and practicality became the criteria for the new dress codes. After the First World War, fashions ignored the natural curves of the female figure, and by 1920 the straight-cut chemise was a popular style. The typical dress had a tank top and a

In the 1960s, fashion houses took the simple cut of the shift and embellished it with geometric designs. Here the American actress Pamela Tiffin poses in a dress by Gayle Kirkpatrick made in 1966 with revolutionary Stretchnit material.

low waist, and legs were uncovered below the knee for the first time in history. This long-line silhouette dominated the dress scene in the early years of the decade, leading by 1925 to the straight-up-and-down shift. Coco Chanel in particular pared away fussy details and adapted male garments to create forward-looking dresses that were simple, untailored and short (just below the knee). Made of viscose, jersey or artificial silk, Chanel's dresses were within the price range of almost everyone, and easy to wear and wash. Although the shift didn't last beyond the economic collapse of 1929 – when fashion went back to being serious – it made a spectacular return two decades later.

During the 1950s the level of the waistline fluctuated, and changes in line and hemline came in quick succession. By the middle of the decade, after years of Dior's nipped-in waists and full skirts, most designers were concentrating on a more linear silhouette. Givenchy's revolutionary 'sack' dress of 1956 bypassed the waist and freed women from tight-fitting, restrictive styles, and it started the trend for straighter, shift-like dresses. From Balenciaga's slimline suits to Dior's 'spindle-line' dresses that resembled nightshirts, the new style

The definition of classic chic, Jacqueline Kennedy Onassis popularized the shift and made it part of her signature look. She is pictured left in 1970.

Whether in a structured 1960s cut or a softer, more fluid waif feel, as in the Calvin Klein dress of 2004 below, the shift is easy to wear and to accessorize, and remains a modern wardrobe staple.

represented youthful modernity, and was the prototype for the early tunic dresses of the following decade.

Simplicity continued to guide fashion in the early 1960s, and the straight shift was one of the most popular shapes. It fell in a clean line from the shoulder to just above the knee and, although similar to the A-line minidress, was a more ladylike alternative to the baby-doll look. Variations on the theme were near-endless, and the dresses were often worn with matching coats and flat pumps or boots. From the ubiquitous Lilly dresses by Lilly Pulitzer in their bright wash-and-wear cotton, to Yves Saint Laurent's range inspired by the work of the Dutch painter Piet Mondrian, the shift gave women a modern, lithe look. During her time as American first lady, Jacqueline Kennedy was known for her elegant shift dresses in pale colours, which she teamed with short jackets and her signature pillbox hat.

Since the 1960s the shift dress has appeared time and again on the catwalk. Calvin Klein's short, strapless and classic shifts, in black, white or beige, made headlines during the 1990s, and were a welcome change from all the fussy detailing of the decade. Today, in a fashion world brimming over with ostentation and raunch appeal, the shift dress is a ladylike breath of fresh air. Whether it is paired with turbo-charged stilettos or with simple ballet flats, the shift always manages to keep the wearer on the sophisticated side of sexy.

48. Loafer

The loafer was central to the preppy look that dominated American fashion for decades. Rock Hudson was one of the many who adopted the crisp but casual look in the 1950s.

When the loafer was launched in the United States in 1933, few could have imagined how popular the slip-on shoe would be. It became the ultimate preppy footwear, and no fashion-conscious American kid was without a pair. Fans have included President John F. Kennedy (who wore his without socks) and Katharine Hepburn, who teamed them with wide-cut trousers.

The origins of the loafer can be traced back to the Native American moccasin, which was made from a single piece of soft leather that was wrapped around the foot. In the early 1930s the American leather company Spaulding marketed a soft slip-on shoe that it called the loafer, because one loafed around in it. Sensible, practical and extremely comfortable, it was popular with both men and women and complemented the casual styles of the era.

Other American shoe manufacturers issued similar shoes, putting their own individual stamp on them. Most loafers have a long upper that reaches high up the foot; a now classic variation is the penny loafer, with a decorative slotted strip on the upper.

In the 1950s American college students of both sexes took to the loafer, the casual style of which perfectly complemented jeans and capri pants. The shoe's status as a fashion item became assured when James Dean made it part of his teenage-rebel uniform of jeans and white T-shirt, and Elvis Presley wore a pair of white buckskin loafers in the musical film *Jailhouse Rock* (1957). The penny loafer in particular was the quintessential American shoe throughout the 1950s and 1960s, worn at the office as well as at weekends. The loafer was taken up by louche European

society gentlemen, the emerging jet set
and glamorous stars of the silver screen
in the early 1960s, when Italian design
house Gucci produced a lighter version,
with a distinctive metal strap in the shape
of a horse's bridle bit straddling the upper.

Since then, the popularity of the loafer
has fluctuated in accordance with catwalk
trends. Designers gave the shoe a chic
makeover in the early 1990s. The
buzzwords were Patrick Cox Wannabe

loafers; launched in 1993, they came in
flat or stack-heeled versions and were an
instant hit with such celebrities as Madonna
and Elton John. In 1995 Chanel introduced
high-heeled loafers that came with specially
minted coins in their slotted strips; at about
the same time loafers by the label Belgian
Shoes (which had been handmade in velvet,
suede or patent leather since the mid-1950s)
became greatly sought after.

As collegiate chic became big fashion
news at the end of the noughties, the loafer
was everywhere on the catwalk. Chanel,
Marc Jacobs and Céline reinterpreted the
classic shoe, and such household names as
Kirsten Dunst and Jessica Alba were among
those who partnered it with skinny jeans,
or cute minidresses and leggings. With the
recent vogue for loafers in such untraditional
colours as bright orange and pink (and even
tartan, as produced by Tommy Hilfiger), it
looks as if the loafer is set to thrive as one
of the most wearable footwear trends.

Fun, freedom and the
supple penny loafer
in the mid-1940s.

49. Combat trousers

First issued by the British military in 1938, combat trousers (also known as cargo pants) were introduced as a response to the growing mechanization of armies. Cut looser than regular army trousers, they were made of heavy khaki serge and featured large pleated side pockets that gave soldiers easy access to maps and other 'cargo'. Modern army combat trousers were born in 1942, when the United States Army started making them in cotton drill and added more pockets.

Some fifty years later, these utilitarian trousers crossed over from the battlefield to street wear. In the early 1990s a mood of apathy and social alienation was sweeping over British and American youth. Shampoo-averse, brooding Generation Xers (people born between the mid-1960s and the early 1980s) adopted a new grunge aesthetic that saw off the glossy, dressy styles of the day and embraced the downbeat, the naturalistic and the tatty. Such subcultural groups as indie and grunge kids raided army-surplus stores for oversized baggy combat trousers, chunky work boots and army coats. The grunge style of the American bands Nirvana, Pearl Jam and Smashing Pumpkins – with their unkempt look of tattered jeans and dirty cargo pants – influenced young people on both sides of the Atlantic.

While grunge fashion had its roots in alienation and poverty, the style that filtered down from the street to the catwalk was altogether different. By the mid-1990s grunge glamour was a trend, and military combat trousers had everyone's sartorial pulses racing. The British girl band All Saints pioneered a new slouchy chic, consisting of baggy combat trousers, pulled down so low on the hips that the

G-string underwear was visible, and teamed with skintight vests and trainers. Such designers as Marc Jacobs and Dolce & Gabbana offered combat trousers in softer fabrics and lighter colours, sometimes with ribbon trim or other embellishments. Ralph Lauren presented silk cargo pants on the runway in 1998, and shapeless, embroidered trousers by the Maharishi brand ('Mahas') were a favourite among

The plain, hard-wearing 'cargo pants' that were part of the field kit for American GIs during the Vietnam War are the direct ancestors of today's fashion combat trousers.

Even without side
pockets, these
alternative combats
retain a suggestion
of their military
background.

the 'beautiful people'. By the end of the
decade, what had once provided an edgy
alternative to jeans had become a standard
choice for all, available in cuts to suit all
shapes and sizes. Middle-aged men and
women took to this comfortable style,
confirming the mainstream status of the
garment. Combat-style clothing, including
three-quarter-length cargo pants, and
miniskirts and dresses with side pockets,
often in colourful camouflage prints, was
popular with everyone.

More recently combat trousers have
been reformulated and revitalized. As
the baggy, grungy look made way for a

sleeker silhouette in the early years of
the twenty-first century, a streamlined
version of the classic combie has been
introduced. A glamorous twist on the
traditional look has been offered by sexy
cargo pants cut leaner on the hips and
tighter on the legs, made in silver lamé
or satin, cropped or ruched high above
the ankle to reveal teetering stilettos.
Houlihans – thigh-clamping, reworked
skinny cargo pants launched in 2010 by
the jeans company J Brand – have been
favoured by such A-listers as the singer
Kylie Minogue and the actress Jessica
Alba. Today it is hard to find a designer
or high-street brand that hasn't produced
a version of the cargo pant. Whether
they are cut loose and baggy or skinny
and figure-hugging, combat trousers
not only have universal appeal, but also
are testimony to the power of simple,
utilitarian fashion.

50. Polo neck

Teamed with jeans and ballet flats, a black polo-neck jumper can create a look that is sharp and sophisticated, with overtones of beatnik cool. The rough, masculine garment worn by nineteenth-century French fishermen and sailors has evolved through the decades to become one of the fashion world's most versatile garments, and a reliable building block to any outfit.

Jumpers entered the fashion scene in the early 1920s, when Coco Chanel introduced her revolutionary black pullover. Her masculine-style jumpers, appropriated from the coarse sailors' roll-neck sweater, had slashed or V necks, but their unadorned style made them a forerunner of today's polo neck. Chanel's jumper was designed to be worn with the yachting trousers or pleated skirts that formed her line of casual, sporty clothes; ultra-modern and youthful, they gave women a new freedom

The 'skinny rib' of this polo neck allows the jumper to hug the body as it moves, giving the top a touch of urban polish. A more rugged, outdoorsy feel emanates from the cable-knit polo neck opposite, with its serpentine two-cable braiding of different widths.

and comfort. Jean Patou's sportswear-influenced jumpers in navy, red or white were also a prototype for the fashions to come. By the mid-1920s the sweater-and-skirt pairing was standard daytime apparel.

During the 1930s the high-neck sweater became fashionable for the bohemian male. One such was Noël Coward, who proudly wrote in his memoir *Present Indicative* (1937) that he had taken to 'wearing coloured turtle-necked jerseys, actually more for comfort than for effect, and soon I was informed by my evening paper that I had started a fashion'. Marlene Dietrich bucked women's fashion trends when she donned a masculine polo neck with a trouser suit, but in the following decade, as women got used to wearing mannish fashions during the Second World War, they took up the high-neck sweater and partnered it with simple skirts or tailored slacks.

The silhouette of the 1950s American 'sweater girl' consisted of the polo neck and a wide belt, which exaggerated the bust and hips, as modelled left by the actress Margaret Hayes.

The pragmatic image of the polo neck was transformed in the 1950s by glamorous images from Hollywood. Shapely 'sweater girls', including Marilyn Monroe, Jane Russell and Lana Turner, radiated a pneumatic sex appeal in their high-neck, tight-fitting jumpers that emphasized the breasts. In New York and San Francisco, the black polo neck was given an air of raffish cool by the freewheeling beatniks in the late 1950s. Such writers, poets and folk singers as Jack Kerouac, Allen Ginsberg and Bob Dylan drank, caroused and shook up the status quo in their signature black high-neck jumpers, black jeans and sneakers. Audrey Hepburn gave the look a fashionable makeover in her outfit of black turtleneck and black pedal pushers in the musical film *Funny Face* (1957).

In 1960 Yves Saint Laurent's dramatic Beat Look collection for the House of Dior sent shockwaves through the fashion press. Outfits of high-neck black-and-white pullovers, caps and leather coats were seen as subversive and anti-feminine but also as exciting and new, and it wasn't long before avant-garde creators followed Saint Laurent's lead. One of the period's dominant looks was the skinny-rib polo neck, by the likes of the London designers Mary Quant, Marion Foale and Sally Tuffin (under the label Foale and Tuffin) or the Scottish knitwear firm John Laing, teamed with straight black jersey trousers or worn under A-line tunics. By the 1970s this style of jumper had become an integral part of the classic American mix-and-match wardrobe. The epitome of wearable chic was a caramel, navy or white polo neck by Calvin Klein, Ralph Lauren or Sonia Rykiel, paired with tailored trousers, knickerbockers or a simple skirt.

The polo neck has remained a mainstay of fashion. With its pared-down shape, it is a viable alternative to the jacket, and is also elegant enough to be worn as evening wear. Whether it a be chunky model with an outdoorsy feel, a casual but classic merino-wool version or a slinky cashmere knit, the high-neck jumper is a reliable backdrop to any outfit and a timeless formula for urban chic.

51. Dungarees

The denim dungarees
of Depression-era
America, as seen in
this photograph of
a Louisiana man in
the 1930s, influenced
the early-1980s
folky farmhand look
of the British band
Dexys Midnight
Runners (below).

Wrath (1940), based on John Steinbeck's novel (1939). Women first wore dungarees during the Second World War, covering their hair with brightly coloured scarves and turbans as they took jobs in factories and worked as land girls in the fields.

Dungarees crossed over from the shop floor to the fashion arena when feminists took them up in the early 1970s. Tough, inexpensive and comfortable, the dungaree was the ultimate anti-fashion garment, bought from army surplus stores and industrial manufacturers. The figure-swamping bib overall swiftly became a symbol of 'women's lib'; it was worn by women who burned their bras, did not shave their legs and railed against men.

While loose, casual clothing had gained acceptance by the mid-1970s, men regarded dungarees as drab and dull, and longed for the return of women in

Brightly coloured dungarees featured in Madrid fashion week collections for 2013. Given the couture treatment, they are emerging as a chic design classic. Shown left is an offering from the Spanish label El Colmillo de Morsa.

When Roland Mouret designed for his Spring/Summer 2010 shows a pair of silk crêpe dungarees (later worn by Demi Moore with nothing underneath), one could be certain that the bib-and-buckle denim dungaree had thrown off its populist workwear associations and feminist shackles. Waist-high blue denim overalls for workmen were introduced by Levi Strauss in San Francisco in about 1875. By the 1930s the bibbed overall had become the uniform of the railway worker and the farmhand eking out a living in Depression-hit America, as seen on Henry Fonda in the dust-bowl epic *The Grapes of*

Dungarees

high heels, lipstick and bras. They had to wait a while. In the wake of the United Nations' International Women's Year of 1975, feminist dressing reached its apogee, and fashion went baggy. Breasts, waists and ankles were concealed; long smock dresses, full dirndl skirts and dungarees did the concealing. Designer labels took up the trend and gave the dungaree a fashion makeover: Kenzo produced exceptionally large striped overalls, Fiorucci created brightly coloured cotton versions, and other top-end designers sent silky, slimmed-down overalls down the catwalks, teamed with high strappy sandals and tiny vest tops. There were even purple crushed-velvet overalls that were gathered at the ankles and worn with flowery shirts.

In the early 1980s the look was brought back to earth by the band Dexys Midnight Runners, whose scruffy, folksy look went with their new Celtic sound. The style reached the mainstream teen market towards the end of the decade, after the Australian TV soap *Neighbours* dressed a young Kylie Minogue (playing mechanic Charlene) in dungarees. Also popular at this time were dungaree shorts. In the 1990s, brightly coloured baggy dungarees, worn with tie-dyed T-shirts and big smiley badges, were the uniform of the acid house ravers who danced until dawn to the pounding Balearic beat.

The early twenty-first-century catwalks were dominated by the trend for body-conscious, streamlined designs, and overalls were a welcome relief when they staged a comeback in 2010. A far cry from the charmless versions of the 1970s, the new-style dungarees were corseted (Jean Paul Gaultier) or made of silk with

delicate prints (Roberto Cavalli), and a variety of different styles and lengths have appeared on the high street. Comfortable and communicating a slouchy sex appeal, modern dungarees can be dressed up with high heels, worn on their own or cropped, in the style of capri pants. At last, the humble dungaree is making all the right fashion noises.

In the early 1990s DKNY took the denim bib and braces and teamed them with high-end accessories, as shown above, bringing a touch of glamour to the utilitarian garment.

52. Kaftan

Imagine lounging by the pool in a Marrakech villa in 1967 with Yves Saint Laurent and Talitha Getty (actress and wife of the oil heir John Paul Getty Jr), or partying in Ibiza in 2005 with Kate Moss and Jade Jagger, and chances are that kaftans feature in that vision. More than any other garment, the kaftan embodies the spirit of sun, freedom and the hippy-luxe lifestyle. This shapeless, colourful

and usually light tunic, which in the West once typified countercultural dress and the 'beautiful people', has become both Everywoman's summer staple and a glamorous fashion trend.

Long, loose-fitting robes and tunics have been standard items of clothing for thousands of years, particularly in the Near East. Ornately decorated versions in fine cotton or silk were worn by the fourteenth-century Ottoman sultans as a marker of prestige, and this style of clothing has long been a staple form of dress in such places as Morocco, India and South-East Asia. The kaftan floated into the European and American fashion landscape in the mid-1960s, when the 'hippy trail' brought global references into general culture. Young people started wearing kaftans and long cheesecloth tunics that they had discovered on their travels, and they teamed them with long strings of beads, Indian jewellery and ankle chains as they drifted around rock festivals and love-ins. Fashion-shoot teams jetted off to Bali and India on exotic assignments, commissioned by such fashion magazines as *Vogue* and *Nova*, to photograph tanned models lazing by the pool in brightly coloured kaftans.

By 1966 leading fashion designers had taken up the trend, and the kaftan became the ultimate in glamorous loungewear. Designers borrowed references from around the world, producing colourful, fluid robes. Long, flowing kaftans in exotic fabrics – often embellished with gold and silver thread – by Yves Saint Laurent, Bill Blass and Pierre Cardin were luxurious enough to translate into evening wear. Particularly popular with royalty and movie stars were the British designer

Page 139: The oil heir John Paul Getty Jr and his wife, Talitha, in Moroccan kaftans on the terrace of their holiday house in Marrakech in 1970.

A slit-fronted cashmere/polyester-mix kaftan designed by Roy Halston in 1972.

Thea Porter's floor-length versions of the kaftan, in a mix of chiffon, velvet and recycled traditional Eastern textiles. In Saint Tropez, the international jet set flocked to the Bedouin palace-inspired shop opened by the designer Jean Bouquin, which was crammed with flowing kaftans, love beads and luxurious pyjama trousers.

The kaftan went on to influence designs in the early 1970s. The soft, flowing lines of Eastern robes were incorporated into all the major collections, resulting in tent dresses with full sleeves, tassels and appliqué, accessorized with floppy hats and long scarves. The British designer Zandra Rhodes, in particular, created kaftan-shaped dresses in floaty chiffon with innovative colourful prints and zigzag hems.

It is no surprise that the kaftan is now the number-one poolside-to-party get-up,

The paisley pattern of the long kaftan pictured far left reflects the late-1960s interest in Eastern cultures. Today many kaftans are intended to be worn at the beach or by the pool, and are short and diaphanous.

and a staple of any woman's summer wardrobe. It is easy to wear, and – when scattered with sequins or such exotic patterns as leopard print – glamorous. It can be slipped on over a bikini after a swim; tunic-length versions can be tied at the waist and worn with jeans; and whatever its length, it can be accessorized with jewelled sandals and chunky beads for the evening.

53. Granny dress

With its long, whirling tiered skirt, tight bodice and high neck, the granny dress projects covered-up chic and homely, earth-mother sex appeal. In the late 1960s and early 1970s a generation of young women flounced around the streets in floral maxidresses as a feminist retort to the flesh-baring hot pants and miniskirts of the era, and the style still carries with it an element of languid romanticism that has ensured its continued popularity.

The granny dress's alternative name, the prairie dress, reflects its roots in the home-made cotton frocks of the nineteenth-century pioneer women of the American Midwest. Floor-length and usually with a pie-crust neck, this modest and feminine design was the blueprint for the long dresses that came into fashion in the mid-twentieth century. In 1966 the

maxidress arrived, signalling a sea change in fashion. In contrast to the angular designs of the earlier part of the decade, a romantic style was established that would last well into the 1970s. Victoriana-style dresses were first embraced by the flower-child hippy. The dresses, which were often bought from second-hand shops, were patterned in flower prints and had flowing skirts; 'love bead' necklaces, bells on the ankles and crushed-velvet maxicoats were frequent accessories to the hippy look.

This style was epitomized by the Welsh designer Laura Ashley, who had started out in the 1950s producing home-printed scarves and tea towels. Her first cotton maxidress, introduced in 1966, had a ruffled skirt, intricate smocking and a sweet Peter Pan collar, and was less about fashion than about a 'back to nature' aesthetic. The look spread rapidly, and the name Laura Ashley became

The American television series *Little House on the Prairie*, adapted from Laura Ingalls Wilder's series of *Little House* books and produced from 1974 to 1983, helped to bring the granny or prairie dress into the mainstream.

The designer Oscar de la Renta, pictured in 1976 with a model in one of his floor-length granny-style creations.

synonymous with long, romantic country-style dresses in flowery calicos and innocent white cottons with crocheted lace inserts.

In London, Barbara Hulanicki – whose first Biba boutique had opened in 1964 – began to design clothes that looked to the

past. Her flowing Empire-line midi- and maxidresses with puffed sleeves, produced in such muted colours as plum and misty brown, were at the epicentre of the new old-fashioned look. By the late 1960s the granny dress had become part of a new other-worldliness that was pervading fashion. Other designers and manufacturers followed: Angela Gore gave us pin-tucked bodices and long, flowing skirts, and Gina Fratini pastel-coloured dresses in butterfly and flower prints that were particularly popular. The granny look, which involved a crocheted shawl, lace-up boots and a suede shoulder bag, became the 'in' style.

In the 1970s Bill Gibb's extravagantly styled and decorative versions, and Yves Saint Laurent's tartan dresses, were among a proliferation of big-skirted maxidresses. The Laura Ashley look remained popular until the early 1980s; her sweet ruffled dresses and pinafores seemed to tap into a lost femininity as power-suited glamazons took over the streets. In 1981, when Lady Diana Spencer's betrothal to Prince Charles made her front-page news, her Laura Ashley outfits contributed to a new generation of women signing up to prairie chic. Since those days, the granny dress has been a mainstay of every maxi fashion that has hit the runway. It was reworked by Marc Jacobs and Chloé in the late noughties, and today slinky young women waft around in ankle-length sprigged cotton dresses, referencing a timeless femininity.

54. A-line minidress

When the French designer Christian Dior launched his groundbreaking A-line collection in spring 1955, a new silhouette was born, one that has remained a fashion mainstay ever since. Dior called it the A-line because his dresses and coats were narrow and fitted at the top, flaring out from the bust or waist in a straight line to the hem just above the knee, in a shape reminiscent of the letter 'A'. *Vogue* called it 'The most wanted silhouette in Paris', adding that 'it is the prettiest triangle since Pythagoras', and women were in awe of the charming simplicity of the outfits. Indeed, the new silhouette was revolutionary, marking a departure from the nipped-in waist and full skirts of Dior's New Look of 1947 to a simpler shape and a de-emphasized waistline. The commercially successful A-line was one of a series of controversial looks of the 1950s that paved the way to a more casual, simple fashion.

In 1958, the year after Dior's death, his successor at his couture house, Yves Saint Laurent, made a strong statement with the launch of his dramatic, wedge-shaped 'trapeze' line. Fashion pundits applauded his triangular dresses and coats that flared out dramatically from the shoulders, creating a dramatic silhouette, and *Vogue* declared the line a triumph.

By the early 1960s, as the 'youthquake' was gathering pace and fashion took on a new freedom of expression, the A-line minidress became one of the major fashion breakthroughs. The variations on the theme were seemingly endless: from the neat office mini pinafore dress by the London label Foale and Tuffin, and the striking mini with a horizontal gap in the middle – the two pieces held together with a large

chain mail and metal – to create distinctly avant-garde minidresses.

By the 1980s A-line garments and flared shapes had gone out of fashion, as shoulder pads – which had first become popular in the 1940s – returned with a vengeance: skirts now had to be tight-fitting to balance the look. Yet the A-line mini shift has continued to drift in and out of vogue, remaining popular with women desiring to show a bit of leg. A variety of A-line mini styles appeared on the catwalks in the late 1990s, and the cut resurfaced again in the international collections for Spring/Summer 2007, with the likes of Lanvin's satin A-line dresses and Chloé's appliquéd mini shifts. Legs had made a dramatic reappearance on the catwalks. Fresh, youthful and feminine, the simple A-line is definitely here to stay.

plastic ring – by the French designer André Courrèges, to Mary Quant's brightly coloured short styles, which often featured big cut-away armholes, oversized patch pockets and pretty necklines reminiscent of children's wear. The minidress was revealing and exciting, yet its clean lines gave it more than a dash of chic. By 1965 the A-line mini shift was worn by everyone, from society belles and the trendiest models to the average woman. The look was encapsulated by the London-born-and-bred model Twiggy, who with her wide-eyed elfin features and thin, angular build set a new girl-in-the-street standard for fashion models and created the British 'dolly bird' look of the era.

The space age had a major influence on fashion, as seen in the Moon Girl collection launched in 1964 by Courrèges. White and silver plastic minidresses, inspired by astronauts' spacesuits and teamed with felt hats and mid-calf white boots, became one of the defining looks of hip young things. As the radical change in womenswear continued, such designers as the Frenchmen Emanuel Ungaro and Pierre Cardin eschewed traditional soft fabrics for more unusual materials – including paper, plastic

The 'face of 1966' (as declared by the *Daily Express*), seventeen-year-old Twiggy heralded a new look with her boyish haircut and slim figure.

55. Mini-crini

In the shows for his ready-to-wear collection of 2003, John Galliano sprinkled 'fairy dust' over his black coat with ruffled trim and crinoline.

Sometimes fashion gives women the Cinderella treatment and creates a dress that is like a fairy tale come true. The mini-crini, with its short, puffed-out skirt and tight-fitting, boned bodice, is candy-floss cute with overtones of Degas ballerina and flouncy rock chick. The crinoline skirt has been reinterpreted, reworked and reconfigured since it whooshed on to the fashion scene in the mid-1980s, to take in puffballs and layered tutus, and in its many variations is retro-modernism at its best.

In the mid-nineteenth century, the fashionable hourglass figure was obtained through the use of a corset, and layers of petticoats to support the wide skirts of the period. Cage crinolines – introduced in the late 1850s and made of cane, baleen (whalebone) or steel – allowed the creation of skirts of unprecedented volume, but symbolized the suffocating, class-bound conformity of the time.

In 1916 the crinoline was briefly revived and reworked as a fashion item. Pioneered in France by Jeanne-Marie Lanvin, Jeanne Paquin and the House of Worth, the *robe de style* featured a wide skirt stiffened with hoops and decorated with lace and crystal embroidery. In contrast to the Victorian versions, the bodices of these 'modern' dresses were unfitted, and the skirts rose to just above the ankle. They were simple and elegant; velvet versions were for the afternoon, and fine, tinted tulles and muslins for the evening. They were soon cast aside, however, as the flapper dress danced its way on to the social scene.

The crinoline came back into fashion in the United Kingdom in the mid-1980s. While the power-dressing craze brought American footballer-sized shoulder pads and mannish suits for women, Vivienne Westwood, inspired by the ballet *Petrushka*, created a full-skirted shape that gave fashion a new silhouette. Her mini-crini of 1985 combined the traditional tutu with an abbreviated form of the Victorian crinoline.

A nineteenth-century illustration depicts one of the drawbacks of 1850s ladies' fashions. A gentleman calls for a gate to be opened so that his companion, who sports a broad crinoline, can exit from a field, as she cannot fit through the opening at the side.

A tutu-style cocktail dress by the French designer Christian Lacroix for his ready-to-wear collection of 1988. This puffed-out silhouette is also seen in his haute couture collections (p. 148).

Mini-crini

At once playful and vampish, it echoed the 1950s party frock, while the nipped-in waist and balletic form were feminine and sexy. As in the Victorian crinoline, the distinctive puffed-out shape was maintained by hidden hoops. Westwood's crinis came in many patterns and colours, from leopard print to polka dots, stars and stripes and even Disney cartoons. Dressed down with over-the-knee socks and clumpy platform shoes, they stopped short of full-on girlie territory. In 1987, the year he started his own label, Christian Lacroix introduced his fantasy-dressing 'le pouf', a short and showy puffball skirt made in brightly coloured satin, and intended to be worn with high stilettos. The shift towards opulent, feminine dressing was confirmed by such high-end labels and designers as Chanel, Balenciaga, Franco Moschino and Emanuel Ungaro, who showed majestic puffed skirts and tutus. High-street versions soon appeared; by the end of the 1980s, teamed with clumpy boots and a cropped jacket, they were a uniform of choice for young women.

The fluffy look was reconfigured in the final years of the twentieth century, as embodied by Sarah Jessica Parker in her outfit of girlie pink tutu and matching leotard as she pranced down the streets of New York in the opening credits of the TV series *Sex and the City*. Mini-crinis paraded down the catwalks in 2009 (Charles Anastase, John Rocha), and today versions of ballet-dancer chic include Christopher Kane's tutus in grown-up shades of black and beige. The pouffy, big-bottomed skirt has became a definitive style statement, and is a hit with women who want to be able to make an entrance without having to go Jessica-Rabbit-hot.

56. Safari suit

On urban streets, the safari look has been a mainstay of chic casual since Yves Saint Laurent turned the utilitarian beige jacket into a sexy fashion item during the 1960s. Over the years the safari look – encompassing the fashion safari suit, the bush jacket and the safari dress – has been continually reworked, repackaged and revitalized. With its practical styling, clean lines and classic neutral colours, it is a favourite unisex style that manages to be both casual and chic at the same time.

The look was devised at the turn of the twentieth century for adventurers going on safari in the African bush, and the lightweight cotton-drill jacket with trench belt and four large patch pockets was both practical and comfortable. By the 1950s,

thanks to such devotees as the tough-guy American writer Ernest Hemingway, who wore safari outfits on many of his escapades, the look had come out of Africa and entered the mainstream.

The style was first adapted for womenswear by Saint Laurent in his Saharienne collection of 1968. His safari jacket with lace tie at the front and tunic-style cut was a clever twist on the colonial look. He managed to create a garment that was not only practical – it retained

The photographer Robert Capa (far left) adopted the utilitarian safari suit style while documenting the Spanish Civil War (1936–39). The look translated well into a structured feminine design, as conceived in the late 1960s by Yves Saint Laurent (pictured left at the opening of his London boutique in 1969).

the large patch pockets – but also feminine and sexy. Cut close to the body with slits at the side, it was long enough to be worn as a very short dress but also suited trousers. Within a few years, designers were churning out beige cotton-drill shirt dresses with large pockets and wide lapels; in the early 1970s the Dejac label produced a button-up wool dress that was immensely popular. Easy to wear and shape-conscious, these safari shirt dresses were conservative enough for the working woman to wear to the office, yet had enough sex appeal to take her through the evening, too. This 'go-anywhere' dress remained a classic throughout the decade and beyond.

The men's suit became the quintessential leisure suit of the debonair action guy. Ted Lapidus produced a sandy-coloured cotton-drill safari suit that swept through the international fashion scene and helped to define the look of the 1970s male; devotees included the actors Roger Moore, Patrick 'The Prisoner' McGoohan and William Holden, and the French crooner Charles Aznavour. The polyester

versions that followed from mainstream producers, featuring jackets (with tabbed patch pockets and double-wide lapels) paired with acrylic slacks, brought the look within the reach of Everyman. Such companies as Lee and Enka showed handsome male models in cream or sky-blue suits teamed with denim shirts and brightly coloured neckerchiefs. Before long boardrooms, parties and television studios were populated by men dressed top to toe in beige and pale blue polyester.

The safari look for men fizzled out as the flamboyant 1970s gave way to the padded shoulders and conservative Armani suits of the following decade. For women, 'Serengeti chic' rose again in the twenty-first century as tailored clothing became a popular city choice. And it's not surprising: from Marc Jacobs's belted safari jackets paired with khaki skirts to Ralph Lauren's button-through beige safari dress (all from 2011), these garments are versatile and flattering. With their easy-to-wear neutral colours and simple shapes, safari-style separates make things simple for the busy woman.

A camel-coloured safari dress with quirkily placed breast pockets, worn cinched at the waist, by Pat Ashley for John Meyer from 1972.

Opposite: The denim safari suit was a defining menswear fashion of the 1970s. The suit lent the wearer an air of flamboyance both in the workplace and at the nightclub. This photograph dates from 1971.

57. Halter-neck dress

With its bold design that bares the shoulders and upper back, the halter-neck dress can ratchet up sex appeal to sizzling point. Loved by the glitterati of the 1970s and tall, slinky models of every era, the halter-neck dresses so frequently seen on the red carpet today all reference the glamour of early Hollywood, where the groundbreaking style was introduced.

In the 1930s and 1940s, owing to the censorship imposed by the American Motion Picture Production Code (popularly know as the Hays Code), the Hollywood film industry had to limit the showing of cleavage. Clothes designers who worked in film during that era, notably Travis Banton, Howard Greer and Adrian Greenberg (most widely known as simply Adrian), invented the halter neck as a means of creating sex appeal without breaking the code. Such stars as Jean Harlow, Ginger Rogers and Joan Crawford all shimmered and danced in these floaty new styles, with shoulders and upper back on show.

Already in the 1930s the world of film heavily influenced fashion, and ordinary women yearned to imitate the stars. Manufacturers took note, producing more affordable versions of the halter-neck evening gown and making them available in department stores. As the cult of sunbathing took hold, pairing a halter-neck top with floaty pyjama trousers was a particularly popular way to show off a fashionably tanned back.

Only in the late 1940s and early 1950s, as modern lifestyle changes started to gather pace and women took a more relaxed attitude to fashion, did the halter-neck dress, with its simple design, become a popular daytime garment. The charming sundresses by the innovative American

Marilyn Monroe in *The Seven Year Itch* (1955), in the famous ivory halter-neck dress designed by William Travilla.

designer Claire McCardell, in which spaghetti straps criss-cross repeatedly to form a halter neck, were considered to be the height of chic, and made regular appearances at poolside parties and barbecues. The halter-neck dress became officially one of the sexiest styles on the planet after a blast of New York subway air lifted Marilyn Monroe's dress in the film *The Seven Year Itch* (1955). That figure-hugging ivory satin gown with a deep décolletage – created by the costume designer William Travilla – has spawned countless copycat designs, and versions of it are still worn at events by such stars as Angelina Jolie and Scarlett Johansson.

Below: A yellow floor-length halter-neck dress, decorated with a bow at the neck, by Nina Ricci from 1982.

Monroe's dress remains the most prized expression of the genre, however: in 2011 it was sold at auction for $4.6 million.

The style took a back seat during the 1960s, but the fantasy glamour of the Hollywood halter neck reappeared a decade later. Reworked with a modernist appeal, figure-revealing halter-neck dresses in such soft fabrics as jersey,

silk crêpe and chiffon shimmered once again on mid-1970s dance floors and at glamorous soirées. The layered look that had been so fashionable in the early part of the decade gave way to clothes that flattered toned and tanned bodies. The American designers Roy Halston, Bill Blass and Geoffrey Beene draped their clients in deconstructed dresses that managed to cling to every curve and made femininity hip again. Halston in particular was known for his 'superclients', such as Bianca Jagger, Joan Collins and Liza Minnelli, who were photographed many times at the hip New York nightclub Studio 54 in his V-neck halter dresses, looking sexy, relaxed and comfortable.

The halter neck has been endlessly reinterpreted. Today a silk halter-neck top can be dressed down with skinny jeans and high platform sandals, or worn with delicate heels for vintage glamour. Long halter gowns in bright pinks and sorbets are perfect for balmy summer nights. Whatever the style, a woman will always stand out from the crowd in a halter neck.

The 'fairy chimneys' rock formations of Cappadocia, Turkey, make a stunning backdrop for this promotional shot of 1966 of a brown linen halter-neck dress by the American label B.H. Wragge.

58. Cowboy boot

It's hard to say just what it is about cowboy boots that immediately gives the wearer an air of gun-toting sex appeal. Perhaps it's the way they make you walk with a certain confident swagger, or simply the fact that they tap into the American nostalgia for the hard-drinking, hard-living cowboy. Whatever the answer, the tough-edged appeal of this boot is hard to resist.

The original working cowboys of the early nineteenth century wore plain boots designed simply to protect them against the elements and harsh terrain. Not until the early twentieth century did stitching across the toe and leather cut-outs start to appear, creating the cowboy boot as we know it. By the 1920s, Texan rodeo riders were wearing calf-high boots ornately decorated with inlaid leather designs, such as half-moons, dice, diamonds and stars. Soon such brightly coloured embellished cowboy boots were available for both men and women in American stores and mail-order catalogues.

As in the case of many other iconic garments, it took Hollywood to put the cowboy boot firmly on the fashion map. By the 1930s and 1940s the West may have been won, but cowboy movies were popularizing the myth of the heroic gunslinger, and such stars as Gene Autry ('the Singing Cowboy'), John Wayne and Gary Cooper were giving the cowboy a shot of hip-swaggering, whisky-swilling sex appeal that has endured ever since. Women got in on the act, too, in the early 1950s. The cowgirl with her embroidered shirt, full skirt and ankle-high cowboy boots made an appearance not only in

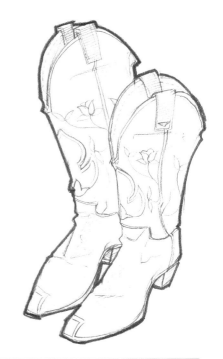

films, but also in glamorous photo shoots. Marilyn Monroe, Betty Grable and other starlets posed in provocative playsuits with matching decorative cowboy boots and a Stetson for a shot of tomboy appeal.

Western style had crossed over from the Great Plains of America and been fully absorbed into the fashion mainstream by the 1960s. The cowboy boot's gritty authenticity and macho braggadocio made it a favourite of country and western singers, rabble-rousing rock fans and American presidents alike. In 1969 the actor Dennis Hopper represented a generation of young people when he rode into the American consciousness in the film *Easy Rider*, his well-used cowboy boots and Harley Davidson emblems of his freewheeling anti-conformity. By the following decade the clothes of the hard-working cowboy – jeans, denim jacket and scruffy brown cowboy boots – had become the everyday casual wear of young men and women who had never seen a live horse.

In the early 1980s fashion tapped into American nostalgia. Blouses were teamed with short rah-rah skirts and brightly coloured cowboy boots, and the pairing of rah-rah and boots became one of the key looks of the decade. Today the cowboy boot is once again a high-fashion item. From Marc Jacobs's metallic pair and Miu Miu's funky boots in black, to a myriad of high-street varieties, the cowboy boot still carries a touch of outlaw chic. On women, they toughen up floaty dresses and look great when partnered with cut-off shorts. Whether as a blocked-heel ankle boot or the full-on country and western style, a pair of good ol' cowboy boots is the ultimate in frontier fashion.

The boots shown below have a slightly lower heel than the traditional cowboy boot; this style was devised for rodeo calf-roping competitions, in which the cowboy (or girl) has to run to tie the calf as well as to ride.

59. Duffel coat

There is something comforting about the duffel coat, with its coarse woollen fabric and rugged, Everyman appeal. Loose-fitting and three-quarter-length with patch pockets, and fastened with toggles (preferably made of buffalo horn), it has been a unisex symbol of social renegades, artists and students ever since the 1950s.

The coat is named after the Belgian town of Duffel, where the cloth was originally made. The duffel coat came into its own when it was taken up by the Royal Navy during the First World War. Sailors and officers alike wore this general-issue item to keep warm and dry on the decks of ships and submarines, and its large toggles were designed to be manipulated easily by cold hands. During the Second World War, images of the military were beamed around the globe. The duffel coat, which featured in wartime newsreels and was glamorized in British propaganda war films (such as *In Which We Serve*, 1942, and *The Cruel Sea*, 1953), was imbued with the rugged heroism of war; it was further popularized when Field Marshal Montgomery was pictured in a beige version, which became known as the Monty.

A generation of British teenagers was influenced by these images. After the war, surplus duffel coats were sold in the United Kingdom by the company Gloverall. The demand was so great that the firm started to manufacture its own, based on the original style. Young men and women wore the duffel coat as much because of its utilitarian origins as for its practical qualities. After thousands of duffel-coated students participated in an anti-nuclear-weapons march from London to the Atomic Weapons Establishment in Aldermaston, Berkshire, in 1958, the coat became a sartorial emblem of protest. Such quintessentially British stars as Richard Burton, Richard Attenborough and Michael Wilding donned the coat, giving it an air of simple but comfortable glamour.

Outside the UK, the duffel coat gained international cult status when it was chosen by left-wing intellectuals and existentialists as an anti-bourgeois statement. Even the avant-garde French writer and film-maker Jean Cocteau was photographed wearing one. In the United States, the no-frills authenticity of the duffel coat made it the apogee of bohemian chic. Greenwich Village beatnik types sat duffel-coated in trendy cafes, with books by Jean-Paul Sartre and Jack Kerouac stuffed into the large pockets; the women's outfits of black polo-neck sweaters and tight capri pants gave the coat a shot of sex appeal. Bob Dylan wore a blue duffel to sing his protest songs, and even Perry Como and Bing Crosby crooned on TV in their beige Montys. Teamed with a button-down shirt, corduroy trousers and penny loafers, the duffel coat became a staple on American campuses, as seen in the film *Carnal Knowledge* (1971), in which two college

The duffel coat was standardized for the British navy in the early twentieth century; its large toggles (rather than buttons) were intended to make it easier to open and close the coat with cold hands. This photograph was taken in 1943 aboard a Norwegian destroyer assisting the Allied forces.

roommates and lifelong friends (played by Jack Nicholson and Art Garfunkel) explore relationships with various women.

The duffel coat crossed over from street fashion on to the catwalk in the 1980s, when male models paraded down the runway with reworked designer duffels and smart woollen trousers by such labels as Katharine Hamnett and Hackett. With today's emphasis on authenticity, the original duffel coat has become a fashion must-have. Such media kittens as Kelly Osbourne, Cheryl Cole and Britney Spears all bring out their inner lad in theirs; the actress Gwyneth Paltrow wears hers out shopping; and the grunge goddess Alexa Chung has chosen her Monty to go out on the town. Whatever the event, the duffel coat offers a unique combination of retro-chic slouchiness and tradition that refuses to go out of fashion.

The American singer-songwriter Taylor Swift sports a warm duffel coat on a visit to London's zoo in early 2012.

Jack Nicholson and Art Garfunkel as duffel-clad university students in the drama film *Carnal Knowledge* (1971).

60. Corset

Madonna stimulated the renewed popularity of the corset by wearing this landmark, highly sexualized pink creation by Jean Paul Gaultier on her Blond Ambition tour of 1990.

The ultimate garment of female subjugation, or a symbol of empowerment and sexual confidence? Whatever the interpretation, the corset has been a fascinating, alluring and controversial item of female clothing since it was first developed more than 400 years ago. From the two-piece stays of the sixteenth century to the tightly laced corsets of the 1800s, these undergarments were designed to squeeze women's torsos into unnatural shapes in order to create the fashionable silhouette of the day.

In the nineteenth century, the desired tiny wasp waist required extremely tightly laced corsets stiffened with whalebone and metal that pressed into the flesh. While today we may think this corset-bound figure is grotesque, at the time it was considered to be a status symbol and a testimony to the leisured life of the wearer. Women were prepared to suffer to look beautiful, and the heaving bosoms and fainting fits caused by the corset only added to the erotic appeal. It took the crusading British suffragettes, and their campaign against these restrictive garments in the early years of the twentieth century, for the corset to start to go out of fashion.

Women continued to shape and compress their torsos with an array of rubberized garments – foundations, girdles, long-line bras – until the mid-1960s, when the miniskirt and the introduction of tights (as an alternative to garters and stockings) finally freed the female form. During the 1980s, when glamour dressing became fashionable, a playful, ironic take on the bustier was initiated by such rebellious designers as Vivienne Westwood and Jean Paul Gaultier, who transformed the undergarment into a visible item of clothing. Westwood created satin corsets in

pretty pastel shades, such as baby blue and pink. Her corsets were provocative, sexy and curve-boosting, but also surprisingly practical: stretch fabrics granted ease of movement, and removable sleeves converted daytime corsets to evening wear. Simultaneously voluptuous and bawdy, the new corset was not the oppressive garment of the nineteenth century, but rather a symbol of the new 'girl power'.

In the 1890s, there was no gentle way of achieving the fashionable waspish waistline. The restrictiveness of the whalebone corset could lead to fainting.

Corset

The ever-popular corset retains a classic shape and fitting similar to that of the nineteenth century, but modern materials technology now makes it less restrictive. This pink and gold brocade version is by John Galliano for Dior's ready-to-wear range of 2002.

After Madonna famously wore a pink corset with conical breasts designed by Gaultier on her extensive Blond Ambition tour in 1990, the corset went global. Various incarnations of the garment made corsets fun, bold and confident. Dolce & Gabbana gave us jewelled versions, Thierry Mugler a blue satin corset evening dress; women wore daring black satin corsets with jeans, or leather corsets over white shirts at work.

Gaultier and Dolce & Gabbana, among others, also popularized the corset dress, based on a traditional girdle. D&G's corset dress of the late 1980s became one of the label's signature pieces; black, clinging and decorated with traditional lingerie features, including hooks and eyes, it was refined yet sexually charged. Whether made of daring red lace, sheer chiffon, bright satin or leopard-print Lycra, the corset has become the dress of choice when women want to look and feel sexy. The slender Sarah Jessica Parker and Kylie Minogue, and the shapely Catherine Zeta-Jones and Beyoncé, have all taken advantage of its curve-enhancing properties.

The trend for these figure-hugging designs shows no sign of dying out. In 2010–11 corsetry could be seen on many catwalks: at Yves Saint Laurent spectacular dresses featuring cinched waists were paired with slouchy cardigans, while at Christian Dior corsets were teamed with silk, lace and 1950s hairstyles. Westwood's Corset Princess dress of 2010 remains a favourite (Helena Bonham Carter is a fan). Sleek and body-focused, the new corset is for the strong, sexy woman who is not afraid to make a statement and showcase her va-va-voom.

The Argentine–American actress Julie Gonzalo in 2004, wearing a leather corset over a polo-neck top, a popular combination that creates an everyday body-conscious silhouette.

61. Pencil skirt

A pencil skirt brings an element of dressed-up chic to an outfit that no pair of trousers ever can. Its high-waisted, long-line shape wraps itself around the hips and thighs, and creates a curvy silhouette that can be both sexy and elegant. Despite its restrictive form (running for the bus when wearing one would be unthinkable), this slim, moulded skirt has been sashaying in and out of fashion since it was launched some sixty years ago.

The pencil skirt originated in the early years of the twentieth century, when the Parisian designer Paul Poiret devised the ankle-length hobble skirt. 'I have freed the bust from prison, but I have put chains on the legs', he said when his new design appeared in 1910. Indeed, in his creation the legs were so tightly encased that a hobble strap or garter had to be worn below the knee to prevent the

material from ripping, making walking difficult for the wearer. In New York, purpose-built steps had to be fitted to trams to allow women to board. The hobble skirt was a short-lived craze that petered out in 1913, but the concept of the tight-fitting skirt was to return to prominence forty years later.

The main themes for women's fashion during the 1950s were femininity and refinement, and clothing that created an elegant silhouette was favoured. The leading French couturiers Jacques Fath, Christian Dior and Pierre Balmain introduced straight, tight-fitting skirts that fell to the knee, and teamed them with low stilettos and either boxy or close-fitting jackets. Relative ease of movement was enabled thanks to the insertion of godets or kick-pleats at the back. This streamlined silhouette was often achieved by artifice,

The hobble skirt, the first incarnation of the pencil skirt (seen here in New York in about 1910), made it tricky to board trolley cars but afforded gentlemen a rare glimpse of ladies' ankles.

Pencil skirt

Opposite: Such clever design features as kick-pleats and slits enable the pencil skirt to retain its slimline silhouette yet grant some freedom of movement. The outfit shown here dates from the mid-1950s.

Left: A Geoffrey Beene ensemble of 1965, with a knee-length black pencil skirt topped by a loose black-and-white cotton tweed jacket.

and roll-on elasticated girdles became a must-have in any woman's wardrobe.

Despite the fact that such practical fashions as slacks and loose-fitting shirtwaisters were prevalent, women were prepared to swap comfort for the sex appeal of the figure-hugging pencil skirt. Mass-market versions were soon available and, along with the beehive hairdo and the twinset, it became a cornerstone of 1950s style. Hollywood loved the pencil skirt, and shapely Marilyn Monroe, Elizabeth Taylor and Kim Novak set pulses racing when they appeared in their tight-fitting skirts both on and off the screen.

The pencil continued to be popular in the first half of the 1960s, but was knocked off its perch when minis swept in. It returned to prominence in the aspirational 1980s, however, when new wealth and conservatism led to 'power suit' status dressing. For women who wanted to project a businesslike appearance tempered with a dash of glamour, an above-the-knee pencil skirt, paired with a jacket with padded shoulders and accessorized with high court shoes and 'big hair', communicated both their ability to compete in the boardroom and their power in the bedroom. Designers obliged: successful working women could flaunt their figures and their salaries in Thierry Mugler's brightly coloured tailored suits or a reworked feminine classic from Dior.

Its glory days may be behind it, but the pencil skirt has never disappeared completely from the fashion scene. It was wheeled out briefly in the late 1990s, with Prada, Anna Molinari and Dolce & Gabbana all showing long, tight-fitting skirts in sensual fabrics, worn with cute sweaters or cropped cardigans; and in

2011 it was a key silhouette in collections from Marc Jacobs, Stella McCartney and Givenchy. Whether in leopard print, leather or just plain black, the pencil skirt is a fashion all-rounder: smart enough for the office and sufficiently on trend to create a stylish look for the evening.

The power-dressing tailoring of the pencil skirt makes it a first choice for celebrities when they want to be taken seriously, as seen here on the actress Nicollette Sheridan as she arrives at a Los Angeles court in 2012.

62. Trainers

It was in April 1980, when an eleven-day subway strike in New York led to thousands of workers putting on their trainers to walk to work, that this humble sports footwear – harder-wearing than the canvas-upper sneaker – began its rise to global domination. After the strike, trendy urbanites were still criss-crossing the city in Nikes or Reeboks and slipping into office-appropriate footwear at their desks. While sports shoes had become popular with the rise of jogging in the 1970s, they had been seen as purely practical items. Once the trainer was out on the streets, however, the major sports-shoe manufacturers Adidas, Nike, Puma and Reebok were forced to improve their stylistic and technological developments, creating bold logos, disco-bright colours and high-tech fabrication methods in the name of fashion.

Another factor in the developing attitude to the wearing of trainers was the emergence of hip-hop culture in the early 1980s. When members of the band Run DMC started wearing the Adidas Campus, street-styled with laces undone and logoed tongues on show, for teenagers everywhere they transformed the trainer from sports shoe to cult object. Run DMC even wrote a song about their favourite brand, 'My Adidas' (1986). Also an important influence in trainers becoming fashion footwear is the link between sport and urban youth. In 1985 the basketball superstar Michael Jordan was hired to endorse Nike's new multicoloured ankle-height high-tops, resulting in a frenzy of interest; the Air Jordan has since become one of the most famous trainer styles. By the end of the 1980s the trainer was universally popular, and such moulded-plastic-and-mesh creations as the Nike Air

Max (with an air-filled cushioning unit at the heel) and the Reebok AeroStep were the sports footwear of choice for gym bunnies and followers of fashion alike.

In the United Kingdom, when hip hop gave way to the softer sounds of acid house and Balearic beat in the 1990s, leaders of street style looked back to the 'old-school' trainer. Training shoes of the 1970s, such as the Puma States and Adidas Campus, had serious street cred, and were favoured by such cult indie bands as the Happy

American presidential candidate George Bush (father of the later US president George W. Bush) dons his trainers for an aerobics workout while campaigning in 1980. The trainer was about to cross over into mainstream fashion.

market. At Chanel, for example, Karl Lagerfeld embellished hip-hop trainers with the unmistakable big 'double C' logo, giving the shoes a glamorous edge. A decade later, Stella McCartney's range for Adidas, with its feminine colours and detailing, was aimed at a more mainstream market.

The trainer now holds an assured position in the fashion industry, and it is not hard to see why. Sports shoes are comfortable, and can make a statement of laid-back cool. The 'old-school' trainer is having another fashion moment. Dressed-down celebrities are wearing scruffy reformulated Nike high-tops (which set off skinny jeans to excellent effect) and Nike Waffle trainers from the 1970s. Such polished women as Goldie Hawn, Sarah Jessica Parker and Kylie Mynogue have all been snapped working the trainers angle. The fancy designer trainer is popular, too, despite its high price tag. From Balenciaga's trainers in lizard and calfskin, to Isabel Marant's high-tops with a concealed wedge, these shoes are far too glamorous to be worn to the gym.

The Girls Aloud singer Sarah Harding (left) in fitness chic, complete with bottled water, in 2012.

The high-end Louboutin trainer shows that there are many angles to the trainer phenomenon, both on and off the field.

Mondays and the Stone Roses. Anti-fashion was in; grunge girls would team their Pumas with second-hand dresses and large woolly jumpers.

Major fashion houses also got in on the trainer act in the 1990s, teaming up with sports-shoe manufacturers to get a key slice of this lucrative

63. Pant suit

It could be argued that there is no fashion concept more fun and becoming than the pant suit. The ultimate in sophisticated comfort, this simple layered look – also known as the dress-over-trousers and distinct from the trouser suit – manages to create a casual but edgy silhouette. A sophisticated version of the T-shirt and leggings, the pant suit flatters the female figure without emphasizing it, and is a fail-safe day-to-evening outfit.

A clue to the origins of the fashion pant suit can be found in South and Central Asia, where both women and men wear the salwar kameez, a traditional ensemble comprised of loose trousers (the salwar) and a long tunic (the kameez). In the mid-1960s this sartorial concept, modest and becoming to any body shape, gained mainstream high-fashion appeal after André Courrèges's Moon Girl collection

The original pant suit, the salwar kameez, originated in Asia. This photograph shows a salwar kameez being modelled in Amer Fort, near Jaipur, India.

featured white gaberdine trousers cut long over the ankles paired with softly styled white tunics. These groundbreaking outfits hit the headlines, and other leading designers created similar ensembles: Pierre Cardin produced pant suits in futuristic fabrics and patterns; op-art suits inspired by the work of the English painter Bridget Riley were a fun take on the look; and sleeveless tunic tops and matching plain trousers by Foale and Tuffin (Marion Foale and Sally Tuffin) were a favourite with celebrities. When the French pop singer Françoise Hardy wore a Courrèges pant suit on stage in 1966, it helped to fuel a trend that endured into the next decade.

Colours ranged from sober black and bright orange to delicate pastels, on either plain or patterned fabrics. The new outfits were tighter than the salwar kameez, and so matt crêpes and jersey were favoured,

The model Veruschka in 1969, in a woollen pant suit with a yellow-and-black gilet by Mila Schön.

as they provided the requisite stretch, but lace made an appearance with Courrèges's white lace suit with straight trousers and tunic-style top. Paired with silver-buckled, low-heeled 'pilgrim shoes' or calf-length boots, pant suits provided women with a way to emphasize the legs without having to wear short skirts. *Vogue* featured lithe models gambolling across the landscape in brightly coloured pant suits, their hair cut in neat geometric bobs.

As fashion shifted towards a more hippy ideal in the late 1960s, richly patterned velvet pant suits were the order of the day. Devotees of the style crossed all social and cultural groups: brightly coloured tunics worn over flared trousers were a favourite outfit for figures as diverse as the rock chick Janis Joplin and the glamourpuss Elizabeth Taylor. In London, Barbara Hulanicki of Biba gave the pant suit a new romanticism with her loose tunic suits in flowery printed rayon, worn with floppy hats and smudgy make-up. By the early 1970s the pant suit had become the quintessential casual outfit in the United States, where chain stores sold more keenly priced alternatives in synthetic fabrics. With its easy-to-wear neatness and such detailing as wide lapels on the tunic top, the outfit was typical of the decade's 'real clothes for real women'.

Having found itself sidelined for much of the 1980s and 1990s, the pant suit made a welcome return as a riposte to high-maintenance looks. After years of body-conscious dresses and nipped-in waists, at last it was time for something easy, flattering and comfortable. In noughties Britain, dresses and skirts worn over tapered trousers or bell-bottoms became

a standard style on the streets; in 2010, the look made it on to the catwalks, with Marni, Stella McCartney, Rag & Bone and Marc Jacobs all spearheading the trend. For women of all ages, the dress-over-trousers remains a classic match and a key look, whether as a simple tunic worn over skinny jeans with Converse sneakers, a flowery chiffon number over flared jeans, or a full-on 1970s pant suit.

In 2003, the American designer Alice Roi showed her trousers paired with a knit dress by Argentina-born Soledad Twombly.

64. Beret

The beret is one of the most versatile pieces of headwear. This plain, circular cap, usually made of felt or woollen cloth and sometimes featuring a leather trim around the edge, was developed by French and Spanish peasants in the eighteenth century. It was traditionally a piece of male headgear, but entered the fashion lexicon in the twentieth century as characteristic of the sultry siren, the existentialist philosopher or the populist revolutionary.

In the late 1920s the French designer Coco Chanel took up the 'Basque' beret (the original style) to create a playful accessory to her unique style of sporty womenswear. She herself often wore one, tilted to one side, teamed with one of her jersey suits and a string of pearls. It was one of her many borrowings from the male wardrobe that epitomized the androgynous look of the era's modern

woman, and it became widely copied, in particular by film stars. Marlene Dietrich scandalized polite society in the early 1930s, when she wore a beret partnered with a trouser suit, shirt and tie as daywear; her deliberate defiance of the status quo not only made her look like a femme fatale with attitude, but also imbued the beret with dramatic chic. Greta Garbo later adopted the look, pulling the beret over her straight blond hair.

While the beret was popular in the 1930s, replacing the cloche hat of the 1920s flapper, it wasn't until the 1940s that it became a key fashion item. During the Second World War, small hat styles were popular: they complemented the era's pared-down silhouette and saved on much-needed materials for the war. As has often happened, fashion turned for inspiration to the military, and the

Bombshell Dorothy Lamour (left) models the classic Hollywood take on the beret in the early 1940s, when plain suits were accessorized with elaborate headwear. A decade later, the style was sharper and neater, as seen (above) in this photograph of a green velvet beret by Mr. John – the American milliner John Pico John – of 1951.

classic army beret was reinterpreted for women: they were to be worn flat, pancake-style, or jauntily tilted to one side, and came in a multitude of colours and materials, from lush velvets and wools to felt and mink. Often embellished with surface decoration, such as flowers, sequins or feathers, the new-style beret managed to lift outfits out of the drab uniformity of wartime fashion.

In the early 1960s, when hats for mature women were still symbols of over-designed affectation, modern style was about simplicity, and nothing looked younger and fresher than a simple beret pulled down low to one side. When, to accessorize her colourful tunics, Mary Quant designed a collection of berets in twelve bright 'Quant' colours, including red, yellow and pink, this simple hat epitomized the new, informal styles. The beret became particularly popular with young women after the release of the film *Bonnie and Clyde* (1967), in which Faye Dunaway portrayed a pistol-toting female gangster, her youthful beret exemplifying the unruly casual chic of the decade.

Many iconic figures, not just fashionable women, have used the beret as a way of defining their image. Artists, bohemians and revolutionaries have adopted it as a gesture of rebellion against the status quo. The black beret came to symbolize the courageous spirit of the French Resistance during the Second World War, and was taken up by Parisian Left Bank cultural figures, such as the philosopher Jean-Paul Sartre and the actress and singer Juliette Gréco. The artist Pablo Picasso wore a beret, as did the writer Ernest Hemingway. In the 1950s, when the Latin American guerrilla leader Che Guevara took to wearing a black beret with a five-pointed star, it became imbued with an edge of danger and rebellion that it has never lost.

The fashionable 1960s beret was designed to sit perfectly on a cropped Vidal Sassoon haircut. The white example shown here, from 1966, is by the American hat-making firm Betmar.

65. Desert boot

You don't need to be near sand to appreciate the desert boot. The appeal of this lightweight, crêpe-soled suede footwear has endured since it was launched in 1950 (originally for men only), and it has been associated with icons through the decades, from the actor Steve McQueen and members of the Beatles to the singer Paul Weller, to name but a few. The original desert boot was developed in the late 1940s by Nathan Clark of the British family shoe business Clarks. He had been inspired by the rough suede boots worn by fellow servicemen during the Western Desert campaign of the Second World War; on his return home, he set about developing the ultra-comfortable, streamlined low boot with its pioneering crêpe sole.

The desert boot struck an original note. With its rugged appearance and utilitarian

appeal, it soon became an integral part of the 1950s American Ivy League look. Hollywood method actors favoured the boot: Anthony Perkins wore a pair with a button-down shirt and chinos in the film *Psycho* (1960), and Paul Newman gave it sex appeal. Never as rebellious as the sneaker nor as obviously aggressive as the thick-soled brothel creeper, the desert boot also communicated a low-key authenticity that made it popular with left-wing intellectuals and serious-minded poets and singers. The beatniks Jack Kerouac and Allen Ginsberg teamed theirs with scruffy jeans, sweatshirts and a dose of post-war malaise, as did Bob Dylan.

The French adored the boots, referring to them as *les Clarks*, and the combination of desert boot and duffel coat became a symbol of rebellious 1960s French student youth. In Britain, nattily dressed Mods

The Clarks centre-seamed Desert Trek boot (left), launched in the 1970s and still popular today.

liked the boots' simple, modern style;
the band the Who partnered them with
double-breasted jackets and slim-fitting
Italian trousers. The desert boot's
adaptability to different styles of clothing
granted it a broader appeal in the 1970s,
making it a staple of middle-class
suburban wardrobes. The suede boot
was reassuringly neutral, a comfortable
alternative to more rigid leather footwear,
and could be worn by Everyman.

There has been no shortage of devotees
in more recent times. Michael Douglas wore
brown suede Clarks desert boots in the
blockbuster *Wall Street: Money Never Sleeps*
(2010), to dress down a smart suit. The
former Oasis frontman, Liam Gallagher,
loves the desert boot so much that he
has collaborated with Clarks to launch his
own version as part of his Pretty Green
clothing brand, established in 2010. Other

fans include the singer Robbie Williams and
the shoe-design supremo Manolo Blahnik.

Fashion came full circle when Clarks
reintroduced the desert boot as part of
its Clarks Originals range in 2010. As
interest in the desert boot was rekindled,
other designers created their own versions,
and trendsetters eagerly snapped up a
pair. Women, too, now favour the desert
boot: contrasting with her high-heel-loving
character in the *Sex and the City* series,
Sarah Jessica Parker was spotted buying
two pairs in a New York shoe shop – one
in brown, one in black. As an antidote to
the towering stilettos and platforms of
the early twenty-first century, the fashion
crowd turned their attention – and their
feet – to flatter, more comfortable styles
of footwear that can 'toughen up' floral
dresses, or give an edge to cut-off shorts
or skinny jeans.

Today the humble desert boot comes
in many forms (including the low-wedged
Clarks Yarra, which quickly became a
cult among female fashionistas after its
launch in 2010), and from many different
labels. Whether in patent leather, denim
or the original suede, it is a favourite
with the cool, the hip and anyone
who doesn't want blisters.

66. Boob tube

Despite its utter simplicity, the boob tube can radiate nuclear levels of sex appeal. Essentially a strapless tube of stretchy material that clings tightly around the torso, it accentuates the bust, stomach and shoulders. Although the roots of the boob tube can be traced back to ancient Egypt, where female athletes would strap pieces of cloth around their chests to allow maximum movement, it wasn't until the early 1970s that the fashion potential of this type of revealing garment was spotted.

The boob tube was 'invented' in the late 1960s by Murray Kleid, owner of the New York womenswear manufacturer S&M Fringing. There had been a mistake in his production line, but Kleid glimpsed the resulting garment's potential and sent samples out to local distributors. These proved so popular that the company was

soon distributing them worldwide. By the mid-1970s fashion designers were taking note and had started to produce boob tubes in various colours and sizes, initially as a sporty, casual garment usually intended to be worn on the beach; with the arrival of the disco craze, the boob tube soon became a key element of the disco uniform.

In the later 1970s discotheques were packed with women shimmying to the pounding beat in skintight satin trousers, leotards or footless tights, all topped by sparkly boob tubes. Pink, purple and electric-blue were popular colours, while satin, lamé and stretch nylon were the preferred fabrics. Disco fashion was a dance-based look, inspired in part by the fitness craze of the early 1970s and the film *Saturday Night Fever* (1977). The boob tube fitted the bill: it was easy to dance in, crease-proof and attention-seeking.

Style of the 1970s: the American photographer and actress Berry Berenson (left) in a striped boob tube; funny-girl Goldie Hawn (above) in a longer, plain version.

Back in 2000, teen songstress Christina Aguilera modelled a pink sequined cropped boob tube that, when paired with jeans, created the classic L.A. look.

By the end of the decade many items of disco wear were crossing over into daywear, and soon everyone was wearing boob tubes and leotards. One popular development was the figure-hugging tube dress in plain colours: in 1978 Mary Quant's fluid boob tube dresses (available in beige, white or black only) were a huge success. The trend for boob tubes continued during the 1980s. Worn under a jacket, and usually in conservative colours, the boob tube became respectable enough to be accepted as office wear. The mid-1990s saw the arrival of the micro tubular top – a cross between a boob tube and a bandeau – as the midriff became that decade's predominant erotic zone. This was a style aimed at the young, who paired the top with ripped jeans or miniskirts.

Disco style made a triumphant comeback in the early years of the twenty-first century; high-street shops were awash with sparkly boob tubes and fluorescent stretchy tube dresses that, while verging on the kitsch, were still highly wearable when teamed with skinny jeans or shorts. Today, as fashion has moved towards a more streamlined look, plain, stretchy tube dresses have taken over. Easy to wear yet infused with erotic appeal, the tube dress – whether glammed up with high heels or toned down with trainers – is the perfect way for the lithe young woman to show off her fit and fabulous figure.

67. Trilby

The trilby is one of the most iconic hats of the twentieth century. Worn dipped over one eye or pushed jauntily on to the back of the head, this (usually) felt titfer, with its low, dented crown and its narrow brim that turns up at the back, has been a signifier of louche living since it made its debut appearance in London in the late nineteenth century. It has graced the heads of gangsters, wisecracking fictional detectives, free spirits and young trendsetters. These days, a hat is no longer a societal must-wear; instead, the trilby is a chirpy addition to any outfit, and gives the wearer an air of rakish cool.

The hat is named after the eponymous heroine of George du Maurier's novel *Trilby* (1895). A thrilling satire set against the backdrop of the bohemian artistic world and the bourgeoisie, the story became a sensation when it was dramatized on the stage in London the following year; a particularly distinctive hat worn in the play was soon referred to as a trilby. It became associated with intellectual bohemianism and the avant-garde, who took to it as a signifier of rebellion against the stultifying dress codes of the age. It must be noted that, at the time, the elegant gentleman would wear a bowler hat or a stiffened homburg.

After the First World War, as unstructured, comfortable clothing became the mark of the modern man, the trilby became the fashionable hat of choice. Along with the new patterned sweaters and wide trousers, this 'jazzy' hat was taken up by students, artists, writers and show-business types. By the 1930s, the trilby-wearing reporter with his rumpled suit and dodgy lifestyle was a popular fixture in black-and-white 'newspaper' movies of the time, such as *The Front Page* (1931). The hat had crossed over to gangsters, hoodlums and the world of shady 'operators', too: the trilby was a smart accessory to the double-breasted suit, waistcoat and spats, and was an integral part of the image and status of the gangland fraternity. The notorious American mobsters Lucky Luciano and Al Capone were ardent trilby wearers. Hollywood latched on to the look, and by the early 1940s every film-noir 'wise guy' and hard-boiled private investigator was identifiable by his trilby and his belted trench coat.

In the years after the Second World War, efforts at reinstating 'normality' led to the creation of the man in grey flannel suit and trilby hat as an emblem of an

Frank Sinatra was rarely seen without a trilby. Here he is pictured in classic pose at his piano in the drama film *Young at Heart* (1954).

The trilby is a fashionista favourite, especially with the boho and music-festival set.

ordered, conformist society. It wasn't until the 1960s, as men started wearing polo necks and slacks instead of the formal suit, that the trilby relinquished its reign. By the time a hatless John F. Kennedy was inaugurated as president of the United States in 1961, hat-wearing was the preserve of the few rather than the majority.

Along with its cheekier cousin the pork-pie hat (so called because of its flattened top shaped like a pork pie), the trilby was favoured by cool jazz types in the 1950s and 1960s. It was also popularized by the sartorial style of the 1960s Jamacian ska musicians, and that of the British Mods of the same decade. Since then the trilby has gone from being a badge of the 'man about town' to becoming the headgear of the subcultural tribe. It became the hat of choice for the Two Tone ska revival in the late 1970s, the finishing touch to the outfits of shiny suits and loafers worn by the Specials and other Two Tone bands. Today the trilby is also a style favourite with trendy celebrities (both Eva Longoria and Britney Spears chose trilbies as part of their travelling outfits in the summer of 2012), funky musicians and anyone who wants to add a touch of Sinatra glamour to their outfit.

The trilby underwent a revival in the 1980s thanks to the Two Tone record label, which signed such ska bands as the Selector (pictured here in 1980).

68. Sloppy joe

Floppy, slightly baggy and worn long over the hips, the sloppy joe sweater is the exemplar of slouchy chic. The oversized 'boyfriend' jumper is an antidote to high-maintenance tailored dressing, the rock 'n' roll of the knitwear world: worn with tapered trousers, shorts or a floaty dress, it somehow manages to looks sexy in a rumpled sort of way.

The heritage of the sloppy joe is based firmly in post-war America and the late-1940s/early 1950s phenomenon of the 'bobby soxer', a teenage girl whose typical outfit was sloppy joes, pedal pushers or jeans, saddle shoes and short, rolled-down 'bobby socks'. Moving around in gangs to a musical background of the likes of Frank Sinatra and Bing Crosby, bobby soxers represented generational change. Their uniform of outsized sweater (often borrowed from a brother's or a boyfriend's

wardrobe) and jeans – as modelled in the comedy film *The Bachelor and the Bobby-Soxer* (1947) – was considered to be scandalous, and was a shift away from the more conventional twinset and pearls.

In the mid-1950s the sloppy joe was taken up by the beatniks. Arty, defiant, anti-fashion and anti-materialistic, they expressed their disdain for all things commercial, in part by the way they dressed. The female beatnik's scruffy outfit of stripy sloppy joe sweater, tight trousers, flat shoes and glass-bead necklace was a celebration of individuality, and a shocking fashion statement at a time when most women wore stockings and knee-length

Audrey Hepburn was no slouch in her roomy jumper in 1957. At a time when high fashion was very structured, the sloppy joe was a comfortable dress-down alternative.

skirts. By the end of the decade, mainstream fashion had incorporated a casual look of loose mohair jumpers paired with tight black ski pants and accessorized with brightly coloured costume jewellery. *Vogue* and other magazines featured baggy jumpers by the likes of Norman Norell (under the label Traina-Norell), in such lively colours as apricot and cherry.

While the sloppy joe slipped off the fashion radar in the 1960s and 1970s as skinny-rib and V-necked jumpers took centre stage, the oversized floppy sweater came back into favour during the 1980s. Large novelty-pattern jumpers teamed with rah-rah skirts, woollen tights and leg warmers made their way to the forefront of fashion as the 'big' look featured in many catwalk collections. This was a decade of extremes, and sloppy woollens with huge shoulder pads were worn over Lycra miniskirts or femme-fatale leather trousers. The sloppy joe also felt the impact of the era's fitness craze, which brought on to the streets styles that had previously been confined to the gym. Particularly influential in this regard was the look displayed by Jennifer Beals in the dance-romance film *Flashdance* (1983): her loose sweatshirt, with one sleeve hanging provocatively off the shoulder, kick-started a trend that would last through the decade. Oversized sweatshirts, in leopard-print and gaudy neon colours, could now be worn cinched with a wide belt, over lacy leggings and high court shoes.

The 1990s grunge girls took to wearing baggy, drab men's sweaters that they bought from second-hand shops, slung over baby-doll dresses and teamed with bovver boots. This anti-fashion style was briefly taken up by Marc Jacobs and other

high-end designers, who created a fashion stir when they promoted the designer grunge look with colourful, baggy jumpers worn over mismatching flares or skirts. Today, updated and reincarnated, the oversized 'boyfriend' jumper is a stylish affair, a fitting balancing act for skinny jeans or leggings; for the workplace, it can be worn belted over a pencil skirt – cocoon fashion at its best.

Looking great with ripped jeans, skinny trousers or leggings, the modern oversized 'boyfriend jumper' is still hugely popular.

177

69. Winkle-picker

Women's winkle-pickers often feature a fine heel, complementing many types of outfit.

In the United Kingdom, the 1950s saw a greater degree of experimentation in male fashions than had been the case in previous decades, and the exaggeratedly pointy-toed winkle-picker – an otherwise plain and slim lace-up shoe with a low heel – was one of the first items of street style to define a section of post-war British youth: the sharply dressed rock-'n'-rolling Teddy boys who emerged out of east London.

The elongated shoes of these young followers of fashion were distant relations of the *poulaines* that had been popular with stylish men of the medieval French courts. As in the case of the *poulaines*, the original winkle-pickers were about style only, and were notoriously difficult to walk in. (The shoe is named after the British seaside tradition of eating winkles, using a sharp pin or 'winkle picker' to extract the flesh from the shell.) As street styles

Winkle-pickers have their origins in the medieval French *poulaines*. The shoes pictured left, photographed at a market in Tallinn, Estonia, in 2006, are broadly similar to the medieval style.

Winkle-picker Chelsea boots (with elasticated sides) were just the thing for this sharp-suited band, snapped at the Cavern Club in Liverpool in 1964. Shoe styles for women were similarly pointy, as can be seen at the bottom of the photograph.

evolved in the early 1960s, the Teddy boys abandoned their pointy-toed footwear in favour of the more aggressive-looking brothel creeper; the sleek winkle-picker was taken up by the dapper Mods as the perfect partner to their sharply tailored suits and smooth hairstyles.

Winkle-pickers had originally been produced in England at factories in Northampton, but the Mods embraced the finer Italian versions that had become available. The shoe had gained some notoriety in its early days in the 1950s as a result of being worn by Teddy boys in gang fights. But although the winkle-picker looks lethal, it would be highly unlikely that a typically stylish Mod would subject his expensive Italian imports to any kind of abuse. As the fashion reached its peak, the heels began to rise and the points to be rounded off. By the mid-1960s

the winkle-picker had evolved into the Chelsea boot, with its higher heel and less exaggerated point.

In common with many street styles, the winkle-picker has provided inspiration for a wide range of fashion designers. Pointy-toed shoes made a comeback in the late 1970s and 1980s with the punks, Rockabillies and Goths. In the early 1980s young women also took up the fashion, teaming pointy-toed ankle boots known as pixie boots with black tights and flounced rah-rah skirts.

Fast-forward to the twenty-first century, and sharply pointed boots and shoes are once again popular with young males because they complement the fashion for skinny suits. Among designer versions are Dolce & Gabbana's black-and-white winkle-pickers that taper to an exaggeratedly sharp apex, a good few inches past the toes. The winkle-picker remains a favourite of such 'edgy' personalities as Mickey Rourke, who wore a bright orange metallic-look pair to a premiere of his film *The Wrestler* (2008), and the 'bad boy' Russell Brand. The enduring popularity of this flamboyant shoe is a testimony to the fact that male vanity lives on.

70. Field jacket

Field jacket

Page 181: Plain field jackets were issued to these American troops, photographed in Vietnam in 1965.

Below: Camouflage uniforms were introduced during the Second World War.

The field jacket, one of the most widely copied pieces of military apparel of the past fifty years, may recently have been reworked as a high-fashion item, but it still carries with it the air of tough, army-surplus chic it acquired in the 1970s. The United States Army issued its first field jacket in the early 1940s; the waist-length design, based on a civilian windbreaker, was stylish, but lacked the necessary practical elements for combat situations, such as warmth and durability. New designs followed over the years, and in 1965 the army introduced the longer M65 field jacket, made of extra-tough fabric and featuring four flap pockets and an insulating lining. It was this jacket, worn extensively by the American forces fighting in the Vietnam War and veterans returning from the conflict, that crossed over into the mainstream in the late 1960s.

It is difficult to overestimate the influence the Vietnam War had on civilian clothing. Army-surplus apparel was already popular, and the field jacket, with its association with combat, was easily romanticized. Daubed with slogans and thrown over a scruffy pair of jeans, it became the standard protest garment for the throngs of young people marching against the atrocities of war. It was also taken up by militants of the African American Black Panther Party, who partnered it with jeans and their signature berets, and it wasn't long before the field jacket, in common with many other protest garments, represented radical chic. When the satirical television series *M*A*S*H*, set in a military field hospital during the Korean War of the early 1950s, was first screened in 1972, the popularity of field jackets grew further. Soon field jackets,

The field jacket lends itself to army-surplus chic. Robert De Niro, in his role in *Taxi Driver* (1976), cemented the garment as an outsider choice.

which had once been regarded as subversive when worn by civilians, had become acceptable daytime wear on American campuses and urban streets. After all, this clothing was inexpensive, practical and extremely hard-wearing.

Al Pacino risked his life in a field jacket in the police-corruption film *Serpico* (1973), and Sylvester Stallone sweated in one as Rambo in the action movie *First Blood* (1982). But it was Robert De Niro, playing the psychotic Vietnam vet Travis Bickle in the film *Taxi Driver* (1976), who gave the jacket an association with every alienated loner standing up against authority. Since those days, the field jacket has been an important dress-down garment for both sexes. The original M65 jacket was among the army-surplus items appropriated by the grunge kids in the 1990s as visual metaphors for their sense of alienation.

In the first decade of the twenty-first century, as combat-themed collections became a directional fashion trend, designers reworked the jacket to appeal to women. Marc Jacobs's tough-chic field jackets, with their slightly shrunken fit, have been particularly popular, as have Banana Republic's pure cotton versions. Today the field jacket is a piece of womenswear, worn to toughen up floaty dresses or to dress down patterned leggings, and its no-fuss practicality makes it an essential item for any woman marching round the city streets.

Miley 'Hannah Montana' Cyrus teams a field jacket with comfy jeans and high-heeled shoes in 2011 for an effortlessly dressed-down look.

Picture Credits

Acknowledgements

This book is dedicated to my wonderful
nephews and niece, Oskar, George, Myles
and Georgia.

Thanks to Merrell Publishers' Claire
Chandler for her support and enthusiasm,
and to the team at Merrell, especially
Marion Moisy, editor, and Nick Wheldon,
picture manager. It has been a pleasure
working with you all.

Thanks also to Billy Berwitz and his
encyclopaedic knowledge of fashions past
and present. Our chats were inspiring.

Index

First published 2013 by
Merrell Publishers, London and New York

Merrell Publishers Limited
81 Southwark Street
London SE1 0HX

merrellpublishers.com

British Library Cataloguing in Publication
Data. A catalogue record for this book is
available from the British Library.

ISBN 978-1-8589-4588-0

Produced by Merrell Publishers Limited
Designed by Nicola Bailey
Drawings by Rebecca Adams
Project-managed by Marion Moisy
Indexed by Vanessa Bird

Printed and bound in China

KATE MULVEY is a fashion writer
and journalist. Her articles on fashion
and lifestyle have appeared in such
publications as *The Times*, the *Sunday
Times*, the *Daily Telegraph*, the *Daily
Mail*, the *Daily Express*, *She* and *Red*.
Her previous books (as co-author)
include *Decades of Beauty* (1998),
Key Moments in Fashion (1998) and
Vintage Fashion (2006).

Front cover: Courrèges dress of 1969
(see page 144)

Back cover (left to right): 1960s
trench coat by Claret (see page 114);
1950s little black dress (see page 10);
1960s bell-bottoms (see page 15);
1970s hot pants (see page 46)